LA MER DU NORD
BELGIQUE
Calais
Boulogne
Lille
Moselle
LUXEMBOURG
Amiens
Havre
Rouen
Seine
Reims
Verdun
Meuse
Metz
Nancy
Marne
VOSGES
Strasbourg
Rhin
Versailles
PARIS
Domrémy
Chartres
Seine
Orléans
Blois
Dijon
JURA
Bourges
Loire
SUISSE
Genève
Rhône
ALPES
Lyon
MASSIF CENTRAL
Grenoble
ITALIE
Rhône
Avignon
Nîmes
Nice
Arles
Cannes
Toulouse
Marseille
Carcassonne
LA MER MÉDITERRANÉE

Beginning French

A CULTURAL APPROACH

BEGINNING FRENCH

William S. Hendrix and Walter Meiden

2—

A Cultural Approach

Third Edition

The Ohio State University

Houghton Mifflin Company · Boston

THE RIVERSIDE PRESS • CAMBRIDGE, MASSACHUSETTS

PRINTED IN THE U.S.A.

Preface

Beginning French is based on four fundamental ideas: (1) the reading material of a foreign language text, even in the most elementary book, must be meaningful, interesting, and written in connected sentences and paragraphs; (2) a language course should give the student knowledge about and appreciation of the country whose language he is studying; (3) the lessons should be presented and taught so that the student feels that it is language he is learning and not grammar; (4) a language can best be learned through a series of activities carried on in that language: questions — direct and indirect, exercises, résumé compositions, blackboard dictation, and conversation.

To that end, the lessons of *Beginning French* are built around reading selections which are designed to give the student some idea of French geography, a bird's-eye view of French history from the seventeenth century on, an insight into various aspects of everyday French life, and an appreciation of the contributions of the French in many fields of human endeavor. From the very first lesson the student deals with meaningful and informational material concerning which he can carry on a conversation. A set of questions in French and a conversational exercise afford him practice in speaking about this material. All-French exercises give him the opportunity to use the new grammatical constructions and vocabulary introduced in the lesson. A set of questions on the new grammatical constructions permits him to approach the grammar inductively if he can, and references to the *Grammaire* allow him to look up the rules if he must.

The following modifications have been introduced into this edition:

(1) Facts concerning France have been brought up to date.

(2) New lessons concerning contemporary aspects of French life have taken the place of certain lessons dealing with World War II.

(3) A greater proportion of the lessons are in dialog, so that now approximately one-third of the lessons consist of conversation.

(4) Many of the lessons have been slightly shortened so as to fit more easily into one class hour.

(5) In each lesson, a special section entitled *Conversation* affords the student drill in conversation and in pattern practice.

(6) The presentation of grammatical principles in the various lessons has been slightly rearranged for greater facility in learning.

(7) In lessons 51–60 there is a new exercise affording practice on verbs which give the English-speaking person difficulty in French.

(8) In the *Supplément* a new oral English-to-French exercise affords the student practice in important basic patterns.

(9) The reviews now come after every five lessons.

(10) Many of the grammar sections have been reworded and, whenever necessary, rules have been changed to conform to actual usage.

(11) In the *Prononciation,* increased emphasis has been given to intonation patterns, rules for *liaison* have been brought up to date, and there is a detailed description of how to learn to pronounce the French *r.*

(12) For laboratory use there are tapes on which the reading material, the questions and answers, and all exercises that lend themselves to pattern practice have been recorded.

We sincerely appreciate the many suggestions of our own colleagues and students at Ohio State and of teachers and students in other schools of the country in which the Revised Edition of *Beginning French* has been used. We wish to thank all the French friends who have aided us in any way in preparing this material and we are particularly grateful to the following, who have read the manuscript in part and made many useful suggestions: Monsieur and Madame Maurice Bigot, Monsieur and Madame Lucien Carle, Cyrille de Brunhoff, Gérard Cleisz, Juliette Lemoine Dallier, Jacques Delécluse, l'Abbé Durosoy, Henri-Gérard Duruisseau, Rémi Kremp, and André Mynard. We are especially indebted to Jean Bonnassies, who went over the entire manuscript in great detail, to our colleague Charles Carlut, who read the Third Edition both in manuscript and in proof and made many helpful suggestions, to Pierre and Monique Léon of the Institut de Phonétique for their most important contributions in the section on pronunciation, in the various phonetic transcriptions, and for their many other useful suggestions, and to Dr. William Holbrook of Northwestern University for his various suggestions on the manuscript. We wish to thank Miss Maude Spitler of Dayton, Ohio for her very careful reading of the entire proof and our colleague Robert Mitchell for his critical reading of the proof of the *Grammaire* and *Vocabulaire.*

The final responsibility for the accuracy of facts and language is assumed by the authors.

W. M.

Table des matières

Introduction au Professeur xvii

Introduction à l'Étudiant xxvi

Leçons

PREMIÈRE LEÇON. La France 1
DEUXIÈME LEÇON. Les continents 4
TROISIÈME LEÇON. Les plaines et les montagnes . . . 7
QUATRIÈME LEÇON. Les frontières de la France . . . 10
CINQUIÈME LEÇON. La Seine et la Loire 13
PREMIÈRE RÉVISION — LEÇONS 1 à 5 17
SIXIÈME LEÇON. La Garonne et le Rhône 20
SEPTIÈME LEÇON. La Bretagne 23
HUITIÈME LEÇON. La Touraine 27
NEUVIÈME LEÇON. La Normandie 31
DIXIÈME LEÇON. Le Midi de la France 34
DEUXIÈME RÉVISION — LEÇONS 6 à 10 39
SUPPLÉMENT — LEÇONS 1 à 10 41
ONZIÈME LEÇON. Deux Américains en France . . . 56
DOUZIÈME LEÇON. Un week-end à la campagne . . . 59
TREIZIÈME LEÇON. Une dictée dans une classe française . 62
QUATORZIÈME LEÇON. Une leçon sur Victor Hugo . . 64
QUINZIÈME LEÇON. Les saisons et les mois de l'année . . 68
TROISIÈME RÉVISION — LEÇONS 11 à 15 71
SEIZIÈME LEÇON. Le lycée français 73
DIX-SEPTIÈME LEÇON. Une journée au lycée 76
DIX-HUITIÈME LEÇON. Les départements français . . . 79
DIX-NEUVIÈME LEÇON. Le Président de la République . . 84

VINGTIÈME LEÇON. Le Premier Ministre et le Parlement . 87

QUATRIÈME RÉVISION — LEÇONS 16 à 20 91

SUPPLÉMENT — LEÇONS 11 à 20 92

VINGT ET UNIÈME LEÇON. Les monopoles de l'État . . 112

VINGT-DEUXIÈME LEÇON. La pension de famille . . . 115

VINGT-TROISIÈME LEÇON. Le Quartier latin 119

VINGT-QUATRIÈME LEÇON. L'Université de Paris . . . 122

VINGT-CINQUIÈME LEÇON. Les cours à l'université . . 125

CINQUIÈME RÉVISION — LEÇONS 21 à 25 129

VINGT-SIXIÈME LEÇON. Le Cité Universitaire 131

VINGT-SEPTIÈME LEÇON. Fontainebleau 134

VINGT-HUITIÈME LEÇON. Le retour en chemin de fer . . 137

VINGT-NEUVIÈME LEÇON. L'Alsace-Lorraine 140

TRENTIÈME LEÇON. Les parties du corps 144

SIXIÈME RÉVISION — LEÇONS 26 à 30 148

SUPPLÉMENT — LEÇONS 21 à 30 150

TRENTE ET UNIÈME LEÇON. Premières impressions de Paris 173

TRENTE-DEUXIÈME LEÇON. La concierge 176

TRENTE-TROISIÈME LEÇON. Les moyens de transport à Paris 180

TRENTE-QUATRIÈME LEÇON. Le repas au restaurant . . 184

TRENTE-CINQUIÈME LEÇON. De l'Étoile à la Concorde . 187

SEPTIÈME RÉVISION — LEÇONS 31 à 35 192

TRENTE-SIXIÈME LEÇON. Les Tuileries et le Louvre . . 194

TRENTE-SEPTIÈME LEÇON. Notre-Dame de Paris . . . 197

TRENTE-HUITIÈME LEÇON. Une soirée au théâtre . . . 201

TRENTE-NEUVIÈME LEÇON. Projets de vacances . . . 205

QUARANTIÈME LEÇON. Les vacances en France . . . 209

HUITIÈME RÉVISION — LEÇONS 36 à 40 213

SUPPLÉMENT — LEÇONS 31 à 40 215

QUARANTE ET UNIÈME LEÇON. La France et l'Europe de 1871 à 1939 235

QUARANTE-DEUXIÈME LEÇON. Madame Bonneville achète un flacon de parfum 239

QUARANTE-TROISIÈME LEÇON. La guerre de 39 et l'occupation 243
QUARANTE-QUATRIÈME LEÇON. La mode 248
QUARANTE-CINQUIÈME LEÇON. La France depuis la guerre 252
NEUVIÈME RÉVISION — LEÇONS 41 à 45 257
QUARANTE-SIXIÈME LEÇON. Y va-t-on ou n'y va-t-on pas? . 259
QUARANTE-SEPTIÈME LEÇON. Comment on fait la connaissance d'une jeune fille française 263
QUARANTE-HUITIÈME LEÇON. Le mariage en France . . 268
QUARANTE-NEUVIÈME LEÇON. La course-cycliste 272
CINQUANTIÈME LEÇON. Le sport en France 276
DIXIÈME RÉVISION — LEÇONS 46 à 50 280
SUPPLÉMENT — LEÇONS 41 à 50 282
CINQUANTE ET UNIÈME LEÇON. Pasteur 302
CINQUANTE-DEUXIÈME LEÇON. Louis XIV 306
CINQUANTE-TROISIÈME LEÇON. Le Château de Versailles . 310
CINQUANTE-QUATRIÈME LEÇON. L'automne 313
CINQUANTE-CINQUIÈME LEÇON. Le dix-huitième siècle . 318
CINQUANTE-SIXIÈME LEÇON. La radio et la télévision en France 323
CINQUANTE-SEPTIÈME LEÇON. Napoléon Ier 330
CINQUANTE-HUITIÈME LEÇON. Noël 334
CINQUANTE-NEUVIÈME LEÇON. Napoléon III 338
SOIXANTIÈME LEÇON. Les Français en Amérique . . . 342
ONZIÈME RÉVISION — LEÇONS 51 à 60 348
SUPPLÉMENT — LEÇONS 51 à 60 351

Grammaire

THE ARTICLE — L'ARTICLE §§ 1–6 367
THE NOUN — LE NOM §§ 7–8 375
THE ADJECTIVE — L'ADJECTIF §§ 10–18 378
THE ADVERB — L'ADVERBE §§ 19–22 392
THE PRONOUN — LE PRONOM §§ 23–40 398

THE PREPOSITION — LA PRÉPOSITION §§ 41–45 . . . 420
THE VERB — LE VERBE §§ 46–89
I. THE ORGANIZATION OF THE FRENCH VERB — L'ORGANISATION DU VERBE FRANÇAIS §§ 46–48 . . 426
II. THE FORMATION AND USE OF TENSES AND OTHER PARTS OF THE VERB — LA FORMATION ET L'EMPLOI DES TEMPS ET DES AUTRES PARTIES DU VERBE §§ 49–87 429
III. SPECIAL TYPES OF VERBS — DES CATEGORIES SPÉCIALES DES VERBES §§ 88–89 470
IV. THE USES OF CERTAIN VERBS — LA FAÇON D'EMPLOYER CERTAINS VERBES §§ 90–94 474
V. THE CONJUGATION OF THE VERB — LA CONJUGAISON DU VERBE § 95 482
MISCELLANY — TRAITS DIVERS §§ 96–97 500

Prononciation

REMARKS ON THE FRENCH LANGUAGE — DIVERSES NOTIONS SUR LA LANGUE FRANÇAISE §§ 1–6 511
PRONUNCIATION — PRONONCIATION §§ 7–12 515
THE PRONUNCIATION OF THE FRENCH LETTERS — LA PRONONCIATION DES LETTRES FRANÇAISES §§ 13–18 . 523
PRONUNCIATION BY PHONETIC SYMBOLS — LA PRONONCIATION PAR LES SYMBOLES PHONÉTIQUES §§ 19–23 . 532

Vocabulaire

THE FAVORITE MISTAKES — LES FAUTES FAVORITES . . 541
ENGLISH-FRENCH VOCABULARY — VOCABULAIRE ANGLAIS-FRANÇAIS 547
FRENCH-ENGLISH VOCABULARY — VOCABULAIRE FRANÇAIS-ANGLAIS 563

Index 617

Table des illustrations

	entre
La Seine traverse Paris La France est sûrement très différente de l'Amérique (*Place du Tertre, Montmartre*) Les montagnes sont des barrières naturelles (*scène dans les Alpes*)	2–3
Même les costumes bretons sont différents des costumes des autres régions de France (*femme bretonne*) Les châteaux du moyen âge sont des forteresses (*château d'Ussé*) Les châteaux de la Renaissance sont des édifices élégants de style italien (*château de Chenonceaux*) Les rues étroites de Rouen sont très pittoresques (*la rue du Gros-Horloge*) Les maisons de Rouen sont de style typiquement normand	34–35
En Provence beaucoup de villes conservent des traces de l'ancienne civilisation romaine A Cannes se trouvent de charmantes plages et d'élégants hôtels (*la plage à Cannes*) Un nombre considérable de Parisiens ont une maison à la campagne Dimanche je vais jouer avec mon ami Pierre	66–67
Je vais à une école de garçons; Marie va à une école de filles — Ouvres vos livres et choisissez un poème pour notre leçon — Moreau, apportez au bureau le livre que vous cachez Les jeunes filles ne vont pas aux mêmes lycées que les jeunes gens Les élèves se réunissent dans ces cours pendant les heures de récréation Mais comme le tabac et les allumettes sont des monopoles de l'État ainsi que les timbres, on peut acheter des timbres dans un bureau de tabac	82–83

	entre
Ensuite, j'entre dans une cabine téléphonique pour donner un coup de téléphone à un camarade	82–83
Tout le long du boulevard se trouvent des cafés typiquement français (*café des Champs-Élysées*)	114–115
Chaque quartier de Paris a ses cafés (*le café de Flore à Saint-Germain des Prés*)	
Les plus grands s'amusent avec leurs petits bateaux au bord du bassin du jardin (*scène au jardin du Luxembourg*)	
Les étudiants et les étudiantes viennent travailler leurs cours dans ce jardin agréable et calme (*scène typique au jardin du Luxembourg*)	
Les Facultés des Lettres et des Sciences se trouvent dans un grand bâtiment près du Boulevard Saint-Michel; la Sorbonne	
La Sorbonne n'est que le bâtiment où se trouvent les Facultés des Lettres et des Sciences (*cour de la Sorbonne*)	
Nous sommes allés attendre un autobus. Bientôt il en est arrivé un (*arrêt près des quais de la Seine*)	
Nous sommes montés dans le train, qui est parti à huit heures dix	146–147
Cette forêt n'est pas une forêt comme les autres (*forêt de Fontainebleau*)	
Nous sommes enfin arrivés devant le château de Fontainebleau, superbe construction de la Renaissance française	
Beaucoup de voyageurs attendaient le train. Quelques-uns d'entre eux causaient, d'autres se promenaient le long du quai	
Dans chaque compartiment il y avait deux banquettes, l'une en face de l'autre	
Strasbourg est une très belle ville (*Place de la Cathédrale, Strasbourg*)	
La Tour Eiffel, construction métallique moderne	
De sa loge la concierge peut surveiller tous les gens qui arrivent	178–179
Il y a partout à Paris des stations de métro, dont l'entrée se trouve sur le trottoir	
. . . le métro, train souterrain qui permet de voyager sans être gêné par la circulation de la rue	

	entre
Nous nous sommes mis à table et le garçon nous a apporté la carte (*au restaurant «A l'orée du Bois»*) Tout le long de la Seine il y a de nombreuses boîtes qui contiennent de vieux livres et des gravures anciennes La Place de la Concorde est une des plus vastes et des plus belles du monde L'avenue des Champs-Élysées est large et animée De nombreuses voitures montent et descendent l'avenue (*vue des Champs-Élysées*)	178–179
C'est un des musées les plus célèbres du monde (*le Louvre*) On y voit des tables de tous les pays et de toutes les époques (*salle du Louvre*) C'est une magnifique cathédrale de l'époque gothique (*Notre-Dame de Paris vue de l'autre côté de la Seine*) Du sommet de la cathédrale nous pouvions voir des monuments de tous les côtés et, à nos pieds, la Seine qui traverse toute la ville (*Paris vu de Notre-Dame*) Nous somme passés devant un grand édifice très ancien: le Palais de Justice —Ça? Cette église toute blanche qui domine la ville des hauteurs de Montmarte? C'est le Sacré-Cœur.	194–195
Les jeunes gens partent souvent en groupe à la mer ou à la montagne Certains d'entre eux passent la nuit dans des établissements réservés spécialement aux jeunes gens Une robe, un manteau ou un chapeau qui vient de Paris a un chic qui ne se trouve nulle part ailleurs Le Tour de France est la course la plus populaire que nous ayons Cette salle, appelée la Galerie des Glaces, est célèbre dans l'histoire (*château de Versailles*) Ces jardins à la française sont dessinés géométriquement (*jardins à Versailles avec le Grand Trianon au fond*) Généralement, le prêtre fait un sermon sur la beauté du mariage Les enfants poussent des cris de joie en voyant ce spectacle et vont prendre leurs jouets dans le sapin (*le matin de Noël*)	210–211

Table des cartes

La France est un pays 1

L'Europe est un continent 4

La France est formée de plaines et de montagnes 7

La Seine est le fleuve le plus connu à l'étranger, mais la Loire est le fleuve le plus long de France 14

La Seine, la Garonne et l'estuaire de la Loire ont une importance économique considérable 21

La France se compose de plusieurs régions qui correspondent à peu près aux anciennes provinces d'autrefois 23

La Bretagne est bordée par la mer au nord, à l'ouest et au sud . 24

La Touraine est une province située à environ deux cents kilomètres au sud-ouest de Paris 27

La Touraine est la région des châteaux de la Loire 28

La Normandie est une des provinces les plus intéressantes du nord-ouest de la France 31

Le sud de la France s'appelle le Midi 35

Grenoble se trouve dans les Alpes, pas loin de l'Italie 56

Il y a quatre-vingt-dix départements dans la France métropolitaine . 80

La région située autour de Paris est l'ancienne province de l'Île-de-France 81

Le Boulevard Saint-Michel est le centre du Quartier latin . . . 119

A la fin de la guerre franco-allemande de 1870, l'Allemagne a enlevé à la France toute l'Alsace et le tiers nord-est de la Lorraine . . 141

Paris a de très nombreux quartiers et chacun d'eux a son charme tout particulier 172

L'Avenue des Champs-Élysées mène de la Place de l'Étoile à la Place de la Concorde 188

C'est l'île de la Cité. C'est là que Paris a été fondé 198

Dès le 17 juin 1940, la France fut coupée en deux parties: la zone occupée par les Allemandes et la zone libre, sous l'autorité du gouvernement du maréchal Pétain à Vichy 244

Le Tour de France est la course la plus populaire que nous ayons . . 273

Au milieu du dix-septième siècle, la France possédait une grande partie du Canada et tout le centre des États-Unis 343

Table des chansons

Chevaliers de la Table Ronde 19

L'Alouette 38

Jean Vagona 55

Frère Jacques 111

Le coucou 128

Au clair de la lune 212

La Marseillaise 234

Le petit navire 256

Minuit Chrétiens 334

Il est né le divin Enfant 365

La Seine 366

ACKNOWLEDGMENTS FOR PHOTOGRAPHS

The sources of the photographs are listed in the order in which they appear in the book, by inserts.

INSERT 1

Ewing Galloway, N.Y.; Berko, Pix; H. Armstrong Roberts; H. Armstrong Roberts; French Government Tourist Office; Samuel Chamberlain

INSERT 2

Philip Gendreau; French Government Tourist Office; Pan American World Airways; Yvon; French Cultural Services; Suquet, Institut Pédagogique National

INSERT 3

Landau, Rapho Guillumette; Suquet, Institut Pédagogique National; Suquet, Institut Pédagogique National; Allard, Institut Pédagogique National; Allard, Institut Pédagogique National; Niepce, Rapho; Suquet, Institut Pédagogique National

INSERT 4

Agip, from Black Star; Viollet; Massar, Pix; Viollon, Rapho; Yvon; Viollet; Ciccione, Rapho

INSERT 5

S.N.C.F.; H. Armstrong Roberts; Samuel Chamberlain; S.N.C.F.; S.N.C.F.; Lechner; Pan American World Airways

INSERT 6

Dumas, Rapho; Schall, Pix; Viollet; Viollet; Viollet; Belzeaux, Rapho Guillumette; Ciccione, Rapho Guillumette; French Government Tourist Office

INSERT 7

Trans World Airlines; Philip Gendreau, N.Y.; Samuel Chamberlain; Pan American World Airways; Belzeaux, Rapho Guillumette; H. Armstrong Roberts

INSERT 8

Suquet, Institut Pédagogique National; Suquet, Institut Pédagogique National; Jack Robinson; Jack Robinson; Paris Match; Ewing Galloway, N.Y.; Schall, Pix; Viollet; Marinier, Rapho

Introduction to the Teacher

Learning a foreign language means many things. It means learning to read rapidly and accurately in the language without recourse to translation; it means learning to speak the language fluently; it means acquiring a good pronunciation, it means being able to write the language correctly; it means understanding the language when it is spoken; it means gaining knowledge and appreciation of the culture and the way of life of the people who use the language. In addition, it means learning something of the nature of language itself and improving one's understanding of English vocabulary and grammar through the study of the foreign language.

If the study of a foreign language is to produce the multiple values which give it an indispensable place in the curriculum as a part of a liberal education, it cannot be simply a course in grammar-translation or only a course in elementary French conversation, or even just a course in the rapid reading of French. To earn a right to be a requirement in the curriculum of a liberal arts college, that course must strive to lead the student into all of the above-mentioned language activities.

Beginning French — A Cultural Approach is designed to enable the teachers who use it to develop all of these skills and appreciations. It contains sufficient vocabulary and syntax for a two-semester college course or for the first two years of high school work. Lessons 1–50 present the basic principles of French grammar; Lessons 51–60 provide a concise review of the materials covered in the preceding lessons. Some teachers find it practical to cover Lessons 51–60 at the end of the first-year college course; others prefer to use them, along with reading texts, during the second-year college course.

The Reading Material

Foreign languages are more easily retained if the fundamentals are presented in rhythmic form, such as poetry; or with melody or sound, such as in songs; or with ideas expressed in meaningful sentences. For this last reason and others, the lessons of this text present the grammar and vocabulary in complete and related sentences embodying information about France — her geography, history, and civilization.

The descriptions given in the lessons are not intended to be complete. They are general outlines which the student can fill in as he learns more of France, and her language, literature, and culture. The lessons begin with present French conditions, which are more familiar to the student than past ones. This procedure of studying the present before the past simplifies the teaching of tenses, since the student uses only the present in the beginning lessons. Many teachers introduce contemporary events in France as collateral material to supplement that in the text. And wisely do they do this, for never before have students been so interested in the peoples of the world as at present. They are realizing what past generations of Americans did not realize: that we cannot understand the world as it is without some knowledge of the countries and people of the world.

The material in this book, then, is timely and to most students; more interesting than simple, trite stories or the dry descriptions of the familiar classroom. Teachers who have found difficulty in stimulating classroom discussion in the foreign language might well try using factual material about foreign countries. Experience shows that this type of material can be used very effectively for conversation from the very first day of the foreign language course. When an elementary foreign language course can give students data which relate history, past and present, to political science and to social and economic problems at the same time that it develops language skills, such a course becomes infinitely more interesting to both teacher and students and is lifted considerably from the uninteresting level of the chair, the table, the dog, and the cat.

VOCABULARY

The vocabulary has been carefully chosen and has an excellent correlation with the French word-counts. Cognates have been included freely, especially in the earlier lessons, since, if used correctly, they help the student grasp meanings of words, the concepts, without recourse to his native tongue. Cognates give the student a sense of power to comprehend the foreign language from the very beginning of his study. This sense of power is stimulating to all students and is most helpful to those who have been led to believe that the study of a foreign language is difficult or boring.

The lesson vocabularies are listed in the *Supplément.* This is to encourage the students to derive the meaning of the new words from the context rather than from immediate consultation of the vocabulary. In preparing this Third Edition, we asked our students if they preferred to have the lesson vocabulary included in the lesson proper. To our surprise, they replied: "No, we like the vocabularies as they are, together in one place, where we can review them easily for tests."

Cognates are listed in the lesson vocabulary without English equivalents. This obliges the student to make the comparison between the two languages and calls to his attention the fact that a large number of words are similar in French and English. It also enables instructors to make special word and pronunciation study of such words.

Grammar

The grammar is presented inductively in carefully graded lessons. For reference and for those who wish to approach grammar analytically, a fairly complete presentation of elementary syntax is to be found in the separate section entitled *Grammaire.* There the material is formulated topically, so that the teacher may develop as little or as much of the grammar as he wishes. Grammatical terms are defined and comparisons are made to English grammar. Grammatical principles are illustrated by examples taken from the reading lessons in which they are introduced. The *Index* gives easy reference to any grammatical point. The questions on grammar at the end of each lesson emphasize the more important syntactical items of the lesson and guide the student to that part of the *Grammaire* where he may consult the rules dealing with these facts. Points of only passing interest are mentioned in the footnotes with a reference to the *Grammaire.*

Special care has been taken to introduce verb forms gradually. In order that the learner may have some opportunity to become acquainted with other aspects of the language and to develop some fluency in their use before the problem of verb inflection is raised, only the third person singular and plural of the present tense are used in the first ten lessons. The most commonly used tenses — the present, the imperfect, and the compound past — are introduced in Lessons 11–30, each in a series of lessons which permit the students to assimilate their forms gradually. The other tenses of the indicative are presented in Lessons 31–45, the subjunctive in Lessons 46–50. The simple past and the imperfect subjunctive are introduced merely for recognition, not for active use.

Pronunciation

A tape recording of the text of each lesson read with intervals of silence for pupil repetition is available for those who wish to teach pronunciation through imitation. For those who wish to study the French sounds formally, the section entitled *Prononciation* treats French pronunciation (a) by conventional French spelling; (b) by the symbols of the International Phonetic Alphabet. The discussions of the various sounds are accompanied by appropriate examples taken from words used in the early lessons of the book so as to permit a close correlation between the pronunciation drills and the first lessons of the text. Special attention has been given to the various types of intonation patterns.

The pronunciation of the words in the French-English vocabulary are indicated in phonetic script. These transcriptions, which were carefully checked by M. and Mme Léon of the Institut de Phonétique in Paris, give the current French pronunciations of the words. Linguistic phenomena such as *harmonisation vocalique* have been recognized. Transcriptions such as *aimer* [eme] and *saisir* [sezir] are not errors but rather attempts to indicate the changes in French pronunciation which are taking place.

Oral-Aural Work and Pattern Practice

With the increasing realization of the necessity for training linguists and with the advent of the language laboratory, in recent years emphasis in language training has shifted back to the acquisition of oral-aural skills. From its inception, *Beginning French* has always provided opportunities for oral-aural practice, but this Third Edition has increased these possibilities, partly through additional exercises in the text itself, partly through the recording on tapes of all the material in each lesson which lends itself to effective laboratory use. Teachers may find it helpful to consider these possibilities for oral drill and pattern practice in the various parts of each lesson.

1. *The reading material*

Every reading lesson lends itself admirably to classroom discussion in French. Adult in the level of ideas but sufficiently elementary in their vocabulary and grammar, these lessons furnish abundant material for discussion or serve as a point of departure for conversation on related topics. About two-thirds of the lessons are expository in nature, which is desirable for the development of reading skill, about one-third of them are in dialog form and contain current conversational expressions.

2. *Questions*

A series of questions in French on the reading texts permits the student to test his comprehension of the lesson. The questions of each lesson have been recorded along with answers in the vocabulary of the text. Students can listen to these recordings over and over in order to develop their comprehension of the vocabulary of the lesson in question.

3. *All-French exercises*

Each lesson contains a number of all-French exercises designed to afford drill on the grammatical principles introduced into the lesson. These exercises are most valuable if the student, after working them out, goes over them orally until he can read them without hesitation. A number of these exercises constitute, in effect, pattern practice. Such exercises have been recorded with intervals of silence. The student is told what to do. He then hears the sentence in its original form, records his own version of the changed form, then hears the corrected version.

4. *Conversation*

One of the most effective devices for developing conversation skill is the indirect question. For instance:

Teacher: Monsieur Smith, demandez à monsieur Jones où *il va* ce soir.

Smith: Monsieur Jones, où *allez-vous* ce soir?

Jones: *Je vais* à la bibliothèque ce soir.

All the students in the class hear the basic pattern three times. But each time, the verb form changes, and it changes from the nature of speech, thus motivating the learning of the changes.

Each lesson of this edition contains a *Conversation* consisting of four indirect questions, which may be used verbatim in the classroom to start the indirect question period. The teacher can then ask other indirect questions, based on the text or on related subjects. The repetition and greater student activity afforded by the indirect question make it a most valuable device for developing conversational skill.

The *Conversations* of Lessons 51–60 are recorded for laboratory use.

5. *Supplementary Exercise B*

In the *Supplément* there is a special English-to-French Exercise B consisting of sentences containing common speech patterns and designed to give the learner an opportunity to learn these patterns through frequent repetition of them in meaningful material. The sentences are so constructed that the patterns are often repeated with slight variations from one sentence to the next. To be of greatest value, this exercise should be prepared by the student orally. He should look at the English sentence but read it over in French again and again until he can say it rapidly and without hesitation. Such preparation will make it possible for him to master the patterns to the point where they will become automatic.

The Organization of the Lessons and the Reviews

Beginning French is a "longer grammar." Actually, a "longer grammar" is not necessarily any longer than a "shorter grammar." It simply divides the essential grammar and vocabulary into more convenient learning units. The "longer grammar" has the tremendous advantage of concentrating the attention of the learner on one or two new grammatical points and on a limited number of new words in any given lesson.

In colleges where the overwhelming majority of students are non-majors and where recognition knowledge of many grammatical points is sufficient, the lessons may be assigned at the rate of one a day, provided that the teacher does not try to cover intensively each point in the reading lesson and each grammatical detail. Schools desiring to impart a more thorough knowledge of the language may, of course, spend two or more days on each lesson.

Reviews occur after each five lessons. These reviews are divided into *Première partie,* which summarizes the cultural content of the preceding lessons, and *Deuxième partie,* which provides exercises involving grammatical principles in those lessons. This division permits the instructor to assign either part separately if he so desires. The review lessons are deliberately limited in length so that teachers who desire can also assign supplementary reading on the same day. Although these reviews come after each five lessons of the text, instructors who prefer can defer the review lessons until the end of the semester or omit them altogether.

The lessons fall into three natural divisions: Lessons 1–30, which introduce the most used tenses (present, imperfect, compound past) and the other commonest grammatical principles: Lessons 31–50, which present the other tenses of the indicative, the subjunctive, and the rest of the basic grammar; and Lessons 51–60, which review the grammar already presented.

It is advisable to supplement the lessons of *Beginning French* with selections from a reader. Teachers may find it advantageous, for instance, to have a period of several weeks of reading after covering the first thirty lessons of the text. Too fast a coverage of the grammar of a language is likely to result in grammatical indigestion. Whenever the students begin to have trouble absorbing grammatical principles at the rate of a lesson a day, the remedy is to intersperse a series of lessons from a reader.

Method

Beginning French lends itself to the various methods of teaching modern languages. For the proponent of the reading method, it has abundant connected and carefully graded reading material; because of the meaningful content of this material, the text is especially suitable for courses which prepare the student to read French rapidly. The teacher who prefers the conversational approach will find many lessons written in dialog form and much to talk about in the informational reading texts of every lesson. There are abundant all-French exercises for those who use only French in class and English-to-French exercises in the *Supplément* for those who prefer that type of work. For schools which have language laboratories there is a complete set of tapes which afford opportunities for pronunciation drill and pattern practice.

This text has been used for many years by the authors and their colleagues with a method which emphasizes varied classroom activities that permit the participation during the class hour of a maximum number of students in all forms of linguistic activity. A short description of that method may be of interest to French teachers.

The First Day

On the very first day of the first semester, although the students have never before seen or heard French and have no book, the class is kept for the entire hour, and the students hear, speak, and write the language they are about to learn.

On entering the class, the instructor obtains the names of his students, writes on the board the title of the textbook, speaks for a very short time on the importance of French as a language, and then sends all the students to the board. He now proceeds as follows:

Instructor: Paris est la capitale de la France. *Répétez.*
Class (in unison): Paris est la capitale de la France.
Instructor: Écrivez.

Everyone writes as much as he can of the sentence. The instructor chooses a sentence with some errors for correction. Perhaps the student has written: *Paree e la capital de la France.* The instructor points out that the first word is written *Paris* but pronounced *Pari,* that the second word is written *est* but pronounced *è,* etc. He asks that all students correct all errors and calls on several of them to read the sentence in French. He then continues the dictation in the same way.

Instructor: Paris est situé sur la Seine. *Répétez.*
Class: Paris est situé sur la Seine.
Instructor: Écrivez.

Everyone writes the sentence. The instructor corrects the sentence of one student, explaining that an acute accent over an *e* indicates a different pronunciation. He then has the class pronounce *sur* in unison and then each pupil individually, to make sure that the *u* is being pronounced accurately.

Instructor: La Seine traverse Paris. *Répétez.*
Class: La Seine traverse Paris.
Instructor: Écrivez. (etc.)

This procedure is continued with each sentence in the first lesson until about twelve minutes of the end of the hour. During the course of the dictation, the instructor briefly explains the existence of two genders and the difference between *le* and *la.*

The students are now sent to their seats, and the first lesson is assigned for the following day. The students are directed to (1) write out the answers to the *Questions* in complete French sentences; (2) do all the exercises, underlining the words they supply in the blanks; (3) go to the language laboratory to listen to the recording of Lesson 1. They are told to go to the board at the beginning of the second class hour and to write on it, in French, a summary of the first lesson from memory.

The remainder of the first hour is spent on questions and answers in French, such as: *Quelle est la capitale de la France? Où est situé Paris?* If he feels that the class understands, the instructor does not hesitate to ask other questions in the same pattern, such as: *Quelle est la capitale du Canada? Où est situé Chicago?*

The Following Days

Each day's work starts with a summary of the lesson in French on the blackboard. The students are encouraged to arrive before the bell rings so that everyone is working at the board at the beginning of the hour. The instructor goes from student to student, correcting errors, indicating in some way how far he has read, so that he begin at that point on his second round of the class. He cannot, of course, spend much time explaining to any individual during this correction period. Students must not write from notes, and the composition period *must not* last for more than ten minutes after the bell has rung, for students tend to grow restless.

The instructor then has the students erase their résumés and he dictates a sentence. The students repeat it after him, then write it. The instructor corrects the sentences of one or two students, and the students correct their sentences from these models. Sentences are dictated at normal speaking speed and in complete units rather than groups of words. Students do not start to write the sentence until they have all repeated the sentence aloud in unison. Sometimes the dictation is used merely to develop comprehension of the vocabulary of the lessons. Other times, it is used very effectively to teach the grammar of the lesson. For instance, when the class is studying the compound past, sentences may be dictated in the present, after which the class can rewrite them in the compound past. The dictation period lasts from ten to twenty minutes per day.

The students then take their seats for the correction of the exercises. This correction is limited to about five minutes of the class hour. The teacher, *not the students,* reads the correct answers while the students correct their errors. The teacher never has each student read one sentence, filling in the blank, since such an activity would take much valuable time which can better be used for conversation and pronunciation drill.

Then follows a conversation period. Various devices are used to develop fluency in the use of the lesson. Among these are the question and answer, the indirect question described on page xxi, having each student in the class volunteer to give some sentence from the text, and having one student start an oral summary of the reading material, which summary is continued by other students. The conversation period is also effectively used for pattern practice. In teaching pronoun objects, for instance, the instructor may announce to the class that he will ask questions with noun objects and that the students are to answer the questions in the same pattern but using a pronoun object.

The last part of the hour is usually devoted to reading aloud. Going around the class rapidly and as often as time permits, each student in turn reads one or two sentences. When a student makes an error, the teacher writes the mispronounced word or sound on the board and briefly drills the entire class on that word or sound. In the introductory course, whatever the lesson assigned, each day the class begins the oral reading at Lesson 1 until every student can read Lesson 1 with correct sounds and intonation. Students develop good reading habits much more readily when using material with which they are very familiar than by using the relatively unfamiliar material in the lesson of the day.

Introduction to the Student

You have often seen French expressions in books and newspapers. You have heard that French is the polite language all over the world, the speech of diplomats. You know that many scientific treatises are written in French, even by scholars whose native language is not French.

You are now to begin the study of that language. Once you have learned French, you will find a new world opened to you. You will discover that your own English language becomes clearer by a knowledge of French vocabulary and French grammar. You will have access to French literature, which is as considerable as your own and distinctly different. You will gain a better understanding of France and of the French people.

French is one of the easiest of foreign languages for us to read, because many French and English words are almost identical, while many others are so similar in form that you will have no trouble in recognizing them. In fact, Alexandre Dumas once said, "English is only French mispronounced."

How to Learn French

Your French book consists of sixty lessons. Each lesson is divided into a reading selection, a set of questions based on this selection, various *devoirs* or exercises, a special set of conversational questions, labeled *Conversation,* and the *Grammaire* or grammar questions. At the end of each tenth lesson is a *Supplément* containing vocabularies and the new verb forms introduced in each lesson.

Various procedures might be used to master these lessons. The following will go far in giving you a command of the language.

First, go over the reading selection to grasp the sense of the material. At this first reading, do not look up the words you do not know and do not translate into English. Concentrate on discovering what the lesson is about. Many words appearing for the first time will disclose their meaning through their use in the sentence (by their context). Now read the selection a second time, turning to the lesson vocabulary in the *Supplément* to find the meaning of the words you do not know or cannot determine from their use in the sentence. Words not in the lesson vocabulary must have occurred in some earlier lesson, but you can also find them in the French-English vocabulary at the end of the book. During the second reading, note any new constructions that appear and try to discover from their use in the lesson just what they mean. If you are unable to do this, turn to the grammar questions at the end of this lesson and try to answer them. If you cannot answer them from your observation of the constructions as they are used in the reading selection, look them up in the section of the *Grammaire* indicated after the question. If you have trouble understanding the grammatical terms used, you will find these terms explained at the beginning of the section in which they are taken up.

Go over the reading selection as many times as is necessary in order to understand it in French without the intervention of English. If this seems hard, do it the more often in order to develop the habit. No one ever reads a language easily or fluently by translating it. One reads it easily and fluently only by reading it in the original language and understanding it without transferring it into English. But do not be satisfied with your preparation of the lesson until you know the meaning of every word in the reading selection.

Study this material until you can write a summary of it in French or give one orally. It helps to copy the reading selection in French. Above all, *never write the English meaning of the words in your book.* Such English words serve as a crutch which hinders rather than helps language learning.

Next, turn to the *Questions.* Read each question aloud and answer it orally in French. Always use a complete sentence for your answer. Go over these questions again and again until you can give the answers rapidly without reference to the lesson itself.

Next, skip down to the last section of the lesson, the *Grammaire.* If you have noted new constructions in your reading selection, you will already know the answers to many of these questions. For the others, turn to the section of the *Grammaire* (pages 367–508) indicated by the references in parentheses after the questions and study the topic in question. Do not be satisfied until you *thoroughly understand and know the facts involved* in the discussion of each topic. For verb forms, consult the pages indicated in the *Supplément.* Always learn these verb forms before you finish your preparation of the lesson.

Now you are ready for the exercises or *devoirs.* Read carefully the French directions above each exercise. In reading them, if you have any difficulty which is not explained in the footnotes, look up the terms you do not know in the French-English vocabulary at the end of the book. Study the model sentences given after the directions and the examples given in the *Grammaire.* These sentences will show you how the exercise is to be done. Write your *devoirs* in a notebook. Copy the entire sentence, underlining the words with which you fill in the blanks. *Do not write in the textbook itself.* Keep it clean for later practice. When you have written your exercises, put them out of sight and now read the same exercises orally from the textbook. Do not be satisfied with your preparation of the lesson until you can read these exercises rapidly and without hesitation.

To prepare the *Conversation,* first read the question as it is in that exercise. Next, pretend to ask the question of someone. Then answer that question aloud yourself. Go over the *Conversation* until you can ask and answer the questions without hesitation.

If your school has recordings of the lessons in its language laboratory, use them every day from the very first lesson. To develop a good pronunciation, repeat during the intervals of silence the sentences or phrases of the reading selection as read by the native speaker. Imitate both his intonation and his manner of making the individual sounds. If your laboratory has play-back equipment, compare your own reading of the lesson with that of the native speaker, note the difference in sound and intonation, and in subsequent readings, bring your sounds and intonation into line with his. Do not be satisfied with your laboratory preparation until you can repeat the reading selection in such a way that it sounds French. To develop comprehension, listen to the recording of the reading selection and to that of the questions and answers until you can understand them readily. To fix patterns of common speech, repeat the sentences of the recorded exercises, making the indicated changes, and then compare them with the correct forms, as given immediately afterward by the native speaker. Go over these exercises again and again until you can read them without hesitation. As far as possible, do these exercises orally without looking at your book, so as to train the ear. Also, use the recordings with intervals of silence for dictation practice. Listen to the reading of the sentence or phrase, then write as much of it as possible during the interval. Replay the recording as often as necessary in order to write the complete reading selection. Then compare what you have written with the printed version in the textbook.

Be sure to learn each lesson thoroughly before going on to the next. If you are having difficulty with any lesson, it is probably because you have not completely mastered the preceding lessons. It is an excellent idea, in that case, to go back to the very first lesson, to read it over for content, being sure that you know every word in it, and to work out its exercises orally; then go over every subsequent lesson until you locate the first one you have not mastered thoroughly. Rework that lesson until you are sure of every word and construction in it, and then continue working out the subsequent lessons in the same manner until you reach the current lesson. To improve your pronunciation, it is likewise an excellent idea to go back to the recordings of Lesson 1 and to work on the reading material of each lesson until you are satisfied that your pronunciation of it is good. By mastering each lesson thoroughly, you assure yourself of a solid basis for all further work in the language you are studying.

La France

Paris est la capitale de la France. Paris est situé sur la Seine. La Seine traverse Paris. Calais est dans le nord de la France. Calais est situé sur la mer du Nord. Strasbourg est dans l'est de la France. Strasbourg est situé sur le Rhin. Marseille est dans le sud de la France. Marseille est sur la Méditerranée. Brest est dans l'ouest de la France. Brest est situé sur l'Atlantique.

La France est un pays

Questions

1. Quelle est la capitale de la France? 2. Quelle est la capitale des[1] États-Unis? 3. Où est situé Paris? 4. Où est situé Washington? 5. Où est Bâton-Rouge? 6. Dans quelle partie de la France est Marseille? 7. Dans quelle partie des États-Unis est San Francisco? 8. Où est situé Strasbourg? 9. Où est Philadelphie? 10. Dans quelle partie de la France est situé Calais? 11. Dans quelle partie des États-Unis est situé Denver? 12. Où est situé Chicago? 13. Quelle est la capitale de l'Ohio? 14. Où est Boston?

Devoirs

A. *Remplacez*[2] *les tirets par le mot convenable indiqué à droite.*[3]
EXEMPLE: Chicago est dans le —— des États-Unis. Chicago est dans le *nord* des États-Unis.

1. Washington est situé dans l' —— des États-Unis. 2. San Francisco est dans l' —— des États-Unis. 3. Atlanta est situé dans le —— des États-Unis. 4. Dans quelle —— des États-Unis est situé Détroit? 5. Indianapolis est la —— de l'Indiana. 6. Montgomery est —— capitale de l'Alabama. 7. —— est la capitale de l'Illinois? 8. Memphis est situé —— le Mississippi. 9. Le Mississippi —— les États-Unis. 10. Paris est —— dans le nord de la France. 11. —— est situé Brest? 12. Calais est situé —— le nord de la France. 13. Dans quelle partie —— la France est situé Bordeaux? 14. Paris —— situé sur la Seine. 15. Chicago est —— dans le nord des États-Unis.

a. capitale
b. dans
c. de
d. est
e. la
f. nord
g. où
h. ouest
i. partie
j. quelle
k. situé
l. sud
m. sur
n. traverse

[1] The word *des* is a contraction of *de les*.

[2] *Fill in the blanks by the proper word listed at the right.*

[3] In this exercise and in similar exercises in other lessons, you are to supply words which will complete the meaning of the sentences. These will always be words used in the lesson for the first time. For your convenience and for the sake of uniformity in correcting, an alphabetical list of the words to be used is given to the right of the exercise. This list contains not only all words to be used in the exercise but also several words which do not fit into any of the sentences. Do not use words which are not in this list, even though they make good sense in the sentence.

La Seine traverse Paris

La France est sûrement très différente de l'Amérique

Les montagnes sont des barrières naturelles

B. Remplacez[1] *les tirets par* ***le, la, ou l'.*** EXEMPLE: Calais est situé sur —— mer du Nord. Calais est situé sur *la* mer du Nord.

1. Washington est —— capitale des États-Unis. 2. Chicago est situé dans —— nord des États-Unis. 3. Paris est situé sur —— Seine. 4. Strasbourg est situé sur —— Rhin. 5. Marseille est dans —— sud de —— France. 6. Brest est situé dans —— ouest de la France sur —— Atlantique. 7. New York est situé dans —— est des États-Unis sur —— Atlantique. 8. Los Angeles est situé dans —— ouest des États-Unis. 9. Calais est situé dans —— nord de —— France.

CONVERSATION

1. Demandez à Monsieur[2] A. où est Marseille. 2. Demandez à Monsieur B. où est situé Paris. 3. Demandez à Monsieur C. quelle est la capitale de la France. 4. Demandez à Monsieur D. dans quelle partie de la France est situé Brest.

VOCABULAIRE — PAGE 41

GRAMMAIRE[3, 4]

1. What three ways of expressing *the* do you find in this lesson? When is each used? (§ 1 A)

2. What two genders are there in French? (§ 7 A)

3. With what types of geographical names is the definite article used in French but ordinarily omitted in English? (§ 4 C)

[1] Remplacez les tirets par *Fill in the blanks with*

[2] The word *Monsieur* is used for the sake of convenience. Supply *Madame* or *Mademoiselle* where applicable.

[3] The reference after each question indicates the paragraph in the ***Grammaire*** (beginning on page 367) in which the answer to the grammatical question may be found.

[4] Be sure to read the *Introduction to the Student,* and turn to page 41 to get acquainted with the *Supplément* to Lesson 1.

DEUXIÈME LEÇON

Les continents

L'Europe est un continent. L'Afrique est aussi un continent. L'Europe est un petit continent. L'Afrique est un grand continent.

La France est un pays. La France est grande. La Belgique est aussi un pays. Mais la Belgique est petite. La France et la Belgique sont en Europe. L'Espagne, le Portugal et l'Italie sont aussi en Europe. Madrid est la capitale de l'Espagne. Rome est la capitale de l'Italie. Rome est une grande ville.

L'Europe est un continent

La Russie est un très grand pays. Une partie de la Russie est située en Europe. Mais une grande partie de la Russie est en Asie.

L'Amérique du Nord est un grand continent. Les États-Unis sont en Amérique du Nord. Le Canada et le Mexique sont aussi en Amérique du Nord.

Questions

1. Est-ce que l'Europe est un continent? (Oui, monsieur, madame, mademoiselle, l'Europe est un continent.) 2. Est-ce que l'Afrique est un grand continent? 3. Est-ce que la France est un pays? 4. Est-ce que la Belgique est un petit pays? 5. Est-ce que la France et la Belgique sont en Europe? 6. Est-ce que le Portugal et l'Italie sont aussi en Europe? 7. Quelle est la capitale de l'Espagne? 8. Est-ce que la capitale de l'Italie est une grande ville? 9. Où est située une grande partie de la Russie? 10. Est-ce que les États-Unis sont un grand pays? 11. Est-ce que le Canada et le Mexique sont en Amérique du Nord? 12. Est-ce qu'une partie de la Russie est située en Europe?

Devoirs

A. Remplacez les tirets par le mot convenable indiqué à droite.

1. Le Mexique est un——. 2. Les États-Unis ——un grand pays. 3. Est-ce que la Russie est aussi——grande? 4. La Belgique est un——pays situé en Europe. 5. Est-ce que le Canada et le Mexique sont——Amérique du Nord? 6. ——, monsieur, le Canada et le Mexique sont en Amérique du Nord. 7. Est-ce que Chicago est une grande——? 8. L'Espagne est en Europe et l'Italie est——en Europe.

a. aussi
b. en
c. grand
d. oui
e. pays
f. petit
g. sont
h. très
i. ville

*B. Remplacez les tirets par **un** ou **une**.*

1. Rome est——ville. 2. L'Afrique est——continent. 3. La Russie est——pays. 4. L'Espagne est——partie de l'Europe. 5. La Méditerranée est——mer.

C. Mettez la forme convenable de l'adjectif indiqué. EXEMPLE: L'Afrique est très (grand). L'Afrique est très *grande.*

1. L'Europe est un (petit) continent. 2. Madrid est une (grand) ville. 3. Dans (quel) partie de la France est situé Strasbourg? 4. La Belgique est (petit). 5. La capitale de la France est (situé) sur la Seine.

6. La Russie est un (grand) pays. 7. (Quel) est le pays situé au nord de la France? 8. Brest est (situé) dans l'ouest de la France.

®[1] *D. Mettez les phrases suivantes à la forme interrogative.* EXEMPLE: Les États-Unis sont en Amérique du Nord. Est-ce que les États-Unis sont en Amérique du Nord?

1. Marseille est sur la Méditerranée. 2. L'Espagne est un grand pays. 3. La Seine traverse Paris et Rouen. 4. L'Afrique est un grand continent. 5. Une[2] partie de la Russie est en Europe. 6. Une grande partie de la Russie est en Asie.

CONVERSATION

1. Demandez à Monsieur E. si la France est un pays. 2. Demandez à Monsieur F. si l'Espagne et le Portugal sont en Europe. 3. Demandez à Monsieur G. si les États-Unis sont en Amérique du Nord. 4. Demandez à Monsieur H. si Rome est une grande ville.

VOCABULAIRE — PAGE 42

GRAMMAIRE[3]

1. What two ways of expressing *a* or *an* do you find in this lesson? When is each used? (§ 3 A)

2. How does the French adjective agree with its noun? (§ 9 A)

3. How do most adjectives form their feminine? (§ 10 A)

4. Note that the feminine form of the interrogative adjective ***quel*** is ***quelle.***

5. What is a conversational way of asking a question in French? (§ 96 A)

6. What is the plural of the verb form ***est?***

7. What form of the verb is used with ***les États-Unis?***

8. Notice that all continents and all countries ending in *-e* (except *le Mexique*) are feminine. All other countries are masculine.

9. The ordinary French word for *in* is ***dans.*** But what word expresses *in* with a continent or a feminine country? (§ 42 B)

[1] An ® indicates that the exercise in question has been recorded.
[2] What happens to *que* in *Est-ce que . . .* when the next word begins with a vowel?
[3] The reference after each question indicates the paragraph in the *Grammaire* (beginning on page 367) in which the answer to the grammatical question will be found. When no reference is given, the answer may be derived from examination of the reading lesson.

La France est formée de plaines et de montagnes

TROISIÈME LEÇON

Les plaines et les montagnes

La France est formée de plaines et de montagnes. Les plaines se trouvent surtout à l'intérieur de la France. Les montagnes se trouvent aux frontières de la France. Les Pyrénées sont des montagnes élevées situées dans le sud-ouest de la France et dans le nord de l'Espagne. Les Pyrénées forment la frontière entre la France et l'Espagne. Les Alpes sont des montagnes très élevées situées dans le sud-est de la France. Les Alpes se trouvent aussi en Suisse et en Italie. Le Jura et les Vosges se trouvent dans l'est de la France. Le Jura et les Vosges sont des montagnes moins élevées que les Alpes et les Pyrénées. Le Massif Central est un grand plateau. Le Massif Central se trouve au centre de la France.

Les États-Unis sont aussi un pays de plaines et de montagnes. Les montagnes des États-Unis se trouvent dans l'est et dans l'ouest du pays. Le centre des États-Unis est une grande plaine. Les montagnes Rocheuses sont dans l'ouest du pays. Les Alleghanys sont dans l'est des États-Unis. Les Alleghanys sont des montagnes moins élevées que les montagnes Rocheuses.

Questions

1. Où se trouvent les plaines de France? 2. Où se trouvent les grandes plaines des États-Unis? 3. Est-ce que les Pyrénées sont des montagnes élevées? 4. Dans quels pays se trouvent les Pyrénées? 5. Dans quels pays se trouvent les Alpes? 6. Dans quelle partie de la France sont situées les Alpes? 7. Citez (Mentionnez) des montagnes élevées de l'ouest des États-Unis. 8. Citez des montagnes moins élevées de l'est des États-Unis. 9. Quel est le grand plateau situé au centre de la France? 10. Dans quelle partie de la France se trouvent le Jura et les Vosges? 11. Dans quelle partie des États-Unis se trouvent les montagnes Rocheuses?

Devoirs

A. Remplacez les tirets par le mot convenable indiqué à droite.

1. Les Andes sont des —— situées dans l'ouest de l'Amérique du Sud. 2. Les Pyrénées forment la frontière —— la France et l'Espagne. 3. Le Jura et les Vosges sont des montagnes —— élevées que les Pyrénées. 4. Dans quelle partie de la France —— trouvent le Jura et les Vosges? 5. Les Alpes sont des montagnes très ——. 6. Les Alpes —— la frontière entre la France et l'Italie. 7. Les plaines se trouvent —— à l'intérieur de la France. 8. Est-ce que les montagnes Rocheuses se trouvent —— l'intérieur des États-Unis? 9. Le Massif Central est moins élevé —— les Pyrénées et les Alpes.

a. à
b. au
c. élevées
d. entre
e. forment
f. intérieur
g. moins
h. montagnes
i. plateau
j. que
k. se
l. surtout

® *B. Mettez au pluriel tous les mots possibles des phrases suivantes.* EXEMPLE: La plaine se trouve à l'intérieur du pays. *Les plaines* se *trouvent* à l'intérieur *des pays.*

1. La ville est située dans la plaine. 2. Quel est le continent situé à l'est de la montagne? 3. Quelle est la montagne située au centre de la plaine? 4. Une montagne forme la frontière du pays. 5. Dans quelle partie du continent est située la plaine? 6. La montagne est une frontière. 7. Quelle est la ville située dans le grand continent? 8. Où se trouve la capitale du pays?

C. Introduisez[1] *dans la phrase les mots entre parenthèses. Faites*[2] *les contractions nécessaires.* EXEMPLE: Les villes (de les) pays sont très grandes. Les villes *des* pays sont très grandes.

1. Paris est la capitale (de la) France. 2. Les montagnes élevées (de les) États-Unis se trouvent dans l'ouest (de le) pays. 3. Les montagnes de la France se trouvent (à les) frontières (de le) pays. 4. La Méditerranée se trouve (à le) sud (de la) France. 5. Est-ce que les montagnes se trouvent (à le) intérieur de l'Espagne? 6. Le Massif Central est situé (à le) centre de la France. 7. Une grande partie (de le) pays est située en Europe. 8. L'Italie est située (à le) sud-est de la France. 9. Strasbourg est une ville (de le) est de la France. 10. Est-ce qu'une partie (de les) villes (de le) pays sont très petites? 11. La Belgique est située (à le) nord (de la) France. 12. La capitale (de le) pays est située (à la) frontière.

CONVERSATION

1. Demandez à Monsieur I. si les Pyrénées sont des montagnes élevées. 2. Demandez à Monsieur J. si le Massif Central se trouve au centre de la France. 3. Demandez à Monsieur K. si les Pyrénées forment la frontière entre la France et l'Espagne. 4. Demandez à Monsieur L. si les plaines se trouvent surtout à l'intérieur de la France.

VOCABULAIRE — PAGES 43–44

GRAMMAIRE

1. What is the plural of *le* and *la?* (§ 1 B)

2. What is the plural of *un* and *une?* How is this plural expressed in English? (§ 3 B)

[1] *Put the words in parentheses into the sentence.*

[2] *Make the necessary contractions.* This includes elisions where the following noun begins with a vowel.

3. How do French nouns generally form their plural? (§ 8 A) What can you say of the plural of nouns whose singular ends in *-s?* (§ 8 B)

4. How do adjectives usually form their plural? (§ 11 A) Give the masculine and feminine singular and plural of ***grand, petit,*** and ***situé.***

5. In French certain forms of ***de*** and the **definite article** and of ***à*** and the **definite article** always contract. What are the contractions of ***de le*** and ***de les?*** of ***à le*** and ***à les?*** (§ 2 A, B)

6. The words ***forme, traverse,*** and ***se trouve*** are third person singular verb-forms. What is the third person plural of these same verb-forms? How does the plural form differ from the singular in pronunciations?

7. What type of action is expressed by verbs such as ***se trouve?*** What grammatical term is used to designate such verbs? (§ 88 E)

QUATRIÈME LEÇON

Les frontières de la France

Les Pyrénées forment la frontière entre la France et l'Espagne. Les Alpes forment la frontière entre la France et l'Italie. Les montagnes sont des barrières naturelles. Elles constituent des frontières excellentes qui sont relativement faciles à défendre.

La Méditerranée limite la France au sud. L'Atlantique limite la France à l'ouest. La Manche limite la France au nord-ouest. Les côtes de la Méditerranée, de la Manche et de l'Atlantique ont des plages magnifiques. Elles ont un intérêt touristique considérable.

Le Rhin est un fleuve qui sépare la France de l'Allemagne. Il forme une partie de la frontière entre les deux pays. Le Rhin est large et profond. Il a une grande importance commerciale. Mais les fleuves sont moins faciles à défendre que les montagnes. Ils sont moins difficiles à traverser que les mers et les montagnes.

La France est limitée au nord par la Belgique et le Luxembourg.

La frontière artificielle entre la France et la Belgique est difficile à défendre. Elle est moins forte que les autres frontières de la France.

Questions

1. La France est-elle un pays? 2. Le Canada et le Mexique sont-ils aussi des pays? 3. Les Pyrénées forment-elles la frontière entre la France et l'Espagne? 4. Les montagnes sont-elles des barrières naturelles? 5. Sont-elles relativement faciles à défendre? 6. La Manche limite-t-elle la France au nord-ouest? 7. Les côtes de la Méditerranée et de l'Atlantique ont-elles des plages? 8. Ont-elles un intérêt touristique? 9. Quelle est la frontière qui sépare le Texas du Mexique? 10. La Méditerranée sépare-t-elle la France de l'Afrique? 11. Le Rhin forme-t-il une partie de la frontière entre la France et l'Allemagne? 12. Le Rhin a-t-il une grande importance commerciale? 13. Les fleuves sont-ils moins faciles à défendre que les montagnes? 14. Par quels pays la France est-elle limitée au nord? 15. Pourquoi la frontière entre la France et la Belgique est-elle difficile à défendre?

Devoirs

A. Remplacez les tirets par le mot convenable indiqué à droite.

1. Le Rio Grande est un —— qui sépare le Mexique du Texas. 2. Les montagnes sont des barrières naturelles; elles sont relativement —— à défendre. 3. Les frontières artificielles sont moins —— que les frontières naturelles; elles sont moins faciles à défendre. 4. La France est un pays d'Europe; le Portugal est un —— pays d'Europe. 5. Les États-Unis sont limités au nord —— le Canada et au sud —— le Mexique. 6. Le Massif Central est un plateau —— se trouve au centre de la France. 7. —— les fleuves sont-ils relativement difficiles à défendre? 8. Les plages —— un intérêt touristique considérable.

a. autre
b. défense
c. difficiles
d. excellente
e. faciles
f. fleuve
g. fortes
h. ont
i. par
j. pourquoi
k. qui
l. relativement
m. séparent

® *B. Remplacez les tirets par **il, elle, ils** ou **elles**.* EXEMPLE: La Russie est très grande. —— est située en Europe et en Asie. *Elle* est située en Europe et en Asie.

1. Le Rhin forme une partie de la frontière entre la France et l'Allemagne. —— a une importance commerciale considérable. 2. La

France est grande. —— est limitée au sud-ouest par l'Espagne. 3. Les montagnes Rocheuses sont très élevées. —— se trouvent dans l'ouest des États-Unis. 4. Des fleuves séparent les deux pays. —— constituent des frontières naturelles. 5. Les mers sont importantes. —— ont un intérêt touristique et commercial. 6. L'Europe est petite. —— se trouve à l'ouest de l'Asie. 7. Les États-Unis sont très grands. —— sont situés au sud du Canada. 8. Le fleuve est au centre du continent. —— sépare deux grands pays. 9. Un fleuve et une montagne constituent les frontières du pays. —— sont relativement difficiles à défendre.

® C. *Mettez les phrases suivantes à la forme interrogative en employant l'inversion.* EXEMPLE: La Seine traverse Paris. La Seine traverse-t-elle Paris?

1. Ils sont en France. 2. Elle est aux États-Unis. 3. Il sépare la France de l'Italie. 4. Elle forme la frontière sud de la France. 5. Les frontières sont difficiles à défendre. 6. Le Rhin sépare la France de l'Allemagne. 7. Les villes de France sont petites. 8. Une mer limite les États-Unis à l'est.[1] 9. Le Mississippi traverse le pays. 10. Les Grands Lacs sont au sud du Canada.

CONVERSATION

1. Demandez à Monsieur M. si les côtes de la Méditerranée ont des plages. 2. Demandez à Monsieur N. si le Rhin a une importance commerciale. 3. Demandez à Monsieur O. par quelles montagnes la France est limitée au sud-ouest. 4. Demandez à Monsieur P. si la frontière artificielle entre la France et la Belgique est difficile à défendre.

VOCABULAIRE — PAGE 45

GRAMMAIRE

1. What are the third person singular subject personal pronouns? the third person plural subject personal pronouns? (§ 23 A)

2. What is the difference between *ils* and *elles?* (§ 23 A)

3. From your observation of questions 5 and 8 in this lesson, what is a method of asking a question the subject of which is a pronoun? (§ 96 B)

4. From your observation of questions 1 to 4 in this lesson, what is a method of asking a question the subject of which is a noun? (§ 96 C)

[1] In the inverted interrogative form, a *-t-* must be placed between the verb and *il* or *elle* even when the final consonant of the verb stem is *-t-* if that verb form ends in *-e.* Thus, the inverted form of *il limite* is *limite-t-il.*

5. From your observation of questions 6, 11, and 12 of this lesson, in inverting the subject and verb, what is done to prevent having to pronounce two vowels together? (§ 96 D)

6. When the masculine singular of an adjective ends in unaccented *-e,* as in *facile* and *difficile,* how is the feminine singular formed? (§ 10 B)

7. When the masculine singular of an adjective ends in *-el,* as in *naturel, artificiel,* and *quel,* how is the feminine singular formed? (§ 10 F)

8. What is the plural of the verb-form *a?*

CINQUIÈME LEÇON

La Seine et la Loire

La Seine est le fleuve de France le plus connu à l'étranger. La Seine est plus connue que les autres fleuves de France, parce que Paris est situé sur la Seine. La Seine traverse Paris. Elle divise la ville en deux parties. Elle est relativement étroite à Paris. La Seine traverse la province de Normandie et se jette dans la Manche. Le Havre est un grand port situé à l'embouchure de la Seine. Le Havre est le port le plus important de la Manche. Il est important pour le commerce avec les États-Unis et l'Angleterre. Cherbourg est un port militaire de la Manche. Souvent les voyageurs américains arrivent en France par Cherbourg et par le Havre.

La Loire est le fleuve le plus long de France. La Loire est donc plus longue que la Seine. La source de la Loire se trouve au centre de la France dans le Massif Central. La Loire coule d'abord vers le nord et ensuite vers l'ouest. Elle se jette dans l'Atlantique près de Nantes. L'estuaire de la Loire a une importance commerciale considérable.

Les villes situées sur la Loire sont moins connues à l'étranger que les villes situées sur la Seine. Orléans, Tours et Nantes sont les trois villes les plus importantes situées sur la Loire.

La Seine est le fleuve le plus connu à l'étranger, mais la Loire est le fleuve le plus long de France

Questions

1. Pourquoi la Seine est-elle le fleuve de France le plus connu à l'étranger? 2. Quel est le fleuve le plus connu des États-Unis? 3. Le Mississippi est-il relativement étroit dans le Minnesota? 4. Quel est le fleuve le plus long et le plus large de l'Amérique du Sud? 5. Où se jette le plus grand fleuve de l'Amérique du Sud? 6. Quel est le port situé à l'embouchure de l'Hudson? 7. Quelle province du nord-ouest de la France la Seine traverse-t-elle? 8. Où se jette la Seine? 9. Citez deux ports importants de la Manche. 10. Pourquoi le Havre est-il important? 11. Par quels ports les voyageurs américains arrivent-ils sou-

vent en France? 12. Citez un port de France situé sur la mer du Nord. 13. Quel est le plus long fleuve de France? 14. Où est la source de la Loire? 15. Où se jette la Loire? 16. Citez trois villes importantes situées sur la Loire.

Devoirs

A. Remplacez les tirets par le mot convenable indiqué à droite.

1. La Seine est très —— à l'étranger. 2. Elle —— vers le nord et se jette dans la Manche au Havre. 3. La Seine est —— à Paris; elle est plus large en Normandie. 4. La Seine est le fleuve de France le plus connu —— Paris est situé sur la Seine. 5. La Loire, qui est moins connue à l'étranger que la Seine, coule d'abord —— le nord et —— vers l'ouest. 6. Elle se jette dans l'Atlantique —— Nantes. 7. Le Havre et Calais sont importants pour le commerce —— l'Angleterre. 8. Est-ce que le Mississippi est très connu ——? 9. La Loire est plus —— que les autres fleuves de France.

a. à l'étranger
b. avec
c. connue
d. coule
e. ensuite
f. étroite
g. longue
h. parce que
i. pour
j. près de
k. source
l. vers

® *B. Répondez*[1] *aux questions suivantes par des phrases complètes. Employez des noms comme sujets. Soulignez les comparatifs et les superlatifs dans vos réponses.* Exemple: La Russie est-elle le plus grand pays d'Europe? Oui, la Russie est le plus grand pays d'Europe.

1. Les Alpes sont-elles les montagnes les plus élevées de France? 2. La Loire est-elle plus longue que la Seine? 3. La Seine est-elle plus étroite à Paris qu'au Havre? 4. Est-ce que Paris est la plus grande ville de France? 5. Est-ce que le Havre et Cherbourg sont plus connus à l'étranger que Tours et Orléans? 6. Les fleuves sont-ils moins faciles à défendre que les montagnes?

C. Mettez le comparatif ou le superlatif de l'adjectif indiqué. Faites l'accord des adjectifs. Exemples: 1. Les pays d'Europe sont (petit) que les pays d'Afrique. Les pays d'Europe sont *plus petits* que les pays d'Afrique. 2. La Russie et l'Allemagne sont

[1] *Answer the following questions in complete sentences. Use noun-subjects. Underline the comparatives and superlatives in your answers.* This type of exercise is useful for rapid drill on a given grammatical point. After writing out the exercise, you should read the questions and answer them orally until you can do it rapidly and without hesitation.

(grand) pays d'Europe. La Russie et l'Allemagne sont *les plus grands* pays d'Europe.

1. La Volga est le fleuve (connu) de Russie. 2. L'Hudson est (important) pour le commerce que le Potomac. 3. L'Amazone est le fleuve (long) de l'Amérique du Sud. 4. La France est (fort) que la Belgique. 5. Les Alpes sont des montagnes (élevé) que le Jura et les Vosges. 6. Londres est (grand) ville d'Angleterre. 7. Les frontières d'Espagne sont (facile) à défendre que les frontières de Belgique. 8. La Loire est (long) que les autres fleuves de France. 9. Les villes situées sur la Loire sont (petit) que Paris. 10. Les fleuves (long) des États-Unis sont au centre du pays.

CONVERSATION

1. Demandez à Monsieur Q. quel est le port de France le plus important de la Manche. 2. Demandez à Monsieur R. quel est le fleuve le plus long de France. 3. Demandez à Monsieur S. quelles sont les trois villes les plus connues situées sur la Loire. 4. Demandez à Monsieur T. où se jette la Loire.

VOCABULAIRE — PAGE 45

GRAMMAIRE

1. How are the comparative and superlative of the French adjective formed? (§ 13 A)

2. How is *than* usually expressed after the comparative form of the adjective? (§ 13 B)

3. What do you note about the position of the definite article with forms of the superlative which follow their noun? (§ 13 C)

4. In English *in* is often used after a superlative; e.g., *The Loire is the longest river* ***in*** *France.* What preposition do the French use after a superlative? (§ 13 D)

5. What is the feminine form of the adjective ***long?*** (§ 10 H) How do you explain this irregularity?

6. In sentences such as *Une partie de* ***la Russie*** *est en Asie,* and *La Seine est un fleuve* ***de France,*** you have sometimes found ***de la*** before a feminine country, sometimes only ***de.*** When ***de*** + **a feminine country** could be expressed by an adjective in English (a river **of France** = a **French** river), only ***de*** is normally used, although ***de la*** is not incorrect. (§ 4 C 2)

7. What type of ***h*** is found in ***le Havre?*** How does it differ from the other type of French ***h?*** (Pages 511–512, § 1 A, B, C)

Cities are usually masculine, but Marseilles, Bruxelles, la Nouvelle Orléans are fem.

Première révision – Leçons 1 à 5

Première partie

A. Répondez en français par des phrases complètes aux questions suivantes.

1. Où est situé Brest? 2. Citez une ville importante de l'est de la France située sur le Rhin. 3. Quel fleuve traverse Paris? 4. Quel est le continent situé au sud de l'Europe? 5. Quelle est la capitale de l'Italie? 6. Dans quels continents se trouve la Russie? 7. Quelles sont les montagnes de France les plus élevées? 8. Citez des montagnes de l'est de la France. 9. Quel est le grand plateau situé au centre de la France? 10. Pourquoi les côtes de la Méditerranée et de l'Atlantique ont-elles un grand intérêt touristique? 11. Pourquoi le Rhin a-t-il une grande importance commerciale? 12. Quelle est la frontière de la France la plus difficile à défendre? 13. Citez les deux ports de la Manche les plus importants pour le commerce? 14. Quel est le plus long fleuve de France? 15. Citez trois villes situées sur la Loire.

B. Expliquez en français par une phrase complète les noms suivants.
EXEMPLE: Italie. L'Italie est un pays d'Europe situé au sud-est de la France.

Alpes	Loire	Paris
Atlantique	Marseille	Pyrénées
Brest	Massif Central	Rhin
Calais	Méditerranée	Seine
Cherbourg	mer du Nord	Strasbourg
Jura	Nantes	Tours
le Havre	Orléans	Vosges

C. Rédigez[1] *une composition sur un des sujets suivants.*

1. Les frontières de la France 2. Les pays d'Europe 3. Les montagnes de la France 4. La Seine

Deuxième partie

A. Remplacez les tirets par la forme convenable de l'article défini ou indéfini selon le cas. (Voir Grammaire §§ 1, 3)

1. — Alpes sont — montagnes très élevées situées dans — sud-est de — France. 2. Elles forment — partie de — frontière entre — France, — Suisse et — Italie. 3. — Massif Central est — grand plateau. 4. — fleuves sont moins faciles à défendre que

[1] *Make up*

—— montagnes. 5. Sur —— Atlantique se trouvent —— plages qui ont —— importance touristique considérable.

B. Mettez la forme convenable de l'adjectif indiqué. (Voir Grammaire §§ 9, 10 A, B, 11 A)

6. Yvetot est une (petit) ville (situé) sur la Seine. 7. La Loire et la Seine sont des fleuves très (connu). 8. (Quel) sont les montagnes de l'est de la France qui sont moins (élevé) que les Alpes? 9. La frontière entre la France et la Belgique est-elle (naturel) ou (artificiel)?

C. Faites la contraction convenable des mots indiqués entre parenthèses. (Voir Grammaire § 2)

10. Est-ce que la capitale (de le) pays est située (à le) centre (de le) continent? 11. Les montagnes (de les) continents se trouvent (à les) frontières (de les) pays.

D. Mettez les phrases suivantes à la forme interrogative en employant ***Est-ce que . . .*** *(Voir Grammaire § 96 A)*

12. La Loire est plus longue que les autres fleuves de France. 13. Elle est située au sud de Paris.

E. Mettez les phrases suivantes à la forme interrogative en employant l'inversion. (Voir Grammaire § 96 B, C, D)

14. Le Rhin est un grand fleuve. 15. Il sépare la France de l'Allemagne. 16. La France a des montagnes magnifiques. 17. La Méditerranée limite la France au sud.

F. Remplacez les tirets par les pronoms personnels convenables. EXEMPLE: Où est la Suisse? —— est au centre de l'Europe. *Elle* est au centre de l'Europe. (*Voir Grammaire* § 23 *A*)

18. La France est en Europe. —— se trouve à l'ouest de l'Allemagne. 19. Les grandes plages de France se trouvent sur la Méditerranée, l'Atlantique et la Manche. —— ont un intérêt touristique considérable. 20. Le Rhin est un fleuve. —— a une grande importance commerciale. 21. Les fleuves sont importants pour le commerce. Mais —— sont moins faciles à défendre que les montagnes.

G. Mettez la forme convenable du comparatif ou du superlatif de l'adjectif indiqué, selon le cas. EXEMPLE: La Loire est (long) que la Seine, mais la Seine est le fleuve (connu) de France. La Loire est *plus longue* que la Seine, mais la Seine est le fleuve *le plus connu* de France. (*Voir Grammaire* § 13 *A, C*)

22. La France est un des pays (important) d'Europe. 23. Elle est (grand) que l'Espagne et le Portugal. 24. Est-ce que le Rhin et la Loire sont les fleuves (connu) de France? 25. La Loire est (long) que les autres fleuves de France, mais elle est (important)[1] pour le commerce que la Seine.

[1] *less important*

Chevaliers de la Table Ronde

1. Chevaliers[1] de la Table Ronde[2], Goûtons[3] voir si le vin est bon. (bis)[4]

Goûtons voir, oui, oui, oui,
Goûtons voir, non, non, non, } (bis)
Goûtons voir si le vin est bon.

2. Si je meurs, je veux qu'on m'enterre[5] Dans la cave[6] où ' y a du bon vin. (bis)

Dans la cave, oui, oui, oui,
Dans la cave, non, non, non, } (bis)
Dans la cave où ' y a du bon vin.

3. Les deux pieds contre la muraille Et la tête sous le robinet[7]. (bis)

Et la tête, oui, oui, oui,
Et la tête, non, non, non, } (bis)
Et la tête sous le robinet.

4. Sur ma tomb'[8] je veux qu'on inscrive[9]: Ici gît[10] le roi des Buveurs[11]. (bis)

Ici gît, oui, oui, oui,
Ici gît, non, non, non, } (bis)
Ici gît le roi des Buveurs.

[1] *knights* [2] *Round* [3] *Let us taste* [4] *repeat* [5] *bury* [6] *cellar*
[7] *faucet* [8] *tomb* [9] *inscribe* [10] *lies* [11] *drinkers*

SIXIÈME LEÇON

La Garonne et le Rhône

La Garonne est un autre fleuve de France. La source de la Garonne n'est pas en France. Elle est dans les Pyrénées espagnoles. La Garonne coule vers le nord-ouest. Elle traverse le sud-ouest de la France et passe par Bordeaux pour former ensuite la Gironde.

La Gironde est l'estuaire de la Garonne. Elle est large et courte. Elle se jette dans l'Atlantique. Bordeaux est situé sur la Garonne près de la Gironde. Bordeaux est un des plus grands ports de France. Il exporte en grande quantité les vins de la région.

Le Rhône est un fleuve qui se jette dans la Méditerranée. La source du Rhône n'est pas en France. Elle est dans les Alpes suisses. Le Rhône traverse le lac de Genève et entre en France à la frontière suisse. Puis, il tourne vers le sud. Il coule dans une grande vallée fertile et se jette dans la Méditerranée. Le Rhône a un courant très rapide. Lyon est une grande ville située sur le Rhône. Lyon est célèbre par l'industrie de la soie.

Marseille est un grand port situé sur la Méditerranée. Le port de Marseille n'est pas situé sur un fleuve. Marseille est la plus grande ville de France après Paris. Le port de Marseille est très important pour le commerce avec l'Afrique du Nord et l'Orient.

La Seine, la Garonne et l'estuaire de la Loire ont une importance économique considérable. Le Rhône et la Loire jusqu'à Nantes n'ont pas une très grande importance commerciale. Ils ne sont pas navigables. La Loire n'est pas assez profonde, et le Rhône a un courant trop rapide.

Questions

1. La source de la Garonne est-elle en France? (Non, monsieur, madame, mademoiselle, la source de la Garonne n'est pas en France.) 2. Où est la source de la Garonne? 3. Où se jette la Gironde? 4. Bordeaux est-il situé sur l'Atlantique? 5. Est-ce que Bordeaux est célèbre par l'industrie de la soie? 6. La source du Rhône est-elle en France? 7. Le Rhône se jette-t-il dans l'Atlantique? 8. Citez une ville célèbre par l'industrie de la soie. 9. Est-ce que Marseille est une petite ville? 10. Où est située la ville de Marseille? 11. La Loire et le Rhône ont-ils une grande importance commerciale? 12. Pourquoi la Loire et le Rhône n'ont-ils pas un grand intérêt économique?

La Seine, la Garonne et l'estuaire de la Loire ont une importance économique considérable

Devoirs

A. Remplacez les tirets par le mot convenable indiqué à droite.

1. La Loire n'est pas navigable; elle n'est pas —— profonde. 2. La Garonne —— en France à la frontière espagnole. 3. La Gironde n'est pas longue; elle est ——. 4. Bordeaux exporte en grande quantité les —— de la région. 5. Le Rhône traverse le lac de Genève; ——, il entre en France. 6. Le Rhône n'est pas navigable; il a un courant —— rapide. 7. Lyon est la plus grande ville de France —— Paris et Marseille.	a. après b. assez c. courte d. entre e. industrie f. puis g. soie h. trop i. vins

® *B. Mettez les phrases suivantes à la forme négative.* EXEMPLES: La capitale de la France est située sur la Garonne. La capitale de la France *n'*est *pas* située sur la Garonne. 2. Est-elle située sur la Seine? *N'*est-elle *pas* située sur la Seine?

1. Le Rhône coule vers le nord. 2. La Méditerranée limite la France à l'est. 3. La France est en Amérique. 4. Madrid est la capitale du Portugal. 5. La Seine se jette dans la Méditerranée. 6. Les Vosges sont plus élevées que les Alpes. 7. Sont-elles plus importantes que le Jura? 8. Le Massif Central se trouve-t-il au centre de la France? 9. Les grandes villes de France sont-elles situées sur la mer? 10. La Seine se jette dans l'Atlantique à Bordeaux. 11. La Garonne entre en France à la frontière suisse. 12. Les voyageurs arrivent à Paris.

CONVERSATION

1. Demandez à Monsieur U. si Marseille est la capitale de la France. 2. Demandez à Monsieur V. si la Seine se jette dans la Méditerranée. 3. Demandez à Monsieur W. si le Rhône a une très grande importance commerciale. 4. Demandez à Monsieur X. si le Rhône et la Loire sont navigables.

VOCABULAIRE — PAGE 48

GRAMMAIRE

1. How is a French sentence made negative? (§ 22 A)

2. What is the position of *ne* and *pas* in a normal declarative sentence? (§ 22 B)

3. What is the position of *ne* and *pas* in an interrogative sentence with a pronoun-subject? with a noun-subject? (§ 22 C)

SEPTIÈME LEÇON

La Bretagne

La France se compose de plusieurs régions qui correspondent à peu près aux anciennes provinces d'autrefois. Chaque région garde encore aujourd'hui des coutumes différentes. Les habitants de chaque région ont un caractère différent. L'architecture des maisons n'est pas la même dans toutes les parties de la France. Aujourd'hui les provinces ne sont plus des

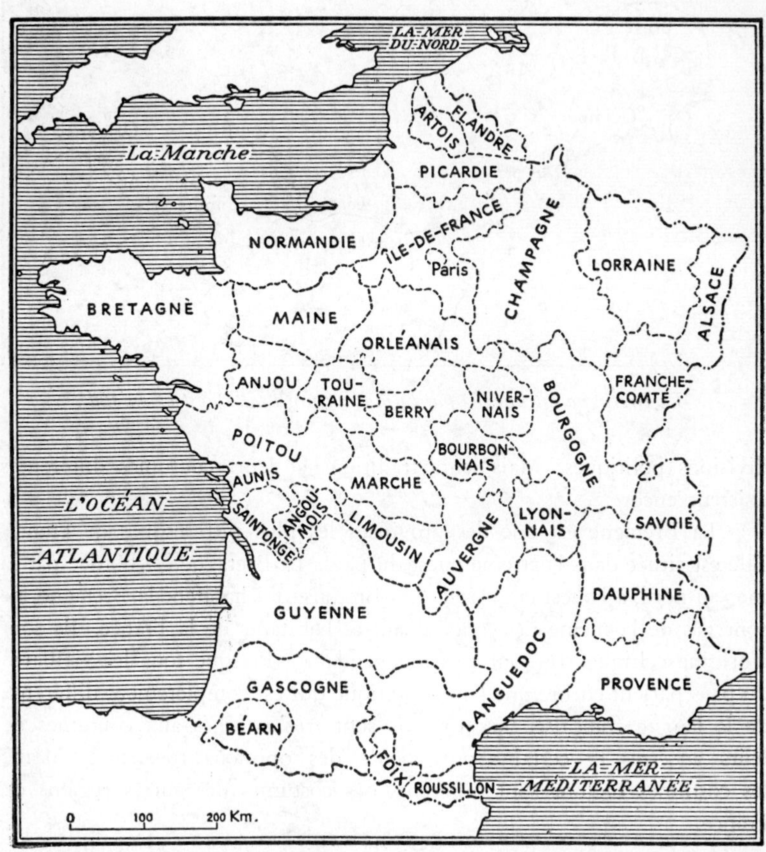

La France se compose de plusieurs régions qui correspondent à peu près aux anciennes provinces d'autrefois

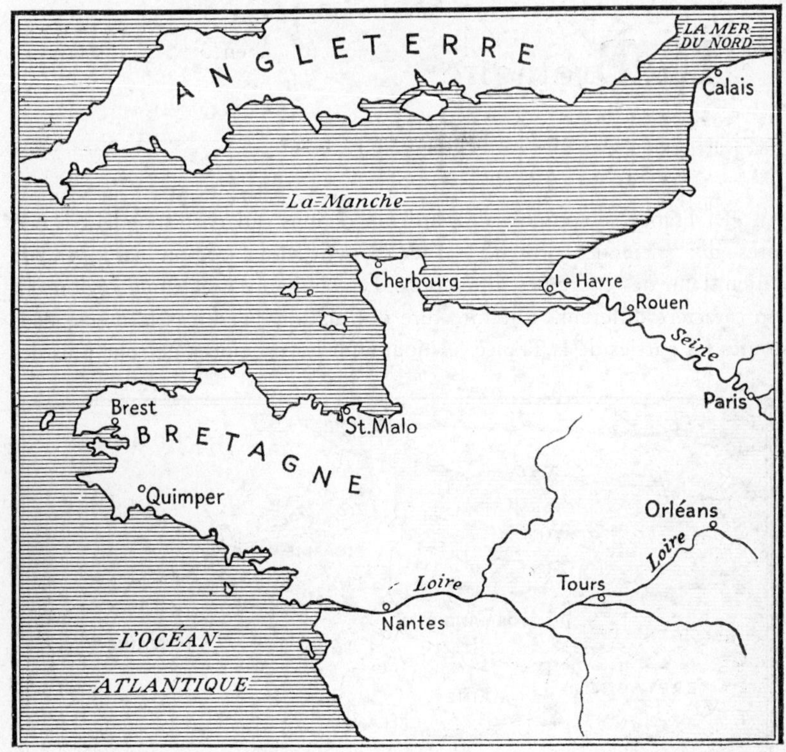

La Bretagne est bordée par la mer au nord, à l'ouest et au sud

divisions politiques. Mais leurs traditions et leurs coutumes différentes existent encore.

La Bretagne est une des provinces les plus pittoresques de France. Elle est située dans l'extrême ouest du pays. La Bretagne est bordée par la mer au nord, à l'ouest et au sud. Les Bretons, qui habitent la Bretagne, ne sont pas de la même race que les autres habitants de la France. Ils sont d'origine celtique. Ils sont très indépendants. Presque tous les vieillards du pays parlent encore une langue celtique qui est complètement différente de la langue française. Les Bretons sont très attachés aux coutumes de leurs ancêtres et certains ont encore des opinions royalistes. Même les costumes bretons sont différents des costumes des autres régions de France.

La Grande-Bretagne est une île située en face de la Bretagne. L'Angleterre est une partie de la Grande-Bretagne.

QUESTIONS

1. Est-ce que les régions de France gardent encore aujourd'hui des coutumes différentes? 2. Est-ce que les habitants de chaque région du pays ont un caractère différent? 3. Où est située la Bretagne? 4. Les Bretons sont-ils de la même race que les autres habitants de la France? 5. De quelle origine sont les Bretons? 6. Quelle langue parlent presque tous les vieillards bretons? 7. A quelles coutumes les Bretons sont-ils très attachés? 8. Les costumes bretons sont-ils les mêmes que les costumes des autres régions de France? 9. Quelle est l'île qui est située en face de la Bretagne? 10. Quel est le pays qui est une partie de la Grande-Bretagne?

DEVOIRS

A. Remplacez les tirets par le mot convenable indiqué à droite.

1. Tous les voyageurs américains ne —— pas français. 2. Les Bretons —— la province qui se trouve dans l'extrême ouest de la France. 3. Ils ne sont pas de la —— race que les autres habitants du pays. 4. L'architecture de leurs —— est très différente. 5. La —— française est plus facile que les autres langues d'Europe. 6. Les vieillards parlent —— une langue celtique. 7. —— provinces ont des costumes pittoresques. 8. Presque —— les Bretons ont un caractère indépendant. 9. Ils gardent encore leurs coutumes d'——.

a. autrefois
b. chaque
c. encore
d. habitent
e. île
f. langue
g. maisons
h. même
i. parlent
j. plusieurs
k. tous

® *B. Indiquez*[1] *le genre des mots suivants. Soulignez la terminaison du mot.* EXEMPLES: 1. division — la division 2. architecture — l'architecture, f.

1. partie 2. ville 3. plateau 4. embouchure 5. industrie 6. quantité 7. région 8. vallée 9. opinion 10. langue

® *C. Introduisez*[2] *les adjectifs indiqués dans la phrase pour modifier le nom en italique. Faites l'accord de l'adjectif.* EXEMPLE: (artificiel) La *frontière* entre la France et la Belgique est difficile à défendre. La *frontière* ***artificielle*** entre la France et la Belgique est difficile à défendre.

[1] *Indicate the gender of the following words. Underline the ending of the word.*
[2] *Put the indicated adjectives into the sentence in such a way that they modify the italicized noun. Make the adjective agree with its noun.*

1. (politique) Les provinces du pays sont des *divisions.* 2. (français) Les habitants de cette ville parlent-ils une langue qui est complètement différente de la *langue?* 3. (royaliste) Est-ce que les Bretons ont encore des *opinions?* 4. (suisse) Le Rhône entre en France à la *frontière.* 5. (commercial) Plusieurs fleuves ont une *importance.* 6. (rapide) Quels fleuves ont un *courant?* 7. (naturel) Les montagnes sont des *frontières.* 8. (magnifique) Les côtes de la Méditerranée ont des *plages.* 9. (élevé) Les Alpes sont des *montagnes.* 10. (difficile) Le français n'est pas une *langue.* 11. (américain) Les *voyageurs* arrivent en France par le Havre. 12. (important) Bordeaux est une *ville.* 13. (fertile) Le Rhône coule dans une *vallée.* 14. (espagnol) Les Basques habitent près de la *frontière.* 15. (indépendant) Les Bretons ont un *caractère.*

D. Introduisez dans la phrase les mots indiqués entre parenthèses. Faites les contractions et les élisions nécessaires.

1. L'architecture (de les) maisons n'est pas la même dans toutes les régions (de le) pays. 2. La province est bordée par la mer (à le) nord, (à le) ouest et (à le) sud. 3. Les habitants (de la) province sont très attachés (à les) coutumes de leurs ancêtres. 4. La source (de le) fleuve est (à le) centre (de la) région.

Conversation

1. Demandez à Monsieur Y. si la Bretagne est bordée au nord par la mer. 2. Demandez à Monsieur Z. si les Bretons parlent la même langue que les autres Français. 3. Demandez à Monsieur A. si la Grande-Bretagne est une île. 4. Demandez à Monsieur B. si l'architecture des maisons est la même dans toutes les parties de la France.

Vocabulaire — page 49

Grammaire

1. Certain endings of French nouns often indicate the gender of these nouns. What is the gender of nouns with these endings: ***–eau, –ée, -ie, -ion, -ment, -té, -ue, -ure?*** of nouns ending in a double consonant + *e?* (§ 7 B 2)

2. What is the regular position of French descriptive adjectives in relation to their nouns? (§ 12 A)

3. Review the very important contractions of ***à le, à les, de le*** and ***de les.*** Must these words be contracted when they occur together? (§ 2)

La Touraine est une province située à environ deux cents kilomètres au sud-ouest de Paris

HUITIÈME LEÇON

La Touraine

La Touraine est une province située à environ deux cents kilomètres au sud-ouest de Paris. Elle occupe le centre de la vallée de la Loire. Cette province est très petite en comparaison des autres provinces de France. Mais elle est très connue. On appelle la Touraine le jardin de la France, parce que la vallée de la Loire est très fertile et parce qu'en Touraine se trouvent des jardins magnifiques.

La Touraine est la région des châteaux de la Loire. Un certain nombre de ces châteaux sont construits dans le style Renaissance; quelques autres datent du moyen âge. Les châteaux du moyen âge sont des forteresses. Ils sont entourés de hautes murailles destinées à empêcher l'ennemi d'approcher. Les châteaux de la Renaissance sont des édifices élégants de style italien.

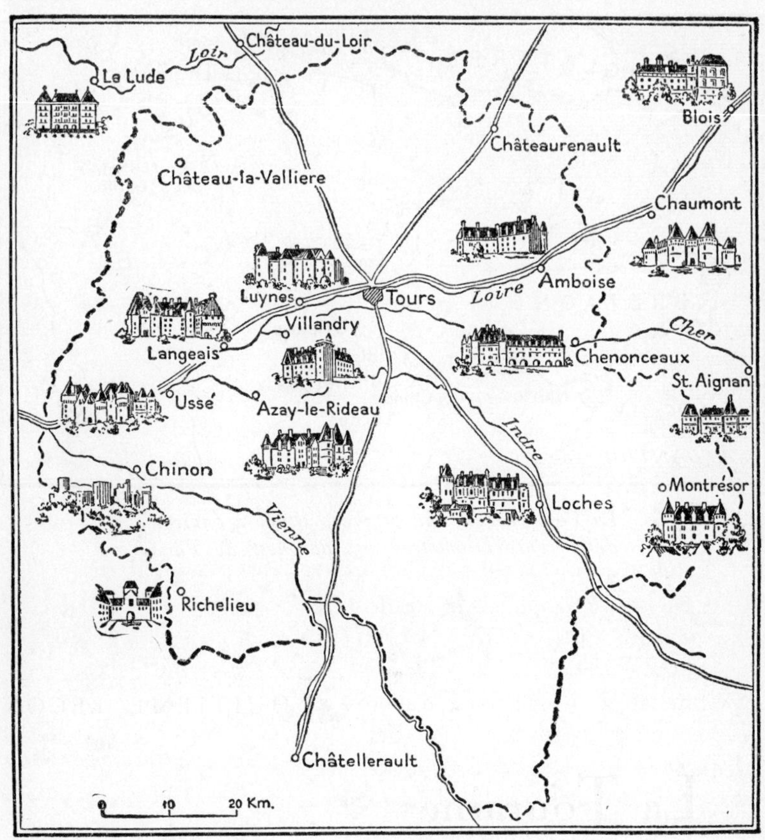

La Touraine est la région des châteaux de la Loire

Chinon est un des plus connus parmi les châteaux du moyen âge. Ce château tombe maintenant en ruines. La ville de Loches a aussi un château fortifié. Cet endroit est connu surtout grâce aux souvenirs du roi Louis XI. Le château de Loches est bien conservé.

Chenonceaux est un magnifique château de la Renaissance. Il y a des tableaux et des tapisseries à l'intérieur de ce château. Ces tapisseries racontent l'histoire des rois de France. On trouve des jardins pittoresques autour de ce château.

Tours est la principale ville de la Touraine. Cette ville est située sur la Loire. Il y a à Tours plusieurs monuments historiques et une cathédrale gothique.

Questions

1. A combien de kilomètres de Paris se trouve la Touraine? 2. Dans quelle vallée est située la Touraine? 3. En comparaison des autres provinces de France, la Touraine est-elle petite ou grande? 4. Comment appelle-t-on la Touraine? 5. Pourquoi appelle-t-on la Touraine le jardin de la France? 6. Dans quelle province se trouvent les châteaux de la Loire? 7. Pourquoi les châteaux du moyen âge sont-ils entourés de hautes murailles? 8. Dans quel style sont construits les châteaux de la Renaissance? 9. Quel château tombe maintenant en ruines? 10. Citez une ville qui a un château fortifié. 11. Pourquoi le château de Loches est-il connu? 12. Citez un château de la Renaissance. 13. Qu'y a-t-il à l'intérieur du château de Chenonceaux? 14. Que racontent les tapisseries de ce château? 15. Que trouve-t-on autour du château de Chenonceaux? 16. Quelle est la principale ville de la Touraine?

Devoirs

A. Remplacez les tirets par le mot convenable indiqué à droite.

1. On —— la Touraine le jardin de la France. 2. —— châteaux de cette région datent du moyen âge. 3. Ces châteaux sont entourés de —— murailles. 4. Ces murailles —— l'ennemi d'approcher. 5. Les châteaux de la Renaissance sont des —— élégants. 6. Ils sont —— de jardins pittoresques. 7. Chenonceaux est un des plus connus —— les châteaux de la Renaissance. 8. A l'intérieur de ce château se trouvent des —— et des tapisseries. 9. Ces tapisseries —— l'histoire des rois de France.

a. appelle
b. édifices
c. empêchent
d. entourés
e. environ
f. hautes
g. parmi
h. quelques
i. racontent
j. tableaux

B. Remplacez les tirets par **ce, cet, cette** *ou* **ces**, *selon le cas.*

1. Tours est une ville située au sud-ouest de Paris. —— ville est la capitale de la province. 2. La ville de Loches a un grand château. —— château date du moyen âge. 3. A l'intérieur de —— édifice il y a des tableaux et des tapisseries. 4. —— tableaux et —— tapisseries racontent l'histoire des rois de France. 5. A Chenonceaux il y a une tapisserie qui raconte l'histoire d'un roi de France. —— histoire est très connue en France. 6. —— roi est très connu aussi. 7. Tours est une ville qui est située sur la Loire. —— endroit est connu grâce aux châteaux de la Loire. 8. Les maisons de —— région sont entourées de jardins. 9. —— jardins sont souvent très élégants.

® *C. Mettez au pluriel les mots en italique.*

1. Il y a *un plateau* au centre de *ce continent.* 2. On trouve *un château* dans *cet endroit.* 3. Il y a *un tableau* dans *ce château.* 4. *Cet édifice a* aussi *une tapisserie.* 5. *Cette tapisserie raconte* l'histoire *du roi.*

® *D. Répondez aux questions suivantes par des phrases complètes. Commencez votre réponse par* **oui** *ou* **non.** *Soulignez*[1] *dans votre réponse les mots en italique.*

1. Appelle-t-*on* les habitants de Bretagne des Bretons? 2. Parle-t-*on* une langue celtique en Bretagne? 3. Trouve-t-*on* des plages en Bretagne? 4. *Y a-t-il* des maisons pittoresques en Bretagne? 5. *Y a-t-il* plusieurs châteaux du moyen âge en Touraine? 6. *Y a-t-il* une cathédrale gothique à Tours?

Conversation

1. Demandez à l'étudiant qui est à[2] votre droite s'il y a une cathédrale à Tours. 2. Demandez à l'étudiant qui est à[3] votre gauche si on trouve des jardins à Tours. 3. Demandez à l'étudiant qui est devant[4] vous si les tapisseries racontent l'histoire des rois du moyen âge. 4. Demandez à l'étudiant qui est derrière[5] vous s'il y a des tableaux à l'intérieur du château de Chenonceaux.

Vocabulaire — pages 50–51

Grammaire

1. French does not normally distinguish between *this* and *that* or *these* and *those.* What are the four forms of the French demonstrative adjective? When is each form used? (§ 15 A, B)

2. How does French form the plural of words ending in *-eau?* (§ 8 C)

3. Explain the use of the indefinite pronoun ***on.*** (§ 40 A)

4. Explain the use of the expression ***il y a.*** (§ 91 A)

[1] *In your reply underline the italicized words.*
[2] *to your right* [3] *to your left* [4] *in front of you* [5] *behind you*

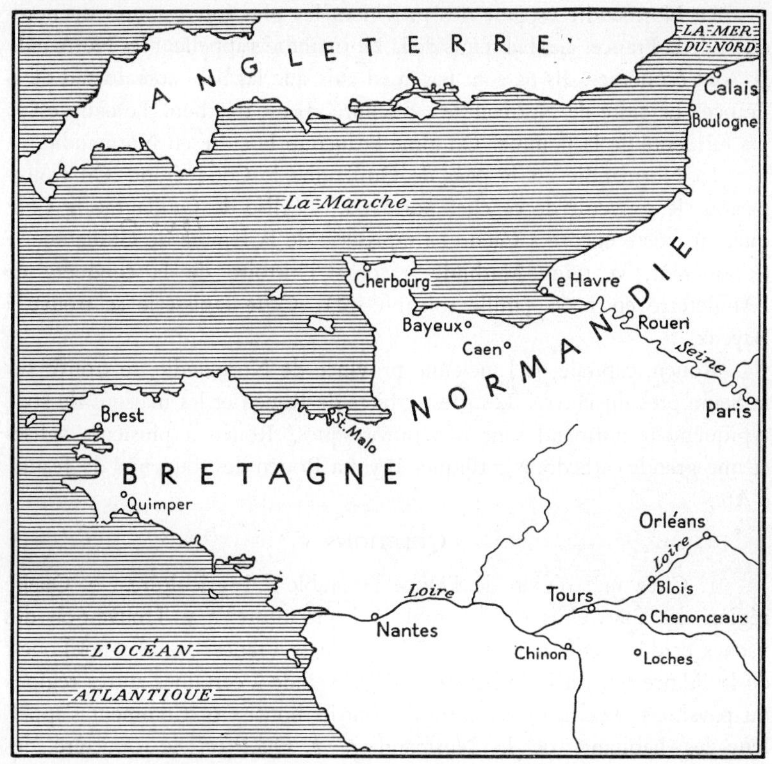

La Normandie est une des provinces les plus intéressantes du nord-ouest de la France

NEUVIÈME LEÇON

La Normandie

Le nord-ouest de la France est une région favorable à l'agriculture. On trouve en grand nombre dans toute la région des vaches, des bœufs et des moutons. Le nord-ouest de la France fournit à certaines autres régions du pays du lait, de la crème, du beurre, du fromage et de la viande. Les fromages français sont très bons. La crème est bonne aussi.

La Normandie est une des provinces les plus intéressantes du nord-ouest de la France. Les habitants de la Normandie s'appellent les Normands. Ils sont économes. Ils ne sont pas aussi gais que les habitants du sud de la France. Le cidre de Normandie est réputé. Il est très bon. Le cidre est le jus fermenté de la pomme. On aime beaucoup le cidre en Normandie.

La Normandie est le pays de Guillaume le Conquérant. On trouve partout le souvenir de ce chef normand. L'église de Guillaume le Conquérant existe encore à Caen. La tapisserie de la femme de Guillaume le Conquérant, la reine Mathilde, raconte l'histoire de la conquête de l'Angleterre en 1066 (mille soixante-six). Cette tapisserie se trouve à Bayeux.

Rouen, capitale de l'ancienne province de Normandie, se trouve sur la Seine près du Havre. Les rues étroites de Rouen et les maisons de style typiquement normand sont très pittoresques. Rouen a plusieurs églises et une grande cathédrale gothique. Il y a à Rouen des souvenirs de Jeanne d'Arc.

Questions

1. Citez une région de France favorable à l'agriculture. 2. Quelle région des États-Unis est favorable à l'agriculture? 3. Trouve-t-on des vaches et des bœufs dans le nord-ouest de la France? 4. Le nord-ouest de la France fournit-il du beurre et de la viande à certaines autres régions du pays? 5. Les fromages français sont-ils bons? 6. Comment s'appellent les habitants de la Normandie? 7. Quel est le caractère des Normands? 8. Dans quelle province de France aime-t-on beaucoup le cidre? 9. Dans quelle ville de Normandie se trouve l'église de Guillaume le Conquérant? 10. Quelle histoire la tapisserie de la reine Mathilde raconte-t-elle? 11. Dans quelle ville de Normandie se trouve la tapisserie de la reine Mathilde? 12. Dans quelle ville y a-t-il des souvenirs de Jeanne d'Arc? 13. Sur quel fleuve est situé Rouen? 14. Près de quel port se trouve Rouen? 15. De quel style sont les maisons de Rouen?

Devoirs

A. Remplacez les tirets par le mot convenable indiqué à droite.

1. Les habitants de la Normandie —— les Normands. 2. —— dans cette province on trouve des vaches et des bœufs. 3. Cette région —— du lait et de la viande à certaines autres régions. 4. A Rouen il y a une cathédrale et plusieurs ——. 5. Les —— des villes normandes sont souvent très étroites.

a. aime
b. s'appellent
c. églises
d. femme
e. fournit
f. lait

6. La tapisserie de la reine Mathilde, —— de Guillaume le Conquérant, se trouve à Bayeux. 7. La femme du roi s'appelle la ——.

g. partout
h. reine
i. rues

B. Remplacez les tirets par ***du, de la, de l'*** *ou* ***des,*** *selon le cas.*

1. La région de Lyon fournit —— soie à toute la France. 2. En Normandie on trouve —— vaches, —— bœufs et —— moutons. 3. Les bœufs, les vaches et les moutons fournissent —— viande aux habitants du pays. 4. Les vaches fournissent —— lait et —— crème à toute la France. 5. Dans les maisons normandes on trouve souvent —— fromage, —— beurre et —— cidre. 6. Dans les autres parties de la France on trouve le plus souvent —— vin. 7. Il y a —— souvenirs de Jeanne d'Arc à Rouen.

C. Remplacez les tirets par la forme convenable de l'article défini ou de l'article partitif, selon le cas.[1]

1. On trouve —— cidre dans toutes les villes normandes. 2. Les Normands aiment —— cidre. 3. Il y a —— lait dans toutes les villes des États-Unis. 4. —— lait est très bon. 5. Y a-t-il —— pommes en France? 6. —— pommes sont bonnes. 7. Les Français aiment beaucoup —— vin. 8. Il y a —— vin dans toutes les régions de France.

D. Mettez la forme convenable de l'adjectif indiqué.

1. (Tout) la région est favorable à l'agriculture. 2. Le (bon) cidre de Normandie est réputé dans (tout) le pays. 3. Certains ports (italien) sont situés sur la Méditerranée. 4. Les opinions du roi sont (bon). 5. (Tout) les vieillards bretons parlent une langue (ancien). 6. La crème est (bon), et les fromages sont (bon) aussi. 7. Les villes (italien) sont célèbres par leur architecture. 8. Les (ancien) provinces ne sont plus des divisions politiques. 9. Presque (tout) les villes de l'intérieur de la France sont situées sur des fleuves. 10. Parmi les (bon) fromages français on cite le Gruyère, le Camembert, le Roquefort et le Brie.

CONVERSATION

1. Demandez à l'étudiant qui est à votre droite s'il y a des vaches en Normandie. 2. Demandez à l'étudiant qui est à votre gauche si on aime beaucoup le cidre en Normandie. 3. Demandez à l'étudiant qui est devant vous si Rouen a plusieurs églises. 4. Demandez à l'étudiant qui est derrière vous où se trouve la tapisserie de la reine Mathilde.

[1] If you can add "in general" after the noun, use the definite article. If the noun indicates an indefinite quantity (i.e., *some*), use the partitive article.

Grammaire

1. List the partitive articles. (§ 5 A)

2. Explain the use of the French partitive article. (§ 5 B)

3. How can one tell whether ***du, de la, de l'***, and ***des*** mean *of the* or *some?* (§ 5 C)

4. Explain the use of the definite article in the sentence: *On aime beaucoup le cidre en France.* (§ 4 B)

5. What is an appositive? Find two examples of appositives in the reading lesson. When is the article used and when omitted before an appositive? (§ 4 E)

6. Give the four forms of the irregular adjectives ***bon*** (§ 10 H) and ***tout*** (§ 11 E). What are the various forms of the adjective ***ancien*** and others ending in ***-en?*** (§ 10 F)

7. The infinitive of ***il fournit*** is ***fournir.*** What is the ***ils*** form of ***fournir?*** (Page 53)

8. In the sentence: *Rouen is as large as Caen,* there is an example of a comparison of equality. Find an example of a comparison of equality in the reading lesson. How is the comparative of equality *as . . . as* expressed in French? (§ 13 F)

9. In Lesson 7 we learned that descriptive adjectives normally follow their nouns in French. In Exercise D of this lesson, certain adjectives precede their nouns. List some adjectives which regularly precede their nouns. (§ 12 D, E)

DIXIÈME LEÇON

Le Midi de la France

Le sud de la France s'appelle le Midi. Le Midi est une région différente du nord de la France. Dans le Midi il y a plus de soleil que dans le nord. Les hivers sont plus courts et les étés plus longs. Le printemps arrive plus tôt dans le Midi que dans le nord, et l'automne arrive plus tard. Le Midi, comme la Normandie, est favorable à l'agriculture. Par contre, il y a peu d'industries dans le Midi.

Dans le Midi il y a beaucoup de fruits et de légumes qui ne se cultivent pas dans le nord. On trouve l'olivier dans le Midi. Il n'y a pas

ême les costumes bretons sont différents des costumes des autres régions de France

Les châteaux du moyen âge sont des forteresses

Les châteaux de la Renaissance sont des édifices élégants de style italien

Les rues étroites de Rouen sont très pittoresques

Les maisons de Rouen sont de style typiquement normand

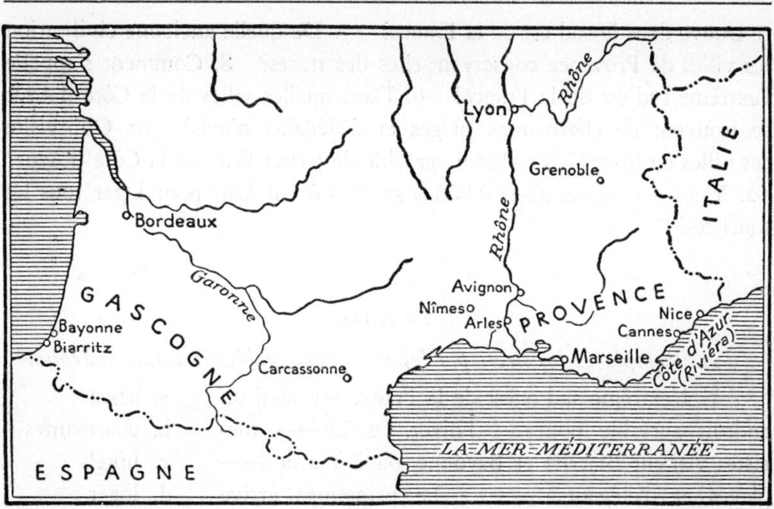

Le sud de la France s'appelle le Midi

d'oliviers dans le nord. On trouve des oranges dans l'extrême sud-est de la France. Il n'y a pas d'oranges dans le nord du pays. Le Midi fournit beaucoup de vin à toute la France.

Dans le sud-est de la France se trouve une ancienne province célèbre dans l'histoire. Elle s'appelle la Provence. La Provence est la *Provincia* des Romains. En Provence beaucoup de villes conservent des traces de l'ancienne civilisation romaine. La Provence est aussi la région des anciens troubadours, célèbres par leurs chansons d'amour.

L'extrême sud-est du Midi de la France s'appelle la Côte d'Azur ou Riviera française. Il y a toujours de nombreux touristes dans cette région. A Nice, à Cannes et dans d'autres villes de la Côte d'Azur se trouvent de charmantes plages et d'élégants hôtels. En hiver beaucoup de gens de tous les pays du monde visitent ces villes. Il est agréable aussi de passer l'été sur la Côte d'Azur, mais il y a quelquefois trop de touristes. En été il n'y a pas toujours assez d'hôtels pour loger tout le monde.

QUESTIONS

1. Comment s'appelle le sud de la France? 2. Y a-t-il de longs hivers dans le Midi de la France? 3. Y a-t-il beaucoup d'industries dans le Midi? 4. Citez des fruits du Midi de la France. 5. Dans quelle partie de la France trouve-t-on des oranges? 6. Quelle ancienne province

se trouve dans le sud-est de la France? 7. De quelle ancienne civilisation les villes de Provence conservent-elles des traces? 8. Comment s'appelle l'extrême sud-est de la France? 9. Dans quelles villes de la Côte d'Azur se trouvent de charmantes plages et d'élégants hôtels? 10. Qui visite ces villes en hiver? 11. Est-il agréable de passer l'été sur la Côte d'Azur? 12. Y a-t-il toujours assez d'hôtels sur la Côte d'Azur pour loger tous les touristes?

Devoirs

A. *Remplacez les tirets par les mots convenables indiqués à droite.*

1. L'extrême sud-ouest de la France est aussi un endroit agréable pour —— l'hiver. 2. De —— touristes visitent Biarritz et Bayonne, où il y a de —— plages et d'élégants ——. 3. Le printemps arrive plus —— en Normandie qu'en Provence. 4. L'automne arrive plus —— en Bretagne que dans le Midi de la France. 5. —— les Américains visitent les ruines romaines de la Provence et la ville fortifiée de Carcassonne.

a. assez
b. charmantes
c. hôtels
d. loger
e. nombreux
f. passer
g. quelquefois
h. tard
i. tôt

B. *Remplacez les tirets par **l'article partitif** ou par **de**.* EXEMPLE:

Il y a —— charmantes plages dans le nord-ouest de l'Espagne.
Il y a *de* charmantes plages dans le nord-ouest de l'Espagne.

1. Il y a —— nombreuses ruines dans le Midi de la France. 2. On trouve —— villes fortifiées qui datent du moyen âge. 3. Beaucoup —— Français visitent la ville fortifiée de Carcassonne, qui a —— hautes[1] murailles. 4. A Nîmes et à Arles il y a —— traces de la civilisation des Romains. 5. Il y a —— murailles autour de la célèbre ville d'Avignon, mais cette ville n'a pas —— monuments romains. 6. En été il n'y a pas assez —— hôtels[1] pour loger les touristes qui arrivent à Biarritz et dans —— autres endroits sur l'Atlantique. 7. Il y a trop —— gens et pas assez —— plages. 8. On ne trouve pas —— hôtels[1] dans ces villes. 9. Y a-t-il —— plages sur les côtes des États-Unis? 10. Il y a plus —— plages dans l'ouest que dans l'est. 11. Mais aux États-Unis on ne trouve pas —— traces de la civilisation des Romains.

[1] Note that the *h* of *haut* is aspirate and that the *h* of *hôtel* is mute. What difference does this make in pronunciation? in linking? in elision? (Pages 511–512, § 1 A, B)

® *C. Répondez aux questions suivantes par des phrases complètes. Commencez votre réponse par Non.*[1] EXEMPLE: Trouve-t-on des troubadours à Rouen? Non, on ne trouve pas de troubadours à Rouen.

1. Y a-t-il des oliviers à Chicago? 2. Trouve-t-on des traces de la civilisation des Romains dans le nord du Canada? 3. Y a-t-il des plages dans le Massif Central? 4. La Bretagne fournit-elle de la soie aux autres régions de la France? 5. La France fournit-elle du lait à la Russie?

® *D. Répondez aux questions suivantes en employant dans la réponse le mot indiqué entre parenthèses.*[2] EXEMPLE: Y a-t-il du soleil en Afrique? (trop) Il y a *trop* de soleil en Afrique.

1. Trouve-t-on des oranges en Californie? (beaucoup) 2. Y a-t-il des touristes en Floride? (trop) 3. Les États-Unis exportent-ils du vin en France? (peu) 4. Trouve-t-on des fruits en Espagne? (assez) 5. Y a-t-il des chansons populaires aux États-Unis? (beaucoup)

E. Mettez[3] *les adjectifs indiqués devant le nom en italique. Faites tous les changements nécessaires dans la phrase.* EXEMPLE: (charmant) A Cannes se trouvent *des plages.* A Cannes se trouvent ***de charmantes*** *plages.*

1. (nombreux) Il y a toujours des *touristes* sur la Côte d'Azur. 2. (grand) On trouve des *hôtels* à Cannes. 3. (autre) Y a-t-il des *villes* sur la Méditerranée? 4. (bon) Il y a des *fromages* en France et en Suisse. 5. (long) Y a-t-il des *hivers* dans le Midi de la France?

CONVERSATION

1. Demandez à l'étudiant qui est à votre droite s'il y a beaucoup de fruits dans le Midi de la France. 2. Demandez à l'étudiant qui est à votre gauche s'il y a assez d'hôtels pour loger tous les touristes. 3. Demandez à l'étudiant qui est devant vous si les hivers sont plus longs dans le nord que dans le Midi. 4. Demandez à l'étudiant qui est derrière vous s'il y a trop de touristes à Cannes en été.

[1] What word normally follows *pas* before a noun? (§ 6 C)
[2] What preposition normally follows adverbs of quantity? (§ 6 B)
[3] *Place the indicated adjectives before the italicized noun. Make all necessary changes in the sentence.*

VOCABULAIRE — PAGES 53–54

GRAMMAIRE

1. The partitive *des* is not normally used before **adjective + plural noun.** What word is used instead of **des**? (§ 6 A)

2. List the expressions of quantity used in your lesson. What preposition is used after these expressions before a noun? (§ 6 B)

3. What preposition normally follows the negative *pas* before a noun? (§ 6 C)

L'Alouette

(Canadian song)

Alouette [1], gentille alouette, Alouette, je te plumerai [2].

1. Je te plumerai la têt', Je te plumerai la têt',
Et la têt', Et la têt', Oh!
Alouette, etc.

2. Je te plumerai le bec [3], Je te plumerai le bec,
Et le bec, Et le bec,
Et la têt', Et la têt', Oh!
Alouette, etc.

3. Je te plumerai les patt's [4] (bis)
Et les patt's (bis)
Et le bec (bis)
Et la têt' (bis)
Oh!
Alouette, etc.

4. le cou 5. le dos [5] 6. les ail's [6] 7. la queue [7] etc.

[1] *lark* [2] *pluck* [3] *bill, beak* [4] *legs* [5] *back* [6] *wings* [7] *tail*

Deuxième révision — Leçons 6 à 10

Première partie

A. Répondez en français par des phrases complètes aux questions suivantes.

1. Où est la source de la Garonne? 2. Quelle grande ville de France est située sur la Garonne? 3. Pourquoi la Loire et le Rhône n'ont-ils pas une très grande importance économique? 4. Où est située la Bretagne? 5. De quelle origine sont les habitants de la Bretagne? 6. Quelle langue parlent les vieillards bretons? 7. Dans quelle vallée est située la Touraine? 8. Quels châteaux sont des édifices de style italien? 9. Que trouve-t-on à l'intérieur du château de Chenonceaux? 10. Dans quelle province de France trouve-t-on beaucoup de souvenirs de Guillaume le Conquérant? 11. Pourquoi beaucoup de gens visitent-ils la ville normande de Bayeux? 12. Quelle est la capitale de l'ancienne province de Normandie? 13. Quelle province de France conserve des traces de l'ancienne civilisation romaine? 14. Citez deux villes de la Côte d'Azur. 15. Pourquoi les touristes passent-ils l'hiver sur la Côte d'Azur?

B. Expliquez en français par une phrase complète les noms suivants.

Bayeux	Côte d'Azur	Mathilde
Bordeaux	Garonne	Nice
Bretagne	Gironde	Normandie
Caen	Guillaume le Conquérant	Provence
Cannes	Loches	Rhône
Chenonceaux	Lyon	Touraine
Chinon		Tours

C. Rédigez une composition sur un des sujets suivants.

1. Le Rhône 2. Quelques provinces de France 3. La Bretagne 4. La Touraine 5. La Normandie 6. Quelques villes de France 7. Le Midi de la France 8. La Côte d'Azur

Deuxième partie

A. Écrivez les phrases suivantes à la forme négative. (Voir Grammaire § 22 *A, B, C)*

1. Le nord de la France s'appelle le Midi. 2. Brest est en Normandie. 3. Est-il au centre de la France? 4. La Côte d'Azur se trouve-t-elle dans l'extrême sud-est de la France? 5. La Loire se jette dans la Méditerranée.

B. Introduisez dans la phrase les adjectifs indiqués de façon à modifier le nom en italique. Faites l'accord de l'adjectif. (Voir Grammaire § 12 A)

6. (italien) Les châteaux de la Renaissance sont des édifices de *style.* 7. (fortifié) Quelle ville a un *château?* 8. (étroit) Toutes les villes normandes ont des *rues.* 9. (romain) Beaucoup de villes conservent la trace de l'ancienne *civilisation.* 10. (magnifique) A Cannes il y a une *plage.*

C. Remplacez le mot en italique par **ce, cet, cette** *ou* **ces,** *selon le cas. (Voir Grammaire § 15 A)*

11. *La* province se trouve au nord-est de la France. 12. *Les* châteaux sont des forteresses. 13. *L'*église est à Caen. 14. *L'*habitant parle français. 15. *Le* pays est très grand.

D. Remplacez les tirets par l'article partitif ou par **de** *selon le cas. (Voir Grammaire §§ 5 A, B; 6 A, B, C)*

16. En Bretagne il y a —— villes très anciennes. 17. Saint-Malo est une ville fortifiée avec —— hautes murailles. 18. Beaucoup —— touristes visitent cette ville au printemps et en été. 19. Il n'y a pas —— touristes à Saint-Malo en hiver, parce que les hivers ne sont pas très agréables en Bretagne. 20. Mais il y a trop —— gens sur la Côte d'Azur. 21. On trouve —— plages partout. 22. Mais il n'y a pas —— hôtels dans ces endroits.

E. Mettez la forme convenable de l'adjectif indiqué. (Voir Grammaire §§ 10 F, H; 11 E)

23. (tout) les pays ont-ils du (bon) fromage et de la (bon) crème? 24. Les (ancien) provinces conservent des traces d'une (ancien) civilisation. 25. Presque (tout) les femmes parlent beaucoup.

Supplément aux Leçons 1 à 10

PREMIÈRE LEÇON

Vocabulaire [a]

l'Atlantique *m.*	la France	le Rhin
Brest	Marseille [b]	la Seine
Calais	la Méditerranée	situé
la capitale	Paris	Strasbourg
	la partie	

dans *in*
de *of*
des *of the* (+ *plural noun*)
est [c] *is*
l'est [d] *m.* *east*
les États-Unis *m.* *the United States*
le, la, l' *the*
la mer *sea*
la mer du Nord *the North Sea*
le nord *north*
où *where*
l'ouest [d] *m.* *west*
quelle *f.* *what, which*
le sud *south*
sur *on*
traverse *crosses*

Verbes

être *to be* Paris *est . . .* COMMANDS *Remplacez . . .*

Devoirs [1]

A.[2] *Write the French equivalent of each of the following sentences.*

1. Calais is situated in the north of France. 2. Madrid is the capital of Spain. 3. Brest is in the west of France. 4. Strasbourg is situated in the east of France. 5. The Seine crosses Paris. 6. What is the capital of France?

[1] If the lesson vocabulary does not contain all the words you need, refer to the English-to-French vocabulary (pages 547–561).

[2] Exercise A is a written exercise designed to test your knowledge of French grammar and vocabulary, especially of the grammatical principles and the vocabulary introduced in the lesson. Read over the lesson, learn the vocabulary, and familiarize yourself with the principles taken up in the *Grammaire* of the lesson before working out this exercise.

[a] The words in each *Vocabulaire* are divided into two groups. In the first group are listed words which resemble English and whose meaning you can determine because of their similarity to English. Such words are called *cognates.* In the second group are words which are distinctly different in the two languages and which are, therefore, defined. These words are called *non-cognates.*

In the *Vocabulaire* the gender of a word is indicated by *le* for a masculine word, *la* for a feminine word. When a noun begins with a vowel (or a mute *h*), *m.* indicates a masculine noun, *f.* a feminine noun.

[b] The French spelling is *Marseille,* the English spelling *Marseilles.*

[c] The verb-form *est* is pronounced [ɛ]. The *-st* is silent.

[d] The *-st* is pronounced in the nouns *est* [ɛst] and *ouest* [wɛst].

7. In what part of France is [1] Paris? 8. What is the capital of‿the [2] United States? 9. In what part of‿the United States is [1] Baton Rouge? 10. Where is the Mediterranean?

[1] *est situé*
[2] This mark indicates that the connected English words are expressed by a single word in French. The indication will be given only the first few times a given expression occurs.

B.[1] *Say aloud rapidly the French equivalent of each of the following sentences.*

1. Where is Calais? 2. Calais is in the north of France. 3. Strasbourg is in the east of France. 4. Paris is situated on the Seine. 5. Strasbourg is situated on the Rhine. 6. Where is Brest [2] situated? 7. In what part of France is Strasbourg [2] situated? 8. In what part of France is Paris [2] situated?

[1] Exercise B is an oral exercise designed to afford you drill on common speech patterns introduced in the lesson. In this first lesson, for instance, are several very common patterns such as (1) *Où est . . .?* (2) *Dans quelle partie de la France est . . .?* (3) *. . . est situé sur. . . .* To prepare Exercise B, say aloud rapidly the French equivalent of each of the English sentences, and do this repeatedly until you can read all the sentences in the exercise very rapidly and without hesitation. When you can do this, the patterns will become automatic and you will be able to use them in conversation. You will find Exercise B easier to do than Exercise A, because in Exercise B the emphasis is on common patterns rather than on grammatical constructions, and because there is always repetition of words and phrases. [2] Place this word at the end of the sentence.

DEUXIÈME LEÇON

Vocabulaire

l'Amérique du Nord *f.*
l'Afrique *f.*
l'Asie *f.*
la Belgique
le Canada
le continent
l'Europe *f.*
l'Italie *f.*
Madrid
le Mexique
le Portugal
Rome
la Russie

aussi *also, too*
en *in*[a]
l'Espagne *f.* *Spain*
et *and*
grand *large; great*
les *the*
madame *f.* *madam, ma'am; Mrs.*
mademoiselle *f.* *Miss*
mais *but*
monsieur *m.* *sir; Mr.*
oui *yes*
le pays *country*
petit *small, little*
quel, quelle[b] *what, which*
sont *are*
très *very*
un, une *a, an*
la ville *city*

[a] The usual word for *in* is *dans.* For the present, use *en* to express *in* only with feminine countries.
[b] When two forms of an adjective are given in the vocabulary, the first is the masculine singular form, the second is the irregular feminine form.

Verbes

être *to be*	L'Espagne et l'Italie *sont* . . . Les États-Unis *sont* . . .
COMMAND FORMS IN *-ez*	*Mettez* . . .

Devoirs

A. Write the French equivalent of each of the following sentences.

1. Russia is a large country. 2. Russia is large. 3. The capital of France is situated on the Seine. 4. Africa is a large continent, but Europe is a small continent. 5. Is Belgium a small country? [1] 6. Is Paris a small city? 7. Is a part of France situated in Africa? [2] 8. Are Canada and Mexico in North America? 9. Is the United States also in North America? 10. In what continent is Italy situated? [3]

[1] For the form of these questions, consult questions 1 to 6 on page 5.
[2] For this question, consult question 12 on page 5.
[3] For the word order of this question, consult question 9 on page 5.

B. Say aloud rapidly the French equivalent of each of the following sentences.

1. Is Europe a continent? 2. Is France a country? 3. France is a large country. 4. France is large. 5. France and Belgium are in Europe. 6. Spain, Portugal, and Italy are also in Europe. 7. Canada and Mexico are in North America. 8. The United States is [1] also in North America.

[1] Not *est.*

TROISIÈME LEÇON

Vocabulaire

les Alleghanys [a]
les Alpes *f.*
l'Amérique du Sud *f.*
le centre
former [b]
la frontière
l'intérieur *m.*
le Jura
le Massif Central
mentionner
la plaine
le plateau
les Pyrénées *f.*
les Vosges *f.*

[a] Pronounce as if it were written *Alléghany.* The accent over the -e- is doubtless lacking because this is a foreign place name.
[b] Verbs in *-er* have an adjectival form in *-é* corresponding to the English past participle in *-ed;* e. g., former (*form*), formé (*formed*). In the vocabulary, such verbs are given in the *-er* (infinitive) form.

à *to, in, at*
au (*contraction of* à le) *to the, in the, at the*
aux (*contraction of* à les) *to the, in the, at the*
citer *mention, give an example of*
des (*contraction of* de les) *of the, from the*
des (*plural of* un *and* une) *some*
du (*contraction of* de le) *of the, from the*
élevé[a] *high, elevated*
entre *between*
moins *less*
la montagne *mountain*
les montagnes Rocheuses *f. the Rocky Mountains*
que *than*
le sud-est *southeast*
le sud-ouest *southwest*
la Suisse *Switzerland*
surtout *especially*
se trouver *be, be located, be found*

Verbes

INFINITIVE	PAST PARTICIPLE	
former *to form*	formé *formed*	La France est formée . . .

INFINITIVE	SINGULAR	PLURAL
former	La montagne forme . . .	Les montagnes forment . . .
se trouver	La ville se trouve . . .	Les villes se trouvent . . .

Devoirs

Use forms of **se trouver** *in these exercises wherever* **is** *or* **are** *may be translated by* **is found, are found, is located,** *or* **are located.**

A. *Write the French equivalent of each of the following sentences.*

1. The mountains of the country are very high. 2. Spain and France are large. 3. The mountains are to the north of the border. 4. The Rocky Mountains are in the west of the United States. 5. The Pyrenees are between France and Spain. 6. Are the Alps less high than the Massif Central? 7. The Vosges are mountains[1] situated in the east of the country. 8. Two of the cities of the continent are to the south of the mountains. 9. Especially the plains are to the north of the mountain.

[1] In French this word must be preceded by the plural form of the indefinite article.

B. *Say aloud rapidly the French equivalent of each of the following sentences.*

1. The mountains are in the south of the country. 2. The mountains are in the north of the continent. 3. The plateau is in‿the[1] center of the country. 4. The plains are in‿the[1] interior of the continent. 5. The mountains are the boundaries of the country. 6. The mountains of the

[1] Express this combination with *à* and the definite article.
[a] The second *-e-* of *élevé* is completely silent [elve].

United States are in the east and in the west of the country. 7. Are the plains of the United States in the[1] center of the country? 8. In what part of the country are the mountains and the plains?

[1] Express this combination with *à* and the **definite article**.

QUATRIÈME LEÇON

Vocabulaire

artificiel, artificielle
la barrière
commercial
considérable
défendre

difficile
excellent
l'importance *f.*
limiter
le Luxembourg
naturel, naturelle

magnifique
profond
relativement[a]
séparer
touristique

a *has*
l'Allemagne *f.* *Germany*
autre *other*
constituer *form, make, constitute*
la côte *seacoast*
deux *two*
elle *it; she*
elles *f.* *they*
facile *easy*
le fleuve *river*
fort *strong*

il *it; he*
ils *m.* *they*
intérêt *m.* *interest*
large *wide*
la Manche *the English Channel*
le nord-ouest[b] *northwest*
ont *have*
par *by; through*
la plage *beach*
pourquoi *why*
qui *which, that; who*

Verbes

avoir *to have* il a ils ont

INTERROGATIVE FORMS

est-il?	forme-t-il?	limite-t-il?	se trouve-t-il?	a-t-il?
sont-ils?	forment-ils?	limitent-ils?	se trouvent-ils?	ont-ils?

Devoirs

Use inverted word order to express the questions in this lesson.

A. Write the French equivalent of each of the following sentences.

1. The Rhine is a river; it separates France from Germany. 2. The beaches of the Mediterranean are magnificent; they have a great importance.

[a] The ending *-ment* in French corresponds to the ending *-ly* in English.
[b] The *-d-* is silent, the *-st* is pronounced in *nord-ouest* [nɔrwɛst].

3. The rivers separate the two countries; they make[1] an excellent border. 4. Are the cities of the country small? 5. Is the Seine deep and wide? 6. Is the capital of the country a large city? 7. Do the mountains have a considerable[2] importance? 8. Do the rivers cross the country? 9. Does the Rhine form a part of the border between France and Germany? 10. Are the rivers less difficult to[3] cross than the mountains?

[1] Use a form of *constituer.*
[2] Look in your reading lesson to determine the position of this adjective in relation to its noun. [3] *à*

B. Say aloud rapidly the French equivalent of each of the following sentences.

1. Mountains[1] are natural boundaries.[2] 2. Rivers[1] are natural boundaries.[2] 3. The coasts of the Mediterranean and of the Atlantic have magnificent beaches.[2] 4. The English Channel has magnificent beaches.[2] 5. The Alps form the boundary between France and Italy. 6. The Rhine forms a part of the boundary between France and Germany. 7. The Rhine has a great commercial importance. 8. Rivers[1] are less easy to[3] defend than mountains.[1]

[1] Use the definite article with this word, which is taken in a general sense.
[2] Use the plural of the indefinite article with this word, which is indefinite. [3] *à*

CINQUIÈME LEÇON

Vocabulaire

américain	important	Orléans
arriver	la Loire	le port
Cherbourg	long, longue	la province
le commerce	militaire	la source
diviser	Nantes	Tours
le Havre[a]	la Normandie	le voyageur

l'Angleterre *f.* England
avec *with*
couler *flow*
connu *known, well-known; famous*
donc *therefore, then*
l'embouchure *f.* *mouth (of a river)*
ensuite *then*
l'estuaire *m.* *estuary (wide mouth of a river where it flows into the sea)*

étroit *narrow*
se jeter[b] dans *empty into*
parce que *because*
plus *more*
pour *for*
près de *near*
souvent *often*
trois *three*
vers *toward*

à l'étranger *abroad*
d'abord *at first*

[a] See page 511, § 1 B for an explanation of the aspirate *h*.
[b] Some verbs in *-eter* double the *-t-* in forms where this *-t-* is followed by a silent *-e* or *-ent*. EXAMPLE: il se jette, ils se jettent.

Verbes

se jeter | il se jette | ils se jettent

Devoirs

A. Write the French equivalent of each of the following sentences.

1. Often the American traveler arrives in France by Cherbourg. 2. Bordeaux is larger than Calais. 3. Is the Loire longer than the Seine? 4. The Loire is the longest river in[1] the country. 5. The Seine is wider than the Loire. 6. What are the two most important cities situated on the Seine? 7. What is the longest river in[1] the United States? 8. The Loire flows toward the west and empties into the Atlantic near Nantes. 9. Le Havre is important for commerce[2] with England. 10. Is Calais less well known than Paris?

[1] What preposition is used after a superlative in French? (§ 13 D)
[2] Use the definite article with this noun. (§ 4 B)

B. Say aloud rapidly the French equivalent of each of the following sentences.

1. What is the most important port on[1] the English Channel? 2. Le Havre is the most important port on[1] the English Channel. 3. The Loire is the longest river in[1] France. 4. The Loire is longer than the Seine. 5. What is the most important city situated on the Loire? 6. Paris is the most important city situated on the Seine. 7. Paris is more important than Cherbourg. 8. Often American travelers[2] arrive in France by Le Havre.

[1] *de* [2] Use the definite article.

THÈME[a]

Leçons 1 à 5

Write the French equivalent of each of the following sentences.

1. Africa is larger than Europe, but it is smaller than Asia. 2. The United States, Canada, and Mexico are in North America. 3. In what part of the country is[1] the capital situated? 4. The Massif Central is a large plateau which is[2] located in[3] the center of France. 5. Belgium is a small country which is[2] located to the north of France. 6. It (Belgium) is smaller than Spain and Portugal. 7. Le Havre and Cherbourg are the most important ports of the English Channel. 8. Often American travelers[4] arrive in France by one of the two ports. 9. The Loire is the longest river in[5] the country. 10. The Loire is therefore longer than the other rivers of the country.

[1] See page 2, question 10, for word order. [2] Use a form of *se trouver.*
[3] in the *au* [4] Use the definite article.
[5] What preposition follows the superlative in French? (§ 13 D)

[a] Each *Thème* offers a review of the vocabulary and grammatical principles of the preceding five lessons through English-to-French translation.

SIXIÈME LEÇON

Vocabulaire

l'Afrique du Nord *f.*	la Garonne	passer
Bordeaux	la Gironde	la quantité
économique	Genève	rapide
entrer	l'industrie *f.*	la région
exporter	Lyon [a]	le Rhône
fertile	navigable	la vallée
	l'Orient *m.*	

après *after*	ne . . . pas *not*
assez *enough*	non *no*
célèbre *famous*	puis *then*
le courant *current*	la soie *silk*
court *short*	suisse *Swiss*
espagnol *Spanish*	tourner *turn*
jusqu'à *up to*	trop *too; too much, too many*
le lac *lake*	le vin *wine*

Verbes

NEGATIVE FORMS

il ne forme pas	il ne se trouve pas	il n'a pas	il n'est pas
ils ne forment pas	ils ne se trouvent pas	ils n'ont pas	ils ne sont pas

NEGATIVE-INTERROGATIVE FORMS

ne forme-t-il pas	ne se trouve-t-il pas	n'a-t-il pas	n'est-il pas
ne forment-ils pas	ne se trouvent-ils pas	n'ont-ils pas	ne sont-ils pas

Devoirs

A. Write the French equivalent of each of the following sentences.

1. The Rhone is not a river of the United States. 2. It does not flow toward the north. 3. Brest is not one of the most famous cities of France. 4. The Garonne is not a river which empties into the English Channel. 5. The Loire is not deep enough[1]. 6. Does not the Loire empty into the Atlantic? 7. Does not Bordeaux export the wines of the region? 8. The current of the Seine is not too rapid. 9. Paris does not export the wines of the region of Bordeaux.

[1] precedes its adjective

[a] The spelling of *Lyon* in French is different from its spelling in English.

CRFL

B. *Say aloud rapidly the French equivalent of each of the following sentences.*

1. Bordeaux is one of the largest ports in[1] France. 2. Marseilles is one of the largest cities in[1] France. 3. Marseilles is the largest city of France after Paris. 4. Marseilles is not the largest city of France. 5. Bordeaux is not situated on the Loire. 6. The Rhone empties into the Mediterranean. 7. The Rhone does not empty into the Atlantic. 8. The Rhine does not form the boundary between France and Spain.

[1] *de* without an article

SEPTIÈME LEÇON

Vocabulaire

l'ancêtre *m.*
l'architecture *f.*
attacher
border
le caractère
celtique
se composer
complètement
correspondre
le costume
la différence
différent
la division
exister
extrême
indépendant
l'opinion *f.*
l'origine *f.*
pittoresque
politique
la race
royaliste
la tradition

ancien, ancienne *former*[a]
aujourd'hui *today*
autrefois *formerly*
la Bretagne *Brittany*
le Breton, la Bretonne *Breton, an inhabitant of Brittany*
certains *certain ones*
chaque *each*
la coutume *custom*
encore *still*
français *French* (adj.)
garder *keep*
la Grande-Bretagne *Great Britain*
l'habitant *m.* *inhabitant*
habiter *live, inhabit, live in*
l'île *f.* *island*
la langue *language*
leur (*m. f. sing.*), leurs (*m. f. pl.*) *their*
la maison *house*
même (adj.) *same;* (adv.) *even*
ne . . . plus *no longer*
parler *speak, talk*
plusieurs *several*
presque *almost*
tout, toute, tous, toutes *all, every*
le vieillard *old man*

à peu près *approximately, about*
en face de *opposite, facing*

Verbes

correspondre (AND OTHER -re VERBS)

il correspond ils correspondent

[a] When *ancien* precedes its noun, it means *former*; when it follows its noun, it means *old.*

Devoirs

Italicized words in the sentences below are indefinite nouns. In French these nouns must be preceded by the plural form of the indefinite article. See § 3 B.

A. Write the French equivalent of each of the following sentences.

1. Each province still keeps different *customs.* 2. The provinces of the country are political *divisions.* 3. Do the old men speak the French language? 4. The inhabitants of the provinces have picturesque *houses.* 5. Almost all the inhabitants of the continent still[1] speak two languages. 6. Great Britain is situated to the north of France. 7. Is Marseilles[2] an important city of the south of the country? 8. The country has natural *boundaries.* 9. All the continents and all the cities have different *languages.*

[1] Place directly after the verb. [2] French spelling differs from English.

B. Say aloud rapidly the French equivalent of each of the following sentences.

1. Today France is composed of several regions. 2. Brittany is a very picturesque province. 3. The French houses are very picturesque. 4. The architecture of the houses is not the same in all[1] parts of France. 5. Who inhabits Brittany? 6. Do the old‿men speak the same language as[2] the other inhabitants of the country? 7. The old‿men speak a different language. 8. Nearly all the old‿men speak the language of their ancestors.

[1] Supply the definite article. [2] *que*

HUITIÈME LEÇON

Vocabulaire

approcher	élégant	Louis XI[a]
la cathédrale	l'ennemi *m.*	le monument
certain	la forteresse	le nombre
Chenonceaux	fortifié	occuper
Chinon	gothique	principal
la comparaison	historique	la Renaissance
conservé	italien, italienne	la ruine
dater	le kilomètre	le style
l'édifice *m.*	Loches	la Touraine

[a] Louis onze

appeler *call*
autour de *around*
bien *well*
ce, cet, cette, ces *this, that, these, those*
cent *hundred*
le château *castle*
combien *how much, how many*
comment *how; what*
construit *constructed*
destiné à *designed to*
empêcher *prevent*
l'endroit *m.* *place*
entouré *surrounded*
environ *about, approximately*
haut *high*
l'histoire *f.* *story; history*
le jardin *garden*
maintenant *now*
la muraille *wall*
on *one* (indefinite pronoun)
onze *eleven*
parmi *among*
que? qu'? *what?*
quelque *some*
raconter *tell*
le roi *king*
le souvenir *remembrance, reminder, recollection*
le tableau *picture, painting*
tomber *fall*
trouver *find*

comment appelle-t-on *what does one call, what do they call*
grâce à *thanks to*
il y a *there is, there are*
le moyen âge *the Middle Ages*

Verbes

ALL VERBS IN **-eler**

appeler il appelle ils appellent

Devoirs

A. Write the French equivalent of each of the following sentences.

1. They [1] call that province the garden of France. 2. There are several castles of the Middle Ages in [2] Touraine. 3. These castles have walls [3]. 4. One finds pictures [3] in this place. 5. These pictures tell the story of a king [4] of France. 6. Chinon is a castle which is falling in [2] ruins. 7. This building is known thanks to the reminders of Joan of Arc. 8. Are there gardens [3] around this castle? 9. Are there pictures [3] which tell the story of Louis XI in this place? 10. Does one speak the French language in that country?

[1] Use *on*. [2] *en*
[3] This indefinite noun must be preceded by the plural of the indefinite article.
[4] a king of France *un roi de France*

B. Say aloud rapidly the French equivalent of each of the following sentences.

1. One finds picturesque gardens[1] around this castle. 2. There are paintings[1] in[2] the interior of the castle. 3. There is a castle at[2] Loches. 4. Is there a cathedral at[2] Tours? 5. Are there castles[1] in that valley? 6. This region is situated at about two hundred kilometers to the southwest of Paris. 7. Brittany is situated at about three hundred kilometers to the west of Paris. 8. One calls the inhabitants of Brittany[3] Bretons[1].

[1] This indefinite noun must be preceded by the plural of the indefinite article.
[2] *à* [3] Use the definite article with this place name.

NEUVIÈME LEÇON

Vocabulaire

l'agriculture *f.*	la crème	normand
Bayeux	économe	les Normands *m.*
Caen[a]	favorable	réputé
le chef	fermenté	Rouen
le cidre	gai	six
la conquête	intéressant	typiquement
	Mathilde	

s'appeler *be called*	le jus *juice*
aimer *like; love*	le lait *milk*
beaucoup *a great deal; much*	mille *thousand*
le beurre *butter*	le mouton *sheep*
le bœuf[b] *steer, ox*	partout *everywhere*
bon, bonne *good*	la pomme *apple*
l'église *f.* *church*	la reine *queen*
la femme[c] *wife; woman*	la rue *street*
fournir *furnish*	soixante-six[d] *sixty-six*
le fromage *cheese*	la vache *cow*
Guillaume *William*	la viande *meat*

aussi . . . que *as . . . as*
Comment s'appelle . . .? *What is . . . called?*
Guillaume le Conquérant *William the Conqueror*
Jeanne d'Arc *Joan of Arc*

[a] Pronounced [kɑ̃].
[b] The final *-f* of *bœuf* is pronounced in the singular [ləbœf], but silent in the plural [lebø].
[c] The word *femme* is pronounced [fam] to rhyme with *dame*.
[d] The *-x-* of *soixante* is pronounced as *s* in the English word *see* [swasɑ̃t].

Verbes

fournir (AND MOST OTHER **-ir** VERBS)

il fournit	ils fournissent

Devoirs

In these exercises, distinguish carefully between nouns used in the general sense, which are preceded by the definite article, and those expressing indefinite quantity, which are preceded by the partitive article.

A. Write the French equivalent of each of the following sentences.

1. One finds cows and sheep in that region. 2. France furnishes wine and silk to all the countries of the world. 3. Is there any butter in the former province of Normandy? 4. Do the Normans like apples and cider a great deal[1]? 5. Cheese and milk are good. 6. Is cream good? 7. Languages are easy. 8. The wife of the king is called the queen. 9. Is William the Conqueror as well[2] known as Joan of Arc?

[1] Follows the verb directly. [2] well known *connu*

B. Say aloud rapidly the French equivalent of each of the following sentences.

1. One finds cows and steers in that region. 2. One finds milk, butter, and cream in those regions. 3. Is there any meat in that region? 4. They[1] like cider a great deal[2] in that country. 5. They[1] like milk a great deal[2] in[3] the United States. 6. That church still[2] exists at Caen. 7. Who is the king's[4] wife? 8. This city has several churches and a cathedral.

[1] *on* [2] Place directly after the verb. [3] in the *aux*
[4] For the French method of expressing possession, see § 41.

DIXIÈME LEÇON

Vocabulaire

agréable	la civilisation	la Provence
Arles	cultiver	la Riviera[a]
l'automne *m.*	le fruit	romain
Avignon	l'hôtel *m.*	les Romains
Bayonne	Nice	le touriste
Biarritz	Nîmes	la trace
Cannes	l'orange *f.*	le troubadour
Carcassonne		visiter

[a] This term was current some years ago, but it has been entirely replaced by *la Côte d'Azur.*

l'amour *m. in sing., f. in pl.* *love*
assez de *enough*
beaucoup de *much; many; a lot of*
charmant *charming*
la chanson *song*
comme *like, as*
la Côte d'Azur *French Riviera*
l'été *m.* *summer*
les gens *m. pl.* *people*
l'hiver *m.* *winter*
le légume *vegetable*
loger *lodge*
le Midi *south (of France)*
le monde *world*
nombreux, nombreuse *numerous*
l'olivier *m.* *olive tree*
passer *spend (time)*
peu de *little; few*
plus de *more*
le printemps *spring*
quelquefois *sometimes*
le soleil *sun*
tard *late*
tôt *soon*
toujours *always*
trop de *too much; too many*

par contre *on the contrary*
tout le monde *everyone, everybody*

Devoirs

In this exercise, use le Midi to express the region known as the south of France.

A. Write the French equivalent of each of the following sentences.

1. In the south there are fruits which are not found[1] in the north. 2. One finds many oranges in the southeast of the country. 3. There are numerous[2] ruins in the south of France. 4. There are more tourists on the Mediterranean than on the English Channel. 5. There are too many people and not enough hotels at Cannes. 6. Are there too many hotels in this city? 7. There are good[2] hotels and numerous[2] beaches on the Riviera. 8. Few cities do not have any monuments. 9. In other places one finds high[2] walls which date from the Middle Ages.

[1] Use a form of *se trouver.* [2] Place the adjective before the noun.

B. Say aloud rapidly the French equivalent of each of the following sentences.

1. There are many fruits in the south of France. 2. One finds many tourists on the Riviera. 3. There aren't any tourists in Brittany in[1] winter. 4. There aren't any beaches near Marseilles. 5. Are there enough hotels in that region? 6. The winters are longer in the north than in the south. 7. There are too many people on the beaches in[1] summer. 8. There are few hotels in that city.

[1] *en*

Thème

Leçons 6 à 10

Write the French equivalent of each of the following sentences.

1. The Loire hasn't a great commercial importance, because it is not very deep. 2. The Rhone does not empty into the Atlantic. 3. These old men inhabit a picturesque country. 4. The inhabitants of this province are different from the inhabitants of the other provinces of the country. 5. There are many castles in that place. 6. One finds magnificent pictures in these buildings. 7. The northwest of France furnishes milk, cream, and butter to those parts of the world. 8. Do the French like cider? 9. Are there good beaches on the Atlantic? 10. There are few hotels but too many people at Cannes in [1] summer.

[1] *en*

Jean Vagona

Jean Vagona savait djoya [1], Jean Vagona savait djoya,
Savait djoya de la clarinette, Savait djoya de la clarina.
Cla-cla-cla de la clarinette, Cla-cla-cla de la clarina.

Bonhomme, bonhomme, tu n'es pas maître en ta maison,
Car nous y sommes, Car nous y sommes.

Jean Vagona savait djoya, Jean Vagona savait djoya,
Savait djoya de la flûtinette, Savait djoya de la flûtina.
Flû-flû-flû de la flûtinette, Flû-flû-flû de la flûtina.
Cla-cla-cla de la clarinette, Cla-cla-cla de la clarina.

Bonhomme, (etc.)

le violon, le trombone, le triangle, la grosse caissette, le violoncelle, etc., etc.

[1] Dialect for *jouer.*

ONZIÈME LEÇON

Deux Américains en France

Je suis Américain, mais je parle couramment le français. J'ai un camarade américain qui s'appelle Robert. Il parle français aussi. Cet été nous visitons la France ensemble. Nous avons une moto et nous voyageons à travers tout le pays. Aujourd'hui nous sommes à Grenoble, ville pittoresque entourée de montagnes. Grenoble se trouve dans les Alpes, pas loin de l'Italie.

Nous passons souvent la nuit dans les auberges de la jeunesse. Ces auberges sont destinées aux jeunes gens qui n'ont pas beaucoup d'argent. Là, nous rencontrons des garçons et des jeunes filles de toutes les nationalités. Nous aimons être au milieu de ces jeunes gens pour avoir la possibilité d'échanger des idées. A table une jeune fille me demande:

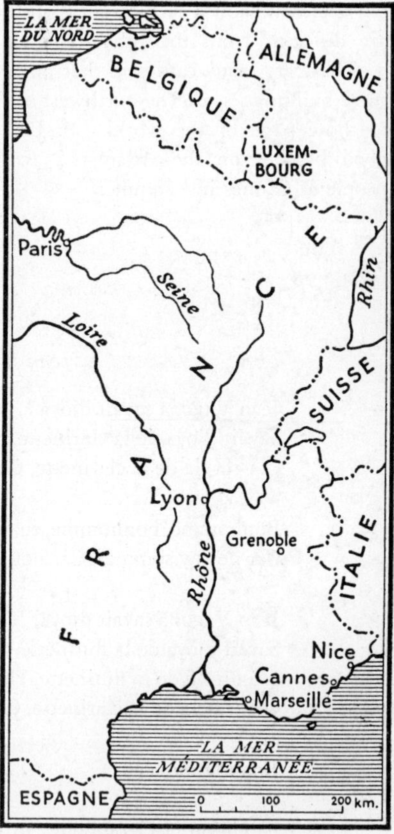

Grenoble se trouve dans les Alpes, pas loin de l'Italie

— Êtes-vous Français?

— Non, je ne suis pas Français. Je suis Américain. Et vous?

— Je suis Française, et pendant les vacances je voyage à bicyclette. Vous avez une moto, n'est-ce pas?

— Oui, et je voyage avec un camarade. Demain nous commençons à explorer les Alpes.

— Comment trouvez-vous la France? Elle est sûrement très différente de l'Amérique.

Questions

1. Où est Grenoble? 2. Quelle langue parlent les Français? 3. A qui sont destinées les auberges de la jeunesse? 4. Qui rencontre-t-on dans les auberges de la jeunesse? 5. Comment voyagent souvent les jeunes gens qui visitent la France?

Devoirs

® *A. Répondez aux questions suivantes en employant* je *dans la réponse.* EXEMPLE: Aimez-vous passer l'été sur la plage? Oui, monsieur, *j'*aime passer l'été sur la plage.

1. Êtes-vous Américain? 2. Parlez-vous français? 3. Avez-vous un camarade français? 4. Visitez-vous la France? 5. Voyagez-vous souvent? 6. Êtes-vous maintenant à Grenoble? 7. Passez-vous souvent la nuit dans un hôtel? 8. Êtes-vous maintenant en vacances? 9. Avez-vous une moto?

® *B. Répondez aux questions suivantes en employant* **vous** *dans la réponse.* EXEMPLE: Est-ce que j'aime le cidre? Oui, mademoiselle, *vous* aimez le cidre.

1. Est-ce que je parle français? 2. Est-ce que nous voyageons en voiture? 3. Est-ce que je trouve la France différente de l'Amérique? 4. Est-ce que j'ai une bicyclette? 5. Suis-je en vacances? 6. Visitons-nous la France? 7. Commençons-nous à parler français? 8. Sommes-nous à Paris aujourd'hui?

C. Remplacez les tirets par le pronom convenable.

1. —— suis Américain. 2. —— êtes Français. 3. —— sommes dans une auberge de la jeunesse. 4. —— parlons de la France et de l'Amérique. 5. —— aimez beaucoup voyager en France. 6. —— ai un camarade qui s'appelle Robert. 7. Avez-—— une bicyclette? 8. Voyagez-—— souvent? 9. —— avons des camarades qui parlent français. 10. —— aiment avoir la possibilité d'échanger des idées avec des amis.

D. Remplacez l'infinitif par le présent du verbe, s'il y a lieu.
EXEMPLE: Vous (parler) français. Vous *parlez* français.

1. Je (être) Américain. 2. J'(avoir) un camarade français qui s'appelle Robert. 3. Nous (aimer) voyager en France. 4. Nous (voyager) dans la région des Alpes. 5. Nous (avoir) une moto. 6. Vous (être) Français, n'est-ce pas? 7. (avoir)-vous une bicyclette? 8. Vous ne (voyager) pas à bicyclette. 9. Je (rencontrer) des jeunes

gens dans les auberges de la jeunesse. 10. Demain vous (commencer) à explorer les Alpes. 11. Aujourd'hui nous (commencer) à parler français. 12. Nous aimons (être) en France. 13. Aimez-vous (avoir) la possibilité de parler français? 14. Nous (être) maintenant à Grenoble.

E. Mettez les phrases suivantes à la forme interrogative. Faites attention surtout à la première personne du singulier. EXEMPLES: 1. Nous avons une bicyclette. Avons-nous une bicyclette? 2. Je parle français. Est-ce que je parle français?

1. Vous avez beaucoup de camarades. 2. J'aime voyager en France. 3. Marie et Robert sont des camarades. 4. Je voyage avec Robert.

CONVERSATION

1. Demandez à l'étudiant qui est devant vous s'il parle français. 2. Demandez à l'étudiant qui est derrière vous s'il est Américain. 3. Demandez à l'étudiant qui est à votre gauche s'il a une moto. 4. Demandez à l'étudiant qui est à votre droite s'il aime voyager.

VOCABULAIRE — PAGES 92–93

GRAMMAIRE

1. What are the French subject personal pronouns? (§ 23 A)

2. The French have two words for *you*: ***tu*** and ***vous***. At present, use only the form ***vous*** to express *you,* whether in the singular or plural. If you wish to learn the distinction between ***tu*** and ***vous,*** read § 23 B.

3. How is the present of ***-er*** verbs regularly formed? (§ 49 A) What are the forms of the present of the regular ***-er*** verbs ***parler, visiter,*** and ***aimer?*** (Page 93)

4. What irregularity do you notice in the present of the ***-cer*** verb ***commencer*** and the ***-ger*** verb ***voyager?*** Conjugate ***commencer*** and ***voyager*** in the present tense. (Page 93)

5. What are the forms of the present of the irregular verbs ***être*** and ***avoir?*** (Page 93)

6. Usually any sentence may be made interrogative either by the use of ***Est-ce que*** . . . or by inverting the subject and the verb. In what form of the present of ***-er*** verbs can only the ***Est-ce que*** form be used? (Page 500, note 2)

7. Normally the definite article is used with names of languages. When is it omitted before the name of a language? (§ 4 F)

8. Give examples of the use of . . . ***n'est-ce pas?*** (§ 96 J)

DOUZIÈME LEÇON

Un week-end à la campagne

Les Français aiment beaucoup la campagne. Un nombre considérable de Parisiens ont une maison à la campagne où ils passent leurs week-ends. Souvent ils y passent aussi leurs vacances. En France beaucoup de magasins ferment non seulement le dimanche, mais aussi le samedi ou le lundi. De nombreux Français passent ainsi deux jours de la semaine à la campagne.

Roger est un petit Français; il a huit ans. Il habite à Paris avec son père, sa mère, ses frères Georges et Paul et sa sœur Marie. Paul a seize ans, Georges douze ans et Marie neuf ans. Dans une lettre à son oncle et à sa tante qui habitent en Amérique Roger raconte sa vie en France. Voici sa lettre:

Paris, le 12 juin

Mon cher oncle et ma chère tante,

Samedi soir, je vais à la campagne avec papa, maman, mes frères et ma sœur. Nous allons y passer le week-end. Dimanche je vais jouer avec mon ami Pierre, et Marie va jouer avec son amie Jacqueline.

Je vais à l'école le lundi, le mardi, le mercredi, le vendredi et le samedi. Nous n'y allons pas le jeudi et le dimanche. Nous sommes libres le jeudi. Je vais à une école de garçons; Marie va à une école de filles, car en France les garçons et les filles vont à des écoles différentes. Mes frères vont au lycée, car ils sont plus âgés. Nos écoles ne se trouvent pas dans la même rue, mais elles sont toutes dans notre quartier.

Je vais très bien. Maman et papa vont bien aussi. Comment allez-vous?

Vos vacances sont-elles au mois de juillet? Nos vacances vont bientôt commencer. Elles durent trois mois.

Bons baisers,

Votre neveu,

ROGER

QUESTIONS

1. Aimez-vous beaucoup la campagne? 2. Avez-vous une maison à la campagne? 3. Passez-vous vos week-ends à la campagne? 4. Aux États-Unis les magasins ferment-ils le lundi? 5. Quel âge a Roger? 6.

Quel âge avez-vous? 7. Où habite Roger? 8. Combien de sœurs a Roger? 9. Combien de frères a Roger? 10. Où habitent l'oncle et la tante de Roger? 11. Où Roger passe-t-il le week-end? 12. Quels jours de la semaine Roger va-t-il à l'école? 13. Quels jours de la semaine allez-vous à l'école? 14. En France les garçons et les filles vont-ils à la même école? 15. A quelle école vont les frères de Roger? 16. Comment allez-vous? 17. Votre frère va-t-il bien? 18. Vos vacances sont-elles en hiver ou en été? 19. Combien de mois durent vos vacances?

Devoirs

A. Écrivez en français.

17, 6, 16, 9, 15, 13, 7, 14, 5, 12

B. Remplacez les adjectifs possessifs anglais par l'équivalent français.

1. Je vais en France avec (*my*) père, (*my*) mère et (*my*) frères. 2. Nous rencontrons (*our*) camarades dans (*our*) quartier. 3. (*Your*) oncle et (*your*) tantes sont à la campagne. 4. Roger raconte (*his*) histoire à (*his*) mère. 5. Marie raconte (*her*) histoire à (*her*) père et à (*her*) mère. 6. Georges et Paul rencontrent (*their*) amis dans une rue de (*their*) quartier. 7. Marie joue avec (*her*) amie Jacqueline et Roger joue avec (*his*) ami Pierre. 8. Maurice parle à (*his*) camarades de (*their*) vie à Paris.

® *C. Remplacez les mots en italique par* ***y***. Exemples: 1. Est-ce que Maurice va à la maison? Oui, il va *à la maison.* Oui, il *y* va. 2. Marie est à l'école. Êtes-vous *à l'école* aussi? *Y* êtes-vous aussi?

1. Allez-vous à la campagne? Oui, je vais *à la campagne* jeudi. 2. Est-ce que nous allons bientôt en France? Oui, nous allons *en France* cet été. 3. Que trouve-t-on en Touraine? On trouve des châteaux *en Touraine.* 4. Les touristes passent-ils l'hiver sur la Côte d'Azur? Oui, ils passent l'hiver *sur la Côte d'Azur.* 5. Est-ce que Roger va à l'école le dimanche? Non, il ne va pas *à l'école* le dimanche. 6. Nous allons à la campagne vendredi. Allez-vous *à la campagne* aussi?

*D. Remplacez les tirets par la forme convenable du présent du verbe **aller**.*

1. Nous —— en France cet hiver. 2. Je —— à la campagne avec mon père. 3. ——-vous à Rouen? 4. Roger —— à l'école tous les jours de la semaine. 5. Georges et Paul ne —— pas à une école de filles. 6. Je —— en Espagne cet été. 7. Marie —— à Paris avec sa mère. 8.

Nous —— au lycée lundi. 9. Vous —— jouer avec votre camarade. 10. Comment —— -vous?

CONVERSATION

1. Demandez à l'étudiant qui est à votre droite quel âge il a. 2. Demandez à l'étudiant qui est devant vous s'il va à l'école le samedi. 3. Demandez à l'étudiant qui est à votre gauche comment il va. 4. Demandez à l'étudiant qui est derrière vous s'il va passer ses vacances à la campagne.

VOCABULAIRE — PAGES 94–95

GRAMMAIRE

1. Count up to 20 in French. (§ 17 A)

2. List the possessive adjectives which occur in the lesson. Compare them with the classified list in § 14 A of the Grammaire.

3. With what does the possessive adjective agree in French? How does this differ from English usage? (§ 14 B)

4. When are ***mon, ton,*** and ***son*** used instead of ***ma, ta,*** and ***sa*** before a feminine singular noun? (§ 14 C)

5. When is the adverb *y* used in French? (§ 29 A) Note that *y* always comes *before* the verb it modifies, whether in a statement or a question.

6. What are the forms of the present of the irregular verb ***aller?*** (Page 95) How does English express that verb in a sentence such as: Je ***vais*** *jouer avec mon ami.* In the idiomatic *Comment **allez**-vous? Je* ***vais*** *bien.*

7. What are the days of the week? (§ 97 A) The article is not usually employed with the days of the week, but it must be used at certain times. Explain when it is used. (§ 4 D)

8. How does one say in French: *How old are you? I am twenty years old.* (90 A)

TREIZIÈME LEÇON

Une dictée dans une classe française

Imaginez que vous êtes les élèves d'une école française. Vous êtes dans une classe où des garçons de onze et douze ans étudient un texte de Victor Hugo.

La salle est grande et claire. Elle a une porte à droite et cinq fenêtres à gauche. Beaucoup de lumière entre par les fenêtres. Devant nous il y a le bureau du professeur et un grand tableau noir. Nous sommes assis à nos places.

—Écoutez, dit le professeur. Il lit à haute voix le texte de Victor Hugo. Il le lit lentement. Les élèves le lisent à voix basse. Il y a un mot difficile. Le professeur l'explique. Puis, il dit:

—Monnot, allez au tableau et copiez le début du texte.

L'élève Monnot écrit au tableau les premières phrases du texte. Il les écrit avec soin.

Maintenant, le professeur dit:

—Dupont, lisez ces phrases à haute voix.

Je les lis lentement. Ensuite, nous les lisons tous ensemble. Le professeur remarque une faute. Il la corrige et dit:

—Lisez cette phrase, Monnot.

L'élève Monnot la lit correctement.

—Effacez le tableau et asseyez-vous, s'il vous plaît.

Ensuite, le professeur explique:

—Je vais vous dicter la première partie du texte. Je vais la dicter lentement. Écrivez, s'il vous plaît. Le Chevalier, taisez-vous et tâchez de faire attention.

Le professeur lit le début du texte. Nous l'écrivons. Je l'écris à l'encre avec mon stylo; en France les élèves n'écrivent pas les devoirs au crayon. Le professeur lit le début du texte une deuxième fois. Puis il continue la dictée.

QUESTIONS

1. Quel âge ont les élèves de la classe? 2. Notre classe est-elle grande et claire? 3. La porte de la salle est-elle à gauche ou à droite? 4. Com-

bien de fenêtres y a-t-il dans notre classe? 5. La lumière entre-t-elle par les fenêtres ou par la porte de la salle? 6. Où est le bureau du professeur? 7. Tous les élèves écrivent-ils au tableau noir? 8. Le professeur lit-il le texte à haute voix ou à voix basse? 9. Les élèves sont-ils assis quand ils écrivent au tableau? 10. Qui explique les mots difficiles aux élèves? 11. Qui corrige les fautes des élèves? 12. Qui efface le tableau? 13. Écrivez-vous les devoirs au crayon ou à l'encre? 14. Qui lit le début du texte aux élèves?

DEVOIRS

® *A. Remplacez les expressions en italique par le pronom complément convenable.* EXEMPLE: J'aime la France et je visite *la France* en été. J'aime la France et je *la* visite en été.

1. Je lis le devoir et je copie *ce devoir* au tableau. 2. J'aime les vacances et je passe *mes vacances* à la campagne. 3. On dit qu'il y a une tapisserie dans le château et qu'on trouve *cette tapisserie* dans la grande salle. 4. Le professeur écrit au tableau un mot difficile et il explique *ce mot* aux élèves. 5. Monnot copie une phrase. Efface-t-il *cette phrase* ensuite? 6. Le professeur remarque une faute et il corrige *cette faute.* 7. Les élèves trouvent le texte et ils lisent *le texte* à voix basse. 8. Nos amis vont à Grenoble et nous rencontrons *ces amis* dans une auberge de la jeunesse. 9. Beaucoup de gens visitent les villes de la Côte d'Azur. Visitent-ils *ces villes* en été ou en hiver? 10. La Touraine est très jolie et on appelle *la Touraine* le jardin de la France. 11. Mon camarade écrit les phrases au tableau et puis il lit *les phrases* à ses amis. 12. Le professeur lit le texte et les élèves écoutent *le texte.*

B. Remplacez l'infinitif par l'impératif. EXEMPLE: (regarder) le tableau. Regardez le tableau.

1. (parler) français en classe. 2. (corriger) vos fautes. 3. (effacer) les phrases. 4. (aller) au tableau et (écrire) cinq mots. 5. (lire) les mots à haute voix.

C. Remplacez l'infinitif par la forme convenable du présent ou par l'impératif, selon le cas.

1. (écrire) tous les mots difficiles. 2. Je (lire) ces mots à haute voix. 3. Qui (écrire) au tableau? 4. (lire) toutes les phrases au professeur. 5. (écrire)-vous avec un stylo? 6. Les deux élèves (lire) le texte. 7. Nous (écrire) très lentement. 8. (lire)-vous avec soin? 9. J'(écrire) toutes les phrases au tableau. 10. Ne (lire) pas ces fautes.

11. Les élèves (lire) les phrases du texte. 12. Qui (lire) les mots difficiles du texte?

CONVERSATION

1. Demandez à l'étudiant qui est assis près de la porte s'il écrit ses devoirs à l'encre. 2. Demandez à l'étudiant qui est assis près de la fenêtre s'il lit le texte à haute voix. 3. Demandez à l'étudiant qui est assis à votre droite s'il aime écrire au tableau. 4. Demandez à l'étudiant qui est devant vous s'il écrit la dictée au crayon.

VOCABULAIRE — PAGES 96–97

GRAMMAIRE

1. What are the direct object pronouns? (§ 24 A) How are they used? (§ 24 B)

2. What is the usual position of object-pronouns with respect to the verb? (§ 30 A)

3. What happens to the forms of ***me, te, le,*** and ***la*** when they directly precede a verb beginning with a vowel or a mute-h? (Page 399, note 1)

4. In your reading lesson find verbs ending in ***-ez*** which have no subject-pronoun. What function do such verbs perform? What grammatical term describes this function? (§ 79 A)

5. What are the imperative forms of ***parler, regarder, écrire,*** and ***lire?*** (Page 97)

6. Give the forms of the present tense of the irregular verbs ***écrire*** and ***lire.*** (Page 97)

QUATORZIÈME LEÇON

Une leçon sur Victor Hugo

Pendant la dictée, je constate que mon stylo est vide. Je le remplis. Nous remplissons toujours nos stylos avec de l'encre bleue.

Le professeur finit la lecture du texte. Les élèves finissent de l'écrire. Puis le professeur leur parle de Victor Hugo. Il leur dit:

— Victor Hugo est un des écrivains les plus connus de la littérature française. Il est célèbre non seulement par ses romans, mais aussi par ses poèmes et ses pièces de théâtre. Ses romans *Notre-Dame de Paris* et *Les Misérables* sont connus dans tous les pays du monde. Maintenant, nous allons lire un poème de Victor Hugo. Ouvrez vos livres et choisissez un poème pour notre leçon.

Nous choisissons un poème sur la mer. Le professeur nous dit que ce poème est très connu. Ensuite, il me dit:

— Dupont, lisez.

Pendant que je lis le poème, le professeur observe la classe. Il remarque l'élève Moreau, qui, assis derrière tous ses camarades, lit un livre qu'il semble cacher. Aussitôt, il ordonne:

— Dupont, arrêtez. Moreau, continuez.

L'élève Moreau, confus, ne réussit pas à trouver le passage. Le professeur lui dit:

— Apportez au bureau le livre que vous cachez. Ah! Vous lisez un roman policier pendant que nous étudions un poème de Victor Hugo. Les autres élèves m'obéissent toujours. Je ne les punis jamais. Vous, vous ne m'obéissez pas. Donc, je vous punis. Copiez ce poème cinq fois dans votre cahier.

Moreau baisse la tête et réfléchit. Il pense à sa punition méritée.

QUESTIONS

1. Quand remplissez-vous votre stylo? 2. Avec quoi remplissez-vous votre stylo? 3. Qui finit la lecture du texte? 4. Qui finit d'écrire le texte? 5. De quel écrivain le professeur parle-t-il aux élèves? 6. Pourquoi Victor Hugo est-il très connu? 7. Citez deux romans de Victor Hugo. 8. Pendant que l'élève Dupont lit à haute voix un poème de Victor Hugo, que lit l'élève Moreau? 9. Où est assis l'élève Moreau? 10. Quand le professeur lui dit de continuer la lecture du poème, l'élève Moreau réussit-il à trouver le passage? 11. Le professeur punit-il les élèves qui lui obéissent? 12. Pourquoi le professeur punit-il l'élève Moreau? 13. Combien de fois l'élève Moreau copie-t-il le poème dans son cahier? 14. A quoi pense l'élève Moreau?

DEVOIRS

® *A. Remplacez les expressions en italique par un pronom complément.*

EXEMPLE: Le professeur, qui est devant les élèves, parle *aux élèves* de Victor Hugo. Le professeur, qui est devant les élèves, *leur* parle de Victor Hugo.

1. Un élève qui parle au professeur dit *au professeur* que son stylo est vide. 2. Roger, qui écrit une lettre à sa tante, raconte *à sa tante* qu'il va passer le week-end à la campagne. 3. Le professeur dit aux élèves: — Ouvrez vos livres, et lit *aux élèves* un poème de Victor Hugo. 4. Le professeur remarque que l'élève Moreau lit un roman policier et ordonne *à Moreau* de lire à haute voix. 5. Vous parlez à Georges et à Marie. Parlez-vous *à Georges et à Marie* d'un roman de Victor Hugo? 6. Le professeur parle à Hélène. Explique-t-il le texte *à Hélène?* 7. Maurice parle à Louise et à Yvonne, et il dit *à Louise et à Yvonne* que les vacances commencent demain. 8. Quand je parle à mes camarades, je raconte *à mes camarades* mon voyage en France. 9. Quand nous écrivons une lettre, nous écrivons *la lettre* à l'encre.

® *B. Répondez aux questions suivantes en employant des pronoms compléments* ***indirects.*** EXEMPLE: Expliquez-vous le texte à votre sœur? Oui, monsieur, je *lui* explique le texte.

1. Lisez-vous ce poème à vos camarades? 2. Écrivez-vous une lettre à votre mère? 3. Parlez-vous souvent à votre professeur? 4. Racontez-vous cette histoire à votre oncle? 5. Le professeur explique-t-il la leçon aux élèves?

C. Remplacez l'infinitif par la forme convenable du présent du verbe indiqué ou par l'impératif, selon le cas.

1. Quand (remplir)-vous votre stylo? 2. Nous (finir) la lecture du poème. 3. (choisir) un roman policier. 4. Les élèves ne (réussir) pas à trouver le passage dans le texte. 5. Qui (obéir) au professeur? 6. Je (punir) Roger quand il n'écrit pas une lettre à son oncle. 7. Ensuite, il baisse la tête et (réfléchir). 8. Nous (choisir) une bonne voiture. 9. Maurice et sa sœur (finir) de copier le poème dans leur cahier. 10. Ma mère me (punir) quand je ne lui (obéir) pas. 11. Je (réussir) à trouver mon stylo. 12. (punir)-vous les élèves qui lisent des romans policiers en classe?

D. Remplacez les tirets par le pronom relatif ***qui, que ou qu'.***

1. Nous allons choisir un poème —— est très connu. 2. Le poème —— nous choisissons est de Victor Hugo. 3. Le professeur ne punit pas les élèves —— lui obéissent. 4. L'élève —— le professeur punit ne lui obéit jamais. 5. L'élève Moreau lit un livre —— il semble cacher.

En Provence beaucoup de villes conservent des traces de l'ancienne civilisation romaine

A Cannes se trouvent de charmantes plages et d'élégants hôtels

Un nombre considérable de Parisiens ont une maison à la campagne

Dimanche je vais jouer avec mon ami Pierre

6. Marie écrit une dictée —— elle trouve difficile. 7. Les élèves —— arrivent en classe après le professeur vont au tableau. 8. Le professeur corrige les phrases —— ils écrivent. 9. Rouen est une ville —— est sur la Seine. 10. Les gens —— vous rencontrez dans les auberges de la jeunesse parlent toutes les langues.

CONVERSATION

1. Demandez à Monsieur A. s'il aime les romans policiers. 2. Demandez à Monsieur B. s'il obéit toujours à sa mère. 3. Demandez à Monsieur C. si le professeur lui explique souvent la leçon. 4. Demandez à Monsieur D. s'il copie sa leçon dans son cahier.

VOCABULAIRE — PAGE 98

GRAMMAIRE

1. How does French express the indirect object pronouns *to me, to you, to him, to her, to us,* and *to them?* (§ 25 A) How are these pronouns used? (§ 25 B)

2. What is the usual position of the indirect object pronoun in respect to the verb? (§ 30 A)

3. What happens to the forms of ***me*** and ***te*** when they directly precede a verb beginning with a vowel or a mute-h? (Page 400, note 1)

4. In French the second conjugation is made up of verbs whose infinitive ends in ***-ir.*** What endings are added to the stem of this verb to form the present tense? (§ 49 B) What ***-ir*** verbs do you find in this lesson?

5. Give the forms of the present tense of the ***-ir*** verbs ***finir*** and ***remplir.*** (Page 98)

6. What is a relative pronoun? (§ 39) In French, the two commonest relative pronouns are ***qui*** and ***que.*** When is ***qui*** used? (§ 39 B) When is ***que*** used? (§ 39 C) When does ***que*** become ***qu'?*** (§ 39 C)

7. In the sentence *Moreau baisse* ***la*** *tête,* how is ***la*** expressed in English? Comment on this use of the article in French. (§ 4 G)

QUINZIÈME LEÇON

Les saisons et les mois de l'année

Il y a quatre saisons dans l'année. Ce sont le printemps, l'été, l'automne et l'hiver. Au printemps il fait beau en France. En été il fait chaud, particulièrement dans le Midi. En automne il fait parfois mauvais temps. Le ciel est souvent couvert. En hiver, il fait froid et il neige, surtout dans les Alpes et les Pyrénées. Mon frère aime beaucoup l'hiver, car lui et ses amis font souvent du ski à la montagne. Moi, j'aime mieux l'été, mais lui aime beaucoup les sports d'hiver.

Il y a douze mois dans l'année. Janvier est le premier mois, février est le deuxième. Pendant cette période il fait souvent mauvais temps. Mars est le troisième mois de l'année. En mars il y a beaucoup de vent. Avril est le quatrième mois. Il pleut souvent en avril. Pâques tombe en mars ou en avril. On donne quinze jours de vacances aux élèves et aux étudiants à cette époque. Pendant ces vacances, nous faisons toujours un voyage quelque part. Un de mes camarades fait le voyage avec nous, et c'est lui qui conduit la voiture. Il aime mieux conduire que moi. Mai est le cinquième mois de l'année. C'est le mois des fleurs. Juin est le sixième mois de l'année. Ma sœur aime beaucoup juin. Pour elle, c'est le plus beau des mois. Juillet est le septième mois. En France le 14 juillet est la fête nationale. Les Parisiens aiment beaucoup cette fête qui est pour eux l'occasion de danser le soir dans les rues. Août est le huitième mois de l'année. C'est la période des vacances. Au mois d'août il fait généralement beau. Septembre est le neuvième mois. En septembre il fait doux. Le 15 septembre les élèves rentrent en classe. Octobre est le dixième mois. Il fait frais en octobre. Novembre est le onzième mois. En novembre les étudiants recommencent leurs cours dans les universités et les grandes écoles. Décembre est le dernier mois de l'année. C'est le mois des vacances de Noël.

Questions

1. Combien y a-t-il de saisons dans l'année? 2. Quelles sont les saisons de l'année? 3. Pour vous, quel est le plus beau mois de l'année?

4. Quel temps fait-il en France au printemps? 5. En quelle saison fait-il chaud? 6. Dans quelle région de France surtout fait-il chaud en été? 7. Dans quelle partie des États-Unis fait-il chaud en été? 8. Quand fait-il mauvais temps? 9. En quelle saison neige-t-il beaucoup? 10. Combien y a-t-il de mois dans l'année? 11. Quel est le premier mois de l'année? 12. Neige-t-il en janvier et en février? 13. En quel mois y a-t-il beaucoup de vent? 14. En quel mois pleut-il beaucoup? 15. Avez-vous des vacances à Pâques? 16. Où faites-vous un voyage pendant les vacances de Pâques? 17. Voyagez-vous en voiture ou à bicyclette? 18. Pourquoi aimez-vous beaucoup le mois de mai? 19. Pourquoi le 14 juillet est-il une date importante en France? 20. Pourquoi août est-il le mois des vacances en France? 21. En quel mois les élèves des lycées français rentrent-ils en classe? 22. Quand recommencent vos cours à l'université? 23. En quel mois recommencent les cours des universités françaises? 24. Pourquoi le 4 juillet est-il une date importante en Amérique?

Devoirs

A. *Remplacez par l'équivalent français les expressions de temps qui se trouvent entre parenthèses.*

1. En hiver (*it is cold*). 2. (*It rains*) très souvent en avril. 3. En décembre (*it snows*). 4. Souvent (*it is cloudy*) en Angleterre. 5. En novembre (*the weather is bad*). 6. En quel mois (*is it hot*)? 7. En automne (*it is mild*). 8. En mars (*it is very windy*). 9. (*What kind of weather is it*) au printemps? 10. Dans le Midi de la France (*the weather is good*). 11. (*It is cool*) en novembre.

B. *Remplacez par les équivalents français les pronoms indiqués entre parenthèses.*

1. Maurice et (*I*) allons à la montagne pendant les vacances de Noël. 2. C'est (*he*) qui aime les sports d'hiver. 3. (*He*) et ses camarades font du ski dans les Alpes. 4. Qui est là? (*I*). 5. Vous êtes avec (*them*) tout le temps. 6. Pour (*us*) l'automne est la saison la plus intéressante de l'année. 7. Nous arrivons souvent après (*you*). 8. Marie n'est pas là, et j'ai un livre pour (*her*). 9. Qui est assis près d' (*them*, f.)? 10. Paul n'est pas là. Pourquoi parlez-vous de (*him*)? 11. (*He*), il ne parle jamais français. 12. C'est (*I*) qui vais en Suisse. 13. (*They*), ils vont en Espagne. 14. Qui va en Italie? (*She*). 15. Gérard et (*I*) aimons mieux l'hiver que (*he*).

C. Remplacez les infinitifs entre parenthèses par la forme convenable du présent du verbe. Tous ces verbes sont irréguliers.

1. A Noël je (faire) souvent un voyage en Angleterre. 2. Il (pleuvoir) beaucoup en Angleterre. 3. Je (conduire) ma voiture tous les jours de la semaine. 4. En hiver nous (faire) du ski à la montagne. 5. Madame Dallier (conduire)-elle bien? 6. Vous ne (faire) pas toujours les devoirs. 7. Mais les autres élèves les (faire). 8. (conduire)-vous votre voiture à l'université? 9. Il (faire) beau en été. 10. (pleuvoir)-il en automne? 11. Nous (faire) un voyage en voiture. 12. Nous (conduire) la voiture jusqu'à la frontière de ce pays. 13. Ces jeunes filles ne (conduire) pas bien. 14. Tous les élèves (faire) un voyage pendant les vacances.

D. Écrivez en français.

1st, 8th, 10th, 12th, 7th, 2d, 5th, 3d

Conversation

1. Demandez à l'étudiant qui est assis à côté de vous s'il neige beaucoup en hiver. 2. Demandez à l'étudiant qui est près de la porte s'il pleut beaucoup en avril. 3. Demandez à l'étudiant assis devant vous s'il fait beau au mois de juillet. 4. Demandez à l'étudiant assis derrière vous s'il conduit sa voiture pour aller à l'université.

Vocabulaire — page 99

Grammaire

1. List the expressions of weather used in this lesson and make sentences with them. What verb is used impersonally in most expressions of weather? (§ 92 B and page 100)

2. List the disjunctive pronouns. (§ 27 A)

3. In what sort of positions are disjunctive pronouns used? Mention six ways in which they are used. (§ 27 B)

4. In sentences such as *C'est le mois des vacances, C'est lui qui conduit la voiture, Ce sont les élèves qui aiment les sports d'hiver, Ce sont eux qui vont à la montagne,* how are *C'est* and *Ce sont* expressed in English? This construction will be taken up in detail later. For the present it is sufficient to know that *C'est* and *Ce sont,* when followed by a noun or pronoun, are often expressed in English by **It is.**

5. How are ordinals usually formed? Count to 12 by ordinals. (§ 18 A, B)

6. Give the forms of the present of the irregular verbs *faire* and *conduire* and the *il*-form of the impersonal verb *pleuvoir.* (Page 100)

Troisième révision – Leçons 11 à 15

Première partie

A. Répondez en français par des phrases complètes aux questions suivantes.

1. Citez une ville du sud-est de la France qui n'est pas loin de l'Italie. 2. Où les jeunes gens qui voyagent en France passent-ils quelquefois la nuit? 3. Pourquoi les jeunes gens trouvent-ils intéressantes les auberges de la jeunesse? 4. Où les Parisiens passent-ils parfois leurs week-ends? 5. Quels jours de la semaine les élèves français vont-ils à l'école? 6. Pourquoi Roger et Marie ne vont-ils pas à la même école en France? 7. A l'école, qui explique la leçon aux élèves? 8. Si un élève parle trop, qui lui dit: «Taisez-vous»? 9. Le bureau du professeur est-il devant ou derrière les élèves? 10. Qui est Victor Hugo? 11. Victor Hugo est-il célèbre seulement par ses romans? 12. Quels élèves le professeur punit-il? 13. En quels mois neige-t-il beaucoup? 14. En quelle saison fait-on du ski à la montagne? 15. Quelle est la date de la fête nationale de la France?

B. Expliquez en français par une phrase complète les noms suivants.

Grenoble	Les Misérables	Victor Hugo
	Notre-Dame de Paris	

C. Rédigez une composition sur un des sujets suivants.

1. Une conversation entre un Français et un Américain dans une auberge de la jeunesse 2. La salle de classe 3. Une leçon dans une classe française[1] 4. Les mois de l'année 5. La saison que j'aime le mieux

[1] In French there are two ways of saying *a French class.* The expression *une classe française* means *a class in France,* while *une classe de français* indicates *a class in which French is taught.*

Deuxième partie

A. Remplacez les mots entre parenthèses par l'équivalent français. (*Voir Grammaire* § *14*)

1. (*My*) père et (*my*) mère visitent (*their*) pays. 2. (*Your*) oncle et (*your*) tantes habitent dans la même ville. 3. (*Our*) professeur a (*his*) livre et (*his*) cahiers dans (*his*) classe.

B. Remplacez les expressions en italique par des pronoms compléments. Exemple: Roger écrit une lettre *à Jacqueline.* Roger *lui* écrit une lettre. (*Voir Grammaire* §§ *24, 25, 29 A, B, 30 A*)

4. Le professeur arrive *dans la classe* après les élèves. 5. Il lit *toutes les phrases* à Marie. 6. Explique-t-il *la leçon* à ses élèves? 7. Lit-il un poème de Victor Hugo *aux élèves?* 8. Nous passons le week-end *à la campagne.*

C. *Remplacez par l'équivalent français les pronoms relatifs indiqués en anglais.* (*Voir Grammaire* § *39 B, C*)

9. Aimez-vous le roman (*which*) nous lisons? 10. Nous lisons *Notre-Dame de Paris,* (*which*) est un roman célèbre de Victor Hugo.

D. *Remplacez par l'équivalent français les pronoms anglais entre parenthèses.* (*Voir Grammaire* § *27*)

11. (*They*), ils vont avec (*us*) à la campagne. 12. Marie et (*I*) parlons mieux que (*he*). 13. Qui fait les devoirs pour (*you*)? (*He*).

E. *Remplacez l'infinitif par le présent. Ces verbes sont réguliers.* (*Voir Grammaire* § *49 A, B et les pages 93 et 98*)

14. Je (parler) français et vous m'(écouter). 15. Nous (aimer) voyager en France. 16. Je (finir) d'écrire une phrase pendant que vous (remplir) votre stylo.

F. *Remplacez l'infinitif par le présent. Ces verbes sont irréguliers à la première personne du pluriel du présent.* (*Voir Grammaire* § *89 A, B et la page 93*)

17. Aujourd'hui nous (commencer) à lire *Notre-Dame de Paris.* 18. Nous (corriger) les fautes.

G. *Remplacez l'infinitif par le présent ou l'impératif. Ces verbes sont tous irréguliers.* (*Voir les pages 93 à 100*)

19. Je (aller) en Angleterre, Roger (aller) en France et nos autres amis (aller) en Suisse. 20. Vous (être) en Suisse et demain vous (faire) un voyage en Italie, n'est-ce pas? 21. Ma mère (conduire) bien, mais vous (conduire) mieux. 22. Paul (écrire) un poème dans son cahier pendant que nous (écrire) des devoirs au tableau. 23. (écrire) tous les devoirs de la leçon et (lire) ces devoirs à haute voix. 24. Nous (avoir) un poème à copier dans nos cahiers et vous (avoir) un roman policier à lire. 25. Je (être) en France et demain mes camarades (faire) un voyage en Allemagne.

SEIZIÈME LEÇON

Le lycée français

Le lycée est une école de l'État qui prépare les élèves aux universités et aux grandes écoles. On y entre à dix ou onze ans. Les études au lycée durent sept ans. Elles donnent aux élèves une culture générale plutôt qu'une formation pratique.

Tous les élèves du lycée étudient le français, l'histoire et la géographie, les sciences et les mathématiques et au moins une langue étrangère. L'étude des langues est considérée comme très importante pour la formation intellectuelle. Quelques élèves apprennent le latin, le grec et une langue vivante. D'autres choisissent le latin et deux langues vivantes. D'autres encore n'étudient qu'une langue vivante. Mais tous apprennent au moins une langue.

Au lycée le travail est très sérieux. L'élève y apprend non seulement à écrire correctement le français mais aussi à perfectionner son style. Chaque année, il étudie la littérature française ainsi que l'histoire de France et l'histoire des autres pays du monde.

Pour obtenir un diplôme il ne suffit pas de suivre des cours au lycée pendant plusieurs années. A la fin de la sixième année d'études, l'élève est obligé de passer un examen d'État, appelé *première partie du baccalauréat* ou *premier bachot,* qui comporte des épreuves écrites sur toutes les matières et des épreuves écrites et orales sur les langues vivantes. Les sujets[1] des épreuves écrites sont choisis par le Ministère de l'Éducation Nationale; dans les épreuves orales les élèves ne sont pas interrogés par leurs propres professeurs mais par des professeurs d'autres établissements. Si un élève échoue aux épreuves, il est obligé de redoubler sa classe.

Les élèves qui réussissent à la première partie du baccalauréat passent encore un an au lycée. Pendant cette dernière année ils continuent les études des années précédentes, mais ils se spécialisent en philosophie, en mathématiques ou en sciences. A la fin de cette septième année, ils passent

[1] In France the written examination usually consists of a choice of three subjects of composition. The candidate develops as completely as possible the subject he has chosen in the three or four hours allotted him. He is judged not only on his comprehension of the topic but also on his ability to express himself effectively in French. In France, examinations of the objective type have never enjoyed any measure of popularity.

un second examen d'État, appelé *deuxième partie du baccalauréat* ou *deuxième bachot.* Les élèves qui réussissent à cet examen ont le droit de commencer leurs études supérieures dans les universités ou dans les grandes écoles. Ils ont une culture étendue et une formation intellectuelle sérieuse.

Mais le baccalauréat, qui n'est pas une simple formalité administrative, est très difficile, et souvent plus de la moitié des candidats échouent à cet examen.

Questions

1. Qu'est-ce qu'un lycée? 2. A quel âge entre-t-on au lycée? 3. Combien d'années durent les études au lycée? 4. Quelles matières apprend-on au lycée? 5. L'étude de quelle matière est considérée comme très importante pour la formation intellectuelle? 6. Qu'est-ce qu'une langue vivante? 7. Quelles langues les élèves du lycée apprennent-ils? 8. Le travail du lycée est-il sérieux? 9. Est-ce que l'élève du lycée apprend à bien écrire le français? 10. Est-ce que l'élève américain apprend à bien écrire l'anglais? 11. Qu'est-ce que c'est que le baccalauréat? 12. Quelles épreuves l'élève du lycée est-il obligé de passer à la fin de la sixième année d'études? 13. Par qui sont choisis les sujets des épreuves écrites? 14. Par qui sont interrogés les élèves dans les épreuves orales? 15. Entre quelles matières l'élève choisit-il la dernière année de lycée?

Devoirs

A. Remplacez les tirets par la forme convenable du mot ***an*** *ou* ***année.***

1. Un élève américain entre au lycée à quatorze ——. 2. Pendant la première —— de lycée, il étudie l'anglais, l'algèbre, la biologie et le latin. 3. La deuxième —— il étudie l'anglais, l'histoire, la géométrie et le latin. 4. Il passe quatre —— au lycée. 5. Il étudie l'anglais pendant plusieurs ——. 6. Apprend-il les mathématiques chaque ——? 7. Pendant combien d' —— l'élève américain apprend-il les sciences? 8. Un élève qui passe quelques —— au lycée apprend à écrire l'anglais. 9. Dans beaucoup de lycées les élèves sont obligés de passer des épreuves écrites tous les ——.

B. Remplacez les tirets par la forme convenable de l'adjectif interrogatif ***quel.*** Exemple: —— études donnent à l'élève une culture générale? *Quelles* études donnent à l'élève une culture générale?

1. A —— âge apprend-on le latin? 2. Dans —— école apprend-on à lire? 3. —— est la science la plus importante? 4. —— sont les

langues vivantes qui sont les plus connues? 5. —— est la capitale de la France? 6. —— sont les lycées où les élèves se spécialisent en sciences?

C. Remplacez les tirets par ***Qu'est-ce que . . . , Qu'est-ce que c'est que . . .*** *ou par une forme de* ***quel.***

1. —— est la plus grande ville du Canada? 2. —— sont les écrivains les plus connus du Canada? 3. —— la philosophie? 4. —— une auberge de la jeunesse? 5. —— la science? 6. —— sont les sciences les plus importantes? 7. —— une province? 8. —— est la province la plus connue du pays?

D. Mettez la forme convenable de l'adjectif indiqué entre parenthèses.

1. Le lycée français donne à l'élève une culture (général) et une formation (intellectuel). 2. Les études du lycée sont très (sérieux). 3. Pendant la (premier) année de lycée on commence à apprendre le latin. 4. Pendant les (dernier) années on apprend les sciences. 5. L'étude des langues (étranger) est considérée comme très importante en France. 6. En France le baccalauréat est très difficile; ce n'est pas une formalité (administratif). 7. La civilisation française est très (ancien).

Conversation

1. Demandez à l'étudiant qui est à votre droite ce que c'est qu'un lycée. 2. Demandez à l'étudiant assis près de la fenêtre quelles sont les matières qu'on apprend dans un lycée français. 3. Demandez à l'étudiant assis derrière vous s'il passe des examens à la fin de l'année. 4. Demandez à Monsieur X. s'il réussit toujours à ses examens.

Vocabulaire — pages 101–102

Grammaire

1. In this lesson, both ***an*** and ***année*** are used to express the English word *year.* When is each used? (§ 98 — *year*)

2. What is an interrogative adjective? (§ 16) Arrange the interrogative adjectives into a table. (§ 16 A) How do interrogative adjectives agree with the noun they modify? (§ 16 B)

3. When used with a form of the verb ***être,*** what function does the interrogative adjective often serve? (§ 16 C)

4. How do the French express the English *What is . . .* in order to ask for the definition of a word? Study questions 1, 6 and 11 of this lesson and ***Grammaire*** § 38 F.

5. How does one form the feminine of certain adjectives whose masculine form ends in *e* + **consonant?** (§ 10 C) What is the feminine form of the adjectives ***étranger, premier,*** and ***dernier?***

6. How does one form the feminine of a French adjective whose masculine form ends in *-f?* (§ 10 D) of an adjective whose masculine form ends in *-x?* (§ 10 E)

7. How does one form the feminine of an adjective whose masculine form ends in ***-el, -eil,*** or ***-ien?*** (§ 10 F)

8. Conjugate in the present tense the irregular verbs ***apprendre, obtenir,*** and ***suivre.*** (Page 103)

DIX-SEPTIÈME LEÇON

Une journée au lycée

Il y a beaucoup de lycées à Paris. Mon ami Maurice va au lycée Louis-le-Grand, ainsi appelé en souvenir du roi Louis XIV. Un matin je le rencontre dans la rue. Il me dit bonjour et me demande:

— Quelle heure est-il?

Je regarde ma montre et lui réponds:

— Il est huit heures moins le quart.

— Oh! Ma classe commence à huit heures!

— Comment! Vos cours commencent à huit heures du matin? Dans notre école ils ne commencent qu'à huit heures et demie! Je n'arrive jamais au lycée avant huit heures et quart.

— Moi, j'arrive à Louis-le-Grand presque toujours à huit heures moins cinq.

— A quelle heure déjeunez-vous?

— A midi ou à midi et demi selon les jours. Les classes recommencent à une heure et demie ou à deux heures selon les lycées et durent jusqu'à quatre heures ou quatre heures et demie de l'après-midi.

— Évidemment, vous n'avez pas de classes le samedi.

— Si, nous avons des classes le samedi matin. En France, c'est le jeudi qui est jour de congé. Mais le travail du lycée semble vous intéresser. Voulez-vous m'y accompagner? Vous pouvez assister aux cours ce matin.

— Avec plaisir.

— Bon. Allons, j'entends d'ici la cloche.

Au lycée, nous voyons beaucoup de jeunes gens qui arrivent à bicyclette. Il n'y a que des garçons car, en général, les jeunes filles ne vont pas aux mêmes lycées que les jeunes gens. A l'intérieur du lycée il y a plusieurs grandes cours. Les élèves s'y réunissent pendant les heures de récréation. Nous montons au premier étage. Quarante élèves attendent le professeur devant la porte de la classe. Pendant que nous attendons, le professeur arrive. Maurice lui dit:

— Je vous présente un camarade américain qui désire voir un lycée français.

Le professeur veut bien et me donne alors la permission d'assister à son cours.

Dans la salle, je vois au mur deux cartes — une carte de l'ancienne France divisée en provinces et une carte de la France contemporaine divisée en départements. J'entends le professeur dire:

— Aujourd'hui, nous allons parler des départements français.

Il est huit heures. La classe commence.

Questions

1. Quelle heure est-il maintenant? 2. A quelle heure commence votre classe? 3. A quelle heure commence la classe de Maurice? 4. A quelle heure les deux jeunes gens arrivent-ils au lycée? 5. A quelle heure recommencent les classes de l'après-midi? 6. Les jeunes gens arrivent-ils souvent au lycée à bicyclette? 7. Pourquoi ne voyez-vous pas de jeunes filles à Louis-le-Grand? 8. Qu'y a-t-il à l'intérieur du lycée? 9. A quel étage se trouve la classe de Maurice? 10. Pouvons-nous entrer dans la classe avant le professeur? 11. Que désire voir le camarade de Maurice? 12. Qu'est-ce que Maurice demande au professeur? 13. Qu'est-ce que ce jeune Américain voit au mur? 14. Que dit le professeur? 15. A quelle heure commence la classe?

Devoirs

A. Écrivez en français.

Il est 9:00, 11:30, 3:15, 7:45, 2:05, 6:55, 2:00, 12:30, 1:00, 8:30.

B. Remplacez les infinitifs par la forme convenable du présent du verbe. Ce sont des verbes réguliers en ***-re.***

1. J'(attendre) le professeur. 2. Mon camarade (attendre) son ami Maurice. 3. Nous (entendre) les élèves qui se réunissent dans la cour. 4. Maurice me demande si j'(entendre) la cloche qui sonne. 5. Je lui (répondre) que ses camarades (attendre) le professeur. 6. (entendre)-vous Louise? 7. (attendre)-vous votre mère? 8. Je (répondre) que j' (attendre) ma sœur.

C. Remplacez les infinitifs par la forme convenable du présent du verbe. Tous ces verbes sont irréguliers.

1. Je (voir) Maurice. 2. Il me (voir) aussi. 3. Si je (pouvoir), je (vouloir) assister aux cours du lycée. 4. On (apprendre) beaucoup de choses. 5. (vouloir)-vous m'accompagner au lycée? 6. Vous (pouvoir) y aller. 7. Mes camarades (vouloir) voyager en province. 8. Ils (pouvoir) nous accompagner. 9. Nous (pouvoir) voir le Midi de la France. 10. Si nous (vouloir) voir la Côte d'Azur, nous (pouvoir) aller à Nice. 11. Je ne (dire) pas qu'il y a un hôtel à Nice. 12. Vous (dire) que les plages sont charmantes.

D. Remplacez les tirets par ***Que . . . , Qu' . . .*** *ou* ***Qu'est-ce que . . .*** (What . . .) *selon la construction de la phrase:*

1. —— vous écrivez? 2. —— lisez-vous? 3. —— dit le professeur? 4. —— Maurice apprend au lycée? 5. —— nous allons lire? 6. —— apprend-on au lycée? 7. —— vous voulez voir?

Conversation

1. Demandez à l'étudiant qui est assis à côté de vous quelle heure il est. 2. Demandez à l'étudiant qui est assis derrière vous à quelle heure commence sa classe de français. 3. Demandez à l'étudiant qui est devant vous s'il entend la cloche. 4. Demandez à l'étudiant qui est assis à votre gauche à quelle heure il arrive en classe.

Vocabulaire — pages 103–104

Grammaire

1. How is the present of *-re* verbs formed? (§ 49 D) Use in sentences the forms of the present of ***attendre, entendre,*** and ***répondre.*** (Page 105)

2. What are the forms of the present of the irregular verbs ***dire, pouvoir, voir,*** and ***vouloir?*** (Page 105) [1]

3. To express the interrogative *What . . .?* as the object of the sentence, both ***Que . . .?*** and ***Qu'est-ce que . . .?*** are used, but the word order of the sentences differs. When is each used? (§ 38 D)

4. From the material in the lesson, organize a table which contains the principles of time-telling in French. (§ 97 D)

5. What do you note about the expressions containing the adjective ***demi?*** (§ 97 E)

6. How do the French and most other non-English-speaking peoples indicate the afternoon and evening hours in time-tables and formal announcements? Compare the convenience of this method with that of the American system. (§ 97 F)

7. The most usual way of expressing *yes* in French is ***oui.*** What other word is used to express *yes* in this lesson? When is this word used to express *yes* in French? (§ 98 — *yes*)

DIX-HUITIÈME LEÇON

Les départements français

Le professeur pose des questions aux élèves. Il les leur pose pendant toute l'heure.

— Aujourd'hui, nous allons étudier les divisions administratives de la France. Quelles sont ces divisions?

— La France est divisée en départements.

— Combien y a-t-il de départements?

— Il y a quatre-vingt-dix départements dans la France métropolitaine.

— Qui est à la tête du département?

[1] What common pattern do you notice in the last three of these irregular verbs? Read over § 49 E and try to develop a system for learning the present of irregular verbs.

Il y a quatre-vingt-dix départements dans la France métropolitaine

— A la tête de chaque département il y a un préfet nommé par le Président de la République. Le préfet est chargé de l'exécution dans le département des lois et des décrets votés par le gouvernement.

— La division de la France en départements est-elle très ancienne?

— Elle date de la Révolution française, c'est-à-dire de 1789 [1].

— Voici deux cartes de France. Le professeur nous les montre. Cette carte-ci représente la France d'aujourd'hui. Cette carte-là représente l'ancienne France. Quelle est la carte des départements?

Les élèves la lui indiquent, et je constate que les départements

[1] dix-sept cent quatre-vingt-neuf

La région située autour de Paris est l'ancienne province de l'Île-de-France

français sont beaucoup plus petits que les états des États-Unis. Le professeur nous montre le département de la Seine, où est situé Paris. Il nous le montre sur la carte de la France d'aujourd'hui. Il ne nous le désigne pas sur la carte de l'ancienne France.

— Cette carte-ci est divisée en quatre-vingt-dix départements. Savez-vous en quoi est divisée cette carte-là?

— Elle est divisée en trente-deux provinces.

— Voilà Paris. La région située autour de Paris est l'ancienne province de l'Île-de-France. C'est le berceau de la langue française et du gouvernement de la France.

Maurice me demande:

— Vous comprenez ces explications, n'est-ce pas?

Je lui réponds que je les comprends. Maurice cherche un livre avec les deux cartes, et il me le donne. Il me dit:

— Regardez cette carte-là. Voici Paris. Voilà l'Île-de-France.

Je regarde l'Île-de-France, qui me semble très petite. Je ferme le livre, et je le lui rends. Je sais que l'état du Texas est plus grand que la France entière, mais je ne le lui dis pas.

Questions

1. Qui pose les questions aux élèves? 2. Comment est divisée la France d'aujourd'hui? 3. Combien y a-t-il de départements en France? 4. Comment sont divisés les États-Unis? 5. Combien d'états y a-t-il aux États-Unis? 6. Les départements français sont-ils grands ou petits? 7. Qui est à la tête de chaque département? 8. Par qui est nommé le préfet? 9. De quoi est chargé le préfet? 10. Quelle est la date de la Révolution française? 11. Vous comprenez toujours les explications du professeur, n'est-ce pas? 12. Vous savez dans quel département se trouve Paris, n'est-ce pas? 13. Qu'est-ce que c'est que l'Île-de-France? 14. Pourquoi l'Île-de-France est-elle importante dans l'histoire de France? 15. Après l'Alaska, quel est le plus grand état des États-Unis? 16. Cet état-là est-il plus grand que la France entière?

Devoirs

*A. Remplacez les tirets par **il y a** ou **voilà**, selon le sens.*

1. —— beaucoup d'hôtels sur la Côte d'Azur. 2. Regardez! —— un très grand hôtel. 3. —— le camarade qui veut parler avec vous. Je vous le présente. 4. —— trente-deux élèves dans ma classe de français. 5. —— plusieurs cartes de France dans les salles de notre école. 6. Taisez-vous. —— le professeur. 7. —— notre voiture. La voyez-vous? 8. —— trop de voitures dans les rues des grandes villes.

B. Écrivez en français.

100, 10, 70, 31, 20, 61, 90, 41, 81, 50, 71, 40, 91

*C. Remplacez les tirets par la forme convenable de l'adjectif démonstratif en employant . . . **-ci** et . . . **là** où il faut.* Exemple: —— leçon est plus difficile que —— leçon. *Cette* leçon-*ci* est plus difficile que *cette* leçon-*là*.

1. —— professeur est plus sévère que —— professeurs. 2. ——

Je vais à une école de garçons; Marie va à une école de filles

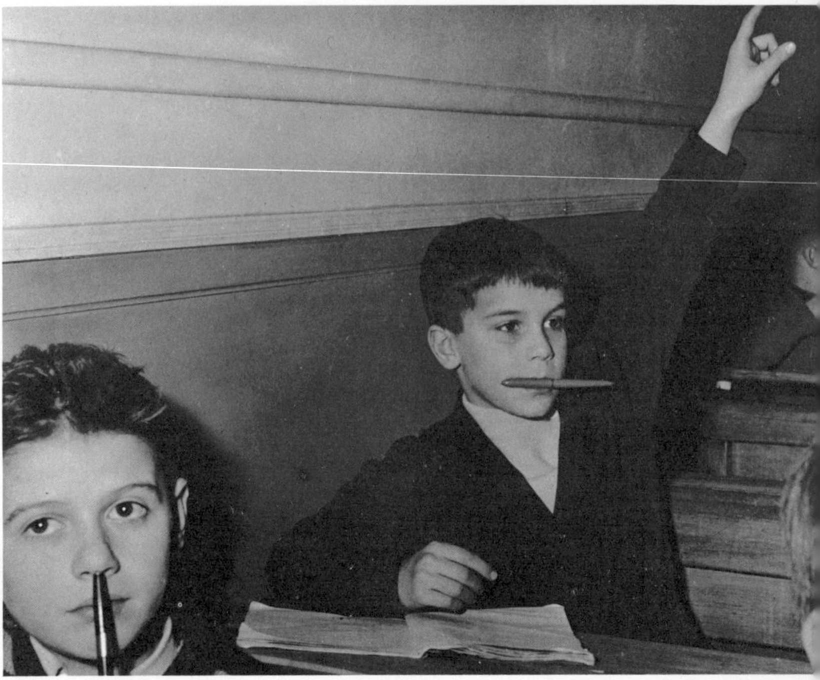

— *Ouvrez vos livres et choisissez un poème pour notre leçon*

— *Moreau, apportez au bureau le livre que vous cachez*

Les jeunes filles ne vont pas aux mêmes lycées que les jeunes gens

Les élèves se réunissent dans ces cours pendant les heures de récréation

Mais comme le tabac et les allumettes sont des monopoles de l'État ainsi que les timbres, on peut acheter des timbres dans un bureau de tabac

Ensuite, j'entre dans une cabine téléphonique pour donner un coup de téléphone à un camarade

élèves apprennent plus que —— élèves. 3. —— état est plus grand que —— état. 4. —— province est plus pittoresque que —— provinces.

® D. *Remplacez les expressions en italique par des pronoms compléments.* EXEMPLES: 1. Maurice me montre *cette carte.* Maurice me *la* montre. 2. Lisez-vous *la leçon à Robert? La lui* lisez-vous?

1. Le professeur me montre *mes fautes.* 2. Il indique *la province aux élèves.* 3. Louise donne *le cahier à ses sœurs.* 4. Écrivez-vous *cette lettre à votre oncle?* 5. Nous montrons *le poème à notre tante.* 6. Vous rend-elle *ce poème?* 7. Qui nous explique *la leçon?* 8. Je lis *les phrases à Roger.* 9. Raconte-t-il *cette histoire à ses amis?* 10. Allez-vous souvent *en France?*

® E. *Mettez les phrases du devoir D à la forme négative.* EXEMPLES: 1. Maurice ***ne*** *me la* montre ***pas.*** 2. ***Ne*** *la lui* lisez-vous ***pas?***

® F. *Répondez aux questions suivantes en employant deux pronoms compléments.* EXEMPLE: Maurice pose-t-il les questions aux élèves? Oui, il *les leur* pose.

1. Louise donne-t-elle ces livres à sa mère? 2. Charles vous montre-t-il ses devoirs? 3. Les élèves racontent-ils cette histoire au professeur? 4. Qui vous explique la leçon?

CONVERSATION

1. Demandez à l'étudiant qui est à votre gauche combien il y a de départements en France. 2. Demandez à l'étudiant qui est à votre droite s'il comprend les explications du professeur. 3. Demandez à l'étudiant assis derrière vous qui pose les questions aux élèves. 4. Demandez à l'étudiant assis devant vous s'il veut assister à une classe française.

VOCABULAIRE — PAGES 105–106

GRAMMAIRE

1. Count by 10's up to 100. Beginning with 11, count by 10's up to 101. (§ 17 A, C)

2. Explain the difference between ***il y a*** and ***voilà.*** (§ 91 A, B)

3. How does one distinguish *this* from *that* in French? (§ 15 B, C)

4. What is the position of object pronouns in relation to the verb? (§ 30 A)

5. When there are two object pronouns, what is their order? (§ 31 C, D)

6. What is the position of *ne* in a negative sentence containing object pronouns? (§ 22 B) in a negative question containing object-pronouns? (§ 22 C)

7. What are the forms of the present of the irregular verbs *comprendre* and *savoir?* (Page 106)

DIX-NEUVIÈME LEÇON

Le Président de la République

La France et les États-Unis sont des républiques. Mais l'organisation du gouvernement français est différente de l'organisation de notre gouvernement.

Selon la Constitution de 1958[1], la France est une République indivisible, laïque, démocratique et sociale. Cette République assure l'égalité devant la loi de tous les citoyens sans distinction d'origine, de race ou de religion. Elle respecte toutes les croyances. La devise de la République est Liberté, Égalité, Fraternité. Son principe est: gouvernement du peuple, par le peuple et pour le peuple.

Le système gouvernemental français comprend le Président de la République, qui assure le fonctionnement régulier de l'État, le Gouvernement[2] proprement dit, c'est-à-dire le Premier Ministre, qui, avec le Conseil des Ministres, détermine et conduit la politique de la Nation, et le Parlement, qui vote les lois. Il existe aussi le Conseil Constitutionnel, qui veille à la constitutionnalité des lois, et un Conseil Économique et Social, qui donne au Gouvernement son avis dans les domaines économiques et sociaux.

Le Président de la République est à la tête du gouvernement. Il est élu pour sept ans au suffrage universel, c'est-à-dire par tous les Français qui ont le droit de voter.

[1] dix-neuf cent cinquante-huit

[2] When the term *le Gouvernement* is capitalized in the lessons on French government, it indicates the special sense of the word, that is, the executive branch at the head of which is the Prime Minister.

La Constitution de 1958[1] donne au Président de la République beaucoup de pouvoirs. C'est lui qui est, en effet, le chef de l'État.

Le Président de la République nomme le Premier Ministre. Il préside le Conseil des Ministres. Il est chef des armées. Il promulgue les lois votées par le Parlement. Il n'a pas le droit de veto, mais il peut demander au Parlement une nouvelle délibération d'une loi ou de certains de ses articles, et cette nouvelle délibération ne peut pas être refusée. Dans certains cas il peut dissoudre l'Assemblée Nationale et proclamer de nouvelles élections. Quand la sécurité de la Nation est menacée, il peut prendre les mesures exigées par les circonstances.

Questions

1. *Qui* est à la tête du gouvernement français? 2. *Qui* le Président de la République nomme-t-il? 3. Par *qui* le Président de la République est-il élu? 4. *Qu'est-ce qui* donne beaucoup de pouvoirs au Président de la République? 5. *Que* vote le Parlement? 6. *Qu'est-ce que* la République assure à tous les citoyens français? 7. De *quoi* le Président de la République est-il le chef? 8. Quelle est la date de la Constitution française? 9. Qu'est-ce que la France selon la Constitution de 1958? 10. Quelle est la devise de la République? 11. Est-ce que la République respecte toutes les croyances? 12. Quel est le principe de la République? 13. *Qui* assure le fonctionnement régulier de l'État? 14. *Qui* détermine et conduit la politique de la Nation? 15. *Qui* veille à la constitutionnalité des lois? 16. *Qui* donne au gouvernement son avis dans les domaines économiques et sociaux? 17. Le Président de la République a-t-il le droit de veto? 18. Le Président de la République peut-il dissoudre l'Assemblée Nationale? 19. Quand la sécurité de la Nation est menacée, *que* peut faire le Président de la République?

Devoirs

A. Remplacez les tirets par les mots convenables indiqués à droite.

1. La France assure l'égalité devant la loi de tous les —— de la République. 2. Elle respecte toutes les ——. 3. Le Conseil Économique et Social donne au gouvernement son —— dans les domaines économiques et sociaux. 4. Quand la sécurité de la Nation est menacée, le Président de la République peut —— les mesures exigées par les circonstances. 5. Dans certains cas il peut dissoudre l'Assemblée Nationale et proclamer de —— élections.

a. avis
b. citoyens
c. conduit
d. croyances
e. devises
f. nouvelles
g. prendre
h. sans
i. veiller

[1] dix-neuf cent cinquante-huit

B. Remplacez les tirets par le pronom interrogatif qui veut dire Who . . .? *ou* Whom . . .?

1. —— a un frère? 2. —— finit cette dictée? 3. —— le professeur punit-il? 4. Avec —— Roger va-t-il en classe? 5. De —— les élèves parlent-ils aujourd'hui? 6. —— Maurice et Paul rencontrent-ils dans la rue?

C. Remplacez les tirets par le pronom interrogatif qui veut dire What . . .?

1. —— nous faisons? 2. Avec —— écrivez-vous? 3. —— dit le professeur? 4. —— lisent les jeunes filles? 5. —— le président écrit? 6. —— est sur le bureau du professeur? 7. —— est devant les élèves?

D. Remplacez le mot indiqué entre parenthèses par l'équivalent français.

1. (*Who*) est votre camarade? 2. Avec (*whom*) parlez-vous? 3. (*Whom*) le professeur voit-il? 4. (*What*) est derrière le professeur? 5. De (*what*) Roger parle-t-il à sa sœur? 6. (*What*) corrige le professeur? 7. (*What*) nous écrivons au tableau? 8. (*Who*) vous attend? 9. (*What*) voyez-vous au tableau? 10. Avec (*what*) écrivez-vous? 11. (*What*) entre dans la salle quand la fenêtre est ouverte? 12. (*What*) nous prononçons après le professeur? 13. Par (*whom*) le Président des États-Unis est-il élu? 14. (*Whom*) entendons-nous à la porte?

Conversation

1. Demandez à Monsieur A. qui est le chef de l'État français. 2. Demandez à Monsieur B. ce [1] que le Président de la République peut faire quand la sécurité de la Nation est menacée. 3. Demandez à Monsieur C. ce [1] que le système gouvernemental français comprend. 4. Demandez à Monsieur D. ce [1] que la Constitution de 1958 donne au Président de la République.

[1] Note from the examples that follow how a direct question is converted into an indirect question.

DIRECT QUESTION	INDIRECT QUESTION
Que fait Roger?	Demandez à Monsieur A. *ce que* fait Roger.
Qu'est-ce qu'il écrit?	Demandez à Monsieur B. *ce qu*'il écrit.

The *que* and *qu'est-ce que* of the direct question are replaced by *ce que* in the indirect question.

VOCABULAIRE — PAGES 107–108

GRAMMAIRE

1. What is an interrogative pronoun? (§ 38)

2. From observation of the questions in this lesson, which interrogative pronoun may always be used when referring to persons? (§ 38 A)

3. Which interrogative pronoun refers to a thing used as the subject? as the object? as the object of a preposition? (§ 38 A, B)

4. Both *Que . . .?* and *Qu'est-ce que . . .?* are used as the object of a verb in referring to a thing, but a different word-order is used with each. Explain this difference. (§ 38 D)

5. Conjugate the verb ***prendre*** in the present tense. (Page 108)

6. Review the present tense of the verbs ***conduire*** (page 100) and ***comprendre*** (page 106). The verbs ***prendre, apprendre,*** and ***comprendre*** constitute a verb family; they are all conjugated in the same pattern.

VINGTIÈME LEÇON

Le Premier Ministre et le Parlement

Le Gouvernement détermine et conduit la politique de la Nation. C'est le Premier Ministre qui dirige l'action du Gouvernement. Il est responsable de la Défense Nationale. Il assure l'exécution des lois. Dans beaucoup de domaines il peut gouverner par ordonnance ou décret, de sorte qu'il a aussi un certain pouvoir législatif.

Le Premier Ministre et les autres ministres constituent le Conseil des Ministres. Le Conseil des Ministres correspond au Cabinet des États-Unis. Chaque ministre est à la tête d'un ministère. Il y a beaucoup de ministres, par exemple, le Ministre de la Justice, des Affaires Étrangères, de l'Intérieur, des Forces Armées, de l'Éducation Nationale, de l'Agriculture, de l'Information, etc. Selon la Constitution de 1958, les ministres ne peuvent pas être en même temps membres du Parlement.

Le Parlement comprend l'Assemblée Nationale et le Sénat. Les membres de l'Assemblée Nationale s'appellent les députés. Il y a environ cinq cent quarante-cinq députés. Quatre cent soixante-cinq de ces députés représentent la France métropolitaine. Les députés sont élus directement par les électeurs. Les membres du Sénat s'appellent les sénateurs. Ils sont élus au suffrage indirect. La France métropolitaine est représentée par deux cent cinquante-cinq sénateurs. Il y a d'autres sénateurs qui représentent les citoyens français des territoires d'outre-mer.

Le Parlement se réunit chaque année pour une période de six mois au maximum. Les deux chambres du Parlement ne se réunissent pas au même endroit. L'Assemblée Nationale se réunit au Palais Bourbon, qui se trouve sur la rive gauche de la Seine en face de la Place de la Concorde. Le Sénat se réunit au Palais du Luxembourg, qui se trouve dans le jardin du même nom.

Le Parlement exerce le pouvoir législatif, c'est-à-dire qu'il vote les lois. Le Parlement seul a le pouvoir de déclarer la guerre.

Si la majorité des membres du Parlement sont contre la politique du Premier Ministre, le Parlement peut désapprouver son programme ou adopter une motion de censure. A ce moment-là, le Premier Ministre doit remettre au Président de la République la démission du Gouvernement. Mais si l'Assemblée Nationale abuse de son droit de renverser le Gouvernement, le Président de la République peut la dissoudre et décider que de nouvelles élections doivent avoir lieu.

La Constitution de 1958, qui remplace la Constitution de 1946, est la base de la Cinquième République.

Questions

1. Qui détermine la politique de la France? 2. Qui dirige l'action du Gouvernement? 3. De quoi est responsable le Premier Ministre? 4. Qui assure l'exécution des lois? 5. Qui compose le Conseil des Ministres? 6. Qui dirige les ministères? 7. Citez quelques ministres. 8. Est-ce qu'un ministre peut être en même temps membre du Parlement? 9. Quelles sont les deux chambres qui constituent le Parlement? 10. Comment s'appellent les membres de l'Assemblée Nationale? 11. Environ combien de députés y a-t-il? 12. Par qui sont élus les députés? 13. Par qui sont élus les sénateurs? 14. Environ combien de sénateurs représentent la France métropolitaine? 15. Où se réunit l'Assemblée Natio-

nale? 16. Où se réunit le Sénat? 17. Qui vote les lois en France? 18. Qui a le pouvoir de déclarer la guerre? 19. Si la majorité des membres du Parlement sont contre la politique du Gouvernement, que peuvent-ils faire? 20. Si l'Assemblée Nationale abuse de son droit de renverser le Gouvernement, qu'est-ce que le Président de la République peut faire? 21. Quelle constitution est à la base de la Cinquième République?

DEVOIRS

A. Remplacez les tirets par les mots convenables indiqués à droite.

1. La nouvelle constitution —— l'ancienne. 2. Le Palais Bourbon se trouve sur la —— gauche de la Seine. 3. C'est le Premier Ministre qui —— l'action du Gouvernement. 4. Une partie des députés sont généralement pour la politique du Premier Ministre, les autres sont —— sa politique. 5. Si le Parlement est contre la politique du Gouvernement, le Premier Ministre —— remettre sa démission au Président de la République. 6. Aux États-Unis, qui a le pouvoir de déclarer la ——? 7. En France, le Parlement —— a le pouvoir de déclarer la guerre. 8. Quel est le —— du jardin où se trouve le Palais du Luxembourg?

a. contre
b. démission
c. dirige
d. doit
e. guerre
f. lieu
g. moment
h. nom
i. palais
j. remplace
k. renversent
l. rive
m. seul

B. Écrivez en chiffres. EXEMPLE: vingt-trois — 23

treize, trente-deux, quarante-deux, soixante-cinq, quatre-vingt-treize, soixante-dix-huit, quarante-six, quatre-vingt-onze, soixante-neuf, vingt et un, soixante, quatre-vingt-neuf, cinquante et un, soixante-treize, seize, quatre-vingt-quatre, vingt-neuf, quarante-quatre, cent soixante et onze, trois cent vingt-huit, mille deux cent quatre-vingt-cinq.

C. Écrivez en français.

100 députés, 200 sénateurs, 340 membres, 150 kilomètres, 500 habitants, 945 livres, 1000 maisons.

D. Écrivez en français.

34, 49, 62, 362, 78, 80, 13, 70, 16, 688, 19, 48, 92, 953, 14, 12, 75, 99, 15, 779, 95, 21, 76, 44, 247, 596, 90, 88, 65, 140, 680, 265, 17, 98, 116, 870, 171, 72, 56, 1356, 1948, 34, 2139

E. Écrivez en français les dates suivantes.

1875, 1914, 1492, 1215, 1939, 1685, 1776, 1553, 1861, 1066, 1946, 1973, 43 B.C., 490 B.C., 476 A.D., 800 A.D.

CONVERSATION

1. Demandez à l'étudiant assis près de la fenêtre où se réunissent les deux chambres du Parlement. 2. Demandez à l'étudiant assis près de la porte qui vote les lois. 3. Demandez à l'étudiant assis devant vous qui a le pouvoir de déclarer la guerre. 4. Demandez à l'étudiant assis derrière vous s'il veut lire la Constitution de 1958.

VOCABULAIRE — PAGES 109–110

GRAMMAIRE

1. Count from 1 to 100 in French until you can do so rapidly. (§ 17 A, B, C)

2. When does ***quatre-vingt(s)*** have an *-s* and when not? (§ 17 C)

3. When does ***cent*** require *-s* in the plural? (§ 17 D)

4. How does French express such numbers as 152 and 1152? (§ 17 E)

5. How are dates between 1100 and 1999 expressed in French? (§ 17 F)

6. How are B.C. and A.D., when referring to dates, expressed in French? (§ 17 F)

7. What are the forms of the present of ***devoir*** and ***remettre?*** (Page 110)

Quatrième révision – Leçons 16 à 20

Première partie

A. Répondez en français par des phrases complètes aux questions suivantes.

1. Pour avoir une culture générale en France, à quelle école doit-on aller? 2. Quel examen l'élève du lycée passe-t-il après les six premières années d'études? 3. Quels élèves de lycée redoublent leur classe? 4. A quelle heure déjeunez-vous? 5. Où se réunissent les élèves de lycée pendant les heures de récréation? 6. Les États-Unis sont divisés en états; quelles sont les divisions administratives de la France? 7. Quelle province est le berceau de la langue française? 8. Quelles sont les plus petites divisions administratives: les provinces ou les départements? 9. Pourquoi la date 1789 est-elle importante dans l'histoire de France? 10. Pour combien de temps le Président de la République est-il élu? 11. Combien de membres y a-t-il dans le collège électoral français? 12. Qui préside le Conseil des Ministres? 13. En France, qui est responsable de la Défense Nationale? 14. Où se trouve le Palais Bourbon? 15. Qui peut dissoudre l'Assemblée Nationale et décider que de nouvelles élections doivent avoir lieu?

B. Expliquez en français par une phrase complète les noms suivants.

Assemblée Nationale
baccalauréat
Conseil des Ministres
département
France métropolitaine
Île-de-France
Louis-le-Grand
lycée
Palais Bourbon
Palais du Luxembourg
Place de la Concorde
Parlement
préfet
Premier Ministre
Président de la République
Révolution française
Sénat

C. Rédigez une composition sur un des sujets suivants.

1. Le lycée français 2. Une classe de lycée 3. La Constitution de 1958 4. Le gouvernement de la France

Deuxième partie

A. Mettez la forme convenable de l'adjectif indiqué entre parenthèses. (Voir Grammaire § 10 C, D, E, F)

1. J'ai beaucoup de travail pendant les (dernier) semaines de l'année. 2. (quel) sont les saisons de l'année? 3. Le département est une division (administratif). 4. Les villes (italien) sont très pittoresques. 5. Les études en France sont-elles très (sérieux)?

B. Remplacez les mots indiqués en anglais par l'équivalent français. (*Voir Grammaire* §§ *16 C, 38 F*)

6. (*What is*) le fleuve le plus long de France? 7. (*What is*) la littérature?

C. Remplacez les expressions en italique par des pronoms compléments. EXEMPLE: Roger écrit *cette lettre à ses frères.* Roger *la leur* écrit. (*Voir Grammaire* §§ *30 A, 31 C, D*)

8. Maurice nous indique *l'ancienne province.* 9. Vous explique-t-il *la leçon?* 10. Louise me montre *les deux voitures.* 11. Lit-elle *la lettre à ses amies?* 12. Je donne *les cahiers aux élèves.*

D. Remplacez les pronoms interrogatifs anglais par l'équivalent français. (*Voir Grammaire* § *38 A, B, D*)

13. (*What*) Maurice explique à Roger? 14. De (*what*) parle-t-il à sa mère? 15. (*Whom*) Louise voit-elle à Tours? 16. (*What*) faites-vous ce matin? 17. (*Who*) doit copier le poème cinq fois?

E. Remplacez l'infinitif par le présent. Ce sont des verbes réguliers en -re. (*Voir Grammaire* § *49 D et la page 105*)

18. Je (répondre) à Maurice que nous (attendre) nos camarades. 19. — (entendre)-vous la cloche? me (répondre)-il.

F. Remplacez l'infinitif par le présent. Ces verbes sont tous irréguliers. (*Voir Grammaire* § *49 E et les pages 103 à 110*)

20. (pouvoir)-vous me dire qui (vouloir) aller avec nous? 21. Je (devoir) finir mon travail. 22. Quand vous (voir) le professeur, vous lui (dire) toujours bonjour, n'est-ce pas? 23. Je (savoir) que vous (apprendre) beaucoup de mots dans cette classe. 24. Je (suivre) un cours très intéressant cette année. 25. Je (prendre) la voiture le lundi, et mes sœurs la (prendre) les autres jours de la semaine.

Supplément aux Leçons 11 à 20

ONZIÈME LEÇON

Vocabulaire

Américain
l'Amérique *f.*
la bicyclette
le camarade
commencer

explorer
Grenoble
l'idée *f.*
me
la nationalité

la possibilité
Robert
la table
visiter
voyager

l'argent *m.* *money*
l'auberge *f.* *inn*
*avoir *have*
comment *how*
couramment *fluently*
demain *tomorrow*
demander *ask*
échanger *exchange*
*être *be*
ensemble *together*
la fille[a] *girl*
le Français *Frenchman*
le garçon *boy*
jeune *young*

à bicyclette *by bicycle, on a bicycle*
à table *at the table*
à travers *across*
au milieu *in the midst of, among*
l'auberge de la jeunesse[d] *f.* *youth hostel*

la jeunesse *youth*
je *I*
joli *pretty*
là *(over) there*
le milieu *middle; midst*
la moto (*abbr. for* la motocyclette)[b] *motorcycle*
nous *we*
la nuit *night*
pendant *during*
rencontrer *meet*
sûrement *surely*
les vacances *f.* *vacation*[c]
vous *you*

la jeune fille[e] *girl*
les jeunes gens[f] *m.* *young people; young men*
en vacances *on a vacation*
n'est-ce pas *isn't that so? don't you? etc.*

Verbes

parler[g]	**commencer**	**voyager**	**avoir**	**être**
je parl*e*	je commenc*e*	je voyag*e*	j'ai	je suis
tu parl*es*	tu commenc*es*	tu voyag*es*	tu as	tu es
il parl*e*	il commenc*e*	il voyag*e*	il a	il est
nous parl*ons*	nous commen*çons*	nous voyag*eons*	nous avons	nous sommes
vous parl*ez*	vous commenc*ez*	vous voyag*ez*	vous avez	vous êtes
ils parl*ent*	ils commenc*ent*	ils voyag*ent*	ils ont	ils sont

* An asterisk (*) placed before a verb indicates that this verb is irregular. The forms that you will be required to know are listed after the vocabulary.

[a] Usually *fille* means *daughter,* but in certain expressions it means *girl.* From the age of about eleven to seventeen, a *girl* is called a *jeune fille.*

[b] The dictionary lists only *motocyclette,* but everyone says *moto,* so that *motocyclette* now sounds strange to the French ear.

[c] In French the word *vacation* is always expressed by the plural form *les vacances.*

[d] In France *youth hostels* are called both *des auberges de la jeunesse* and *des auberges de jeunesse.* In fact, the official association title is *auberges de jeunesse.* However, both forms are so current that either can be considered correct.

[e] It is best for the American student always to use the expression *jeune fille* to express the equivalent of the English word *girl.*

[f] The expression *les jeunes gens* means *young people,* but in addition it is the usual plural of *le jeune homme* and often means *young men.* The expression *les jeunes hommes* can be found but is very rare in French.

[g] The verb parler may be considered as a model for regular -er verbs. The complete conjugation of *parler* may be found in § 95, no. 1.

Devoirs

A. Write the French equivalent of each of the following sentences.

1. I speak French with Maurice. 2. You spend the night in a youth hostel. 3. There we meet boys and girls of every[1] nationality. 4. I like to be in France. 5. We do not have much money. 6. Do you have much money? 7. We are not French. 8. Am I French? 9. Do I speak French? 10. I have a bicycle, and I am visiting France with an American friend.

[1] Use the plural form with the definite article.

B. Say aloud rapidly the French equivalent of each of the following sentences.

1. I am American. 2. You are American. 3. You are not French. 4. I speak French. 5. Do you speak French? 6. We are French. 7. I have an American friend whose[1] name is Robert. 8. Do you have a French friend whose[1] name is Robert?

[1] whose name is *qui s'appelle*

DOUZIÈME LEÇON

Vocabulaire

Georges
Jacqueline
la lettre

la maman
Marie
le papa
Paul

le quartier
Roger
le week-end[a]

âgé *old*
ainsi *thus*
*aller *go*
l'ami *m.* *friend*
l'amie *f.* (*girl*) *friend*
l'an *m.* *year*
le baiser *kiss*
bientôt *soon*
la campagne *country* (*opposite of city*)
car *for* (*because*)
cher, chère *dear*
durer *last*

l'école *f.* *school*
fermer *close*
le frère *brother*
jouer *play*
le jour *day*
juillet *July*
juin *June*
libre *free*
le lycée *high school* (*with academic course for students from 11 to 19 years of age*)
le magasin *store*
la mère *mother*

* An asterisk (*) placed before a verb indicates that this verb is irregular. The forms that you will be required to know are listed after the vocabulary.

[a] The French language has taken over a certain number of English words and expressions.

le mois *month*
le neveu *nephew*
l'oncle *m.* *uncle*
le père *father*
Pierre *Peter*
la semaine *week*
seulement *only*
le soir *evening*
la tante *aunt*
la vie *life*
voici *here is, here are*
y *there* [a]

à la campagne *in (to) the country*
à l'école *in (to) school*
non seulement *not only*
Comment allez-vous *How are you?*
Je vais très bien. *I am very well*
Quel âge avez-vous? *How old are you?*
J'ai dix ans. *I am ten (years old).*
Je vais [b] jouer. *I am going to play.*

With Lesson 12, learn also: the numbers up to 20 (§ 17 A)
the days of the week (§ 92 A)
the possessive adjectives (§ 14 A)

Verbes

aller

je vais	nous allons
tu vas	vous allez
il va	ils vont

Devoirs

A. Write the French equivalent of each of the following sentences.

1. I am going to the country with my mother and my brothers. 2. We spend the week end there.[1] 3. How old are you? 4. His sister is ten years old. 5. In France, the stores close on [2] Saturdays or on Mondays. 6. Her brother goes to school, but we do not go there.[1] 7. Do you go to school with your friend and his brother? 8. Her uncle and his aunt live in France with their nephew. 9. Her father and her mother live in Spain with your friend. 10. Our brother and our sisters go to the country and spend five days there.

[1] Since the place has already been mentioned, what word is used to express *there*?
[2] For the manner of expressing this construction, see line 4 of the reading lesson.

[a] To express *there* use the adverb *y* only when the place has been mentioned previously. The adverb *là*, which also means *there*, points out and is much stronger.

[b] When the present tense of the verb *aller* is followed directly by an infinitive, it is normally expressed in English by the progressive (*-ing*) form. In both English and French it is often used as a substitute for the future. EXAMPLE: I am going to play = I'll play.

B. Say aloud rapidly the French equivalent of each of the following sentences.

1. I am going to the country with my father. 2. Are you going to the country with your sister? 3. We go to school Monday, Tuesday, Wednesday, Thursday, and Friday. 4. My brothers do not go to school Saturday and Sunday. 5. I am going to play with my friend. 6. How are you? 7. I am very well. 8. Our friends are well also. 9. Our vacation[1] is in[2] the month of July.

[1] Use the plural form in French. [2] in the *au*

TREIZIÈME LEÇON

Vocabulaire

la classe
continuer
copier
correctement
Dupont
imaginer
Le Chevalier
Monnot
la place[a]
le professeur[b]
regarder
remarquer
le texte
Victor Hugo

assis, *seated*
bas, basse *low*
le bureau *desk*
clair *clear*
corriger *correct*
le crayon *pencil*
le début *beginning*
deuxième *second*
devant *before; in front of*
le devoir *exercise*
la dictée *dictation*
dicter *dictate*
la droite *right*
écouter *listen (to)*
*écrire *write*

effacer *erase*
l'élève[c] *m. and f. pupil*
l'encre *f. ink*
étudier *study*
expliquer *explain*
la faute *mistake*
la fenêtre *window*
la fin *end*
la fois[d] *time*
la gauche *left*
la *her, it*
le *him, it*
lentement *slowly*
les *them*
*lire *read*

* An asterisk (*) placed before a verb indicates that this verb is irregular. The forms that you will be required to know are listed after the vocabulary.

[a] The French word *place* often has the meaning, *a place to sit down; endroit* is the common word for the English *place.*

[b] The term *professeur* indicates a secondary school or college teacher. The terms *instituteur* and *institutrice* are used to designate the elementary school teacher.

[c] The word *élève* refers to the grade and high school pupil, whereas *étudiant* is used for the college student.

[d] In French there are several words to express the English *time.* The word *fois* is used to enumerate: e.g., la première fois (*first time*), trois fois (*three times*), etc.

la lumière *light*
le mot *word*
noir *black*
la phrase *sentence*
la porte *door*
premier, première *first*
que (*conj.*) *that*
la salle (*class*) *room*
si *if*
le soin *care*
le stylo *fountain pen*
le tableau (noir) (*black*) *board*
tâcher *try*
la voix *voice*

à droite *to the right*
à gauche *to the left*
à haute voix *aloud*
à voix basse *in a low voice, in a whisper*
asseyez-vous *sit down*
écrire à l'encre *write in ink*
écrire au crayon *write with a pencil*
faire attention *pay attention; watch out*
il dit *he says*
jusqu'à *up to*
s'il vous plaît *please*
taisez-vous *keep still, be still*

Verbes

écrire		lire	
j'écris	nous écrivons	je lis	nous lisons
tu écris	vous écrivez	tu lis	vous lisez
il écrit	ils écrivent	il lit	ils lisent

IMPERATIVES

INFINITIVE	parler	regarder	écrire	lire
IMPERATIVE	parlez	regardez	écrivez	lisez

Devoirs

A. Write the French equivalent of each of the following sentences.

1. Speak to the girl. 2. Go to the country. 3. Read the sentences. 4. Write five words. 5. The teacher reads the sentences and explains them to the pupils. 6. The pupils correct their mistakes and erase them. 7. The boys notice a mistake and correct it. 8. I write a sentence on[1] the board and the other pupils read it. 9. You read the text and we write it.

[1] on the *au*

B. Say aloud rapidly the French equivalent of each of the following sentences.

1. Go to the board and copy the text. 2. Read this sentence. 3. I read it slowly. 4. Do you read it aloud? 5. Erase the board and sit down, please. 6. Write the sentences, please. 7. Be still. 8. The teacher reads the sentences and we write them.

QUATORZIÈME LEÇON

Vocabulaire

ah!
bleu
littéraire
Moreau
observer
la page
le passage
le poème
le théâtre

apporter *bring*
arrêter *stop*
aussitôt *immediately*
baisser *lower*
cacher *hide*
le cahier *notebook*
choisir *choose*
confus *embarrassed*
constater *ascertain; notice*
derrière *behind*
l'écrivain *m.* *writer*
finir *finish*
la leçon *lesson*
la lecture *reading*
leur *to them*
le livre *book*
lui *to him, to her*
mériter *deserve*
ne ... jamais *never*
obéir *obey*
ordonner *order*
pendant *during*
pendant que *while*
penser *think;* penser à *think of*
la pièce *play*
punir *punish*
la punition *punishment*
que (*relative pron.*) *whom, which, that*
réfléchir *reflect*
remplir *fill*
réussir *succeed*
le roman *novel*
sembler *seem*
la tête *head*
vide *empty*

Ouvrez ... *Open ...*

Verbes

finir [a]

je fin*is*	nous fin*issons*
tu fin*is*	vous fin*issez*
il fin*it*	ils fin*issent*

Devoirs

A. Write the French equivalent of each of the following sentences.

1. One pupil fills his fountain pen while the other chooses a poem. 2. The teacher tells them that Victor Hugo is one of the most famous writers of French literature.[1] 3. We finish the reading of the poem which we are studying. 4. Do you obey your father? [2] 5. He punishes me when

[1] French requires the definite article.

[2] In French the verb *obéir* requires an indirect object.

[a] The verb *finir* may be considered a model for most *-ir* verbs. The complete conjugation of *finir* may be found in § 95, no. 2.

I do not obey him.[1] 6. The teacher explains the lesson to us. 7. Who tells him to[2] bring his notebook to the teacher's[3] desk? 8. The book which he is reading is a detective story. 9. The girls who are seated in the classroom choose a novel of Victor Hugo.

[1] In French the verb *obéir* requires an indirect object.
[2] *d'* [3] For the French method of expressing possession, see § 41.

B. Say aloud rapidly the French equivalent of each of the following sentences.

1. Open your books, please. 2. Bring the book to the desk. 3. Bring to the desk the book that you are hiding. 4. Open the book and read the lesson. 5. Copy the lesson six times. 6. When my fountain pen is empty, I fill it. 7. We fill our fountain pen with blue ink. 8. We write our exercises in our notebook with blue ink.

QUINZIÈME LEÇON

Vocabulaire

danser
généralement
national
particulièrement
la période
recommencer
le ski
le sport
l'université *f.*
le voyage

l'année *f.* *year*
beau, belle[a] *beautiful*
ce (*pronoun*) *it*
chaud *warm; hot*
le ciel *sky*
*conduire *drive; lead*
le cours *course*
couvert *covered*
dernier, dernière *last*
doux, douce *mild, soft*
l'époque *f.* *time*
l'étudiant[b] *m. and f.* *student*
*faire *do; make*
la fête *holiday*
la fleur *flower*
frais, fraîche *fresh, cool*
froid *cold*
mauvais *bad*
mieux *better* (adv.)
neiger *snow*
Noël *Christmas*
l'occasion *f.* *opportunity*
Pâques *Easter*
parfois *sometimes*
*pleuvoir *rain*
rentrer *return; return home; return to school*
la saison *season*
le temps *weather*
le vent *wind*
la voiture *car, automobile*

* An asterisk (*) placed before a verb indicates that this verb is irregular. The forms that you will be required to know are listed after the vocabulary.
[a] The adjective *beau* has a slight peculiarity which will be taken up in a later lesson.
[b] The word *étudiant* refers to a college student; the word *élève* refers to a pupil in high school or in the elementary grades.

SEASONS

au printemps *in spring*
en été *in summer*
en automne *in autumn*
en hiver *in winter*

QUESTIONS

En quel mois . . . ? *In what month . . . ?*
En quelle saison . . . ? *In what season . . . ?*

Quel temps fait-il? *What kind of weather is it?*

MISCELLANEOUS EXPRESSIONS

à la montagne *in the mountains, to the mountains*
aimer mieux *like better, prefer*
conduire une voiture *drive a car*
faire du ski *go skiing*
faire un voyage *take a trip*
les grandes écoles *schools of the level of our American colleges, such as engineering, dentistry, and education, which in France do not belong to the university*
quelque part *somewhere*
quinze jours [a] *two weeks*

WEATHER

le ciel est couvert *it is cloudy*
il fait beau *it is good weather*
il fait chaud *it is warm (hot)*
il fait doux *it is mild*
il fait frais *it is cool*
il fait froid *it is cold*
il fait mauvais temps *it is bad weather*
il y a beaucoup de vent [b] *it is very windy*

With this lesson also learn (a) the months of the year (§ 97 B)
(b) the disjunctive pronouns (§ 27 A)
(c) the ordinals up to 12th (§ 18 A, B)

Verbes

faire	**pleuvoir** [c]	**conduire**
je fais		je conduis
tu fais		tu conduis
il fait	il pleut	il conduit
nous faisons		nous conduisons
vous faites		vous conduisez
ils font		ils conduisent

Devoirs

A. Write the French equivalent of each of the following sentences.

1. It is mild in [1] spring, it is warm in [1] summer, it is cool in [1] autumn, and it is cold in [1] winter. 2. It is very windy in [2] the month of March, and

[1] See the vocabulary above for the way of rendering this expression in French.
[2] in the *au*

[a] To express *two weeks*, the French often use *quinze jours* instead of *deux semaines*, which is also heard.
[b] The French equivalent of *It is windy* is *Il y a du vent* or *Il fait du vent.*
[c] This is an impersonal verb, that is, it has only *il* forms.

it rains in April. 3. At that time[1] the weather is bad, for it is cloudy. 4. I do my exercises, but you do not do your exercises. 5. Maurice and I go[2] to school with her. 6. Mary drives better than they. 7. Are you speaking of him or of us? 8. Paul likes to drive better than I. 9. At that time[1] we take[3] a trip to the mountains, and my friend drives the car for me.

[1] Use *époque* [2] The verb is the first person plural.
[3] See p. 100 for the way of rendering this expression in French.

B. Say aloud rapidly the French equivalent of each of the following sentences.

1. When the weather is good, I drive the car to the mountains. 2. When the weather is bad, we do not drive well. 3. I like to drive better than he. 4. I like to drive in spring when it is mild. 5. In summer it is hot and sometimes it rains. 6. When it is hot, we take a trip to the mountains. 7. I take a trip to the mountains in August, because August is the month of[1] vacations. 8. We have a vacation[2] at Christmas too.

[1] Supply the definite article. [2] Use the plural form.

Thème

Leçons 11 à 15

Write the French equivalent of each of the following sentences.

1. I am American; do I speak English? 2. We have a motorcycle, and we travel in France in summer. 3. My uncle and my aunt write me a letter each week. 4. We go to school while our friends go to the country. 5. Write a letter to your teacher. 6. We write it, and our teacher reads it. 7. The pupil tells them that she is finishing her exercises. 8. We fill our fountain pens, and another pupil finishes his letter. 9. They take a trip to the mountains because it is very warm. 10. Charles and I like to drive better than they.

SEIZIÈME LEÇON

Vocabulaire

administratif, administrative	la géographie	perfectionner
le candidat	le grec	la philosophie
considérer	intellectuel, intellectuelle	préparer
la culture	interroger	la science
le diplôme	le latin	second[b]
l'éducation[a] *f.*	les mathématiques *f.*	sérieux, sérieuse
l'examen *m.*	le ministère	simple
la formalité	obliger	se spécialiser
général	oral	le sujet

[a] In this lesson *éducation* is the equivalent of the English *education*, but usually *éducation* means *bringing up* rather than *education*.
[b] The *-c-* of *second* is pronounced *-g-*. [səgõ] or [zgõ].

*apprendre *learn*
le baccalauréat *baccalaureate degree obtained by French lycée student after passing two series of state examinations*
le bachot *popular term for baccalauréat*
choisi (*pp of choisir*) *chosen*
comporter *include*
donner *give*
le droit *right*
échouer *fail*
écrit (*pp of* écrire) *written*
l'ensemble *m.* *whole, total*
l'épreuve *f.* *test*
l'établissement *m.* *establishment*
l'état *m.* *state;* l'État *government*
étendu *extensive*
étranger, étrangère *foreign*
l'étude *f.* *study*
la fin *end*
la formation *training*
la matière *subject (of study)*
la moitié *half*
ne . . . que[a] *only*
*obtenir *obtain*
ou *or*
plutôt *rather*
pratique *practical*
précédent *preceding*
propre *own*
redoubler *repeat (a year of school)*
*suffire *suffice;* il suffit *it suffices*
*suivre *follow*
supérieur *higher; advanced*
tous[b] (*pronoun*) *all, everyone*
le travail *work*
vivant *living*

ainsi que *as well as*
au moins *at least*
échouer à un examen *fail an examination*
les études supérieures *advanced studies*
la langue vivante *modern language*
le Ministère de l'Éducation Nationale *Ministry of Education*
passer un examen *take an examination*
redoubler la classe *take over a year of school work*
réussir à un examen *pass an examination*
réussir dans un cours *pass a course*
suivre un cours *take a course*

* An asterisk (*) placed before a verb indicates that this verb is irregular. The forms that you will be required to know are listed after the vocabulary.

[a] The use of *ne* before the verb and *que* after, meaning *only*, is very common in French: *D'autres encore n'étudient qu'une langue vivante* means *Still others study only one modern language.*

[b] The word *tous* not followed by a noun is a plural pronoun meaning *all* or *everyone* and is followed by a plural verb form. When used as a pronoun, *tous* is pronounced [tus], the final *-s* being sounded. When used as an adjective, *tous* is pronounced [tu], the final *-s* being silent.

Verbes

apprendre	**obtenir**	**suivre**
j'apprends	j'obtiens	je suis
tu apprends	tu obtiens	tu suis
il apprend	il obtient	il suit
nous apprenons	nous obtenons	nous suivons
vous apprenez	vous obtenez	vous suivez
ils apprennent	ils obtiennent	ils suivent

Devoirs

A. Write the French equivalent of each of the following sentences.

1. What is the school that prepares the pupil for[1] the universities? 2. Which is the foreign language that is considered[2] the most difficult? 3. What are the principal cities of France? 4. What is geography? 5. What is a foreign language? 6. The first language that the pupils learn is French.[3] 7. The pupils spend seven years in[4] the lycée and several years at the university. 8. There are numerous[5] tests during the last part of the year, and these examinations are not a simple[6] administrative formality. 9. The studies in[4] the lycée are very serious, for the intellectual training of the pupil is considered[2] very important.

[1] for the *aux* [2] Supply *comme* after forms of *considérer.*
[3] Use the definite article with names of languages. [4] in the *au*
[5] This adjective precedes its noun. What word must precede the adjective?
[6] This adjective precedes its noun.

B. Say aloud rapidly the French equivalent of each of the following sentences.

1. What is a lycée? 2. What is philosophy?[1] 3. What is an intellectual training? 4. Does the study of languages give an intellectual training to the pupils? 5. What are the most important subjects?[2] 6. Which are the languages that the pupils learn in[3] the lycée? 7. I take an examination today. 8. If I pass[4] the examination, I continue my studies at the university.

[1] Use the definite article with this noun. [2] *matières* [3] in the *au*
[4] Do not use the verb *passer.* See the list of expressions at the end of the vocabulary on page 102.

DIX-SEPTIÈME LEÇON

Vocabulaire

accompagner	désirer	oh
contemporain	diviser	la permission
le département	intéresser	la récréation
	Louis XIV	

allons! *let's go!*
alors *then*
l'après-midi *m. and f.* *afternoon*
assister à *attend, be present at*
attendre *wait for*
bonjour *good day, good morning*
la carte *map*
la cloche *bell*
Comment! *What!*
le congé *day off, vacation*
la cour *court, courtyard, patio*
déjeuner[a] *eat the noon meal; lunch*
demander *ask*
demi *half*
*dire *say*
entendre *hear*
l'étage *m.* *floor, story (of a building)*
évidemment *obviously; evidently*
l'heure *f.* *time; hour; o'clock*
ici *here*
Louis-le-Grand *Louis the Great, i.e., Louis XIV*
le matin *morning*
midi *noon*
monter *go up, climb*
la montre *watch*
le mur *wall*
le plaisir *pleasure*
*pouvoir *be able, can*
présenter *present, introduce*
quarante *forty*
répondre *reply*
se réunir *meet, assemble*
selon *according to*
si *yes*[b]
*voir *see*
*vouloir *want, wish, be willing*

en souvenir de *in memory of*
les jeunes gens *young people; young men*[c]
le premier étage *the second floor*[d]

TIME PATTERNS

Quelle heure est-il?	*What time is it?*
Il est huit heures.	*It is eight o'clock.*
Il est huit heures trois.	*It is three minutes after eight.*
Il est huit heures et quart.	*It is quarter after eight.*
Il est huit heures et demie.	*It is half past eight.*
Il est neuf heures moins le quart.	*It is quarter of nine.*
Il est neuf heures moins cinq.	*It is five minutes to nine.*
A quelle heure . . . ?	*At what time?*

* An asterisk (*) placed before a verb indicates that this verb is irregular. The forms that you will be required to know are listed after the vocabulary.

[a] Since the noon meal in France is normally the biggest meal of the day, it is not quite accurate to render *déjeuner* as *lunch.*

[b] The word *si* has several meanings. The common word for *yes* is *oui.* For when to use *si* as *yes,* see § 98 — *yes.*

[c] The plural of *le jeune homme* is *les jeunes gens.*

[d] The French call the ground floor the *rez-de-chaussée* and the floor above the ground the *premier étage.*

Verbes

répondre [a]	**dire**	**pouvoir** [c]	**voir** [c]	**vouloir** [c]
je répond*s*	je dis	je peux [d]	je vois	je veux
tu répond*s*	tu dis	tu peux	tu vois	tu veux
il répond [b]	il dit	il peut	il voit	il veut
nous répond*ons*	nous disons	nous pouvons	nous voyons	nous voulons
vous répond*ez*	vous dites	vous pouvez	vous voyez	vous voulez
ils répond*ent*	ils disent	ils peuvent	ils voient	ils veulent

Devoirs

A. *Write the French equivalent of each of the following sentences.*

1. What time is it? 2. It is three o'clock. 3. It is half past four. 4. I want to see my brother at quarter after ten. 5. I am waiting for [1] my friend in the courtyard. 6. He cannot see his mother at quarter of two. 7. Maurice answers that he does not wish to arrive at noon. 8. What do you see on [2] the second floor? 9. We reply that we see a map [3] of France on [2] the wall.

[1] Included in the French verb. [2] on the *au* [3] map of France *carte de France*

B. *Say aloud rapidly the French equivalent of each of the following sentences.*

1. Maurice says good morning to me. 2. He asks me: "What time is it?" 3. I tell him [1] that it is quarter after ten. 4. He asks me: "At what time do you want to lunch?" 5. I answer him [1] that I want to lunch at half past twelve. 6. Do you want to go to [2] class with me? 7. I can hear the bell from here, and now we can go to [2] class. 8. What do you see on [3] the wall?

[1] What kind of object is this? [2] to class *en classe* [3] on the *au*

DIX-HUITIÈME LEÇON

Vocabulaire

charger	métropolitain	représenter
l'exécution *f.*	le président	la révolution
le gouvernement	la question	voter
	la république	

[a] The verb *répondre* may be considered a model for *-re* verbs. The complete conjugation of an *-re* verb (*perdre*) may be found in § 95, no. 3.

[b] A few verbs, whose stems do not end in *-d*, add *-t* here. EXAMPLE: *rompre* (break), *il rompt.*

[c] What type of irregularity is common to these three verbs?

[d] There is an alternate form, *je puis,* which is used especially in the interrogative.

le berceau *cradle*
chercher *look for; go and get*
*comprendre *understand*
le décret *decree*
désigner *designate, indicate*
entier, entière *entire*
l'explication *f.* *explanation*
l'Île-de-France *ancient French province of which Paris is the center*
indiquer *point out, indicate*
la loi *law*
montrer *show*

nommer *name; nominate*
poser *put*
le préfet *prefect*
quatre-vingt-neuf *eighty-nine*
quatre-vingt-dix *ninety*
quoi *what* (interrogative pronoun used after a preposition)
rendre *return* (*something to someone*)
*savoir *know*
trente-deux *thirty-two*
voilà *there is, there are*

c'est-à-dire *that is to say*
la France métropolitaine *France proper, European France, referring to France without her overseas territories*

le Président de la République [a] *the President of France*
la Révolution française *the French Revolution*
toute l'heure *the whole hour*

With Lesson 17, learn to count by 10's to 100. (§ 17 A)
First begin with 10: 10, 20, 30, etc.
Then begin with 11: 11, 21, 31, etc.

Verbes

savoir	**comprendre** [b]
je sais	je comprends
tu sais	tu comprends
il sait	il comprend
nous savons	nous comprenons
vous savez	vous comprenez
ils savent	ils comprennent

Devoirs

A. Write the French equivalent of each of the following sentences.

1. This country is larger than that country. 2. Do you understand the explanation of the teacher? I understand it. 3. The boy gives me the notebooks. He gives them to me. 4. I show the book to the pupils. I show

* An asterisk (*) placed before a verb indicates that this verb is irregular. The forms that you will be required to know are listed after the vocabulary.

[a] The President of France is always spoken of as *Le Président de la République;* one never hears *Le Président de la France.*

[b] Notice that *comprendre* is conjugated like *apprendre* (page 103) and *prendre* (§ 95, no. 36).

it to them. 5. Roger does not read this lesson to the teacher. He does not read it to him. 6. Does he return[1] your fountain pen to you? Does he return it to you? 7. The teacher asks[2] those pupils the questions. He asks them of[3] them. 8. My brother does not tell me that story. He does not tell it to me. 9. Do you know the lesson? I know it.

[1] Use a form of *rendre.*
[2] Use a form of the expression *poser une question à quelqu'un.*
[3] An indirect object in French.

B. *Say aloud rapidly the French equivalent of each of the following sentences.*

1. Do you know if this state is larger than that state? 2. I do not know if this province is more important than that province. 3. Do you understand the explanations of the other pupils? 4. Yes, I understand them. 5. Roger looks for[1] the book and shows it to me. 6. Does he give it to me? 7. Yes, he gives it to me, and I return[2] it to him. 8. No, I do not return it to him, because I want to look at[1] it.

[1] Included in the French verb. [2] Use a form of *rendre.*

DIX-NEUVIÈME LEÇON

Vocabulaire[a]

l'article *m.*	économique	l'organisation *f.*
l'assemblée *f.*	l'élection *f.*	le Parlement
assurer	électoral	présider
la circonstance	le fonctionnement	le principe
le collège	gouvernemental	proclamer
la constitution	indivisible	refuser
la constitutionnalité	la liberté	régulier
constitutionnel	le membre	la religion
la délibération	menacer	respecter
démocratique	la mesure	la sécurité
déterminer	le ministre	social
la distinction	la nation	le système
le domaine		le veto

[a] Words, expressions, and irregular verbs occurring for the first time in this lesson will be repeated in the lesson vocabulary of the first subsequent lesson in which they occur.

l'armée *f.* *army*
l'avis *m.* *opinion*
le cas *case*
le citoyen *citizen*
*comprendre *comprise; understand*
*conduire *conduct; lead; drive*
le conseil *council; advice*
la croyance *belief*
la devise *motto*
*dissoudre *dissolve*
l'égalité *f.* *equality*
*élire (*pp* élu) *elect*
exiger *require, demand*

la fraternité *brotherhood*
laïque *secular, lay, not ecclesiastic*
nouveau, nouvelle[a] *new*
le peuple *people; the masses*
la politique *policy, policies*
le pouvoir *power*
*prendre *take*
promulguer *promulgate, put into execution*
sans *without*
veiller à *look after, watch out for, keep an eye on*

l'Assemblée Nationale *the National Assembly* (*lower house of the French Parliament*)
le collège électoral *electoral college*
le Conseil Constitutionnel *the Constitutional Council, a body which decides on the constitutionality of French laws*
le Conseil des Ministres *the Council of Ministers* (*the French Cabinet*)
le Conseil Économique et Social *the Economic and Social Council*
en effet *in fact*
le Premier Ministre *the Prime Minister*
proprement dit *properly speaking*

Verbes

prendre

je prends	nous prenons
tu prends	vous prenez
il prend	ils prennent

Devoirs

Before working out this exercise, study carefully the questions in Lesson 19. Analyze the word order used in each of the first seven sentences and with each type of interrogative pronoun. Also see § 96 H, I.

* An asterisk (*) placed before a verb indicates that this verb is irregular. Learn the conjugation of the present tense of the irregular verb *prendre*, which follows. You have already learned the present of *comprendre* in connection with Lesson 18 (page 106) and the present of *conduire* in connection with Lesson 15 (page 100). The irregular verb *dissoudre* is used only in the infinitive in this lesson; its present tense need not be learned.

[a] The adjective *nouveau* has a slight peculiarity which will be taken up in a later lesson.

A. Write the French equivalent of each of the following sentences.

1. Who is at the head of the government? 2. What is the teacher saying? 3. With what is he writing? 4. What is on the teacher's desk? 5. With whom does this boy go to class? 6. What do the pupils correct? 7. To whom does he show his book? 8. Whom does he meet on the street? 9. What prevents the teacher from punishing[1] the pupil?

[1] Use the infinitive form of the verb after prepositions.

B. Say aloud rapidly the French equivalent of each of the following sentences.

1. Who is at the door? 2. Who is in front of the class? 3. What is the teacher doing? 4. With what is he correcting the exercises? 5. With whom do you go to school? 6. Whom do you see? 7. What do you want? 8. What does your friend want?

VINGTIÈME LEÇON

Vocabulaire[a]

abuser
l'action *f.*
adopter
l'affaire *f.*
armé
la base
Bourbon
le cabinet
la censure
la chambre
décider
déclarer
la défense
le député
désapprouver
directement
l'électeur *m.*
etc. (et cetera)
l'exemple *m.*
exercer
la force
gouverner
indirect
l'information *f.*
la justice
législatif, législative
la majorité
le maximum
la motion
l'ordonnance *f.*
le programme
responsable
le Sénat
le sénateur
le suffrage
le territoire

contre *against*
la démission *resignation*
*devoir *must, have to*
diriger *direct*
la guerre *war*
le lieu *place*
le moment *moment, time*
le nom *name*
outre-mer *abroad, beyond the seas*
le palais *palace*
la place *public square*
*remettre *hand (something to someone)*
remplacer *replace, take the place of*
renverser *overthrow*
la rive *(river) bank*
seul *alone, only*

* An asterisk (*) placed before a verb indicates that this verb is irregular. The forms that you will be required to know are listed after the vocabulary.

[a] Words, expressions, and irregular verbs occurring for the first time in this lesson will be repeated in the lesson vocabulary of the first subsequent lesson in which they occur.

avoir lieu *take place*
de sorte que *so that*
en même temps *at the same time*
par exemple *for example*
à ce moment-là *at that time*
au maximum *at the most*
au suffrage indirect *by indirect suffrage*

la Cinquième République *the Fifth French Republic (government brought into France in 1958 by General de Gaulle, which took the place of the Fourth Republic)*
le Palais Bourbon *the building where the Assemblée Nationale meets*
le Palais du Luxembourg *the building located in the Luxembourg Garden where the Senate meets*
la Place de la Concorde *famous square in Paris situated between the Champs-Élysées and the Tuileries Gardens and directly opposite the Palais Bourbon*

Ministre des Affaires Étrangères *Minister of Foreign Affairs (corresponds to the Secretary of State in the United States)*
Ministre de l'Agriculture *Minister of Agriculture*
Ministre des Forces Armées *Minister of Defense*
Ministre de l'Information *Minister of Information*
Ministre de l'Intérieur *Minister of the Interior*
Ministre de la Justice *Minister of Justice*

Verbes

devoir	**remettre**
je dois	je remets
tu dois	tu remets
il doit	il remet
nous devons	nous remettons
vous devez	vous remettez
ils doivent	ils remettent

Devoirs

A. Write the French equivalent of each of the following sentences.

1. Today there are about five hundred forty-five deputies in[1] the National Assembly. 2. There are fifty-nine teachers and six hundred seventy-five pupils in that school. 3. Ninety-three cities are located in the east of the country. 4. Two hundred students are gathering in the courtyard. 5. Three hundred fifty pupils are waiting in front of the door. 6. There are three thousand six hundred inhabitants in that place. 7. There are eighty-three books and seventy-eight notebooks in that classroom. 8. These dates

[1] à

are important: 1066, 1789, 1812, 1914, 1945. 9. We have ten thousand six hundred ninety-five students in our university.

B. Say aloud rapidly the French equivalent of each of the following sentences.

1. Are you against the policies[1] of the president? 2. You must hand your exercises to the teacher. 3. You must hand the letter to my mother. 4. Hand in your exercises. 5. You must hand in your exercises today. 6. Who directs the policies[1] of the government? 7. The Parliament alone has the power to[2] declare war[3]. 8. Are there about five hundred forty-five deputies in France?

[1] This word is singular in French. [2] *de* [3] Supply the definite article.

THÈME

Leçons 16 à 20

Write the French equivalent of each of the following sentences.

1. The first year at school[1] is very interesting. 2. What is a foreign language? 3. I am waiting for[2] my friend who wishes to[3] go to[4] class with me. 4. We reply that we can make the trip. 5. I find Robert's[5] pencil and I give it to him. 6. He returns it to me. 7. This language is more difficult than those languages. 8. What are you reading? 9. Whom do you see? 10. What is behind that building?

[1] Supply the definite article. [2] In French, this word is part of the verb.
[3] Not expressed in French. [4] *en* [5] How is possession expressed in French? (§ 41)

Frère Jacques

Frère Jacques, Frère Jacques,
Dormez-vous? Dormez-vous?
Sonnez les matines[1], Sonnez les matines,
Ding, din, don! Ding, din, don!

[1] *morning bells*

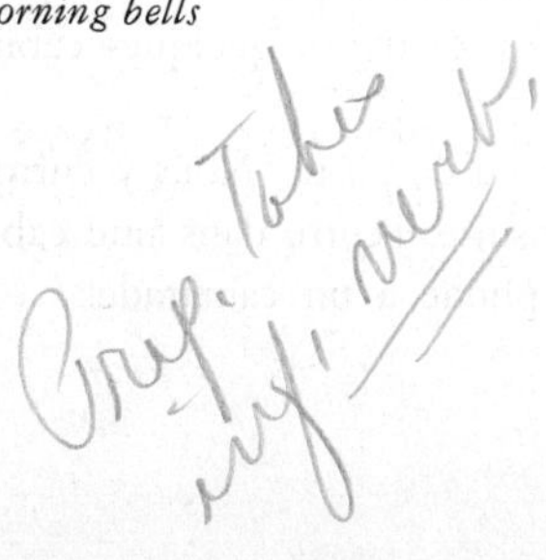

VINGT ET UNIÈME LEÇON

Les monopoles de l'État

— J'ai besoin d'un timbre pour envoyer une lettre. En avez-vous chez vous?

— Je n'en ai pas chez moi, mais allons au bureau de tabac qui est à côté.

— Au bureau de tabac? Mais je ne veux pas de tabac. Je n'en ai pas besoin. Je ne fume pas. Je veux seulement mettre une lettre à la poste.

— Eh bien, venez. Chez nous, on peut acheter des timbres au bureau de tabac.

Tout étonné, j'entre avec mon ami dans une petite boutique où l'on[1] vend du tabac, des cigares, des cigarettes, des allumettes, etc. Maurice me demande:

— Combien de timbres voulez-vous?

— J'en veux un — pour envoyer une lettre aux États-Unis.

— Je dois en acheter aussi. J'en veux cinq.

Maurice demande des timbres, et on lui en donne six. Puis, mon camarade me dit:

— Cette boîte bleue que vous voyez là-bas est une boîte aux lettres. Il faut mettre votre lettre dans cette boîte.

— N'y a-t-il pas de bureaux de poste à Paris?

— Mais si! Il y en a beaucoup. Il y a aussi une grande poste centrale rue du Louvre. Mais comme le tabac et les allumettes sont des monopoles de l'État ainsi que les timbres, on peut acheter des timbres dans un bureau de tabac. D'ailleurs, on peut en acheter aussi dans beaucoup de cafés.

— Ah! J'ai aussi besoin de téléphoner. D'où peut-on téléphoner?

— Pour cela, il faut aller à la poste. En France le télégraphe et le téléphone sont également des monopoles de l'État. On envoie les télégrammes de la poste. Il y a aussi des téléphones publics à la poste. Cependant, on en trouve aussi dans les cafés, et il y a quelques cabines téléphoniques dans la rue.

Maurice et moi arrivons devant un bureau de poste. Nous y entrons, et je cherche le numéro dans l'annuaire. Ensuite, j'entre dans une cabine téléphonique pour donner un coup de téléphone à un camarade.

[1] For the use of *l'on* see § 40B.

QUESTIONS

1. Pourquoi avez-vous besoin d'un timbre? 2. Avez-vous des timbres chez vous? 3. Fumez-vous? 4. Où peut-on acheter des timbres en France? 5. Que peut-on acheter dans un bureau de tabac français? 6. Combien de timbres désire Maurice? 7. Combien de timbres donne-t-on à Maurice dans le bureau de tabac? 8. Y a-t-il beaucoup de bureaux de poste à Paris? 9. Pourquoi peut-on acheter des timbres dans un bureau de tabac? 10. Où faut-il aller en France pour téléphoner? 11. Pourquoi faut-il aller à la poste pour envoyer un télégramme? 12. Y a-t-il des cabines téléphoniques dans les rues de Paris? 13. Où faut-il chercher le numéro de téléphone d'un ami? 14. Dans la poste, comment fait-on pour donner un coup de téléphone?

DEVOIRS

® *A. Suivez*[1] *les indications.* EXEMPLE: Dites à Robert que vous ne fumez pas. Robert, je ne fume pas.

1. Dites à Maurice que vous avez besoin d'un timbre. 2. Dites à Louise que vous voulez envoyer une lettre en France. 3. Dites à Charles que vous allez chercher son numéro de téléphone dans l'annuaire.

® *B. Répondez aux questions suivantes en employant je et en dans la réponse.* EXEMPLE: Voulez-vous des allumettes? Oui, *j'en* veux.

1. Avez-vous des timbres? 2. Voulez-vous du lait? 3. Avez-vous beaucoup d'argent? 4. Combien de stylos avez-vous? 5. Combien de timbres avez-vous chez vous?

® *C. Répondez aux questions suivantes en employant* **en** *dans la réponse.*

1. Les étudiants ont-ils beaucoup de travail? 2. Votre père a-t-il besoin d'une voiture? 3. Combien de fenêtres y a-t-il dans la classe? 4. Combien d'états y a-t-il aux États-Unis? 5. Y a-t-il trop de voitures dans la rue?

® *D. Remplacez les expressions en italique par des pronoms compléments.*

1. Si vous voulez des timbres, j'ai *des timbres* à la maison. 2.

[1] *Follow the instructions.* In this type of exercise, you are required to tell someone something. Simply follow the instructions. What you say will indicate whether you understand the instructions. For instance, if someone should say to you in English: *Tell John that you are going to class,* you would say: *John, I am going to class.*

Maurice a deux sœurs et moi, j'ai trois *sœurs*. 3. Je n'écris jamais de lettres, mais mon frère écrit beaucoup *de lettres*. 4. Je cherche un crayon, et je trouve *des crayons* sur le bureau du professeur. 5. Robert demande de l'argent à son père, parce qu'il n'a pas *d'argent*. 6. Nous ne voyons pas de fleurs dans ce jardin. Voyez-vous *des fleurs*[1]? 7. Je n'ai pas de moto. Avez-vous une *moto*[1]?

® *E. Remplacez les expressions en italique par des pronoms compléments. Attention à l'ordre des pronoms.*

1. Si votre ami veut du lait, il y a *du lait* chez nous. 2. Mes camarades cherchent des romans policiers, et je leur donne *des romans policiers*. 3. Prenez ce crayon, car il y a assez *de crayons* pour tout le monde. 4. Roger lit toutes ces histoires, et puis il me raconte beaucoup *d'histoires*. 5. Nous avons plusieurs timbres; je vais vous donner deux *timbres*. 6. Quand j'ai besoin d'argent, ma mère me donne *de l'argent*.

® *F. Remplacez les expressions en italique par les pronoms compléments convenables. Distinguez entre* ***en, le, la*** *et* ***les***.[2]

1. Nous avons *des livres*. 2. Vous avez *les livres*. 3. J'ai deux *lettres*. 4. J'ai *vos lettres*. 5. Marie cherche une *carte de France*. 6. Marie trouve *cette carte*. 7. Écrivez-vous beaucoup *de lettres?* 8. Écrivez-vous toujours *les devoirs?*

G. Remplacez l'infinitif par la forme convenable du présent du verbe indiqué.

1. Pour téléphoner, il (falloir) aller à la poste. 2. Je (mettre) ma lettre dans la boîte aux lettres. 3. (envoyer)-vous souvent des lettres en France? 4. Roger (envoyer) un télégramme à sa tante. 5. Qui (venir) vous voir cet après-midi? 6. Marie et Louise (venir) ce matin et vous (venir) cet après-midi, n'est-ce pas? 7. Je (devoir) lire ma leçon, et vous (devoir) écrire vos devoirs.

Conversation

1. Demandez à l'étudiant assis devant vous s'il a besoin d'un timbre. 2. Demandez à l'étudiant assis près de la porte d'où on peut téléphoner

[1] What is the position of the object pronoun in relation to the verb? (§ 30 A)

[2] One way of determining whether the pronoun is *en* or *le, la* or *les* is to put the sentence into English with the noun and then change the English noun to a pronoun. If the English pronoun is *some* or *any* or an expression ending in *of it* or *of them*, French will use *en*. If the English object is *him, her, it*, or *them*, French will use *le, la* or *les*.

Tout le long du boulevard se trouvent des cafés typiquement français

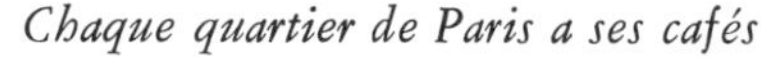

Chaque quartier de Paris a ses cafés

Les plus grands s'amusent avec leurs petits bateaux au bord du bassin du jardin

Les étudiants et les étudiantes viennent travailler leurs cours dans ce jardin agréable et calme

Les Facultés des Lettres et des Sciences se trouvent dans un grand bâtiment près du Boulevard Saint-Michel: la Sorbonne

La Sorbonne n'est que le bâtiment où se trouvent les Facultés des Lettres et des Sciences

Nous sommes allés attendre un autobus. Bientôt il en est arrivé un

aux États-Unis. 3. Demandez à l'étudiant assis près de la fenêtre où il faut aller pour acheter un timbre. 4. Demandez à l'étudiant assis à côté de vous s'il y a un bureau de poste près de l'école.

VOCABULAIRE — PAGES 150–151

GRAMMAIRE

1. How is the French pronoun ***en*** expressed in English? (§ 28 A)

2. Study carefully the examples given in § 28 B. When is a noun direct object replaced by the pronoun *en* rather than by the pronouns *le, la* or *les?* (§ 28 B and page 114, note 2)

3. What is the position of ***en*** in the sentence? (§ 31 A) What is its position in relation to *y?* (§ 31 B) What is its position in relation to any other pronoun object, such as ***nous, me, lui,*** or ***leur?*** (§ 31 C)

4. What are the forms of the present of the irregular verbs ***devoir, envoyer, falloir, mettre,*** and ***venir?*** (Page 151)

VINGT-DEUXIÈME LEÇON

La pension de famille

Il y a beaucoup de pensions de famille en France. Les gens qui travaillent loin de chez eux, les célibataires, les étudiants de province qui font leurs études à Paris s'installent presque tous[1] dans des pensions de famille. Dans ces pensions on trouve une certaine atmosphère familiale. La propriétaire de la pension s'occupe de la maison et s'intéresse, parfois même trop, à la vie de ses pensionnaires. Quelques pensionnaires habitent à l'hôtel et ne viennent à la pension que pour les repas; d'autres ont dans la maison une chambre où ils travaillent et où ils couchent[2]. On sert les

[1] When *tous* is used as a pronoun, the *-s* is pronounced [tus].

[2] Distinguish between *coucher,* which means *to spend the night,* and *se coucher,* which means *to go to bed.*

repas dans la salle à manger: le petit déjeuner le matin, le déjeuner à midi et le dîner vers sept heures et demie ou huit heures du soir. Après le dîner les pensionnaires restent souvent dans la salle à manger à causer une heure ou deux. Dans les romans d'un grand écrivain du dix-neuvième siècle, Honoré de Balzac, on trouve de vivantes descriptions de la pension de famille et de la vie des pensionnaires.

Jean, étudiant en médecine, et Jacques, son petit frère qui va au lycée Louis-le-Grand, habitent à Paris dans une pension. Leur mère leur écrit de Melun:

«Êtes-vous bien à la pension? Combien de temps dormez-vous? A quelle heure vous levez-vous? A quelle heure vous couchez-vous? Sortez-vous beaucoup? Vous sert-on[1] de bons repas? Quand partez-vous en vacances?»

Jean lui répond dans une lettre:

«La vie à la pension n'est pas désagréable. Je me sens presque chez moi ici. Je me réveille vers six heures et demie du matin. Je me lève tout de suite. Puis, je me lave, je m'habille et je prends le petit déjeuner. Jacques se lève plus tard. Je l'appelle vers sept heures et quart. Je sors de bonne heure. Je rentre à la pension vers midi. Je reste ici l'après-midi pour travailler ou bien je me promène. Après le dîner, Jacques et moi sortons souvent ensemble. Nous nous promenons le long de la Seine. Parfois nous allons au cinéma. Jacques se couche vers dix heures. Je me couche un peu plus tard. Jacques dort environ neuf heures. Moi, je dors environ huit heures. Tout le monde est très gentil à la pension. Les repas sont bons. Je pars en vacances la semaine prochaine . . . »

Questions

1. Qui trouve-t-on dans les pensions de famille? 2. De quoi la propriétaire de la pension s'occupe-t-elle? 3. A quoi la propriétaire s'intéresse-t-elle? 4. Dans quelle salle sert-on les repas? 5. Comment s'appellent les repas? 6. Quel est le grand écrivain français du dix-neuvième siècle qui donne dans ses romans de vivantes descriptions de la pension de famille? 7. Combien d'heures dormez-vous? 8. A quelle heure vous levez-vous? 9. A quelle heure vous couchez-vous? 10. Sortez-vous beaucoup? 11. Vous sert-on de bons repas? 12. Partez-vous souvent en vacances?

[1] From *servir:* Do they serve you . . . ?

Devoirs

® *A. Suivez les indications.*

1. Dites à Jacques que vous vous couchez toujours de bonne heure. 2. Dites à Hélène que vous ne dormez pas assez. 3. Dites à Jean que vous vous sentez très bien.

B. Remplacez l'infinitif par le présent.

1. Je (dormir) neuf heures. 2. Je (sortir) vers huit heures. 3. Vous (servir)-on de bons repas? 4. Les pensions (servir) d'assez bons repas. 5. Vous (dormir) trop. 6. Tous les élèves (dormir) beaucoup. 7. Nous (sortir) après le dîner. 8. Mon petit frère ne (sortir) pas. 9. Je (partir) souvent en vacances.

C. Remplacez l'infinitif par le présent. EXEMPLES: 1. Nous (se lever) à huit heures. Nous *nous levons* à huit heures. 2. (s'occuper)-vous de vos cours? *Vous occupez*-vous de vos cours?

1. Nous (se réveiller) vers sept heures. 2. (se laver)-vous immédiatement? 3. Jean (s'occuper) de la maison. 4. Les autres élèves (s'intéresser) à leurs études. 5. Je (s'habiller) vite. 6. Je (se sentir) très bien chez moi. 7. (se spécialiser)-vous en mathématiques? 8. Est-ce que nous (se tourner) vers le tableau? 9. Votre mère (se réveiller)-elle avant vous? 10. Vos parents (se sentir)-ils bien?

D. Remplacez l'infinitif par le présent. Attention à l'orthographe et aux accents.

1. Il (se lever). 2. Elle (se promener). 3. Vous (s'appeler) Jean. 4. Nous (s'appeler) Dupont. 5. Je (se promener). 6. Nous (se lever) immédiatement. 7. Il (s'appeler) Benoît. 8. Elles (se promener) le long de la Seine. 9. Vous (s'appeler) Marie. 10. Vous (se promener) souvent.

Conversation

1. Demandez à l'étudiant qui est près de la porte à quelle heure il se couche. 2. Demandez à l'étudiant qui est derrière vous à quelle heure il se lève. 3. Demandez à l'étudiant qui est à côté de vous s'il sort beaucoup le soir. 4. Demandez à l'étudiant qui est devant vous s'il va souvent au cinéma.

VOCABULAIRE — PAGES 152–153

GRAMMAIRE

1. You have already studied the present of *-ir* verbs such as ***finir.*** Most *-ir* verbs are conjugated like ***finir*** and may be called ***-ir* verbs of the first class.** There is an important group of six very common *-ir* verbs which we shall call ***-ir* verbs of the second class.** These six verbs differ in three tenses from *-ir* verbs of the first class. What are these six verbs? [1] How do they form their present tense? (§ 49 C)

2. Use in sentences forms of the present of ***dormir, partir, servir, sortir,*** and ***sentir.*** (Page 153)

3. What is a reflexive verb? Give examples of sentences with reflexive verbs in English. How do French reflexive verbs differ from other French verbs? (§ 88 A, B, C)

4. List the reflexive objects. (§ 26 A)

5. Examine the reflexive verbs used interrogatively in the text and in questions 2, 3, 8 and 9. What is the position of the reflexive pronoun object? of the subject and the verb? Are these positions contrary to the general rules for pronoun objects? for interrogative word order?

6. Use in sentences the forms of the present of the reflexive verbs ***se laver, se coucher,*** and ***se sentir.*** (Page 153)

7. What are the forms of the present of the verbs ***se lever, acheter,*** and ***appeler?*** (Page 153) Explain why there are changes in the ***je, tu, il,*** and ***ils*** forms of these verbs but not in the ***nous*** and ***vous*** forms. (§ 89 D, F)

8. Use in sentences the forms of the present of the irregular verb ***prendre.*** (Page 153)

[1] *-ir* verbs of this class are marked (2) in the vocabulary. Other *-ir* verbs are not marked.

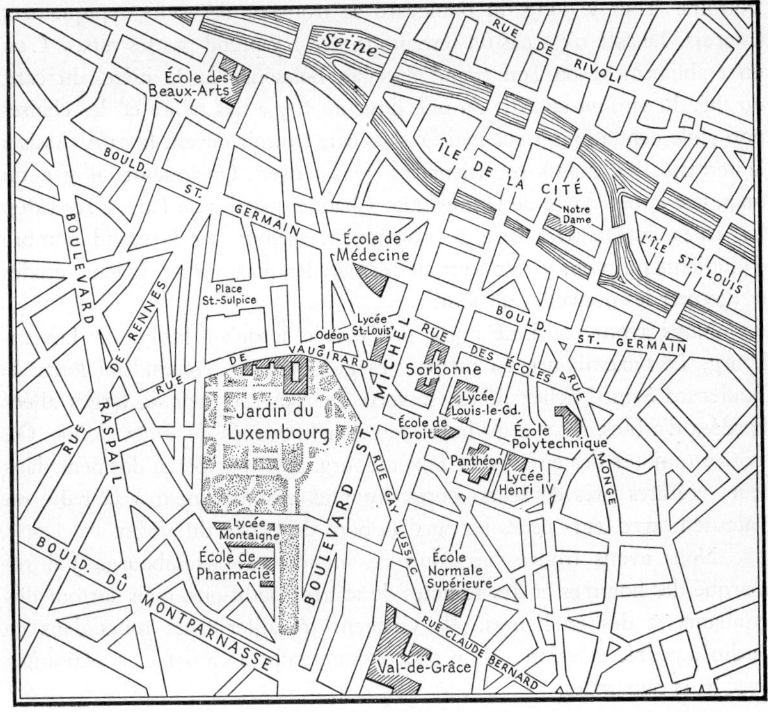

Le Boulevard Saint-Michel est le centre du Quartier latin

VINGT-TROISIÈME LEÇON

Le Quartier latin

A quatre heures et demie Maurice a fini sa journée au lycée. Nous avons attendu son camarade Jacques un moment. Ensuite, nous avons quitté le lycée et nous avons marché ensemble jusqu'au Boulevard Saint-Michel.

Le Boulevard Saint-Michel, appelé «Boul' Mich'» par les étudiants, est le centre du Quartier latin. De nombreux étudiants se promènent sur les trottoirs. Tout le long du boulevard se trouvent des cafés typiquement français. Le café n'est pas un restaurant. On n'y prend pas ses repas. C'est un établissement où l'on prend diverses boissons: de la bière, du café, du thé, du vin, un apéritif ou une liqueur. Il y a des tables et des chaises non seulement à l'intérieur mais aussi sur le trottoir devant le café. Assis à la terrasse, les clients regardent les gens passer. Quelquefois il y a un orchestre et on écoute de la musique. Chaque quartier de Paris a ses cafés. Les cafés du Quartier latin se distinguent surtout par le grand nombre d'étudiants qui vont y retrouver des camarades pour parler de leurs études et discuter les nouvelles du jour.

Nous avons continué notre promenade jusqu'au Jardin du Luxembourg. Le Luxembourg est un parc magnifique, très étendu, qui longe le Boulevard Saint-Michel. Il est traversé en tous sens par de larges allées bordées d'arbres. Il y a de nombreux massifs ornés de jolies fleurs. On trouve toujours des enfants au Luxembourg. Les tout petits dorment dans leurs voitures près de leurs mères, les plus grands jouent à la balle ou s'amusent avec leurs petits bateaux au bord du bassin du jardin.

Nous avons trouvé beaucoup de monde au Luxembourg. J'ai remarqué des hommes et des femmes de toutes conditions, mais surtout des étudiants et des étudiantes. Ils viennent travailler leurs cours dans ce jardin agréable et calme. Ils y restent longtemps à causer et à plaisanter avec leurs camarades.

Questions

1. A quelle heure Maurice a-t-il fini sa journée au lycée? 2. Qui avons-nous attendu? 3. Jusqu'où avons-nous marché? 4. De quel quartier le Boulevard Saint-Michel est-il le centre? 5. Qu'est-ce qu'un café? 6. Prend-on ses repas au café? 7. Quelles boissons prend-on au café? 8. Où se trouvent les tables des cafés français? 9. Comment les cafés du Quartier latin se distinguent-ils des autres cafés de Paris? 10. Qu'est-ce que le Luxembourg? 11. Qui avons-nous trouvé au Luxembourg? 12. A quoi jouent les enfants qui viennent au Luxembourg? 13. Pourquoi les étudiants viennent-ils au Luxembourg? 14. Qu'est-ce que les étudiants font au Luxembourg?

Devoirs

® *A. Suivez les indications.*

1. Dites à Paul que vous avez quitté le lycée à trois heures et demie. 2. Dites à Louise que vous avez répondu à sa lettre. 3. Dites à Robert que vous avez fini la lecture d'un roman très intéressant.

® *B. Mettez au présent les verbes des phrases suivantes.* EXEMPLE: Vous avez entendu de la musique. Vous *entendez* de la musique.

1. Maurice a fini sa lettre. 2. Il a cherché un bureau de poste. 3. Il a demandé un timbre à l'employé. 4. L'employé lui a donné un timbre. 5. Il lui a rendu cinq francs. 6. Vous avez téléphoné de la poste. 7. Nous avons obéi à notre mère. 8. J'ai attendu mes camarades devant la poste.

® *C. Mettez au passé composé les verbes des phrases suivantes.* EXEMPLE: Nous traversons la rue. Nous *avons traversé* la rue.

1. Ce jeune homme parle français. 2. Je lui réponds en français. 3. Nous entendons de la musique au café. 4. Je choisis une boisson. 5. Mes camarades quittent le lycée vers trois heures. 6. Vous remplissez votre stylo. 7. Ma mère punit mon frère. 8. Mon frère obéit à mon père. 9. Je réponds à la question. 10. Nous finissons nos devoirs en classe. 11. Nous achetons des timbres dans un bureau de tabac. 12. Les enfants causent dans le parc. 13. Ils jouent à la balle. 14. Je discute les nouvelles du jour avec Henri.

CONVERSATION

1. Demandez à l'étudiant assis devant vous s'il a fini ses devoirs. 2. Demandez à l'étudiant assis à côté de vous s'il a trouvé beaucoup de monde dans le parc. 3. Demandez à l'étudiant assis près de la fenêtre s'il a attendu son camarade ce matin. 4. Demandez à l'étudiant assis près de la porte à quelle heure il a quitté sa maison ce matin.

VOCABULAIRE — PAGES 154–155

GRAMMAIRE

1. What is a compound tense? (§ 60)

2. Of what two parts is the French *passé composé* (**compound past**) made up? (§ 61 A)

3. With what auxiliary verb is the *passé composé* usually conjugated? (§ 61 B)

4. How is the past participle of a regular English verb formed? How are the past participles of French verbs in *-er* formed? in *-ir?* in *-re?* (§ 75 A)

5. What type of action does the *passé composé* ordinarily express? (§ 63 A)

6. Conjugate in the *passé composé* the verbs ***donner, finir,*** and ***attendre.*** (Page 155)

VINGT-QUATRIÈME LEÇON

L'Université de Paris

Avez-vous entendu parler de l'Université de Paris? Moi, j'ai toujours voulu savoir comment elle est organisée. J'ai donc été très content de faire la connaissance de Jean Perrot, étudiant en médecine à Paris qui connaît aussi l'organisation de nos universités. En effet, il a eu la chance de passer un an dans une université américaine. Il a pu faire ainsi la comparaison des deux systèmes. J'ai donc profité de cette occasion pour lui demander:

— L'Université de Paris est-elle divisée en plusieurs facultés comme nos universités?

— Oui, il y en a cinq: Lettres, Sciences, Droit, Médecine et Pharmacie.

— Où se trouve l'Université de Paris?

— Elle est dans le Quarticr latin, mais les différentes facultés qui composent l'université sont séparées. Les Facultés des Lettres et des Sciences se trouvent dans un grand bâtiment près du Boulevard Saint-Michel: la Sorbonne. Plus loin, tout près du Panthéon, se trouve la Faculté de Droit. Quant aux bâtiments de la Faculté de Médecine, il y en a un de l'autre côté du Boulevard Saint-Michel et d'autres beaucoup plus loin. La Faculté de Pharmacie se trouve à cinq cents mètres de la Sorbonne.

— La Sorbonne n'est pas l'Université de Paris?

— Non, la Sorbonne n'est que le bâtiment où se trouvent les Facultés des Lettres et des Sciences. Mais elle n'a pas toujours été le siège de ces facultés. Elle a été fondée en 1253 pour faciliter aux étudiants pauvres les études de théologie. Pendant longtemps elle n'a été que la Faculté de Théologie.

J'ai été étonné d'apprendre que l'Université de Paris ne comprend que cinq facultés. J'ai demandé à Jean où l'on fait ses études pour devenir ingénieur, dentiste, etc. Il m'a expliqué qu'à côté de l'Université de Paris il y a beaucoup d'instituts comme l'École Polytechnique et l'École Centrale, où l'on se prépare à devenir ingénieur, l'École des Beaux-Arts, où l'on apprend la peinture, la sculpture et l'architecture, l'École Normale Supérieure, qui forme d'excellents professeurs, etc. Ces instituts s'appellent *les grandes écoles.*

Questions

1. Avez-vous entendu parler de la Sorbonne? 2. Avez-vous entendu parler de la vie des étudiants à Paris? 3. Connaissez-vous l'organisation des universités françaises? 4. Avez-vous eu la chance de passer un an dans une université française? 5. Quelles sont les cinq facultés de l'Université de Paris? 6. Qu'est-ce que la Sorbonne? 7. La Sorbonne a-t-elle toujours été le siège des Facultés des Lettres et des Sciences? 8. Quand la Sorbonne a-t-elle été fondée? 9. Pourquoi la Sorbonne a-t-elle été fondée? 10. Qu'est-ce que l'École Polytechnique? 11. Qu'est-ce que l'École Normale Supérieure? 12. Connaissez-vous des étudiants français? 13. Savez-vous le nom de la rue où se trouve la Sorbonne? 14. Connaissez-vous un professeur français?

Devoirs

*A. Remplacez les tirets par la forme convenable du présent de **savoir** ou **connaître**, selon le sens.*

1. Vos camarades —— que vous êtes ici. 2. ——-vous Jean? 3. ——-vous si Jean est à Paris? 4. Nous —— les romans de Balzac. 5. ——-vous où est Marie? 6. ——-nous Marie? 7. Elle —— l'anglais. 8. Je —— ma leçon. 9. Yvonne —— très bien Paris. 10. Je —— monsieur Dupont.

*B. Remplacez l'infinitif entre parenthèses par la forme convenable du participe passé. Les participes passés de tous ces verbes sont **irréguliers.***

1. Avez-vous (comprendre) les explications du professeur? 2. Tous les élèves ont (lire) des romans de Balzac. 3. Est-ce que vous avez (voir) le Luxembourg? 4. Nous avons (avoir) beaucoup de difficulté à comprendre cette leçon. 5. Jean a (être) en Amérique pendant un an. 6. Oui, Gérard a (recevoir) une lettre ce matin. 7. J'ai (mettre) mes devoirs sur le bureau du professeur. 8. Avez-vous (apprendre) les participes passés des verbes irréguliers? 9. J'ai (écrire) ces participes passés cinq fois. 10. Qu'est-ce que vous avez (faire) ce matin? 11. Je n'ai pas (pouvoir) venir vous voir ce matin. 12. Qui a (prendre) mon stylo?

® *C. Mettez au passé composé les verbes des phrases suivantes. Les participes passés de tous ces verbes sont **irréguliers.***

1. Je veux acheter un timbre. 2. Vous comprenez l'employé.

3. Ma mère écrit beaucoup de lettres. 4. Il peut trouver sa maison. 5. Vous dites son nom. 6. Nous avons une voiture. 7. Elle met la lettre à la poste. 8. Jean lit un livre intéressant. 9. Qui est à Paris? 10. Nous voyons les Champs-Élysées.

® *D. Mettez au passé composé les verbes des phrases suivantes. Ces phrases sont toutes à la forme négative.*

1. Je ne parle pas de la vie des étudiants. 2. Vous ne finissez pas votre phrase. 3. Ils n'entendent pas la musique. 4. Nous ne remarquons pas les étudiants assis à la terrasse du café. 5. Elle n'attend pas son frère. 6. Je ne choisis pas de boisson.

® *E. Mettez au passé composé les verbes des phrases suivantes. Ces phrases sont toutes à la forme interrogative.*

1. Trouvez-vous votre stylo? 2. Punit-il l'élève? 3. Répondent-elles à la question? 4. Roger rend-il la lettre à Marie? 5. Louis montre-t-il le Luxembourg à ses camarades? 6. Les élèves réussissent-ils à comprendre le texte?

CONVERSATION

1. Demandez à Monsieur A. s'il a eu la chance de passer un an à Paris. 2. Demandez à Monsieur B. s'il a pu voir la Sorbonne. 3. Demandez à Monsieur C. s'il a été en France. 4. Demandez à Monsieur D. s'il a lu la leçon aujourd'hui.

VOCABULAIRE — PAGES 156–157

GRAMMAIRE

1. Both ***savoir*** and ***connaître*** mean *to know.* Yet, they cannot usually be used interchangeably, for in French their meanings are distinct. Study the use of these two verbs in your reading lesson and state what the difference is. (§ 94 — *know*)

2. Make sentences with the forms of the present of ***connaître*** and ***devenir.*** (Page 157)

3. Many past participles are irregular in French. What is the ending of the past participles of ***-oir*** verbs and of many irregular verbs? (§ 75 A, B)

4. What are the irregular past participles of ***appartenir, apprendre, avoir, comprendre, connaître, courir, devenir, dire, écrire, être,***

faire, falloir, lire, mettre, offrir, pouvoir, prendre, recevoir, savoir, venir, voir, and *vouloir?* (Page 157)

5. When a sentence written in the *passé composé* is negative, the *ne* comes exactly where it would in the present. (§ 22 B) What is the position of *pas?* (§ 22 D)

6. What is the interrogative word order in the *passé composé* when there is a pronoun-subject? (§ 62 B) a noun-subject? (§ 62 C)

VINGT-CINQUIÈME LEÇON

Les cours à l'université

—Je vais vous expliquer l'organisation des cours, mais allons d'abord nous asseoir à la terrasse de ce café.

Jean et moi avons choisi une table à la terrasse. Jean a commandé deux bières que le garçon nous a apportées tout de suite. Nous les avons bues et Jean a continué:

—Chez vous, pour avoir un diplôme, vous suivez un certain nombre de cours. Ces cours sont souvent organisés en petits groupes de vingt-cinq à trente étudiants. Vous êtes obligés d'assister aux cours. On vous interroge sur la leçon, et vous passez des examens de temps en temps. A la fin du semestre vous passez un examen écrit sur les matières que vous avez choisies. Peu d'étudiants américains échouent aux examens.

En France les étudiants qui, après le lycée, désirent poursuivre leurs études sont obligés, pour certaines facultés, de suivre pendant un an des cours supplémentaires qui les préparent directement aux études qu'ils veulent faire.[1] Une fois admis à la faculté, l'étudiant en lettres ou en

[1] In recent years, the various colleges of the French universities have considered the students insufficiently prepared to take their courses in the university directly and have imposed a year of preparation between the *baccalauréat* obtained after the *lycée* and matriculation in the university itself. This year is called *propédeutique.* The studies of *l'année propédeutique* have a special name, depending on the nature of the courses. For some scientific students it is the MPC (*mathé-*

sciences travaille d'ordinaire trois ans pour obtenir son premier diplôme, qui s'appelle la licence. Pour l'avoir, il doit connaître un certain nombre de matières qui constituent le programme. Il s'inscrit aux cours, mais il n'est pas obligé de les suivre. Il peut se préparer chez lui ou à la bibliothèque. Les cours eux-mêmes sont souvent de simples conférences. La plupart du temps plusieurs centaines d'étudiants sont inscrits à un seul cours. J'ai vu des cours suivis par huit cents étudiants.

Mais ces cours ne traitent qu'une petite partie du programme. L'étudiant est obligé d'apprendre les autres questions lui-même. Un étudiant en psychologie, par exemple, peut suivre un cours sur la mémoire, mais à la fin de l'année il passe un examen écrit et un examen oral sur un programme beaucoup plus vaste; il est donc obligé de préparer tout seul beaucoup d'autres questions de psychologie: intelligence, instincts, passions, sensations, perceptions, habitudes, etc. Les professeurs français sont sévères; un assez grand nombre d'étudiants échouent à leurs examens. Mais les étudiants qui réussissent ont une bonne connaissance de leur programme.

A ce moment-là, Jean a aperçu un camarade sur le boulevard. Il lui a fait signe. Le jeune homme nous a vus; il nous a salués amicalement. Alors, Jean a appelé le garçon, lui a demandé: «Combien est-ce que je vous dois?» et lui a donné de l'argent. Sur la somme que Jean lui a donnée, le garçon a rendu la monnaie. Nous la lui avons laissée pour le service.

Questions

1. Quelle boisson Jean a-t-il choisie? 2. Combien d'étudiants y a-t-il dans votre cours de français? 3. Êtes-vous obligé d'assister au cours? 4. Qui vous interroge sur la leçon? 5. Qu'est-ce que vous passez à la fin du semestre? 6. Est-ce que beaucoup d'étudiants américains échouent aux examens? 7. Est-ce que l'étudiant français est obligé de suivre les cours? 8. En quoi consistent les cours des facultés

---

matiques, physique, chimie), for others SPCN (*sciences physiques, chimiques et naturelles*), for literary students it is the ELG (*études littéraires générales*).

French universities do not limit the number of students admitted to medical school. After the *lycée*, the student desiring to study medicine first spends one year in a course called PCB (*physique, chimie, biologie*), after which he enters medical school directly. There are six years of general medicine, at the end of which most medical students spend several years interning in hospitals. In France, it is very difficult to get an internship; medical students must pass difficult competitive examinations in order to secure them.

françaises? 9. Combien d'étudiants y a-t-il dans certains cours des facultés françaises? 10. Qu'est-ce que l'étudiant est obligé de passer à la fin de l'année? 11. Vos professeurs sont-ils sévères? 12. Les étudiants américains que vous connaissez travaillent-ils beaucoup? 13. Les cours que vous suivez sont-ils difficiles? 14. Pourquoi Jean et son ami ont-ils laissé de l'argent au garçon?

Devoirs

® *A. Suivez les indications.*

1. Dites à Charles que vous avez aperçu un camarade de l'autre côté de la rue. 2. Dites à Henri qu'il doit travailler beaucoup pour réussir à son examen. 3. Dites à Claire que vous n'avez pas échoué à votre examen.

B. Remplacez l'infinitif par le participe passé. Attention à l'accord du participe passé. Exemple: Il a (raconter) l'histoire qu'il a (lire). Il a *raconté* l'histoire qu'il a *lue.*

1. Avez-vous (répondre) aux questions que le professeur a (poser)? 2. Nous avons (visiter) toutes les provinces. Les avez-vous (voir)? 3. Savez-vous bien les langues que vous avez (apprendre)? 4. J'ai bien (comprendre) la phrase que mon camarade a (écrire). 5. Où est la carte que nous avons (mettre) sur votre bureau? 6. J'ai les lettres que cet élève a (recevoir).

® *C. Mettez au passé composé les verbes en italique. Faites l'accord du participe passé où il faut.* Exemple: Nous avons commandé la bière que le garçon *apporte.* Nous avons commandé la bière que le garçon *a apportée.*

1. La rue qu'elle *traverse* est dans le Quartier latin. 2. Quelles nouvelles *entendez*-vous? 3. L'examen que je *passe* est difficile. 4. Aimez-vous ces jolies fleurs que Maurice *achète?*

® *D. Remplacez les expressions en italique par des pronoms compléments. Faites l'accord du participe passé où il faut. Distinguez entre* **le, la, les** *et* **en.** Exemple: Nous avons montré *les livres à ma mère.* Nous *les lui* avons montrés.

1. Marie a écouté *la musique.* 2. Nous avons visité *ces anciennes villes.* 3. Avez-vous acheté *ce stylo?* 4. Il m'a donné *la lettre.* 5. Ont-ils raconté *cette nouvelle à leurs parents?* 6. Il a suivi deux *cours.* 7. Avez-vous reçu *des lettres?* 8. J'ai écrit tous *les devoirs.* 9. Avons-

nous fini *la leçon?* 10. Il a acheté *le lait et le café.* **11.** Nous avons trouvé *des livres* dans la bibliothèque.

Conversation

1. Demandez à Monsieur E. s'il est obligé de travailler beaucoup pour réussir aux examens. 2. Demandez à Monsieur F. s'il a échoué à son examen de français. 3. Demandez à Monsieur G. si les professeurs américains sont sévères. 4. Demandez à Monsieur H. si les étudiants américains qui réussissent ont une bonne connaissance de leur programme.

Vocabulaire — pages 158–159

Grammaire

1. Past participles of verbs conjugated with ***avoir*** in the *passé composé* do not usually change their forms. Under what circumstances do they change their forms and with what do they agree? (§ 77 A)

2. Does the past participle agree with a preceding ***en?*** (§ 77 A)

3. Conjugate in the present the verbs ***apercevoir, s'asseoir,*** and ***boire.*** What are the past participles of these irregular verbs? (Page 159)

4. In this reading lesson are the forms ***lui-même*** and ***eux-mêmes.*** What form of the personal pronoun is used with ***-même?*** (§ 27 B 7)

Le coucou

Dans la forêt lointaine [1], On entend le coucou;
Du [2] haut de son grand chêne [3], Il répond au hibou [4].

Coucou, coucou, coucou, coucou, coucou;
Coucou, coucou, coucou, coucou, coucou.

Dans la forêt lointaine, etc.

This may be sung as a round, the second group starting "Dans la forêt . . ." when the first group sings "Coucou, coucou . . ."

[1] *distant* [2] *top* [3] *oak* [4] *owl*

Cinquième révision — Leçons 21 à 25

Première partie

A. Répondez en français par des phrases complètes aux questions suivantes.

1. Citez des monopoles de l'État en France. 2. Si on veut envoyer un télégramme en France, où faut-il aller? 3. Quels sont les endroits d'où on peut téléphoner en France? 4. Qui est Balzac? 5. Où habitent beaucoup d'étudiants de province qui font leurs études dans une grande ville? 6. Quel repas prend-on en France le matin? 7. Comment s'appelle le quartier de Paris où se trouvent les diverses facultés de l'Université de Paris? 8. Comment s'appelle le grand jardin du Quartier latin où les étudiants passent des heures à travailler et à causer avec leurs camarades? 9. Quel est le boulevard de Paris où on rencontre le plus d'étudiants? 10. Combien de facultés l'Université de Paris comprend-elle? 11. Dans quelles écoles de Paris peut-on apprendre à devenir ingénieur? 12. Quelle est l'école de Paris la plus célèbre pour la formation des professeurs? 13. En général, où y a-t-il le plus d'étudiants dans un cours, en France ou en Amérique? 14. Comment l'étudiant français se prépare-t-il aux examens? 15. Quand on quitte un café, pourquoi laisse-t-on de l'argent sur la table?

B. Expliquez en français par une phrase complète les noms suivants.

Boulevard Saint-Michel	École Polytechnique	licence
École Centrale	Honoré de Balzac	Quartier latin
École des Beaux-Arts	Jardin du Luxembourg	Sorbonne
École Normale Supérieure		Université de Paris

C. Rédigez une composition sur un des sujets suivants.

1. Les monopoles de l'État 2. La pension de famille en Amérique 3. Le Quartier latin 4. La Sorbonne 5. Le Luxembourg

Deuxième partie

A. Remplacez les expressions en italique par le pronom complément convenable. Attention à l'ordre des pronoms compléments. (*Voir Grammaire* §§ *28 A, B; 30 A; 31 A, B*)

1. Demandez de l'argent à votre oncle. A-t-il beaucoup *d'argent?* 2. Combien de timbres Georges vous a-t-il envoyés? Il m'a envoyé cinquante *timbres.* 3. Je ne trouve pas de crayons. Il y a *des crayons* sur le bureau de votre père.

B. Remplacez l'infinitif par le présent du verbe. (*Voir Grammaire §§ 49 C, E; 88 A, C; 89 D, F; pages 151–159*)

4. Je (dormir) tous les matins jusqu'à dix heures. 5. A quelle heure (se réveiller)-vous? 6. Mon camarade (se lever) avant moi. 7. Nous (se promener) le matin et ils (se promener) le soir. 8. Quand on ne nous (servir) pas, nous (se servir). 9. Il (falloir) téléphoner de la poste. 10. Je (s'appeler) Robert et vous (s'appeler) Jean. 11. Paul (sortir) un moment et puis nous (partir) pour Dijon. 12. Je (devoir) attendre mon camarade, mais vous (devoir) partir tout de suite. 13. Je (venir) chercher votre voiture. 14. (prendre) votre bicyclette pour aller à la poste.

C. Mettez les verbes au passé composé. Tous ces verbes sont réguliers. (*Voir Grammaire §§ 22 D; 61 A; 62 A, B, C; 75 A*)

15. Nous trouvons beaucoup de monde au Luxembourg. 16. Les étudiants choisissent plusieurs livres. 17. Je n'entends pas la cloche d'ici. 18. Finissez-vous la lecture de ce roman aujourd'hui?

D. Mettez les verbes au passé composé. Tous ces verbes ont un participe passé irrégulier. (*Voir Grammaire § 75 B*)

19. Qu'est-ce que vous apprenez à l'école? 20. Je ne comprends pas les explications du professeur. 21. Les garçons mettent les chaises sur le trottoir. 22. Ne pouvez-vous pas venir cet après-midi? 23. Je suis content de votre travail.

E. Remplacez l'infinitif par le participe passé. Attention à l'accord du participe passé. (*Voir Grammaire § 77 A*)

24. Quels devoirs avez-vous (écrire)? 25. J'ai (trouver) votre lettre et je l'ai (lire).

La Cité Universitaire

—En France l'étudiant est beaucoup plus libre qu'en Amérique. Non seulement il n'est pas obligé d'assister aux cours, mais sa vie privée n'est pas du tout surveillée. Même les étudiantes conservent une indépendance entière. Elles habitent où elles veulent, elles sortent quand elles veulent, et elles rentrent quand elles veulent. En France, on considère l'étudiant et l'étudiante comme assez grands pour prendre leurs propres responsabilités.

—Vous n'êtes pas obligé d'habiter dans une chambre recommandée par l'université, même au début?

—Oh, non! Moi, je suis sorti du lycée à dix-sept ans. Mon père est mort cette année-là. Je suis venu à Paris au mois de novembre. Pendant deux ans j'ai habité dans une pension; maintenant, j'ai une chambre à l'hôtel. Mais beaucoup d'étudiants sont logés à la Cité Universitaire.

—Qu'est-ce que c'est que la Cité Universitaire?

—Vers 1923, on a commencé à construire au sud de Paris un groupe de bâtiments pour les étudiants étrangers et les étudiants de province qui viennent à Paris faire leurs études. Plus de trente nations y sont représentées. Beaucoup de ces maisons sont construites dans le style de leur pays. Les chambres et les repas coûtent beaucoup moins cher à la Cité Universitaire qu'ailleurs. Si vous voulez, nous pouvons aller la voir.

Nous sommes allés attendre un autobus. Bientôt il en est arrivé un. Nous sommes montés; il nous a menés rapidement vers le Boulevard Jourdan. Nous sommes descendus et nous sommes entrés dans un très grand parc où nous avons vu de nombreux bâtiments: la maison suisse, la maison du Canada, le pavillon belge, la Fondation des États-Unis et beaucoup d'autres. Pour les étudiants français qui viennent de province il y a une immense Maison des Provinces françaises.

Les cinq mille étudiants français et étrangers qui habitent à la Cité Universitaire occupent des chambres dans les différentes maisons. Il y a aussi une grande Maison Internationale où se trouvent des restaurants, une bibliothèque, des salles de danse, de musique, de jeu et une piscine. Les étudiants de tous les pays du monde s'y retrouvent et peuvent apprendre à mieux se connaître. Nous y sommes restés plusieurs heures. Enfin, nous sommes revenus par l'autobus au Quartier latin.

QUESTIONS

1. L'étudiant français est-il obligé d'assister aux cours? 2. La vie privée de l'étudiant français est-elle surveillée? 3. Les étudiantes américaines conservent-elles une indépendance entière? 4. A quel âge Jean est-il sorti du lycée? 5. Quand son père est-il mort? 6. En quel mois Jean est-il venu à Paris? 7. Où a-t-il habité à Paris pendant les deux premières années? 8. Qu'est-ce que c'est que la Cité Universitaire? 9. Dans quel style sont construites les maisons de la Cité Universitaire? 10. Où sommes-nous allés? 11. Où sommes-nous descendus de l'autobus pour voir la Cité Universitaire? 12. Combien d'étudiants sont logés à la Cité Universitaire? 13. Où habitent les étudiants français qui viennent de province? 14. Qu'est-ce qu'il y a dans la Maison Internationale? 15. Pendant combien de temps sommes-nous restés à la Cité Universitaire?

DEVOIRS

® *A. Suivez les indications.*

1. Dites à André que vous êtes resté à Paris tout l'été. 2. Dites à Michel que vous êtes allé chez votre camarade. 3. Dites à Charlotte que vous êtes sorti à huit heures du soir.

® *B. Mettez au passé composé les verbes des phrases suivantes.*

EXEMPLE: Nous sortons du lycée à quatre heures. Nous *sommes sortis* du lycée à quatre heures.

1. Maurice va chez son ami. 2. Il y arrive vers huit heures moins dix. 3. Nous descendons de l'autobus au Luxembourg. 4. Marie entre dans la salle avec sa sœur. 5. Les étudiants partent vers cinq heures du soir.

® *C. Mettez au passé composé les verbes des phrases suivantes. Ces phrases sont toutes à la forme négative.*

1. Vous ne montez pas dans l'autobus avec nous. 2. Je ne reste pas à Paris tout l'été. 3. Ces gens ne meurent pas tout de suite. 4. Louise et Hélène ne viennent pas ce matin.

® *D. Mettez au passé composé les verbes des phrases suivantes. Ces phrases sont toutes à la forme interrogative.*

1. Vos sœurs retournent-elles à Dijon? 2. Reviennent-elles à Paris? 3. Jean sort-il cet après-midi? 4. Marie descend-elle de l'autobus devant la maison?

E. Remplacez les tirets par l'auxiliaire convenable. EXEMPLE: Les étudiants —— compris cette explication. Les étudiants *ont* compris cette explication.

1. Nous —— été à Tours. 2. —— -vous vu ces châteaux? 3. Je —— allé à Blois. 4. Notre professeur nous —— lu l'histoire du château de Blois. 5. Les étudiants américains —— venus en Touraine apprendre la langue française. 6. —— -nous restés longtemps dans ce pays? 7. Mon camarade —— entré dans le château. 8. Nous —— commandé du thé. 9. Quand —— -vous revenu à Tours? 10. Jean —— mis la carte de France sur la table.

CONVERSATION

1. Demandez à Monsieur I. s'il est allé au cinéma hier. 2. Demandez à Monsieur J. s'il est resté chez lui ce matin. 3. Demandez à Monsieur K. à quelle heure il est sorti ce matin. 4. Demandez à Monsieur L. à quelle heure il est rentré chez lui dimanche soir.

VOCABULAIRE — PAGES 160–161

GRAMMAIRE

1. What type of verb do you find conjugated with *être* as an auxiliary in this lesson? (§ 61 C)

2. Give a list of the intransitive verbs of motion conjugated with *être* in the compound tenses. (§ 61 D)

3. With what do the past participles of intransitive verbs of motion conjugated with *être* always agree? (§ 77 B)

4. When ***vous*** is the subject of a verb conjugated with ***être*** in a compound tense, is the past participle singular or plural? (§ 77 C)

5. Conjugate the verb ***arriver*** in the *passé composé.* (Page 162)

6. Give the present and the past participle of the irregular verbs ***construire, mourir,*** and ***revenir.*** (Page 162)

Fontainebleau

Dans l'autobus, Jean m'a demandé:

— Avez-vous déjà visité Fontainebleau?

— Non, je ne sais même pas où c'est.

— Fontainebleau est une petite ville située à soixante kilomètres au sud-est de Paris. Elle est intéressante à cause de son château et de la célèbre forêt qui l'entoure. Il y a là aussi une école d'art et de musique où de jeunes Américains viennent étudier sous la direction des meilleurs professeurs et artistes français. Voulez-vous y aller demain?

— Je veux bien.

Ce soir-là, je me suis couché vers dix heures. Le lendemain matin je me suis levé de bonne heure. Je me suis vite habillé, et vers huit heures moins le quart, j'ai retrouvé Jean à la gare de Lyon. Nous avons pris nos billets, et nous sommes montés dans le train, qui est parti à huit heures dix.

Après une heure de voyage, nous sommes arrivés à Fontainebleau. Nous avons marché un peu; bientôt nous sommes arrivés dans une grande forêt où nous nous sommes promenés pendant des heures. Cette forêt n'est pas une forêt comme les autres: elle est beaucoup plus étendue, et dans plusieurs endroits d'énormes rochers donnent un air sauvage à la forêt. Il y a partout de très jolis paysages que des peintres comme Corot et Millet ont rendus célèbres.

Nous sommes restés dans la forêt toute la matinée. Nous en sommes sortis à midi. Nous avons traversé la ville, et nous sommes enfin arrivés devant le château de Fontainebleau, superbe construction de la Renaissance française, qui est devenu un musée national. Nous y sommes entrés avec un guide.

Le château contient entre autres choses des souvenirs de Napoléon Ier, l'empereur des Français né en Corse en 1769 et mort à Sainte-Hélène en 1821. On y trouve des appartements splendides, des meubles admirables et une riche bibliothèque.

Vers quatre heures et demie, nous nous sommes dirigés vers la gare. Nous avons couru pour ne pas manquer le train de cinq heures.

Questions

1. Où est Fontainebleau? 2. Pourquoi Fontainebleau est-il intéressant? 3. Quelle école y a-t-il à Fontainebleau? 4. A quelle heure vous êtes-vous couché hier soir? 5. A quelle heure vous êtes-vous levé ce matin? 6. Où Jean et son camarade ont-ils pris leurs billets? 7. A quelle heure le train est-il parti de la gare? 8. Combien de temps le voyage de Paris à Fontainebleau a-t-il duré? 9. Où Jean et son camarade se sont-ils promenés à Fontainebleau? 10. En quoi la forêt de Fontainebleau est-elle différente des autres? 11. Quels peintres ont rendu célèbres les paysages de la forêt? 12. De quelle époque est le château de Fontainebleau? 13. Qu'est-ce que ce château est devenu? 14. Quand est né Napoléon? 15. Quand est-il mort? 16. Que trouve-t-on dans le château de Fontainebleau? 17. Vers quelle heure Jean et son camarade se sont-ils dirigés vers la gare? 18. Pourquoi ont-ils couru?

Devoirs

® *A. Suivez les indications.*

1. Dites à Maurice que vous vous êtes couché à onze heures du soir. 2. Dites à Gérard que vous vous êtes levé de bonne heure ce matin. 3. Dites à Henri que vous vous êtes promené dans la forêt près de votre maison.

® *B. Mettez au passé composé les verbes des phrases suivantes. Toutes ces phrases sont à l'affirmatif.*

1. Marie se couche de bonne heure. 2. Elle se réveille vers six heures du matin. 3. Elle se lève vers six heures et demie. 4. Elle s'habille dans sa chambre. 5. Elle s'occupe de la maison. 6. Vous vous intéressez à beaucoup de choses. 7. Je me spécialise en histoire. 8. Les étudiants se dirigent vers le fleuve.

® *C. Mettez au passé composé les verbes des phrases suivantes. Ces phrases sont au négatif ou à l'interrogatif.*

1. Je ne m'intéresse pas à la vie privée des pensionnaires. 2. Marie ne se spécialise pas en philosophie. 3. Nous ne nous réveillons pas avant midi. 4. Vous ne vous couchez pas à dix heures. 5. Vous habillez-vous dans votre chambre? 6. Nous occupons-nous de nos cours? 7. Les étudiants se voient-ils à la bibliothèque? 8. Jean et Robert se retrouvent-ils au café?

® *D. Mettez au passé composé les verbes des phrases suivantes. Attention à l'auxiliaire.*

1. A quelle heure déjeunez-vous? 2. Je vais en classe avec Louise. 3. Nous arrivons en classe après nos camarades. 4. Tous les élèves écrivent leurs devoirs. 5. Nous nous levons quand le professeur entre dans la salle. 6. Qui corrige les fautes des élèves? 7. Le professeur nous lit un poème de Victor Hugo. 8. Les élèves se tournent vers lui. 9. Nous rentrons à midi. 10. Vous vous voyez jeudi, n'est-ce pas?

E. Remplacez les tirets par **à cause de** *ou* **parce que** *selon le cas.*

1. Fontainebleau est intéressant —— son château. 2. Tours est pittoresque —— cette ville est située dans la vallée de la Loire. 3. Je ne vous ai pas écrit —— je n'ai pas beaucoup de temps. 4. Monsieur Maurois doit aller à Cannes —— sa femme. 5. Je ne suis pas allé au cinéma —— j'ai beaucoup à faire.

F. Remplacez les tirets par une forme de **meilleur** *s'il faut un adjectif et par* **mieux** *s'il faut un adverbe.*

1. Molière et Flaubert sont parmi les —— écrivains de la littérature française. 2. J'aime —— le printemps que l'hiver. 3. Bernard est un —— élève que Roger. 4. Il comprend —— que son frère. 5. Victor Hugo écrit bien, mais il y a d'autres écrivains qui écrivent —— que lui. 6. Quels sont les —— livres sur les provinces françaises?

Conversation

1. Demandez à Monsieur M. à quelle heure il s'est couché. 2. Demandez à Monsieur N. en quelle année il est né. 3. Demandez à Monsieur O. s'il s'est réveillé de bonne heure ce matin. 4. Demandez à Monsieur P. s'il s'est promené dans la forêt cette semaine.

Vocabulaire — page 163

Grammaire

1. With what auxiliary verb are reflexive verbs conjugated in the compound tenses? (§ 61 E)

2. The past participle of a reflexive verb almost always agrees with the reflexive object. When does the past participle of a reflexive verb not agree with its reflexive object? (§ 77 D)

3. From observation of questions 4, 5, 9 and 17 of this lesson, note

carefully the word order of questions containing reflexive verbs which are in the *passé composé.*

4. Point out two intransitive verbs of motion which are conjugated with ***avoir.*** They are used in this lesson.

5. What is the difference between ***meilleur*** and ***mieux?*** between ***parce que*** and ***à cause de?*** (§ 98 — *because, better*)

6. In the sentence *Nous avons couru pour **ne pas** manquer le train de cinq heures,* why do ***ne*** and ***pas*** both precede the verb? (§ 22 H)

7. Conjugate the reflexive verb ***se coucher*** in the *passé composé.* Watch the agreement of the past participle. (Page 164)

8. Conjugate in the present and *passé composé* the irregular verbs ***contenir, courir,*** and ***naître.*** (Page 164)

VINGT-HUITIÈME LEÇON

Le retour en chemin de fer

Il était déjà presque cinq heures quand nous sommes arrivés à la gare. Un employé se tenait près de la porte qui donne accès aux quais. Nous lui avons montré nos billets et nous sommes passés sur le quai. Beaucoup de voyageurs attendaient le train. Quelques-uns d'entre eux causaient, d'autres se promenaient le long du quai. Jean, qui voulait arriver à Paris pour six heures, s'impatientait.

Enfin, nous avons entendu siffler le train; il était encore loin, mais il approchait à toute vitesse. Il est arrivé, s'est arrêté et quelques voyageurs sont descendus. Les gens qui attendaient sur le quai sont montés dans les wagons. Il y avait quelques wagons très confortables de première classe et beaucoup de wagons de deuxième. Il y avait aussi un wagon-restaurant où des voyageurs dînaient.

Nous sommes montés dans un wagon; nous y avons trouvé deux places. Comme la plupart des wagons français, il était divisé en compartiments. Dans chaque compartiment il y avait deux banquettes, l'une en face de l'autre, avec des places pour quatre voyageurs sur chacune. Tout le long du wagon un couloir donnait accès aux compartiments.

Notre wagon était plein de voyageurs. Les gens qui n'avaient pas de place dans les compartiments se tenaient dans le couloir. Ils étaient debout ou assis sur leurs valises. Dans notre compartiment une femme causait avec son mari, une jeune fille lisait un roman policier, un enfant mangeait du pain et du chocolat, sa petite sœur dormait et un vieillard qui parlait avec un accent prononcé disait à une dame:

—Oui, je suis Alsacien. J'habitais autrefois Mulhouse. Je finissais mes études à Strasbourg quand la guerre de 14 a éclaté. Nous faisions partie de l'Allemagne à ce moment-là et j'ai été obligé de servir pendant quatre ans dans l'armée allemande.

Il est toujours facile de causer dans un compartiment et bientôt j'ai profité de l'occasion pour poser à ce monsieur des questions sur l'Alsace. Il commençait à m'en parler quand le contrôleur est venu demander les billets. Il les a vus, mais il ne les a pas gardés, car en France on remet les billets seulement quand on sort de la gare.

Questions

1. Quelle heure était-il quand nous sommes arrivés à la gare? 2. A qui a-t-il fallu montrer nos billets à la gare? 3. Qui attendait le train sur le quai? 4. Que faisaient les voyageurs qui attendaient le train? 5. A quelle heure Jean voulait-il arriver à Paris? 6. Qui est descendu du train? 7. Où dînaient certains voyageurs? 8. En quoi étaient divisés les wagons? 9. Combien de banquettes y avait-il dans chaque compartiment? 10. Qui était dans le couloir? 11. Qui mangeait du pain dans le compartiment? 12. Que faisait la petite sœur de l'enfant qui mangeait du pain et du chocolat? 13. Pourquoi le vieillard avait-il un accent? 14. Où habitait-il autrefois? 15. Que faisait-il quand la guerre de 14 a éclaté? 16. Pourquoi a-t-il été obligé de servir pendant quatre ans dans l'armée allemande? 17. De quoi ce monsieur commençait-il à parler quand le contrôleur est venu? 18. Pourquoi le contrôleur n'a-t-il pas pris les billets?

Devoirs

® *A. Suivez les indications.*

1. Dites à Charlotte que vous écoutiez la radio quand elle a téléphoné de la poste. 2. Dites à Claude que vous écriviez une lettre quand son

frère est arrivé. 3. Dites à Suzanne que vous finissiez votre travail quand la cloche a sonné.

® *B. Mettez les verbes suivants à l'imparfait.*

1. vous finissez 2. j'entends 3. je sers 4. il a traversé 5. je veux 6. il choisit 7. je cause 8. vous avez parlé 9. ils sont 10. vous vous habillez 11. il va 12. je mange 13. nous nous promenons 14. il y a 15. j'ai 16. vous partez 17. elle se dirige 18. nous effaçons 19. vous êtes 20. nous avons eu 21. je dors 22. il a été 23. je commence

® *C. Mettez les verbes des phrases suivantes à l'imparfait ou au passé composé selon le sens. Ces phrases forment un récit.*

1. Un matin d'octobre je rencontre Maurice dans la rue. 2. Il porte ses livres et son cahier. 3. Il est très gai. 4. Je lui demande où il va. 5. Il me répond qu'il va à l'école. 6. Notre école n'est pas loin. 7. Nous y allons ensemble. 8. Bientôt nous arrivons dans une cour où jouent les élèves. 9. Nous montons au premier étage et quand nous entrons dans la classe nos camarades causent avec d'autres élèves. 10. La salle de classe est agréable; il y a cinq fenêtres d'un côté et un tableau noir de l'autre. 11. Le professeur arrive après nous. 12. Ensuite, la cloche sonne. 13. Le professeur commence à parler aux élèves de l'histoire des châteaux de la Loire. 14. Enfin il nous lit un texte. 15. Pendant qu'il lit le texte, un élève lui pose une question. 16. Il répond à la question et puis il continue la lecture du texte.

CONVERSATION

1. Demandez à Monsieur Q. s'il parlait français quand le professeur est entré dans la classe. 2. Demandez à Monsieur R. s'il y avait un wagon-restaurant dans le train. 3. Demandez à Monsieur S. s'il habitait à la campagne quand il était jeune. 4. Demandez à Monsieur T. s'il parlait français quand il était en France.

VOCABULAIRE — PAGE 165

GRAMMAIRE

1. How is the imperfect of most verbs formed? (§ 51 A)

2. How is the imperfect of the first class of *-ir* verbs formed? (§ 51 B)

3. How may the stem of the imperfect of all verbs (except ***être*** and ***falloir***) be found? (§ 51 C)

4. In the imperfects of ***-cer*** and ***-ger*** verbs what is done to retain the soft sounds of *c* and *g?* (§ 89 A, B)

5. What are the forms of the imperfect of ***donner, finir, sortir, perdre, manger, commencer, avoir,*** and ***être?*** the forms of the present, imperfect, and *passé composé* of the irregular verbs ***remettre*** and ***se tenir?*** (Pages 166, 151, and 164)

6. Why is the imperfect so called? In general, what sort of states and actions is the imperfect used to express? (§ 52 A)

7. What are the two common uses of the imperfect to form a background for the principal actions? (§ 52 B 1, 2)

8. What tense is used in French to express customary, habitual, or repeated action in the past? (§ 52 C)

9. Explain the use of each imperfect in your reading lesson.

VINGT-NEUVIÈME LEÇON

L'Alsace-Lorraine

Quand le contrôleur est parti, j'ai repris ma conversation avec mon compagnon de voyage.

—Puisque l'Alsace faisait partie de l'Allemagne quand la guerre a éclaté en 1914, elle n'a donc pas toujours été française?

—Non. Vous savez que l'Alsace se trouve sur la rive ouest du Rhin qui la sépare de l'Allemagne actuelle. Elle a souvent été un champ de bataille au cours des luttes entre Français et Allemands, si bien que depuis le dix-septième siècle, elle a été tantôt française, tantôt allemande.

—Quand l'Alsace est-elle devenue française pour la première fois?

—A l'origine l'Alsace était un état germanique. Après Charlemagne, elle est devenue une partie du Saint Empire romain germanique. Au dix-septième siècle les armées de Louis XIV l'ont occupée et elle est devenue

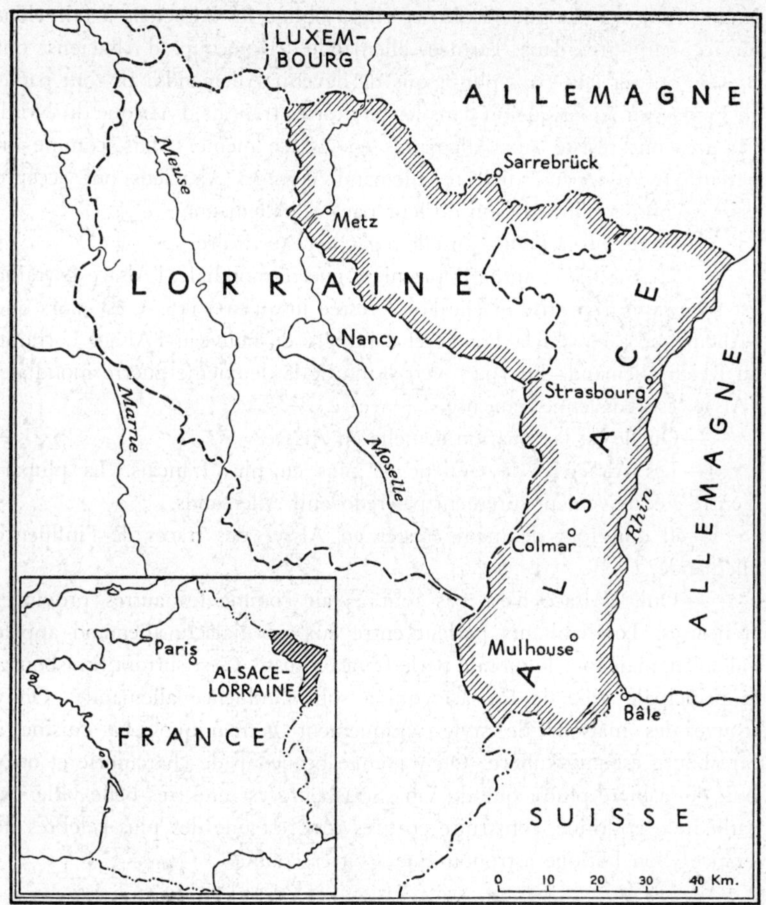

A la fin de la guerre franco-allemande de 1870, l'Allemagne a enlevé à la France toute l'Alsace et le tiers nord-est de la Lorraine

une province française. Elle est restée française depuis cette époque jusqu'à la guerre franco-allemande de 1870. L'Allemagne a gagné cette guerre et a enlevé à la France toute l'Alsace et le tiers nord-est de la Lorraine; c'est ce territoire qu'on appelle l'Alsace-Lorraine.

—Qu'est-ce qui s'est passé alors? Est-ce que les Alsaciens ont accepté ce changement?

—L'Allemagne a essayé d'effacer en Alsace-Lorraine toutes les traces de la culture et des influences françaises. Elle a interdit l'emploi de la langue française dans les écoles et elle a obligé les Alsaciens à faire leur service militaire dans l'armée allemande. Beaucoup d'Alsaciens ont préféré quitter leur pays plutôt que de devenir Allemands. Ils sont partis en France, en Amérique ou dans les territoires français d'Afrique du Nord. D'autres ont résisté aux Allemands en Alsace même. Mais, comme on parlait en Alsace un dialecte allemand, certains Alsaciens ont accepté assez volontiers l'intégration de leur pays à l'Allemagne.

— Comment la France a-t-elle regagné ce territoire?

— En 1918, à la fin de la première guerre mondiale, l'Alsace-Lorraine est redevenue française et elle l'est[1] restée jusqu'en 1940. C'est alors que l'Allemagne a envahi la France et a intégré de nouveau l'Alsace-Lorraine au Reich allemand. En 1945, vers la fin de la deuxième guerre mondiale, l'Alsace est redevenue française.

— Quelle est la situation actuelle en Alsace?

— Les Alsaciens deviennent de plus en plus français. La plupart d'entre eux ne veulent sûrement pas redevenir Allemands.

— Il doit tout de même rester en Alsace des traces de l'influence allemande?

— Oui, l'Alsace n'est pas tout à fait comme les autres provinces françaises. Les habitants parlent entre eux un dialecte allemand appelé l'alsacien, mais tout le monde parle français aussi. C'est surtout Strasbourg, la principale ville de l'Alsace, qui a subi l'influence allemande. On y trouve des maisons de style typiquement germanique. La cuisine à Strasbourg est particulière. On y mange beaucoup de charcuterie et on y boit de la bière plutôt que du vin. Strasbourg est une très belle ville. Sa cathédrale gothique, construite en grès rose, est une des plus célèbres de France. Son horloge astronomique est très connue.

Questions

1. Où est située l'Alsace? 2. Quand l'Alsace est-elle devenue française pour la première fois? 3. Quelle sorte d'état était l'Alsace à son origine? 4. De quoi l'Alsace faisait-elle partie après Charlemagne? 5. Comment l'Alsace est-elle devenue une partie de la France? 6. Quand l'Allemagne a-t-elle enlevé l'Alsace à la France? 7. Qu'est-ce que l'Alsace-Lorraine? 8. Qu'est-ce que les Alsaciens ont fait quand l'Alsace est devenue allemande en 1871? 9. Quand la France a-t-elle regagné ce territoire? 10. Quelle est la situation actuelle en Alsace? 11. Quelles langues parle-t-on en Alsace? 12. Quelle est la principale ville de

[1] *remained French* (lit. *remained it*)

l'Alsace? 13. En quoi la ville de Strasbourg est-elle différente des autres villes de France? 14. Pourquoi la cathédrale de Strasbourg est-elle célèbre?

Devoirs

® *A. Suivez les indications.*

1. Dites à Bernard que vous avez essayé d'aller en France. 2. Dites à André que vous êtes partis en France l'année dernière. 3. Dites à Claude que vous parliez français quand vous étiez petit.

B. Mettez les verbes indiqués au passé composé ou à l'imparfait. Ces phrases forment un récit.

1. De 1607 à 1776 notre pays (être) une colonie anglaise. 2. Les habitants (être) d'origine anglaise. 3. On (parler) anglais et on (conserver) les coutumes anglaises. 4. Mais l'Amérique (être) loin de l'Angleterre. 5. Les Américains (avoir) des idées de liberté et d'indépendance. 6. En 1776 ils (se séparer) de l'Angleterre. 7. L'Angleterre (envoyer) une armée en Amérique. 8. Washington (être) à la tête des armées américaines. 9. A cette époque La Fayette (venir) offrir ses services aux treize colonies. 10. La guerre (durer) de 1776 à 1783. 11. Enfin les Américains (gagner) la guerre. 12. Les colonies américaines (devenir) les États-Unis.

® *C. Écrivez ces phrases au passé composé ou à l'imparfait selon le sens. Ces phrases forment un récit.*

1. Ce matin je me réveille de bonne heure. 2. Il fait très beau. 3. Le soleil entre par ma fenêtre ouverte. 4. Je me lève bien vite et je m'habille. 5. Je descends au jardin où m'attendent ma mère et ma sœur Madeleine. 6. Au moment où j'arrive, ma mère lit une lettre à Madeleine. 7. Ensuite nous sortons tous en voiture. 8. Les rues sont pleines de monde. 9. Nous allons dans un magasin où nous achetons des fruits. 10. Enfin, nous retournons à la maison vers midi.

Conversation

1. Demandez à Monsieur U. ce[1] qu'il faisait quand vous lui avez téléphoné. 2. Demandez à Monsieur V. ce qu'il écrivait quand le professeur lui a dit de lire. 3. Demandez à Monsieur W. ce qu'il mangeait

[1] The *ce que* of the indirect question may be expressed by *Qu'est-ce que* in the direct question, e.g., ***Qu'est-ce que** vous faisiez quand je vous ai téléphoné?*

quand le professeur est entré dans la classe. 4. Demandez à Monsieur X. quelle langue il parlait quand il était jeune.

VOCABULAIRE — PAGES 167–168

GRAMMAIRE

1. Americans tend to use the imperfect in French where the *passé composé* is required. Explain when the imperfect and when the *passé composé* is used in a narration. (§ 53 A)

2. When an action takes place within a definitely limited period of time, whether it be one minute or a hundred years, must the imperfect or the *passé composé* be used? (Page 433, note 1)

3. Review the uses of the imperfect (§ 52 A, B, C; 53 B) and those of the *passé composé.* (§ 63 A, B, C)

4. Analyze each verb of this lesson which is in the imperfect or the *passé composé,* explaining why one tense or the other is used.

5. Give the past participle of the irregular verb ***interdire*** and the present and past participle of the irregular verbs ***redevenir*** and ***reprendre.*** (Page 168)

6. How does English express ***un compagnon de voyage?*** (§ 6 E)

TRENTIÈME LEÇON

Les parties du corps

Chaque année beaucoup d'étrangers viennent en France. Pour ceux qui veulent apprendre le français quelques universités françaises ont créé des cours de grammaire, de prononciation, de conversation et de littérature. Il y en a à Paris, à Tours, à Dijon, à Grenoble, à Nancy, etc.

Une Suédoise et une Anglaise parlent des cours qu'elles suivent à Grenoble. Celle-ci s'intéresse surtout à la littérature, celle-là aux cours pratiques. La Suédoise dit:

— Moi, je préfère les cours de conversation à ceux de grammaire.

Ces derniers sont plus difficiles et moins intéressants que les autres. Nous avons un excellent professeur de conversation. Tous les jours il nous apprend un vocabulaire très utile. Voulez-vous assister à son cours?

Les deux étudiantes entrent dans la salle juste au moment où le professeur commence une leçon sur les différentes parties du corps.

— Aujourd'hui, nous allons apprendre les mots français qui désignent les différentes parties du corps humain. Sur la tête, qui est la partie supérieure du corps, se trouvent les cheveux. La figure ou le visage se compose du front, des yeux, du nez, de la bouche, des joues et du menton. De chaque côté de la tête se trouvent les oreilles. Nous entendons avec les oreilles, nous voyons avec les yeux, nous sentons avec le nez. Celui qui ne voit pas est aveugle. Celui qui n'a qu'un œil est borgne. Le pluriel d'*œil* est *yeux*. On dit en français *un œil* mais *deux yeux*. Celui qui n'entend pas est sourd et celui qui ne peut pas parler est muet. Celui qui ne peut ni entendre ni parler est sourd-muet. Dans la bouche se trouvent la langue, avec laquelle nous goûtons, et les dents, avec lesquelles nous mâchons. La langue, les dents et les lèvres font partie du mécanisme avec lequel nous parlons.

Le cou unit la tête au tronc. Le tronc contient entre autres organes importants les poumons, le cœur et l'estomac. Le cœur sert à faire circuler le sang, qui coule dans les artères et dans les veines. Les poumons, qui sont nécessaires à la respiration, se trouvent dans la poitrine.

Les membres du corps humain sont les bras et les jambes. Le bras comprend deux parties qui sont réunies par le coude. Il se termine par la main, qui a cinq doigts. La jambe comprend deux parties qui sont réunies par le genou. Elle se termine par le pied.

Les os, les muscles, le cerveau et les nerfs sont aussi des parties du corps.

Questions

1. Qu'est-ce que les universités françaises ont créé pour ceux qui viennent en France apprendre le français? 2. Dans quelles villes de France y a-t-il des cours pour les étrangers? 3. Pourquoi préférez-vous les cours de conversation à ceux de grammaire? 4. Où la Suédoise mène-t-elle l'Anglaise? 5. Avec quoi parle-t-on? 6. Avec quoi sent-on? 7. Avec quoi entendons-nous? 8. Avec quoi voit-on? 9. Quelle est la différence entre un aveugle et un borgne? 10. Avec quoi mâchez-vous? 11. Avec quoi marchez-vous? 12. A quoi sert le cœur? 13. A quoi servent les poumons? 14. Qu'est-ce qui unit la tête au tronc? 15. Où

se trouvent les poumons? 16. Qu'est-ce qui coule dans les artères et dans les veines? 17. Quel organe du corps fait circuler le sang? 18. Comment s'appelle celui qui ne peut pas entendre? 19. Qu'est-ce qu'un muet? 20. Avec quoi pense-t-on?

Devoirs

A. Remplacez les tirets par le mot désignant la partie du corps qu'il faut.

1. On entend avec les——. 2. On sent avec le——. 3. Nous parlons avec la——. 4. Les——sont nécessaires à la respiration. 5. Les deux parties du——sont réunies par le coude. 6. On écrit avec la——. 7. Celui qui n'a qu'un——est borgne. 8. On voit avec les——. 9. Le——sert à faire circuler le sang. 10. On pense avec le——.

B. Remplacez les tirets par la forme convenable du pronom démonstratif, en mettant -ci et -là quand[1] *il y a lieu.*

1. ——qui ne peut pas voir est aveugle. 2. ——qui vont à l'école sont des élèves. 3. ——qui ne peut pas entendre est sourde. 4. ——qui ne parlent pas sont muettes. 5. Cette leçon-ci est plus longue que——. 6. Ces nations-ci sont plus riches que——. 7. J'aime mieux lire l'histoire de France que——d'Allemagne. 8. Ce professeur-ci parle plus vite que——. 9. Les montagnes de France sont plus élevées que——d'Angleterre. 10. La capitale de la France est plus connue que——de la Suède. 11. Les fleurs du midi sont-elles moins belles que——du nord? 12. Cette jeune fille-ci travaille moins que——que vous avez vue dans l'autre salle. 13. Ces étudiants-ci sont-ils plus jeunes que——? 14. Ces livres-ci sont moins bien écrits que——que vous avez trouvés à Paris. 15. Les lycées de Paris sont plus connus que——de Tours. 16. Ce cours-ci est plus pratique que——.

C. Remplacez les tirets par une forme convenable du pronom relatif.

1. Où est le stylo avec——vous avez écrit cette lettre? 2. Il est sur la table——se trouve à gauche de la porte. 3. La lettre——j'ai écrite y est aussi. 4. Fermez la porte par——vous êtes entré. 5. Les villes dans——il y a beaucoup d'habitants n'ont pas assez d'hôtels. 6. Cherchez-vous les timbres——vous avez achetés hier? 7. Ceux——je cherche étaient sur la table dans ma chambre. 8. Mais je ne vois plus les livres sous——je les ai mis.

[1] *when it is necessary.*

Nous sommes montés dans le train, qui est parti à huit heures dix

Cette forêt n'est pas une forêt comme les autres

Nous sommes enfin arrivés devant le château de Fontainebleau, superbe construction de la Renaissance française

Beaucoup de voyageurs attendaient le train. Quelques-uns d'entre eux causaient, d'autres se promenaient le long du quai

Dans chaque compartiment il y avait deux banquettes, l'une en face de l'autre

Strasbourg est une très belle ville

La Tour Eiffel, construction métallique moderne

Conversation

1. Demandez à Monsieur Y. s'il aime mieux la conversation que la grammaire. 2. Demandez à Monsieur Z. s'il préfère un cours de français à un cours d'anglais. 3. Demandez à Monsieur A. s'il voit avec les yeux. 4. Demandez à Monsieur B. avec quoi il parle.

Vocabulaire — pages 169–170

Grammaire

1. What is a demonstrative pronoun? (§ 33)

2. What are the French definite demonstrative pronouns? With what do they agree? (§ 33 A, B)

3. By what must the definite demonstrative pronoun be followed? (§ 33 C)

4. When may the demonstrative pronouns not be followed by ***-ci*** or ***-là?*** (§ 33 C)

5. How is the demonstrative pronoun used to express *the former* and *the latter?* What other method may be used to express *the latter?* (§ 33 D)

6. You have already learned that the relative ***qui*** is used as the subject of a dependent clause and that the relative ***que*** is used as the object of a dependent clause. What relative pronoun, found for the first time in this lesson, is used after a preposition? (§ 39 D)

7. In this lesson the verb ***préférer*** is used. Conjugate the verb ***préférer*** in the present and imperfect tenses. (Page 170) What happens in the present tense to verbs whose stem ends in *-é-* + **a single consonant?** (§ 89 E)

8. Explain the use of the definite articles in the sentence *Nous entendons avec **les** oreilles, nous voyons avec **les** yeux, nous sentons avec **le** nez.* (§ 4 G)

Sixième révision–Leçons 26 à 30

Première partie

A. Répondez en français par des phrases complètes aux questions suivantes.

1. En quoi l'étudiant français est-il plus libre que l'étudiant américain? 2. Comment s'appelle le groupe de bâtiments construits pour les étudiants au sud de Paris? 3. Citez quelques pays qui ont construit des bâtiments à la Cité Universitaire. 4. Comment s'appelle la petite ville au sud-est de Paris qui est célèbre par sa forêt et son château? 5. Où va-t-on se promener en général à Fontainebleau? 6. Les souvenirs de quel empereur trouve-t-on au château de Fontainebleau? 7. Combien de classes y a-t-il dans les trains français? 8. Quand il n'y a pas de place pour s'asseoir dans les compartiments d'un wagon, où se mettent les voyageurs? 9. En France, à quel moment le voyageur remet-il son billet de chemin de fer? 10. Quelles sont les armées qui ont occupé l'Alsace au dix-septième siècle? 11. Pourquoi les Alsaciens ont-ils quitté l'Alsace en grand nombre après la guerre franco-allemande? 12. Que boit-on à table le plus souvent à Strasbourg? 13. Où y a-t-il des cours pour les étrangers en France? 14. Quel est le pluriel d'*œil?* 15. Combien de doigts avez-vous à chaque main?

B. Expliquez en français par une phrase complète les noms suivants.

Alsace	Corse	Millet
Alsace-Lorraine	Dijon	Nancy
Boulevard Jourdan	Fontainebleau	Napoléon Ier
Charlemagne	Lorraine	Saint Empire romain germanique
Cité Universitaire	Maison des Provinces françaises	Sainte-Hélène
Corot	Maison Internationale	

C. Rédigez une composition sur un des sujets suivants.

1. Un voyage en chemin de fer 2. L'Alsace-Lorraine 3. Les parties du corps 4. La vie d'un étudiant français 5. Fontainebleau

Deuxième partie

A. Mettez au passé composé les verbes des phrases suivantes. (Voir Grammaire § 61)

1. Quand nous arrivons à Dijon, nous cherchons un autobus. 2. Je me promène dans la rue principale. 3. Je vois des camarades, et je cours

pour les retrouver. 4. Je ne m'arrête pas un seul moment. 5. Nous revenons à Paris le soir. 6. Tout le monde se couche de bonne heure.

B. Écrivez ces phrases au passé composé ou à l'imparfait selon le sens. Ces phrases forment un récit. (*Voir Grammaire* § 53)

7. Bernard, un Américain de seize ans qui (apprendre) encore le français au lycée, (partir) pour la France au début de juin. 8. Quand il (arriver) à Paris, il (chercher) tout de suite le Quartier latin. 9. Beaucoup d'étudiants (se promener) le long du Boulevard Saint-Michel, d'autres (être) assis à la terrasse des cafés. 10. Bernard (se présenter) à un étudiant et lui (demander) où (être) le Luxembourg. 11. L'étudiant lui (répondre) que le Luxembourg (se trouver) de l'autre côté du Boulevard Saint-Michel. 12. Bernard (entrer) dans le Luxembourg et il (regarder) un moment plusieurs enfants qui (jouer) à la balle. 13. Ensuite il (s'asseoir) et (commencer) à lire un roman policier.

C. Remplacez par l'équivalent français les pronoms démonstratifs indiqués en anglais. (*Voir Grammaire* § 33)

14. Apportez en classe votre livre et (*that*) de votre ami. 15. Je peux vous vendre ces timbres-ci, pas (*those*). 16. Le professeur a d'abord corrigé les fautes de Maurice, et puis (*those*) des autres élèves. 17. Préférez-vous ce roman-ci ou (*the one*) que vous avez lu la semaine dernière?

D. Remplacez les tirets par ***mieux*** *ou par la forme convenable de* ***meilleur.*** (*Voir Grammaire* § 98 — *better*)

18. Charles comprend —— que Claude. 19. Peut-on dire que Balzac est un —— écrivain que Victor Hugo?

E. Remplacez les tirets par ***à cause de*** *ou* ***parce que.*** (*Voir Grammaire* § 98 — *because*)

20. Hugo est connu —— ses poèmes. 21. Balzac est connu —— il nous donne un admirable tableau de la vie du dix-neuvième siècle.

F. Remplacez les pronoms relatifs indiqués en anglais par l'équivalent français. (§ 39 B, C, D)

22. Où est la chaise sur (*which*) vous avez mis les cahiers? 23. Le livre (*which*) vous avez lu doit être intéressant.

G. Mettez à l'imparfait les verbes des phrases suivantes. (Voir Grammaire § 51)

24. Le professeur punit souvent les élèves qui ne lui obéissent pas.
25. Quand nous entendons la cloche, nous entrons en classe.

Supplément aux Leçons 21 à 30

VINGT ET UNIÈME LEÇON

Vocabulaire

central
le cigare
la cigarette
etc. (et cetera)
Louvre
le monopole
le numéro
public, publique
le tabac
le télégramme
le télégraphe
le téléphone
téléphoner
téléphonique

acheter[a] *buy*
l'allumette *f.* *match*
l'annuaire *m.* *telephone directory*[b]
le besoin *need*
la boîte *box*
la boutique *shop; store*
le bureau *office*
la cabine *booth*
le café *establishment which serves coffee, tea, chocolate, beer, etc.*
cela *that*
cependant *however*
chez[c] *at the house of*
*devoir *have to, must*
eh bien *well, very well*
en *some, any, of it, of them*
*envoyer *send*
étonner *surprise*
*falloir *to be necessary*
fumer *smoke*
là-bas *over there, down there*
*mettre *put*
la poste *post office*
le timbre *stamp*
tout (*adv.*)[d] *very, quite*
vendre *sell*
*venir *come*

* An asterisk (*) placed before a verb indicates that this verb is irregular. The forms that you will be required to know are listed after the vocabulary.

[a] Forms of the present of *acheter* whose last syllable contains mute *e* place a grave (`) accent over the *e* in the second syllable to indicate that it is pronounced; e.g., *j'achète, il achète, ils achètent;* but *nous achetons, vous achetez.* This spelling change will be taken up in Lesson 22.

[b] Strictly speaking, the word *annuaire* means *yearbook*, but the telephone book is always referred to as *l'annuaire,* so that this is the most common meaning that *annuaire* has come to have.

[c] There is no exact English equivalent of the French preposition *chez.* Depending on the context, it may mean *at the house of, at the place of business of, in the country of.* Thus, in one context *chez nous* might mean *at our house,* but in a different context, it might mean *in our country.*

[d] As an adverb, *tout* is usually invariable. For cases in which it agrees, see § 11 E.

à côté *next door, nearby*
avoir besoin *need*
la boîte aux lettres *mailbox*
le bureau de poste *post office*
le bureau de tabac *tobacco shop*
la cabine téléphonique *telephone booth*
chez [a] nous *at our house; in our country*
le coup de téléphone *telephone call*
d'ailleurs *besides, moreover*
donner un coup de téléphone *make a telephone call*
mettre (une lettre) à la poste *mail (a letter)*

Verbes

devoir	**envoyer**	**falloir**	**mettre**	**venir**
je dois	j'envoie		je mets	je viens
tu dois	tu envoies	il faut	tu mets	tu viens
il doit	il envoie		il met	il vient
nous devons	nous envoyons		nous mettons	nous venons
vous devez	vous envoyez		vous mettez	vous venez
ils doivent	ils envoient		ils mettent	ils viennent

Devoirs

When **some** *or* **any** *modifies a noun, it is usually expressed in French by the partitive construction. When* **some** *or* **any** *replaces a noun, it is usually expressed by* **en.**

A. *Write the French equivalent of each of the following sentences.*

1. There are tobacco shops in the large cities, and there are some in the small towns also. 2. Robert comes to [1] my house with some cigarettes and gives one of them to my father. 3. Maurice needs several stamps, and I need some too. 4. How many brothers have you? I have three [2]. 5. We buy one [3] hundred stamps, and I send some to my mother. 6. It is necessary to go to the post office to [4] telephone. 7. I look for [5] the telephone book, and I find two [2] on the desk. 8. Where are the matches? There are some in that shop. 9. My friend asks for [5] some matches and they [6] give him ten [2].

[1] Use *chez* with the proper pronoun. [2] Supply *of them.* [3] Omit in French. [4] *pour* [5] Included in the verb in French. [6] *on*

B. *Say aloud rapidly the French equivalent of each of the following sentences.*

1. Do you have any stamps? Yes, I have some. 2. How many brothers

[a] There is no exact English equivalent of the French preposition *chez.* Depending on the context, it may mean *at the house of, at the place of business of, in the country of.* Thus, in one context *chez nous* might mean *at our house,* but in a different context, it might mean in our country.

do you have? I have two [1]. 3. People [2] like cigarettes, and we sell many of them. 4. Do you need some matches? Yes, I need some. 5. He likes cigarettes. Does he smoke too many [1]? 6. To [3] telephone it is necessary to go into a café. 7. I go to the post office and I enter [4] a telephone booth. 8. I make a telephone call to a friend.

[1] Supply *of them.* [2] *On* [3] *Pour* [4] In French *entrer* is followed by *dans.*

VINGT-DEUXIÈME LEÇON

Vocabulaire

l'atmosphère *f.*
désagréable
la description
le dîner
la famille
Honoré de Balzac
s'intéresser
la médecine
Melun
servir (2)

A (2) after an *-ir* verb indicates that it belongs to the second class of *-ir* verbs. (§ 49 C)

bien *comfortable, well-off*
causer *chat*
le célibataire *bachelor*
la chambre *bedroom*
le cinéma *movie*
coucher *spend the night*
se coucher *go to bed*
le déjeuner *noon meal; lunch* [a]
dix-neuvième *nineteenth*
dormir (2) *sleep*
familial *family* (adj.)
gentil, gentille [b] *nice*
s'habiller *dress oneself, get dressed*
s'installer *settle*
Jacques *Jack*
Jean *John*
se laver *wash oneself*
se lever *get up*
manger *eat*
s'occuper de *busy oneself with, be in charge of*
partir (2) *go away, leave* [c]
la pension *boarding house*
le, la pensionnaire *boarder*
le petit déjeuner *breakfast*
*prendre *take*
prochain *next*
se promener *go for a walk, take a walk*
le, la propriétaire *landlord, landlady; owner*
rentrer *return to the house, return home*

* An asterisk (*) placed before a verb indicates that this verb is irregular. The forms that you will be required to know are listed after the vocabulary.

[a] Since the noon meal in France is normally the biggest meal of the day, it is not quite accurate to render *le déjeuner* as *lunch.*

[b] The *-l* in gentil is completely *silent* [ʒɑ̃ti]. The feminine *gentille* is pronounced [ʒɑ̃tij].

[c] The verbs *sortir* and *partir* both mean *to leave,* but *sortir* has the connotation of *going out for a short time,* whereas *partir* means *to leave in a more general sense.* The verb *sortir* also means *to go out with someone.* Both *sortir* and *partir* are always followed by *de* before a place. EXAMPLES: Nous *partons de* Paris. Je *sors de* la maison.

le repas *meal*
rester *remain*
se *oneself; himself; herself; themselves*
se réveiller *wake up*
se sentir (2) *feel*
le siècle *century*
sortir (2) *go out, leave*[a]
travailler *work*
vers[b] *about, approximately*

A (2) after an *-ir* verb indicates that it belongs to the second class of *-ir* verbs. (§ 49 C)

de bonne heure *early*
être bien *be comfortable*
l'étudiant en médecine *medical student*
faire des études *carry on studies*
le long de *along*
ou bien *or indeed*
la pension de famille *boarding house*
prendre[c] le petit déjeuner *have one's breakfast*
rester à causer *stay and talk*
la salle à manger *dining room*
tout de suite *immediately*

Verbes

REFLEXIVE VERB	*-ir* VERBS OF THE SECOND CLASS		IRREGULAR VERB
se laver	**dormir**	**sortir**	**prendre**
je me lave	je dor*s*	je sor*s*	je prends
tu te laves	tu dor*s*	tu sor*s*	tu prends
il se lave	il dor*t*	il sor*t*	il prend
nous nous lavons	nous dorm*ons*	nous sort*ons*	nous prenons
vous vous lavez	vous dorm*ez*	vous sort*ez*	vous prenez
ils se lavent	ils dorm*ent*	ils sort*ent*	ils prennent

VERB IN . . . e - er	VERB IN -eler
acheter	**appeler**
j'achète	j'appelle
tu achètes	tu appelles
il achète	il appelle
nous achetons	nous appelons
vous achetez	vous appelez
ils achètent	ils appellent

[a] The verbs *sortir* and *partir* both mean *to leave,* but *sortir* has the connotation of *going out for a short time,* whereas *partir* means *to leave in a more general sense.* The verb *sortir* also means *to go out with someone.* Both *sortir* and *partir* are always followed by *de* before a place. EXAMPLES: Nous *partons de* Paris. Je *sors de* la maison.

[b] The preposition *vers* is used with time expressions with the meaning of *about* or *approximately.* EXAMPLE: Je rentre *vers* neuf heures. I return home *at about* nine o'clock.

[c] The verb *prendre* is used with all nouns referring to meals. EXAMPLES: prendre le dîner *to have dinner;* prendre un repas *have a meal.*

Devoirs

A. Write the French equivalent of each of the following sentences.

1. We often[1] go‿out after dinner[2]. 2. I go‿to‿bed, I sleep nine hours, I get‿up at eight o'clock in‿the[3] morning, and I go‿out. 3. You wake‿up, you get‿up, and you dress yourself. 4. He calls his brother, but you do not call your brother. 5. Does one serve good meals at the boarding house? 6. We have our[4] breakfast in our room[5]. 7. I feel very good in[6] the evening. 8. Do you wake up early in[6] the morning?

[1] Place directly after the verb. [2] Supply the definite article. [3] *du* [4] *le*
[5] *chambre* [6] Omit in translation.

B. Say aloud rapidly the French equivalent of each of the following sentences.

1. At what time do you go‿to‿bed? 2. I go‿to‿bed at[1] ten o'clock in the evening. 3. At what time do you get‿up? 4. We get‿up at[2] quarter after seven in the morning. 5. How do you feel? 6. I feel well. 7. At what time do you go‿out? 8. I go‿out at half past eight in the morning.

[1] at ten o'clock in the evening *à dix heures du soir*
[2] at quarter after seven in the morning *à sept heures et quart du matin*

VINGT-TROISIÈME LEÇON

Vocabulaire

la balle
le boulevard
Boul' Mich'
calme
discuter[a]
se distinguer
la liqueur
le moment
la musique
l'orchestre[b] *m.*
le parc
le quartier
le restaurant
Saint-Michel
la table

l'allée *f.* *path, walk*
s'amuser *have a good time*
l'apéritif *m.* *appetizer, drink taken before the meal to stimulate the appetite*
l'arbre *m.* *tree*
le bassin *basin, pool, fountain*
le bateau *boat*
la bière *beer*
la boisson *drink*
le bord *edge*
le café *coffee*
la chaise *chair*
le client *customer*
la condition *circumstance, walk of life*
divers *different*
l'enfant *m. and f.* *child*

[a] In French *discuter* means *discuss* but also *argue over.*
[b] The *-ch-* of *orchestre* is pronounced like *k* [ɔrkɛstr].

l'étudiante *f.* *girl student*
l'homme *m.* *man*
la journée [a] *day*
longer *skirt, border*
longtemps *a long time*
marcher *walk*
le massif *flower bed*
le monde [b] *people*
la nouvelle [c] *news*
orner *ornament, decorate*
passer *pass by*
plaisanter *joke*
la promenade *walk*
quitter *leave*
retrouver *meet*
le sens *direction*
la terrasse *part of café on sidewalk*
le thé *tea*
le trottoir *sidewalk*
la voiture *carriage*

beaucoup de monde *many people*
le Boulevard Saint-Michel *main street of the Latin Quarter*
de toute condition *of every walk of life*
en tous sens *in every direction*
le Jardin du Luxembourg *the Luxembourg Garden*
prendre un repas *have a meal*
le Quartier latin *the Latin Quarter*
tout le long *all along*
les tout petits *the very small ones*
travailler un cours *work on a course*

Verbes

A. THE PAST PARTICIPLE

CLASS		INFINITIVE	PAST PARTICIPLE
Regular verbs in	*-er*	donn*er*	donn*é*
	-ir	fin*ir*	fin*i*
	-re	attend*re*	attend*u*

B. LE PASSÉ COMPOSÉ

donner	**finir**	**attendre**
j'ai donné	j'ai fini	j'ai attendu
tu as donné	tu as fini	tu as attendu
il a donné	il a fini	il a attendu
nous avons donné	nous avons fini	nous avons attendu
vous avez donné	vous avez fini	vous avez attendu
ils ont donné	ils ont fini	ils ont attendu

[a] The word *jour* is much more common and should normally be used for *day.* The word *journée* stresses the duration of the day.
[b] The word *monde,* whose basic meaning is *world,* sometimes means *people.* The expression *beaucoup de monde,* meaning *many people,* is common.
[c] In the singular *la nouvelle* refers to *a piece of news; les nouvelles* means *news in general.*

Devoirs

A. Write the French equivalent of each of the following sentences.

1. We walked on the sidewalk. 2. They served the dinner in[1] the garden. 3. He finished his work. 4. I answered[2] the teacher's question. 5. You discussed the news[3] of the day. 6. We found many people seated in‿front‿of the tables. 7. They dined in a restaurant of the Latin Quarter. 8. I left[4] the café at six o'clock. 9. On the sidewalk there‿are[5] tables and chairs.

[1] in the *au* [2] The verb *répondre* requires *à* before the noun it governs.
[3] Use the plural. [4] Use a form of *quitter.* [5] Use a form of *se trouver.*

B. Say aloud rapidly the French equivalent of each of the following sentences.

1. I finished my work at half past three. 2. The students finished their work at four o'clock. 3. The students walked up to the garden. 4. We heard music in[1] the café. 5. The children played ball[2]. 6. There are many people on the boulevard. 7. There are tables and chairs on the sidewalk in front of the café. 8. The customers are seated in front of the café.

[1] in the *au* [2] *à la balle*

VINGT-QUATRIÈME LEÇON

Vocabulaire

composer
content
le dentiste
faciliter
l'institut *m.*
Jean Perrot
l'organisation *f.*
organiser
le Panthéon
la pharmacie
se préparer
la sculpture[a]
la Sorbonne
le système
la théologie

le bâtiment *building*
la chance *luck*
comprendre *comprise; understand*
la connaissance *acquaintance*
*connaître *be acquainted with, know; become acquainted with*
le côté *side*
*devenir *become*
le droit *law (study of, practice of)*
la faculté[b] *school, college*
former *train*
l'ingénieur *m.* *engineer*
les lettres *f. pl.* *literature and art, "letters"*
le mètre *meter, 39.37 inches*

* An asterisk (*) placed *before* a verb indicates that this verb is irregular. The forms that you will be required to know are listed after the vocabulary.
[a] The *-p-* in *sculpture* [skyltyr] is silent.
[b] The term *faculté* refers to the faculty and buildings of any school of a university. Its meaning is broader than that of the English word *faculty.* It is also used to indicate the various schools or colleges which comprise a university. Thus: *Faculté des Lettres, Faculté de Médecine, Faculté de Droit,* etc.

l'occasion *f.* *opportunity; occasion*
pauvre *poor*
la peinture *painting*

à côté de *beside, next to*
de l'autre côté *on the other side*
l'École des Beaux-Arts *famous Paris School of Fine Arts*
l'École Centrale *engineering school*
l'École Normale Supérieure *élite Normal School which trains select students to be teachers*

profiter de *profit by, take advantage of*
quant à *as for*
le siège *seat*

l'École Polytechnique *élite engineering school which trains its students to be both engineers and army officers*
en effet *in fact, as a matter of fact*
entendre parler de *hear of*

Verbes

connaître	**devenir**
je connais	je deviens
tu connais	tu deviens
il connaît	il devient
nous connaissons	nous devenons
vous connaissez	vous devenez
ils connaissent	ils deviennent

LE PASSÉ COMPOSÉ

à l'interrogatif	**au négatif**	**au négatif de l'interrogatif**
ai-je donné	je n'ai pas donné	n'ai-je pas donné
as-tu donné	tu n'as pas donné	n'as-tu pas donné
a-t-il donné	il n'a pas donné	n'a-t-il pas donné
avons-nous donné	nous n'avons pas donné	n'avons-nous pas donné
avez-vous donné	vous n'avez pas donné	n'avez-vous pas donné
ont-ils donné	ils n'ont pas donné	n'ont-ils pas donné

PAST PARTICIPLES OF IRREGULAR VERBS

infinitive	**past participle**	**infinitive**	**past participle**
appartenir	appartenu	falloir	fallu
apprendre	appris	lire	lu
avoir	eu	mettre	mis
comprendre	compris	offrir	offert
connaître	connu	pouvoir	pu
courir	couru	prendre	pris
devenir	devenu	recevoir	reçu
dire	dit	savoir	su
écrire	écrit	venir	venu
être	été	voir	vu
faire	fait	vouloir	voulu

Devoirs

A. Write the French equivalent of each of the following sentences.

1. We spoke French in Paris. We did not speak French in Paris. Did we speak French in Paris? 2. They explained the organization of the university to us. They did not explain the organization of the university to you. Did they explain the organization of the university to him? 3. Your mother saw that building. Your mother did not see that building. Did your mother see that building? 4. I wrote three letters. I did not write any [1] letters. Did you write a letter to them? 5. I understood your explanation. They did not understand our explanation. Did you understand his [2] explanation? 6. We were obliged to dine in a restaurant. Were you obliged to dine in a restaurant? I was not obliged to dine in a restaurant. 7. Paul wanted to read that book. He did not want to read that book. Did Paul want to read that book? 8. Do you know that student? 9. Does he know that you are going to [3] the dentist?

[1] What construction is used after a negative? (§ 6 C) [2] *son* (§ 14 C) [3] *chez*

B. Say aloud rapidly the French equivalent of each of the following sentences.

1. I know a student who had the luck to [1] spend six months in [2] Paris. 2. Do you know that student? 3. Does he know that Paris is one of the largest cities of Europe? 4. He learned to [2] speak French in [2] Paris. 5. Did you read a novel of Balzac? 6. We did not receive your letter this morning. 7. Did you see the Law [3] School? 8. I was obliged to [1] remain in that city.

[1] *de* [2] *à* [3] Law School *Faculté de Droit*

VINGT-CINQUIÈME LEÇON

Vocabulaire

directement
l'exemple *m.*
le groupe
l'instinct *m.*
l'intelligence *f.*

la mémoire
la passion
la perception
la psychologie
le semestre
la sensation

le service
sévère
le signe
supplémentaire
vaste

*admettre *admit;* admis *admitted*
amicalement *in a friendly way*
*apercevoir *notice, perceive;* aperçu *noticed, perceived*

*s'asseoir *sit down;* assis *seated*
assez *rather; enough*
la bibliothèque *library*

* An asterisk (*) placed before a verb indicates that this verb is irregular. The forms that you will be required to know are listed after the vocabulary. In this lesson, for instance, the verbs *admettre, s'inscrire,* and *poursuivre* should be learned as vocabulary, but they are not common enough to warrant your learning their conjugation.

*boire *drink;* bu *drank*
la centaine *hundred*
commander *order*
la conférence *lecture*
*devoir *owe;* dû *owed*
le garçon *waiter; boy*
l'habitude *f.* *habit*
*s'inscrire *enroll;* inscrit *enrolled*
laisser *leave*
la licence *first college degree in the French university*
la monnaie *change; small change*
-même [a] *-self*
la plupart *most, greater part; majority*
*poursuivre *pursue, continue;* poursuivi *pursued, continued*
le programme [b] *curriculum, course of study*
saluer *greet*
seul *single; alone*
la somme *sum*
traiter *treat; deal with, take up*

à ce moment là *at that moment; at that time*
de temps en temps *from time to time*
faire signe à *motion to, beckon to, make a sign to*
par exemple *for example*
une fois *once*

Verbes

apercevoir, aperçu [c]	s'asseoir, assis [c, d]	boire, bu [c]
j'aperçois	je m'assois	je bois
tu aperçois	tu t'assois	tu bois
il aperçoit	il s'assoit	il boit
nous apercevons	nous nous asseyons	nous buvons
vous apercevez	vous vous asseyez	vous buvez
ils aperçoivent	ils s'assoient	ils boivent
j'ai aperçu, *etc.*	je me suis assis, *etc.* [e]	j'ai bu, *etc.*

Review devoir, dû — page 151.

* An asterisk (*) placed before a verb indicates that this verb is irregular.

[a] *-même* means *-self* when combined with disjunctive pronouns; e.g., moi-même, *myself;* lui-même, *himself;* eux-mêmes, *themselves.*

[b] The term *programme* sometimes indicates a group of courses required for a given degree, sometimes a list of topics or works a student is required to know when preparing for a given examination.

[c] From now on, the infinitive, past participle, and the first person singular of the *passé composé* of each new irregular verb will be given.

[d] This verb has two distinct conjugations in most of the simple tenses. These may be found in § 95, no. 12. The forms of the present given here are the most commonly used in conversation. The imperative of *s'asseoir* is *asseyez-vous.*

[e] The *passé composé* of reflexive verbs is conjugated with the auxiliary *être* and is studied in Lesson 27.

Devoirs

A. Write the French equivalent of each of the following sentences.

1. We called the waiter. We called him. 2. Have you read those books? Have you read them? 3. We ordered some beer. We ordered some (of it). 4. There are the flowers which she sold us. 5. The books which we found are on the desk. 6. Which letters did you write? 7. The table which we chose is near a window. 8. He spoke to the children that we saw on [1] the street. 9. Did he receive the letters which we wrote this morning? 10. Where is the student who learned French [2] at school [2]?

[1] *dans* [2] Supply the definite article.

B. Say aloud rapidly the French equivalent of each of the following sentences.

1. We ordered some tea. 2. The waiter brought us the tea which we ordered. 3. I drank the tea at once. 4. Did you fail [1] the examination? 5. Few students fail [1] their examinations. 6. I was obliged to [2] go to the library. 7. Did you take [3] an examination at the library? 8. A student can prepare himself at [4] home or at the library.

[1] Use a form of *échouer à.* [2] *de* [3] Not a form of *prendre.*
[4] Use a phrase beginning with *chez.*

THÈME

Leçons 21 à 25

Write the French equivalent of each of the following sentences.

1. Jack needs a stamp and John needs five (of them). 2. I do not send any [1] books to the teacher, for he has enough (of them). 3. Roger goes to bed at ten o'clock, sleeps nine hours, and gets up at seven o'clock. 4. I wash myself at once and then I go out. 5. We finished our work, and then we walked up to the Luxembourg. 6. I found many students seated in front of the café. 7. They were very glad to make the acquaintance of a student who knows the president. 8. We did not have the luck to [2] spend a year in France. 9. The waiter brought us the meals which we ordered. 10. Which lessons did you learn?

[1] What construction is used after *pas?* (§ 6 C) [2] *de*

VINGT-SIXIÈME LEÇON

Vocabulaire

l'autobus *m.*	l'indépendance *f.*	rapidement
la danse	international, internationaux	recommander
descendre	Jourdan	la responsabilité
immense	la nation	universitaire

ailleurs *elsewhere*
belge *Belgian*
la cité [a] *city*
*construire *construct;* construit *constructed*
enfin *finally*
la fondation [b] *foundation*
grand *big; grown-up*
le jeu *game*
mener *lead; take (a person)*
*mourir *die;* mort *dead*
le pavillon [c] *building*
la piscine *swimming pool*
privé *private*
se retrouver *meet each other; be; gather*
*revenir *come back, return;* revenu *came back, returned*
se [d] *each other*
surveiller *watch*

le Boulevard Jourdan *boulevard on which the* Cité Universitaire *is located*
la Cité Universitaire *extensive living quarters for French and foreign university students situated in the southern part of Paris*
de province *from the provinces*
descendre d'un autobus *get off a bus*
la Fondation des États-Unis *the United States House at the* Cité Universitaire
la Maison des Provinces françaises *the building at the* Cité Universitaire *which houses French students coming from the provinces*
la Maison Internationale *the International House at the* Cité Universitaire
monter dans un autobus *get on a bus*
pas du tout *not at all*
prendre sa responsabilité *assume one's own responsibility*
la salle de danse (de musique, de jeu, *etc.*) *dance hall (music room, game room, etc.)*

* An asterisk (*) placed before a verb indicates that this verb is irregular. The forms that you will be required to know are listed after the vocabulary.

[a] The term *cité* is not the ordinary word for *city* and should not be used as such. It indicates a group of people living within a given area, and sometimes refers to a walled or fortified city such as Carcassonne or Aigues-Mortes. The common word for *city* is *ville.*

[b] Used in this lesson to designate certain buildings in the *Cité Universitaire.*

[c] The term *pavillon* is not the ordinary word for *building.* In this lesson it is used to designate certain buildings in the *Cité Universitaire.* The common words for *building* are *bâtiment* and *édifice.*

[d] In its reflexive sense the pronoun *se* means *oneself, himself, herself, themselves.* It means *each other* in its reciprocal sense.

Verbes

LE PASSÉ COMPOSÉ

arriver [a]

je suis arrivé(e)	nous sommes arrivé(e)s
tu es arrivé(e)	vous êtes arrivé(e)(s)
il est arrivé	ils sont arrivés
elle est arrivée	elles sont arrivées

construire, construit	**mourir, mort**	**revenir, revenu** [b]
je construis	je meurs	je reviens
tu construis	tu meurs	tu reviens
il construit	il meurt	il revient
nous construisons	nous mourons	nous revenons
vous construisez	vous mourez	vous revenez
ils construisent	ils meurent	ils reviennent
j'ai construit, *etc.*	je suis mort(e), *etc.*	je suis revenu(e), *etc.*

Devoirs

A. Write the French equivalent of each of the following sentences.

1. We went to the university. 2. I arrived there at 6:15. 3. They got on the bus. 4. Where did you get off the bus? 5. She stayed at the university for [1] a year. 6. They entered [2] the house. 7. We came back with your friend. 8. The bus took [3] us to the Latin Quarter. 9. I left [4] school [5] at [6] the age of fourteen.

[1] *pendant* [2] The verb *entrer* requires *dans* before the noun it governs.
[3] Use a form of *mener.* [4] Use a form of *sortir de.* [5] Supply the definite article.
[6] at the age of fourteen *à quatorze ans*

B. Say aloud rapidly the French equivalent of each of the following sentences.

1. I went to the movie. 2. Did you go to the movie? 3. We entered [1] the movie at eight o'clock. 4. They left [2] the movie at nine thirty. 5. She remained at the movie an hour and a half. 6. Did you come back by bus [3]? 7. I got on the bus at ten o'clock. 8. We got off the bus at quarter after ten. 9. My father died last summer.

[1] The verb *entrer* requires *dans* before the noun it governs.
[2] Use a form of *sortir de.* [3] Supply the definite article.

[a] This is a model of the conjugation of an intransitive verb of motion in the *passé composé.*
[b] Notice that *revenir* is conjugated exactly like *venir.* Compound verbs are usually conjugated like the simple verbs from which they are derived.

VINGT-SEPTIÈME LEÇON

Vocabulaire

admirable
l'appartement *m.*
l'art *m.*
l'artiste *m. and f.*
la construction
Corot
la direction
l'empereur *m.*
énorme
Fontainebleau
la forêt
le guide
Millet
le musée
Napoléon Ier [a]
riche
Sainte-Hélène
splendide
superbe
le train

l'air *m.* *air; appearance*
le billet *ticket*
la chose *thing*
*contenir *contain;* contenu *contained*
la Corse *Corsica*
*courir *run;* couru *ran*
se diriger *go, direct one's steps*
entourer *surround*
la gare *railroad station*
le lendemain *next day*
la matinée *morning*
meilleur (*comparative of* bon) *better*
le meuble *piece of furniture;* les meubles *furniture*
*naître *be born;* né *born*
le paysage *landscape, countryside*
le peintre *painter*
rendre + *adjective* [b] *make + adjective*
le rocher *rock*
sauvage *wild; savage*
sous *under*
vite *quickly*

à cause de *because of*
la gare de Lyon *the Paris railroad station from which trains leave for Lyons, Marseilles, and the Riviera*
le lendemain matin *the next morning*
monter dans un train *get on a train*
prendre un billet *buy a ticket, get a ticket*
le peintre rend le paysage célèbre *the painter makes the landscape famous*

* An asterisk (*) placed before a verb indicates that this verb is irregular. The forms that you will be required to know are listed after the vocabulary.

[a] Napoléon premier [b] Un peintre *rend* un endroit *célèbre.* A painter *makes* a place *famous.*

Verbes

LE PASSÉ COMPOSÉ

se coucher [a]

je me suis couché(e)	nous nous sommes couché(e)s
tu t'es couché(e)	vous vous êtes couché(e)(s)
il s'est couché	ils se sont couchés
elle s'est couchée	elles se sont couchées

contenir, contenu	**courir, couru**	**naître, né**
je contiens	je cours	je nais
tu contiens	tu cours	tu nais
il contient	il court	il naît
nous contenons	nous courons	nous naissons
vous contenez	vous courez	vous naissez
ils contiennent	ils courent	ils naissent
j'ai contenu, *etc.*	j'ai couru, *etc.*	je suis né(e), *etc.*

Devoirs

A. *Write the French equivalent of each of the following sentences.*

1. The artist ran toward the forest. 2. The president was born in 1732 and died in 1799. 3. The castle contains furniture [1] of the different [2] periods in [3] French [4] history. 4. You went to bed at ten o'clock. You did not go to bed early. Did you go to bed at eleven o'clock? 5. We got up early. We did not get up early. Did you get up early? 6. They dressed before breakfast [5]. They did not dress before breakfast. Did they dress before breakfast? 7. She went [6] toward the railroad station. 8. Louise woke up the next [7] morning. Did Louise wake up the next [7] morning? Louise did not wake up at seven o'clock. 9. We got [8] our tickets at the railroad station.

[1] Use the plural of this noun. [2] Use a form of *différent* before the noun. [3] *de*
[4] French history *l'histoire de France* [5] Supply the definite article. [6] Use a form of *se diriger.* [7] the next morning *le lendemain matin* [8] Use a form of *prendre.*

B. *Say aloud rapidly the French equivalent of each of the following sentences.*

1. I got up early. 2. At what time did you get up? 3. At what time did you go to bed? 4. I went to bed at ten o'clock. 5. They got [1] their tickets at the railroad station. 6. We got on the train at once. 7. We took [2] a walk in the forest. 8. Did you run in the forest?

[1] Use a form of *prendre.* [2] take a walk *se promener*

[a] This is a model of the conjugation of a reflexive verb in the *passé composé.* Only verbs whose reflexive objects are indirect do not take these agreements.

VINGT-HUITIÈME LEÇON

Vocabulaire

l'accent *m.*
l'accès *m.*
l'Alsace *f.*
l'Alsacien *m.*
le chocolat
le compartiment
confortable
dîner
l'employé *m.*
Mulhouse
prononcer
la valise

l'armée *f.* *army*
s'arrêter *stop*
la banquette *bench, seat*
le chemin *road*
le contrôleur *conductor*
le couloir *passage, corridor*
la dame *lady*
debout *standing*
déjà *already*
éclater *break out*
le fer *iron*
la guerre *war*
s'impatienter[a] *become impatient*
le mari *husband*
le monsieur *gentleman*
le pain *bread*
plein *full*
le quai *platform*
quelqu'un *someone*
*remettre[b] *turn in, hand back;* remis *turned in, handed in, handed back*
le retour *return*
siffler *whistle*
*se tenir *stand, be;* tenu *stood*
la vitesse *speed*
le wagon *coach, railroad car*
le wagon-restaurant *dining car*

à toute vitesse *at full speed*
le chemin de fer *railroad*
descendre d'un train *get off a train*
faire partie de *be part of*
la guerre de 14[c] *World War I (1914–18)*
quelques-uns d'entre eux[d] *some of them*

* An asterisk (*) placed before a verb indicates that this verb is irregular. The forms that you will be required to know are listed after the vocabulary.

[a] French often uses the reflexive form of the verb to indicate what in English is expressed by *become* (*get*) + adjective, e.g., se fâcher *get angry;* se fatiguer *get tired;* s'irriter *become irritated.*

[b] The French express *Hand in your papers* by *Remettez vos copies.*

[c] Originally, World War I was called *la Grande Guerre.* Now it is called *la guerre de 14* or *la première guerre mondiale.*

[d] The expression *d'entre* + disjunctive pronoun is often used to express *of* + pronoun.

Verbes

THE IMPERFECT[a]

-er *verbs*	*most* **-ir** *verbs*	*2d class* **-ir** *verbs*	**-re** *verbs*
je donn*ais*	je finiss*ais*	je sort*ais*	je perd*ais*
tu donn*ais*	tu finiss*ais*	tu sort*ais*	tu perd*ais*
il donn*ait*	il finiss*ait*	il sort*ait*	il perd*ait*
nous donn*ions*	nous finiss*ions*	nous sort*ions*	nous perd*ions*
vous donn*iez*	vous finiss*iez*	vous sort*iez*	vous perd*iez*
ils donn*aient*	ils finiss*aient*	ils sort*aient*	ils perd*aient*

avoir	**être**	**falloir**
j'avais	j'étais	
tu avais	tu étais	
il avait	il était	il fallait
nous avions	nous étions	
vous aviez	vous étiez	
ils avaient	ils étaient	

-cer *verbs*	**-ger** *verbs*
commencer	**manger**
je commençais	je mangeais
tu commençais	tu mangeais
il commençait	il mangeait
nous commencions	nous mangions
vous commenciez	vous mangiez
ils commençaient	ils mangeaient

remettre, remis — *conjugated like* mettre — (§ 95, no. 28)
se tenir, tenu — *conjugated like* contenir — (§ 95, no. 40)

Devoirs

In these exercises, distinguish carefully between verbs which must be in the imperfect and verbs which must be in the **passé composé.**

Groups of English words which are expressed by a single word in French are linked.

A. *Write the French equivalent of each of the following sentences.*

1. It was ten o'clock when I arrived at the station. 2. The employee was‿standing[1] near the door. 3. Several travelers were‿waiting on the platform. 4. Some[2] of‿them[3] were‿chatting, others[4] were‿walking

[1] Use a form of *se tenir.* [2] *Quelques-uns* [3] *d'entre eux* [4] *d'autres*

[a] The conjugation of the imperfect of regular and irregular verbs may be found in § 95, column 3.

up‿and‿down[1] the platform. 5. Finally, the train arrived, some travelers got off, others[2] got‿on[3] the train. 6. In my compartment an old man was‿reading a novel, a little boy was‿eating some bread, and a girl was‿sleeping. 7. A man was‿beginning to[4] speak of the war when the conductor came. 8. He looked at our tickets, but he did not take them. 9. One must hand the tickets to an employee when one leaves[5] the station.

[1] *le long de* [2] *d'autres* [3] use a form of *monter dans* [4] *à* [5] Use a form of *sortir.*

B. Say aloud rapidly the French equivalent of each of the following sentences.

1. Many passengers were‿waiting‿for the train. 2. The people who were‿waiting on the platform got‿on the train. 3. The train was full of passengers. 4. There were eight passengers in each compartment. 5. There were also some passengers in the aisles. 6. These passengers were‿eating bread. 7. It was already two o'clock when the train arrived. 8. I was‿finishing my studies when the war broke out.

VINGT-NEUVIÈME LEÇON

Vocabulaire

accepter
l'Afrique du Nord *f.*
l'Alsace-Lorraine *f.*
astronomique
la bataille
le changement
Charlemagne
le dialecte
l'empire *m.*
germanique
l'influence *f.*
l'intégration *f.*
la Lorraine
préférer
résister
rose
la situation
le territoire

actuel, actuelle *present*
l'Allemand *m.* *German*
allemand *German*
le champ *field*
la charcuterie[a] *pork, pork products, sausage meat; market where pork is sold*
le compagnon *companion*
la cuisine *cooking*
depuis *since*
l'emploi *m.* *use*
enlever *take away, take from*
envahir *invade*
essayer *try*
gagner *win*
le grès *sandstone*
l'horloge *f.* *clock*
*interdire *forbid;* interdit *forbidden*
la lutte *struggle*
mondial (adj.) *world, world-wide*
particulier, particulière *special, particular*

* An asterisk (*) placed before a verb indicates that this verb is irregular. The forms that you will be required to know are listed after the vocabulary.

[a] In France pork is not usually sold in the ordinary meat markets, but rather in special markets called *charcuteries.*

se passer *happen*
puisque *since*
redevenir *become again;* redevenu *became again*
regagner *regain*
le Reich (*German*) *empire*
reprendre *resume, begin again, continue* repris *resumed, began again, continued*
la rive (*river*) *bank*
saint *holy*
subir *undergo*
tantôt . . . tantôt *now . . . now, sometimes . . . other times*
le tiers *third*
volontiers *willingly, with pleasure*

à l'origine *originally*
de nouveau *again*
de plus en plus *more and more*
en Alsace même *in Alsace itself*
entre eux *among themselves*
la guerre franco-allemande *the Franco-Prussian War* (*1870–71*)
la première guerre mondiale *World War I* (*1914–18*)
la deuxième guerre mondiale *World War II* (*1939–45*)
le Saint Empire romain germanique *the Holy Roman Empire* (*800–1806*)
si bien que *so that*
tout à fait *completely*
tout de même *all the same*

Verbes

interdire, interdit — *conjugated like* dire — (§ 95, no. 21)
redevenir, redevenu — *conjugated like* devenir — (§ 95, no. 43)
reprendre, repris — *conjugated like* prendre — (§ 95, no. 36)

Devoirs

In these exercises, distinguish carefully between verbs which must be in the imperfect and verbs which must be in the passé composé.

Groups of English words which are expressed by a single word in French are linked.

A. Write the French equivalent of each of the following sentences.

1 When I entered [1] the restaurant, I saw many students who were‿chatting among themselves. 2. They were‿eating while the waiters served some other customers. 3. When I was younger, I used‿to‿live in [2] Paris. 4. I was‿finishing my courses in [2] the Law School and my brother was‿carrying [3]‿on his studies in [2] the Medical School. 5. One morning while my brother was still sleeping, I left [4] the house to go to the Luxembourg. 6. We often [5] used‿to‿read in that garden. 7. That [6] morning I re-

[1] This verb is followed by *dans* in French. [2] *à*
[3] carry on his studies *faire ses études* [4] Use a form of *sortir de.*
[5] Place directly after the verb. [6] that morning *ce matin-là*

turned [1] to the house at [2] about nine o'clock. 8. My brother was getting up when I came in. 9. I stayed in my room for [3] two hours.

[1] Use a form of *rentrer*. [2] at about *vers* [3] *pendant*

B. Say aloud rapidly the French equivalent of each of the following sentences.

1. Alsace became a French province in [1] the seventeenth century. 2. It remained French until the Franco-Prussian war. 3. Germany won the Franco-Prussian war. 4. At the end of the Franco-Prussian war Germany took [2] from France all Alsace and the northeast third of Lorraine. 5. What happened then? 6. Germany forbade the use of the French language in the schools. 7. She obliged the young Alsatians to [3] do their military service in the German army. 8. Many Alsatians preferred to leave [4] Alsace rather than to [5] become German.

[1] in the *au* [2] take from *enlever à* [3] *à* [4] Use a form of *quitter*. [5] *de*

TRENTIÈME LEÇON

Vocabulaire

l'artère *f.*
circuler
Dijon
humain
juste
le mécanisme
le membre
le muscle
muet, muette
Nancy
nécessaire
le nerf
l'organe *m.*
le pluriel
la prononciation
la respiration
unir
la veine
le vocabulaire

l'Anglaise *f.* *English girl*
*apprendre *teach; learn;* appris *taught; learned*
aveugle *blind*
borgne *blind in one eye*
la bouche *mouth*
le bras *arm*
celui, celle, ceux, celles *this, that, these, those; the one, the ones*
le cerveau *brain*
les cheveux *m.* *hair* (the singular form, *le cheveu,* indicates one single hair)
le cœur *heart*
le corps *body*
le cou *neck*
le coude *elbow*
créer *create, make*
la dent *tooth*
le doigt *finger*
l'estomac *m.* *stomach*
l'étranger *m.* *foreigner*
la figure *face*
le front *forehead*
le genou *knee*

* You have already learned the present of the irregular verb *apprendre* with its meaning *to teach* in Lesson 16. Review its conjugation on page 103.

goûter *taste*
la grammaire *grammar*
la jambe *leg*
la joue *cheek*
la langue *tongue*
lequel, laquelle, lesquels, lesquelles (*relative pronoun used after prepositions*) *which*
la lèvre *lip*
mâcher *chew*
la main *hand*
le menton *chin*
le nez *nose*
ni . . . ni . . . ne *neither . . . nor*
l'œil *m. sing.* (*pl.* les yeux) *eye*
l'oreille *f.* *ear*
l'os[a] *m.* *bone*
où (§ 39 F) *when*
le pied *foot*
la poitrine *chest*
le poumon *lung*
réunir *join, unite*
le sang *blood*
sentir (2) *feel*
sourd *deaf*
sourd-muet *deaf-mute*
la Suédoise *Swedish girl*
se terminer *finish, end*
le tronc *trunk*
utile *useful*
le visage *face*
les yeux *m. pl.* (*sing.* l'œil) *eyes*

A (2) indicates an *-ir* verb of the second class. (§ 49 C)

au moment où *at the time when*
ce dernier *the latter*
de chaque côté *on each side*
servir à *be used to*
tous les jours *every day*

Verbes

VERB IN . . . é -er

préférer

PRESENT	IMPERFECT
je préfère	je préférais
tu préfères	tu préférais
il préfère	il préférait
nous préférons	nous préférions
vous préférez	vous préfériez
ils préfèrent	ils préféraient

Devoirs

A. Write the French equivalent of each of the following sentences.

1. Do you eat with your[1] mouth? 2. We hear with our[1] ears, we see with our[1] eyes, and we smell with our[1] nose. 3. He[2] who cannot see

[1] How does French express the possessive adjective before parts of the body? (§ 4 G)
[2] Use a form of the demonstrative pronoun.

[a] *un os* [œ̃ɔs]: the *-s* is pronounced in the singular; *des os* [dezo]: the *-s* is silent in the plural.

is blind. 4. Those who cannot hear are deaf. 5. Did you notice the pencil with which I am writing? 6. These courses are easier than those. 7. The city in which my friend works is larger than the one in which I work. 8. This university is nearer Baton Rouge than that one. 9. Do you prefer these novels to those of Balzac?

B. Say aloud rapidly the French equivalent of each of the following sentences.

1. Those who wish can learn French at the university. 2. Why do you prefer conversation [1] courses to grammar courses [2]? 3. There are courses in France for those who wish to learn French. 4. If you know all the parts of the human body, raise your [3] hand. 5. Are the parts of the body with which one eats more important than those with which one walks? 6. He [4] who cannot hear is deaf. 7. Those who cannot see are blind. 8. Do you pronounce with your [3] lips?

[1] How does French express this adjectival noun? (§ 6 E)
[2] Use a demonstrative pronoun instead of repeating *courses.*
[3] How does French express the possessive adjective before parts of the body? (§ 4 G)
[4] Express this word by a form of the demonstrative pronoun.

Thème

Leçons 26 à 30

Write the French equivalent of each of the following sentences.

1. He [1] who has visited the region of the Loire must be acquainted with its castles. 2. We lived near Tours from January to November. 3. Every day we used to take walks along the river. 4. One morning we got up early. 5. We left [2] the house at eight o'clock and went to the station. 6. At the station many people were talking to their friends. 7. We got on the train at once. 8. When the train arrived at Blois, it stopped, and those who were waiting in the aisles got off.

[1] Use a demonstrative pronoun in French. [2] Use a form of *sortir de.*

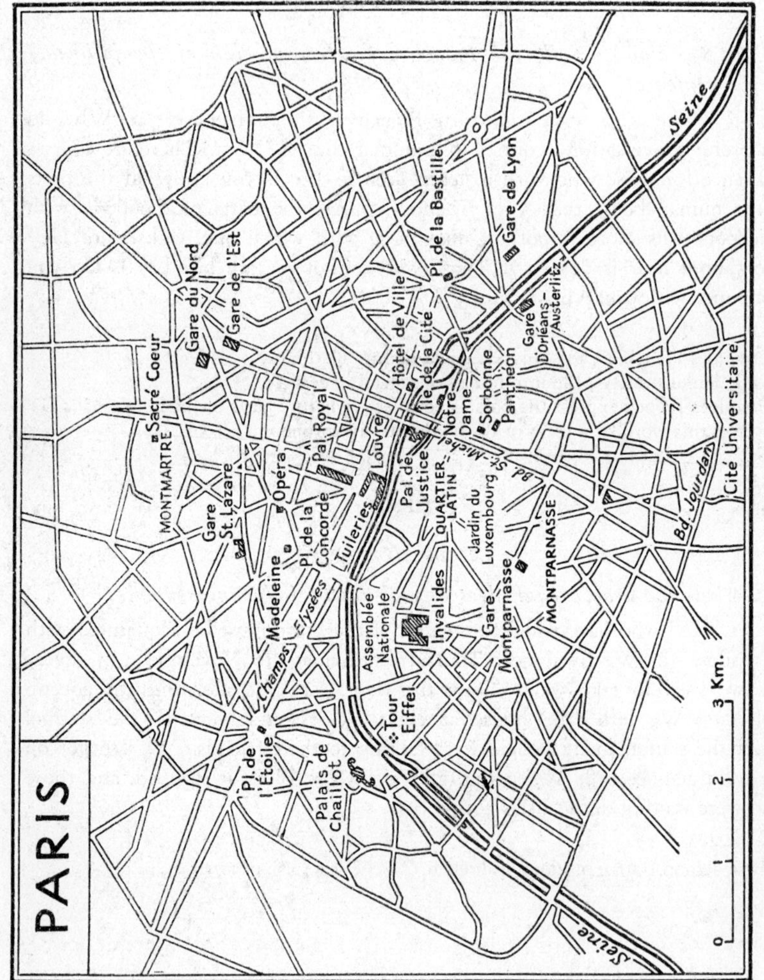

Paris a de très nombreux quartiers et chacun d'eux a son charme tout particulier

Premières impressions de Paris

Paris, le 17 juillet

Chers Barry et Keith,

Je suis arrivé à Paris le 20 juin, mais j'espère que vous me pardonnerez de[1] vous écrire aujourd'hui seulement. Quand vous saurez combien Paris est magnifique, vous me comprendrez — les jours ne sont pas assez longs pour tout voir et pour tout admirer. Que de merveilles! Aucune autre ville au monde ne ressemble à Paris! Aucune n'est aussi jolie!

Lorsque vous aurez des économies suffisantes, il faudra absolument venir. Paris vous enchantera aussitôt que vous y serez et vous l'aimerez tout de suite. Vous ne finirez pas de contempler les splendeurs qu'il y a partout. Vous[2] penserez avoir tout vu et vous découvrirez encore d'autres richesses. Chaque promenade que vous ferez dans les rues de Paris vous apportera de merveilleuses surprises!

Paris a de très nombreux quartiers et chacun d'eux a son charme tout particulier: l'Opéra avec les grands boulevards; le Quartier latin, si animé avec ses étudiants; Montparnasse avec ses cafés et ses artistes; Montmartre et ses boîtes de nuit; le quartier ouvrier de la Bastille; l'Étoile, si riche en souvenirs de l'histoire de France — et tant d'autres encore . . . !

L'architecture des monuments de Paris est également très variée: Notre-Dame, magnifique cathédrale de style gothique; l'église de la Madeleine, qui ressemble à un temple grec; le Sacré-Cœur, église de style byzantin; la Tour Eiffel, construction métallique moderne, etc. Mais vous ne trouverez pas ici de gratte-ciel, style d'architecture si caractéristique de New York.

Dès que vous serez à Paris, vous remarquerez aussi des choses qui vous paraîtront très curieuses. L'aspect des rues parisiennes, notamment, vous étonnera beaucoup. Ces rues sont très différentes des rues américaines et les maisons vous sembleront étranges. Elles ont presque toutes plusieurs étages et comprennent de nombreux appartements. Elles bordent le

[1] *for waiting until today to write you.*

[2] *You will think that you have seen everything.* (lit., *You will think to have seen everything.*) The past infinitive of *voir* is *avoir vu.*

trottoir; il n'y a pas d'espace entre les maisons et le trottoir. Il n'y a pas d'espace entre les maisons non plus; elles se[1] touchent.

Quand vous viendrez en France, tâchez donc de passer le 14 juillet à Paris. Cela vous intéressera certainement. Ce jour-là, la ville est très gaie; il y a beaucoup de monde et on entend de la musique partout. La veille et le soir du 14 juillet vous verrez les gens danser sur les places et aux carrefours.

(*à suivre*)[2]

Questions

1. Quand Robert est-il arrivé à Paris? 2. Pourquoi n'a-t-il pas écrit plus tôt à ses amis en Amérique? 3. Quand j'irai à Paris, quels quartiers intéressants de la ville est-ce que je pourrai visiter? 4. Quel monument de style gothique est-ce que je verrai à Paris? 5. Quel est le style d'architecture que je ne trouverai pas à Paris? 6. Si nous allons à Paris, quelle construction métallique moderne verrons-nous? 7. Est-ce que nous trouverons les rues de Paris différentes des rues des villes américaines? 8. Y a-t-il de l'espace entre les maisons et le trottoir à Paris? 9. Si vous passez la veille et le soir du 14 juillet à Paris, qu'est-ce que vous verrez dans les rues? 10. Qu'est-ce que vous entendrez dans les rues de Paris ces soirs-là?

Devoirs

® *A. Suivez les indications.*

1. Dites à Suzanne que vous partirez pour Paris le 8 juin. 2. Dites à Henriette que quand vous serez à Paris, vous lui écrirez une longue lettre. 3. Dites à Guy que quand vous arriverez en France, vous lui enverrez un roman policier français.

® *B. Mettez au futur les verbes en italique. Tous ces verbes sont réguliers.* EXEMPLE: Nous *avons cherché* un bon restaurant. Nous *chercherons* un bon restaurant.

1. Claude *parle* de son voyage en France. 2. Nous *nous sommes habillés* rapidement. 3. Vous *finissiez* votre lettre à ce moment-là. 4. Ils *ont dormi* toute la nuit. 5. Je *sors* tous les soirs. 6. *Perdiez*-vous votre stylo? 7. J'*ai entendu* de la musique dans les cafés. 8. *Sont*-elles *parties* de bonne heure? 9. *Se sont*-ils *couchés* tard?

[1] *each other.* Here, *se* is a reciprocal pronoun.
[2] *to be continued.*

® *C. Mettez au futur les verbes suivants. Tous ces verbes sont* ***irréguliers*** *au futur.* EXEMPLE: pouvait-elle — pourra-t-elle

1. elle reçoit 2. il est 3. je vais 4. vous avez fait. 5. elles avaient 6. j'ai voulu 7. il voyait 8. elles sont mortes 9. je suis venu 10. il doit 11. il pleut 12. vous avez couru 13. a-t-il envoyé 14. je sais 15. nous avons pu

® *D. Mettez le récit suivant au futur.*

1. Cet été j'ai visité Bordeaux. 2. Quand nous étions dans cette ville, nous sommes allés chez nos amis. 3. Ils nous attendaient chez eux. 4. Dès qu'ils nous ont vus, ils nous ont parlé de l'Amérique. 5. Il y avait beaucoup de monuments à voir à Bordeaux. 6. Lorsque nous y étions, nous avons entendu de la musique dans les cafés. 7. On nous a servi de la bière dans ces cafés. 8. Êtes-vous allé voir le port de Bordeaux? 9. Il y avait des bateaux sud-américains. 10. J'ai vu plusieurs lycées dans la ville. 11. Les élèves du lycée obéissent à leurs professeurs. 12. Le soir nous nous sommes couchés à onze heures. 13. Ma mère a très bien dormi. 14. Elle était contente d'être à Bordeaux. 15. Aussitôt qu'elle est venue nous voir, je l'ai envoyée chez vous.

CONVERSATION

1. Demandez à l'étudiant assis devant vous quand il ira en France. 2. Demandez à l'étudiant assis près de la porte s'il parlera français quand il sera en France. 3. Demandez à l'étudiant assis près de la fenêtre s'il vous écrira une lettre dès qu'il arrivera à Paris. 4. Demandez à l'étudiant assis à côté de vous quels monuments il ira voir lorsqu'il sera à Paris.

VOCABULAIRE — PAGES 215–216

GRAMMAIRE

1. How is the future of a French verb regularly formed? (§ 54 A)

2. What are the forms of the future of ***donner, finir, servir,*** and ***perdre?*** (Page 216)

3. Relatively few verbs are irregular in the future, and the verbs that are irregular form a pattern. Learn the future of the irregular verbs ***aller, avoir, courir, devoir, envoyer, être, faire, falloir, mourir, pleuvoir, pouvoir, recevoir, savoir, tenir, valoir, venir, voir*** and ***vouloir,*** given in § 54 B.

4. What is the general use of the future? (§ 55 A)

5. In which cases is the future used in French where a present is required in English? (§ 55 B)

6. Use in sentences the present, imperfect, future and *passé composé* of ***découvrir*** and ***paraître.*** (Page 216)

TRENTE-DEUXIÈME LEÇON

La concierge

(*suite*)

Ce qui m'a le plus étonné en France, c'est d'y trouver des habitudes différentes des nôtres. Prenez, par exemple, les immeubles de Paris. Dans ces grandes maisons il y a de nombreux appartements. Mais comment y trouver un locataire? La plupart du temps, les noms des locataires ne sont affichés ni à l'entrée de l'immeuble ni sur les portes des appartements. Pour savoir où habite un locataire, on est donc obligé de s'adresser à la concierge. D'ordinaire, la concierge demeure au rez-de-chaussée dans sa loge, qui est une petite pièce située près de la porte de l'immeuble. De là elle peut surveiller tous les gens qui arrivent. C'est elle qui indique à quel étage et dans quel appartement habite la personne qu'on vient voir. Presque toutes les grandes maisons de Paris ont une concierge. Elle balaie les couloirs, nettoie les escaliers, reçoit le courrier et le distribue aux locataires. Elle sait tout ce qui se passe dans la maison et tous les locataires la respectent ou la craignent.

Ce qui est surtout curieux, c'est la façon d'entrer dans un immeuble la nuit. En effet, la concierge ferme la porte de l'immeuble vers dix heures du soir. Même les locataires n'ont pas la clé de cette porte. Ceux qui veulent entrer appuient sur un bouton électrique qui ouvre la porte automatiquement. Mais la concierge surveille même pendant la nuit, et ceux qui entrent doivent dire leur nom quand ils passent devant la loge. De cette façon, la concierge sait qui est entré.[1]

Voilà mes premières impressions de la France. Lisez-les et dites-moi ce que vous en pensez. Je n'ai pas le temps d'écrire à tout le monde. Allez donc chez nos camarades avec ma lettre et montrez-la-leur, s'il vous plaît. Allez aussi chez notre professeur et racontez-lui ce que je vous ai écrit, mais ne lui montrez pas la lettre. Ne la lui montrez pas; vous savez bien pourquoi.

Écrivez-moi ce que vous faites en Amérique pendant les vacances. Racontez-le-moi en détail. Ne me dites pas que vous n'avez pas le temps. Je vous en prie, ne me le dites pas. Répondez à ma lettre tout de suite. Envoyez votre réponse à l'adresse que je vous ai donnée avant mon départ. J'attends de vos nouvelles avec grande impatience. Envoyez-les-moi par avion.

Je vous serre bien cordialement la main à tous les deux,

ROBERT

QUESTIONS

1. Qu'est-ce qu'un immeuble? 2. Pourquoi est-il difficile de trouver un locataire dans un appartement parisien? 3. A qui faut-il s'adresser pour savoir dans quel appartement habite un locataire? 4. Qu'est-ce que c'est qu'une concierge? 5. Où habite-t-elle? 6. Quel travail fait la concierge dans l'immeuble? 7. Vers quelle heure la concierge ferme-t-elle la porte de l'immeuble le soir? 8. Est-ce que les locataires ont la clé de la porte de l'immeuble? 9. Que fait-on pour entrer dans un immeuble la nuit? 10. Que faut-il dire quand on passe devant la loge de la concierge la nuit? 11. A qui Barry et Keith doivent-ils montrer la lettre? 12. Pourquoi ne doivent-ils pas montrer la lettre au professeur? 13. Robert veut-il une réponse à sa lettre? 14. Pourquoi dit-il à Barry et Keith d'envoyer la réponse par avion?

[1] The method of gaining admittance to a Paris apartment house during the night is in a state of flux. Up to World War II, the person wishing to enter rang the doorbell, which awakened the *concierge,* who pulled a cord or pressed a button which opened the door. This system is still in force in some apartment buildings. But in many, the door opens automatically when the caller rings the bell and the *concierge,* if awakened, watches while the late-comer goes by her *loge.*

Some apartment buildings have eliminated the *concierge.* In such buildings, the tenants have keys to the outside door of the apartment house, and their names are posted on the mailboxes in the outside hall of the first floor of the building.

Devoirs

® *A. Suivez les indications.*

1. Dites à Jacques de vous écrire tout de suite. 2. Dites à François d'aller chez le professeur avec sa lettre et de la lui montrer. 3. Dites à Victor d'apporter sa lettre en classe et de nous la lire.

® *B. Remplacez les mots en italique par des pronoms compléments. Ensuite, mettez la phrase à la forme négative.* Exemple: Montrez-moi *la lettre.* (a) Montrez-*la*-moi. (b) Ne me *la* montrez pas.

1. Donnez-moi *votre adresse.* 2. Montrez-moi *sa voiture.* 3. Envoyez *les fleurs à Marie.* 4. Dites-nous *son nom.* 5. Rendez-moi *ces lettres.* 6. Lisez-moi *ce*[1] *que vous écrivez.* 7. Racontez-nous *ce*[1] *que vous faites.*

® *C. Remplacez les mots en italique par des pronoms compléments. Ensuite, mettez la phrase à la forme affirmative.* Exemple: Ne racontez pas *ce*[1] *que vous faites à votre mère.* (a) Ne *le lui* racontez pas. (b) Racontez-*le-lui.*

1. Ne donnez pas *la lettre au professeur.* 2. Ne me montrez pas *cette maison.* 3. Ne nous dites pas *la date.* 4. N'envoyez pas *ces livres à Paul.* 5. Ne m'expliquez pas *ces choses.* 6. Ne lisez pas *à Robert ce*[1] *que vous écrivez.*

D. Remplacez les tirets par la forme convenable de l'expression française qui exprime what[2].

1. Il me dit toujours —— il fait. 2. —— vous lisez est intéressant. 3. Dites-moi —— votre frère a trouvé sur le trottoir. 4. —— m'a le plus étonné, c'est le repas français. 5. Écrivez-vous —— vous pensez? 6. —— j'aime surtout, c'est la musique. 7. Il ne sait pas —— il veut. 8. Savez-vous —— vous voulez? 9. J'aime lire —— n'est pas trop difficile. 10. Écrivez-moi —— vous faites.

E. Mettez les verbes indiqués (a) *au présent* (b) *au futur.* Exemple: Nous (appuyer) sur le bouton. (a) Nous *appuyons* sur le bouton. (b) Nous *appuierons* sur le bouton.

1. Les concierges (balayer) le couloir et (nettoyer) l'escalier. 2. Qui (nettoyer) la salle? 3. Vous (appuyer) sur le bouton.

[1] Entire expressions such as these are replaced by *le* (it).

[2] In such constructions, English usage requires either *what* or *that which;* French uses the *that which* form. These blanks require two words each.

De sa loge la concierge peut surveiller tous les gens qui arrivent

y a partout à Paris des stations
: métro, dont l'entrée se trouve
r le trottoir

. . . le métro, train souterrain qui permet de voyager sans être gêné par la circulation de la rue

Nous nous sommes mises à table et le garçon nous a apporté la carte

Tout le long de la Seine il y a de nombreuses boîtes qui contiennent de vieux livres et des gravures anciennes

La Place de la Concorde est une des plus vastes et des plus belles du monde

L'avenue des Champs-Élysées est large et animée

De nombreuses voitures montent et descendent l'avenue

Conversation

1. Demandez à Louis s'il a le temps de vous écrire. 2. Demandez à Robert s'il habite dans un appartement. 3. Demandez à Henri de vous montrer la lettre qu'il a reçue de son camarade. 4. Demandez à Albert ce qu'il fait pendant les vacances.

Vocabulaire — pages 217–218

Grammaire

1. What is the general rule for the position of object pronouns with reference to the verb? (§ 30 A) When does the object pronoun follow the verb? (§ 30 B)

2. What happens to the weak object pronoun ***me*** when it is placed after the verb? Why? (§ 30 B) What happens to the strong form ***moi*** when it is placed before the verb? Why?

3. What is the relative order of object pronouns when one of them begins with ***l***-? when both begin with ***l***-? (§ 31 C, D)

4. How is the relative pronoun *what* expressed as the subject of its clause? as the direct object of its clause? (§ 39 G)

5. Give the forms of the present, imperfect, *passé composé,* and future of the irregular verbs ***craindre, ouvrir,*** and ***recevoir.*** (Page 218)

6. What are the forms of the present and future of the verbs ***balayer, nettoyer,*** and ***appuyer?*** (Page 218) What governs the use of -*i*- or -*y*- as the final vowel of the stem of these verbs? (§ 89 C)

Les moyens de transport à Paris

Paris, le 6 août

Mes chères tantes,

Juste au moment où je partais pour Dijon j'ai reçu la lettre dans laquelle vous me demandez quelques détails sur la vie à Paris. Je suis en France depuis six semaines et il y a un mois que je suis seule dans une pension dont la propriétaire est très gentille.

Vous me demandez notamment quels sont les moyens de transport à Paris. Il y a, bien entendu, de nombreux taxis, assez bon marché, du reste. Mais les moyens de transport les plus utilisés sont l'autobus, dans lequel on peut se déplacer très rapidement, et le métro, train souterrain qui permet de voyager sans être gêné par la circulation de la rue.

Il y a partout à Paris des stations de métro, dont l'entrée se trouve sur le trottoir. A chaque entrée, de larges escaliers donnent accès à une vaste salle souterraine où les voyageurs peuvent prendre leurs billets et parfois même acheter un journal. Partout dans les couloirs du métro, des plans de Paris indiquent très clairement le parcours des trains.

Pour arriver sur le quai où s'arrête le train que l'on veut prendre, il faut suivre un couloir souterrain. Au bout du couloir se trouve un portillon (petite porte) automatique. Dès que le train entre dans la station, ce portillon se ferme automatiquement pour empêcher les voyageurs de se précipiter sur le quai pendant que le train est là. Au moment où le train s'en va, le portillon s'ouvre et les voyageurs peuvent à nouveau passer sur le quai où ils attendent le train suivant.

On n'arrive pas souvent à destination sans changer de train: il faut prendre une correspondance. Prendre une correspondance veut dire changer de train. On est parfois obligé de prendre plusieurs correspondances.

Marie Deschamps, dont vous connaissez la famille, est l'amie avec qui je sors le plus souvent à Paris. Hier, je suis allée Place de l'Opéra avec elle et son frère. Nous avons pris le métro à une heure où il y avait beaucoup de monde. Nous sommes allés de la station Montparnasse à Châtelet, où nous avons dû prendre la correspondance. A Châtelet nous avons suivi de longs couloirs voûtés pour arriver jusqu'à notre quai. Nous y avons attendu le train. Marie s'impatientait:

— Voici trois minutes que nous attendons et le train n'est pas encore là, disait-elle.

Le métro est arrivé plein de voyageurs. Heureusement, il n'y a que quatre stations entre Châtelet et Opéra. Nous sommes sortis du métro Place de l'Opéra.

(*à suivre*)

QUESTIONS

1. Depuis combien de semaines parlez-vous français? 2. Les taxis de Paris sont-ils bon marché? 3. Quels sont les principaux moyens de transport à Paris? 4. Qu'est-ce que le métro? 5. Quelles sont les villes des États-Unis qui ont un métro? 6. Où se trouve l'entrée du métro? 7. Où distribue-t-on les billets de métro? 8. Qu'est-ce qui indique le parcours des trains dans le métro parisien? 9. Qu'est-ce qui empêche les voyageurs de se précipiter sur le quai pendant qu'un train est dans la station? 10. Que veut dire *prendre la correspondance?* 11. Qui est Marie Deschamps? 12. A quelle station Louise et ses amis ont-ils pris le métro? 13. A quelle station ont-ils pris la correspondance? 14. Pourquoi Marie s'impatientait-elle à Châtelet? 15. Où les jeunes gens sont-ils sortis du métro?

DEVOIRS

® *A. Suivez les indications.*

1. Dites à Georges que vous êtes dans la classe depuis vingt minutes. 2. Dites à Gilbert que vous apprenez le français depuis trois mois. 3. Dites à Yvonne que vous êtes arrivé à la gare au moment où le train partait.

® *B. Écrivez les phrases suivantes en employant* (1) ***il y a*** (2) ***depuis.***

EXEMPLE: Voilà deux semaines que nous sommes à Paris. (1) *Il y a* deux semaines que nous sommes à Paris. (2) Nous sommes à Paris *depuis* deux semaines.

1. Voilà une heure que je travaille. 2. Voici plusieurs mois que nous prenons cet autobus. 3. Voilà vingt minutes que mademoiselle Lequin parle au téléphone.

C. Introduisez dans la phrase les mots indiqués entre parenthèses. EXEMPLE: La France est un pays (*whose inhabitants*) aiment la liberté. La France est un pays *dont les habitants* aiment la liberté.

1. Où est la chambre (*whose windows*) sont ouvertes? 2. Nous avons rencontré un jeune homme (*whose wife*) est en vacances. 3. Nous connaissons des écoles (*whose pupils*) sont tous contents.

D. Introduisez dans la phrase les mots indiqués entre parenthèses. EXEMPLE: (*whose name*) Avez-vous écrit à l'employé . . . je vous ai donné . . .? Avez-vous écrit à l'employé *dont* je vous ai donné *le nom?*

1. (*whose history*) Il est intéressant de visiter un pays . . . on a lu . . . 2. (*whose owner*) Mais il est surtout agréable de passer quelques jours dans une maison . . . vous connaissez bien . . . 3. (*whose car*) Est-ce que Marcel vous a parlé de ce monsieur . . . il a trouvé . . .?

E. Remplacez les tirets par la forme convenable[1] *du pronom relatif.*

1. Cet après-midi Paul va chez un camarade —— a acheté une voiture. 2. Il veut voir cette voiture —— son camarade lui a parlé. 3. Il veut lui demander aussi —— il va faire lundi soir. 4. La rue —— se trouve la maison de son camarade est dans un quartier peu connu. 5. L'autobus —— Paul prend n'est pas celui —— va dans ce quartier. 6. Au moment —— il commence à causer avec un voyageur, Paul s'aperçoit qu'il doit changer de direction. 7. Il prend un autre autobus —— le mène près de la maison de son camarade. 8. Cet ami, —— s'appelle René, travaille chez lui. 9. René ouvre la porte et mène Paul dans la pièce —— il travaille. 10. Ensuite, il lui montre la voiture —— il a achetée. 11. Il explique à Paul tout[2] —— l'intéresse. 12. Les jeunes gens sortent dans la voiture et visitent des endroits —— Paul ne savait rien. 13. Les rues dans —— se trouvent ces endroits sont très jolies. 14. Paul demande à René s'il sait —— l'a étonné le plus dans la ville. 15. Paul et René rencontrent une jeune fille avec —— René parle pendant plusieurs minutes. 16. Il lui dit: — Dites-moi —— vous avez fait ces derniers jours.

[1] Some of these blanks will require two words (*ce qui, ce que* or *ce qu'*) to complete the meaning of the sentence. Note especially the expressions *tout ce qui* and *tout ce que.*

[2] What relative pronoun is used in French to express *everything that?* (Page 418, note 1)

CONVERSATION

1. Demandez à l'étudiant qui est à côté de vous depuis quand il est dans votre classe. 2. Demandez à l'étudiant qui est derrière vous depuis combien de mois il parle français. 3. Demandez à l'étudiant qui est assis près de la porte s'il a pris un autobus pour venir en classe. 4. Demandez à l'étudiant qui est assis près de la fenêtre s'il a dû prendre la correspondance pour venir en classe en autobus.

VOCABULAIRE — PAGES 219–220

GRAMMAIRE

1. Explain the idiomatic use of ***depuis, il y a . . . que, voici . . . que,*** and ***voilà . . . que*** with the present tense. (§ 50 B)

2. You have already learned that the relative ***qui*** is used as the subject of its clause, that the relative ***que*** is used as the object of its clause, and that the relative ***lequel*** is used after a preposition, especially to refer to things. What two relative pronouns, referring to persons, are used after prepositions? (§ 39 B, C, D)

3. Explain the use of the relative pronoun ***dont.*** Give examples of two types of sentences in which ***dont*** is used. (§ 39 E)

4. What is the relative pronoun of place and time? How is the relative of time expressed in English? (§ 39 F)

5. How is the relative pronoun *what* expressed in French? (§ 39 G)

6. Present in outline form all the relative pronouns, including the indefinites ***ce qui*** and ***ce que.*** (§ 39 A)

7. Study the irregular verbs ***s'en aller*** and ***permettre.*** Like what simple verbs are they conjugated? (Page 220)

Le repas au restaurant

(*suite*)

En sortant du métro, nous nous sommes trouvés devant l'Opéra. Maurice m'a dit en regardant sa montre:

— Voulez-vous déjeuner avec nous?

Après avoir cherché un peu dans le quartier, nous avons trouvé un restaurant avec des tables non seulement à l'intérieur mais aussi sur le trottoir. En entrant, nous avons vu beaucoup de personnes à table. De nombreux garçons les servaient. Chacun d'eux s'occupait d'un certain nombre de clients.

Nous nous sommes mis à table et le garçon nous a apporté la carte (le menu). Avant de choisir, Maurice nous a demandé si nous voulions boire du vin. Il est d'usage en France de boire du vin aux repas, mais parfois on boit de la bière, du cidre ou de l'eau minérale.

Le repas de midi, c'est-à-dire le déjeuner, commence d'ordinaire par un hors-d'œuvre: radis, olives, œufs durs, tomates, sardines, pâté. Puis on choisit un plat du jour: poisson ou viande. On sert les légumes avec ou après la viande. On mange, par exemple, des pommes de terre frites avec un bifteck, des haricots verts avec une côtelette de porc. Après la viande et les légumes, on prend généralement une salade. La salade de laitue, entre autres, est très appréciée en France. On la prépare en la mélangeant dans un grand saladier avec du sel, du poivre, de l'huile et du vinaigre. Après la salade, on mange du fromage. Les fromages de France, tels que le Roquefort, le Camembert, le Brie et le Gruyère, sont réputés et les Français en mangent à presque tous les repas. Avec chaque plat on mange du pain. Au dessert on prend souvent des fruits ou de la pâtisserie. Il y a parfois une glace, mais on en mange beaucoup moins souvent en France que chez nous.

Le repas [1] du soir s'appelle le dîner. Il est plus léger que le déjeuner. Au lieu de commencer par un hors-d'œuvre, il commence souvent par un

[1] What is said concerning the evening meal is true especially in the ordinary French family and since the first World War. In restaurants and in the family when there are guests, the evening meal is usually as complete as or more complete than the noon meal.

potage ou par de la soupe. Après, on sert un ou deux légumes, quelquefois des œufs, de la salade, du fromage et un dessert, mais en général ni viande ni poisson.

Après avoir fini de manger, Maurice a demandé l'addition au garçon, qui la lui a apportée. Il l'a payée en laissant un pourboire[1] de dix pour-cent. Le «dix pour-cent pour le service» est une coutume française.

J'ai beaucoup d'autres choses à vous raconter, mais je dois vous quitter sans écrire davantage aujourd'hui. Je termine, espérant recevoir bientôt de vos bonnes nouvelles, en vous envoyant mes sentiments affectueux.

LOUISE

QUESTIONS

1. En quoi les restaurants français sont-ils différents des restaurants américains? 2. Qui sert les clients d'un restaurant? 3. Qu'est-ce que le garçon a apporté aux jeunes gens? 4. Que boit-on aux repas en France? 5. Par quoi commence le déjeuner? et le dîner? 6. Citez quelques hors-d'œuvre. 7. En quoi consiste le plat du jour? 8. Comment prépare-t-on la salade de laitue? 9. Citez des fromages appréciés en France. 10. Que mange-t-on au dessert? 11. En quoi le dîner français est-il différent du déjeuner? 12. Que demande-t-on au garçon après avoir mangé? 13. Pourquoi laisse-t-on dix pour-cent de l'addition au garçon?

DEVOIRS

® *A. Suivez les indications.*

1. Dites à Denise que vous lui téléphonerez avant de sortir. 2. Dites à Yves que vous irez le voir après avoir terminé votre travail. 3. Dites à Philippe que vous l'avez vu en sortant de la bibliothèque.

B. Écrivez (1) la première personne pluriel du présent (2) le participe présent des verbes suivants. EXEMPLE: 1. vous écoutez — nous écoutons — écoutant 2. il s'est arrêté — nous nous arrêtons — s'arrêtant.

1. il habite 2. nous perdrons 3. elle choisit 4. il a pris 5. nous avons eu 6. vous avez été 7. elle lisait 8. avez-vous envoyé 9. elle meurt 10. je veux 11. il mange 12. il sait 13. je bois 14.

[1] This sum which is left for the waiter should perhaps not be called a tip, since in many restaurants and cafés it constitutes his only compensation. Since the second World War, some of the Parisian restaurants have been asking twelve and even fifteen per cent of the price of the meal for the service.

elle a vu 15. il dit 16. elle a commencé 17. il met 18. je viens 19. j'ai reçu

C. Remplacez, s'il[1] *y a lieu, le présent de l'infinitif par le participe présent ou le passé de l'infinitif.*

1. En (marcher) vite, nous sommes arrivés tôt au restaurant. 2. Avant d'(aller) à Tours, il faut lire l'histoire de la Renaissance. 3. (obéir) à ses parents, il a suivi des cours à la Faculté de Droit. 4. Au lieu de (prendre) un billet au guichet, il a causé avec une jeune fille. 5. Avant de (dire) son nom, il a demandé qui j'étais. 6. (savoir) qu'il était là, je ne pouvais rien dire. 7. Après (voir) le professeur, il a annoncé son intention de partir pour Toulouse. 8. En (sortir) de la maison, Mme Paquet a rencontré sa sœur. 9. Avant de (recevoir) l'argent, Maurice a dû apporter les livres. 10. Après (regarder) sa montre, Charles a dit qu'il fallait se dépêcher. 11. Sans (parler) de son travail, il a quitté la maison. 12. Après (arriver) à la gare, il m'a téléphoné.

D. Dans chacune des phrases suivantes, on aurait un participe présent en anglais. En français, on n'emploie pas un participe présent dans ces phrases. Introduisez les mots entre parenthèses dans les phrases et expliquez ce qu'on emploie au lieu du participe présent:

1. Nous (*are writing*) une lettre. 2. Ils (*were eating*) de la glace quand Charles est entré dans la salle. 3. Avant de (*receiving*) son ami, il a fermé la porte de la chambre. 4. Après (*reading*) le journal, il est monté dans sa chambre. 5. Ils sont allés au cinéma sans (*knowing*) où vous étiez.

Conversation

1. Demandez à l'étudiant assis près de la porte s'il est sorti ce matin sans avoir pris son petit déjeuner. 2. Demandez à l'étudiant assis près du bureau du professeur ce qu'il fera après avoir terminé ses études. 3. Demandez à l'étudiant assis derrière vous s'il commencera à travailler avant de terminer ses études. 4. Demandez à l'étudiant assis à votre droite qui il a vu en entrant dans la classe.

[1] *if necessary*

VOCABULAIRE — PAGES 221–222

GRAMMAIRE

1. What is the ending of the English present participle? (§ 73) of the French present participle? (§ 73 A)

2. On what stem is *-ant* added to form the French present participle? (§ 73 B)

3. What three verbs have irregular present participles? (§ 73 B)

4. Give the present participles of ***donner, finir, dormir, répondre, être, avoir,*** and ***savoir.*** (Page 222)

5. What sort of action does the present participle indicate? Give examples of sentences with a present participle. (§ 74 A)

6. With what preposition is the present participle sometimes used? In such cases, to what does the action of the present participle refer? (§ 74 B)

7. When and with what does the present participle agree? (§ 74 C)

8. What verbal construction is used after all prepositions except *en?* (§ 78 A)

9. How does French express the very common *before —ing?* (§ 78 B 1) the very common *after —ing?* (§ 78 B 2)

10. In English the present participle is often used to form the progressive tenses. We say: *I am reading, he was writing.* Such forms do not exist in French. How does French express these progressive tenses? (§ 50 A, § 52 B 2)

TRENTE-CINQUIÈME LEÇON

De l'Étoile à la Concorde

Paris est vraiment pittoresque. Tout le long de la Seine il y a des quais où se trouvent de nombreuses *boîtes*[1] qui contiennent de vieux

[1] The word *boîte* means *box.* In this lesson it refers to the large boxes set up on the parapet of the walls overlooking the wharves along the Seine; in them are displayed books and etchings for sale to passers-by.

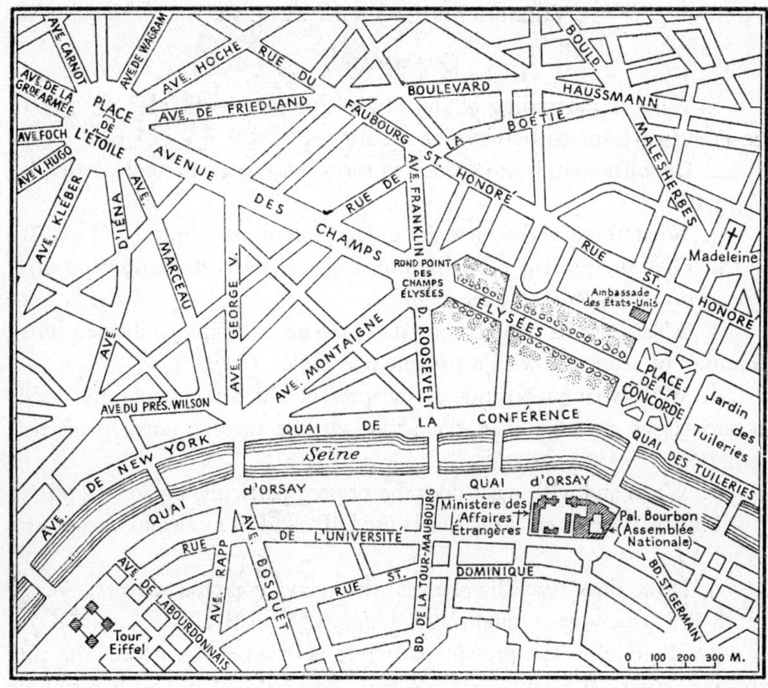

L'Avenue des Champs-Élysées mène de la Place de l'Étoile à la Place de la Concorde

livres et des gravures anciennes. Toutes sortes de gens feuillettent ces vieilles éditions qui ont quelquefois une assez grande valeur. Un vieil homme, le bouquiniste, surveille parfois plusieurs boîtes et renseigne les curieux sur le prix des livres.

La Seine divise Paris en deux parties: la rive gauche où se trouvent de vieux quartiers et de vieilles rues et la rive droite où se trouvent les nouveaux quartiers élégants des Champs-Élysées et de l'Opéra avec de larges avenues modernes.

Un après-midi, je me trouvais Place de l'Étoile avec Maurice. Cette place s'appelle ainsi parce que de son centre partent de larges avenues dans toutes les directions, ce qui lui donne la forme d'une étoile. Plusieurs de ces avenues portent le nom des grandes victoires et des généraux de Napoléon. Au centre de la place il y a un immense monument érigé en l'honneur des armées de Napoléon: l'Arc de Triomphe. Sous ce bel arc de triomphe se trouve le tombeau du soldat inconnu, sur lequel brûle continuellement une flamme en souvenir des soldats tués pendant la guerre de 14.

L'avenue des Champs-Élysées, qui mène de la Place de l'Étoile à la Place de la Concorde, est large et animée. De chaque côté il y a de belles maisons, des magasins luxueux et de grands cafés. De nombreuses voitures montent et descendent l'avenue et la foule se promène sur les trottoirs en regardant les vitrines des magasins.

— Promenons-nous, m'a dit Maurice.

En descendant l'avenue, nous avons vu beaucoup de gens assis aux terrasses des cafés. Près de la Place de la Concorde nous avons admiré les beaux jardins qui bordent, de chaque côté, l'avenue des Champs-Élysées.

La Place de la Concorde est une des plus vastes et des plus belles du monde. Au centre se trouvent des fontaines, des statues et un vieil obélisque rapporté d'Égypte en 1831. Les voitures passent sur la place si rapidement dans tous les sens qu'il est difficile de la traverser à pied.

Arrivé au centre de la place, Maurice m'a dit:

— Voici devant nous le Jardin des Tuileries et le Louvre.

J'ai vu, en effet, un beau parc et, au loin, un immense édifice.

— Tournez-vous à gauche.

A gauche, au bout de la rue Royale, nous avons vu l'Église de la Madeleine, belle construction de style classique.

— Tournez-vous à droite.

A droite et de l'autre côté de la Seine, j'ai vu le Palais Bourbon, lui aussi de style classique, où se réunit l'Assemblée Nationale.

— Et maintenant, retournez-vous.

Je me suis retourné pour regarder de nouveau les Champs-Élysées et, au loin, le bel Arc de Triomphe.

Questions

1. Qu'est-ce qui se trouve à Paris le long des quais de la Seine? 2. Qui surveille les *boîtes?* 3. Sur quelle rive de la Seine se trouvent les vieux quartiers? 4. Pourquoi la Place de l'Étoile s'appelle-t-elle ainsi? 5. Quel monument se trouve au centre de la Place de l'Étoile? 6. Qu'est-ce qui se trouve sous l'Arc de Triomphe? 7. Décrivez les Champs-Élysées. 8. Qu'y a-t-il au centre de la Place de la Concorde? 9. Pourquoi est-il difficile de traverser la Place de la Concorde à pied? 10. Quand on est au centre de la Place de la Concorde en regardant les Champs-Élysées, qu'y a-t-il à droite? à gauche? derrière?

Devoirs

® *A. Répondez aux questions suivantes par une phrase complète, en commençant par* ***oui*** *ou* ***non.***

1. Un vieil homme renseigne-t-il les gens sur le prix des livres? 2. Les vieilles rues et les vieux quartiers se trouvent-ils sur la rive gauche de la Seine? 3. La flamme du souvenir brûle-t-elle en souvenir des soldats tués pendant les guerres de Napoléon? 4. Est-il facile de traverser la Place de la Concorde à pied? 5. L'Arc de Triomphe est-il un beau monument? 6. La Place de l'Étoile est-elle belle?

B. Remplacez les tirets par les formes convenables de (1) ***beau*** (2) ***vieux*** (3) ***nouveau.*** Exemple: les —— maisons (1) les *belles* maisons (2) les *vieilles* maisons (3) les *nouvelles* maisons.

1. un —— quartier 2. la —— église 3. les —— rues 4. de —— villes 5. le —— arc 6. les —— livres 7. de —— avenues 8. un —— tableau 9. le —— édifice 10. un —— ami

C. Donnez les impératifs (1) ***nous*** (2) ***vous*** *des verbes suivants.* Exemple: choisir (1) choisissons (2) choisissez.

1. écouter 2. obéir 3. dormir 4. répondre 5. se tourner 6. se promener 7. se laver

® *D. Mettez les phrases suivantes à la forme négative.* Exemple: Promenons-nous au bord de la Seine. Ne nous promenons pas au bord de la Seine.

1. Couchez-vous à neuf heures. 2. Levons-nous tout de suite. 3. Spécialisez-vous en mathématiques. 4. Réunissons-nous dans la cour.

E. Écrivez les quatre premiers temps[1] *primitifs des verbes suivants.* Exemple: monter — montant — monté — je monte.

1. chercher 2. entendre 3. partir 4. punir 5. boire 6. être 7. écrire 8. faire 9. lire 10. mettre 11. ouvrir 12. prendre 13. savoir 14. venir

[1] Principal parts of an irregular verb may be found by turning to § 95 of the *Grammaire* and consulting the first two columns. See, for instance, *aller:* in the first column are *aller, allant, allé,* the first three principal parts, and the first form in the second column is *je vais,* the fourth principal part.

Conversation

1. Demandez à l'étudiant qui est à votre droite s'il aime les vieux livres et les vieilles gravures. 2. Demandez à l'étudiant qui est à votre gauche s'il y a de beaux paysages et de belles maisons près de la ville où il est né. 3. Demandez à l'étudiant qui est devant vous de se lever et d'aller au tableau. 4. Demandez à l'étudiant qui est derrière vous de se taire.

Vocabulaire — page 223

Grammaire

1. What are the three singular forms of ***beau?*** of ***vieux?*** of ***nouveau?*** When is each used? What are the plural forms of these adjectives? Note that ***fou*** and ***mou*** also have three singular forms. (§ 10 G)

2. To what forms of the present indicative does the ordinary ***vous*** imperative correspond? (§ 79 A) the ***nous*** or "let us" imperative? (§ 79 B) Give the ***nous*** and ***vous*** imperatives of ***donner, finir, dormir,*** and ***vendre.*** (Page 224)

3. How is the imperative of reflexive verbs written? the negative imperative? (§ 79 D) Give the ***nous*** and ***vous*** imperatives of ***se tourner*** and ***se promener.*** (Page 224)

4. Each English verb has three principal parts, as *use, used, used; write, wrote, written.* Each of these principal parts is used to form certain tenses. Each French verb has five principal parts. You have already studied four of these principal parts. What are they? (§ 48 A 1–4) What are the first four principal parts of ***donner? finir? dormir? perdre?*** (§ 48 B and page 224)

5. Which tense you have studied is derived from the infinitive? which tenses you have studied are derived from the present participle? from the past participle? (§ 48 C)

6. Study the regular verbs ***parler*** and ***finir*** with their first four principal parts and the tenses you already know, as in the outline in § 48 D.

7. Notice that ***beau, vieux,*** and ***nouveau*** precede their nouns. Which French adjectives regularly precede their nouns? (§ 12 E)

Septième révision — Leçons 31 à 35

Première partie

A. Répondez en français par des phrases complètes aux questions suivantes.

1. Quand vous serez à Paris pour la première fois, quels monuments irez-vous voir? 2. Quelle est la différence d'aspect entre une rue de Paris et une rue de votre ville? 3. Pourquoi est-il intéressant de passer le 14 juillet à Paris? 4. Qui balaie les couloirs et nettoie les escaliers des immeubles parisiens? 5. A Paris, pourquoi faut-il s'adresser à la concierge de l'immeuble pour trouver l'appartement d'un locataire? 6. Comment la concierge sait-elle qui entre dans l'immeuble la nuit? 7. Pourquoi le portillon automatique se ferme-t-il dès qu'un train entre dans une station de métro à Paris? 8. Si le métro n'est pas direct, que faut-il faire? 9. Où prend-on les billets de métro? 10. Citez les différents plats d'un déjeuner français. 11. Quelle est la salade la plus appréciée en France? 12. Que laisse-t-on au garçon après un repas dans un restaurant français? 13. Quelle est la différence entre les quartiers de la rive gauche et ceux de la rive droite à Paris? 14. Quels noms portent les avenues qui partent de la Place de l'Étoile? 15. Décrivez la Place de la Concorde.

B. Expliquez en français par une phrase complète les noms suivants.

Brie	Madeleine	Palais Bourbon
Camembert	Montmartre	Roquefort
Concorde	Montparnasse	Sacré-Cœur
Gruyère		Tour Eiffel

C. Rédigez une composition sur un des sujets suivants.

1. Paris 2. L'immeuble parisien 3. Le métro parisien 4. Un repas français

Deuxième partie

A. Remplacez l'infinitif par la forme convenable du verbe. Faites attention surtout au temps. (Voir Grammaire §§ 50 B, 54, 55, 73, 74, 78 A, B, 89 C)

1. Nous (travailler) depuis une demi-heure. 2. Quand Gérard (arriver), nous lui montrerons ce que nous avons écrit. 3. En (corriger) les fautes, il nous expliquera la grammaire. 4. Avant de les lui (remettre), il faut les lire. 5. Je sortirai après (téléphoner) à ma mère. 6. Dès que je (voir) mon camarade, je lui dirai que vous êtes ici. 7. Il y a

déjà un an que nous (aller) à cette école. 8. Au lieu de (rester) à Paris, nous passerons quelques jours en province. 9. J'(appuyer) sur le bouton de l'immeuble, j'entre et je vois la concierge qui (nettoyer) le couloir.

B. Écrivez les impératifs (1) ***vous*** (2) ***nous.*** EXEMPLE: (effacer) le tableau. (1) *Effacez* le tableau. (2) *Effaçons* le tableau. (*Voir Grammaire* § *79 A, B*)

10. (finir) ce devoir et (remettre)-le. 11. (chercher) le plan de Paris et (montrer)-le-leur. 12. (sortir) tout de suite, n'(attendre) pas.

C. Remplacez les tirets par la forme[1] *convenable du pronom relatif.* (*Voir Grammaire* § *39*)

13. Le jour —— il arrivera, je m'en irai. 14. C'est une lettre de l'oncle —— les enfants sont à la campagne. 15. Il a acheté avant la guerre la voiture dans —— vous l'avez vu. 16. Savez-vous —— mon père a fait hier? 17. Il nous a montré le tableau —— un excellent artiste lui a envoyé. 18. Dites-moi —— est sous le livre.

D. Remplacez l'expression en italique par un pronom complément. Ensuite, mettez la phrase à la forme négative. EXEMPLE: Dites-nous *l'heure.* (1) Dites-*la*-nous. (2) Ne nous *la* dites pas. (*Voir Grammaire* §§ *30, 31*)

19. Donnez-moi *cette clé.* 20. Montrez-nous *ces fautes.* 21. Lisez *ce journal à votre mère.* 22. Expliquons *la leçon aux élèves.*

E. Remplacez les tirets par la forme convenable de (1) ***nouveau*** (2) ***vieux*** (3) ***beau.*** EXEMPLE: Ces —— voitures coûtent cher. (1) Ces *nouvelles* voitures coûtent cher. (2) Ces *vieilles* voitures coûtent cher. (3) Ces belles voitures coûtent cher. (*Voir Grammaire* § *10 G*)

23. Cette —— école n'est pas loin de chez nous. 24. Avez-vous vu ce —— édifice? 25. Les —— rues et les —— magasins se trouvent dans ce quartier-là.

[1] Some of these blanks will require two words (e.g., *ce qui, ce que*) to complete the meaning of the sentence.

Les Tuileries et le Louvre

De l'autre côté de la Place de la Concorde nous avons aperçu au loin un grand espace planté d'arbres. C'est le jardin des Tuileries. Il est magnifique. C'est un immense parc avec des statues, des fontaines et de larges allées. Il est d'autant plus beau qu'il y a des fleurs partout.

Au bout du Jardin des Tuileries se trouve l'Arc de Triomphe du Carrousel et, plus loin, un vaste palais. C'est le Louvre. C'est un des musées les plus célèbres du monde. Il comprend plusieurs bâtiments construits à des époques différentes. C'est une ancienne résidence des rois de France, commencée au moyen âge.

Les salles du Louvre sont très nombreuses. Elles contiennent des objets d'art de toutes sortes. Ce sont surtout les peintures, les sculptures et les meubles des différentes époques de l'histoire de France qui ont retenu notre attention.

Nous avons vu d'abord les sculptures. Il y en a deux que nous avons beaucoup admirées. Ce sont *la Victoire de Samothrace* et *la Vénus de Milo.*

Ensuite nous avons parcouru les nombreuses salles de peinture. On y voit des tableaux de tous les pays et de toutes les époques. Ce sont surtout les maîtres de la peinture française depuis le moyen âge jusqu'à nos jours qui sont représentés au Louvre. Nous avons vu un excellent portrait de François Ier, roi de France au seizième siècle. C'est lui qui a encouragé les artistes de la Renaissance. Nous avons remarqué beaucoup de paysages des grands peintres du dix-septième siècle, paysages souvent inspirés de sujets antiques. On peut y voir aussi *l'Embarquement pour Cythère* de Watteau, qui exprime l'atmosphère des fêtes élégantes et des plaisirs royaux au dix-huitième siècle. Il y a des œuvres de Corot, de Millet et de beaucoup d'autres artistes du dix-neuvième siècle et du début du vingtième.

Après avoir vu les peintures françaises, nous avons parcouru une longue galerie. D'un côté il y a les œuvres des grands maîtres de la Renaissance italienne: Raphaël, Léonard de Vinci et Michel-Ange; en face, des peintures espagnoles et, plus loin dans d'autres salles, des peintures flamandes, hollandaises, anglaises, allemandes, etc.

Puis, nous avons exploré une longue suite de salles où se trouvent des meubles splendides des différentes époques de l'histoire de France. Les styles Louis XIII, Louis XIV, Louis XV, Louis XVI, Directoire, Empire (époque de Napoléon Ier), etc. y sont représentés.

C'est un des musées les plus célèbres du monde

***On y voit des tableaux** de tous les pays et de toutes les époques*

C'est une magnifique cathédrale de l'époque gothiq

u sommet de la cathédrale ous pouvions voir des monu-ents de tous côtés et, à nos eds, la Seine qui traverse ute la ville

Nous sommes passés devant un grand édifice très ancien: le Palais de Justice

— Ça? Cette église toute blanche qui domine la ville des hauteurs de Montmartre? C'est le Sacré-Cœur.

Questions

1. Quel est le jardin qui se trouve de l'autre côté de la Place de la Concorde? 2. Que trouve-t-on aux Tuileries? 3. Qu'est-ce que le Louvre? 4. Que voit-on dans les salles du Louvre? 5. Quelles sont les sculptures que nous avons surtout admirées? 6. Quel est le roi de France qui a encouragé les peintres de la Renaissance? 7. Citez trois peintres français du dix-neuvième siècle. 8. Citez trois peintres italiens de la Renaissance. 9. De quel style sont les meubles qui se trouvent au Louvre? 10. Y a-t-il un musée de peinture dans la ville que vous habitez? 11. Quels sont les musées de peinture les plus célèbres des États-Unis? 12. Citez un peintre américain célèbre.

Devoirs

® A. *Répondez aux questions suivantes par une phrase complète, en commençant par* **oui** *ou* **non** *et en employant* **ce** *comme sujet de la réponse.* EXEMPLE: Est-ce qu'un café est un établissement où on prend des repas? *Non,* ***ce*** n'est pas un établissement où on prend des repas.

1. Est-ce que le Louvre est un musée? 2. Est-ce que Millet et Corot sont des peintres du seizième siècle? 3. Raphaël et Michel-Ange sont-ils des artistes de la Renaissance italienne? 4. Est-ce que le Roquefort est le nom d'une rue de Paris? 5. Est-ce que Napoléon est un peintre français célèbre? 6. Est-ce que Fontainebleau est une petite ville située au sud-est de Paris? 7. Est-ce que Cannes et Nice sont des villes célèbres par leurs plages?

® B. *Répondez aux questions suivantes par une phrase complète, en commençant la réponse par* ***ce.*** EXEMPLES: 1. Qu'est-ce que c'est que la Cité Universitaire? *C*'est un groupe de bâtiments construits pour loger les étudiants qui viennent à Paris. 2. Qu'est-ce que Cannes et Nice? *Ce* sont des villes de la Côte d'Azur.

1. Qu'est-ce que la France? 2. Qu'est-ce que la Madeleine? 3. Qu'est-ce que c'est que le métro? 4. Qu'est-ce que Strasbourg? 5. Qu'est-ce qu'un lycée? 6. Qu'est-ce que la Normandie et la Bretagne? 7. Qu'est-ce que la Loire et la Garonne? 8. Qu'est-ce que le Luxembourg? 9. Qu'est-ce que les Alpes et les Pyrénées?

*C. Remplacez les tirets par des pronoms personnels (**il, elle, ils, elles**) ou par le pronom démonstratif **ce**.*

1. Voilà un grand édifice; —— est le Louvre. 2. —— est très vaste. 3. —— est un musée. 4. Voici de belles peintures. —— sont des peintures italiennes. 5. —— sont célèbres. 6. —— sont des peintures de Léonard de Vinci. 7. Regardez ces sculptures. —— sont au Louvre depuis peu de temps.

*D. Remplacez les tirets par des pronoms personnels (**il, elle, ils, elles**) ou par le pronom démonstratif **ce**. Expliquez oralement votre choix.*

1. Charles est avec nous. —— est Français. 2. —— est étudiant à la Faculté de Droit. 3. —— est un étudiant sérieux. 4. —— est souvent au Luxembourg. 5. Voilà Paul et Marie. —— sont nos camarades. 6. —— sont Anglais. 7. —— sont avec nous tout le temps. 8. Regardez ces statues. —— sont près de notre école. 9. Voyez-vous ces jeunes gens? —— sont des élèves du lycée Louis-le-Grand. 10. —— sont eux qui se spécialisent en littérature. 11. Qui est là? —— est moi. 12. Qui est à la porte? —— est vous? 13. Qui est de l'autre côté de la rue? —— est ma sœur. 14. —— est jolie, n'est-ce pas? 15. Robert est mon frère. —— est à l'école. 16. —— est lui qui a perdu ses livres. 17. Qui est François Ier? —— est celui qui a encouragé les artistes de la Renaissance.

E. Écrivez en francais.

Francis [1] I; Charles IX; Henry [2] IV; Louis XIII; Louis XIV; Louis XVI; Napoleon [3] III; Napoleon [3] I; George [4] VI.

F. Quels sont les temps primitifs de ces verbes?

1. voir 2. vouloir 3. aller 4. dormir 5. tenir 6. jouer 7. courir 8. choisir

Conversation

1. Demandez à l'étudiant assis près de la porte qui est Balzac. 2. Demandez à l'étudiant assis près du bureau du professeur ce que c'est que la Sorbonne. 3. Demandez à l'étudiant assis derrière vous ce que c'est que les Champs-Élysées. 4. Demandez à l'étudiant assis à côté de vous qui est la reine Mathilde.

[1] *François* [2] *Henri* [3] *Napoléon* [4] *Georges*

VOCABULAIRE — PAGES 225–226

GRAMMAIRE

1. You have already studied the demonstrative pronoun *ce* in Lesson 15. When is *C'est* ... used and when *Ce sont* ... ? (§ 35 A, B)

2. When may the **introductory** *ce* be used before a form of the verb *être?* (§§ 35 C 1, 36 A)

3. When must the personal pronouns *il, elle, ils* and *elles* be used as the subject of a form of the verb *être* instead of the **introductory** *ce?* (§ 36 B)

4. In the sentences *Il est étudiant* and *Elle est Américaine,* why are the personal pronouns *il* and *elle* used before *est* instead of the **introductory** *ce?* (Page 412, note 3)

5. Review the formation of the ordinals. Count by ordinals from 1 to 30. When are ordinals used with dates and with names of kings and emperors? (§ 18 A, B, D, E)

6. Study the verbs *dormir* (§ 95, no. 4) and *perdre* (§ 95, no. 3) with their principal parts and tenses derived therefrom, as indicated in Lesson 35. Like what simple verbs are *parcourir* and *retenir* conjugated?

TRENTE-SEPTIÈME LEÇON

Notre-Dame de Paris

Nous étions restés au Louvre presque deux heures et j'avais vu beaucoup d'œuvres d'art lorsque Maurice m'a rappelé qu'il était déjà quatre heures et qu'il fallait partir.

En sortant du Louvre, je me suis rendu compte que j'avais beaucoup marché et que j'étais fatigué. Nous avons décidé de nous reposer à la terrasse d'un petit café où Maurice était déjà allé plusieurs fois. Ensuite nous avons repris notre promenade.

En route, en longeant les quais, j'ai vu une grande île au milieu de la Seine. J'ai demandé à Maurice:

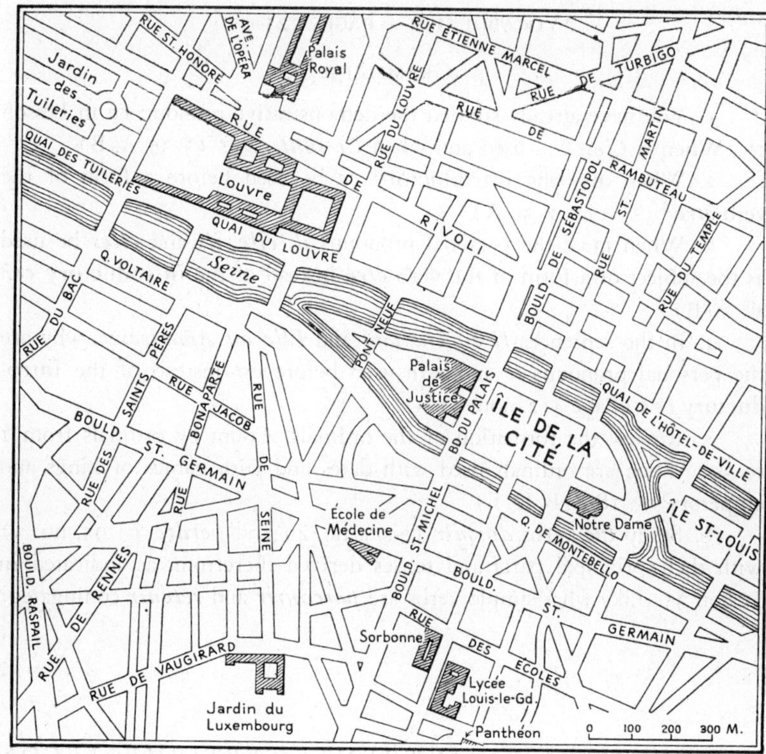

C'est l'île de la Cité. C'est là que Paris a été fondé

— Qu'est-ce que c'est que ça?

— Ça? C'est l'île de la Cité. C'est là que Paris a été fondé. La tribu des Parisii s'y était déjà établie quand César a envahi la Gaule. Plusieurs empereurs romains y ont séjourné. Puis, la ville s'est étendue, d'abord sur la rive gauche, plus tard sur la rive droite.

Pour aller dans l'île de la Cité, nous avons traversé un des ponts qui la relient à la rive droite. Nous sommes passés devant un grand édifice très ancien: le Palais de Justice. Maurice m'a dit qu'il avait été construit au moyen âge, puis détruit et rebâti. Mais avec ses murs sombres et ses tours, il conserve encore aujourd'hui une apparence féodale.

Bientôt nous sommes arrivés sur une grande place devant Notre-Dame de Paris. C'est une magnifique cathédrale de l'époque gothique. Maurice m'a raconté qu'elle avait été commencée au douzième siècle et terminée au treizième sous le règne de Saint-Louis. Nous en avons admiré la façade grandiose avec ses trois immenses portes et ses deux tours symétriques.

Au-dessus de la porte centrale il y a une rosace splendide. Nous avons longuement regardé les sculptures délicates qui entourent ces portes et racontent l'histoire sainte. Puis, nous sommes entrés dans la cathédrale. Des colonnes montent très haut, puissantes et légères. Une odeur d'encens s'élevait dans l'église. Le jour, pénétrant à travers les vitraux, diffusait une lumière douce et colorée. Ces vitraux, très anciens, évoquent des scènes bibliques.

Ensuite, nous sommes montés dans une des tours. Du sommet de la cathédrale, nous pouvions voir des monuments de tous côtés et, à nos pieds, la Seine qui traverse toute la ville. J'avais étudié un plan de la ville et je[1] croyais la connaître. Mais j'avais de la peine à m'orienter et il m'a fallu demander à Maurice:

— Qu'est-ce que c'est que ça?

— Ça? Cette église toute blanche qui domine la ville des hauteurs de Montmartre? C'est le Sacré-Cœur. Ceci? Le dôme des Invalides. Quant à cela, ai-je besoin de vous dire que c'est la Tour Eiffel?

QUESTIONS

1. Qu'est-ce que Maurice et son ami ont vu au Louvre? 2. Pourquoi l'ont-ils quitté à quatre heures? 3. Pourquoi sont-ils allés dans un petit café? 4. Comment s'appelle l'île qui se trouve au milieu de la Seine? 5. Quelle était la tribu qui était établie dans cette île quand César a envahi la Gaule? 6. Quand le Palais de Justice a-t-il été construit? 7. De quelle époque date Notre-Dame? 8. Décrivez la façade de Notre-Dame. 9. Décrivez l'intérieur de la cathédrale. 10. Que racontent les vitraux de Notre-Dame? 11. Quelle est l'église blanche qui domine Paris des hauteurs de Montmartre? 12. Quel dôme peut-on voir de la tour de Notre-Dame?

DEVOIRS

® *A. Suivez les indications.*

1. Dites à Michel qu'il vous a fallu travailler. 2. Dites à Albert que vous vous rendez compte qu'il est déjà tard. 3. Dites à Lucienne que vous étiez déjà sorti quand elle a téléphoné.

B. Mettez les verbes suivants (1) *au passé composé* (2) *au plus-que-parfait.* EXEMPLE: elle fera (1) elle a fait (2) elle avait fait.

1. ils habitaient 2. vous vous rappelez 3. elle partira 4. nous nous reposons 5. il est 6. je vais

[1] *I thought I knew it.*

® *C. Mettez les verbes suivants au plus-que-parfait.*

1. nous écrivons 2. il s'élève 3. elle ne vient pas 4. voulez-vous 5. je ne m'habille pas 6. elles meurent 7. peut-il 8. je dors 9. je ne dis pas 10. nous aurons 11. vous ne vous coucherez pas

D. Remplacez l'infinitif par le plus-que-parfait.

1. Nous (lire) plusieurs romans français avant d'aller en France. 2. (mettre)-vous la lettre à la poste avant son arrivée? 3. Elle (mourir) avant le soir. 4. Il (venir) voir le nouveau professeur. 5. Elle (croire) qu'il était riche. 6. Elles (se voir) à Marseille.

E. Remplacez les tirets par **ceci** *ou* **cela.**

1. Remarquez ——. 2. Préférez-vous —— ou ——? 3. Choisissons-nous —— ou ——? 4. Écrivez ——, n'écrivez pas ——. 5. Regardez ——.

F. Remplacez les tirets par **celui, celle, ceux, celles, ceci** *ou* **cela,** *selon le sens, en ajoutant* **-ci** *ou* **-là** *où il faut.*

1. Faites ——, ne faites pas ——. 2. Ce garçon-ci est plus jeune que ——. 3. Ne lisez pas ——. 4. Lisez ce livre-ci, ne lisez pas ——. 5. Voilà deux chambres. Préférez-vous —— ou ——? 6. Voici trois desserts. Choisissez ——. 7. Ne dites pas ——. 8. Voilà deux restaurants. Dites-moi —— que vous préférez. 9. Ne regardez pas ——. 10. —— prend beaucoup de temps. 11. Voici quelques livres. —— sont plus intéressants que —— qui est sur la table.

Conversation

1. Demandez à l'étudiant qui est assis devant le professeur s'il se rend compte qu'il est déjà tard. 2. Demandez à l'étudiant qui est assis derrière vous s'il avait déjà fait ces devoirs quand il est arrivé en classe. 3. Demandez à l'étudiant qui est à votre gauche s'il faut beaucoup travailler pour apprendre le français. 4. Demandez à l'étudiant qui est à votre droite s'il était déjà sorti quand vous êtes arrivé chez lui.

Vocabulaire — pages 226–227

Grammaire

1. Give an example of an English sentence with the pluperfect (sometimes called the past perfect). How is the pluperfect used in French? (§ 65)

2. Of what two parts does the pluperfect consist? With what auxiliary is it conjugated? (§ 64 A, B) Conjugate in the pluperfect the verbs ***parler, entrer,*** and ***se laver.*** (Page 227)

3. Explain the uses of ***ceci, cela,*** and ***ça.*** (§34 A, B, C)

4. Review the uses of the definite demonstrative pronouns ***celui, celle, ceux,*** and ***celles.*** (§ 33 A, B, C)

5. When does one use a definite and when an indefinite demonstrative pronoun? (§ 34 D)

6. Give the principal parts and study all tenses you have already taken up of the irregular verbs ***avoir*** (§ 95, no. 8) and ***croire*** (§ 95, no. 19). To what family of verbs does ***détruire*** belong? [1]

TRENTE-HUITIÈME LEÇON

Une soirée au théâtre

—Aimeriez-vous aller au théâtre un de ces soirs, Robert?

—Oui, j'irais avec plaisir. A quel théâtre voudriez-vous aller?

—Vous savez, il y a beaucoup de théâtres à Paris comme dans les autres grandes villes d'Europe. Mais il y a aussi cinq théâtres nationaux. Ce sont des théâtres qui appartiennent à l'État et qui sont subventionnés par le gouvernement. Il y a la Comédie-Française, qu'on appelle souvent *le Français,* le Théâtre de France [2], l'Opéra, l'Opéra-Comique et le Théâtre National Populaire [3]. Nous pourrions aller au théâtre un soir. Il serait intéressant d'assister à un spectacle français. D'ailleurs, nous verrions

[1] To determine how an irregular verb is conjugated, look it up in the French-English vocabulary at the end of the book. For instance, for *détruire,* you will find its five principal parts and then "*conj. like* conduire," which means that by looking up the conjugation of *conduire* in § 95, you can arrive at any form you wish of *détruire,* since it follows exactly the same pattern.

[2] *Le Théâtre de France,* established in 1959, is housed on the left bank of the Seine in the former Odéon.

[3] *Le Théâtre National Populaire* is housed in the Palais de Chaillot.

sûrement une bonne pièce, car les acteurs sont toujours excellents dans les théâtres nationaux. Auquel de ces théâtres préféreriez-vous aller?

— J'aimerais voir une pièce de théâtre plutôt qu'un opéra. Quels sont les meilleurs auteurs français? Quel est le Shakespeare français?

— J'aurais du mal à vous répondre, mais je dirais que Corneille et Racine sont nos meilleurs auteurs tragiques, tandis que Molière a écrit nos meilleures comédies. Tous les trois sont du dix-septième siècle. Je crois qu'on joue *le Cid* de Corneille au *Français* demain ou après-demain. Nous pourrions y aller. Mais il vaudrait mieux prendre nos billets à l'avance pour être sûr d'avoir de bonnes places. Nous devrions en retenir dès maintenant.

Le lendemain soir, en arrivant au théâtre, les deux jeunes gens ont remis leurs billets à une ouvreuse, qui les a conduits à leurs places. Ils lui ont donné un pourboire, selon l'usage au théâtre et au cinéma en France.

La représentation du *Cid* était remarquable et la prononciation des acteurs très nette. Robert a été impressionné par la force et la beauté des vers de Corneille dont voici un court exemple:

Jamais nous ne goûtons de parfaite allégresse:
Nos plus heureux succès sont mêlés de tristesse;
Toujours quelques soucis en ces événements
Troublent la pureté de nos contentements.

De tous les usages du théâtre en France, c'est l'entr'acte principal qui, par sa longueur, a le plus étonné Robert. Il y a toujours un entr'acte important de vingt à vingt-cinq minutes qui coupe le spectacle en deux parties. Pendant les entr'actes, les spectateurs peuvent sortir de la salle. Ils vont souvent au foyer, vaste salle où se trouvent les bustes des grands auteurs dramatiques français. C'est là qu'on rencontre les critiques et les auteurs à la mode. Pendant l'entr'acte principal on peut aller fumer ou boire au bar. Mais beaucoup de spectateurs préfèrent aller prendre quelque chose dans un café voisin.

Questions

1. Quels sont les cinq théâtres de Paris qui appartiennent à l'État? 2. Quels sont les meilleurs auteurs tragiques? 3. Connaissez-vous les œuvres de Molière? 4. Lesquelles de ses comédies avez-vous lues? 5. Il y a cinq théâtres nationaux en France. Dans lesquels y a-t-il des représentations d'opéras? 6. Auquel des théâtres nationaux les deux jeunes gens sont-ils allés? 7. Pourquoi ont-ils dû retenir des places à l'avance?

8. A qui ont-ils remis leurs billets en arrivant au théâtre? 9. Pourquoi ont-ils donné un pourboire à l'ouvreuse? 10. Comment Robert a-t-il trouvé la prononciation des acteurs? 11. Selon les vers de Corneille, pourquoi n'est-on jamais parfaitement heureux? 12. Combien de temps dure l'entr'acte principal en France? 13. Qui peut-on rencontrer au foyer du théâtre pendant les entr'actes? 14. Que peut-on faire pendant l'entr'acte principal?

Devoirs

® *A. Répondez par une phrase complète aux questions suivantes. Commencez votre réponse par* **oui** *ou* **non.** *Soulignez les verbes au conditionnel.*

1. Aimeriez-vous aller au théâtre ce soir? 2. Vaudrait-il mieux retenir des places à l'avance? 3. Aurais-je du mal à comprendre le français à Paris? 4. Avez-vous dit que vous seriez heureux de passer un an en France? 5. Croyez-vous que nous entendrions mieux là-bas? 6. Épouseriez-vous une femme qui parle trop?

B. Remplacez les infinitifs par la forme convenable du conditionnel.

1. Marie a dit qu'elle (venir) demain. 2. Je croyais qu'ils (choisir) leur président demain. 3. Vous avez dit que vous (lire) sa lettre tout de suite. 4. Avez-vous dit que vous (aller) au cinéma ce soir? 5. Je croyais qu'il (pleuvoir) pendant la nuit.

® *C. Mettez les verbes suivants au conditionnel.*

1. ils ont reçu 2. vous racontez 3. j'écris 4. elle est morte 5. je perds 6. nous avons vu 7. il faut 8. il est 9. elle dort 10. vous voulez 11. elles doivent 12. elle a fait 13. nous pouvons 14. il a eu 15. vous avez pris 16. je sais

D. Remplacez les tirets par la forme convenable de **lequel.** *Faites la contraction s'il y a lieu.*

1. Il y a cinq théâtres nationaux en France. —— de ces théâtres préférez-vous? 2. *Faust, Phèdre* et *Macbeth* sont des pièces très célèbres. —— de ces pièces est française? 3. Madison, Polk, Lincoln, McKinley, Wilson, Roosevelt et Truman ont été à la tête des États-Unis pendant une guerre. —— de ces présidents ont voyagé en France? 4. Victor Hugo a écrit beaucoup d'œuvres. —— avez-vous lues? 5. Vous m'avez dit que vous connaissez presque tous les pays d'Europe. Dans —— de ces pays

avez-vous voyagé? 6. Il y a plusieurs cinémas dans cette rue. A —— de ces cinémas voulez-vous aller?

E. *Traduisez en anglais la forme du verbe* ***devoir*** *indiquée en italique.* EXEMPLE: Nous *devrions* passer plusieurs heures au Louvre. *devrions* — should

1. Je *dois* acheter des timbres. 2. Vous *devriez* étudier tous les soirs. 3. Mon frère *a dû* sortir à cinq heures. 4. Marie *doit* partir demain. 5. Philippe *doit* être riche. 6. Ces gens *devaient* travailler tout le temps. 7. Nous *devrions* prendre nos billets à l'avance. 8. J'*ai dû* quitter le théâtre. 9. Jacques *devrait* m'écrire, mais il ne m'écrit jamais.

CONVERSATION

1. Demandez à l'étudiant assis à votre gauche s'il aimerait aller au cinéma avec vous ce soir. 2. Demandez à l'étudiant assis derrière vous s'il voudrait devenir professeur de français. 3. Demandez à l'étudiant assis près du bureau du professeur si vous devriez lui téléphoner ce soir. 4. Demandez à l'étudiant assis près de la porte lequel de ses cours il préfère.

VOCABULAIRE — PAGES 228–229

GRAMMAIRE

1. How is the conditional formed? (§ 56) Give the conditional of ***donner, punir,*** and ***répondre.*** (Page 229)

2. Have you noted that both the future and the conditional are formed on the infinitive? If one is irregular, the other will be irregular in the same way. There are eighteen common verbs (and their compounds) which are irregular in the future and conditional. It may help you to learn these irregular tenses by dividing the verbs into classes. Give the irregular conditionals of ***aller, avoir, courir, devoir, envoyer, être, faire, falloir, mourir, pleuvoir, pouvoir, recevoir, savoir, tenir, valoir, venir, voir,*** and ***vouloir.*** (§ 54 B)

3. How is the conditional used? (§ 57 A, B)

4. How is the interrogative pronoun *which one* expressed in French? (§ 38 E)

5. What is the meaning of ***devrions*** in the sentence *Nous* ***devrions*** *retenir des places?* The verb devoir when followed by the infinitive has a number of meanings in its various tenses. What does it mean in the

present? in the imperfect? in the compound past? in the future? in the conditional? (§ 93 B, C, D, E)

6. Study the verbs *se battre* (§ 95, no. 13), ***conduire*** (§ 95, no. 15), and ***valoir*** (§ 95, no. 42). Like what simple verbs are ***appartenir*** and ***combattre*** conjugated?

TRENTE-NEUVIÈME LEÇON

Projets de vacances

Madame Antoine et madame Morel sont deux jeunes femmes d'une trentaine d'années qui sont de très bonnes amies. Une après-midi elles se rencontrent aux Champs-Élysées. Madame Antoine se promène avec son petit chien Chou-Chou.

—Bonjour, Denise.

—Bonjour, Suzanne.

—Comment vas-tu? Tu as l'air un peu fatigué.

—Oui, ce matin j'avais mal à la tête. Il fait très chaud à Paris depuis huit jours.

—Oh oui; moi, j'ai eu chaud cette nuit. Je ne pouvais pas m'endormir. Aussi[1] j'ai sommeil cet après-midi.

—Je crois que nous avons besoin de vacances. Ce sera bientôt la saison. Dès que mon mari sera revenu[2] d'Angleterre, je lui en parlerai.

—Il est parti en Angleterre, ton mari?

—Il est parti il y a quinze jours pour un voyage d'affaires. Il a passé quelques jours en Allemagne, un jour au Danemark, deux jours en Suède et huit jours en Angleterre. Je sais qu'il a également l'intention d'aller en Irlande. Je viens de recevoir une lettre de Londres. Il revient en France la semaine prochaine. Mais où passeras-tu tes vacances cet été?

—Nous avons pensé[3] aller au Portugal. Moi, j'aimerais passer

[1] Meaning? [2] *returns.* This is the *futur antérieur* or future perfect, used much more frequently in French than in English. See §§ 66 and 67.

[3] *thought of going.* Note the meaning of *penser* followed by the infinitive.

quelques semaines dans la vieille Espagne. On est tellement tranquille là-bas. Mais ne restons pas sur ce trottoir. Si[1] nous allions prendre quelque chose dans un café? J'ai soif. Viens, Chou-Chou. Tu as faim? Pauvre petite bête!

A la terrasse d'un élégant café des Champs-Élysées devant une tasse de thé, madame Antoine ajoute:

— Et toi, où vas-tu passer tes vacances?

— Si c'est possible, j'aurais envie d'aller en Amérique. Ce serait merveilleux de passer quelques jours au Canada, de faire un séjour à Québec, de voyager aux États-Unis, de rester huit jours à New York et de voir la Californie. J'ai eu beau en parler plusieurs fois à mon mari, il ne veut pas. Il dit que j'ai tort et je crois que nous finirons par aller tout simplement en Suisse. Du moins, il[2] l'espère. Y es-tu déjà allée?

— Oui. L'été dernier, pour la seconde fois! Nous avons fait le voyage en auto. D'abord nous sommes allés à Chamonix. Nous avons fait quelques excursions dans la région du mont Blanc. Nous avons eu froid là-haut même au mois d'août. Tu n'es jamais allée à Chamonix? Ça en vaut la peine.

— Oh oui! tu as raison. Mais Chamonix est en France. Qu'est-ce que tu as vu en Suisse?

— Chamonix n'est pas loin de Genève. Genève est en Suisse, mais c'est une ville où l'on parle français. Il y a des plages magnifiques sur les bords du lac de Genève. Nous allions nous y baigner tous les jours. Ensuite, nous avons longé le bord du lac en bateau jusqu'à Lausanne.

— Ça a dû être magnifique. A propos de voyages, puisque je te vois, j'en profite pour te demander si tu peux venir dîner chez nous jeudi soir. Il y aura un ami qui vient d'arriver de Chine et du Japon.

— Mais avec plaisir. Oh, il est déjà cinq heures! J'ai honte d'être si bavarde. Je dois rentrer.

— Alors, au revoir. A jeudi.

Questions

1. Où se rencontrent madame Antoine et madame Morel? 2. Comment va madame Morel? 3. Dans quels pays voyage le mari de madame Morel? 4. Où madame Antoine a-t-elle voulu passer ses vacances? 5. Où madame Morel aimerait-elle passer ses vacances? 6. Où madame Antoine et son mari ont-ils passé leurs vacances il y a un an? 7. A-t-on

[1] *How about going to get something in a café?* or *Suppose we go to get something in a café?* French expresses this idea by *si* and the imperfect. [2] *he hopes so.*

froid à la montagne en été? 8. Où est Chamonix? 9. Citez une ville suisse où on parle français. 10. Pourquoi les touristes aiment-ils la ville de Genève? 11. D'où arrive l'ami de madame Antoine?

Devoirs

A. Remplacez les tirets par les mots convenables indiqués à droite.

1. Dans les pays du nord, les habitants ont —— en hiver. 2. Quand j'étais à l'école, j'avais —— du professeur, car il me punissait souvent. 3. Je me coucherai quand j'aurai ——. 4. Ce pauvre élève a —— travailler, il ne réussira pas. 5. Si vous marchez trop, vous aurez —— aux pieds. 6. Oui, vous avez ——; il est mort en 1960. 7. Mais Jean a ——; il n'est pas mort en 1959. 8. Voulez-vous écrire? Avez-vous —— d'un stylo? 9. J'ai échoué à mon examen. J'ai —— de le dire à mes camarades. 10. Voilà le bassin des Tuileries. J'ai —— de jouer avec un petit bateau. 11. On ne devrait manger que quand on a ——. 12. En été on a souvent très ——. 13. Je voudrais boire, car j'ai ——.

a. beau
b. besoin
c. chaud
d. envie
e. faim
f. froid
g. honte
h. mal
i. peur
j. raison
k. soif
l. sommeil
m. tort

B. Remplacez les tirets par la préposition convenable (avec l'article défini s'il y a lieu).

1. Cet été je suis allé —— France. 2. Je suis parti —— États-Unis le 15 juin. 3. Je suis arrivé —— France le 22 juin. 4. Nous ne sommes pas restés —— Cherbourg. 5. Nous sommes allés —— Paris. 6. Nous sommes sortis —— Paris pour faire des voyages —— Versailles, —— Fontainebleau et —— Chartres. 7. Le 30 juin nous sommes partis —— France. 8. Nous sommes allés —— Allemagne, —— Danemark, —— Angleterre et —— Suède. 9. N'êtes-vous pas allés —— Italie, —— Espagne et —— Portugal? 10. Non, mais nous avons rencontré des amis qui venaient —— Portugal et d'autres qui venaient —— Russie. 11. Ils avaient l'intention d'aller —— Chine et —— Japon. 12. Et vous, êtes-vous allés —— Mexique? Oui, nous y avons passé quinze jours. 13. Nous sommes partis —— Mexique le 31 août. 14. L'année prochaine, j'irai —— Canada.

® *C. Remplacez les verbes, les adjectifs et les pronoms de la deuxième personne du pluriel, qui sont en italique, par des verbes, des adjectifs et des pronoms de la deuxième personne du singulier.*

EXEMPLE: *Vous* ne *pouvez* pas trouver *votre* stylo; *prenez* le mien avec *vous.* *Tu* ne *peux* pas trouver *ton* stylo; *prends* le mien avec *toi.*

1. *Vous avez* reçu la lettre que je *vous* ai écrite, n'est-ce pas? 2. *Écrivez*-moi où *vous allez* passer *vos* vacances. 3. *Racontez*-moi l'histoire de *votre* ami. 4. *Serez-vous* à Paris avec *votre* fille? 5. *Vous étiez* à Paris quand *votre* femme y est arrivée. 6. Je serai avec *vous* demain. 7. *Habillez-vous* vite et *sortez* avec *votre* chien. 8. *Aimeriez-vous* aller en Bretagne avec *vos* sœurs?

CONVERSATION

1. Demandez à Monsieur A. s'il a envie d'aller en France cet été. 2. Demandez à Monsieur B. s'il a sommeil. 3. Demandez à Monsieur C. s'il aimerait passer quelques semaines au Japon. 4. Demandez à Monsieur D. combien de temps il est resté à Paris.

VOCABULAIRE — PAGES 230–231

GRAMMAIRE

1. List the personal idiomatic expressions used with ***avoir.*** (§ 90 B)

2. Which countries are masculine? which are feminine? (§ 7 B 4 a)

3. How are *in, at,* or *to* expressed with feminine countries? with masculine countries? with cities? with any place modified by an adjective? [1] (§ 42 A, B, C, D, E)

4. How is *from* expressed with places in French? (§ 43 A, B, C)

5. When do the French use the familiar pronoun ***tu?*** (§ 23 B) Give the ***tu*** forms of present, imperfect, future, conditional, and *passé composé* of ***parler, finir, dormir, perdre, entrer,*** and ***se tourner.*** (Page 232) What can you say of the familiar imperatives? (§ 79 C, D) What are the familiar imperatives of the above verbs?

6. Give the ***tu*** forms of the possessive adjectives (§ 14 A); of the disjunctive pronouns (§ 27 A); of the direct object (§ 24 A); the indirect object (§ 25 A); the reflexive pronouns (§ 26 A).

7. What are the principal parts of ***être*** (§ 95, no. 9) and ***aller*** (§ 95, no. 11)? Study these verbs as in § 48 D.

[1] The construction *dans* + a modified place name is very rare.

QUARANTIÈME LEÇON

Les vacances en France

En France l'été est la saison des grandes vacances. Dès le 1er juin commencent les examens des grandes écoles et des facultés; les universités se vident peu à peu; on n'entend plus personne dans leurs grands couloirs déserts, d'ordinaire si pleins de bruit. Après le 14 juillet ni les écoles primaires ni les lycées ne sont ouverts. Ni étudiants ni professeurs ne fréquentent alors les salles de conférence. On ne voit plus dans les rues les élèves portant négligemment leurs livres sous le bras.

Un élève négligent, ayant oublié [1] son livre d'anglais, se présente au lycée mais n'y trouve que le silence. Racontant cela à un camarade, il demande:

—Devine qui j'ai vu au bout de quelques instants.

—Personne, répond l'autre, qui sait bien qu'il n'y a personne à l'école pendant les vacances.

—Comment, personne? N'y a-t-il pas toujours un concierge même en été?

—Jamais. N'ayant trouvé [1] personne, tu n'as pu rien faire?

—Rien. C'est alors que j'ai décidé de prendre de vraies vacances.

L'été est la saison des vacances non seulement pour les étudiants mais aussi pour les ouvriers, les employés, les commerçants, les domestiques, les fonctionnaires, les femmes de ménage, en somme, pour toutes les classes de la société française. Les vacances prennent une importance de plus en plus grande. Il n'y a guère de Français qui se passe de vacances. Les ouvriers et les employés, entre autres, ont droit à un congé payé de trois semaines par an. Pendant que leur personnel est en vacances, les usines, les bureaux et les magasins cessent le travail et ferment, de sorte que pendant les mois de juillet et d'août il faut parfois chercher longtemps pour trouver un coiffeur, une blanchisseuse ou même un boulanger qui travaille. Le gouvernement a facilité les voyages en créant des billets de congés payés à prix réduits. Tant de personnes quittent Paris l'été qu'on dit: «Il n'y a personne à Paris après le 14 juillet. Il n'y a que des étrangers.» Évidemment, c'est exagéré, mais sans aucun doute, il y a beaucoup moins de Parisiens à Paris en été qu'en hiver.

[1] *having forgotten, having found.* The present participle of the auxiliary and the past participle of the main verb are used to form a compound participle.

Les Français passent leurs vacances en France et à l'étranger. Ils vont à la montagne, au bord de la mer ou à la campagne. Les voyages en Espagne, en Italie et en Suisse sont devenus très à la mode.

Les vacances en famille s'organisent différemment selon les classes sociales, les ressources et les goûts. Beaucoup de personnes qui habitent Paris ont des parents en province. Ces personnes ont souvent l'habitude de passer quelques jours ou quelques semaines chez leurs parents. Elles n'ont que le voyage à payer; aussi[1] les vacances ne leur reviennent-elles pas trop cher. De leur côté, les parents de province leur rendent parfois visite l'hiver quand ils viennent à Paris. Beaucoup de familles partent en voiture; on voit des voitures traînant des remorques de camping.

Les petits Français ont souvent l'occasion d'aller pendant quelques semaines au bord de la mer ou à la campagne même si leurs parents n'ont pas la possibilité de partir avec eux. Des organisations privées et même d'état s'occupent des enfants pendant leurs vacances; sans ces organisations, beaucoup d'entre eux ne connaîtraient jamais ces bons moments de plein air.

Les jeunes gens partent souvent en groupe à la mer ou à la montagne. Il y en a qui vont de ville en ville sur leur scooter ou leur moto. Le sac au dos, ils apprennent ainsi à connaître leur pays mieux que par aucun autre moyen. Certains d'entre eux passent la nuit dans des établissements réservés spécialement aux jeunes gens. Ces établissements s'appellent *les auberges de la jeunesse.* On y vit à très bon marché. Le mouvement *boy-scout* est aussi très répandu en France et permet à beaucoup de jeunes gens de passer des vacances profitables, puisqu'ils apprennent à se rendre utiles tout en faisant un séjour agréable.

Questions

1. Quelle est la saison des grandes vacances en Amérique? 2. Qui entend-on dans les couloirs des lycées en été? 3. Si vous alliez chercher un livre dans un lycée pendant les vacances d'été, qui verriez-vous? 4. Les Français se passent-ils facilement de vacances? 5. A combien de jours de vacances les ouvriers français ont-ils droit? 6. Pourquoi est-il difficile de trouver un coiffeur à Paris pendant le mois d'août? 7. Qui reste à Paris pendant l'été? 8. Où les Français passent-ils leurs vacances? 9. Comment les familles modestes peuvent-elles passer leurs vacances à la campagne? 10. Les Français ont-ils l'habitude de voyager à l'étranger? 11. Où les petits Français peuvent-ils souvent aller passer plusieurs

[1] Meaning of *aussi* in this position? (§ 20 E)

Les jeunes gens partent souvent en groupe à la mer ou à la montagne

ertains d'entre eux passent la nuit dans des éta-issements réservés spécialement aux jeunes gens

Une robe, un manteau ou un chapeau qui vient à Paris a un chic qui ne se trouve nulle part ailleur

Le Tour de France est la course la plus populaire que nous ayons

Cette salle, appelée la Galerie des Glaces, est célèbre dans l'histoire

Ces jardins à la française sont dessinés géométriquement

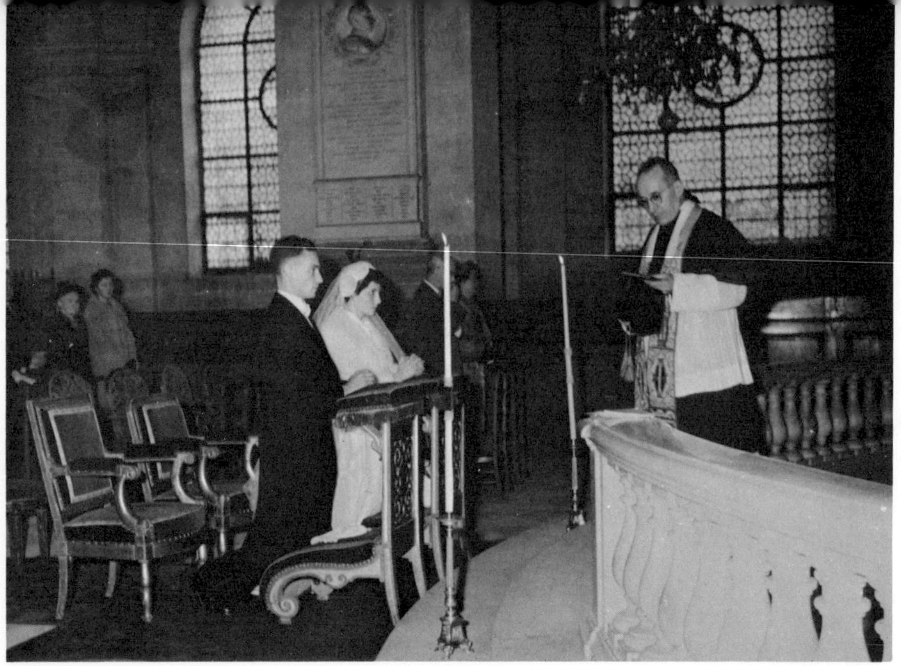

Généralement, le prêtre fait un sermon sur la beauté du mariage

Les enfants poussent des cris de joie en voyant ce spectacle et vont prendre leurs jouets dans le sapin

semaines en été? 12. Qui s'occupe des enfants pendant les vacances? 13. Qu'est-ce que *les auberges de la jeunesse?* 14. Pourquoi le mouvement *boy-scout* est-il utile?

Devoirs

® *A. Suivez les indications.*

1. Dites à Charles que vous n'avez rien oublié. 2. Dites à Gérard que vous n'avez vu personne sur la plage. 3. Dites à Madeleine que vous n'avez ni le temps ni la possibilité de partir cette année.

B. Donnez les adverbes qui correspondent aux adjectifs suivants.

1. vrai 2. négligent 3. relatif 4. particulier 5. agréable 6. récent 7. élégant 8. général 9. évident 10. suffisant

C. Introduisez les mots indiqués entre parenthèses dans les phrases suivantes. Exemple: (*never*) Nous parlons français en classe. Nous *ne* parlons *jamais* français en classe.

1. (*only*) Nous avons quinze jours de vacances. 2. (*scarcely*) Il y a assez de temps pour aller au Canada. 3. (*not at all*) Écrivez-moi[1] cet été. 4. (*never*) J'ai visité Québec. 5. (*no longer*) Il veut passer ses vacances à Montréal. 6. Combien de lettres avez-vous reçues? — (*None.*) 7. Quand irez-vous au Canada? — (*Never.*) 8. Assistez-vous aux cours de l'université? — (*Not any longer*) maintenant. 9. Qui est venu vous voir ce matin? — (*No one*)

D. Remplacez les expressions en italique par les mots indiqués entre parenthèses. Exemple: (*nothing*) Nous cherchons *quelque chose.* Nous *ne* cherchons *rien.*

1. (*no one*) *On* parle allemand au Canada. 2. (*no one*) Nous avons vu *quelqu'un* dans la rue. 3. (*no one*) J'ai donné mon livre à *quelqu'un.* 4. (*nothing*) Il y a *quelque chose* pour vous au courrier. 5. (*nothing*) Il a fait *quelque chose.*[2] 6. (*nothing*) Il y a *quelque chose* sur la table. 7. (*no*) J'ai *une* raison pour le faire. 8. (*no*) *Un* élève a sonné à la porte. 9. Qui est à la porte? — (*No one.*) 10. Qu'est-ce que vous avez? — (*Nothing.*)

[1] What happens to *-moi* in the negative imperative?
[2] What change in word order is necessary?

Conversation

1. Demandez à Monsieur E. s'il a trouvé quelqu'un dans la classe à cinq heures du soir. 2. Demandez à Monsieur F. ce qu'il a écrit au tableau avant l'examen. 3. Demandez à Monsieur G. quand il a passé l'été en France. 4. Demandez à Monsieur H. combien il a d'enfants.

Vocabulaire — pages 232–233

Grammaire

1. How are adverbs usually formed from adjectives? adverbs from adjectives in ***-ant*** and ***-ent?*** (§ 19 A, B)

2. List the negative words commonly used with ***ne.*** Give their English equivalents. (§ 22 E)

3. What can you say of the position of *ne* in the negative sentence? (§ 22 F 1) of ***guère, jamais, plus,*** and ***point?*** (§ 22 F 2) of ***personne*** and ***rien?*** (§ 22 F 3) of ***que?*** (§ 22 F 4) of ***aucun?*** (§ 22 F 5)

4. What can you say of negatives used in a sentence without a verb? (§ 22 G)

5. According to the outline in § 48 D, study the verbs ***boire*** (§ 95, no. 14), ***courir*** (§ 95, no. 17), and ***vivre*** (§ 95, no. 44).

Au clair de la lune

Au clair de la lune [1], Mon ami Pierrot,
Prête [2]-moi ta plume [3], Pour écrire un mot;
Ma chandelle [4] est morte, Je n'ai plus de feu;
Ouvre-moi ta porte, Pour l'amour de Dieu.

Au clair de la lune, Pierrot répondit:
Je n'ai pas de plume, Je suis dans mon lit [5].
Va chez la voisine, Je crois qu'elle y est;
Car dans sa cuisine [6], On bat [7] le briquet.

[1] *moonlight* [2] *lend* [3] *pen* [4] *candle* [5] *bed* [6] *kitchen* [7] *strike a light*

Huitième révision — Leçons 36 à 40

Première partie

A. Répondez en français par des phrases complètes aux questions suivantes.

1. Quel est le musée le plus célèbre de France? 2. Les œuvres de quels peintres trouve-t-on au Louvre? 3. De quel pays sont Raphaël et Michel-Ange? 4. Dans quelle partie de Paris est située Notre-Dame? 5. Quel est le style d'architecture de Notre-Dame? 6. Qu'est-ce qui entoure les portes de Notre-Dame? 7. Qu'est-ce que la Comédie-Française? 8. Qui est Racine? 9. Pourquoi est-il intéressant de se promener au foyer du théâtre pendant les entr'actes? 10. Qu'est-ce que Chamonix? 11. Quelle est la langue qu'on parle à Genève? 12. Où est Lausanne? 13. Pourquoi est-il difficile de trouver une blanchisseuse à Paris au mois d'août? 14. Où les Parisiens passent-ils leurs vacances? 15. Comment les jeunes gens vont-ils souvent de ville en ville pendant leurs vacances?

B. Expliquez en français par une phrase complète les noms suivants.

Carrousel
Chamonix
Cid
Comédie-Française
Corneille
Embarquement pour Cythère
François Ier
Genève
île de la Cité
Invalides
Léonard de Vinci
Lausanne
Louvre
Michel-Ange
Molière
mont Blanc
Notre-Dame
Opéra
Opéra-Comique
Palais de Justice
Racine
Raphaël
Théâtre National Populaire
Tuileries
Vénus de Milo
Victoire de Samothrace
Watteau

C. Rédigez une composition sur un des sujets suivants.

1. Le Louvre 2. L'île de la Cité 3. Le théâtre à Paris. 4. Les vacances en France

Deuxième partie

A. Remplacez les tirets par **il, elle, ils, elles** *ou* **ce.** *Ces phrases forment un récit. (Voir Grammaire § 36)*

1. Voilà Notre-Dame. —— est une cathédrale. 2. —— est située dans l'île de la Cité; —— est magnifique. 3. Connaissez-vous mon frère? —— est lui qui nous a dit de la voir. 4. —— est un auteur bien connu qui connaît l'architecture gothique.

B. Mettez au plus-que-parfait les verbes entre parenthèses. (*Voir Grammaire* §§ *64, 65*)

5. Ma mère (entendre) la bonne nouvelle quand je suis rentré. 6. Ce château (devenir) un musée national au début du siècle.

C. Mettez au conditionnel les verbes entre parenthèses. (*Voir Grammaire* §§ *54, 56*)

7. (vouloir)-vous parler à ma sœur? 8. Georges m'a dit qu'il (avoir) beaucoup à faire dès le 2 mai. 9. Je (être) très content de vous voir.

D. Remplacez les tirets par la forme convenable du pronom démonstratif. (*Voir Grammaire* §§ *33, 34*)

10. —— qui a écrit cette lettre doit l'envoyer. 11. Il ne veut pas faire ——. 12. Il y a trois restaurants dans la rue principale. Lequel préférez-vous? ——? Non, ——.

E. Remplacez les tirets par la préposition convenable. (*Voir Grammaire* §§ *42 A, B, C, D; 43*)

13. Cet été j'irai —— Hollande, —— Belgique, —— Danemark et ensuite —— Bordeaux. 14. L'année dernière je suis allé —— Mexique, —— Brésil et ensuite —— Japon et —— Chine. 15. Mon frère est revenu —— Canada et ma sœur —— France.

F. Remplacez les mots en italique par l'équivalent français des mots anglais indiqués entre parenthèses. Faites les changements nécessaires dans les phrases. (*Voir Grammaire* § *22 E, F*)

16. (*nothing*) J'ai écrit *quelque chose.* 17. (*no one*) Il a vu *quelqu'un.* 18. (*no one*) — Qui est là? — *Un homme.* 19. (*no longer*) Nous y allons *tous les jours.* 20. (*never*) Nous avons *toujours* parlé contre lui. 21. (*no*) Dans cette ville il y a *un* moyen de transport.

G. Remplacez par l'équivalent français les mots anglais indiqués entre parenthèses. (*Voir Grammaire* §§ *19, 38 E; 90 B; 93*)

22. Irving et Bryant sont deux auteurs américains bien connus. (*Which one*) est-ce que tu (*are to*) lire cette semaine? 23. (*Evidently* [1]) tu (*should*) travailler un peu plus pour réussir à tes examens. 24. Tu (*are hungry*); tu (*should*) aller à ce restaurant. 25. Je (*must*) travailler, mais j'(*am sleepy*).

[1] Use the adverbial form of *évident.*

Supplément aux Leçons 31 à 40

TRENTE ET UNIÈME LEÇON

Vocabulaire

absolument
admirer
animé
la Bastille
byzantin
caractéristique
certainement
contempler
curieux, curieuse
Eiffel
enchanter
l'impression *f.*
la Madeleine
merveilleux, merveilleuse
métallique
moderne
Montmartre
Montparnasse
l'Opéra *m.*
pardonner
parisien, parisienne
ressembler [a]
la richesse
la splendeur
la surprise
le temple
toucher

l'aspect *m.* *appearance*
aucun . . . ne (*adj.*) *no*
aucun . . . ne (*pron.*) *none*
aussitôt que *as soon as*
le carrefour *crossroad*
chacun *each one, each* (pron.)
*découvrir *discover;* découvert *discovered*
dès que *as soon as*
les économies *f.* *savings*
l'espace *m.* *space*
espérer *hope*
étonner *surprise, astonish*
étrange *strange*
le gratte-ciel *skyscraper*
grec, grecque *Greek*
lorsque *when*
la merveille *wonder, marvel*
non plus *neither, not . . . either*
notamment *especially, in particular*
ouvrier, ouvrière (*adj.*) *working man's*
*paraître *appear;* paru *appeared*
la place *public square*
suffisant *sufficient*
tant (de) *so much, so many*
la tour *tower*
tout (*pron.*) *everything;* tous (*pl.*) *all*
varié *varied*
la veille *day before, night before, eve*

à suivre *to be continued*
la boîte de nuit *night club*
l'Étoile *f.* *circular public square in Paris in the center of which is the Arc de Triomphe; avenues radiating from it give it the effect of a star*
faire une promenade *take a walk*
les grands boulevards *refers to the wide thoroughfares in the center of Paris*

* An asterisk (*) placed before a verb indicates that this verb is irregular. The forms that you will be required to know are listed after the vocabulary.

[a] The verb *ressembler* requires *à* before the noun it governs, e.g., *La Madeleine ressemble à un temple grec.*

Notre-Dame *Gothic cathedral located on the* île de la Cité *in Paris*
quand vous saurez combien Paris est magnifique *when you learn how magnificent Paris is*
que de merveilles! *how many wonders!*
le Sacré-Cœur *Church of the Sacred Heart, located in the Montmartre section of Paris*
la Tour Eiffel *Eiffel Tower*

Verbes

THE FUTURE

INFINITIVE + present of **avoir**

-er verbs	*-ir verbs*	*-re verbs*
je donner*ai*	je finir*ai*	je perdr*ai*
tu donner*as*	tu finir*as*	tu perdr*as*
il donner*a*	il finir*a*	il perdr*a*
nous donner*ons*	nous finir*ons*	nous perdr*ons*
vous donner*ez*	vous finir*ez*	vous perdr*ez*
ils donner*ont*	ils finir*ont*	ils perdr*ont*

The future of regular and irregular verbs may be found in the tables in § 95.

Learn the future forms of all common irregular verbs. These may be found in convenient groups in § 54 B.

IRREGULAR VERBS

découvrir, découvert; je découvrirai, j'ai découvert — *conjugated like* ouvrir (§ 95, no. 31)
paraître, paru; je paraîtrai, j'ai paru — *conjugated like* connaître (§ 95, no. 16)

Devoirs

A. Write the French equivalent of each of the following sentences.

1. You will pardon me when you know why I have not written to you. 2. As soon as you have enough time, you will come here to see Paris. 3. As soon as my friends arrive in France, they will see things which will seem very curious to them[1]. 4. You will not find any[2] skyscrapers[3] in Europe. 5. When you are in Paris, we shall go to a night club. 6. You will like the Latin Quarter as soon as you see it. 7. I shall not be able to leave[4] before six o'clock. 8. Will your sister be at home when I telephone her[1]? 9. We'll send you a letter as soon as we can.

[1] Indirect object pronoun. [2] What construction is used after *pas?* (§ 6 C)
[3] The plural of *le gratte-ciel* is *les gratte-ciel.* [4] Use a form of *partir.*

B. Say aloud rapidly the French equivalent of each of the following sentences.

1. You have not yet seen Paris; and I [1] either. 2. The streets of Paris do not resemble [2] our streets either. 3. You will not find many skyscrapers in France either. 4. As soon as I can, I'll go to Paris. 5. When I arrive in [3] Paris, I'll write you. 6. As soon as we arrive in [3] Paris, we'll go to the opera. 7. When we are in [3] Paris, we'll see streets which are very different from the American streets. 8. When you are in [3] Paris, you'll take a walk along the Seine.

[1] What sort of pronoun is necessary? (§ 27 B) [2] The verb *ressembler* requires *à*.
[3] *à*

TRENTE-DEUXIÈME LEÇON

Vocabulaire

l'adresse *f.*
automatiquement
le bouton
cordialement
le détail
distribuer
électrique
l'impatience *f.*
la personne
respecter

s'adresser *go and speak to, apply to, go and ask*
afficher *post*
appuyer *press down*
l'avion *m.* *airplane*
balayer *sweep*
bien *very*
ce qui, ce que *what, that which*
la clé [a] *key*
le, la concierge [b] *combination house porter and janitor peculiar to Paris apartment houses*
le couloir *hall, corridor*
le courrier *mail*
*craindre *fear;* craint *feared*
demeurer [c] *live*
le départ *departure*
l'entrée *f.* *entrance*
l'escalier *m.* *stairway*
la façon *manner, way, fashion*
l'immeuble *m.* *apartment house; building*
le locataire *tenant, renter*
la loge *small apartment occupied by the concierge*
nettoyer *clean*
le nom *name*
le nôtre *ours*

* An asterisk (*) placed before a verb indicates that this verb is irregular. The forms that you will be required to know are listed after the vocabulary.
[a] Also spelled *la clef.*
[b] Occasionally, the *concierge* of a Parisian apartment house is a man, but usually it is a woman. For this reason, the lesson is entitled *La concierge.*
[c] The verb *demeurer* is now infrequently used in the sense of *live* and has taken on a slightly archaic flavor. The student is advised to use *habiter* instead.

*ouvrir *open;* ouvert *opened*
la pièce *room*[a]
prier *ask, beg*
*recevoir *receive;* reçu *received*
le rez-de-chaussée *first floor, ground floor*
serrer *press*
la suite *continuation*

de cette façon *in this way*
d'ordinaire *ordinarily*
j'attends de vos nouvelles *I am waiting for news from you*
je vous en prie *I beg of you*
je vous serre la main *I shake your hand*
par avion *by air, by airmail*
par exemple *for example*
tous les deux *both*
tout ce qui[b] *everything that*

Verbes

VERBS IN *-ayer*	VERBS IN *-oyer*	VERBS IN *-uyer*
balayer	***nettoyer***	***appuyer***
	PRESENT	
je balaie	je nettoie	j'appuie
tu balaies	tu nettoies	tu appuies
il balaie	il nettoie	il appuie
nous balayons	nous nettoyons	nous appuyons
vous balayez	vous nettoyez	vous appuyez
ils balaient	ils nettoient	ils appuient
	FUTURE	
je balaierai	je nettoierai	j'appuierai
tu balaieras	tu nettoieras	tu appuieras
il balaiera	il nettoiera	il appuiera
nous balaierons	nous nettoierons	nous appuierons
vous balaierez	vous nettoierez	vous appuierez
ils balaieront	ils nettoieront	ils appuieront

craindre, craint	***ouvrir, ouvert***	***recevoir, reçu***
je crains	j'ouvre	je reçois
tu crains	tu ouvres	tu reçois
il craint	il ouvre	il reçoit
nous craignons	nous ouvrons	nous recevons
vous craignez	vous ouvrez	vous recevez
ils craignent	ils ouvrent	ils reçoivent

* An asterisk (*) placed before a verb indicates that this verb is irregular. The forms that you will be required to know are listed after the vocabulary.

[a] The term *la pièce* is used to indicate a room in a building in general. One says: *C'est une maison de cinq pièces.* The word *pièce* in other contexts indicates a stage play.

[b] For the French equivalent of *everything that,* see page 418, note 1.

je craindrai, *etc.*	j'ouvrirai, *etc.*	je recevrai, *etc.*
j'ai craint, *etc.*	j'ai ouvert, *etc.*	j'ai reçu, *etc.*

Devoirs

A. Write the French equivalent of each of the following sentences.

1. Write me a letter. Write it to me. Don't write it to me. 2. Tell that person [1] your name. Tell it to him. Don't tell it to him. 3. Do not show those exercises to the teacher. Do not show them to him. Show them to him. 4. Read us what you are writing. Read it to us. Don't read it to us. 5. Show her what is in your room. Show it to her. Don't show it to her. 6. Who cleans the halls and sweeps the stairs? 7. We'll clean our room, but we'll not sweep the stairs. 8. We opened the door and we received the mail. 9. He will receive the letter when he opens [2] the door.

[1] Place this indirect object after the direct object in French.
[2] Not the present tense in French.

B. Say aloud rapidly the French equivalent of each of the following sentences.

1. Write me a letter at once. 2. Send it to me by airmail. 3. Tell us what you are doing. 4. Don't tell him what you did. 5. Don't show him what you wrote. 6. I haven't time to write to everyone. 7. Answer [1] my letter at once. 8. Tell me what is on the desk.

[1] The verb *répondre* requires an *à* before its object.

TRENTE-TROISIÈME LEÇON

Vocabulaire

automatique
changer
le Châtelet
la destination
Marie Deschamps
*permettre, permis
la Place de l'Opéra
la station
le taxi
le transport
utiliser

*s'en aller *go away, leave*
le bout *end*
la circulation *traffic*
clairement *clearly*
la correspondance *transfer*
se déplacer *get around*
depuis *since; for*
dont *whose, of which*
se fermer *close*
gêner *impede, hinder*
heureusement *fortunately*
hier *yesterday*
le journal *newspaper*
le métro *subway*
le moyen *means*
*s'ouvrir *open;* ouvert *opened*

* An asterisk (*) placed before a verb indicates that this verb is irregular. The forms that you will be required to know are listed after the vocabulary.

le parcours *route, course*
le plan *map (of a city); plan*
le portillon *(little) door*
se précipiter *rush forward*
sans *without*
souterrain *underground*
suivant *following, next*
voûté *arched*

à nouveau *again*
arriver à destination *arrive at one's destination*
bien entendu *of course*
bon marché *cheap*
changer de train *change trains*
depuis quand *since when, how long*
du reste *besides*
il y a un mois que je suis ici *I have been here for a month*
voici (voilà) un mois que je suis ici *I have been here for a month*
vouloir dire[a] *mean*

Verbes

s'en aller, allé; je m'en irai, je m'en suis allé[b]—*conjugated like* aller. (§ 95, no. 11)
permettre, permis; je permettrai, j'ai permis—*conjugated like* mettre. (§ 95, no. 28)

Devoirs

A. Write the French equivalent of each of the following sentences.

1. I know a teacher whose pupils will send me stamps. 2. We have been reading our mail for an hour. 3. He went off the week when we were in Paris. 4. I have been here for an hour, but the train of which you were speaking has not yet arrived. 5. Yesterday I saw Louise, whose uncle is spending the winter at Nice. 6. He is speaking to the little boy whose mother we saw in the subway. 7. The travelers get[1] their tickets and rush toward the train. 8. The day that I arrived in Paris, I received the letter in which you asked me details concerning[2] French newspapers[3]. 9. How long[4] have you been in France?

[1] Use a form of *prendre.* [2] *sur* [3] Use a form of the definite article.
[4] Model this question after question 1 of the lesson.

B. Say aloud rapidly the French equivalent of each of the following sentences.

1. We have been waiting for[1] the train for an hour. 2. You have been here for ten minutes. 3. How long[2] have you been here? 4. I received

[1] Included in the verb. [2] Model this question after question 1 of the lesson.

[a] Je veux dire que . . . *I mean that . . .* Que veut dire cela? *What does that mean?* Que veut dire le mot **fromage**? *What does the word fromage mean?*
[b] However, the French say: *Je me suis en allé* in the compound past. See Grevisse, *Le bon usage,* § 669, Remarque 2.

your letter just at the moment when I was leaving for Paris. 5. The door closed[1] just at the moment when he arrived. 6. Fortunately we arrived at the station just at the moment when there were taxis. 7. The day that my friend left there were many taxis in the street. 8. What does that word mean[2]? 9. What does the word *métro* mean[2]? 10. The word *métro* means an underground train.

[1] Use the reflexive form of the verb. [2] This verb comes second in the question.

TRENTE-QUATRIÈME LEÇON

Vocabulaire

affectueux, affectueuse
le Brie
le Camembert
le dessert
le Gruyère
le menu
minéral
l'olive *f.*
payer
le porc
le pour-cent
le Roquefort
la salade
la sardine
le sentiment
la soupe
la tomate
le vinaigre

l'addition *f.* *bill, check*
apprécié *popular, well-liked*
avant *before;* avant de + *infinitive before* + present participle
le bifteck *steak*
la carte *menu*
la côtelette *chop*
davantage *more*
dur *hard*
l'eau *f.* *water*
frit *fried*
la glace *ice cream*
le haricot *bean*
le hors-d'œuvre *relish: radishes, tomato salad, sardines, hard-boiled eggs with mayonnaise, etc.*
l'huile *f.* *oil*
la laitue *lettuce*
léger, légère *light*
le lieu *place*
mélanger *mix*
l'œuf[a] *m.* *egg*
le pâté *pastry containing cold spiced meat*
la pâtisserie *pastry*
le plat *course (of a meal); dish (served during a meal)*
le poisson *fish*
le poivre *pepper*
la pomme de terre *potato*
le potage *soup*
le pourboire *tip (for services rendered)*
le radis *radish*
le saladier *salad dish*
le sel *salt*
tel, telle *such;* tel que *such as*
terminer *finish*
la terre *earth*
vert *green*

au lieu de *instead of*
commencer par *begin with*
la côtelette de porc *pork chop*
il est d'usage *it is customary*
se mettre à table *sit down at the table*

[a] The *f* is pronounced in *un œuf* (singular) but silent in *des œufs* (plural) [œ̃nœf, dezø].

l'œuf dur *hard-boiled egg*
le plat du jour *the main course*
les pommes de terre frites *French fried potatoes*
recevoir de vos bonnes nouvelles *receive good news from you*
la salade de laitue *lettuce salad*

Verbes

THE PRESENT PARTICIPLE

	infinitive	*1st person plural present*	*present participle*
-er verbs	donn*er*	nous donn*ons*	donn*ant*
most *-ir* verbs	fin*ir*	nous fin*issons*	fin*issant*
2d class *-ir* verbs	dorm*ir*	nous dorm*ons*	dorm*ant*
-re verbs	répond*re*	nous répond*ons*	répond*ant*

For all verbs, both regular and irregular, one may say that the present participle is formed by dropping the ending *-ons* from the *nous* form of the present indicative and adding *-ant.*

THREE EXCEPTIONS

infinitive	*present participle*
être	étant
avoir	ayant [a]
savoir	sachant

Devoirs

A. Write the French equivalent of each of the following sentences.

1. On arriving in front of a restaurant, we saw waiters who were serving the customers. 2. Before ordering the meal, we asked for [1] the menu. 3. After finishing the first course, we ordered a steak with French-fried potatoes. 4. Then we asked for [1] the bill and we paid it, leaving a tip for the waiter. 5. After leaving [2] the restaurant, we looked for [1] the post office. 6. Seeing that we were foreigners, the employee explained to us that one could send letters by [3] airmail. 7. Instead of buying stamps, we talked with the employee, asking [4] him questions about [5] the service. 8. Looking at [1] my watch, I asked my friend if he wanted to go to the movie. 9. Without waiting for [1] our friend, he said that he was willing to go there.

[1] Included in the verb. [2] Use a form of *sortir de.* [3] by airmail *par avion*
[4] Use a form of *poser une question à quelqu'un.* [5] *sur*

[a] Pronounced [ɛjɑ̃].

B. Say aloud rapidly the French equivalent of each of the following sentences.

1. I have many things to[1] tell you. 2. After looking[2], we found a restaurant. 3. I found a restaurant on leaving[3] the subway. 4. We sat[4] down at the table. 5. Before ordering, we asked for[5] a menu. 6. Instead of beginning[4] with the main[4] dish, we began[4] with a soup. 7. After finishing[6] eating, we asked for[5] the bill. 8. Instead of leaving[3] the restaurant at once, we spoke for[7] some minutes with the other customers.

[1] *à* [2] Use a form of *chercher.* [3] Use a form of *sortir de.*
[4] Consult the lesson vocabulary for this expression. [5] Included in the verb.
[6] Use a form of *finir de.* [7] *pendant*

TRENTE-CINQUIÈME LEÇON

Vocabulaire

l'arc *m.*
l'assemblée *f.*
l'avenue *f.*
Bourbon
les Champs-Élysées
classique
la Concorde
continuellement
l'édition *f.*
l'Égypte *f.*
la flamme
la fontaine
la forme
le général, les généraux
l'honneur *m.*
l'obélisque *m.*
Royal
la sorte
la statue
le triomphe
les Tuileries *f.*
la victoire

beau, bel, belle *beautiful*
la boîte *box (along the Seine used to display books and etchings)*
le bouquiniste *the one who tends these boxes*
brûler *burn*
descendre *go down*
ériger *erect*
l'étoile *star*
feuilleter *leaf through, peruse rapidly*
la foule *crowd*
la gravure *etching*
inconnu *unknown*
luxueux, luxueuse *luxurious*
nouveau, nouvel, nouvelle *new*
le palais *palace*
le prix *price*
le quai *dock, wharf*
rapporter *bring back*
renseigner *inform*
se retourner *turn around again*
le soldat *soldier*
sur *concerning; on*
le tombeau *tomb*
se tourner *turn around*
tuer *kill*
la valeur *value*
vieux, vieil, vieille *old*
la vitrine *show window*
vraiment *truly*

à pied *on foot*
au loin *in the distance*
l'Assemblée Nationale *the National Assembly (lower house of the French Parliament)*
le Palais Bourbon *the Bourbon Palace (building where the* Assemblée Nationale *meets)*

Verbes

IMPERATIVES

infinitive	***nous*** *imperative*	***vous*** *imperative*
donner	donnons	donnez
finir	finissons	finissez
dormir	dormons	dormez
vendre	vendons	vendez
se promener	promenons-nous	promenez-vous
	ne nous promenons pas	ne vous promenez pas
se tourner	tournons-nous	tournez-vous
	ne nous tournons pas	ne vous tournez pas

THE PRINCIPAL PARTS

infinitive	*present participle*	*past participle*	*present*
donner	donnant	donné	je donne
finir	finissant	fini	je finis
dormir	dormant	dormi	je dors
perdre	perdant	perdu	je perds

Study *parler* and *finir* according to the outline in § 48 C, D (pages 428–429). If you are not sure of the forms, consult the paradigms in § 95, nos. 1 and 2 on pages 482–483.

Devoirs

A. Write the French equivalent of each of the following sentences.

1. Near the old quarter there is a beautiful garden, a new building, and some[1] old houses. 2. Let‿us‿ask this old man[2] the price of those new books. 3. Look‿at those old streets. 4. Let‿us‿burn this old letter. 5. Get‿up. No, don't‿get‿up. 6. Let‿us‿walk[3] along[4] this new avenue. Let‿us‿not‿walk along[4] that old wharf. 7. Stop[5] in‿front‿of those beautiful buildings. 8. Let‿us‿visit those old ruins and that old castle. 9. Let‿us‿ask the new prices of those editions.

[1] How is this construction expressed? (§ 6 A) [2] Supply *à* before this expression. [3] Use a form of *se promener.* [4] *le long de* [5] Use a form of *s'arrêter.*

B. Say aloud rapidly the French equivalent of each of the following sentences.

1. Let's go to Paris. 2. Let's walk along the Seine. 3. Let's walk along the boulevard. 4. Turn to the right. 5. Turn to the left. 6. I turned to the right. 7. I saw a beautiful garden with some beautiful flowers. 8. It is difficult to cross the street on foot.

THÈME

Leçons 31 à 35

Write the French equivalent of each of the following sentences.

1. When I am in[1] Paris, I'll walk along the Seine. 2. As soon as we see the wide avenues, we'll look for[2] a large café. 3. Show the letter to them, but don't give it to them. 4. Don't write me the news; tell it to me. 5. They have been in the station for an hour. 6. On leaving the station, they began to[1] look for[2] a restaurant. 7. After finishing their meal, they asked for[2] the bill. 8. Get up early, and then let's visit the old quarters of this beautiful city.

[1] *à* [2] Included in the verb.

TRENTE-SIXIÈME LEÇON

Vocabulaire

antique
l'attention *f.*
Carrousel
l'Empire *m.*
encourager
François Ier
la galerie
hollandais
inspirer
Léonard de Vinci
Louis XIII
Louis XV
Louis XVI
Michel-Ange[a]
l'objet *m.*
planter
le portrait
Raphaël
la résidence
royal, royaux
Samothrace
Vénus de Milo
Watteau

anglais *English*
le Directoire *Directory*
exprimer *express*
la fête *festivity*
flamand *Flemish*
le maître *master*
l'œuvre *f.* *work*
*parcourir *go through;* parcouru *went through*
*retenir *hold;* retenu *held*
la suite *series*

l'Arc de Triomphe du Carrousel *triumphal arch located at one end of the Tuileries Gardens just before the Louvre*
d'autant plus . . . que *so much the more . . . since*
d'un côté *on one side*
depuis . . . jusqu'à *from . . . to*
l'Embarquement pour Cythère *the Embarkation for Cytherea, a well-known painting of Watteau*

* An asterisk (*) placed before a verb indicates that this verb is irregular. The forms that you will be required to know are listed after the vocabulary.
[a] The *-ch-* is pronounced like *k* [mikɛlɑ̃ʒ].

retenir l'attention *attract attention*
la Vénus de Milo *famous ancient statue now in the Louvre*
la Victoire de Samothrace *the Winged Victory, a famous ancient statue now in the Louvre*

Verbes

parcourir, parcourant, parcouru, je parcours—*conjugated like* courir (§ 95, no. 17)
retenir, retenant, retenu, je retiens—*conjugated like* tenir (§ 95, no. 40)

Devoirs

A. Write the French equivalent of each of the following sentences.

1. There is Louis. 2. He is near the door. 3. He is a good pupil. 4. He is very young. 5. He is a Frenchman. 6. Who is with you? 7. It is Susan. 8. She is Mr. Dupont's daughter. 9. She is with Marie. 10. Where are Charles and Maurice? 11. They are in the library. 12. They are our friends. 13. They are Americans. 14. It is they who are going to Paris this summer.

B. Say aloud rapidly the French equivalent of each of the following sentences.

1. Have you seen the Louvre? It is a museum. 2. Do you know Charles? He is a friend of my brother. 3. Who is Louise? She is Charles' sister. 4. She is very pretty. 5. Did you meet Jack and Roger? 6. They are friends of the family. 7. They are very young. 8. Who is there? It is I. 9. Where is Robert? It is he who must accompany us.

TRENTE-SEPTIÈME LEÇON

Vocabulaire

l'apparence *f.*
César
coloré
décider de
délicat
diffuser
le dôme
dominer
l'encens *m.*
fatigué
la Gaule
grandiose
les Invalides *m.*
la justice
l'odeur *f.*
les Parisii *m.*
pénétrer
Saint-Louis
la scène
sombre
le sommet
symétrique
la tribu

au-dessus *above*
biblique *biblical*
blanc, blanche *white*
ça *that*
ceci *this*
la colonne *column*

*croire *believe;* cru *believed*
*détruire *destroy;* détruit *destroyed*
s'élever *rise*
s'établir *establish*
s'étendre *expand; stretch out; spread*
évoquer *evoke, call up (from memory), conjure up*
la façade *front, façade*
féodal *feudal*
la hauteur *height*
le jour *day; daylight*
longuement *for a long time*
s'orienter *see where one is, ascertain one's position*
la peine *difficulty, trouble*
le pont *bridge*
puissant *powerful*
rappeler *remind*
rebâtir *rebuild, reconstruct*
le règne *reign*
relier *link*
se reposer *rest*
la rosace *rose window*
la route *road*
séjourner *sojourn, make a stay, spend some time*
les vitraux (*pl. of* le vitrail) *stained glass windows*

en route *on the way*
l'histoire sainte *f. Bible stories, Bible history*
il me faut + *infinitive*[a] *I have to, I must*
l'île de la Cité *island in the Seine on which Notre-Dame cathedral stands*
le Palais de Justice *the courthouse on the* île de la Cité
qu'est-ce que c'est que ça? *what's that?*
se rendre compte *realize*

Verbes

THE PLUPERFECT

ALL VERBS conjugated with avoir	VERBS OF MOTION conjugated with être	REFLEXIVE VERBS conjugated with être
j'avais parlé	j'étais entré(e)	je m'étais lavé(e)
tu avais parlé	tu étais entré(e)	tu t'étais lavé(e)
il avait parlé	il était entré	il s'était lavé
elle avait parlé	elle était entrée	elle s'était lavée
nous avions parlé	nous étions entré(e)s	nous nous étions lavé(e)s
vous aviez parlé	vous étiez entré(e)(s)	vous vous étiez lavé(e)(s)
ils avaient parlé	ils étaient entrés	ils s'étaient lavés
elles avaient parlé	elles étaient entrées	elles s'étaient lavées

* An asterisk (*) placed before a verb indicates that this verb is irregular. From now on, you will be expected to look up and learn the principal parts of new irregular verbs in § 95. If a given irregular verb is not conjugated in § 95, there will be a reference in the French-English vocabulary at the end of the book to a verb which is conjugated in the same way. In Lesson 37, for instance, you will find *croire* in § 95 (no. 19). The verb *détruire* is conjugated like the verb *conduire,* which you will find in § 95 (no. 15).

[a] In this construction, *il faut* is constant; the pronoun changes: e.g., il me faut *I have to;* il te faut *you have to;* il lui faut *he (she) has to;* il nous faut *we*

Devoirs

A. Write the French equivalent of each of the following sentences.

1. Read this, don't read that. 2. Don't do that. 3. Had the soldiers already destroyed the bridge? 4. We had come to the middle of the river when we noticed the cathedral. 5. She had already washed herself when you telephoned. 6. They had gone to the restaurant and had rested before crossing the bridge. 7. He believed that they had‿decided‿to[1] destroy the road. 8. When I am[2] tired, I shall rest. 9. Do you believe that? I believe it.

[1] Use a form of *décider de* [2] What tense is used?

B. Say aloud rapidly the French equivalent of each of the following sentences.

1. We realized that it was late. 2. I realized that my friend had already left. 3. We had decided to[1] rest. 4. I had studied the map of the city, and I believed[2] that the church was on[3] an island. 5. What's that? 6. This? No, that. 7. It is necessary to leave. 8. It was necessary to go to Paris. 9. On the way, we saw a bridge and a large church.

[1] *de* [2] The imperfect is used to indicate mental states in the past. [3] *dans*

TRENTE-HUITIÈME LEÇON

Vocabulaire

l'acteur *m.*
le bar[a]
la beauté
le buste
le *Cid*
la comédie
la Comédie-Française
le contentement
Corneille
le critique
dramatique
la force
le Français
impressionner
la mode
Molière
l'opéra *m.*
l'Opéra *m.*
l'Opéra-Comique *m.*
Racine
remarquable
Shakespeare[b]
le spectateur
le succès
le Théâtre de France
le Théâtre National Populaire
tragique
troubler

---

have to; il vous faut *you have to;* il leur faut *they have to.* Especially in the present tense, the construction seems to be going out of use. Students should learn it for reading purposes only.

[a] The French word *bar,* borrowed from English, has somewhat but not exactly the same connotation. In the French *bar,* the drinks are not exclusively alcoholic, and one can get a snack there. The word *bar,* although not yet admitted into the dictionary, is very common in France.

[b] Pronounced [ʃɛkspir] in French.

l'allégresse *f.* *joy*
*appartenir *belong;* appartenu *belonged*
après-demain *the day after tomorrow*
auquel (à + lequel) *to which*
l'auteur *m.* *author*
*conduire *lead;* conduit *led*
couper *cut*
dès[a] *from . . . on, as early as*
devrais (*conditional of* devoir) *should, ought to*
l'entr'acte *m.* *intermission*
l'événement[b] *m.* *event*
le foyer *lobby*
heureux, heureuse *happy*
lequel, laquelle *which one, which*
la longueur *length*

à l'avance *in advance*
à la mode *in vogue, in style*
le lendemain soir *the next evening*
prendre quelque chose *have something* (*in an eating place*)

le mal *difficulty, trouble; evil*
mêler *mix*
net, nette *clear*
l'ouvreuse *f.* *usher* (*female*)
parfait *perfect*
la place *seat* (*in a theater*)
la pureté *pureness*
la représentation *performance*
la soirée *evening*
le souci *care*
le spectacle *performance; play*
subventionner *support, subsidize*
sûr *sure*
tandis que[c] *while, whereas*
la tristesse *sorrow, sadness*
*valoir *be worth;* valu *was worth*
le vers *line* (*of poetry*)
voisin (*adj.*) *neighboring*

retenir une place *reserve a seat*
tous les trois *all three*
valoir mieux *be better;* il vaut mieux *it is better;* il vaudrait mieux *it would be better*

Verbes

THE CONDITIONAL

INFINITIVE + IMPERFECT ENDINGS

-er verbs	*-ir verbs*	*-re verbs*
je donner*ais*	je punir*ais*	je répondr*ais*
tu donner*ais*	tu punir*ais*	tu répondr*ais*
il donner*ait*	il punir*ait*	il répondr*ait*
nous donner*ions*	nous punir*ions*	nous répondr*ions*
vous donner*iez*	vous punir*iez*	vous répondr*iez*
ils donner*aient*	ils punir*aient*	ils répondr*aient*

* An asterisk (*) placed before a verb indicates that this verb is irregular.

[a] It is rather difficult to express the immediacy of *dès* in English. The expression *dès maintenant,* for instance, means *from now on,* with the implication of *immediately.*

[b] Pronounced [evɛnmɑ̃].

[c] The English word *while* is expressed by *pendant que* when there is an idea of time, but by *tandis que* when there is an idea of contrast. One might say that *tandis que* means *while on the other hand.* It is pronounced both [tɑ̃dikə] and [tɑ̃diskə].

IRREGULAR FUTURES AND CONDITIONALS

Futures and conditionals of regular verbs may be found in § 95, col. 5 and 6, of irregular verbs in § 95, col. 6 and 7.

Study the forms of the common verbs irregular in the future and conditional as outlined in § 54 B.

Devoirs

A. Write the French equivalent of each of the following sentences.

1. Would you like[1] to go to the post office with me? 2. He said that he would be in France in April. 3. I should like[1] to[2] speak French in France. 4. He said that you ought to read the works of the best French writers. 5. It would be better to see a performance of the *Cid*. 6. Where are those books? He said that I would know which one belonged to him. 7. There are many theaters in this city. You are to tell me which ones you prefer. 8. He should see that play. 9. We must go to the opera.

[1] Use a form of *vouloir*. [2] Omit in translation.

B. Say aloud rapidly the French equivalent of each of the following sentences.

1. You should go to the theater. 2. Should I show the letter to my father? 3. It would be better to go to the movies. 4. I should like to see that play. 5. Would you like to go to the movies with me? 6. Which of the theaters do you prefer? 7. I must[1] leave at once. 8. We are[1] to spend the evening[2] at the theater.

[1] Use a form of *devoir*. [2] *soirée*

TRENTE-NEUVIÈME LEÇON

Vocabulaire

Antoine	l'excursion *f.*	Morel
l'auto *f.*	l'intention *f.*	le Portugal
la Californie	l'Irlande *f.*	possible
Chamonix	le Japon	le projet
la Chine	Lausanne	Québec
Chou-Chou	Londres	simplement
le Danemark	le mont Blanc	Suzanne
Denise		tranquille[a]

[a] Pronounced [trãkil].

les affaires *f. pl.* *business*
aussi . . .[a] *so, therefore*
ajouter *add*
se baigner *bathe, go bathing*
bavard *talkative*
la bête *beast*
le chien *dog*
l'envie *f.* *desire*
s'endormir (2) *go to sleep*
la faim *hunger*
la honte *shame*
là-haut *up there*
la raison *reason*
le séjour *stay, sojourn*
la soif *thirst*
le sommeil *sleep*
la Suède *Sweden*
la tasse *cup*
tellement *so*
le tort *wrong*
la trentaine *about thirty*
tu *you*

A (2) after an *-ir* verb indicates that it belongs to the second class of *-ir* verbs. (§ 49 C)

à jeudi *until Thursday*
à propos de *speaking of*
au revoir *goodbye*
cette nuit *last night*
du moins *at least*
finir par + *infinitive* *finally* + verb[b]
huit jours *a week*
il y a[c] une semaine *a week ago*
tous les jours *every day*
valoir la peine *be worth the trouble*
venir de + *infinitive* *have just* + verb[d]
le voyage d'affaires *business trip*

PERSONAL EXPRESSIONS WITH *avoir*[e]

j'ai l'air de *I seem to*
j'ai beau parler *I speak in vain*[f]
j'ai chaud *I am warm*
j'ai envie de *I feel like*
j'ai faim *I am hungry*
j'ai froid *I am cold*
j'ai honte *I am ashamed*
j'ai l'intention de *I intend to*
j'ai mal *I hurt*
j'ai mal à la tête *I have a headache*
j'ai raison *I am right*
j'ai soif *I am thirsty*
j'ai sommeil *I am sleepy*
j'ai tort *I am wrong*

Verbes

Up to this lesson, the *tu*-forms of the verb have not been used in the text. In this lesson you meet these forms. You should learn to recognize the tenses in which these forms are frequently used, but you should avoid using the *tu*-form yourself at this stage of learning French.

[a] When *aussi* is placed at the beginning of an independent clause, it means *so* or *therefore;* elsewhere, it means *also.*
[b] Roger a fini par sortir. *Roger finally went out.*
[c] When *il y a* is followed by a time expression, it usually means *ago.*
[d] Roger vient de sortir. *Roger has just gone out.*
Roger venait de sortir. *Roger had just gone out.*
[e] Any person or tense may be used. The *je* form of the present is given here to illustrate the use of the pronoun with the expression.
[f] Denise a beau parler à son mari. *Denise speaks in vain to her husband.*

	-er *verb*	-ir *verb*	-ir (2d)	-re *verb*	*intransitive verb of motion*	*reflexive verb*
PRESENT	tu demandes	punis	dors	réponds	entres	te tournes
IMPERFECT	tu demandais	punissais	dormais	répondais	entrais	te tournais
FUTURE	tu demanderas	puniras	dormiras	répondras	entreras	te tourneras
CONDITIONAL	tu demanderais	punirais	dormirais	répondrais	entrerais	te tournerais
COMPOUND PAST	tu as demandé	as puni	as dormi	as répondu	es entré(e)	t'es tourné(e)
FAMILIAR IMPERATIVE	demande	punis	dors	réponds	entre	tourne-toi

Devoirs

A. Write the French equivalent of each of the following sentences.

1. Last summer I went to England, to France, to Germany, to Denmark, and to Sweden. 2. Do you feel like seeing my friends in Paris? 3. We intend to leave[1] France on[2] January 30,[3] and we shall go to London. 4. I never have a headache, but I am often sleepy in summer. 5. Did you leave[1] China or Japan in 1941? 6. He arrived in Canada, went to the United States, and now he lives in St. Louis. 7. You are right, we were hot last night[4]. 8. She speaks in vain to her husband; he always takes‿a‿trip[5] to Portugal in winter. 9. You are wrong; he did not go from Italy to Germany.

[1] Use a form of *partir de.* [2] Omit in translation.
[3] See § 18 E for French method of writing dates. [4] last night *cette nuit*
[5] Use a form of *faire un voyage.*

B. Say aloud rapidly the French equivalent of each of the following sentences.

1. I feel like going to France. 2. I have just returned[1] from France. 3. My friend is asleep; he has just finished his work. 4. My husband went to Portugal a week ago. 5. A year ago he returned from Canada. 6. Every day I have a headache. 7. Are you hungry? 8. Goodbye. 9. Until Sunday.

[1] Use a form of *revenir.*

QUARANTIÈME LEÇON

Vocabulaire

agréable
le boy-scout
le camping
cesser
désert
différemment
exagérer
l'instant *m.*
le mouvement
négligemment
négligent
s'organiser
le personnel
se présenter
profitable
réserver
la ressource
le scooter
le silence
social
la société
spécialement
la visite

la blanchisseuse *washwoman, laundress*
le bord *shore*
le boulanger *baker*
le bruit *noise*
le bureau *office*
le coiffeur *barber*
le commerçant *merchant*
deviner *guess*
le, la domestique *servant*
le dos *back*
le doute *doubt*
l'employé *clerk; employee*
le fonctionnaire *government employee, civil service worker, civil servant*
fréquenter *go to regularly; frequent*
le goût *taste*
guère (ne) *scarcely*

le ménage *household, family*
oublier *forget*
ouvert (*pp of* ouvrir) *open*
l'ouvrier *m. working man*
le parent *relative; parent*
se passer de *do without, get along without*
personne (ne) *no one*
porter *carry*
primaire *primary*
*réduire *reduce;* réduit *reduced*
la remorque *trailer*
répandu *common*
rien (ne) *nothing*
le sac *knapsack*
traîner *pull; drag*
l'usine *f. factory*
se vider *empty*
*vivre *live;* vécu *lived*
vrai *true*

à bon marché *cheap*
à prix réduit *at a reduction*
le congé payé *vacation with pay*
de leur côté *on their part*
de plus en plus grand *greater and greater*
de sorte que *so that*
de ville en ville *from city to city*
en province *in the provinces, outside of Paris*
en somme *in short*

entre autres *among others*
la femme de ménage *maid, cleaning woman*
peu à peu *little by little*
plein air *open air*
rendre visite à quelqu'un *visit someone*
revenir cher *be expensive*
la salle de conférence *lecture room*

Devoirs

A. Write the French equivalent of each of the following sentences.

1. No one is carrying his knapsack. 2. Evidently she never learned that language. 3. He has written nothing. 4. At[1] present, we have only one office. 5. They saw no one on[2] the street. 6. We no longer forget that. 7. Neither the clerks nor the working men remain in Paris during the vacation. 8. Who made that noise? No one. 9. No Frenchman does without vacations.

[1] Use the adverbial form of *actuel.* [2] *dans*

* An asterisk (*) placed before a verb indicates that this verb is irregular.

B. Say aloud rapidly the French equivalent of each of the following sentences.

1. There is no one in the room. 2. We found no one at[1] the barber's. 3. I learned nothing in the course. 4. What did you learn in the course? Nothing. 5. I never forgot that. 6. We have only one servant. 7. We no longer have any[2] servant. 8. Guess who is at the door. No one.

[1] *chez* [2] *de*

Thème

Leçons 36 à 40

Write the French equivalent of each of the following sentences.

1. Do you see that building? It is a famous museum. 2. Who is Corneille? He is a French writer of the seventeenth century. 3. I had gone to the theater and we had given a tip to the usher. 4. Would you like to spend your vacation in Rome? 5. I should attend a performance at the Opéra-Comique. 6. Our relatives went to Germany and to Denmark last summer. 7. My husband was hungry when he arrived from England. 8. No one goes to Canada in winter. 9. We found nothing on the desk.

La Marseillaise

Allons, enfants de la patrie[1]
Le jour de gloire[2] est arrivé;
Contre nous de la tyrannie[3]
L'étendard[4] sanglant[5] est levé[6],
Entendez-vous dans ces campagnes
Mugir[7] ces féroces soldats?
Ils viennent jusque dans nos bras
Égorger[8] nos fils, nos compagnes[9]!

Aux armes, citoyens! formez vos bataillons[10]!
Marchons, marchons!
Qu'un sang impur abreuve[11] nos sillons[12].

[1] *fatherland* [2] *glory* [3] *tyranny* [4] *standard* [5] *bloody* [6] *raised*
[7] *bellow* [8] *slaughter* [9] *wives* [10] *battalion* [11] *water* [12] *fields, furrows*

La France et l'Europe de 1871 à 1939

Après la guerre franco-allemande de 1870, à part quelques conflits locaux, il y eut dans toute l'Europe une période de plus de quarante ans de paix. En France on fonda la Troisième République et, en 1875, on établit la constitution qui resta la base du gouvernement français jusqu'à la défaite de 1940.

Les premières années du vingtième siècle furent marquées par une grande rivalité entre les principales nations d'Europe, qui, toutes, voulaient dominer les petits pays européens et les riches territoires africains. Chacune des grandes puissances cherchait à obtenir la suprématie économique et politique. Toutes les nations, mais surtout l'Allemagne, se préparaient à la guerre. Ces rivalités et ces préparatifs rendaient un conflit presque inévitable. Pourtant, tout semblait calme en 1914 lorsqu'un jeune Serbe assassina l'archiduc-héritier d'Autriche-Hongrie. Voulant profiter de cet incident pour dominer enfin le sud-est de l'Europe, l'Autriche-Hongrie déclara la guerre à la Serbie. En peu de temps, les nations, les unes après les autres, furent entraînées dans le conflit. Aussi, au bout de dix jours, l'Autriche-Hongrie et l'Allemagne se trouvèrent-elles en état de guerre avec la Russie, la France et l'Angleterre, qu'on appela les «Alliés».

Pour gagner la guerre le plus vite possible, l'Allemagne décida d'attaquer la France par le nord. Les armées allemandes, violant le traité qui garantissait la neutralité de la Belgique, traversèrent rapidement ce petit pays, pénétrèrent en France, et, dès les premières semaines de la guerre, arrivèrent tout près de Paris. Heureusement les Français réussirent à les arrêter sur la Marne et un front de plus de mille kilomètres s'établit de la mer du Nord à l'Alsace-Lorraine.

Ce fut pendant quatre ans une lutte épuisante qui coûta la vie à des millions d'hommes et détruisit une grande partie du nord et du nord-est de la France. Mais finalement, avec l'aide des États-Unis d'Amérique, qui entrèrent en guerre en 1917, les Alliés remportèrent la victoire. Par le traité de Versailles, qui mit fin à la guerre de 14, l'Allemagne perdit de nombreux territoires en Europe ainsi que toutes ses colonies.

La défaite fut durement ressentie par l'Allemagne. Le traité de Versailles lui avait imposé d'énormes réparations; l'Allemagne cherchait un moyen de ne pas les payer. Très vite, elle commença a réorganiser son industrie et à reconstituer son commerce. Mais quand arriva la crise financière mondiale de 1929, il y eut en Allemagne beaucoup de chômage. Des milliers de personnes restaient sans travail, sans moyen d'existence et le pays, mécontent, s'agitait. En 1933, les nationaux-socialistes profitèrent de ces circonstances pour s'emparer du pouvoir et leur chef, Hitler, imposa sa dictature. Dès lors, les Allemands n'eurent plus que deux buts: dénoncer le traité de Versailles et devenir les maîtres de l'Europe.

Pendant ce temps, la France subissait, elle aussi, une crise économique qui amena en 1936 un gouvernement de «front populaire». Ce fut une réelle victoire de la classe ouvrière. Ce gouvernement entreprit beaucoup de réformes sociales et créa notamment la semaine de quarante heures et les congés payés. Mais cette période fut marquée par des grèves et des difficultés politiques, et le gouvernement négligea la défense nationale et en particulier l'aviation.

L'Allemagne, qui avait annexé en 1937 l'Autriche et une partie de la Tchécoslovaquie, s'appliquait à devenir la première puissance aérienne du monde. Pendant tout l'été de 1939, elle menaça de s'emparer de la ville libre de Dantzig, port de première importance pour la Pologne. La France et l'Angleterre comprirent enfin l'esprit de domination et les ambitions de conquête d'Hitler. Elles virent qu'il devenait dangereux de laisser l'Allemagne s'étendre davantage et conclurent avec la Pologne un traité d'assistance mutuelle.

Questions

1. Après la guerre franco-allemande, combien d'années de paix a-t-on eues en Europe? 2. Quelles sont les dates de la Troisième République? 3. Par quoi les premières années du vingtième siècle ont-elles été marquées? 4. Que voulait chaque grande nation européenne pendant les premières années du vingtième siècle? 5. Qui a assassiné l'archiduc héritier d'Autriche-Hongrie? 6. Pourquoi l'Allemagne a-t-elle décidé de violer la neutralité de la Belgique? 7. Où les Français ont-ils arrêté les Allemands? 8. Quelles sont les parties de la France qui ont été détruites pendant la guerre de 14? 9. Qui a gagné la guerre de 14? 10. Quel est le traité qui a mis fin à cette guerre? 11. Quels territoires l'Allemagne a-t-elle perdus par le traité de Versailles? 12. Pourquoi l'Allemagne cherchait-elle un moyen de ne pas payer les réparations imposées par le traité de Versailles? 13. Pourquoi y avait-il de l'agitation en Allemagne

pendant la crise financière qui avait commencé en 1929? 14. Quel parti s'est emparé du pouvoir en Allemagne en 1933? 15. Quel a été le but des Allemands dès 1933? 16. Quel gouvernement la crise économique a-t-elle amené en France en 1936? 17. Quels sont les pays que l'Allemagne a annexés? 18. Quelle ville l'Allemagne a-t-elle menacé de prendre pendant l'été de 1939? 19. Pourquoi la France et l'Angleterre ont-elles conclu un traité d'assistance mutuelle avec la Pologne?

Devoirs

® *A. Suivez les indications.*

1. Dites à Francine que vous voulez lire l'histoire de la guerre de 14. 2. Dites à Michel que vous commencez à comprendre le français. 3. Dites à Guy que vous avez refusé d'accompagner votre petit frère au cinéma.

® *B. Les verbes des phrases suivantes sont au passé simple. Mettez ces verbes au passé composé. Tous ces verbes sont réguliers.*

1. Cette dame arriva à Paris vers neuf heures. 2. Nous nous décidâmes à partir le lendemain. 3. Les Allemands traversèrent la Belgique pour entrer en France. 4. Jean finit son travail avant de sortir. 5. Les professeurs punirent les élèves. 6. Nous entendîmes la cloche. 7. Cette dame répondit à la lettre. 8. Les soldats se dirigèrent vers le centre de la ville. 9. Le garçon servit les clients. 10. L'armée s'établit dans le pays.

® *C. Les verbes des phrases suivantes sont au passé simple. Mettez-les au passé composé. Tous ces verbes sont irréguliers au passé simple.*

1. Les premières années du vingtième siècle furent marquées par une grande rivalité entre les principales nations d'Europe. 2. Nous bûmes pendant toute la nuit. 3. Ils conduisirent les soldats devant le général. 4. Elle crut entendre des voix. 5. Le professeur dut punir les mauvais élèves. 6. Elles mirent les livres sur le bureau. 7. L'étudiant ouvrit la porte. 8. Il suivit son chef. 9. Le Président vint vers neuf heures. 10. Je voulus voir le Président. 11. Ce poète vécut au seizième siècle.

D. Remplacez les tirets par une préposition s'il[1] y a lieu.

1. Nous avons cherché —— voir notre camarade. 2. Mais nous n'avons pas pu —— le trouver. 3. J'ai dû —— rentrer vers neuf heures. 4. Avez-vous réussi —— le trouver? 5. Je voudrais —— voyager en

[1] *if one is necessary*

France. 6. Nous avons été obligés —— partir tout de suite. 7. Je me suis décidé —— faire le voyage. 8. N'avez-vous pas oublié —— fermer la porte? 9. J'ai refusé —— sortir. 10. Les enfants ont appris —— parler français. 11. Je regrette —— vous dire cela. 12. Le professeur nous a permis —— traverser la forêt.

Conversation

1. Demandez à l'étudiant qui est à côté de vous s'il apprend à parler français. 2. Demandez à l'étudiant qui est derrière vous s'il a réussi à trouver son camarade. 3. Demandez à l'étudiant qui est devant vous s'il veut aller au cinéma avec vous ce soir. 4. Demandez à l'étudiant qui est près de la fenêtre s'il a oublié d'écrire ses devoirs.

Vocabulaire — pages 282–283

Grammaire

1. How is the *passé simple* of regular verbs in *-er, -ir, -re,* and *-oir* formed? (§ 58 A) What orthographical changes would be necessary in the *passé simple* of verbs in *-cer* and *-ger?* (§ 89 A, B)

2. What does the *passé simple* of many irregular verbs resemble? (§ 58 B 1)

3. Study the *passé simple* of the verbs ***parler, finir, perdre, recevoir, effacer, manger, avoir,*** and ***être.*** (Page 283)

4. Learn to recognize the *passé simple* of the common irregular verbs. (§ 58 B 1, 2)

5. The *passé simple* constitutes the fifth of the principal parts of the French verb. (§ 48 C, D) To find the *passé simple* of irregular verbs, consult the fourth column of the tables in § 95.

6. The *passé simple* is not used in conversation. It is a literary tense. When and how is it used? (§ 59 A, B)

7. In English, we say *I can go, I want* ***to*** *go,* and *I insist* ***on*** *going,* without any apparent reason. Likewise in French, certain verbs are followed by an infinitive without any intervening preposition, others require ***de*** before the infinitive, others ***à,*** and certain others different prepositions. In order to speak French currently, it is necessary to learn these constructions. In your reading lesson, find examples of verbs followed by infinitives with or without an intervening preposition. Then study § 44 A, B, C, D of the ***Grammaire.***

Madame Bonneville achète un flacon de parfum

Les parfums français, célèbres dans le monde entier, s'achètent partout. Ils sont faits avec des extraits de fleurs qui ont été cultivées par des spécialistes dans d'immenses terrains, notamment sur la Côte d'Azur, et qui ont été soumises, dans des laboratoires et des usines, à de multiples manipulations. D'énormes quantités de fleurs sont ainsi utilisées pour obtenir un poids infime d'extrait au moyen duquel le parfum est réalisé. Certains extraits sont importés des pays exotiques. Comme des parfums faits seulement d'extraits de fleurs coûteraient très cher, on y mélange aussi d'autres substances odorantes d'origine chimique, organique et végétale. Associées et combinées, ces substances servent également à parfumer les savons, les poudres, les crèmes et les eaux de Cologne.

Connaissant ces détails, on ne s'étonne plus de constater que ces parfums se vendent si cher dans les parfumeries et les grands magasins. Et lorsqu'il s'agit d'acheter un parfum pour offrir, ce n'est pas une petite affaire. Écoutez plutôt.

Voulant faire un cadeau à une amie, madame Bonneville, femme d'un certain âge, entre dans une parfumerie. Elle regarde avec intérêt les différentes marques et les petits flacons aux[1] formes artistiques. La vendeuse s'approche:

—Vous[2] désirez, madame?

—Un flacon de parfum, mademoiselle. C'est pour offrir. Voudriez-vous me faire voir ce que vous avez?

—C'est pour une personne[3] jeune?

—Oui, pour une dame d'une trentaine d'années.

—Brune ou blonde?

—Blonde.

1 *made up in artistic forms.* In French, the preposition *à* often introduces a phrase indicating a characteristic belonging to the noun it modifies.

2 This is the stock way of asking what a customer wishes to buy.

3 Note the difference of age depending on whether *jeune* precedes or follows its noun; e.g., *un jeune homme* might be from 17 to 22 years of age, whereas *un homme jeune* might be from 23 to 30 years of age.

—Avez-vous une marque préférée? Nous les avons toutes. En ce moment, *Péché mignon* de Carlorelli et *C'est si bon* de Balthazar se vendent beaucoup.

—Non, je préfère quelque chose de[1] moins commun.

Madame Bonneville se fait présenter de nombreux flacons et commence à faire son choix. Elle demande à sentir différents parfums. La vendeuse apporte des échantillons, les ouvre et les fait respirer à madame Bonneville qui réfléchit longuement. Elle hésite à se décider. La jeune fille répand un peu de parfum sur le dos de sa main.

—Celui-ci me plaît, mais je préférerais quelque chose de[1] plus frais. En avez-vous d'autres?

La vendeuse va chercher d'autres échantillons.

—J'aimerais un parfum plus discret que ceux que vous m'avez fait sentir, dit[2] madame Bonneville.

Après plusieurs essais, elle hésite encore entre deux ou trois parfums.

—Combien coûte celui-ci?

—Celui-ci? Il est d'un prix moyen. Celui-là coûte un peu plus cher. En voilà un autre plus cher encore mais de toute[3] première qualité. Il existe aussi en flacon plus grand.

—Qu'est-ce que vous me conseillez?

—Pour une blonde de trente ans, celui-ci, sans hésiter.

—Oui, c'est aussi mon avis, mais il est bien cher. En avez-vous un autre, du même genre, meilleur marché?

Après avoir tourné et retourné, senti et respiré toutes sortes de petits flacons pendant une demi-heure, madame Bonneville finit par se décider pour celui qui lui avait été recommandé par la vendeuse. Elle demande si le magasin peut faire envoyer ce flacon à la personne à qui elle veut l'offrir. La vendeuse prépare alors un joli paquet trois fois plus gros que le flacon et dit:

—Voulez-vous passer à la caisse, s'il vous plaît? Par ici . . .

Madame Bonneville règle à la caisse, et la vendeuse, avant de retourner à son rayon, sourit à sa cliente et lui dit:

—Merci, madame. A une autre fois.

[1] The preposition *de* is always placed between an indefinite and a following adjective; e.g., *quelqu'un d'intéressant, rien de bon.* This *de* is not expressed in English.

[2] When following part or all of a direct quotation, French expressions meaning *he says, he asks,* etc., always invert the verb and subject.

[3] For the agreement of *tout* as an adverb, see § 11 F.

Questions

1. Avec quoi sont faits les parfums? 2. Où sont cultivées les fleurs dont on fait des extraits de parfums? 3. Quels autres produits contiennent ces mêmes extraits? 4. Les parfums se vendent-ils cher? 5. A qui madame Bonneville veut-elle offrir un flacon de parfum? 6. Pourquoi madame Bonneville n'achète-t-elle pas les parfums qui se vendent beaucoup? 7. Madame Bonneville achète-t-elle un flacon de parfum tout de suite? 8. Après avoir fait son choix, à qui madame Bonneville fait-elle envoyer ce flacon de parfum? 9. Quelle sorte de paquet la vendeuse prépare-t-elle? 10. Où madame Bonneville va-t-elle pour régler? 11. Que dit la vendeuse à sa cliente avant de retourner à son rayon?

Devoirs

® *A. Répondez aux questions suivantes par des phrases complètes, en commençant la réponse par* ***oui*** *ou* ***non.*** *Soulignez tous les verbes qui sont à la voix passive.* EXEMPLE: Est-ce que le Palais de Justice a été construit au moyen âge? Oui, il a été construit au moyen âge.

1. Est-ce que les parfums sont faits avec des extraits de fleurs? 2. Est-ce que ces fleurs sont cultivées par des spécialistes? 3. Est-ce que le parfum que madame Bonneville a acheté a été recommandé par la vendeuse? 4. Est-ce que ce parfum sera envoyé à l'amie de madame Bonneville?

B. Remplacez les infinitifs entre parenthèses par la forme passive du passé composé. EXEMPLE: Cette église (terminer) l'année dernière. Cet église *a été terminée* l'année dernière.

1. La Louisiane (vendre) en 1803. 2. La lettre (recevoir) vers la fin du mois. 3. Ces événements (raconter) avec beaucoup de détails. 4. La cathédrale (commencer) vers le douzième siecle. 5. Ces voitures (vendre) hier. 6. Ces villes (attaquer) par l'ennemi. 7. Beaucoup de soldats (tuer) pendant la guerre.

® *C. Remplacez la forme active du verbe par la forme passive. Faites les autres changements nécessaires dans la phrase.* EXEMPLE: Dix soldats défendaient le château. Le château était défendu par dix soldats.

1. Le peuple proclamera une nouvelle république. 2. Les Français et les Anglais exploraient le nouveau monde. 3. La concierge avait

ouvert la porte. 4. On a créé des cours pour les étrangers. 5. Tout le monde admirait les peintures du Louvre. 6. Le Président des États-Unis nomme les hauts fonctionnaires du gouvernement. 7. Un chien avait trouvé l'enfant. 8. La Russie attaquerait-elle les petits pays d'Europe? 9. L'ennemi a pris plus de mille soldats. 10. Les troupes occuperont nos maisons. 11. On a renversé le gouvernement.

D. *Mettez les phrases suivantes à la forme active.* EXEMPLES: 1. Ces lettres ont été écrites par ma mère. Ma mère a écrit ces lettres. 2. Le livre sera vendu. On vendra le livre.

1. Ces personnes ont été tuées près du pont. 2. Des fleurs sont employées pour faire des parfums. 3. Ces paquets ont été envoyés en France par notre client. 4. Des extraits de fleurs sont importés des pays exotiques.

E. *Traduisez en anglais les phrases suivantes. Attention au verbe faire.*

1. Nous ferons construire une maison. 2. On a fait envoyer le paquet à la cliente. 3. La vendeuse fait respirer le parfum à madame Bonneville. 4. Le professeur fait ouvrir la fenêtre. 5. J'ai fait laver ma voiture.

CONVERSATION

1. Demandez à l'étudiant assis devant vous s'il va faire laver sa voiture. 2. Demandez à l'étudiant assis près de la porte si les voitures se vendent bien cette année. 3. Demandez à l'étudiant assis derrière vous si on achète beaucoup de parfum en France. 4. Demandez à l'étudiant assis à côté de vous si le parfum français coûte cher.

VOCABULAIRE — PAGES 284–285

GRAMMAIRE

1. Give examples of the English passive voice. With what auxiliary is it conjugated? With what auxiliary is the French passive formed? (§ 86 A, B) Conjugate the verb ***choisir*** in the passive voice of the present, imperfect, and *passé composé.* (Page 285)
2. How does the past participle of the passive verb agree? (§ 86 C)
3. How is the passive voice used in French? (§ 87 A)
4. How do the French avoid the use of the passive? (§ 87 B)
5. How is *by* expressed in French after the passive verb? (§ 87 C)

6. In a sentence such as *I have my watch repaired,* we use the verb *have* to indicate the idea of *having something done.* What verb do the French use to indicate the same idea? (§ 92 A)

7. Study the verbs ***devoir*** (§ 95, no. 20) and ***dire*** (§ 95, no. 21) according to the outline in § 48 D.

QUARANTE-TROISIÈME LEÇON

La guerre de 39 et l'occupation

Le 1er septembre 1939, l'Allemagne envahit la Pologne et bombarda ses villes. Deux jours après, l'Angleterre et la France déclarèrent la guerre à l'Allemagne. Pendant les huit premiers mois, les opérations militaires à l'ouest restèrent très limitées. Les Français, n'étant pas suffisamment forts pour attaquer, prirent position derrière la ligne Maginot, système de défenses établi le long de la frontière franco-allemande. Mais, en avril 1940, les Allemands envahirent le Danemark et la Norvège, et soudain le 10 mai ils attaquèrent la Hollande et la Belgique, avec lesquelles ils avaient conclu des traités de non-agression. Les troupes allemandes atteignirent rapidement la frontière franco-belge et, au grand désespoir des Français, contournèrent la ligne Maginot à Sedan. A l'intérieur de la France ils avaient constitué une «cinquième colonne» qui répandait de fausses nouvelles et facilitait la désorganisation des armées françaises. Aidées par leur aviation, les forces blindées allemandes avancèrent rapidement. Les troupes françaises se trouvaient continuellement dépassées au cours de leur retraite.

En moins d'un mois les Allemands arrivèrent à la Loire, et toute résistance parut impossible. Le 17 juin 1940, le maréchal Pétain demanda l'armistice. Dès lors, la France fut coupée en deux parties: la zone occupée par les Allemands et la zone libre, sous l'autorité du gouvernement du maréchal Pétain à Vichy. Ces deux zones subsistèrent jusqu'au moment de l'invasion de l'Afrique du Nord par les troupes anglaises et américaines, car à ce moment-là les Allemands occupèrent toute la France.

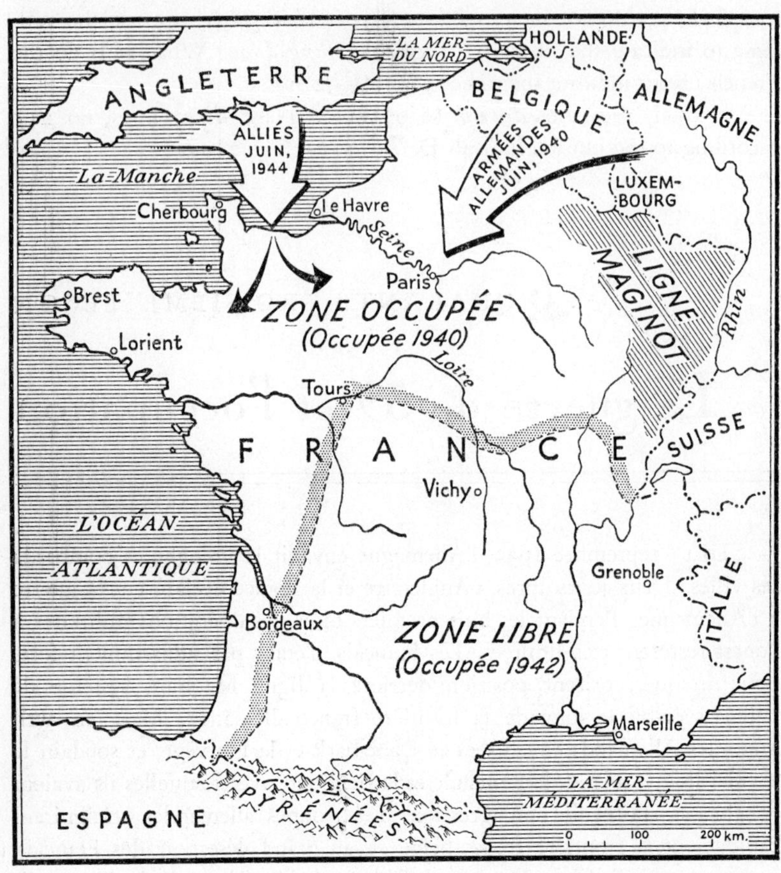

Dès le 17 juin 1940, la France fut coupée en deux parties: la zone occupée par les Allemands et la zone libre, sous l'autorité du gouvernement du maréchal Pétain à Vichy

L'occupation fut très dure pour les Français. Plus d'un million d'entre eux restaient prisonniers de guerre en Allemagne. Beaucoup d'autres furent déportés pour travailler dans des usines allemandes. D'autres encore furent fusillés ou bien enfermés dans des camps de concentration, tantôt simplement pour leurs opinions politiques, tantôt pour leur activité dans la «Résistance». Ils moururent bien souvent de faim, de froid, de mauvais traitements ou même des tortures qu'on leur infligeait. De plus, la guerre continuait, et les alliés bombardaient sans cesse les villes françaises, détruisant les centres industriels, les ports, les ponts et les moyens de communication.

Les Français n'ont jamais admis l'occupation. Des patriotes s'organisèrent pour lutter secrètement contre l'ennemi. Ces organisations formèrent la «Résistance». Elles recevaient des armes parachutées et cherchaient à combattre les Allemands par tous les moyens: sabotages, attentats, transmission de renseignements aux alliés, etc. Les résistants se groupaient dans des régions isolées pour s'entraîner à l'action militaire. D'autres s'échappèrent en Afrique du Nord ou en Angleterre où, depuis l'armistice du 18 juin 1940, le général de Gaulle commandait les «Forces françaises libres».

Pendant ce temps, l'Angleterre et les États-Unis préparaient l'invasion du continent, cette invasion que les Français attendaient depuis si longtemps avec tant d'impatience. Enfin, le 6 juin 1944 ce fut le grand débarquement sur la côte française de Normandie. Après de violents combats, les armées américaines et britanniques s'établirent solidement. La France paya son tribut à cette gigantesque entreprise car, durant la bataille acharnée que les alliés durent soutenir pour enfoncer les défenses allemandes, un grand nombre de villes et de villages furent complètement détruits. Mais bientôt, sous la puissante pression des troupes anglo-américaines, les Allemands durent battre en retraite.

Vers la fin de l'été 1944, la plus grande partie de la France était libérée, mais les Allemands continuèrent à résister. C'est seulement après que les armées américaines, anglaises, françaises et russes eurent envahi l'Allemagne qu'au mois de mai 1945 les chefs nazis se suicidèrent et que quelques généraux allemands signèrent la capitulation sans conditions de l'Allemagne d'Hitler.

QUESTIONS

1. Comment a commencé la guerre de 39? 2. Pourquoi la France et l'Angleterre ont-elles déclaré la guerre à l'Allemagne? 3. Pourquoi les Français n'ont-ils pas attaqué l'Allemagne dès le début de la guerre? 4. Quand l'Allemagne a-t-elle envahi le Danemark et la Norvège? 5. Quels pays l'Allemagne a-t-elle attaqués le 10 mai 1940? 6. Où la ligne Maginot a-t-elle été contournée par les Allemands? 7. Par qui une *cinquième colonne* avait-elle été constituée en France? 8. A quel fleuve les armées allemandes sont-elles arrivées? 9. Quand le maréchal Pétain a-t-il demandé l'armistice? 10. Comment la France a-t-elle été divisée? 11. A quel moment les Allemands ont-ils occupé toute la France? 12. Pourquoi les Français ont-ils été déportés en Allemagne? 13.

Pourquoi les Français ont-ils été enfermés dans des camps de concentration? 14. Par qui les villes françaises ont-elles été bombardées pendant l'occupation? 15. Qu'est-ce que c'était que «la Résistance»? 16. Qui commandait les «Forces françaises libres»? 17. Quand les troupes anglo-américaines ont-elles envahi la France? 18. Quel a été le résultat du débarquement? 19. Quand est-ce que les généraux allemands ont signé la capitulation de l'Allemagne?

Devoirs

® *A. Suivez les indications.*

1. Demandez quand l'Allemagne a attaqué la Pologne. 2. Demandez où l'Allemagne a contourné la ligne Maginot. 3. Demandez où le maréchal Pétain a signé l'armistice. 4. Demandez comment les Français ont résisté aux Allemands pendant l'occupation. 5. Demandez combien d'années la guerre a duré. 6. Demandez quelles armées ont envahi l'Allemagne. 7. Demandez pourquoi les Allemands ont déporté des Français en Allemagne.

® *B. Écrivez les questions suivantes sans employer . . . est-ce que . . .*

EXEMPLE: Pourquoi est-ce que la France a déclaré la guerre à l'Allemagne? Pourquoi la France a-t-elle déclaré la guerre à l'Allemagne?

1. Où est-ce que Vichy se trouve? 2. Quand est-ce que la guerre a commencé? 3. Comment est-ce que le général est parti? 4. Pourquoi est-ce que les alliés ont bombardé les villes françaises? 5. Quand est-ce que les Allemands ont envahi le Danemark? 6. Quels pays est-ce que l'Allemagne a attaqués le 10 mai? 7. A quel fleuve est-ce que les armées allemandes sont arrivées? 8. Pourquoi est-ce que les Français ont été enfermés dans des camps de concentration?

® *C. Écrivez les questions suivantes en employant . . . est-ce que . . .*

EXEMPLE: Comment la France a-t-elle gagné la guerre? Comment est-ce que la France a gagné la guerre?

1. Quand arrivera votre frère? 2. Pourquoi le professeur n'a-t-il pas corrigé les devoirs? 3. Où votre oncle habite-t-il?

D. Remplacez les tirets par une préposition, s'il[1] *y a lieu.*

1. Aimeriez-vous —— apprendre le français? 2. Nous commencerons —— étudier une pièce de théâtre. 3. Ou préféreriez-vous ——

[1] *if one is necessary*

lire un roman? 4. Si vous hésitez —— choisir, regardez les livres de français de votre professeur. 5. Il essaiera —— vous montrer plusieurs pièces de théâtre. 6. Il faut vous habituer —— lire des romans. 7. Vous devez —— lire rapidement. 8. Si vous pouvez —— comprendre sans chercher les mots dans le vocabulaire, vous lirez avec plus de facilité. 9. Le professeur vous dira —— choisir plusieurs livres. 10. Avez-vous réussi —— comprendre la grammaire française? 11. Oseriez-vous —— aller en France tout seul? 12. N'oubliez pas —— répéter les phrases après le professeur. 13. Cela vous aidera —— prononcer mieux. 14. N'ayez pas peur —— causer. 15. Si vous refusez —— parler, vous n'apprendrez jamais —— parler.

CONVERSATION

1. Demandez à l'étudiant assis à votre gauche quand il est arrivé à l'université. 2. Demandez à l'étudiant assis à votre droite pourquoi il étudie le français. 3. Demandez à l'étudiant assis devant vous où il prend ses repas. 4. Demandez à l'étudiant assis derrière vous comment il est venu en classe aujourd'hui.

VOCABULAIRE — PAGES 286–287

GRAMMAIRE

1. Examine the questions in this lesson in order to discover the word order used in a question with a noun-subject when the question begins with ***où, comment, quand, combien*** or ***quel*** modifying a noun. How does a direct object in such a sentence limit the word order? What about questions which begin with ***pourquoi?*** (§ 96 F, G)

2. What types of word order may be used in asking a question with a pronoun subject which begins with ***où, comment, combien, quand, pourquoi,*** or ***quel*** modifying a noun? (§ 96 E)

3. Study the list of prepositions governing dependent infinitives. (§ 44)

4. Study the irregular verbs ***écrire*** (§ 95, no. 22) and ***envoyer*** (§ 95, no. 23) according to the outline in § 48 D.

5. How do the French use the imperfect with ***depuis*** and ***il y avait . . . que?*** How are these constructions expressed in English? Find two examples of ***depuis*** and the imperfect in the reading lesson. (§ 52 D)

6. In line 54 of the reading lesson you will find ***eurent envahi.*** Of what two parts is it composed? What tense is it? How is it formed? (§ 68) When is this tense used? (§ 69 A)

QUARANTE-QUATRIÈME LEÇON

La mode

Dans le domaine de la mode, c'est la France qui donne [1] le ton au monde entier. Une robe, un manteau ou un chapeau qui vient de Paris a un chic qui ne se trouve nulle part ailleurs. La mode change deux fois par an. C'est indispensable à cause des saisons. Il est intéressant d'étudier comment une nouvelle mode est lancée.

Ce sont les grands couturiers [2] de Paris qui créent la nouvelle mode. Parmi les plus connus on peut citer Balmain, Dior, Lanvin-Castillo, etc. [3] La création d'une mode comporte une longue série d'opérations. Le créateur [4], à la recherche d'une idée [5] directrice pour sa «collection» [6], commence par faire des centaines d'esquisses. Il s'inspire aussi des innombrables croquis qui lui sont présentés par des dessinateurs [7] et des modélistes [8] de sa maison. Sur des mannequins il drape des tissus de différentes façons pour [9] voir ce que cela donne. Il finit par adopter une ligne [10] générale, et après bien d'autres opérations encore, les ateliers confectionnent les modèles [11] inspirés de cette ligne. Pendant ce temps, tout le personnel de la maison est tenu au secret professionnel, c'est-à-dire qu'il n'a le droit de révéler à personne quoi que ce soit sur la nouvelle tendance. C'est naturel, du reste. Le secret de la mode est gardé aussi jalousement en France que le secret d'un nouveau modèle de voiture aux États-Unis. Chaque couturier [12] a ses idées, mais par une sorte de mystère, les grandes maisons [13] de couture semblent chaque année être d'accord sur la ligne [10] générale de la mode.

Enfin arrive le moment de présenter les nouvelles créations: c'est le jour [14] de la collection. Des acheteurs viennent du monde entier pour acquérir le droit de reproduire les modèles [11] qui les intéressent. Les mannequins [15], c'est-à-dire les jeunes femmes qui portent les nouvelles

[1] donne le ton *sets the pace* [2] *fashion designers* [3] Actually, these are the names of fashion houses, but in most cases although not all, the fashion house is named after the leading fashion designer of the establishment. [4] *designer* [5] idée directrice *theme* [6] *collection of coats and dresses (to be presented in the coming season)* [7] *model designer* [8] *modelist, pattern stylist* [9] pour voir ce que cela donne *to see how they look* (lit. *to see what result that gives*) [10] ligne générale *general theme* [11] *patterns* [12] *fashion designer* [13] maisons de couture *fashion houses* [14] le jour de la collection *the opening exclusive style show* [15] *models*

créations, défilent devant les clients pour les leur montrer. Il est très impressionnant de voir le défilé des mannequins [1] à la présentation [2]. Ce jour-là, les invités peuvent prendre des notes, mais ils n'ont le droit ni de faire des croquis ni de prendre des photographies. En France, il est interdit par la loi de reproduire un modèle sans avoir payé de droits à la maison [3] de couture qui l'a créé.

Les modèles [4] coûtent très cher, et il n'y a que quelques femmes très riches qui peuvent les acheter. Souvent, ce sont des clients étrangers qui acquièrent le droit de reproduire le modèle [4]. La mode étant lancée, les maisons [5] de confection commencent à faire des robes et des manteaux qui, bien que légèrement différents, restent [6] dans la même note. Ainsi s'établit la mode de la saison, qui est suivie par les grandes entreprises qui fabriquent [7] des vêtements en série à plus bas prix.

Les chapeaux sont créés à peu près de la même façon par les modistes [8], et ils sont présentés en même temps que la collection [9] de couture.

Comment s'explique le succès des créations françaises dans le monde entier? C'est difficile à dire, mais cela tient en partie au sens artistique du Français et à la longue tradition des grands couturiers [10] parisiens. C'est ce qui se paie si cher, comme le démontre l'anecdote suivante:

Une dame élégante avait besoin d'un chapeau pour aller avec une certaine robe qu'elle voulait porter le lendemain soir. Elle court chez la modiste [11], qui, en [12] veine d'inspiration, prend un ruban et lui en fait un chapeau. La cliente, ravie par la nouvelle création, est enchantée jusqu'au moment où elle en demande le prix. Devant le chiffre très élevé que lui indique la modiste, elle s'étonne:

— Oh, mais c'est beaucoup trop cher pour un petit morceau de ruban!

Sur quoi, la modiste [11] reprend le chapeau, le défait, plie le morceau de ruban, le tend à la cliente et lui dit avec un gracieux sourire:

— Le ruban est gratuit, madame, emportez-le.

QUESTIONS

1. Quel pays donne le ton au monde entier dans le domaine de la mode? 2. Tous les combien change la mode? 3. Qui crée les nouvelles

[1] *models* [2] *style show* [3] maison de couture *fashion house* [4] *patterns* [5] maisons de confection *dressmaking establishments* [6] restent dans la même note *follow the same pattern* [7] fabriquent des vêtements en série *make garments in quantity* [8] *milliners* [9] collection de couture *collection of dresses* [10] *fashion designers* [11] *milliner* [12] en veine d'inspiration *in a moment of inspiration*

modes? 4. Qu'est-ce que Dior et Balmain? 5. Comment fait le créateur qui cherche une idée pour sa «collection»? 6. Qu'est-ce que le personnel de la maison de couture n'a pas le droit de révéler? 7. Comment s'appelle la présentation des nouvelles créations? 8. Qui assiste à la collection? 9. Qui présente les nouvelles robes et les nouveaux manteaux? 10. Pourquoi seules les femmes riches peuvent-elles acheter les nouveaux modèles? 11. Quelles sortes de robes sont faites par les maisons de confection? 12. A quel moment sont présentés les nouveaux chapeaux? 13. Comment s'explique le succès des créations françaises dans le monde entier? 14. Pourquoi la femme élégante ne voulait-elle pas prendre le chapeau que la modiste avait fait pour elle? 15. Qu'a fait la modiste quand cette femme a protesté à cause du prix élevé? 16. Si le ruban dont le chapeau était fait était gratuit, pourquoi le prix du chapeau était-il si élevé?

Devoirs

® *A. Suivez les indications.*

1. Dites à Paul qu'il est très difficile de vivre avec ce que vous gagnez. 2. Dites à Marie qu'il est intéressant de voir une maison de couture. 3. Dites à Gérard qu'il est impossible d'aller en France sans beaucoup d'argent.

*B. Remplacez les tirets par **ce** ou **il**, selon le cas.*

1. La mode change deux fois par an. —— est indispensable. 2. Avez-vous vu défiler les mannequins? —— est impressionnant à voir. 3. Nous irons à la présentation. —— sera intéressant de voir les mannequins. 4. Le personnel des ateliers n'a pas le droit de révéler la nouvelle tendance. —— est interdit par la loi. 5. Les acheteurs n'ont pas le droit de prendre des photographies le jour de la collection. —— est naturel. 6. Pouvez-vous m'accompagner au cinéma? —— est impossible. 7. Mais demain, —— sera possible d'y aller. 8. —— est vrai que nous partons ce soir. 9. Non, je pars demain. —— est vrai. 10. —— est facile de trouver de petites voitures en Europe. 11. Jean a passé la soirée à étudier. —— est rare. 12. Maintenant, —— est possible de voyager partout en Europe. 13. Gagne-t-il beaucoup d'argent? —— est possible. 14. Cet artiste travaille neuf heures par jour. —— est très difficile à faire.

C. Remplacez par l'équivalent français les expressions indiquées en anglais entre parenthèses. EXEMPLE: Madame Bonneville demande (*the saleswoman to*) lui montrer des parfums. Madame Bonneville demande *à la vendeuse de* lui montrer des parfums.

1. Jacques a écrit (*his mother to*) le retrouver à la gare. 2. Le professeur dit (*the pupils to*) finir leurs devoirs. 3. Nous avons promis (*our teacher to*) beaucoup travailler. 4. La vendeuse a conseillé (*Mrs. Bonneville to*) prendre un parfum très cher. 5. J'ai demandé (*my friends to*) m'écrire souvent. 6. Monsieur Dupont a téléphoné (*his wife to*) lui envoyer de l'argent. 7. Dites (*Charles to*) bien fermer la porte. 8. Demandez (*Helen to*) ouvrir la fenêtre.

D. *Remplacez les tirets par* de *ou* des *s'il y a lieu. Ne mettez rien où il ne faut rien.*

1. La salle était pleine —— gens. 2. Beaucoup —— Français ont été enfermés dans —— camps —— concentration pendant l'occupation. 3. Ils sont souvent morts —— faim. 4. Il n'y a pas —— ouvriers dans ces usines. 5. Bien —— pays ont eu —— guerres et —— autres difficultés. 6. Pendant —— nombreuses années la France a dû soutenir une lutte continuelle. 7. Pierre est arrivé en classe sans —— livres. 8. Y a-t-il assez —— soldats près de la frontière? 9. Combien avez-vous payé votre chambre —— hôtel? 10. On a besoin —— argent. 11. L'État s'est mis à construire —— immeubles. 12. Autrefois, la France se composait —— provinces. 13. Il reste —— fruits sur la table. 14. Pendant la crise financière de 1929 il y avait peu —— travail. 15. A Paris il n'y a ni —— maisons ni —— appartements à louer[1]. 16. Après —— violents combats, les armées se sont établies dans le pays.

Conversation

1. Demandez à l'étudiant assis près de la fenêtre s'il est difficile d'apprendre le français. 2. Demandez à l'étudiant assis derrière vous s'il est vrai qu'il va en France cet été. 3. Demandez à l'étudiant assis à votre gauche s'il est facile de conduire une voiture. 4. Demandez à l'étudiant assis à votre droite s'il est possible de louer une voiture en France.

Vocabulaire — pages 288–289

Grammaire

1. What grammatical name is given to the *il* in a sentence such as ***Il** est intéressant d'étudier comment une nouvelle mode este lancée?* to the ***ce*** in *Oui, c'est vrai?* (§ 37)

[1] *rent*

2. Give examples of sentences with the *indefinite ce;* with the *impersonal il.* (§ 37)

3. When is the *indefinite ce* used? (§ 37 A)? the *impersonal il?* (§ 37 B)

4. A certain number of common French verbs are followed by *à* before a personal object and *de* before a following infinitive. These might be called the *à + de verbs.* What are the most common of these verbs? Give examples of sentences in which this construction is used. (§ 45 E)

5. Indefinite nouns are normally preceded by the partitive construction. (§ 5 B) Cite two cases where an indefinite noun is used directly after certain words. (§ 5 D)

6. In French indefinite nouns are often preceded by *de.* In which cases are nouns preceded by *de* in French? (§ 6 A, B, C, D, E)

7. Study the verbs *mettre* (§ 95, no. 28) and *mourir* (§ 95, no. 29) according to the outline in § 48 D.

QUARANTE-CINQUIÈME LEÇON

La France depuis la guerre

A la fin de la Deuxième Guerre mondiale, la France dut faire face à la tâche énorme du retour à la vie normale. Si elle n'avait eu qu'à réparer les destructions subies au cours des années de guerre et d'occupation, cela aurait déjà été un travail considérable. Mais elle eut à résoudre encore d'autres problèmes: d'abord se transformer d'un pays de caractère largement agricole en un pays de plus en plus industrialisé, ensuite modifier la structure de son économie et s'adapter à une nouvelle conception du rôle social de l'État, et enfin apaiser une agitation sérieuse dans certaines régions de son empire d'outre-mer. En effet, dans diverses parties de l'Union française, des nationalistes avaient cherché à profiter des circonstances pour rendre leur pays indépendant. A cause de ces mouvements nationalistes, pendant de nombreuses années après la guerre, la France dut soutenir une lutte continuelle dans une région ou dans une autre du monde, et ces luttes épuisèrent ses ressources. Si elle n'avait pas été obligée de dépenser des milliards de francs pour ces guerres incessantes, elle aurait pu utiliser cet argent pour améliorer les conditions d'existence des Français. Si les Français eux-mêmes avaient été d'accord sur la solution du problème colonial, la situation aurait été plus facile. Mais l'opinion du pays à ce sujet était divisée. De plus, pendant toute cette époque, le coût de la vie était assez élevé tandis que les salaires des ouvriers et les traitements des fonctionnaires et des employés restaient à un niveau relativement bas; en outre, il y avait une crise sérieuse du logement, due aux destructions faites pendant la guerre, au contrôle des loyers, au déplacement des populations vers les villes et à l'augmentation de la natalité. Enfin, le franc perdait continuellement de sa valeur par l'inflation, ce qui posait d'autres problèmes au pays. Cependant, malgré toutes les difficultés passées et celles qui subsistent, le relèvement du pays a été extraordinaire.

Dans le domaine du gouvernement, la France cherche encore la solution idéale. Si, à la fin de la guerre, elle avait bien voulu accepter un chef d'État très fort, celui-ci aurait peut-être réussi à résoudre plus rapidement les difficultés du moment. Mais sous la Quatrième République (1947–58), le pouvoir politique était aux mains d'une Assemblée Nationale toute puissante qui renversait constamment le gouvernement. Enfin, quand en 1958, à cause de l'irresponsabilité et de l'inertie du Parlement, le pays se trouva au bord de la guerre civile, on fit appel au Général de Gaulle, et quelques mois plus tard, on institua la Cinquième République, dont la constitution donne des pouvoirs très étendus à son Président. Le Général de Gaulle, premier Président de la nouvelle République, commença tout de suite à prendre des mesures énergiques.

Les changements intervenus en France depuis le début du siècle sont considérables, et les Français ne sont pas toujours d'accord sur leur importance. Écoutez plutôt cette conversation qui eut lieu un soir après dîner dans une famille parisienne:

—Vous savez, dit un des invités, on était beaucoup plus heureux autrefois. Si je pouvais vivre de nouveau en 1900, j'accepterais tout de suite.

—Je ne suis pas de votre avis, répondit un autre. S'il fallait vivre dans les conditions où l'on se trouvait il y a cinquante ans, on serait bien malheureux. Si vous comparez le niveau de vie au début du siècle et la facilité de la vie actuelle, vous serez obligé de reconnaître les progrès énormes qu'on a faits. Comme on vivait simplement au temps de mes parents! Aujourd'hui, au contraire, le Français a envie de profiter de toutes les nouveautés qui ont été mises à sa portée, et il en profite. Le plus modeste fonctionnaire possède un poste de radio, de télévision, un frigidaire et une voiture ou un scooter. De plus, tout travailleur dispose de trois semaines de congés payés, et à cette occasion d'un billet de chemin de fer à tarif réduit, il est assuré contre le chômage, et en cas de maladie, les frais lui sont remboursés à quatre-vingts pour-cent. S'il a des enfants, il touche des allocations familiales qui augmentent sensiblement son salaire. Enfin, le travailleur français bénéficie d'une retraite à l'âge de soixante-cinq ans.

—Les progrès déjà faits sont énormes, dit un troisième, et sous la Cinquième République on avance rapidement. Si la France continue à travailler avec toutes les ressources dont elle dispose, elle deviendra sûrement un des pays les plus prospères d'Europe.

Questions

1. Quels sont les problèmes auxquels la France a dû faire face à la fin de la Deuxième Guerre mondiale? 2. Pourquoi la France a-t-elle dû soutenir des luttes dans diverses parties de son empire d'outre-mer? 3. A quoi était due la crise du logement? 4. Quel a été le résultat de l'inflation en France? 5. A qui appartenait le pouvoir politique sous la Quatrième République? 6. A qui a-t-on fait appel en 1958 quand la France était au bord d'une guerre civile? 7. A qui la constitution de la Cinquième République donne-t-elle des pouvoirs très étendus? 8. Qui a été élu le premier Président de la Cinquième République? 9. Combien de semaines de congés payés le travailleur a-t-il en France? 10. A quelle occasion a-t-il un billet de chemin de fer à tarif réduit? 11. En cas de maladie, quel pourcentage des frais médicaux rembourse-t-on aux Français? 12. A quel âge le travailleur français bénéficie-t-il d'une retraite?

Devoirs

® *A. Suivez les indications.*

1. Dites à René que vous seriez très content d'aller en France si vous aviez le temps. 2. Dites à Denise que si elle avait travaillé, elle aurait réussi à son examen. 3. Dites à Thérèse que si elle va en France, elle trouvera beaucoup de choses intéressantes à voir.

® *B. Mettez les verbes suivants au conditionnel passé.* EXEMPLE: je viens — je serais venu.

1. il parlera 2. nous finirons 3. elle perdait 4. vous devriez 5. elle a fait 6. ils se couchent 7. je viendrai 8. nous irons 9. elle

s'était arrêtée 10. elle se lavait 11. vous offriez 12. nous recevrons 13. je verrais 14. vous croyez 15. elle écrira 16. je peux 17. vous pourrez

C. Remplacez l'infinitif par le temps convenable.

1. Si nous avons le temps, nous (aller) à la campagne ce week-end. 2. Si vous ne (venir) pas, nous saurons que vous êtes malade. 3. Si ma sœur était ici, elle (jouer) avec votre fille. 4. Si Jean (avoir) assez d'argent, il irait en Europe cet été. 5. Si vous aviez vu les châteaux de la Loire, vous (pouvoir) en parler hier. 6. Si nous (être) en France, nous aurions acheté des tableaux et des livres à Paris. 7. Ma sœur ne travaillerait pas si elle (être) à l'université. 8. Qu'est-ce que vous auriez fait si vous (savoir) cela? 9. Si nous (finir) ce devoir avant neuf heures, nous irons au cinéma. 10. S'il (parler) à son camarade, il lui aurait dit cette nouvelle.

D. Mettez les infinitifs au temps convenable.

1. Si la France (avoir) un président puissant, elle aurait pu résoudre plus rapidement les difficultés du pays. 2. Les Russes verraient comment nous vivons s'ils (venir) aux États-Unis. 3. Si l'armée française ne s'était pas rendue en 1940, une grande partie du pays (être) détruite. 4. Si les États-Unis n'avaient pas envoyé de troupes en France en 1917, est-ce que l'Allemagne (gagner) la guerre? 5. Si les Français se rendent compte des problèmes du pays, ils (travailler) davantage. 6. Vous serez très étonné si vous (voyager) dans un train français. 7. Si j'avais pris le métro, je (arriver) avant vous.

® *E. Indiquez le genre des mots suivants en mettant **le** ou **la** devant chaque mot. Expliquez oralement comment on peut reconnaître le genre de chaque mot.* EXEMPLE: bateau — le bateau

1. village 2. fromage 3. quantité 4. muraille 5. bureau 6. question 7. chimie 8. gouvernement 9. forteresse 10. solution 11. potage 12. moitié 13. monument 14. laitue 15. tableau 16. difficulté 17. voiture 18. changement 19. vallée 20. pension 21. traitement

CONVERSATION

1. Demandez à l'étudiant assis devant vous ce qu'il ferait s'il avait beaucoup d'argent. 2. Demandez à l'étudiant assis à votre droite ce qu'il aurait fait s'il n'avait pas préparé sa leçon aujourd'hui. 3. Demandez à

l'étudiant assis à votre gauche où il irait s'il n'avait rien à faire. 4. Demandez à l'étudiant assis derrière vous ce qu'il aurait dit si on lui avait demandé cent dollars.

VOCABULAIRE — PAGES 290–291

GRAMMAIRE

1. How is the past conditional formed? With what auxiliary verbs is it conjugated? (§ 70) Conjugate ***demander, entrer,*** and ***se laver*** in the past conditional. (Page 291)

2. How is the past conditional used? (§ 71)

3. Of what two parts does a conditional sentence consist? Outline and illustrate three types of conditional sentences common in French. (§ 72 A, B)

4. The gender of a French word can often be determined by its ending. List four common masculine endings and seven common feminine endings. (§ 7 B 2)

5. Study the verbs ***faire*** (§ 95, no. 24) and ***lire*** (§ 95, no. 27) according to the outline in § 48 D.

Le petit navire

Il était un petit navire [1], il était un petit navire,
Qui n'avait ja-ja-jamais navigué,
Qui n'avait ja-ja-jamais navigué, Ohé! Ohé!

Il partit pour un long voyage, (bis)
Sur la mer Mé-Mé-Méditerranée, (bis) Ohé! Ohé!

Au bout de cinq à six semaines, (bis)
Les vivres [2] vin-vin-vinrent à manquer [3]. (bis) Ohé! Ohé!, etc.

[1] *boat* [2] *provisions* [3] *be lacking*

Neuvième révision—Leçons 41 à 45

Première partie

A. Répondez en français par des phrases complètes aux questions suivantes.

1. Comment a commencé la guerre de 14? 2. Pourquoi les Allemands ont-ils accepté en 1933 la dictature des nationaux-socialistes? 3. Quelles sont les réformes votées en France par le gouvernement de *front populaire?* 4. Par qui sont cultivées les fleurs dont on fait des extraits de parfums? 5. Citez des produits fabriqués en France qui sont parfumés par les extraits de fleurs et par d'autres substances odorantes. 6. Dans quelles sortes de magasins peut-on acheter des parfums à Paris? 7. Qu'est-ce qui s'est passé en Europe le 1er septembre 1939? 8. Par quels moyens les Allemands ont-ils pu pénétrer si rapidement en France en 1940? 9. Comment les Français ont-ils résisté aux Allemands pendant l'occupation? 10. Pourquoi le personnel de la maison de couture n'a-t-il le droit de révéler à personne la nouvelle tendance de la mode? 11. En général, qui achète les nouvelles créations des couturiers? 12. Quelle est la différence entre un couturier et une modiste? 13. Pourquoi la France a-t-elle été obligée de dépenser des milliards de francs dans les années après la fin de la Deuxième Guerre mondiale? 14. Pourquoi pendant la Quatrième République le gouvernement français n'a-t-il pas pu résoudre les difficultés du moment? 15. Quels avantages les Français d'aujourd'hui ont-ils sur ceux qui vivaient en 1900?

B. Expliquez en français par une phrase complète les noms suivants.

Alliés	ligne Maginot	traité de Versailles
Cinquième République	Pétain	Troisième République
front populaire	Quatrième République	Union Française
de Gaulle	Résistance	Vichy

C. Rédigez une composition sur un des sujets suivants.

1. Madame Crozier achète une robe dans un grand magasin 2. Les parfums français 3. Comment la mode est lancée 4. La guerre de 14 5. La Deuxième Guerre mondiale 6. La France d'aujourd'hui

Deuxième partie

A. Remplacez les expressions entre parenthèses par l'équivalent français. Tous ces verbes sont à la voix passive. (Voir Grammaire § 86)

1. La ville (*was taken*) par les soldats hier. 2. La maison de son père

(*will be sold*) demain. 3. Ces fleurs (*are cultivated*) par des spécialistes.

B. Les verbes suivants sont au passé simple. Écrivez-les au passé composé. (*Voir Grammaire* §§ *58, 61*)

4. (a) ils firent (b) elle lut (c) nous allâmes (d) il vint

C. Écrivez les questions suivantes sans . . . ***est-ce que.*** (*Voir Grammaire* § *96 E, F, G*)

5. Quand est-ce que le roi est mort? 6. Pourquoi est-ce que les Allemands ont traversé la Belgique?

D. Remplacez l'infinitif par la forme convenable du verbe indiqué. (*Voir Grammaire* § *72 A, B*)

7. Si les élèves français faisaient plus de sport, ils n'(apprendre) peut-être pas autant de latin et de grec. 8. Jacques (parler) anglais s'il avait su que votre camarade ne comprenait pas le français. 9. Je vous (voir) ce soir si mon père me laisse sortir. 10. Si vous (voir) le Quartier latin, vous auriez été très impressionnés par ses écoles et ses jardins.

E. Indiquez le genre des mots suivants en mettant ***le*** *ou* ***la*** *devant chaque nom.* (*Voir Grammaire* § *7 B*)

11. (a) dictature (b) domination (c) renseignement (d) sabotage

F. Remplacez les tirets par une préposition s'il y a lieu. (*Voir Grammaire* § *44 A, B, C, D*)

12. Avez-vous appris —— conduire une voiture, et allez-vous —— faire un voyage en voiture cet été? 13. Voulez-vous —— passer quelques jours au Canada? 14. N'oubliez-pas —— voir les monuments de Québec. 15. Nous espérons que vous continuerez —— lire des livres français.

G. Remplacez les expressions anglaises entre parenthèses par l'équivalent français. (*Voir Grammaire* § *45 E*)

16. J'ai dit (*Charles to read*) un roman du vingtième siècle. 17. Il a demandé (*his aunt to*) lui donner de l'argent.

H. Remplacez les tirets par ***ce*** *ou* ***il,*** *selon le cas.* (*Voir Grammaire* § *37*)

18. —— est nécessaire d'aller en France pour bien connaître les

Français. 19. Il neige. —— est évident. 20. Les parfums coûtent cher. —— est vrai.

I. Remplacez les tirets par ***de*** *ou* ***des****, selon le cas.* (*Voir Grammaire* §§ *5 B, 6*)

21. Est-ce que vous suivez un cours —— conversation? 22. Mon bureau est couvert —— livres. 23. Il y a —— gens qui ne font rien.

J. Traduisez les phrases suivantes en anglais. (*Voir Grammaire* § 92 *A*)

24. La propriétaire a fait nettoyer sa chambre. 25. Quand j'aurai assez d'argent, je ferai construire une grande maison.

QUARANTE-SIXIÈME LEÇON

Y va-t-on ou n'y va-t-on pas?

Il y a quelques mois maintenant que vous apprenez le français. Vous savez déjà beaucoup de mots. Vous lisez facilement. Mais il faut que vous appreniez des expressions tout à fait usuelles si vous voulez parler couramment. Il est peu probable que vous trouviez ces expressions-là dans la littérature, mais il est impossible que vous compreniez une conversation courante sans les connaître. Il est bon que vous sachiez saluer un ami, prendre un billet de cinéma, etc. Il est nécessaire aussi que vous étudiiez le subjonctif. Le subjonctif s'emploie très peu en anglais, mais on s'en sert souvent en français. Le subjonctif marque le doute et indique des actions ou des états vagues, des désirs, des craintes, etc. Par conséquent, il faut employer le subjonctif après des verbes tels que *vouloir, désirer, douter* et *craindre,* et après des expressions telles que *c'est dommage, il faut, il est possible, il est peu probable, il est nécessaire, il est bon,* etc.

Je voudrais que vous imaginiez une conversation entre Jacques Dupont et Roger Leblanc, deux jeunes Français qui se rencontrent dans la rue. Ils se serrent la main, car d'ordinaire les Français se serrent la main en se rencontrant et en se quittant. Écoutez leur conversation:

«Bonjour, mon vieux, comment ça va?

— Ça va bien, et toi?

— Moi, aussi.

— Qu'est-ce que tu fais en ce moment?

— Je vais en classe, je travaille un petit peu, je me promène et je m'amuse comme je peux.

— Qu'est-ce que tu fais ce soir?

— Mon père veut que je reste à la maison, mais je voudrais bien aller au cinéma.

— Moi, aussi, j'ai envie de voir le film qui passe au *Rex.* Il paraît qu'il est épatant! Mais j'ai des devoirs à faire.

— Qu'est-ce que tu décides, alors?

— Il vaudrait mieux que je finisse mon travail avant de sortir. Il est peu probable que je sorte avant neuf heures et demie. Mais après, il est possible que j'aille au cinéma quand même.

— Avec qui?

— Je n'en sais rien. Veux-tu venir avec moi?

— Je voudrais bien. Il est possible que je sois libre à cette heure-là. Veux-tu que je te donne un coup de téléphone ce soir vers neuf heures et quart? Je te dirai si je peux sortir.

— Oui, c'est ça.

— D'accord. A tout à l'heure.

* * * * * * * * * * * *

Le soir arrive. Jacques, qui s'attend à recevoir un coup de téléphone de Roger, est installé dans le salon à sa table de travail sur laquelle tous ses papiers de classe sont rangés avec ordre. Il songe qu'il va peut-être passer une bonne soirée avec son camarade. Son père, assis dans un fauteuil, jette un coup d'œil sur le journal. Sa maman, de son côté, écoute à la radio *La Tribune de Paris,* émission au cours de laquelle une vive discussion sur les problèmes du jour s'élève entre les meilleurs journalistes des grands quotidiens. Mais la transmission est mauvaise et elle éteint (ferme) l'appareil.

Vers neuf heures le téléphone sonne. Jacques se précipite et saisit le récepteur:

— Allô!

— C'est toi, Jacques?

— Oui; tu as fini ton travail?

— Oui, si tu veux aller au cinéma, allons-y tout de suite, car il faut que je sois à la maison à onze heures et demie.

— Bon; je vais te chercher chez toi. A tout à l'heure.

— A tout à l'heure.

Questions

1. Depuis quand apprenez-vous le français? 2. Que faut-il que vous appreniez pour parler couramment? 3. Pourquoi faut-il connaître des expressions courantes? 4. Le subjonctif s'emploie-t-il plus souvent en anglais qu'en français? 5. Quelles sortes d'actions le subjonctif indique-t-il? 6. Après quels verbes le subjonctif s'emploie-t-il? 7. Après quelles expressions le subjonctif s'emploie-t-il? 8. Comment Jacques et Roger se saluent-ils? 9. Qu'est-ce que Roger veut faire le soir? 10. Qu'est-ce que son père veut qu'il fasse? 11. Vaudrait-il mieux que Jacques finisse ses devoirs avant de sortir? 12. Vaudrait-il mieux que vous fassiez vos devoirs avant de venir en classe? 13. Est-il nécessaire que vous ayez vos devoirs avec vous quand vous venez en classe? 14. Où est installé Jacques le soir? 15. A quoi s'attend-il? 16. A quoi songe-t-il? 17. Où est assis son père? 18. Que fait son père? 19. Quelle émission sa mère écoute-t-elle à la radio? 20. Pourquoi éteint-elle l'appareil? 21. Qu'est-ce que Jacques entend sonner vers neuf heures du soir? 22. Roger a-t-il fini son travail? 23. A quelle heure faut-il que Roger revienne à la maison?

Devoirs

® *A. Suivez les indications.*

1. Dites à Jean qu'il faut que vous soyez à la maison avant onze heures. 2. Dites à Louise que vous ne voulez pas qu'elle parte. 3. Dites à Denise qu'il vaudrait mieux que vous finissiez les devoirs.

® *B. Mettez **il faut que** devant chacun des verbes suivants et mettez les verbes à la forme convenable.* EXEMPLE: il a entendu, il faut qu'il entende.

1. je raconte 2. tu as puni 3. elle entendra 4. vous saviez 5. nous sommes restés 6. il a obéi 7. il sert 8. elle avait appris 9. ils choisiraient 10. vous avez attendu 11. je pars 12. nous aurons 13. tu es 14. j'ai pris 15. tu es sorti 16. j'ai perdu 17. vous avez salué 18. je vais 19. nous serons 20. vous faites

C. Remplacez l'infinitif par une forme du subjonctif s'il y a lieu.

1. Il est possible de (partir) à neuf heures. 2. Voulez-vous que je (rester) à la maison? 3. Il faut que je (sortir) tout à l'heure. 4. Il faut

(donner) un coup de téléphone à votre mère. 5. Il est important que nous (savoir) s'il viendra. 6. Il vaudrait mieux (payer) un peu plus. 7. M. Dupont veut que ses enfants (apprendre) le français. 8. Il veut (aller) en France avec eux. 9. Faut-il que nous (être) là? 10. Il est possible que votre professeur (aller) à Détroit. 11. Est-il possible qu'il (finir) son travail avant le mois de mars? 12. Il est bon que vous (être) en classe. 13. Je voudrais (aller) au cinéma. 14. Il est peu probable que nous (comprendre) ce monsieur.

D. *Écrivez l'équivalent français des expressions entre parenthèses.*[1]
EXEMPLE: Il est nécessaire (*for them to go*) à Lyon. Il est nécessaire *qu'ils aillent* à Lyon.

1. Il vaudrait mieux (*for me to leave*) tout de suite. 2. Il est impossible (*for you to understand*) cette situation. 3. Il faut (*for us to be*) à la gare à huit heures dix. 4. Il n'est pas possible (*for me to take*) l'avion. 5. Il est important (*for us to know*) où il est. 6. Il est naturel (*for you to finish*) votre travail avant de sortir.

E. *Écrivez l'équivalent français des expressions entre parenthèses.*[2]
EXEMPLE: Nos amis (*want us to arrive*) vers six heures du soir. Nos amis *veulent que nous arrivions* vers six heures du soir.

1. Mon père (*wants me to be*) à la maison à neuf heures. 2. Je (*want you to do*) un bon travail. 3. Vous (*want him to come*), n'est-ce pas? 4. Ils (*want us to know*) la leçon. 5. Nous (*want Louis to hear*) cela.

CONVERSATION

1. Demandez à l'étudiant assis derrière vous s'il veut que vous alliez au cinéma avec lui. 2. Demandez à l'étudiant assis près de la porte s'il veut que vous soyez devant la bibliothèque à neuf heures du soir. 3. Demandez à l'étudiant assis près de vous s'il veut que vous buviez une tasse de café avec lui. 4. Demandez à l'étudiant assis à côté de vous s'il veut que vous lui écriviez une lettre de Paris.

[1] Think as follows: (1) Il est nécessaire (*for them to go*) à Lyon. (2) Il est nécessaire (*that they go*) à Lyon. (3) Il est nécessaire *qu'ils aillent* à Lyon.

[2] Think as follows: (1) Nos amis (*want us to arrive*) vers six heures du soir. (2) Nos amis (*want that we arrive*) vers six heures du soir. (3) Nos amis *veulent que nous arrivions* vers six heures du soir.

Vocabulaire — pages 292–293

Grammaire

1. What is the nature of the subjunctive? (§ 83) How is the subjunctive of regular verbs formed? (§ 80 A) Give the forms of the present subjunctive of ***donner, punir, dormir,*** and ***répondre.*** (Page 294)

2. How is the subjunctive of irregular verbs formed? (§ 80 B) Give the forms of the subjunctive of ***boire, devoir, mourir, prendre,*** and ***venir.*** (Page 294)

3. There are a certain number of subjunctives whose stems are completely irregular. Learn these verbs. What are the forms of the subjunctive of the verbs ***aller, avoir, être, faire, falloir, pouvoir, savoir, valoir,*** and ***vouloir?*** (§ 80 C)

4. What two uses of the subjunctive do you find in this lesson? (§ 83 A, B)

5. When does one use the infinitive instead of the subjunctive after impersonal expressions and after verbs of wishing? (§ 85 A, B)

6. Study the verbs ***pouvoir*** (§ 95, no. 35) and ***prendre*** (§ 95, no. 36) according to the outline in § 48 D. Add the present subjunctive to your outline.

QUARANTE-SEPTIÈME LEÇON

Comment on fait la connaissance d'une jeune fille française

Depuis quelques jours, ce jeune Américain cherche à faire la connaissance d'une jeune fille française qui veuille bien sortir avec lui. Mais il ne connaît personne qui puisse lui indiquer comment faire. Enfin, il rencontre Charles.

— J'aimerais bien connaître quelqu'un qui me dise comment faire en

France la connaissance d'une jeune fille. Je m'étonne que cela ne soit pas plus facile. Je serais très content de sortir avec une Française. J'ai essayé au moins dix fois, mais je doute que ces jeunes filles aient approuvé ma façon de me présenter, et j'ai peur maintenant de les effrayer. Vous allez rire de moi, mais j'ose à peine le leur proposer. Je crains d'être mal jugé.

—Eh bien! C'est dommage que vous ne m'ayez pas demandé cela plus tôt. J'aurais pu vous donner des indications. Je regrette que les choses soient si différentes à cet égard de ce qui se passe chez vous. Oui, je crains qu'il soit plus difficile ici de faire la connaissance de jeunes filles de bonne famille, mais je m'étonne que vous n'en ayez pas déjà eu l'occasion. Ce n'est pourtant pas impossible, croyez-moi, puisque—et je suis heureux de vous en faire part—je vais épouser bientôt la plus charmante d'entre elles.

—Allons donc! Ah mais . . . tous mes compliments! Et puis-je vous demander où vous avez fait la connaissance de votre fiancée?

—Oh, nous sommes des amis d'enfance. Du reste, mes parents et les siens sont eux-mêmes de vieux amis et ils ne s'étonnent certainement pas du tout de voir notre amitié aboutir au mariage. Mais cela ne résoud pas votre problème, car vos amies d'enfance à vous[1] sont en Amérique. Voyons . . . je serais très heureux que vous acceptiez de venir à mon mariage le 1er juillet prochain, et là, je vous présenterai à plusieurs jeunes filles.

—Je vous remercie beaucoup, mais je suis désolé de ne pas avoir su cela plus tôt, car je vais sur la Côte d'Azur et il ne me sera pas possible d'assister à la cérémonie.

—Eh bien! justement, les vacances sont une excellente occasion de faire des connaissances. Au bout de quelques jours à la plage ou à la montagne, tout le monde se connaît. Les jeunes filles y sont beaucoup plus libres qu'à la ville. Je suis sûr que vous aurez bien des occasions d'en voir, de danser et d'aller vous promener avec elles. Je ne doute pas que plus d'une vous plaise. N'ayez pas peur de leur demander si vous pouvez les revoir à votre retour à Paris. Je doute que cela se fasse encore beaucoup, mais il serait peut-être préférable de demander la permission aux parents des jeunes filles. Cela ne m'étonnerait pas qu'ils vous accompagnent la première fois que vous sortirez[2] avec leur fille. Enfin, soyez patient. Vos amies vous emmèneront alors à des soirées dansantes chez leurs amis. Vous y verrez beaucoup de jeunes Françaises.

(*à suivre*)

[1] The *à vous* is used to emphasize *vous*. In English, we should italicize *your* in writing and stress it in speaking to gain the same effect.

[2] How would you explain this use of the future?

QUESTIONS

1. Que cherche ce jeune Américain? 2. Pourquoi a-t-il peur d'effrayer les jeunes filles françaises? 3. Est-il plus difficile de faire la connaissance d'une Française que d'une Américaine? 4. Comment Charles a-t-il connue sa fiancée? 5. Les parents de Charles s'étonnent-ils que leur fils se marie avec cette jeune fille? 6. Quand aura lieu le mariage de Charles? 7. Pourquoi cet Américain ne peut-il pas assister au mariage? 8. Pourquoi les vacances sont-elles une très bonne occasion de faire des connaissances? 9. Comment l'Américain aura-t-il l'occasion de revoir à Paris ses amies de vacances? 10. Serait-il préférable de demander la permission des parents avant de sortir avec une Française? 11. Est-ce que cela vous étonnerait que les parents accompagnent leur fille quand vous sortez avec elle?

DEVOIRS

® *A. Suivez les indications.*

1. Dites à Suzanne que vous cherchez à connaître une Française qui veuille bien sortir avec vous. 2. Dites à Marc que vous seriez content de connaître un Français. 3. Dites à René que vous n'aimeriez pas que le père de la jeune fille française sorte avec vous.

® *B. Mettez les verbes suivants* (1) *au présent du subjonctif* (2) *au passé du subjonctif.* EXEMPLE: elle dormait (1) qu'elle dorme (2) qu'elle ait dormi.

1. nous avons trouvé 2. elle finira 3. nous avons 4. vous partez 5. ils entendent 6. elle viendra 7. vous pouvez 8. il a été 9. nous nous tournons 10. elle se dirigeait

C. Remplacez l'infinitif par le présent ou le passé du subjonctif selon le cas.[1]

1. Lucienne a peur que son mari (apprendre) bientôt la mauvaise nouvelle. 2. Lucienne a peur que son mari (apprendre) la mauvaise nouvelle hier. 3. C'est dommage que vous ne (pouvoir) pas nous accompagner après-demain. 4. C'est dommage que vous ne (pouvoir) pas nous accompagner jeudi dernier. 5. Nous sommes contents que nos amis (aller) en France l'été prochain. 6. Nous sommes contents que nos

[1] In this exercise, there is always some indication in the sentences themselves as to whether the action of the dependent clause takes place before, at the same time as, or after the action of the verb of the independent clause. In the first sentence, the word *bientôt,* and in the second the word *hier* indicate the time.

amis (aller) en France l'été dernier. 7. Je regrette que vous (partir) ce soir. 8. Je regrette que vous (partir) hier.

D. Remplacez l'infinitif par le présent ou le passé du subjonctif s'il y a lieu.

1. Nous cherchons un Français qui (pouvoir) nous expliquer la Constitution française. 2. Je crains que vous n'en (trouver) pas facilement. 3. Êtes-vous content de (rester) ici tout le temps? 4. C'est dommage que votre tante (être) à Tours hier. 5. Il pleuvait tant que j'avais peur de (sortir) de la maison. 6. Mon père est désolé que nous (aller) en Europe l'année prochaine. 7. Nous regrettons de (quitter) New York demain. 8. Avez-vous peur de (traverser) l'Atlantique? 9. Nous craignons qu'il y (avoir) trop de monde sur le bateau si nous partons au mois de juin. 10. C'est dommage que vous (voyager) sur un bateau américain la dernière fois. 11. Nous allons voir si nous pouvons trouver une chambre qui (avoir) l'eau chaude et froide.

E. Écrivez l'équivalent français des mots entre parenthèses.[1]
EXEMPLE: Je suis heureux (*that I work*) dans un bureau. Je suis heureux de travailler dans un bureau.

1. Marie est contente (*that she knows*) votre nom. 2. Nous regrettons (*that we are*) sans moyen de transport. 3. Avez-vous peur (*that you will see*) ce professeur? 4. Ils craignent (*that they will make*) une faute. 5. Il est étonné (*that he can*) conduire sans difficulté. 6. Les étudiants sont heureux (*that they had*[2]) un jour de congé. 7. Je suis étonné (*that I found*[2]) le cahier. 8. Ils sont désolés (*that they arrived*[2]) après le dîner.

F. Écrivez l'équivalent français des mots entre parenthèses.

1. Je regrette (*that I am*) sans argent. 2. Je regrette (*that you are*) sans argent. 3. Nous avons peur (*that we will lose*) ces livres. 4. Nous avons peur (*that you will lose*) ces livres. 5. Les enfants sont contents (*that they have*) un jour de congé. 6. Les enfants sont contents (*that we have*) un jour de congé.

[1] Think as follows: (1) Je suis heureux (*that I work*) dans un bureau. (2) Je suis heureux (*to work*) dans un bureau. (3) Je suis heureux *de travailler* dans un bureau. Remember that expressions of emotion take *de* before an infinitive.

[2] Since the verb is in the past tense, French will require a compound past infinitive

Conversation

1. Demandez à l'étudiant qui est à votre gauche s'il est content que vous partiez tout de suite. 2. Demandez à l'étudiant qui est à votre droite s'il a peur qu'on ait pris sa voiture. 3. Demandez à l'étudiant qui est derrière vous s'il cherche une femme qui sache parler français. 4. Demandez à l'étudiant qui est devant vous s'il est étonné que vous ayez fait vos devoirs.

Vocabulaire — page 295

Grammaire

1. What types of verbs and expressions used in this lesson are followed by the subjunctive in a dependent clause? (§ 83 C, D)

2. When is the subjunctive and when is the infinitive used after such verbs and expressions? Give examples of sentences with each type of construction. (§ 85 A, B, C)

3. In a sentence such as *J'aimerais connaître quelqu'un qui me **dise** comment faire la connaissance d'une jeune fille,* why would the subordinate verb *dise* be put in the subjunctive? (§ 83 E)

4. What kind of time is expressed by the *passé du subjonctif?* (§ 84 B) How is the *passé du subjonctif* formed? (§ 82 A) Conjugate ***donner, entrer,*** and ***se laver*** in the *passé du subjonctif.* (Page 295)

5. Study the verbs ***rire*** (§ 95, no. 37) and ***venir*** (§ 95, no. 43) according to the outline in § 48 D.

Le mariage en France

(*suite*)

—Vous voyez qu'il est nécessaire d'avoir des parents ou des amis pour faire des connaissances intéressantes. C'est le plus sûr moyen qu'il y ait. Les parents [1] jouent aussi un plus grand rôle qu'en Amérique dans les préliminaires du mariage. Ainsi cela vous amusera peut-être de savoir que souvent le jeune homme qui veut se marier ne consulte pas d'abord les parents de la jeune fille mais plutôt les siens. Ce sont eux qui vont chez les parents de la jeune fille pour la demander en mariage, car eux seuls peuvent régler les questions de détails.

—Je crains de ne pas savoir ce que vous entendez par questions de détails.

—Il y a très souvent des questions d'argent comme la dot [2], vous savez, la somme d'argent que la jeune fille apporte à son mari au moment du mariage. Elle doit être en rapport avec la situation financière du jeune homme. C'est la question la plus délicate qui soit à régler.

—Je m'étonne que ces questions d'argent interviennent dans un mariage d'amour comme le vôtre. Ou bien, est-ce qu'on ne se marie pas par amour en France?

—Je crains de ne pas vous avoir donné suffisamment d'explications. Autrefois, quand les différences entre les classes sociales étaient plus marquées, le mariage était souvent une alliance entre familles de condition égale. On épousait souvent une jeune fille pour sa dot ou un jeune homme pour sa position sociale. Les jeunes gens suivaient alors aveuglément les désirs de leurs parents, et ils se mariaient souvent sans s'aimer. Aujourd'hui, les mariages de convenance, qui se faisaient pour des raisons uniquement financières ou sociales, ont à peu près disparu. Mais la coutume de la dot s'est parfois maintenue. J'ai peur que vous ne compreniez pas son but. Elle constitue la plus grande sécurité que l'on puisse donner au mariage. Elle permet au mari de vivre à l'aise avec sa femme et de s'établir solide-

[1] Some years ago, it was necessary by law to have the permission of the parents in a marriage up to the age of twenty-five. Now the age is twenty-one.

[2] In some circles of French society, the dowry has disappeared entirely. In others, it still exists. It is much less common now than formerly.

ment dans ses affaires en attendant qu'il puisse gagner assez d'argent pour économiser et mettre de côté à son tour une dot pour leurs enfants quand ils en auront.

— Je comprends. Mais est-ce qu'on reste longtemps fiancé en France?

— Généralement d'un à six mois. Il y a d'abord les fiançailles, célébrées au cours d'un grand dîner de famille, où l'on félicite les fiancés et où le jeune homme offre à la jeune fille la plus jolie bague qu'il ait pu acheter. Ensuite, quand la date du mariage approche, les bans, c'est-à-dire l'annonce du mariage, sont publiés à l'église et à la mairie.

— Et comment se passe la cérémonie du mariage?

— En France, il y a deux cérémonies: le mariage civil, établi par le Code Napoléon, et le mariage religieux, si on le désire. Le mariage civil est célébré dans une salle spéciale de la mairie qui s'appelle *la salle des mariages*. Le maire lit aux jeunes gens les articles du Code civil relatifs aux devoirs et aux droits des époux, puis il leur demande s'ils veulent être mari et femme. Ils répondent «oui» et signent un registre devant deux témoins. Le même jour ou un autre jour, si l'on désire le mariage religieux, une grande cérémonie a lieu à l'église. Généralement, le prêtre fait un sermon sur la beauté du mariage. Ensuite, tous les invités assistent à un grand repas souvent suivi d'un bal, généralement chez les parents de la jeune fille.

— Je vois que vos coutumes sont assez différentes des nôtres. Merci bien de vos conseils. Je tâcherai de les suivre dès que je serai sur la Côte d'Azur.

Questions

1. Quand il veut se marier, le Français consulte-t-il d'abord les parents de la jeune fille ou les siens? 2. En Amérique, quand vous voulez vous marier, consultez-vous les parents de la jeune fille ou les vôtres? 3. Qu'est-ce que la dot? 4. A quoi sert la dot? 5. Qu'est-ce que le mariage de convenance? 6. Combien de temps reste-t-on fiancé en France? 7. Qu'est-ce que les fiançailles? 8. Où sont publiés les bans? 9. Quelles sont les deux cérémonies de mariage en France? 10. Où a lieu le mariage civil? 11. Que lit le maire pendant la cérémonie du mariage civil? 12. De quoi est suivie la cérémonie du mariage?

Devoirs

® *A. Suivez les indications.*

1. Dites à Philippe que vous craignez de ne pas comprendre l'utilité de la dot. 2. Dites à Gérard que vous vous étonnez de ne pas avoir vu

sa femme. 3. Dites à Charles que ses parents sont plus jeunes que les vôtres.

B. Écrivez l'équivalent français des mots entre parenthèses. Attention à la position de ne . . . pas. EXEMPLES: 1. Il a peur (*that he does not know*) la leçon. Il a peur *de ne pas savoir* la leçon. 2. Êtes-vous content (*that you did not go up*) dans notre chambre? Êtes-vous content *de ne pas être monté* dans notre chambre?

1. Je m'étonne (*that I do not understand*) ces personnes. 2. Michel craint (*that he does not have*) assez d'argent pour faire le voyage. 3. Nous regrettons (*that we will not be able*) voir cette pièce. 4. Nous sommes heureux (*that we did not arrive*) trop tôt. 5. Ma mère est désolée (*that she did not see*) Paris. 6. Je regrette (*that I did not work*) cette année.

C. Remplacez les infinitifs par la forme convenable de l'indicatif ou du subjonctif.[1]

1. *Quatre-vingt-treize* est le dernier roman que Victor Hugo (écrire[2]). 2. Est-ce que *Notre-Dame de Paris* est le dernier roman de Victor Hugo qui (être[3]) intéressant? 3. Est-ce que *le Cid* est la plus belle pièce de Corneille que vous (lire[2])? 4. Nice est la seule ville que nous (visiter[2]) pendant notre voyage sur la Côte d'Azur. 5. Je dirais que Corneille est le premier écrivain français de tragédies qui (être[3]) connu partout dans le monde. 6. Quelle est la meilleure pièce de théâtre que vous (connaître[3])?

® *D. Remplacez les expressions en italique par des pronoms possessifs.* EXEMPLES: 1. Sa sœur est plus âgée que *ma sœur.* Sa sœur est plus âgée que *la mienne.* 2. Je préfère nos villes *à vos villes.* Je préfère nos villes *aux vôtres.*

1. Votre bibliothèque est différente de *ma bibliothèque.* 2. Leur appartement est plus grand que *mon appartement.* 3. Mon stylo n'a pas d'encre. Donnez-moi *votre stylo.* 4. La littérature française est aussi intéressante que *notre littérature.* 5. Les coutumes des Bretons sont différentes de *nos coutumes.* 6. Ma chambre est plus petite que *votre chambre.* 7. Sa maison est plus grande que *leur maison.* 8. Je donnerai

[1] Remember that the indicative is used if you are stating an objective fact in sentences such as these. But if the verb of the dependent clause embodies the concept of a subjective attitude, an educated Frenchman would tend to use the subjunctive.

[2] in the past [3] at present

de l'argent à mon frère; donnez-en à *votre frère.* 9. L'Arabe portait un costume différent de *nos costumes.*

E. Exprimez chaque phrase de deux façons différentes. EXEMPLE: Ce chien est le mien. 1. Ce chien est à moi. 2. Ce chien m'appartient.

1. Cette encre est la sienne. 2. Ces livres sont à eux. 3. Ce stylo est à vous. 4. Ces maisons m'appartiennent.

CONVERSATION

1. Demandez à l'étudiant assis à côté de vous si sa voiture est plus longue que la vôtre. 2. Demandez à un des étudiants assis près de la fenêtre si son stylo a coûté plus cher que le vôtre. 3. Demandez à un des étudiants assis derrière vous s'il regrette de ne pas avoir étudié l'espagnol. 4. Demandez à un des étudiants assis devant vous s'il a peur de ne pas travailler suffisamment.

VOCABULAIRE — PAGES 296–297

GRAMMAIRE

1. What types of words sometimes require a subjunctive in a following modifying clause? What determines whether the indicative or subjunctive is used? (§ 83 F)

2. When are ***ne*** and ***pas*** placed immediately before the verb? Does this rule hold in case of a past infinitive? (§ 22 H)

3. Give an English sentence containing a possessive pronoun. What are the French possessive pronouns? (§ 32 A) Distinguish in pronunciation between the possessive adjectives ***notre*** and ***votre*** and the possessive pronouns ***nôtre*** and ***vôtre.*** (§ 32 B)

4. With what and how do possessive pronouns agree? (§ 32 C)

5. What are various methods of indicating possession in French? (§ 32 D)

6. Study the verbs ***voir*** (§ 95, no. 45) and ***vouloir*** (§ 95, no. 46) according to the outline in § 48 D.

La course-cycliste

Un jour, en me promenant dans une petite ville de France avec un camarade, j'ai vu une grande foule qui se massait des deux côtés de la rue. Des gendarmes empêchaient les gens de traverser.

— Dépêche-toi, à moins que tu veuilles rester ici, m'a dit mon camarade. Il y en a pour un quart d'heure avant que nous puissions continuer notre promenade.

— Ça m'est égal si c'est quelque chose d'intéressant. Mais que font tous ces gens-là?

— Ils attendent les coureurs du «Tour de France». Tu vois ces gendarmes? Ils dégagent la route jusqu'à ce que les coureurs soient passés. Dépêche-toi pour que nous traversions la route tout de suite — à moins que tu préfères rester ici.

— Pourvu que ça ne dure pas trop longtemps, j'aimerais bien voir passer les coureurs. Mais explique-moi de quoi il s'agit. Je n'y connais rien.

— Tu n'as jamais entendu parler des courses de bicyclettes? Bien que les Français ne soient pas aussi sportifs que les autres peuples d'Europe, ils aiment bien suivre les résultats de ces courses. La course-cycliste est un des sports les plus populaires que je connaisse. On désigne généralement les courses par le nom de la ville où le départ a lieu et celui de la ville où a lieu l'arrivée. Il y a, par exemple, Paris-Lille, Paris-Nice, Bordeaux-Paris, le Tour de France, etc. Certaines courses ne durent qu'un jour, d'autres durent plusieurs jours et se font par étapes de cent à trois cents kilomètres.

Les coureurs partent dans la matinée, et la course dure jusqu'à la fin de l'après-midi. Le Tour de France, qui est la course la plus populaire que nous ayons, dure trois semaines. Il finit toujours à Paris. L'itinéraire, qui fait à peu près le tour de tout le pays et passe en Suisse et en Italie, n'est pas toujours le même. L'année dernière, les coureurs sont passés par Lille, Metz, Belfort, Évian, Aix-les-Bains, Grenoble, Digne, Nice, Cannes, Marseille, Montpellier, Pau, Bordeaux, La Rochelle, Nantes, Caen et Paris. Les courses-cyclistes sont organisées en général par des journaux sportifs. Il y aurait beaucoup d'accidents si on ne dégageait pas la route pendant le passage des coureurs. Mais attention! Les voilà!

Le Tour de France est la course la plus populaire que nous ayons

Pendant dix minutes nous avons vu défiler les coureurs. Un grand nombre de voitures de publicité précédaient le peloton. Il y en avait de toutes les tailles et de toutes les couleurs, formant une vraie caravane. Il y avait des voitures commerciales qui avaient acheté le droit de suivre la course. On offre une somme d'argent au coureur qui arrive le premier en haut des plus grandes côtes du parcours. La valeur publicitaire des courses est énorme.

Sur tout le parcours la foule se masse le long de la route. Les paysans quittent leur travail aux champs pour voir le passage des coureurs et pour encourager leur favori.

Après le passage des coureurs, la foule s'est dispersée et mon camarade m'a dit:

— Tu as vu ta première course-cycliste. Mais ce n'est pas le seul sport que nous pratiquions. Quoique les Français ne fassent pas autant de sports que les Anglais et les Américains, ils en font. Écoute.

(*à suivre*)

Questions

1. Qui empêchait les jeunes gens de traverser la route? 2. Qu'est-ce que ces gens attendaient? 3. Quel est le sport le plus populaire aux États-Unis? 4. Citez quelques courses-cyclistes. 5. Quelle est la course-cycliste la plus populaire en France? 6. Combien de jours durent ces courses? 7. Comment sont organisées les courses qui durent plusieurs jours? 8. Qu'est-ce qui suit le peloton des coureurs? 9. Qu'est-ce qu'on offre au coureur qui arrive le premier en haut des plus grandes côtes du parcours?

Devoirs

® *A. Suivez les indications.*

1. Dites à Michel que vous partirez à moins qu'il veuille que vous restiez. 2. Dites à Jeanne que vous lui donnerez un coup de téléphone avant qu'elle sorte. 3. Dites à Jacques que votre mère a acheté une voiture pour que vous puissiez partir en vacances.

B. Remplacez l'infinitif par la forme convenable du verbe.

1. Avant que nous (partir), je voudrais vous dire son nom. 2. Je vous le dis pour que vous (pouvoir) lui écrire. 3. Bien que vous (apprendre) le français, vous ne pourrez pas lire facilement un écrivain du seizième siècle. 4. J'irai à Chamonix faire des excursions dans les Alpes à moins que ma mère nous (attendre) à Paris. 5. Continuez à travailler jusqu'à ce qu'on vous (dire) de vous arrêter. 6. On vous verra pourvu que vous y (être). 7. Quoique vous (avoir) beaucoup à faire, vous venez toujours me voir à l'hôpital. 8. Ne partez pas sans que votre père vous (donner) la permission. 9. Autant que je (savoir), il me la donnera. 10. Quoi que vous (faire), il ne sera pas très content. 11. Il m'a envoyé ce livre afin que je le (lire).

C. Écrivez l'équivalent français des expressions entre parenthèses.[1]

Exemple: Hélène montrera ces livres à tout le monde (*before*

[1] Think as follows: (1) Hélène montrera ces livres à tout le monde (*before she leaves.*) (2) Hélène montrera ces livres à tout le monde (*before leaving*). (3) Hélène montrera ces livres à tout le monde *avant de partir.*

she leaves). Hélène montrera ces livres à tout le monde *avant de partir.*

1. Marie restera à la maison (*in order that she may hear*) cette histoire. 2. Paul vous donnera de l'argent (*before he writes*) à votre père. 3. Je téléphonerai à mes parents (*in order that I may know*) où est Suzanne. 4. Jean prendra les billets (*before he goes*) à la gare.

D. Écrivez l'équivalent français des expressions entre parenthèses.

1. Je lui en parlerai (*before I do*) le travail. 2. Je lui en parlerai (*before he does*) le travail. 3. Charles travaillera cet été (*in order that he may buy*) une voiture. 4. Charles travaillera cet été (*in order that we may buy*) une voiture.

Conversation

1. Demandez à l'étudiant assis près de vous s'il veut vous donner votre cahier avant que vous partiez. 2. Demandez à l'étudiant assis derrière vous s'il a fermé la porte pour pouvoir mieux entendre. 3. Demandez à l'étudiant assis devant vous s'il restera à l'université jusqu'à ce que vous finissiez tout votre travail. 4. Demandez à l'étudiant assis près de la fenêtre s'il a écrit les devoirs au tableau pour que vous puissiez corriger vos fautes.

Vocabulaire — page 298

Grammaire

1. After what subordinate conjunctions is the subjunctive used in French? (§ 83 H)

2. When must a **preposition + an infinitive** be used instead of a **subordinate conjunction + a subjunctive?** (§ 85 D)

3. By what prepositions are the following subordinate conjunctions replaced: ***afin que, pour que, à moins que, avant que, sans que?*** (§ 85 D)

4. Study the irregular subjunctives of the common simple verbs. (Page 299)

5. Study the verbs ***savoir*** (§ 95, no. 38) and ***suivre*** (§ 95, no. 39) according to the outline in § 48 D.

Le sport en France

(*suite*)

—A propos de sports, il faut distinguer entre le sport des professionnels et le sport des amateurs, entre les sports qui se jouent par équipes, comme le football et le basket-ball, et ceux qui sont individuels et auxquels chacun peut participer pour son compte personnel. Je crois qu'en France nous nous intéressons presque autant aux sports professionnels que dans les autres pays, mais je ne crois pas qu'il y ait autant de gens qui fassent du sport. Il est certain en tout cas que nous portons plus d'intérêt aux sports aujourd'hui qu'auparavant.

—Crois-tu que le football, par exemple, soit aussi populaire en France qu'en Amérique?

—Il est très difficile de faire une comparaison, parce que l'organisation et même la façon de jouer sont tout à fait différentes. Il est certain, d'ailleurs, qu'après les courses-cyclistes, le football professionnel est le sport le plus populaire et le plus répandu chez nous. Avant 1932 le football était uniquement un sport d'amateurs. A ce moment-là il a été organisé comme sport professionnel. Je ne crois pas qu'il soit tout à fait comme votre football américain. Chez nous la saison commence vers la fin d'août et ne se termine qu'au mois de mai. Les équipes sont organisées par les villes ou par les clubs plutôt que par les écoles. Et puis, je crois que la façon de jouer au football français est différente. En France, c'est vraiment avec les pieds qu'on joue. On n'a pas le droit de toucher le ballon avec les mains. Je pense que votre football américain ressemble au rugby, qui se joue aussi en France.

—Et le basket-ball?

—Le basket-ball se joue surtout l'hiver. Il est organisé par des équipes d'amateurs.

—Et le base-ball?

—Il est presque inconnu en France. Je suis sûr que la plupart des Français n'ont jamais entendu parler du base-ball.

—Y a-t-il d'autres sports d'équipe?

—Le hockey se joue l'hiver. Mais peut-être que c'est l'athlétisme qui est le plus populaire. L'athlétisme consiste en course[1] à pied, saut[2], lancement du poids[3], du javelot[4], du marteau[5], etc. L'athlétisme est généralement organisé par des clubs.

— Mais les lycées et les grandes écoles? Je suis sûr qu'on fait du sport dans les écoles. Chez nous, c'est une partie du programme.

— Je ne crois pas que tu comprennes bien la mentalité française. Ces dernières années, les autorités des lycées ont commencé à s'intéresser aux loisirs des élèves. Autrefois dans beaucoup de lycées et dans les grandes écoles[6], les sports qui existaient étaient organisés par les élèves eux-mêmes et tolérés par l'administration. Des équipes de football, par exemple, organisaient des rencontres entre elles, mais sans qu'intervienne l'administration. Aujourd'hui, cette administration s'intéresse de plus en plus à l'organisation officielle des sports.

— Ça m'étonne. Je n'aurais pas pensé que les Français soient si peu sportifs. En tout cas, le tennis et le golf doivent se jouer couramment.

— Je suis sûr que tu verras souvent jouer au tennis en France. Mais on y joue parmi les gens d'un certain milieu. Il est beaucoup moins répandu qu'en Amérique. Je ne crois pas qu'il y ait beaucoup de joueurs de golf dans le pays. Le golf existe, évidemment, mais on n'y joue pas beaucoup; les hommes d'affaires français ne s'y habituent pas.

— D'où vient cette différence?

— Chaque peuple a sa façon de s'amuser. Le Français est plus individualiste. Et pourtant, n'oublie pas que c'est un Français, Pierre de Coubertin, qui a fondé en 1894 les nouveaux Jeux Olympiques.

QUESTIONS

1. Après les courses-cyclistes, quel est le sport le plus répandu en France? 2. Le football français est-il un sport amateur ou professionnel? 3. Quelle est la différence entre le football américain et le football français? 4. A quoi ressemble le football américain? 5. Est-ce qu'on joue au basket-ball en France l'hiver? 6. Les Français ont-ils entendu parler du baseball? 7. Citez d'autres sports d'équipe qui se jouent en France. 8. Comparez l'importance des sports dans les écoles américaines et dans les écoles françaises. 9. Qui est Pierre de Coubertin?

[1] *track* [2] *high jump* [3] *shot-put* [4] *javelin* [5] *hammer-throw*
[6] *higher institutions of learning,* including universities and technical schools

Devoirs

® *A. Répondez aux questions suivantes par une phrase complète, en commençant la phrase par oui.*[1]

1. Croyez-vous que le football soit plus intéressant que le basket-ball? 2. Le professeur pense-t-il que les étudiants sachent bien la leçon? 3. Croyez-vous que nous puissions aller en France cet été? 4. Votre frère pense-t-il que vous ayez beaucoup d'argent? 5. Croyez-vous que votre compagnon ait bu un peu trop de vin?

B. Remplacez l'infinitif par l'indicatif ou le subjonctif. Expliquez oralement votre choix. Attention au temps des verbes.

1. Nous croyons que notre ami Gabriel (être) en France. 2. Est-il certain que Maurice (pouvoir) nous accompagner? 3. Je suis sûr qu'on ne (faire) pas de football dans les écoles françaises. 4. Je crois que Paul (venir) nous voir la semaine prochaine. 5. Pensez-vous que Louise (comprendre) ce que nous disons? 6. Je ne crois pas que ces élèves (savoir) tout. 7. Il est probable qu'il (neiger) demain. 8. Je pense que vous (pouvoir) aller à Dijon. 9. Croyez-vous que Marie (sortir) hier soir? 10. Êtes-vous sûr que Jean (partir) demain?

® *C. Introduisez les adverbes entre parenthèses dans les phrases suivantes.* Exemple: (bien) Vous avez parlé. Vous avez *bien* parlé.

1. (hier) J'ai voulu voir votre équipe de football. 2. (encore) Je ne l'ai pas vu. 3. (lentement) J'ai marché jusqu'au bout de la rue. 4. (peut-être) Je verrai des joueurs de tennis. 5. (déjà) J'en avais vu à Paris. 6. (demain) Vous verrez le club de la ville. 7. (certainement) Il y aura de bons joueurs de golf. 8. (toujours) Mon oncle a joué au golf et au tennis. 9. (souvent) Il disait qu'il voudrait passer toute sa vie à faire du sport. 10. (tard) Je suis arrivé chez moi. 11. (beaucoup) J'avais travaillé tout l'après-midi. 12. (trop) Vous avez écrit. 13. (assez) C'est parce que je n'ai pas pensé à ce que j'écrivais. 14. (aujourd'hui) Je suis allé voir le lycée. 15. (ici) Non, je ne suis pas venu. 16. (peut-être) Vous viendrez demain. 17. (hier) Êtes-vous allé à votre cours de littérature? 18. (aussi[2]) Vous avez entendu la conférence sur le roman contemporain.

[1] Before doing this exercise, reread § 83 G, which discusses the mode used after affirmative verbs of thinking and believing.

[2] Used in the sense of *therefore.*

Conversation

1. Demandez à l'étudiant assis près de la fenêtre s'il croit que vous savez la leçon. 2. Demandez à l'étudiant assis près de la porte s'il croit que vous allez en France. 3. Demandez à l'étudiant assis à côté de vous s'il est sûr que vous puissiez conduire une voiture. 4. Demandez à l'étudiant assis derrière vous s'il pense que vous partirez ce soir.

Vocabulaire — page 300

Grammaire

1. The subjunctive is never used after verbs of thinking and believing in an affirmative declarative sentence. What mode is always used after verbs of thinking and believing in such sentences? (§ 83 G)

2. When may one use the subjunctive after expressions of thinking and believing? after expressions such as ***Je suis sûr que,*** etc.? (§ 83 G)

3. How do you account for the occasional use of the subjunctive after verbs of thinking and believing used negatively and interrogatively but not affirmatively?

4. What is the difference in time between the present and past subjunctive in clauses following such verbs? (§ 84 A, B, E)

5. What is the usual position of adverbs in a French sentence? (§ 20 A)

6. Where is the adverb most often placed in sentences with compound tenses? in negative sentences with compound tenses? (§ 20 B) What can be said about the position of adverbs in ***-ment*** in sentences with compound tenses? (§ 20 C)

7. What about the position of adverbs of time and place in sentences with compound tenses? (§ 20 D)

8. What special word order is often found with ***peut-être*** and ***aussi*** (*so*)? (§ 20 E)

9. Study the verbs ***tenir*** (§ 95, no. 40) and ***vivre*** (§ 95, no. 44) according to the outline in § 48 D.

Dixième révision — Leçons 46 à 50

Première partie

A. Répondez en français par des phrases complètes aux questions suivantes.

1. Quand les Français se serrent-ils la main? 2. Quand on prépare ses leçons, vaut-il mieux que la radio soit ouverte ou fermée? 3. Si vous êtes étudiant à l'université, que devez-vous faire avant d'aller au cinéma le soir? 4. Comment un jeune homme français peut-il faire la connaissance d'une jeune Française de bonne famille? 5. Pourquoi est-il plus facile de faire la connaissance d'une Française pendant les vacances? 6. A qui un jeune homme doit-il demander la permission avant de sortir avec une jeune Française? 7. Quel est le rôle des parents dans le mariage en France? 8. Comment sont célébrées les fiançailles en France? 9. Qui marie les fiancés dans la salle des mariages? 10. Qu'est-ce que le Tour de France? 11. Qui dégage la route pour les coureurs-cyclistes? 12. Les Français font-ils autant de sport que nous? 13. Quel est le sport, très populaire en Amérique, qui est presque inconnu en France? 14. Citez les principaux sports que pratiquent les Français. 15. Qui a fondé les Jeux Olympiques modernes?

B. Expliquez en français par une phrase complète les noms suivants.

Code civil	Jeux Olympiques	Pierre de Coubertin
Code Napoléon		Tour de France

C. Rédigez une composition sur un des sujets suivants.

1. Le mariage en France 2. Le football en France 3. Le Tour de France 4. Les sports dans les écoles françaises

Deuxième partie

A. Remplacez les infinitifs par la forme convenable du présent de l'indicatif ou du subjonctif selon le cas. (Voir Grammaire § 83)

1. Il n'y a personne qui (pouvoir) m'aider. 2. Je crois que vous (avoir) tort. 3. Il est vrai que mon frère (être) ici. 4. Bien que vous ne (savoir) pas où aller, je ne (pouvoir) pas vous recevoir. 5. J'ai un ami qui (vouloir) partir pour la France. 6. Je vous téléphonerai avant que nous (venir) chez vous.

B. Remplacez les infinitifs par la forme convenable du présent ou du passé du subjonctif selon le cas. (Voir Grammaire § 84 A, B)

7. Il y a quinze jours de vacances à Noël pour que les étudiants

(pouvoir) aller voir leurs parents. 8. Il est peu probable que votre frère (apprendre) le français quand il voyageait en France. 9. Il se peut que Roger (venir) demain. 10. Je regrette que vous (trouver) la porte fermée quand vous avez sonné hier soir. 11. Continuez à copier ces phrases jusqu'à ce que je vous (dire) de me les remettre. 12. Est-ce le seul homme qui (faire) cela jusqu'ici?

C. *Remplacez les expressions entre parenthèses par l'équivalent français. Choisissez entre l'infinitif et le subjonctif.* (*Voir Grammaire* § 85)

13. Nous sommes très contents (*that we are learning*) le français. 14. Jacques s'étonne (*that you do not know*) où il habite. 15. J'ai peur (*that my father will write*) à mon professeur. 16. Nous avons fermé la porte (*in order that we might hear*) leur conversation. 17. Je téléphonerai à Hélène (*before I sell*) la maison. 18. Je vous explique cela (*in order that you may understand*) ce que j'ai fait.

D. *Remplacez les expressions en italique par un pronom possessif.* (*Voir Grammaire* § 32)

19. Nos sports se jouent par équipe; *vos sports* sont individuels. 20. Voici ma radio. Où est *la radio de Georges?* 21. Ma voiture est plus vieille que *la voiture de madame Lemercier.*

E. *Introduisez les adverbes indiqués dans les phrases suivantes.* EXEMPLE: (déjà) Il a fait ses devoirs. Il a *déjà* fait ses devoirs (*Voir Grammaire* § 20)

22. (encore) Jacques n'a pas écrit cette lettre. 23. (bientôt) Nous serons en France. 24. (demain) Vous verrez vos parents. 25. (peut-être) Ils viendront avec leur voiture.

Supplément aux Leçons 41 à 50

QUARANTE ET UNIÈME LEÇON

Vocabulaire

africain
l'aide *f.*
l'ambition *f.*
annexer
s'appliquer
l'archiduc *m.*
l'assistance *f.*
attaquer
l'aviation *f.*
la base
la circonstance
la colonie
la crise
dangereux, dangereuse
Dantzig
déclarer
dénoncer

la dictature
la difficulté
la domination
européen, européenne
l'existence *f.*
finalement
financier, financière
le front
garantir
Hitler
imposer
l'incident *m.*
inévitable
local, locaux
la Marne
marquer

menacer
le million
mutuel, mutuelle
le national-socialiste
négliger
la neutralité
réel, réelle
la réforme
réorganiser
la réparation
la rivalité
le Serbe
la Serbie
la suprématie [a]
la Tchécoslovaquie
Versailles
violer

aérien, aérienne *air* (adj.), *aerial*
s'agiter *be restless, be in a turmoil*
les Alliés *m.* *the Allies, i.e., France, England, Italy and the other nations who fought against Germany in World War I*
amener *bring about; take* (*a person*)
l'Autriche *f.* *Austria*
l'Autriche-Hongrie *f.* *Austria-Hungary*
le but [b] *aim*
chercher à *seek to, try to*
le chômage *unemployment*
*conclure *conclude;* conclu *concluded*
le conflit *conflict*
la défaite *defeat*

durement *severely*
s'emparer de *seize, take possession of*
entraîner *draw in, drag in*
*entreprendre *undertake;* entrepris *undertaken*
épuisant *exhausting*
l'esprit *m.* *spirit*
établir *establish*
l'état *m.* *state*
la grève *strike*
lors *then, at that moment*
mécontent *unhappy, dissatisfied*
le millier *thousand* (*noun*)
la paix *peace*
perdre *lose*
la Pologne *Poland*
pourtant *however*
le pouvoir *power*

* An asterisk (*) placed before a verb indicates that this verb is irregular.
[a] The ending *-tie* is pronounced as English *see* [sypremasi].
[b] Pronounced either [by] or [but].

le préparatif *preparation*
la puissance *power*
reconstituer *build up*
remporter *carry off, bring back*
ressentir *feel; resent*
le traité *treaty*

à part *except for*
l'archiduc-héritier *crown prince*
la crise financière *depression*
le front populaire *popular front*
mettre fin à *put an end to*
ne . . . plus que *no longer anything but*
le pays s'agitait *there was unrest in the country*
remporter la victoire *win, carry off the victory*
tout près *quite near*
le traité de Versailles *the treaty made at Versailles after World War I*

Verbes

THE SIMPLE PAST

-er *verbs*	-ir *verbs*	-re *verbs*	-oir *verbs*
je parl*ai*	je fin*is*	je perd*is*	je reç*us*
tu parl*as*	tu fin*is*	tu perd*is*	tu reç*us*
il parl*a*	il fin*it*	il perd*it*	il reç*ut*
nous parl*âmes*	nous fin*îmes*	nous perd*îmes*	nous reç*ûmes*
vous parl*âtes*	vous fin*îtes*	vous perd*îtes*	vous reç*ûtes*
ils parl*èrent*	ils fin*irent*	ils perd*irent*	ils reç*urent*

avoir	être	-cer *verbs*	-ger *verbs*
j'eus	je fus	j'effaçai	je mangeai
tu eus	tu fus	tu effaças	tu mangeas
il eut	il fut	il effaça	il mangea
nous eûmes	nous fûmes	nous effaçâmes	nous mangeâmes
vous eûtes	vous fûtes	vous effaçâtes	vous mangeâtes
ils eurent	ils furent	ils effacèrent	ils mangèrent

Devoirs

The instructor will indicate to the class whether to express simple past action by the literary **passé simple** *or by the conversational* **passé composé** *in this exercise.*

A. Write the French equivalent of each of the following sentences.

1. In 1914 Germany decided to attack France from[1] the north. 2. The German armies crossed Belgium. 3. The French succeeded in stopping the Germans. 4. After four years, France and her allies won the war. 5. By the Treaty of Versailles, which put an end to World War I,

[1] *par*

Germany lost all her colonies. 6. But she began to reorganize her industry. 7. Hitler seized the power in 1933. 8. In France, the depression brought about another government. 9. This government neglected national defense.

B. Say aloud rapidly the French equivalent of each of the following sentences.

1. Germany declared war on [1] France. 2. In 1917 the United States declared war on Germany. 3. The Allies succeeded in winning the war. 4. Which treaty put an end to the war? 5. There was a great deal of unemployment in the country. 6. Were there many strikes in the country at that time? 7. Germany threatened to seize several countries. 8. France and England finally [2] understood Hitler's ambitions.

[1] *à* [2] See § 20 B for the position of the adverb.

QUARANTE-DEUXIÈME LEÇON

Vocabulaire

s'approcher	exotique	multiple
artistique	hésiter	organique
blond	importer	le parfum
Bonneville	l'intérêt *m.*	parfumer
Cologne	le laboratoire	la qualité
combiner	la manipulation	le spécialiste
discret, discrète		la substance

associer *associate, mix*
l'avis *m.* *opinion*
brun *brunette*
le cadeau *gift*
la caisse [a] *the cashier's*
chimique *chemical*
le choix *choice*
conseiller *advise*
se décider à *make up one's mind to*
la demi-heure *half hour*
l'échantillon *m.* *sample*
l'essai *m.* *try, attempt*
s'étonner *be surprised*
l'extrait *m.* *extract*
le flacon [b] *bottle*
le genre *kind, type*
gros, grosse *big, large*
infime *tiny, very minute, immeasurably small, infinitesimal*
la marque *brand, trade mark*
merci *thank you*

* An asterisk (*) placed before a verb indicates that this verb is irregular.
[a] There is no exact English equivalent for *la caisse.* It indicates the place in the establishment where money is taken in and given out by the cashier.
[b] A *flacon* is usually a bottle with a glass stopper, in contrast to a *bouteille,* which is often larger and less artistic.

mignon, mignonne *darling*
moyen, moyenne *average, moderate*
odorant *odoriferous, fragrant*
*offrir[a] *offer;* offert *offered*
le paquet *package*
la parfumerie *perfume store*
le péché *sin*
*plaire *please;* plu *pleased*
le poids *weight*
la poudre *powder*
quelque chose *something*
répandre *spread*
le rayon *department (of a store)*
régler *pay (a bill), settle (an account)*
respirer *breathe; inhale*
retourner *return, go back; turn again*
le savon *soap*
*soumettre *submit;* soumis *submitted*
*sourire *smile;* souri *smiled*
le terrain *tract of land, field*
végétal *vegetable (adj.)*
la vendeuse *saleswoman; clerk (in a store)*

à mon avis *in my opinion*
il s'agit de *it is a question of*
coûter cher *be expensive, cost a great deal*
d'un certain âge *middle-aged*
l'eau de Cologne *perfumed toilet water*
écouter plutôt *listen for yourself*
en ce moment *at this time, right now*
faire un cadeau *give a gift*
le grand magasin *department store*
meilleur marché *cheaper*
par ici *this way*
quelque chose de frais *something fresh*

Verbes

THE PASSIVE VOICE

The passive voice consists of the auxiliary verb *être* with the past participle of the verb. This past participle agrees in gender and number with the subject.

PRESENT PASSIVE	IMPERFECT PASSIVE	COMPOUND PAST PASSIVE
je suis choisi(e)	j'étais choisi(e)	j'ai été choisi(e)
tu es choisi(e)	tu étais choisi(e)	tu as été choisi(e)
il est choisi	il était choisi	il a été choisi
elle est choisie	elle était choisie	elle a été choisie
nous sommes choisi(e)s	nous étions choisi(e)s	nous avons été choisi(e)s
vous êtes choisi(e)(s)	vous étiez choisi(e)(s)	vous avez été choisi(e)(s)
ils sont choisis	ils étaient choisis	ils ont été choisis
elles sont choisies	elles étaient choisies	elles ont été choisies

The passive of all other tenses is formed in a similar manner. Consult § 86 B.

* An asterisk (*) placed before a verb indicates that this verb is irregular.
[a] Often, as in this lesson, *offrir* is used in the sense of offering a gift.

Devoirs

A. Write the French equivalent of each of the following sentences.

1. These perfumes are imported from several other countries. 2. Those flowers were being cultivated by specialists[1]. 3. Enormous[2] quantities of flowers have been utilized to[3] obtain that extract. 4. His choice will be made tomorrow. 5. Those packages were brought to this post office by my brother this morning. 6. American cars[4] are bought[5] everywhere. 7. He had his car[6] washed yesterday. 8. The saleswoman will have the perfume[6] sent to the customer. 9. I had the bottle[6] of perfume opened.

[1] How does French indicate that a noun is indefinite? (§ 5 B)
[2] How does French indicate that a plural noun preceded by an adjective is indefinite? (§ 6 A)
[3] *pour* [4] How does French designate an object taken in a general sense? (§ 4 B)
[5] How does French often express the English passive when the action is general? (§ 87 B 2)
[6] In the causative construction, the noun object follows the infinitive in French.

B. Say aloud rapidly the French equivalent of each of the following sentences.

1. Do you wish some perfume? What is your favorite[1] brand? 2. This way, please. 3. How much does this perfume cost? 4. This brand is sold[2] a great deal. 5. Do you have another[3] of the same type? 6. I should prefer something[4] different. 7. We should prefer something[4] more expensive. 8. Would you prefer something[4] cheaper? 9. There is nothing[4] interesting in the library.

[1] *préféré* [2] Since the action is general, use the reflexive form of the verb.
[3] Begin the sentence with *En.*
[4] Separate this indefinite from the following adjective by the preposition *de.*

QUARANTE-TROISIÈME LEÇON

Vocabulaire

l'activité *f.*
aider
anglo-américain
l'arme *f.*
l'armistice *m.*
l'autorité *f.*
avancer
bombarder
britannique
le camp
la capitulation
le combat
combattre
la communication
la concentration
la défense
déporter
la désorganisation
l'entreprise *f.*
franco-belge
de Gaulle
gigantesque
se grouper
la Hollande
industriel, industrielle
l'invasion *f.*
isoler
libérer
limité
nazi
la non-agression
l'occupation *f.*
l'opération *f.*

parachuter
le patriote
Pétain
la position
le prisonnier
la résistance [a]
le résistant
le sabotage
secrètement
Sedan
signer
solidement
subsister
la torture
la transmission
le tribut
la troupe
Vichy
violent
la zone

acharné *desperate, obstinate, intense*
*admettre *admit;* admis *admitted*
*atteindre *reach, attain;* atteint *reached, attained*
l'attentat *m.* *assassination*
blindé *armored, Panzer*
la cesse *ceasing*
la colonne *column*
contourner *outflank, go around*
contre *against*
le débarquement *landing* [b]
dépasser *pass by; by-pass*
le désespoir *despair*
durant *during*
s'échapper *escape*
enfoncer *break into, penetrate*
s'entraîner *train oneself*
faux, fausse *false*
fusiller *shoot*
infliger *inflict*
la ligne *line*
lutter *struggle*
le maréchal *marshal*
la Norvège *Norway*
la pression *pressure*
le renseignement [c] *information*
la retraite *retreat*
russe *Russian*
soudain *suddenly*
*soutenir *sustain;* soutenu *sustained*
suffisamment *sufficiently*
se suicider *commit suicide*
le traitement *treatment*

au cours de *in the course of*
battre en retraite *retreat*
le camp de concentration *concentration camp*
la cinquième colonne *fifth column*
d'entre eux [d] *of them*
de plus *in addition, moreover*
la guerre de 39 *World War II* (1939–45)
sans cesse *ceaselessly, without stopping*

* An asterisk (*) placed before a verb indicates that this verb is irregular.

[a] With the ordinary meaning of *résistance,* during the occupation of 1940–1944 *la Résistance* designated in particular the resistance in France to German occupation and the group which was leading that resistance.

[b] Used by the French to indicate the landing of the American and English troops on the Norman coast of France on June 6, 1944.

[c] le renseignement *the piece of information;* les renseignements *information in general*

[d] Used in expressions such as *deux d'entre eux, quelques-uns d'entre eux.*

Devoirs

Use the **passé composé** *rather than the* **passé simple** *in these exercises. Do the sentences in each exercise* (a) *using . . .* **est-ce que** *. . .* (b) *without using . . .* **est-ce que** *. . .*

A. Write the French equivalent of each of the following sentences.

1. How did the Germans attain their aim? 2. Why did France and England declare war on [1] Germany? 3. How many countries did Germany attack? 4. When did Germany invade Poland? 5. Where did the American troops arrive in France? 6. To [2] what part of the country did France send soldiers? 7. In [3] what year did the generals decide to invade the country? 8. Why did the French resist the [4] troops which were occupying their country? 9. Where did the war begin?

[1] *à* [2] *Dans* [3] *En* [4] *aux*

B. Say aloud rapidly the French equivalent of each of the following sentences.

1. How did the war begin? 2. Why didn't France attack Germany at the beginning of the war? 3. When did Germany begin to attack France? 4. At what time [1] did the Germans occupy all France? 5. By whom were the French cities bombed during the occupation? 6. When did the American soldiers arrive in France? 7. Why did the German authorities shut up the French in concentration camps? 8. By whom were the French cities liberated?

[1] *moment*

QUARANTE-QUATRIÈME LEÇON

Vocabulaire

adopter	indispensable	la photographie
l'anecdote *f.*	s'inspirer	professionnel, professionnelle
la création	le mannequin [a]	révéler
le domaine	le mystère	le secret
draper	la note [b]	la série
gracieux, gracieuse		la tradition

[a] In this lesson, *le mannequin* has two meanings: (1) that of the English *mannequin* (a manufactured figure used to display clothing); (2) *a woman hired to display gowns by wearing them.*

[b] In this lesson, *la note* has two meanings: (1) that of the English *note* in the expression *to take notes;* (2) in the expression *dans la même note,* meaning *in the same pattern.*

l'acheteur *m.* *buyer*
*acquérir *acquire;* acquis *acquired*
l'atelier *m.* *workshop*
bien des[a] *many*
bien que *although*
le chapeau *hat*
le chic *elegance, smartness*
le chiffre *figure*
confectionner *manufacture*
la couture *sewing*
le croquis *first sketch, rough draft*
d'accord *in agreement*
défiler *parade, march past*
démontrer *demonstrate, prove, point out*
*défaire *undo;* défait *undone*
emporter *take away, carry off*
l'esquisse *f.* *sketch*
fabriquer *manufacture*
impressionnant *impressive*
innombrable *innumerable*
l'invité *m.* *guest*
jalousement *jealously*
lancer *launch*
légèrement *slightly*
le manteau *coat*
le morceau *piece*
nul, nulle *no* (adj.)
plier *fold*
porter *carry; wear*
quoi que *whatever*
ravi *enchanted, delighted*
la recherche *search*
*reproduire *reproduce;* reproduit *reproduced*
la robe *dress, gown*
le ruban *ribbon*
le sourire *smile*
la tendance *trend*
tendre *hold out, extend*
*tenir *hold; have;* tenu *held; had*
le tissu *cloth, fabric*
le vêtement *garment, clothing*

à la recherche de *in search of*
à plus bas prix *at a lower price*
de la même façon *in the same way*
être d'accord *be in agreement*
le lendemain soir *the next evening*
nulle part ailleurs *nowhere else*
payer un droit *pay for the right*
quoi que ce soit *anything whatever* (lit., *whatever it may be*)
sur quoi *whereupon*
cela tient à *that is due to, that depends on*
tous les combien *how often*

Devoirs

A. Write the French equivalent of each of the following sentences.

1. Do you need pencils? 2. Don't smoke in the subway. It's forbidden. 3. He promised his wife to buy a car. 4. Many students arrived without books. 5. It is difficult to understand the people who speak rapidly. 6. Do you speak French? It's easy. 7. I told my friend to wear a hat. 8. Did you ask Charles to close the door? 9. It is interesting to spend some weeks in the south of France.

* An asterisk (*) placed before a verb indicates that this verb is irregular.

[a] When *bien* is followed by any form of the partitive construction, it generally has the meaning of *many.* Thus, *bien d'autres choses* means *many other things.*

B. Say aloud rapidly the French equivalent of each of the following sentences.

1. It is easy to learn to speak French. 2. It is easy to do. 3. It is interesting to travel. 4. Let's leave tomorrow. It's impossible. 5. I told my mother to telephone me. 6. I told her to open the window. 7. He asked his friends to wait for[1] him. 8. He asked them to telephone him[2].

[1] Included in the verb. [2] Indirect object.

QUARANTE-CINQUIÈME LEÇON

Vocabulaire

s'adapter
agricole
l'allocation *f.*
bénéficier
civil
colonial
comparer
continuel, continuelle
le contraire
le contrôle
la destruction
l'économie *f.*
énergique
extraordinaire
la facilité
familial
le franc
le frigidaire
idéal (*adj.*)
incessant
industrialiser
l'inertie *f.*
l'inflation *f.*
instituer
l'irresponsabilité *f.*
largement
médical
la mesure
modeste
modifier
le nationaliste
normal
le Parlement
poser
le problème
le progrès[a]
prospère
la radio
réparer
le rôle
le salaire
la solution
la structure
la télévision
se transformer

l'agitation *f.* *agitation, restlessness, unrest*
améliorer *better*
apaiser *calm*
l'appel *m.* *call*
assurer *insure*
l'augmentation *f.* *increase*
augmenter *increase*
avoir à (+ *inf.*) *have to*
le cas *case*
constamment *constantly*
le coût *cost*
dépenser *spend*
le déplacement *moving*
disposer de *have at one's disposition*
dû, due (*pp of* devoir) à *due to*
épuiser *exhaust*
les frais *m. pl.* *expenses*
*intervenir *occur;* intervenu *occurred*
le logement *housing*
le loyer *rent*
la maladie *sickness*

* An asterisk (*) placed before a verb indicates that this verb is irregular.
[a] This word is often used in the plural; e.g., On a fait des progrès énormes.

malgré *in spite of*
malheureux, malheureuse *unhappy*
le milliard *billion*
la natalité *birth rate*
le niveau *level, standard*
la nouveauté *novelty, new thing*
outre-mer *overseas, beyond the seas*
la population *people*
posséder *possess*
le poste [a] *(radio, television) set*
*reconnaître *recognize;* reconnu *recognized*
le relèvement *recovery*
rembourser *reimburse*
renverser *overthrow, overturn*
*résoudre *resolve;* résolu *resolved*
la retraite *retirement; retirement pension*
sensiblement *considerably*
la tâche *task*
le tarif *rate*
toucher *receive (money)*
le traitement *pay (of civil servants and certain others)*
le travailleur *worker*

à ce sujet *on this subject*
à sa portée *at his disposition; within range of him*
à tarif réduit *at a reduced price*
l'allocation familiale [b] *family allowance*
au contraire *on the contrary*
le coût de la vie *cost of living*
en outre *moreover*
faire appel à *call on*
faire face à *confront*
le niveau de vie *standard of living*
le poste de radio *radio set*
le poste de télévision *television set*

Verbes

THE PAST CONDITIONAL

ALL VERBS *conjugated with* avoir	VERBS OF MOTION *conjugated with* être	REFLEXIVE VERBS *conjugated with* être
j'aurais demandé	je serais entré(e)	je me serais lavé(e)
tu aurais demandé	tu serais entré(e)	tu te serais lavé(e)
il aurait demandé	il serait entré	il se serait lavé
elle aurait demandé	elle serait entrée	elle se serait lavée
nous aurions demandé	nous serions entré(e)s	nous nous serions lavé(e)s
vous auriez demandé	vous seriez entré(e)(s)	vous vous seriez lavé(e)(s)
ils auraient demandé	ils seraient entrés	ils se seraient lavés
elles auraient demandé	elles seraient entrées	elles se seraient lavées

* An asterisk (*) placed before a verb indicates that this verb is irregular.

[a] Distinguish between *le poste,* meaning *police station, radio or television set,* or *position, job,* etc., and *la poste,* meaning *post office.*

[b] In addition to his base pay the French worker receives a certain extra sum for each child as well as certain other benefits at the time of the birth of the child and later.

Devoirs

A. Write the French equivalent of each of the following sentences.

1. If it rains, they will not go out. 2. What would you have done if your wife had gone to the theater? 3. If we spoke French well, we would travel in France. 4. If the pupils write the exercises, they will learn that language. 5. If France had had a different constitution, she would have made more progress after the war. 6. Will you go to Paris if you do not receive that letter? 7. If I had the time, I would read many books. 8. If we had opened the door, our friends would have come in. 9. Marie would sell her car if she could find a buyer.

B. Say aloud rapidly the French equivalent of each of the following sentences.

1. If you speak French, you will be able to go everywhere in Europe. 2. If you had spoken French, you would have been able to go everywhere in Europe. 3. If we were in France, we would speak French. 4. Who would come to see you if you were alone? 5. If you had come to see me, I would have helped you. 6. If I had had the time, I would have done the work. 7. If that workman has the time, he will do the work. 8. If I should lose my money, I would not be able to take the train.

THÈME

Leçons 41 à 45

Write the French equivalent of each of the following sentences.

1. Why did that woman wish to buy some perfume? 2. She will have a gift sent to her daughter. 3. Does she drive well? It is difficult to do. 4. If they knew the name of the street, they would be able to find her house. 5. Gérard told his father to send him the fountain pen. 6. Their houses were sold last week. 7. How did those soldiers die? 8. It is impossible to earn much money in a small town. It's true. 9. That is no longer done[1] today. 10. If you had found enough time, you would have been able to read some novels.

[1] Since this is a general statement, how is the English passive idea expressed in French? (§ 87 B 2)

QUARANTE-SIXIÈME LEÇON

Vocabulaire

l'action *f.*	l'expression *f.*	le papier	usuel, usuelle
le désir	le film	probable	vague
la discussion	le journaliste	le Rex[a]	le verbe
douter	l'ordre *m.*	le subjonctif	

[a] A popular name for movie houses in France. Pronounced [rɛks].

allô *exclamation used in answering the telephone in France, equivalent to our "hello"*
l'appareil *m.* (*radio*) *set; apparatus*
s'attendre à *expect*
courant *current*
la crainte *fear*
l'émission *f. program, broadcast*
employer *use;* s'employer *be used*
épatant *fine, "swell"*
*éteindre *turn off;* éteint *turned off*
facilement *easily*
le fauteuil[a] *chair with arms*
installer *settle, set up, install*
Jacques *Jack; James*
jeter *throw*
peut-être *perhaps*
le quotidien *daily newspaper*
ranger *arrange*
le récepteur *telephone mouthpiece and receiver*
saisir *seize*
le salon *living room*
se servir de (2) *use*
songer *think; dream*
sonner *ring*
la transmission *radio reception*
vif, vive *lively*

A (2) indicates an *-ir* verb of the second class. (§ 49 C)

à tout à l'heure *until later, so long*
ça va bien *that's fine, everything's going along well*
c'est ça *that's right*
c'est dommage *it's too bad*
comme je peux *however I can*
comment ça va? *How are things? How are you?*
le coup d'œil *glance*
d'accord *OK*
le film passe au Rex *the film is on at the Rex*
je n'en sais rien *I know nothing of it*
mon vieux *old top, old man (familiar greeting, used between intimate friends of any age)*
par conséquent *therefore*
un petit peu *a little bit*
peu probable *unlikely*
quand même *even so*
la table de travail *work table*
tout à l'heure (with future) *in a little while;* (with past) *just now, a little while ago*
la Tribune de Paris *popular radio program consisting of a discussion of current events by leading French journalists*

* An asterisk (*) placed before a verb indicates that this verb is irregular.
[a] The traditional translation of *armchair* gives a false impression of the nature of a *fauteuil.* Actually, it is any chair with arms, as distinguished from *une chaise,* which is a chair without arms.

Verbes

THE PRESENT SUBJUNCTIVE

a. Regular verbs:

-er *verbs*	*most* **-ir** *verbs*	*2d class* **-ir** *verbs*	**-re** *verbs*
que je donn*e*	que je puniss*e*	que je dorm*e*	que je répond*e*
que tu donn*es*	que tu puniss*es*	que tu dorm*es*	que tu répond*es*
qu'il donn*e*	qu'il puniss*e*	qu'il dorm*e*	qu'il répond*e*
que nous donn*ions*	que nous puniss*ions*	que nous dorm*ions*	que nous répond*ions*
que vous donn*iez*	que vous puniss*iez*	que vous dorm*iez*	que vous répond*iez*
qu'ils donn*ent*	qu'ils puniss*ent*	qu'ils dorm*ent*	qu'ils répond*ent*

***b. Irregular verbs following principle given in* § 80 B:**

	boire	**devoir**	**mourir**	**prendre**	**venir**
que je	boive	doive	meure	prenne	vienne
que tu	boives	doives	meures	prennes	viennes
qu'il	boive	doive	meure	prenne	vienne
que nous	buvions	devions	mourions	prenions	venions
que vous	buviez	deviez	mouriez	preniez	veniez
qu'ils	boivent	doivent	meurent	prennent	viennent

c. Verbs completely irregular in the present subjunctive:

The verbs *aller, avoir, être, faire, pouvoir, savoir, valoir,* and *vouloir* are completely irregular in the present subjunctive. The forms of the present subjunctive of these verbs are listed in § 80 C and may also be found in the next to the last column of the paradigms in § 95.

Devoirs

A. Write the French equivalent of each of the following sentences.

1. It is necessary that he leave[1] immediately. 2. It is possible that I shall finish my work before nine o'clock. 3. It is good that you should know the lesson. 4. It is‿better[2] that he should learn those verbs. 5. I want to understand French[3]. 6. He wants me to understand French[3]. 7. We want to answer[4] the letter. 8. We want him to answer[4] the letter. 9. It is unlikely that he will sleep ten hours.

[1] Use a form of *partir*. [2] Use a form of *valoir mieux*. [3] Supply the definite article. [4] This verb requires *à* before its object.

B. [1] *Say aloud rapidly the French equivalent of each of the following sentences.*

1. You must[2] go to Paris. 2. He wants me to go to Paris. 3. It would be better for you to stay at home. 4. I should like to have you stay at

[1] Before doing this exercise, reread the note on page 162.
[2] Say this sentence with *il faut.*

home. 5. It is possible that these students know what you are doing. 6. It is important that we do our work. 7. It is important that you be in class every day. 8. It would be better for you to be in class.

QUARANTE-SEPTIÈME LEÇON

Vocabulaire

approuver
la cérémonie
Charles
le compliment
la fiancée
juger
le mariage
patient
préférable
proposer
regretter

aboutir à *end up in, result in*
l'amitié *f.* *friendship*
dansant *dancing*
désolé *sorry*
effrayer *frighten*
l'égard *m.* *regard, respect*
emmener *take (a person), take along (a person), lead away*
l'enfance *f.* *childhood*
épouser *marry*
la Française *French girl, French woman*
l'indication *f.* *directions, "tips," information; indication, instruction*
justement *precisely*
oser *dare*
la peur *fear*
remercier *thank*
*revoir *see again;* revu *seen again*
*rire *laugh;* ri *laughed*
le sien, la sienne *his; hers; its*
voyons! *look here; let's see*

à cet égard *in this respect*
à peine *scarcely*
allons donc! *well, for goodness sakes! you don't say!*
avoir peur *be afraid*
faire la connaissance de *get acquainted with*
faire part à quelqu'un *inform someone, announce to someone*
la soirée dansante *dance*

Verbes

THE PAST SUBJUNCTIVE

ALL VERBS	VERBS OF MOTION	REFLEXIVE VERBS
conjugated with avoir	*conjugated with* être	*conjugated with* être
que j'aie donné	que je sois entré(e)	que je me sois lavé(e)
que tu aies donné	que tu sois entré(e)	que tu te sois lavé(e)
qu'il ait donné	qu'il soit entré	qu'il se soit lavé
qu'elle ait donné	qu'elle soit entrée	qu'elle se soit lavée
que nous ayons donné	que nous soyons entré(e)s	que nous nous soyons lavé(e)s
que vous ayez donné	que vous soyez entré(e)(s)	que vous vous soyez lavé(e)(s)
qu'ils aient donné	qu'ils soient entrés	qu'ils se soient lavés
qu'elles aient donné	qu'elles soient entrées	qu'elles se soient lavées

* An asterisk (*) placed before a verb indicates that this verb is irregular.

Devoirs

A. Write the French equivalent of each of the following sentences.

1. I am afraid that they will be too‿far‿away[1]. I am afraid that they were too‿far‿away[1]. 2. We are afraid that we will have too much work. We are afraid that we had too much work. 3. He is glad that you are selling the house. He is glad that you sold the house. 4. We are glad that we will travel in Spain. We are glad that we traveled in Spain. 5. It is too‿bad that he is not coming. 6. Are you sorry that she will be here? Are you sorry that she is here? Are you sorry that she was here? 7. Are you sorry that you are here? Are you sorry that you were here? 8. We have a teacher who knows Russian. We are looking for a teacher who knows Russian. 9. There is no one who can tell us the name of that monument.

[1] *trop loin*

B. Say aloud rapidly the French equivalent of each of the following sentences.

1. I am glad that you are here. 2. I am glad that you were with us at[1] that time. 3. He is afraid that she will go to[2] Russia. 4. He is afraid that she went to[2] Russia. 5. The pupils regret that the teacher knows their secret. 6. They regret that the teacher wrote a letter to their parents. 7. The tourists regret that they are leaving[3] Paris. 8. They regret that they left[3] France.

[1] *à ce moment-là* [2] *en* [3] Use a form of *quitter.*

QUARANTE-HUITIÈME LEÇON

Vocabulaire

l'alliance *f.*
amuser
l'article *m.*
célébrer
le bal
le code

consulter
la date
le préliminaire
publier
le registre

relatif, relative
religieux, religieuse
la sécurité
le sermon
spécial
uniquement

l'aise *f.* *ease, comfort*
l'annonce *f.* *announcement*
aveuglément[a] *blindly*
la bague *ring*
le ban *banns, public announcement or proclamation of marriage*

le conseil *piece of advice;* les conseils *advice (in general)*
la convenance *convenience*
le devoir *duty*
*disparaître *disappear;* disparu *disappeared*
la dot[b] *dowry*

* An asterisk (*) placed before a verb indicates that this verb is irregular.
[a] For the use of *-ément* to form adverbs, see § 19 C.
[b] Pronounce the final *-t* [dɔt].

économiser *save, economize*
égal *equal*
l'époux *m. spouse;* les époux *husband and wife*
féliciter *congratulate*
les fiançailles *f. official promise of marriage, engagement*
le fiancé *betrothed, engaged person*
fiancer *become engaged*
le lieu[a] *place*
*maintenir *maintain;* maintenu *maintained*
le maire *mayor*
le prêtre *priest*
le rapport *relation*
régler *settle, arrange*
le témoin *witness*
le tour *turn*

à l'aise *at (one's) ease*
à son tour *in (his) turn*
avoir lieu *take place*
le Code civil *civil code*
le Code Napoléon *civil code made by Napoleon*
en attendant que *until*
être en rapport *be in relation*
le mariage de convenance *marriage of convenience, marriage for money and position*
mettre de côté *put aside, save*
qu'entendez-vous par *what do you understand by*
suffisamment de *enough*

Devoirs

A. Write the French equivalent of each of the following sentences.

1. Is Latin[1] the most difficult language that there is? 2. This ring belongs to my sister; mine have disappeared. 3. What is the most interesting novel that you have read? 4. He is surprised that he has not received the announcement of their engagement. 5. Your room[2] is very small; ours is larger. 6. Who is the best teacher that you know? 7. Are you glad that you are no longer in England? 8. Our customs are different from theirs. 9. Their marriage will take place tomorrow, but I am afraid that I shall not attend the ceremony. 10. He is glad that he has been able to save enough to[3] buy a car.

[1] Use the article with names of languages. [2] *chambre* [3] *pour*

B. Say aloud rapidly the French equivalent of each of the following sentences.

1. I am glad that I am not obliged to[1] go to the evening party. 2. I am glad that I did not read that article. 3. We are afraid that we did not arrive[2] soon[3] enough. 4. We are afraid that we will not arrive soon[3]

[1] *de* [2] With what auxiliary verb are intransitive verbs of motion conjugated?
[3] soon enough *assez tôt*

* An asterisk (*) placed before a verb indicates that this verb is irregular.
[a] The word *lieu* is rarely used except in expressions such as *avoir lieu* (to take place), *au lieu de* (in place of), *chef-lieu* (seat of government of a *département*), etc. The common word for *place* is *endroit.*

enough. 5. He regrets that he does not understand you. 6. He regrets that he did not understand you. 7. Is Paris the most beautiful city that you know[1]? 8. What is the most interesting film that you have seen?

[1] Use a form of *connaître*.

QUARANTE-NEUVIÈME LEÇON

l'accident *m.*
Aix-les-Bains[a]
Belfort
la caravane
Digne
se disperser
Évian
l'itinéraire *m.*
La Rochelle
Lille
Metz
Montpellier
Pau
le peuple
populaire
le résultat
sportif, sportive

à moins que *unless*
l'Anglais *m.* *Englishman*
l'arrivée *f.* *arrival*
attention! *look out!*
autant (de) *as much, as many*
la côte *hill, slope*
la couleur *color*
le coureur *racer*
la course *race*
la course-cycliste *bicycle race*
dégager *free, clear*
se dépêcher *hurry*
l'étape *f.* *stage*
le favori *favorite*
le gendarme *(state) police*
jusqu'à ce que *until*
se masser *crowd, mass, get together in a group*
le paysan *peasant*
le peloton *group, company, line of racers*
pourvu que *provided that*
pratiquer *practice, engage in*
publicitaire *advertising* (adj.)
la publicité *publicity, advertising*
quoique *although*
la taille *size, height*

ça m'est égal *that's all the same to me*
des deux côtés *on both sides*
en haut *at the top*
faire du sport *engage in sports, take part in sports*
il y en a pour un quart d'heure avant que *it will be a quarter of an hour before*
je n'y connais rien *I'm not acquainted with it at all, I don't know anything about it*
pratiquer un sport *engage in a sport*
qui arrive le premier *who is the first to arrive*
le Tour de France *name of the most popular bicycle race in France*

[a] Pronounced [ɛkslebɛ̃].

Verbes

The following simple verbs follow the principles given in § 80 B to form their irregular present subjunctives. You can also find the complete present subjunctive of these verbs by consulting the next to the last column of the paradigms in § 95.

INFINITIVE	PRESENT SUBJUNCTIVE		INFINITIVE	PRESENT SUBJUNCTIVE	
	que je	**que nous**		**que je**	**que nous**
boire	boive	buvions	mettre	mette	mettions
connaître	connaisse	connaissions	mourir	meure	mourions
courir	coure	courions	naître	naisse	naissions
craindre	craigne	craignions	ouvrir	ouvre	ouvrions
croire	croie	croyions	plaire	plaise	plaisions
devoir	doive	devions	pleuvoir	(il) pleuve	
dire	dise	disions	recevoir	reçoive	recevions
écrire	écrive	écrivions	suivre	suive	suivions
envoyer	envoie	envoyions	tenir	tienne	tenions
falloir	(il) faille		vivre	vive	vivions
lire	lise	lisions	voir	voie	voyions

Devoirs

A. Write the French equivalent of each of the following sentences.

1. We are going to France in order that my sister may get acquainted with Paris. We are going to France in order that we may get acquainted with Paris. 2. He will tell me the result of the examination before you leave[1]. He will tell me the result of the examination before he leaves. 3. Although I understand the grammar, I do not know the words of that language. 4. Stay here until I tell you his name. 5. They will not buy that house unless you approve their choice. 6. We'll go to the movie provided that it does not rain. 7. Hurry unless you wish to stay here. 8. The hour of his departure will be put in the newspapers so that the people can go to the station. 9. He will work until I tell him to stop.

[1] Use a form of *partir.*

B. Say aloud rapidly the French equivalent of each of the following sentences.

1. I stayed home in order to work. 2. I stayed home so that you could go out. 3. Telephone me before you go out. 4. One of my friends will telephone me before I go out. 5. Write me before your departure. 6. Stay here until we arrive. 7. Although you do not like games, you engage in sports, don't you? 8. You can go out provided that you come back before the arrival of the guests.

CINQUANTIÈME LEÇON

Vocabulaire

l'administration *f.*
l'amateur *m.*
le base-ball
le basket-ball
le club
consister
distinguer
le football
le golf
le hockey
individualiste
individuel, individuelle
officiel, officielle
Olympique
Pierre de Coubertin
participer
personnel, personnelle
le professionnel
le rugby
le tennis
tolérer

l'athlétisme *m.* *track and field*
auparavant *formerly*
le ballon *football*
le compte *account; count; benefit*
couramment *currently, commonly; fluently*
l'équipe *f.* *team*
s'habituer *become accustomed to*
le joueur *player*
le loisir *leisure;* les loisirs *leisure time*
la mentalité *nature, psychological make-up (of a person or people)*
le milieu *class, environment; center*
Pierre *Peter*
la rencontre *meeting*

autant que[a] *as much as; as far as*
d'où *from where, whence*
en tout cas *in any case*
faire du sport *engage in sports*
l'homme d'affaires *business man*
les Jeux Olympiques *Olympic games*
porter plus d'intérêt *have more interest*
pour son compte *personally; for his own benefit*

Devoirs

A. Write the French equivalent of each of the following sentences.

1. I am sure that you have already done that work. 2. I believe that sports are important at the university. 3. Do you think that they[1] will have a team next year? 4. We do not think that you will find a great deal of golf in France. 5. Are you sure that he knows how[2] to play[3] tennis? 6. He thinks that they traveled a great deal while they were in Europe. 7. We believe that professional football[4] will be more common later. 8. Per-

[1] *on* [2] Included in the verb. [3] Before a game, the verb *jouer* requires the preposition *à* + article. [4] Supply the definite article with this noun.

[a] Although *autant que* is usually followed by the indicative, it takes the subjunctive in the expression *autant que je sache,* etc.

haps you will find French football[1] different from ours. 9. We ate too much yesterday.

[1] Supply the definite article with this noun.

B. Say aloud rapidly the French equivalent of each of the following sentences.

1. I think that our guests left yesterday. 2. I do not think that the mayor will come to see us tomorrow. 3. Do you think that he will speak French with us? 4. We think that he will go to France soon. 5. I do not think that he knows when he will leave. 6. Do you think that it will rain? 7. Perhaps it will rain tomorrow. 8. I have worked a great deal. 9. I have not yet begun to work.

Thème

Leçons 46 à 50

Write the French equivalent of each of the following sentences.

1. I am glad that they can travel. I am glad that they have been able to travel. 2. We are afraid that they will lose their money. We are afraid that we will lose our money. 3. He wants me[1] to write him[2] a letter. 4. We'll read that article so that we may learn something about[3] that subject. 5. I believe that he already has bought the furniture. 6. Although you have seen their flowers, you have not yet seen ours. 7. Perhaps he will tell us the date of his arrival in order that we may know when he will get married. 8. Hurry unless you wish to stay at home. 9. Is there someone here who can go to the city hall with me?

[1] How do the French say this construction? See page 262, note 1. [2] indirect object
[3] *sur*

Pasteur

La science et ses découvertes sont bien plus importantes dans l'évolution du progrès humain que les rois, les luttes politiques, les manœuvres diplomatiques et les guerres. La science n'a pas de patrie. Ses bienfaits se[1] font sentir partout. Chaque nation y a apporté sa contribution. En France, aucun savant n'est plus célèbre que Pasteur.

Avant Pasteur on n'avait qu'une idée très vague de la cause des maladies contagieuses. Les recherches de ce savant bouleversèrent les connaissances scientifiques de son époque. Grâce à ses travaux et à ceux de savants anglais et allemands, beaucoup de vies humaines furent sauvées.

Pasteur consacra sa vie à la science. Professeur de chimie à l'Université de Strasbourg, il commença par des études sur la fermentation du lait et des alcools qui lui firent découvrir un nouveau procédé de stérilisation appelé *pasteurisation.* Plus tard, il établit la théorie des germes et en détermina l'application en médecine.

A ce moment-là, beaucoup d'animaux domestiques mouraient d'une maladie contagieuse contre laquelle Pasteur venait de[2] découvrir un vaccin. La Société d'Agriculture de Melun voulant des preuves de l'efficacité de ce vaccin, proposa de faire une expérience publique de la nouvelle méthode. Vingt-cinq moutons et six vaches devaient être vaccinés; on leur inoculerait ensuite la maladie, ainsi qu'à vingt-cinq autres moutons et quatre vaches non-vaccinés. Pasteur accepta. L'expérience fut couronnée de succès, car tous les animaux vaccinés survécurent, tandis que tous les autres moururent.

Or, Pasteur n'avait jamais oublié l'impression que lui avait faite dans son enfance une personne mordue par un chien enragé. Il se mit à étudier la rage. Il expérimentait une méthode de traitement qu'il avait déjà appliquée à des animaux, quand le 6 juillet 1885 une femme vint frapper à sa porte avec son enfant Joseph Meister, âgé de neuf ans. L'enfant avait été sérieusement mordu le 4 juillet. Le chien avait été examiné et on avait vu qu'il était enragé.

Pasteur savait que son traitement avait déjà guéri des chiens malades.

[1] *are felt*

[2] *had just.* The imperfect of the idiom *venir de* is expressed by a pluperfect in English.

La question se posa: avait-il le droit d'essayer un tel traitement sur un être humain? L'enfant ne portait pas moins de[1] quatorze blessures et il était condamné. Seul restait le secours éventuel du vaccin.

Pasteur hésita encore. Après avoir pris l'avis d'un médecin, affirmant que le malheureux enfant ne pouvait pas échapper à la rage, il se décida à tenter l'expérience qui avait jusqu'alors réussi sur les chiens.

Les inoculations furent faites chaque jour du 7 au 16 juillet; treize inoculations furent faites en quinze jours[2]. Pendant tout le traitement Pasteur fut très inquiet. Le jour il passait de longues heures à marcher seul dans les bois. Mais ce fut un grand succès: le vaccin avait produit l'effet espéré et Joseph Meister ne présenta plus le moindre symptôme de rage. A partir de ce jour la méthode de Pasteur se pratiqua couramment.

QUESTIONS

1. Pourquoi la science est-elle plus importante dans l'évolution du progrès humain que les rois et les guerres? 2. Quel est le nouveau procédé de stérilisation découvert grâce aux études de Pasteur sur la fermentation du lait? 3. Racontez l'expérience de Pasteur sur les animaux de Melun. 4. Qui est venu frapper chez Pasteur le 6 juillet 1885? 5. Pourquoi Pasteur a-t-il hésité à appliquer son traitement à Joseph Meister? 6. Qu'est-ce qui l'a décidé à tenter l'expérience sur un être humain? 7. Combien d'inoculations ont été faites en quinze jours? 8. Quels ont été les résultats de ce traitement?

DEVOIRS

® *A. Indiquez le genre des noms suivants en écrivant* **le** *ou* **la** *devant chaque nom.* EXEMPLES: *la* stérilisation; *le* village (*Voir Grammaire* § 7 *B*)

1. contribution 2. médecin 3. tristesse 4. tableau 5. patrie 6. Norvège 7. mariage 8. dictée 9. renseignement 10. mécanisme 11. statue 12. samedi 13. blessure 14. maladie 15. nuage 16. Canada 17. théorie 18. femme 19. traitement 20. Belgique 21. printemps 22. formation

® *B. Écrivez le pluriel des noms suivants.* EXEMPLE: le général — les généraux (*Voir Grammaire* § 8)

1. le prix 2. la cause 3. le travail 4. le bateau 5. le nez 6. le jour 7. l'animal 8. le feu 9. le bois 10. le journal 11. le succès

[1] For the use of *de* to express *than,* see § 13 B. [2] meaning?

C. Écrivez les quatre formes des adjectifs suivants. EXEMPLE: important, importante, importants, importantes. (*Voir Grammaire §§ 10, 11*)

1. malheureux 2. quel 3. scientifique 4. enragé 5. malade 6. inquiet 7. sportif 8. égal 9. bon 10. blanc 11. doux 12. frais 13. gentil 14. faux

D. Introduisez les adjectifs indiqués dans la phrase pour modifier le nom en italique. Expliquez oralement pourquoi on met l'adjectif avant ou après le nom. EXEMPLE: (nouveau) Il a proposé de faire une expérience de la *méthode.* Il a proposé de faire une expérience de la ***nouvelle*** *méthode.* (*Voir Grammaire § 12*)

1. (domestique) Beaucoup d'*animaux* mouraient d'une maladie inconnue. 2. (blanc) Le médecin habitait à Strasbourg dans une *maison.* 3. (isolé) Une femme qui habitait dans une *région* de France avait un enfant qui avait été mordu par un chien. 4. (malheureux) L'*enfant* ne pouvait pas échapper à la rage. 5. (pauvre) La *femme* est venue frapper à la porte de Pasteur. 6. (vieux) Ce *savant* savait que l'enfant était condamné. 7. (excellent) Il avait une *raison* pour essayer son traitement. 8. (français) Les travaux des *savants* ont sauvé de nombreuses vies. 9. (long) Auriez-vous fait un *voyage* pour voir un grand médecin? 10. (étranger) Seriez-vous allé dans un *pays?*

E. Remplacez les tirets par la forme convenable du comparatif ou du superlatif des adjectifs indiqués. EXEMPLE: Bismarck a organisé une des armées (fort) d'Europe. Bismarck a organisé une des armées *les plus fortes* d'Europe. (*Voir Grammaire § 13 A, C*)

1. Est-ce que Montréal est la (grand) ville du Canada? 2. Il est (important) de voyager que de lire. 3. Quelle est la (bon) façon d'apprendre une langue étrangère? 4. Pasteur est le savant (connu) de France. 5. Il est (célèbre) que tous les autres savants français.

F. Remplacez les tirets par le mot convenable. Expliquez oralement la raison. (*Voir § 13 B, D*)

1. La Belgique est plus petite —— la France. 2. Montmartre est le quartier le plus animé —— Paris. 3. Les femmes parlent-elles plus —— les hommes? 4. J'ai lu plus —— quinze pages de votre livre. 5. Aucun élève n'a fait moins —— deux fautes.

G. Remplacez les tirets par la forme convenable du présent de **savoir** *ou* **connaître**, *selon le cas. (Voir Grammaire § 94*—know)

1. ——-vous mon professeur de français? 2. Nous —— que vous partez ce soir. 3. Mes frères —— mademoiselle Dupuy. 4. Je —— les œuvres de Zola. 5. Ce petit garçon a appris ce poème; il le —— maintenant. 6. Nous —— bien la région près de Bordeaux. 7. Le père de Robert est sénateur; il —— le Président de la République. 8. Ce jeune homme —— jouer au football.

® CONVERSATION

1. Demandez à Monsieur A. s'il connaît l'œuvre de Pasteur. 2. Demandez à Monsieur B. s'il sait jouer au tennis. 3. Demandez à Monsieur C. s'il connaît Paris. 4. Demandez à Monsieur D. s'il sait tous les mots de cette leçon.

VOCABULAIRE — PAGES 351–352

GRAMMAIRE [1]

A. The gender of nouns. (§ 7)
B. The plural of nouns. (§ 8)
C. The feminine and plural of adjectives. (§§ 10, 11)
D. The position of adjectives. (§ 12)
E. The comparison of adjectives. (§ 13 A, C, E)
F. Ways of expressing *than* with the comparative and *in* with the superlative. (§ 13 B, D)
G. Ways of expressing *know* in French. (§ 94)

[1] Because of the broad nature of the review exercises, the grammar is stated topically instead of in questions. The letters indicating the topics correspond to the letters at the head of the exercises. You will know many of these principles from your former lessons. If you can do the exercises without reference to the grammar, this indicates that you have mastered the principles involved. If you cannot, read over the grammar references before doing the exercises.

Louis XIV

La France n'a pas toujours été une république. Du règne de Clovis (481–511) à la Révolution française (1789–94), elle a été gouvernée par des rois. Pendant de longs siècles, et surtout au moyen âge, ces rois avaient peu de pouvoir. Chaque province était alors gouvernée par un seigneur féodal qui se considérait comme le chef absolu de son propre territoire et qui était parfois aussi puissant que le roi lui-même. A cette époque la France n'était pas encore une très grande nation. Mais peu à peu, les rois unifièrent le royaume et la France acquit de plus en plus de prestige parmi les nations du monde.

C'est sous le règne de Louis XIV (1643–1715) que la France parvint à l'apogée de sa gloire et de sa puissance. Elle possédait de vastes territoires en Amérique; elle avait une forte armée qui lui permettait d'être la première puissance militaire et politique d'Europe; sa littérature, arrivée grâce à Corneille, Racine et Molière à son plus haut degré de perfection, servait de modèle à tous les écrivains du continent; son art et son architecture étaient célèbres et imités partout. Le français était devenu la langue diplomatique et on le parlait dans tous les milieux cultivés d'Europe.

En même temps, le pouvoir personnel du roi s'étendit de plus en plus. C'est ainsi qu'au dix-septième siècle le pouvoir royal devint absolu et que le roi gouverna seul. Louis XIV, qui dirigea personnellement les affaires du royaume pendant cinquante-quatre ans et acheva la centralisation du pouvoir, fut le plus absolu de tous les rois de France. On disait alors que la monarchie était de droit divin, que le roi était le représentant de Dieu sur la terre. Louis XIV, cependant, eut l'intelligence et la sagesse de s'entourer de ministres dont certains furent pour lui de remarquables conseillers. A l'intérieur du pays, il s'appliqua à rétablir l'ordre dans l'administration; il encouragea l'agriculture, l'industrie et les travaux publics; il créa une marine, réorganisa l'armée et fortifia les frontières; enfin et surtout, il acheva l'unification territoriale du pays. A l'étranger, il entreprit une longue série de guerres qui assurèrent à la France un grand prestige.

Mais si le règne de Louis XIV représente l'apogée de la gloire française, on peut y trouver aussi les germes de son déclin. Louis XIV fut un roi despotique et, à partir de 1685, sa haine contre les protestants, dont il voulait interdire la doctrine, entraîna de violentes querelles religieuses. La cour, dont il aimait s'entourer, comprenait de dix-sept à dix-huit mille personnes et son entretien absorbait une grande partie des revenus du royaume. Ces luttes religieuses, les dépenses extravagantes qu'occasionnaient le train de vie et les fêtes de la cour, la corruption de la cour elle-même, les guerres lointaines si coûteuses, tout cela finit par affaiblir le pays.

Questions

1. Quand la France a-t-elle été gouvernée par des rois? 2. Les rois de France avaient-ils beaucoup de pouvoir au moyen âge? 3. Par qui étaient gouvernées les provinces au moyen âge? 4. Qu'est-ce qui permettait à la France d'être la première puissance militaire et politique d'Europe sous le règne de Louis XIV? 5. A qui la littérature française servait-elle alors de modèle? 6. Où étaient imités l'architecture et l'art français? 7. Qu'était devenue la langue française et où la parlait-on pendant le règne de Louis XIV? 8. Dans quel continent les milieux cultivés parlent-ils encore le français? 9. Quelles sont actuellement les langues diplomatiques? 10. Quand le pouvoir royal est-il devenu absolu en France? 11. A quelle époque la France a-t-elle atteint l'apogée de sa gloire et de sa puissance? 12. De qui disait-on que le roi était le représentant sur la terre? 13. De qui Louis XIV s'est-il entouré? 14. Quelles ont été les grandes réformes de Louis XIV? 15. Quelle unification a été achevée sous son règne? 16. Qu'ont assuré à la France les guerres de Louis XIV? 17. Quelle doctrine Louis XIV voulait-il interdire? 18. Qu'occasionnaient le train de vie et les fêtes de la cour de Louis XIV?

Devoirs

A. Remplacez[1] *les tirets par l'article défini ou indéfini s'il y a lieu. Expliquez oralement chaque emploi ou omission de l'article.* (*Voir Grammaire* § 4)

1. Aimez-vous —— musique et —— art? 2. Nous commencerons un nouveau roman —— mercredi. 3. Monsieur Lefort est —— bon professeur. 4. Pierre est resté à Chamonix, —— petite ville de France près du mont Blanc. 5. Le mari de madame Perrot est —— médecin. 6. Est-ce que —— commerce et —— industrie sont importants aux

[1] *Fill out the blanks with the definite or indefinite article where necessary.* The expression *s'il y a lieu* implies that some blanks require no word to complete the meaning of the sentence.

États-Unis? 7. Avez-vous déjà visité —— Suisse? 8. Non, j'ai passé mes vacances en —— France. 9. Pasteur était —— professeur à l'Université de Strasbourg. 10. Nous n'avons jamais de classe —— samedi. 11. Quand madame Delécluse et son mari ne veulent pas que les enfants comprennent la conversation, ils parlent en —— anglais. 12. Généralement madame Laffont va voir sa mère —— lundi. 13. Mademoiselle Deslandes, —— professeur de lycée à Rouen, est allée passer un an au Canada. 14. Nous irons voir le Louvre —— vendredi. 15. Je ne parle pas —— allemand, mais j'ai appris —— français très jeune.

B. *Remplacez les tirets par l'article partitif ou par* de. *Expliquez oralement l'emploi ou l'omission de chaque article partitif.* (*Voir Grammaire* §§ 5, 6)

1. Pendant —— longs siècles la France a été gouvernée par —— rois qui avaient peu —— pouvoir. 2. Au dix-septième siècle elle possédait —— vastes territoires en Amérique. 3. Avez-vous besoin —— argent? 4. La gare était pleine —— voyageurs. 5. Ce paysan habitait une maison —— bois. 6. Voulez-vous —— bon lait? 7. Il n'y a pas —— beurre sur la table. 8. Ce ne sont pas —— hommes, ce sont —— bêtes. 9. La plupart —— étudiants aiment chanter les chansons françaises. 10. Les touristes rapportent bien —— choses avec eux. 11. Y a-t-il assez —— encre dans votre stylo? 12. Notre maison est entourée —— fleurs. 13. Le bureau du professeur est couvert —— livres. 14. Il y a beaucoup —— avions près des grandes villes. 15. On ne peut pas trouver —— riz en France. 16. Nous avons vu —— belles femmes à Paris. 17. Nous sommes allés au cinéma bien —— fois.

C. *Remplacez les tirets par la préposition qui veut dire* in, at *ou* to. (*Voir Grammaire* § 42)

1. J'irai d'abord —— Londres, ensuite —— Paris. 2. Nous resterons —— France deux mois, ensuite, nous irons —— Espagne, —— Portugal, —— Italie, —— Allemagne, —— Danemark et —— Angleterre. 3. Allez-vous aussi —— Amérique? 4. Oui, je vais —— Amérique du Nord. 5. Avez-vous été —— États-Unis et —— Mexique? 6. Non, je suis resté —— Canada. 7. Je passerai l'hiver —— Marseille ou —— Nice.

D. *Remplacez les tirets par la préposition qui exprime* from. (*Voir Grammaire* § 43)

1. Votre oncle est-il revenu —— États-Unis et —— Canada? 2. Il

est parti —— Angleterre hier, il reviendra —— Suisse la semaine prochaine et —— Portugal au mois de décembre. 3. Cette dame-ci vient —— Russie, celle-là vient —— Japon.

E. Remplacez les mots anglais par l'équivalent français. N'ajoutez pas de préposition où il n'y en a pas dans la phrase française. Écrivez left *au passé composé. (Voir Grammaire* §94 — leave)

1. Cet étudiant (*goes out*) beaucoup. 2. Nous (*left*) la voiture dans le garage. 3. Yvonne (*left*) son amie après une longue conversation. 4. Le professeur (*left*) de la salle un moment. 5. Nous ne pouvons rien faire; je (*am leaving*). 6. Georges (*went out*) avec Louise Dupré. 7. Votre mère (*left*) de l'argent sur la radio. 8. Charles (*left*) l'université à cinq heures. 9. Les Perrot (*left*) pour l'Italie ce matin. 10. Leurs enfants (*left*) de Paris hier.

® CONVERSATION

1. Demandez à Monsieur E. s'il est sorti avec des camarades hier soir. 2. Demandez à Monsieur F. s'il va partir pour la France à la fin du mois. 3. Demandez à Monsieur G. à quelle heure il a quitté l'école. 4. Demandez à Monsieur H. où il a laissé son livre de français.

VOCABULAIRE — PAGE 353

GRAMMAIRE

A. The uses and omission of articles. (§ 4)
B. The use of the partitive article and of *de.* (§ 5, 6)
C. The prepositions of place *to, in, at.* (§ 42)
D. The preposition of place *from.* (§ 43)
E. Ways of expressing *leave* in French. (§ 94)

CINQUANTE-TROISIÈME LEÇON

Le Château de Versailles

La cour de Louis XIV était la plus brillante du continent. C'est pour donner à cette cour une résidence digne de son éclat que Louis XIV construisit à vingt kilomètres de Paris le château de Versailles.

Dès qu'on le voit, ce château donne une impression de majesté grandiose, avec sa vaste cour d'honneur entourée de hautes grilles. Son immense façade semble encore agrandie par la perspective des deux ailes. Derrière le château on aperçoit de magnifiques jardins au delà desquels une vaste forêt s'étend à perte de vue. Cette forêt, ces jardins et le château lui-même évoquent non seulement l'époque de Louis XIV mais encore bien d'autres souvenirs de l'histoire de France.

Le château contient de très nombreuses salles. Dans les unes on peut admirer des peintures qui représentent les principaux épisodes de l'histoire de France, dans d'autres il y a des statues de rois et de reines de France, dans d'autres enfin on voit les meubles des styles les plus purs des différentes époques.

La plus belle salle du château est une longue pièce éclairée par dix-sept grandes fenêtres donnant sur les jardins. En face de ces fenêtres se trouvent dix-sept grands miroirs. Cette salle, appelée la Galerie des Glaces, est célèbre dans l'histoire pour deux raisons principales: d'abord, c'est là qu'en 1871 le roi de Prusse fut proclamé empereur d'Allemagne et que naquit l'Empire allemand; ensuite, c'est là que fut signé en 1919 le traité de Versailles qui mit fin à la guerre de 1914.

Les jardins de Versailles sont caractéristiques de l'époque où fut construit le château. Il est impossible de dire à quel point la vue de ces jardins aux [1] lignes régulières évoque la beauté du passé! Ces jardins à la française sont dessinés géométriquement avec deux grandes allées centrales perpendiculaires. De chaque côté de ces allées, des massifs et des parterres de fleurs sont disposés avec une symétrie parfaite. Les jardins de ce genre sont l'expression du goût classique du dix-septième siècle. Ils montrent comment la nature devait être ordonnée pour plaire aux Français de cette époque. Ils font contraste avec les jardins de style *rock garden,* qui sont

[1] *with straight lines.* The preposition *à* is often used to introduce a phrase indicating a characteristic quality of the noun it modifies.

l'expression du romantisme du dix-neuvième siècle. Les jardins de Versailles furent imités partout en Europe: en Angleterre, en Allemagne et en Espagne.

Dans le parc se trouve le Grand Trianon, magnifique édifice en marbre de couleur, construit par Louis XIV lorsqu'il s'aperçut que le grand château manquait d'intimité. Tout près de là se trouve le Petit Trianon où habita jadis la femme de Louis XVI, la reine Marie-Antoinette.

Aujourd'hui, le château est devenu un musée national. Chaque jour, des centaines de touristes le visitent et reviennent à Paris vivement impressionnés par sa beauté et par les vestiges du passé qu'ils y rencontrent à chaque pas.

Questions

1. Dans quel but Louis XIV a-t-il construit le château de Versailles? 2. Quelle impression a-t-on en regardant la façade du château? 3. Que contiennent les différentes salles du château? 4. Quels sont les deux événements qui ont rendu célèbre la Galerie des Glaces? 5. Comment sont dessinés les jardins à la française? 6. Quel goût expriment les jardins à la française? 7. Dans quels pays les jardins de Versailles ont-ils été imités? 8. Quand Louis XIV a-t-il construit le Grand Trianon? 9. Quelle est la reine qui a habité autrefois le Petit Trianon? 10. Qu'est devenu aujourd'hui le château de Versailles? 11. Qu'est-ce qui impressionne les touristes qui visitent ce château?

Devoirs

A. Mettez au présent les verbes indiqués entre parenthèses. Ils sont tous réguliers. (*Voir Grammaire* §§ *49 A, B, C, D, 95*)

1. Quand on est à Paris, on (visiter) les monuments et les musées. 2. J'(entendre) la voix du professeur. 3. Robert (dormir) toujours jusqu'à dix heures du matin. 4. Nous (se dépêcher) parce que nous avons beaucoup à faire. 5. Les membres du collège électoral (choisir) le Président de la République. 6. Les élèves (répondre) aux questions du professeur. 7. Je (partir) ce matin et les autres (partir) cet après-midi.

® *B. Indiquez le temps des verbes suivants et mettez-les au présent de l'indicatif. Ces verbes sont tous irréguliers au présent.* Exemple: elle aurait vu (conditionnel passé): elle voit. (*Voir Grammaire* §§ *49 E, 95*)

1. il faudra 2. ils pourraient 3. ils avaient cru 4. il sut 5.

elles viendraient 6. j'étais 7. elle est morte 8. il tint 9. j'enverrais 10. j'ai pris 11. nous avons connu 12. elles reçurent 13. j'aurais lu 14. vous vous êtes assis 15. vous direz 16. elle s'est mise 17. ils firent 18. ils iront 19. je devrais

C. Donnez les trois formes de l'impératif des verbes suivants. EXEMPLE: (manger) cette pomme. (1) Mange cette pomme. (2) Mangeons cette pomme. (3) Mangez cette pomme. (*Voir Grammaire* §§ 79, 95)

1. (regarder) ce tableau. 2. Ne (punir) pas cet enfant. 3. (partir) tout de suite. 4. (répondre) à la question. 5. (se dépêcher); il faut partir. 6. (être) là à huit heures du matin. 7. N'(avoir) pas peur.

D. Remplacez les expressions anglaises par l'équivalent français. (*Voir Grammaire* § 50)

1. Charles (*is laughing*) parce que Madeleine (*is running*) à l'école. 2. Nous (*have been*) à Lyon depuis trois jours. 3. Je (*am reading*) un bon livre. 4. Voilà dix minutes que le professeur (*has been writing*) au tableau. 5. Il y a un an que vous (*have been learning*) le français.

E. Remplacez l'infinitif par la forme convenable du verbe, s'il y a lieu. (*Voir Grammaire* §§ 74, 78)

1. En (passer) devant la loge la nuit, on est obligé de (dire) son nom à la concierge. 2. Avant d'(entrer) dans la maison, il faut sonner à la porte. 3. Après (sonner), on attend que la concierge se réveille. 4. Au lieu d'(ouvrir) la porte avec une clé, on attend devant la maison. 5. (savoir) que Paul était malade, je suis allé le voir. 6. Sans (regarder) sa mère, le garçon est monté dans sa chambre. 7. Après (arriver) à la gare, j'ai cherché un taxi. 8. Avant de (monter) dans le taxi, j'ai demandé où était la rue principale. 9. Au lieu de (prendre) l'autobus, le vieux professeur a décidé d'aller à pied. 10. (avoir) peur que le train parte, j'ai couru à la gare.

*F. Remplacez les tirets par la forme convenable du présent de **vivre** ou **d'habiter**, selon le cas.* (*Voir Grammaire* § 94—live)

1. Où —— -vous? 2. Jean —— près de l'école. 3. Est-ce que cet enfant —— encore? 4. De quoi —— ces gens? 5. Nous —— à Dijon. 6. Monsieur Dupré —— facilement de ce qu'il gagne. 7. Quand nous sommes à Paris, nous —— toujours au Quartier latin.

® CONVERSATION

1. Demandez à Monsieur I. si Louis XIV a vécu au dix-septième siècle. 2. Demandez à Monsieur J. où il habite. 3. Demandez à Monsieur K. s'il vit de ce qu'il gagne. 4. Demandez à Monsieur L. où la reine Marie-Antoinette a habité à Versailles.

VOCABULAIRE — PAGES 354–355

GRAMMAIRE

A. The present indicative of regular verbs. (§§ 49 A, B, C, D; 95)
B. The present indicative of irregular verbs. (§§ 49 E; 95)
C. The imperative. (§§ 79, 95)
D. Uses of the present tense. (§ 50)
E. Constructions of verbs used after prepositions. (§§ 74, 78)
F. Ways of expressing *live* in French. (§ 94)

CINQUANTE-QUATRIÈME LEÇON

L'automne

Avec l'automne tout le monde rentre de vacances pour se remettre au travail. Les jours deviennent plus courts et les nuits sont, au contraire, plus longues. A la campagne les champs sont déserts, car la moisson [1] est déjà rentrée [2]. Très haut dans le ciel les oiseaux de passage volent vers le sud. Les feuilles des arbres prennent des couleurs jaunes, rouges et dorées [3] et tombent aussi bien sur les grands boulevards de Paris que dans les forêts solitaires ou dans les chemins de campagne.

Pour les écoliers [4] l'automne a un sens tout particulier, car c'est au début de l'automne que les élèves des écoles primaires, des collèges [5] et des lycées retournent à leurs études. Pour les uns la rentrée [6] est l'occasion

[1] *harvest* [2] *gathered* [3] *golden* [4] *schoolboys*
[5] *private high schools* [6] *reopening of school*

de revoir leurs camarades de classes, pour les autres c'est surtout l'obligation de se remettre au travail.

Le célèbre romancier[1] Anatole France, dans un style très délicat, évoque ses souvenirs d'enfance encore imprégnés[2] de la beauté mélancolique de l'automne et de la tristesse de la rentrée[3]:

> Je vais vous dire ce que me rappellent, tous les ans, le ciel agité de l'automne, les premiers dîners à la lampe et les feuilles qui jaunissent[4] dans les arbres qui frissonnent[5]; je vais vous dire ce que je vois quand je traverse le Luxembourg dans les premiers jours d'octobre, alors qu'il est un peu triste et plus beau que jamais; car c'est le temps où les feuilles tombent une à une sur les blanches épaules des statues. Ce que je vois alors dans ce jardin, c'est un petit bonhomme[6] qui, les mains dans les poches et sa gibecière[7] au dos, s'en va au collège[8] en sautillant[9] comme un moineau[10]. Ma pensée seule le voit; car ce petit bonhomme[6] est une ombre; c'est l'ombre du moi[11] que j'étais il y a vingt-cinq ans...
>
> Il y a vingt-cinq ans, à pareille époque, il traversait, avant huit heures, ce beau jardin pour aller en classe. Il avait le cœur un peu serré[12]: c'était la rentrée[3].

Tout le monde éprouve plus ou moins la mélancolie de l'automne. Paul Verlaine, pour qui la poésie était avant tout une musique, chante la profonde tristesse de son âme dans *Chanson d'automne.*

Les sanglots[13] longs
Des violons[14]
De l'automne
Blessent mon cœur
D'une langueur[15]
Monotone.

Tout suffocant[16]
Et blême[17], quand
Sonne l'heure,
Je me souviens

[1] *novelist* [2] *imbued* [3] *reopening of school* [4] *turn yellow*
[5] *tremble* [6] *fellow* [7] *book bag* [8] *private high school*
[9] *jumping about* [10] *sparrow* [11] *being* [12] *heavy* [13] *sobs*
[14] *violins* [15] *languor* [16] *stifling* [17] *pale*

Des jours anciens
Et je pleure.

Et je m'en vais
Au vent mauvais
Qui m'emporte
Deçà [1], delà,
Pareil à la
Feuille morte.

L'automne est aussi la saison des vendanges [2] et de la chasse. A cette époque-là les vendangeurs [3] coupent les grappes [4] de raisin [5] qu'on transporte ensuite à la ferme pour les écraser et en faire du bon vin. De leur côté, les chasseurs parcourent les prés [6] et les bois.

A plusieurs points de vue, l'automne est la plus belle saison de l'année en France.

Questions

1. En quelle saison l'aspect de la nature inspire-t-il de la mélancolie? 2. Quels sont les aspects caractéristiques de l'automne? 3. Quand les écoliers rentrent-ils à l'école? 4. Qui est Anatole France? 5. Quel jardin de Paris traverse-t-il dans les premiers jours d'octobre? 6. Qui voit-il dans le jardin? 7. Qui est le petit bonhomme qu'il voit? 8. Pourquoi ce petit bonhomme avait-il le cœur un peu serré? 9. Qui est Paul Verlaine? 10. Pour Paul Verlaine, qu'est-ce que la poésie? 11. Que font les vendangeurs en automne? 12. Que fait-on des grappes de raisin coupées?

Devoirs

A. *Remplacez les tirets par le pronom qui convient au sens.* Exemple: Cherchez-vous des pommes? Non, j'——ai trouvé et je——ai achetées. Non, j'*en* ai trouvé et je *les* ai achetées. (*Voir Grammaire* §§ *24, 25, 27, 28, 29*)

1. Voilà Henri. Dites-——que nous——verrons ce soir. 2. N'avez-vous pas vu mes cahiers? Je——cherche depuis hier. 3. Je connais ces enfants; je——ai donné des timbres. 4. Maurice est très heureux, car ses parents——ont promis une nouvelle bicyclette. 5. Marie est heureuse aussi, car ses parents——ont promis une robe. 6.

[1] Deçà, delà *here and there* [2] *grape harvest* [3] *grape gatherers*
[4] *bunches* [5] *grapes* [6] *meadows*

Elle —— a déjà cinq. 7. Si Jean le veut bien, vous pouvez aller avec —— au cinéma. 8. Paul et Pierre sont partis. Je ne sais pas ce que je ferai sans ——.

® *B. Répondez aux questions suivantes en employant des pronoms compléments. Soulignez les pronoms.* EXEMPLE: Allez-vous en classe demain? Oui, j'y vais. (*Voir Grammaire §§ 24, 25, 27, 28, 29*)

1. Aimez-vous l'automne? 2. Faites-vous des promenades en automne? 3. Combien de pièces françaises avez-vous lues? 4. Connaissez-vous Anatole France? 5. Allez-vous à la campagne avec Hélène dimanche? 6. Avez-vous vu des nuages dans le ciel? 7. Y a-t-il des chasseurs dans les champs? 8. Restez-vous longtemps chez vos amis?

C. Introduisez les pronoms compléments dans les phrases, en les mettant dans l'ordre convenable. EXEMPLE: (la, me) Il expliquera. Il *me l'*expliquera. (*Voir Grammaire §§ 30, 31*)

1. (le, lui) Nous avons donné. 2. (les, me) Vous montrerez. 3. (les, nous) Envoyez. 4. (la, leur) Lisez. 5. (les, lui) Ne demandez pas. 6. (en, lui) Jean a donné. 7. (en, me) Envoyez. 8. (en, leur) Demandons. 9. (y) Allez. 10. (y) Ne restez pas.

® *D. Remplacez les expressions en italique par des pronoms compléments.* (*Voir Grammaire §§ 30, 31*)

1. Mon père a cherché le tableau et il nous a montré *ce tableau.* 2. J'ai acheté des timbres pour ma mère et moi et j'ai donné *des timbres à ma mère.* 3. Roger ne comprend pas cette phrase. Expliquerez-vous *cette phrase à Roger?* 4. Vous lisez un roman? Apportez-moi *ce roman.* 5. Mettez le stylo sur le bureau; ne m'apportez pas *le stylo.* 6. Vos amis vous ont demandé cet article. Lisez *cet article à vos amis.* 7. Pierre a beaucoup de chiens; il m'a donné deux *chiens.* 8. J'aime Paris et je vais *à Paris* tous les ans. 9. Si ma propriétaire a du beurre, elle nous donnera *du beurre.* 10. Roger a pris des photos de ses camarades; il montrera *ces photos à ses camarades.*

® *E. Remplacez par un pronom les expressions en italique. Expliquez oralement pourquoi vous employez ce pronom.* (*Voir Grammaire § 27*)

1. Mon frère a une grande maison; j'habite chez *mon frère.* 2. Il faut parler à Louise et Marie. Ce sont *Louise et Marie* qui vont en France cet été. 3. Qui ouvrira la porte? *Richard.* 4. Ce chien n'est pas pour

vous; il est pour *Charles et moi.* 5. Jean conduit bien, mais vous conduisez mieux que *Jean.* 6. Il n'y a que des enfants dans ce jardin; *les enfants* seuls peuvent y jouer.

® F. *Remplacez les expressions en italique par des pronoms, en faisant les autres changements nécessaires dans la phrase.* (*Voir Grammaire* §§ *28C; 29 C, D*)

1. Notre propriétaire pose beaucoup de questions à ses pensionnaires; elle s'intéresse beaucoup à *ses pensionnaires.* 2. Je lis ce livre parce que je m'intéresse à *ce livre.* 3. Notre ancien professeur va partir. Vous vous souvenez de *ce professeur,* n'est-ce pas? 4. J'ai habité dans cette ville pendant longtemps; je me souviens bien de *cette ville.* 5. Parce que son camarade l'a beaucoup aidé, Louis pense souvent à *son camarade.* 6. Mais Louis n'aime pas ses leçons, et il pense rarement à *ses leçons.* 7. Votre sœur semble être une jeune fille intéressante; parlez-moi de *votre sœur.* 8. Notre voyage n'était pas bien agréable; ne parlons plus de *notre voyage.* 9. Le professeur vous a posé une question; répondez au *professeur.* 10. Je vous ai posé une question; répondez à *ma question.*

G. *Écrivez les phrases suivantes avec* (a) ***épouser;*** (b) ***se marier avec.*** EXEMPLE: Mon frère (*will marry*) Hélène. (a) Mon frère *épousera* Hélène. (b) Mon frère *se mariera avec* Hélène. (*Voir Grammaire* § *94* — marry)

1. Jean (*married*) Yvonne le 25 janvier. 2. Si Solange (*marries*) Jacques, elle ne sera pas heureuse. 3. Robert va (*marry*) la fille d'un voisin. 4. Si j'avais beaucoup d'argent, je (*would marry*) une jeune fille pauvre. 5. Vous (*married*) une jeune fille charmante.

® CONVERSATION

1. Demandez à Monsieur M. quand il va se marier. 2. Demandez à Monsieur N. s'il va se marier avec une jeune fille riche. 3. Demandez à Monsieur O. s'il aimerait se marier avec une Française. 4. Demandez à Monsieur P. si son ami a épousé une Française.

VOCABULAIRE — PAGES 355–356

GRAMMAIRE

A, B. Direct and indirect object pronouns, disjunctive pronouns, *y* and ***en.*** (§§ 24, 25, 27, 28, 29)

C, D. Position and order of object pronouns. (§§ 30, 31)
E. Disjunctive pronouns. (§ 27)
F. Special uses of the pronouns *y* and ***en.*** (§§ 28 C, 29 C, D)
G. Ways of expressing *marry* in French. (§ 94)

CINQUANTE-CINQUIÈME LEÇON

Le dix-huitième siècle

Au dix-huitième siècle l'absolutisme royal avait conduit à de véritables abus. Il n'y avait plus ni liberté de parole, ni liberté de la presse, ni liberté de religion. La noblesse et le clergé jouissaient de nombreux privilèges. Seul le peuple payait les impôts et, comme ils étaient très lourds, la misère était générale. La prodigalité extravagante de la cour et l'incompréhension totale des besoins du peuple, qui ont caractérisé la fin de l'Ancien régime, ruinaient peu à peu le pays.

Cet absolutisme du pouvoir royal et tous les abus qu'il entrainaît amenèrent les penseurs de l'époque à mettre en doute les principes mêmes sur lesquels reposait l'Ancien régime. Ils arrivèrent, malgré les difficultés qu'il y avait à le faire, à les critiquer ouvertement. Les œuvres de Montesquieu, de Voltaire et de Rousseau notamment répandirent la notion des Droits de l'homme. Malgré les efforts du gouvernement royal pour empêcher la diffusion des idées nouvelles, elles ne tardèrent pas à se répandre et gagnèrent même l'étranger. En Amérique elles influencèrent profondément les auteurs de la Déclaration d'indépendance et ceux de la Constitution américaine. En France, elles contribuèrent beaucoup à amener la chute de l'Ancien régime.

L'autorité royale reçut un coup décisif en 1789. Louis XVI, voyant le trésor vide, dut convoquer les États-Généraux, assemblée nationale qui n'avait pas été réunie depuis 1614. Les représentants du peuple, qui formaient dans ces États-Généraux ce qu'on appelait le *tiers état,* refusèrent de voter les nouveaux impôts que demandait le roi si, en échange, quelques libertés n'étaient pas accordées au peuple. Les membres du tiers état se séparèrent des représentants de la noblesse et du clergé, se constituèrent en assemblée nationale et jurèrent de ne pas se séparer avant d'avoir établi une constitution. Devant cette attitude du tiers état, le roi se décida à agir et rassembla des troupes. Il était trop tard. Déjà le peuple de Paris commençait à se soulever contre l'autorité royale et l'on sentait partout une atmosphère de révolution.

Le 14 juillet 1789, le peuple marcha sur la Bastille, s'empara de cette prison qui était le symbole de l'autorité royale et libéra les prisonniers politiques qui s'y trouvaient enfermés. A la suite de cette première victoire du peuple, les États-Généraux votèrent l'abolition des privilèges, détruisant ainsi la base de l'Ancien régime. Peu après, la famille royale fut emprisonnée. Vers 1791 se forma le parti républicain, qui demanda l'abolition de la monarchie. En 1792 une nouvelle assemblée révolutionnaire, la Convention nationale, proclama la République et prépara une constitution. Elle condamna Louis XVI à la guillotine. Avec la mort du roi, presque tout l'ordre établi disparut. On changea le calendrier, on adopta le système métrique des poids et mesures et on substitua à Dieu la déesse Raison.

Alors commença la Terreur. Le Comité de Salut public envoya chaque jour de nombreuses victimes à la guillotine. Les prisons étaient pleines de *suspects,* c'est-à-dire de tous ceux que l'on soupçonnait de ne pas aimer la République. Parmi bien d'autres, le jeune poète André Chénier et Lavoisier, fondateur de la chimie moderne, moururent guillotinés.

La Terreur prit fin en 1795 avec l'établissement du Directoire. Mais le changement de régime politique avait alarmé les rois des autres pays d'Europe qui craignaient de voir s'introduire chez eux les idées nouvelles de liberté. Dès la proclamation de la République en France, ils avaient commencé à s'armer contre elle. Gouvernée à l'intérieur par un Directoire faible et menacée à l'extérieur sur ses frontières, la France était en danger. C'est alors qu'apparut Napoléon.

Questions

1. A quels abus l'absolutisme royal avait-il conduit? 2. Qui payait les impôts sous l'Ancien régime? 3. Qu'est-ce qui a ruiné la France pendant le dix-huitième siècle? 4. Citez des écrivains du dix-huitième siècle dont les œuvres ont répandu la notion des Droits de l'homme. 5. Quels sont les Droits de l'homme? 6. Qui les idées de Voltaire et de Rousseau ont-elles influencé en Amérique? 7. Pourquoi le roi Louis XVI a-t-il dû convoquer les États-Généraux? 8. Qu'est-ce que les États-Généraux? le tiers état? 9. A quelle condition le tiers état aurait-il voté

de nouveaux impôts? 10. Que sentait-on partout à Paris à ce moment-là? 11. Qu'est-ce que la Bastille? 12. Qu'ont fait les États-Généraux pour détruire la base de l'Ancien régime? 13. Comment est mort Louis XVI? 14. Qu'a fait la Convention nationale pour changer l'ordre établi? 15. Qu'est-ce que la Terreur? 16. Citez des hommes célèbres guillotinés pendant la Terreur. 17. Pourquoi les rois des autres pays d'Europe ont-ils commencé à s'armer contre la France? 18. Qui est apparu à ce moment-là?

Devoirs

A. *Remplacez l'infinitif par la forme convenable du passé composé. Attention à l'auxiliaire.* (*Voir Grammaire* § *61*)

1. Jacques (se réveiller) de bonne heure ce matin. 2. Il (se lever) tout de suite. 3. D'abord il (prendre) son petit déjeuner. 4. Ensuite il (sortir) de la maison. 5. Il (marcher) jusqu'à la maison de son ami Louis. 6. Il (frapper) à la porte. 7. Louis lui (ouvrir) la porte. 8. Jacques et Louis (aller) en classe ensemble.

B. *Remplacez l'infinitif par le participe passé de ces verbes conjugués avec* ***avoir.*** *Attention à l'accord du participe passé.* (*Voir Grammaire* § 77 *A*)

1. Avez-vous (voir) les beaux tableaux que nous avons (acheter)? 2. Quelle nouvelle avez-vous (entendre) à la radio? 3. Où est la maison que cet homme d'affaires vous a (vendre)? 4. Nous avons (parler) des livres que nous avions (lire). 5. Cet enfant a (prendre) la pomme que j'avais (mettre) sur la table et l'a (manger).

C. *Remplacez l'infinitif par le participe passé de ces verbes de mouvement conjugués avec* ***être.*** (*Voir Grammaire* § 77 *B, C*)

1. Nous sommes (revenir) à la maison à quatre heures. 2. La reine Victoria est (mourir) en 1901. 3. Nos amis sont (aller) voir les chiens de chasse. 4. Êtes-vous (arriver) à Orléans hier matin? 5. Les voyageurs sont (partir) de Blois en auto.

D. *Remplacez l'infinitif par le participe passé de ces verbes pronominaux.* (*Voir Grammaire* § 77 *D*)

1. Ces dames se sont (installer) dans un compartiment. 2. Nous nous sommes (laver) la figure. 3. Georges et Paul se sont (parler) pendant deux heures. 4. Nous nous sommes (souvenir) de cet incident. 5. Les colonies américaines se sont (séparer) de l'Angleterre.

E. Remplacez les infinitifs de ce récit par la forme convenable de l'imparfait ou du passé composé, selon le cas. (*Voir Grammaire* §§ *52 A, B, C, 53, 63*)

Hier soir, je (aller) au cinéma avec mon camarade Jacques. Comme le cinéma est loin de chez nous, nous (prendre) un autobus. Nous (monter) dans l'autobus rue Montpellier et nous en (descendre) avenue Lafayette. Quand nous (arriver) devant l'entrée du cinéma, il y (avoir) déjà beaucoup de monde devant le guichet. Il (faire) froid dehors. Nous (attendre) dix minutes pour prendre nos billets. Pendant que nous (attendre), nous (causer). Enfin, nous (pouvoir) entrer dans le cinéma.

Nous (trouver) une place et nous (s'asseoir). Il y (avoir) à côté de nous une femme, son mari et un enfant de six ans. Pendant qu'on (montrer) le film, cette femme (parler) continuellement. L'enfant (manger) du chocolat. Il (demander) souvent à son père de lui expliquer ce qui (se passer) dans le film.

Nous (rester) là deux heures. Le film (être) bon. Il me (plaire). Enfin, nous (sortir) et nous (reprendre) l'autobus.

Autrefois, je (aller) souvent au cinéma. Je (aimer) voir les films. Je (attendre) avec impatience le samedi après-midi.

F. Remplacez les verbes en italique par le passé composé ou l'imparfait selon le sens. (*Voir Grammaire* §§ *52 A, B, C, 53, 63*)

Un soir d'hiver, un voyageur *entre* dans une auberge. Il *est* fatigué et il *a* faim. Il *neige* dehors et comme il *fait* très froid, beaucoup de gens *sont* assis autour du feu dans la grande salle de l'auberge, de sorte qu'il n'y *a* plus de place. Ces personnes *discutent* entre elles et ne *font* pas attention au nouveau venu.

Le voyageur *se demande* comment trouver une place près du feu. Enfin il *dit* tout haut:

— Garçon, veuillez [1] apporter un plat d'huîtres [2] à mon cheval.

Cela *étonne* le garçon, car il *sait* que les chevaux ne mangent pas d'huîtres. Il lui *répond:*

— Mais, monsieur, votre cheval ne mangera pas d'huîtres.

Très calme, le voyageur lui *dit:*

— Apportez-les à mon cheval. Vous verrez.

Les autres *entendent* ces paroles et *veulent* voir un cheval qui mange des huîtres. Ils *se lèvent* et *vont* avec le garçon.

[1] *please.* This is the imperative of *vouloir.* [2] *oysters*

Dès qu'ils *sortent,* le voyageur *se met* près du feu. Après un moment, tout le monde *revient* dans la salle. Le voyageur *est* assis près du feu.

— Monsieur, *dit* le garçon, ne vous ai-je pas dit que votre cheval ne mangerait pas d'huîtres?

Le voyageur le *regarde* d'un air surpris et amusé et lui *répond:*

— Eh bien, apportez-les-moi. Je les mangerai moi-même.

G. Remplacez les mots anglais par l'équivalent français. (*Voir Grammaire* § *94* — meet)

1. Je n'ai pas vu M. et Mme Leland depuis des années, mais ce matin je les (*met*) à la bibliothèque. 2. Si vous voulez, je peux vous (*meet*) devant ce restaurant. 3. Hier nous (*made the acquaintance of*) Mme Duval. 4. Je vous (*will meet*) ce soir à dix heures.

® CONVERSATION

1. Demandez à Monsieur Q. s'il a rencontré des amis dans la rue ce matin. 2. Demandez à Monsieur R. à quelle heure il peut vous retrouver devant la bibliothèque. 3. Demandez à Monsieur S. s'il a déjà fait la connaissance du nouveau professeur. 4. Demandez à Monsieur T. où il a retrouvé son ami hier soir.

VOCABULAIRE — PAGES 357–358

GRAMMAIRE

A. The formation of the *passé composé* with various auxiliaries. (§ 61)

B. The agreement of the past participle of verbs conjugated with ***avoir.*** (§ 77 A)

C. The agreement of the past participle of intransitive verbs of motion conjugated with *être.* (§ 77 B, C)

D. The agreement of the past participle of reflexive verbs. (§ 77 D)

E, F. The use of the *passé composé* and the imperfect in the same paragraph (§§ 52 A, B, C; 53, 63)

F. Ways of expressing *meet* in French. (§ 94)

La radio et la télévision en France

Lancée vers 1920, la radio est aujourd'hui d'un usage très courant en France. Chaque famille a son poste, même dans les fermes les plus isolées au fond des campagnes. Dans presque toutes les maisons, surtout à l'heure des repas et le soir après dîner, on met (ouvre, allume) la radio pour écouter en famille les programmes qu'on aime.

La télévision, d'origine plus récente, est loin d'être aussi répandue que la radio, mais elle commence à se voir de plus en plus. Quand on va chez des amis le soir, on se trouve souvent obligé de regarder la télévision au lieu de passer la soirée à bavarder comme autrefois.

A l'heure actuelle, les programmes de la radio et de la télévision françaises sont très variés, et chacun peut trouver une émission à son goût. Les conférences et les causeries littéraires, artistiques ou scientifiques sont destinées à l'élite intellectuelle. Ceux qui aiment la grande musique peuvent assister, chez eux, aux concerts magnifiques que donnent les grands orchestres français et étrangers ou encore aux retransmissions [1] d'opéras et d'opérettes. Les amateurs de théâtre ont la possibilité de suivre toutes sortes de pièces. Les jeunes gens trouvent leur plaisir dans les heures de jazz que leur offrent les meilleurs orchestres de danse de Paris. Le grand public se passionne pour les émissions [2] de variétés dans lesquelles les airs à la mode, l'esprit des chansonniers [3] et les jeux [4] radiophoniques font oublier pendant quelques heures les soucis quotidiens. Avec la radio ou la télévision on peut suivre les reportages [5] des grands matches de football, de rugby, de tennis, les principaux combats [6] de boxe, les grandes courses-cyclistes et notamment le Tour de France, auquel sont consacrées plusieurs émissions par jour pendant les trois semaines qu'il dure. Fréquemment dans la journée, des bulletins d'informations donnent les dernières nouvelles, tandis que les revues de presse citent et commentent des extraits d'articles de journaux français et étrangers. Le Président de la

[1] *broadcasts* [2] émissions de variétés *variety shows* [3] *popular song artists* [4] jeux radiophoniques *quiz shows* [5] *reporting* [6] combats de boxe *boxing bouts*

LA TÉLÉVISION

FRANCE

LUNDI 14

12.30 Télé-Paris. - 13. Journal. - 13.30 Fin. - 19.15 Histoires sans paroles : Les joies du camping. - 19.30 Art et magie de la cuisine. - 20. Journal. - 20.35 La vie des animaux. - 20.55 SHOW CLAUDE BESSY-GENE KELLY. - 21.40 Panorama mexicain : Rites de la Semaine Sainte. - 21.55 Musique pour vous : Le pianiste japonais Toyoaki Matsuura, grand prix du Concours Long-Thibaud. - 22.25 Journal.

MARDI 15

12.30 Télé-Paris. - 13. Journal. 13.30 Fin. - 19.30 Magazine de l'Aviation. - 20. Journal. - 20.35 « TOUS LES DEUX », pièce de Michel Dulud, avec Maria Mauban et Jean Deschamps. - 21.50 L'envers du décor (l'actualité théâtrale parisienne). - 22.20 LE CRITERIUM DU FILM : Comment voter. - 22.50 Journal.

MERCREDI 16

12.30 La vie qui va : L'actualité en mouvement. - 13. Journal. - 13.30 Fin. - 19.15 Nos amis les bêtes. - 19.30 Service d'été : Bienvenue aux jeunes étrangers. - 20. Journal. - 20.30 Me Henri Torrès. - 20.35 Variétés, par. Badel. - 21.5 « MONSIEUR KAHN », émiss. de J.-M. Coldefy, commentaires de G. de Caunes. - 21.40 Lectures pour tous. - 22.30 Journal.

JEUDI 17

12.30 Télé-Paris. - 13. Journal. - 13.30 Fin. - 17.30 Pic et pic et colegram. - 17.45 Les aventures de Nicolas et Virginie. - 18. Dessins animés. - 18.15 Parade du jeudi. - 19. Faites-le vous-même. - 19.15 Feuilleton : « Un gars du Canada ». - 19.30 Magazine féminin. - 20. Journal. - 20.35 TIC TAC DOU, émiss. de jeux. - 21.35 Petit théâtre : « L'ESCALE », de J. Celham. - 21.50 Panorama mexicain : Ciudad Mexico. - 22.20 Journal.

VENDREDI 18

12.30 Discorama. - 13. Journal. - 13.30 Fin. - 19.15 Lectures pour nous. - 19.50 Dessins animés. - 20. Journal. - 20.35 LES CINQ DERNIERES MINUTES : « Dans le pétrin », émiss. policière. - 22.5 Panorama mexicain : Tierras Mexicanas. - 22.20 Eurovision : VOLLEY-BALL : Tournoi des trois continents. - 23. Journal.

SAMEDI 19

12.30 Télé-Paris. - 13. Journal. - 13.30 Fin. - 16.30 « LA VEUVE DE L'INNOCENT », film d'André Cerf avec Jean Desailly, Sophie Desmarets, Saturnin Fabre, Jean Tissier, Raymond Bussières, Marcel Peres, Duvaleix, Betty Daussmond. - 18. Voyage sans passeport. - 18.15 La femme chez elle. - 18.30 Jeux et variétés. - 19. Silhouettes animées. - 19.25 Magazine du temps passé : La Pologne. - 20. Journal. - 20.35 LE GROS LOT, émiss. de jeux. - 21.35 Chez vous ce soir. - 22.20 Eurovision : VOLLEY-BALL: Tournoi des trois continents. - 23. Journal.

LUXEMBOURG

DIMANCHE 13

17.2 « LE CORSAIRE NOIR », film d'aventures avec Pedro Armandariz et Dolorès del Rio. - 18.30 Aigle Noir, - 19. Bon anniversaire. - 19.5 Faits divers. - 19.25 Orchestre Mantovani. - 19.55 Psychoroscope. - 20. Nouvelles. - 20.10 « RUY BLAS », film de Pierre Billon avec J. Marais, D. Darrieux. - 21.50 Ciné-Actualités. - 22.20 Fin.

LUNDI 14

19.17 Bon anniversaire. - 19.20 « CHARLOT VEUT SE MARIER », film de Charlie Chaplin. - 19.38 Sports-Actualités. - 19.55 Psychoroscope. - 20. Journal. - 20.20 « CHANTAGE », film de Guy Lefranc, avec Raymond Pellegrin et Magali Noël. - 21.50 Journal.

MARDI 15

19.17 Bon anniversaire. - 19.20 Chasse en Afrique. - 19.46 Vedette à vos ordres. - 19.55 Psychoroscope. - 20. Journal. - 20.20 LES AVENTURES DE L'INSPECTEUR BLAISE. - 20.50 Vedettes à vos ordres (suite). - 21.20 Catch. - 21.50 Documentaires filmés (Arts et Sciences). - 22.15 Journal.

MERCREDI 16

18.47 Kit Carson. - 19.15 Bon anniversaire. - 19.20 La recette du chef. - 19.40 Votre bébé et vous.

Programme de télévision hebdomadaire

RADIO-TÉLÉVISION

JEUDI - 17 SEPTEMBRE

TÉLÉVISION

DOCUMENTAIRES

8. *Nat.* La vie intellectuelle.
9.40 *Nat.* L'Université
13.6 *Nat.* La vie des lettres.
21.40 *Nat.* Nouvelles musicales. — *Int.* Etranger, mon ami.
22. *Nat.* L'art et la vie.
22.30 *Int.* Masque et Plume.
23.10 *Nat.* Idées et hommes.

THEATRE

14.24 *Nat.* Festival de Carcassonne : « Guillaume d'Orange »
20.26 *Rég.* « On ne saurait penser à tout », de Musset.
21. *Lux et RMC* « Le Héros et le Soldat », de Bernard Shaw.

LYRIQUE

10.10 *Nat.* L'art vocal.
12.5 *Nat.* Concert lyrique.
22. *M.F.* « Le Rossignol », de Strawinsky.
22.10 *Rég.* Lyrique à la carte.
22.25 *Nat.* Anna-Maria Iriarte.
23. *Int.* Concert Puccini.

MUSIQUE

11.18 *Int.* La lyre d'Orphée.
17.15 *Nat.* Récital d'orgue.
17.30 *Int.* Petit concert, — *M.F.* Les grands musiciens.
19.11 *Nat.* Musique russe.
20. *Nat., Int. et M.F.* Orch. Radio-symphonique.
23. *M.F.* Orchestre de Nice.
23.55 *Nat.* Marcelle de Lacour.

VARIETES

20. *Eur.* Musicorama.
20.5 *Lux., RMC.* C'est décidé!
20.30 *Lux., RMC.* Nanette.

RADIO

FRANCE I

6.15 Inf. - 6.25 Disques présentés par Jean Yschard (à 7.15, 8.15 et 9.15 Inf.). - 9.18 Une fleur pour vous, mesdames, Disques présentés par Denise Alberti. (Vers 10.15 Inf). - 10.45 Travaillez en musique ! - 11.15 Inf. - 11.18 La Lyre d'Orphée, par Jen Witold. - 11.55 Disques présentés par Jean Fontaine.

12.15 Inf. - 12.20 Disques présentés par Jean Fontaine. - 13.20 Disques présentés par Jean Fontaine (à 14.15 et 15.15 Inf.). - 15.18 Disques présentés par René Raymond (à 16.15 et 17.15 Inf.). - 17.30 Petit concert. - 18.15 Inf. - 18.20 Guitare. - 18.35 Variétés dernière heure. - 19.15 Paris vous parle.

20. ORCH. RADIO-SYMPH. (voir France III). - 21.40 ETRANGER, MON AMI, de Dominique Arban. - 22.30 LE MASQUE ET LA PLUME : lettres, théâtre, cinéma.

LUXEMBOURG

6.35 Bonjour le monde (à 6.40 et 7.30 Inf.). - 8.33 Inf. -8.43 Ménage en musique. - 10.30 Messe des malades.

11.30 Journal de Mickey. - 11.41 Festival de midi. - 21.11 Inf. agricoles. - 12.29 Le personnage mystérieux. - 12.34 La chose. - 13. Inf. - 13.33 Champion ! - 14.24 Feuilletons. - 14.54 En musique. - 16.5 Haut les cœurs ! - 16.20 Cric et Crac. - 17.30 Magazine féminin. - 18.30 La fête à tout le monde. - 19. Musique à la Clay. - 19.15 Inf. - 19.31 Dix millions d'auditeurs. - 19.56 La famille Duraton.

20.5 C'EST DECIDE ! - 20.31 Découvertes de Nanette. - 20.46 Où est la vérité ? - 21. Théâtre : « LE HEROS ET LE SOLDAT », de Bernard Shaw, avec François Périer. - 22.15 Bal (à 23. Inf.). - 24. Inf. et Radio-Minuit.

Programme de radio et de télévision quotidien

République et les principaux ministres ont pris l'habitude de s'adresser au pays à la radio et à la télévision. Ils expliquent aux Français les mesures importantes prises ou à prendre en matière politique, financière ou sociale. La télévision en particulier permet de suivre des offices religieux, des films et des documentaires, comme par exemple des fabrications industrielles ou des opérations chirurgicales. En semaine il n'y a pas actuellement de programmes de télévision pendant les heures de travail. Mais il y a quelques émissions de radio d'une portée particulière: leçons de culture physique le matin, cours de langues vivantes, causeries médicales, financières et agricoles, ou encore des émissions destinées aux mères de famille, aux enfants, aux malades des hôpitaux, etc.

La Radiodiffusion-Télévision[1] française (R.T.F.) est un monopole d'État. Chaque foyer français qui possède un récepteur[2] est obligé de payer un impôt aussi bien pour la radio que pour la télévision. En effet, c'est l'État qui subventionne entièrement la R.T.F. et ceci a des conséquences importantes: il n'y a aucune sorte de publicité ni à la radio ni à la télévision nationales, car la R.T.F. n'a pas à ménager d'intérêts commerciaux quelconques. Ses programmes ne sont pas établis en vue d'attirer à tout prix le plus grand nombre possible d'auditeurs ou de spectateurs. Elle peut ainsi offrir pour le plus grand agrément et le meilleur profit de ceux qui suivent ses émissions des programmes de haute qualité, tant au point de vue culturel qu'artistique ou documentaire. Par contre, ce monopole ne favorise pas un développement rapide de la télévision, dont les programmes restent encore très limités en nombre, et les informations que donne la R.T.F. sont toujours inspirées et contrôlées par le gouvernement.

A côté des différentes chaînes[3] de la R.T.F., quelques autres postes[4] émetteurs de langue française sont très écoutés en France. Parmi eux il y a Radio-Luxembourg et Europe N° 1. Ces deux stations appartiennent à des sociétés privées et, pour des raisons financières évidentes, leurs programmes comportent beaucoup de publicité. En revanche, leur journal parlé et les commentaires de leurs chroniqueurs[5] politiques échappent à l'influence des pouvoirs publics. Cette indépendance leur vaut d'être suivis par un large public, avide d'informations que lui refusent parfois, surtout en période de crise, les émetteurs nationaux.

[1] *Radio Broadcasting and Television* [2] *receiving set* [3] *networks*
[4] postes émetteurs *broadcasting stations* [5] *chroniclers*

QUESTIONS

1. Quand la radio a-t-elle été lancée? 2. Est-ce la radio ou la télévision qui est la plus répandue en France? 3. Quels sont les programmes destinés à l'élite intellectuelle? 4. Quels programmes de musique peut-on entendre à la radio française? 5. Quels reportages sur le sport peut-on suivre à la radio et à la télévision? 6. Comment le Président de la République et les principaux ministres se servent-ils de la radio et de la télévision? 7. Quels programmes spéciaux peut-on suivre à la télévision? 8. Citez quelques émissions de radio qui ont lieu en semaine pendant les heures de travail. 9. Pourquoi le Français est-il obligé de payer un impôt pour son poste de radio ou de télévision? 10. Pourquoi n'y a-t-il pas de publicité à la radio et à la télévision française? 11. À votre avis, vaut-il mieux que la radio et la télévision soient des entreprises financées par des sociétés privées ou un monopole d'État? 12. En quoi Radio-Luxembourg et Europe N° 1 sont-ils différents des autres postes émetteurs de radio en France? 13. Pourquoi les programmes de Radio-Luxembourg et d'Europe N° 1 comportent-ils beaucoup de publicité? 14. Pourquoi les Français écoutent-ils parfois les informations données par Radio-Luxembourg et Europe N° 1?

DEVOIRS

A. Remplacez par l'équivalent français les expressions entre parenthèses. (Voir Grammaire §§ 14, 32)

1. Comment s'appelle (*your*) camarade et quelle est (*his*) origine? 2. Où est (*his*) voiture? 3. (*mine*) est derrière la maison. 4. J'ai acheté (*my*) poste de radio il y a un an. 5. Quand avez-vous acheté (*yours*)? 6. Avez-vous compris (*my*) explication? 7. (*Theirs*) est plus facile à comprendre. 8. Avez-vous vu (*his*) frère et (*his*) sœur? 9. (*Our*) oncle et (*our*) tantes de province viennent nous voir dimanche. 10. (*Their*) professeur va en Espagne voir (*his*) parents. 11. Paul a trouvé (*my*) journaux et (*my*) carte de France sur (*my*) bureau. 12. Où avez-vous trouvé (*his*)? 13. Avez-vous vu (*her*) élégante robe? 14. Avez-vous vu (*ours*)?

B. Remplacez le mot en italique par le mot entre parenthèses, en faisant les changements nécessaires. EXEMPLE: (rien) Nous avons lu *un livre.* Nous n'avons *rien* lu. (*Voir Grammaire § 22 D, E, F*)

1. (personne) *Denise* est devant la porte. 2. (personne) Nous

avons vu *un homme* derrière la maison. 3. (rien) J'ai écrit *une phrase* au tableau. 4. (rien) Paul avait vu *beaucoup de voitures* dans la rue. 5. (aucun) Mes parents ont *une bonne* raison de partir. 6. (aucun) Je connais *un* moyen d'aller à Paris. 7. (plus) Ces enfants jouent *toujours* sur les plages. 8. (jamais) Ils ont parlé *constamment* de leurs vacances.

C. Remplacez les tirets de ce récit par les pronoms relatifs qui conviennent au sens. (Voir Grammaire § 39)

Un paysan —— un chien avait mordu est allé voir un avocat[1] —— était son voisin. Il lui a dit:

— J'ai été mordu par un chien et je sais à —— il appartient. Que faut-il faire pour obtenir des réparations?

— C'est très facile, a répondu l'avocat. Vous pouvez réclamer vingt francs à la personne —— le chien vous a mordu.

— Eh bien, a répondu le paysan —— cette réponse a enchanté, c'est votre chien —— m'a mordu. Donnez-moi donc les vingt francs —— vous me devez.

— Certainement, a répondu l'avocat, à —— cette idée n'a pas plu, je le ferai. Mais il faut me payer quarante francs les conseils —— je vous ai donnés.

D. Remplacez les tirets par le pronom relatif qui convient. (Voir Grammaire § 39)

1. Dites-moi —— font ces gens. 2. Voilà la dame —— vous avez vu le mari. 3. Où est la lettre —— vous m'avez écrite? 4. Les voitures —— je parlais sont déjà parties. 5. Je voudrais vous parler des camarades avec —— votre fils joue tous les jours. 6. Avez-vous retrouvé le stylo avec —— vous avez écrit vos devoirs? 7. Le jour —— nous avons commencé un autre travail, ce professeur est parti en vacances. 8. N'oubliez pas —— vous m'avez promis. 9. Au moment —— ces troupes arriveront, j'irai ailleurs. 10. Dites-lui —— vous empêche de travailler.

E. Mettez les verbes en italique au temps indiqué entre parenthèses. (Voir Grammaire § 89 A, B)

1. (présent) Nous *avons changé* d'appartement mardi. 2. (imparfait) Je *mange* souvent avant de me coucher. 3. (présent) Nous *effacions* toujours le tableau. 4. (imparfait) Le jeune garçon *commence* à comprendre son professeur.

[1] *lawyer*

F. Mettez les verbes en italique au temps indiqué entre parenthèses. (Voir Grammaire § 89 C, D, E, F)

1. (présent) Les enfants *essayaient* d'apprendre le poème. 2. (présent) Vous *vous êtes levé* de bonne heure. 3. (futur) Vous *avez payé* ce parfum très cher. 4. (futur) La concierge *nettoyait* l'escalier toutes les semaines. 5. (futur) Nous *avons essuyé* la table. 6. (présent) J'*ai mené* mon frère au cinéma. 7. (présent) Jeanne *espérait* se marier en juin. 8. (futur) Les élèves *répètent* après le professeur. 9. (futur) Nous *appelions* les enfants vers huit heures du matin. 10. (présent) Tous les fleuves *se jetaient* dans la mer.

G. Remplacez les mots anglais par l'équivalent français. (Voir Grammaire § 94—must)

1. (*You must speak*) français. 2. (*I must write*) une lettre à ma mère. 3. Quand vous serez à Paris, (*you must*[1] *visit*) les Invalides. 4. Vous avez une belle voiture! (*You must be*) riche! 5. Nous ne pouvons pas rester; (*we must go*) à notre classe de français. 6. Regardez Maurice qui entre dans cette maison. (*He must know*) monsieur Abel.

® CONVERSATION

1. Demandez à Monsieur U. si vous devez rester plus longtemps. 2. Demandez à Monsieur V. s'il faut que vous fassiez ce travail aujourd'hui. 3. Demandez à Monsieur W. si votre ami doit partir demain. 4. Demandez à Monsieur X. s'il faut que votre frère aille se reposer.

VOCABULAIRE — PAGE 359

GRAMMAIRE

A. Possessive adjectives and pronouns. (§§ 14, 32)
B. Negative adverbs. (§ 22 D, E, F)
C, D. Relative pronouns. (§ 39)
E. Orthographical changing verbs in *-cer* and *-ger.* (§ 89 A, B)
F. Orthographical changing verbs in *-yer, -e-er,* and *-é-er.* (§ 89 C, D, E, F)
G. Ways of expressing *must* in French. (§ 94)

[1] Since this action will take place at some future date, French uses the future tense here.

Napoléon Ier

Si Napoléon Bonaparte était né un an plus tôt, il aurait été Italien, car il naquit en Corse en 1769 un an après que cette île fut devenue française. Il était général à vingt-quatre ans, et à vingt-sept il commandait en chef l'armée d'Italie. Il remporta une série de victoires sur l'empereur d'Autriche au cours de la campagne d'Italie. A son retour à Paris il fut l'objet de l'admiration générale. Il proposa au Directoire d'aller conquérir l'Égypte, d'où les Français pourraient menacer les possessions anglaises de l'Inde. Le Directoire, jaloux des succès de Bonaparte, lui donna une armée pour se débarrasser de lui et l'envoya en Égypte. Mais là, Bonaparte gagna la célèbre bataille des Pyramides et revint en France plus populaire que jamais.

En 1799, Bonaparte, profitant de la faiblesse du Directoire et de la situation extérieure devenue grave, fit un coup d'état et prit le pouvoir. Il fut alors nommé premier consul.

Les guerres d'Italie continuaient. Une fois victorieux, Bonaparte s'occupa de l'administration de la France, car s'il menaça la paix de l'Europe par ses ambitions de conquête, il fit beaucoup de réformes heureuses à l'intérieur du pays. Il réunit toutes les règles du droit français dans ce qu'on appelle le Code Napoléon ou le Code civil. Ce code constitue encore aujourd'hui la base du droit civil en France, en Belgique, en Hollande, en Suisse et même en Louisiane. Bonaparte établit un nouveau système financier, dont la Banque de France fut l'organisme le plus important. Il rétablit l'ordre dans les départements. Il conclut avec le pape un concordat rétablissant la religion catholique en France. En 1802 il se fit nommer consul à vie et en 1804 il se proclama empereur et prit le nom de Napoléon Ier.

L'Angleterre, la Russie, la Suède et l'Autriche, craignant le développement de sa puissance, s'unirent pour le combattre. Napoléon aurait aimé faire passer ses armées en Angleterre, mais la flotte française n'était pas assez forte. Napoléon dut se contenter de faire la guerre sur le continent, à l'Autriche et à la Russie, alliées de l'Angleterre. Par une série de victoires, il sépara l'Autriche et la Prusse de l'Angleterre. Il entra à Berlin et devint le maître des états allemands. Il établit le blocus continental contre les Anglais, en interdisant à tous les autres pays de vendre leurs produits à l'Angleterre. En 1808 il fit monter son frère Joseph sur le trône d'Espagne. Au nord il prit possession de la Hollande. En 1812 il envahit la Russie. Mais au lieu d'accepter la bataille, les Russes reculèrent toujours, brûlant tout dans leur retraite. En arrivant à Moscou, les troupes de Napoléon ne trouvèrent rien à manger. Vaincu par le froid et la faim, Napoléon décida de battre en retraite. Harcelée par les Russes, une petite partie seulement de la Grande Armée réussit à rentrer en France. Victor Hugo décrit d'une manière saisissante la retraite de Russie dans son œuvre *l'Expiation*:

Il neigeait. On était vaincu par sa conquête.
Pour la première fois l'aigle [1] baissait [2] la tête.
Sombres jours! l'empereur revenait lentement,
Laissant derrière lui brûler Moscou fumant [3].
Il neigeait. L'âpre [4] hiver fondait [5] en avalanche.
Après la plaine blanche une autre plaine blanche.
On ne connaissait plus les chefs ni le drapeau [6].
Hier la grande armée, et maintenant troupeau [7].

Épuisé, Napoléon continua la lutte contre les armées des pays d'Europe. Peu à peu ses forces militaires diminuèrent, et il fut enfin vaincu à la bataille de Leipzig en 1813. Les alliés victorieux poursuivirent Napoléon jusqu'au Rhin et la France fut alors envahie à son tour. Enfin Napoléon abdiqua et les alliés l'exilèrent à l'île d'Elbe, dans la Méditerranée. Six mois après, il parvint à revenir en France. Rassemblant des troupes il reprit Paris à Louis XVIII, frère du roi Louis XVI et réorganisa l'armée. Mais il fut battu en 1815, cette fois définitivement, à la bataille de Waterloo. On l'exila à Sainte-Hélène, île perdue au milieu de l'Atlantique, où il devait mourir en 1821. Louis XVIII reprit son trône et la France redevint un royaume.

Certes, Napoléon fut vaincu, mais il inspire toujours de l'admiration à bien des Français et reste pour eux un des plus grands héros de la France.

Questions

1. Où est né Napoléon? 2. S'il était né un an plus tôt, quelle aurait été sa nationalité? 3. A quel âge est-il devenu général? 4. Qu'a-t-il proposé au Directoire? 5. Pourquoi le Directoire lui a-t-il donné une

[1] *eagle* [2] *lowered, bowed* [3] *smoking* [4] *harsh* [5] *rushed forth as* [6] *flag* [7] *herd*

armée? 6. Quelle est la bataille que Napoléon a gagnée en Égypte? 7. Quand Napoléon a-t-il été nommé premier consul? 8. Qu'est-ce que le Code Napoléon? 9. Dans quels pays le Code Napoléon est-il la base du droit civil? 10. Pourquoi les autres pays d'Europe se sont-ils unis contre Napoléon? 11. Pourquoi Napoléon n'a-t-il pas envahi l'Angleterre? 12. Qu'est-ce que le blocus continental? 13. Racontez la campagne de Russie. 14. Quelle est l'œuvre de Victor Hugo qui décrit la retraite de Russie? 15. A quelle bataille Napoléon a-t-il été vaincu? 16. Où a-t-il été exilé? 17. Qu'a-t-il fait six mois après? 18. Qui était roi de France à ce moment-là? 19. Où Napoléon a-t-il été battu de nouveau? 20. Où a-t-il été exilé la deuxième fois?

Devoirs

® *A. Mettez les verbes suivants* (1) *au futur* (2) *au futur antérieur.* (*Voir Grammaire* §§ *54, 66*) Exemple: il trouvait: il trouvera — il aura trouvé:

1. il voit 2. nous avions fait 3. vous êtes 4. j'écris 5. elle se couche 6. tu sais 7. ils reviennent 8. je pouvais

® *B. Mettez les verbes suivants* (1) *au conditionnel* (2) *au conditionnel passé.* (*Voir Grammaire* §§ *56, 70*) Exemple: nous avons perdu: nous perdrions — nous aurions perdu

1. il pleut 2. je voulais 3. ils vont 4. nous sommes morts 5. vous avez envoyé 6. il fallait

C. Remplacez l'infinitif par la forme convenable du verbe. (*Voir Grammaire* § *72*)

1. Si ces gens (pouvoir) prendre leurs billets, ils seraient partis tout de suite. 2. Si vous ne travaillez pas, vous ne (réussir) pas à votre examen. 3. Si vous (rester) avec nous, vous verrez l'exposition de Paris. 4. S'il avait plu, nous (passer) l'après-midi à la maison. 5. Si nous (voyager) toute la journée, nous arriverons à Marseille vers neuf heures du soir. 6. Si j'étais dans certains pays du monde, je (être) probablement surveillé.

D. Remplacez les mots entre parenthèses par l'équivalent français. (*Voir Grammaire* §§ *55, 67*)

1. Quand nous (*were*) en France, nous avons visité la forêt de Fontainebleau. 2. Quand je (*am*) en France, je vais toujours à Tours. 3. Quand vous (*are*) en France, vous verrez certainement la Tour Eiffel. 4. Dès que je (*see*) Jacques, je lui parlerai de vous. 5. Lorsque vous

(*have*) assez d'argent, achetez une voiture. 6. Quand nous (*finish*) notre travail, nous sortirons tout de suite. 7. Dès que nous (*have read*) le journal, nous téléphonerons à Madeleine. 8. Quand Marie (*has learned*) à parler français, elle fera un voyage en France.

® *E. Introduisez dans la phrase l'adverbe indiqué entre parenthèses.* EXEMPLE: (bien) Vous avez travaillé ce matin. Vous avez *bien* travaillé ce matin. (*Voir Grammaire* § 20)

1. (toujours) Ces jeunes gens s'arrêtent devant notre maison. 2. (aujourd'hui) Les voyageurs sont arrivés à l'auberge. 3. (beaucoup) Nous avons travaillé cette année. 4. (souvent) Les Français écoutent les émissions de la radio. 5. (rarement) Vous allez à Cherbourg. 6. (hier) Michel est parti pour Tours. 7. (déjà) Les étudiants ont pris leurs billets. 8. (encore) Nous ne sommes pas montés dans les tours de la cathédrale. 9. (peut-être) Nous reviendrons demain. 10. (lentement) Nous avons marché le long de la Seine. 11. (aussi[1]) Nous ne sommes pas fatigués.

F. Remplacez les tirets par la forme convenable du mot français qu'il faut pour exprimer return. (*Voir Grammaire* § 94—return)

1. Maurice est allé à Tours; il—— ici demain soir. 2. Il avait le livre dont vous parlez, mais il—— ce livre à la bibliothèque hier. 3. Marie a passé huit jours ici; elle—— chez elle jeudi dernier. 4. Hier soir je suis sorti à sept heures, je—— vers minuit et ensuite, je me suis couché. 5. Vous sortez? A quelle heure—— -vous?

® CONVERSATION

1. Demandez à Monsieur A. à quelle heure il est rentré hier soir. 2. Demandez à Monsieur B. quand il retournera en Europe. 3. Demandez à Monsieur C. quand il reviendra en classe. 4. Demandez à Monsieur D. s'il a rendu les livres à la bibliothèque.

VOCABULAIRE — PAGES 360–361

GRAMMAIRE

A. Formation of the future and the future perfect. (§ 54, 66)
B. Formation of the conditional and the past conditional. (§§ 56, 70)
C. Conditional sentences. (§ 72)
D. Uses of the future and the future perfect. (§ 55, 67)
E. Position of adverbs. (§ 20)
F. Ways of expressing *return* in French. (§ 94)

[1] *therefore*

CINQUANTE-HUITIÈME LEÇON

Noël

Il fait déjà froid en décembre: c'est l'époque des longues soirées au coin du feu où l'on entend le vent siffler sous la porte et où dehors, le sol et les toits sont souvent recouverts de neige. C'est l'époque aussi des fêtes de Noël. Dans les écoles, les vacances de Noël commencent le 23 décembre après la classe et durent jusqu'au 3 janvier. Les élèves et les étudiants rejoignent leurs familles. En effet, parmi les grandes fêtes de l'année, Noël est avant tout la fête de la famille et, comme ailleurs, c'est pour les enfants surtout que Noël est un grand jour.

Noël est en même temps une très grande fête religieuse et la tradition veut que l'on se rende, la veille de Noël, à la messe [1] de minuit. Vous ne pouvez pas vous figurer avec quelle émotion on entend soudain, dans le silence d'une nuit de décembre, toutes les cloches de toutes les églises qui appellent les fidèles à venir célébrer la naissance du Christ! L'église est brillamment illuminée et on chante des cantiques [2] de Noël, dont le plus connu est:

Minuit! Chrétiens, c'est l'heure solennelle
Où l'homme Dieu descendit jusqu'à nous
Pour effacer la tache [3] originelle
Et de son Père arrêter le courroux [4].
Le monde entier tressaille [5] d'espérance
A cette nuit qui lui donne un Sauveur [6]!
Peuple à genoux, attends ta délivrance,
Noël! Noël! Voici le Rédempteur [7]!
Noël! Noël! Voici le Rédempteur [7]!

Au * retour de la messe [1] l'arbre de Noël attend les enfants. C'est un petit sapin [8] illuminé de bougies [9] multicolores, orné d'étoiles d'or et d'argent et chargé de cadeaux. Les enfants poussent des cris de joie en

* Christmas customs differ considerably in different families. Some families receive the gifts on Christmas eve, others on Christmas morning, still others on Christmas afternoon.

[1] *mass* [2] *carols* [3] *blemish* [4] *anger* [5] *tremble* [6] *Savior* [7] *Redeemer* [8] *pine tree* [9] *candles*

voyant ce spectacle et vont prendre leurs jouets[1] dans le sapin[2]. Ensuite, la famille se réunit autour d'une table pour le réveillon[3]. Généralement, c'est un repas léger où l'on mange surtout de la charcuterie et des gâteaux, mais, dans certaines maisons, c'est à ce moment-là qu'a lieu le véritable repas de Noël et la fête se prolonge alors très tard dans la nuit.

Les tout petits, trop jeunes pour assister à la messe[4] de minuit, sont couchés depuis longtemps. Il y a déjà plusieurs semaines qu'ils ont écrit au Père Noël pour lui demander les cadeaux dont ils ont le plus envie. Car c'est aussi la veille de Noël pendant la nuit que le Père Noël descend dans les cheminées pour y déposer des jouets[1], des bonbons[5] et des gâteaux. Le matin de Noël, les petits enfants se précipitent vers la cheminée où ils avaient mis leurs sabots[6] ou leurs souliers bien propres et bien rangés. C'est pour eux une joie sans pareille de découvrir parmi les paquets l'auto mécanique ou la poupée[7] dont ils rêvaient depuis si longtemps. Et les parents ne sont pas moins heureux à la vue de cet enthousiasme que fait naître chaque année le mystère enfantin[8] des jouets[1] venus du ciel.

Le jour de Noël, au déjeuner, la famille se réunit pour manger une dinde[9] ou une oie[10] rôtie[11] et, au dessert, la traditionnelle bûche[12] de Noël, gâteau au chocolat qui ressemble à une grosse branche d'arbre et dont chacun reçoit un grand morceau. Dans l'après-midi, des amis ou des voisins viennent se joindre au cercle de famille et les enfants dansent des rondes[13] et chantent des chansons de Noël.

En France, on n'envoie pas de vœux pour Noël. C'est à l'occasion du jour de l'an, le 1er janvier, qu'on envoie des vœux de «bonne année» et qu'on fait de nombreuses visites.

Questions

1. En quelle saison le sol est-il recouvert de neige? 2. Où les étudiants passent-ils généralement les vacances de Noël? 3. Où va-t-on la veille de Noël? 4. Comment est illuminé l'arbre de Noël? 5. Qu'est-ce que le réveillon? 6. Où les enfants mettent-ils leurs souliers la veille de Noël? 7. Que leur apporte le Père Noël? 8. Pourquoi les parents sont-ils aussi heureux que les enfants le matin de Noël? 9. Que mange-t-on au déjeuner le jour de Noël? 10. Qu'est-ce que la bûche de Noël? 11. A quoi ressemble-t-elle? 12. Qui vient se joindre à la famille l'après-

[1] *toys* [2] *pine tree*
[3] *lunch or dinner eaten after midnight mass on Christmas eve* [4] *mass*
[5] *candy* [6] *wooden shoes* [7] *doll* [8] *childish* [9] *turkey* [10] *goose*
[11] *roasted* [12] *log* [13] *rounds*

midi? 13. La fête de Noël est-elle l'occasion d'échanges de vœux? 14. Quand envoie-t-on des vœux en France?

DEVOIRS

A. Remplacez les tirets par une préposition où il y a lieu. (Voir Grammaire § 44 A, B, C, D)

1. N'oubliez pas —— mettre votre nom sur les lettres que vous enverrez. 2. Mon père vous invite —— passer quelques jours chez nous. 3. Michel m'a dit —— me dépêcher. 4. Désirez-vous —— venir avec moi? 5. Non, je préfère —— aller avec René. 6. La sœur de Denise commencera —— travailler demain. 7. Elle espère —— voir toutes ses amies là-bas. 8. Je veux —— vous voir un moment. 9. Oui, Jean a hésité —— venir nous voir. 10. Vous n'osez pas —— le lui dire, n'est-ce pas? 11. Pourquoi continuez-vous —— y aller? 12. Demandez au Père Noël —— vous apporter beaucoup de jouets. 13. Nous avons essayé —— passer nos vacances de Noël chez nos parents. 14. Pourquoi le professeur a-t-il refusé —— vous permettre —— prendre des vacances à Noël? 15. Oh, je vais réussir —— partir la veille de Noël.

B. Remplacez les expressions entre parenthèses par l'équivalent français. (Voir Grammaire § 45 B)

1. Nous (*are waiting for*) mon oncle, qui nous mènera au musée. 2. Je (*am looking for*) quelqu'un qui puisse m'aider. 3. Qui (*asked for*) cet argent? 4. Les élèves (*listen to*) les explications du professeur. 5. Nous avons payé (*two dollars for this book*). 6. Elle (*looked at*) son mari tout étonnée.

C. Remplacez les tirets par la préposition convenable en y ajoutant l'article où il y a lieu. (Voir Grammaire § 45 C, D et Vocabulaire français-anglais)

1. Avez-vous assisté —— votre classe de français ce matin? 2. Je me suis approché —— la table pour écrire. 3. Je préfère jouer —— tennis tandis que Marie préfère jouer —— violon. 4. Vous ressemblez beaucoup —— votre père. 5. Le professeur a essayé d'apprendre —— élèves à parler français. 6. Paul s'est aperçu —— son erreur et il a corrigé sa faute. 7. Dans cette classe nous ne manquons pas —— travail. 8. Je pense souvent —— mes amis français et ils pensent souvent —— moi. 9. Que pensez-vous —— cet homme? 10. Le Père Noël n'apporte rien aux enfants qui n'obéissent pas —— leurs parents. 11. Profitez —— l'occasion de connaître ce savant. 12. Les enfants ont demandé —— leurs parents des automobiles mécaniques. 13. Ils ont remercié leurs

parents —— beaux cadeaux qu'ils avaient reçus à Noël. 14. Anatole France se souvient —— son enfance et —— ses promenades au Luxembourg. 15. Tous mes amis se servent —— ma voiture. 16. Vous occupez-vous —— vos leçons? 17. J'ai prié —— mon ami de m'envoyer des timbres. 18. Qui est entré —— votre chambre? 19. Il faut plaire —— gens. 20. Je n'ai pas encore répondu —— sa lettre.

D. Remplacez par l'équivalent français les expressions entre parenthèses. Attention aux prépositions. (*Voir Grammaire* § 45 *E*)

1. Nous avons dit (*our friends to*) nous attendre. 2. Le professeur permettait (*the pupils to*) lire des romans policiers tous les lundis. 3. J'ai demandé (*Charles to*) me téléphoner. 4. La mère a interdit (*the children to*) jouer dans la rue. 5. Nous avons promis (*Marie to*) lui donner de l'argent. 6. Le médecin a conseillé (*my brother to*) prendre des vacances. 7. Je (*will ask him to*) fermer la porte. 8. Qui (*advised them to eat*) beaucoup de pain? 9. Je (*told her to*) rester à la maison. 10. Nous (*permit them to*) jouer dans la cour. 11. J'écrirai (*my sister to*) venir tout de suite.

E. Remplacez par l'équivalent français les mots entre parenthèses. (*Voir Grammaire* § 94 — spend)

1. Nous (*spent*) nos vacances à la plage. 2. Nous (*spent*) beaucoup d'argent pendant les vacances. 3. Mon frère (*will spend*) huit jours à la campagne. 4. Il (*will spend*) tout ce qu'il a gagné cet été. 5. Vous (*spend*) trop. 6. Je (*spend*) mon temps à laver ma voiture.

® CONVERSATION

1. Demandez à Monsieur E. s'il a passé ses vacances de Noël chez ses parents. 2. Demandez à Monsieur F. s'il a dépensé beaucoup d'argent à Noël. 3. Demandez à Monsieur G. où il a passé la veille de Noël. 4. Demandez à Monsieur H. combien d'argent il a dépensé pour des cadeaux de Noël.

VOCABULAIRE — PAGES 361–362

GRAMMAIRE

A. Prepositions governing dependent infinitives. (§ 44)
B. Verbs governing nouns without a preposition. (§ 45 A, B)
C. Verbs governing nouns with a preposition. (§ 45 A, C, D)
D. The *à* + *de* verbs. (§ 45 E)
E. Ways of expressing *spend* in French. (§ 94)

CINQUANTE-NEUVIÈME LEÇON

Napoléon III

Le dix-neuvième siècle fut une période de révolutions et de troubles. En 1815, après la chute de Napoléon Ier, les grandes puissances d'Europe remirent Louis XVIII sur le trône de France. En 1830 le peuple se révolta contre Charles X, frère de Louis XVIII, et prit Louis-Philippe pour roi. En 1848, le chômage amena une crise économique et le peuple, mécontent, se révolta encore une fois. On proclama la Deuxième République. Louis Napoléon, neveu de Napoléon Ier, fut élu président de cette république. Mais il était ambitieux comme son oncle. Il s'empara du pouvoir et en 1852 se proclama empereur. Ce fut le Second Empire.

Le règne de Napoléon III fut marqué par des progrès matériels considérables. Ce fut pour la France une des périodes les plus prospères de son histoire. L'empereur fit embellir Paris. Il fit construire une partie des grands boulevards qu'on admire tant aujourd'hui. C'est à cette époque qu'un Français, Ferdinand de Lesseps, fit percer le canal de Suez, et la France contrôla cet important ouvrage pendant plusieurs années. C'est l'époque aussi où elle commença à acquérir l'empire colonial qui la rendait si puissante avant la guerre de 39.

Mais la France n'était pas la seule nation qui augmentait alors sa puissance. A la même époque, l'Allemagne, qui était restée longtemps une confédération d'états indépendants, parvenait peu à peu à s'unifier sous l'autorité du roi de Prusse. Bismarck, homme d'état très habile, y organisait une des plus fortes armées du monde. Entre 1864 et 1870, il libéra l'Allemagne des puissances étrangères. A ce moment-là Bismarck rêvait d'une guerre qui achèverait l'unification des états allemands du nord et du sud.

L'occasion se présenta bientôt. En 1868 les Espagnols avaient renversé leur reine Isabelle II. Ils avaient offert la couronne à un cousin du roi de Prusse, qui avait accepté. Le gouvernement français protesta; le prince retira sa candidature. Mais quand la France demanda à l'Allemagne la promesse de ne jamais[1] mettre ce prince sur le trône d'Espagne, l'Allemagne refusa à son tour. La France interpréta ce refus comme une insulte et déclara la guerre à l'Allemagne.

[1] Why are the negatives together? (§ 22 H)

Commencée en 1870, la guerre dura moins d'un [1] an. La France ne pouvait rien contre l'immense organisation militaire de Bismarck. Elle dut céder l'Alsace et une partie de la Lorraine à l'Allemagne et payer une indemnité de guerre de cinq milliards de francs [2].

Pendant la guerre, les Français renversèrent le Second Empire. Napoléon III se sauva en Angleterre. On fonda la Troisième République, et en 1875, on établit la constitution qui fut la base du gouvernement français jusqu'à la défaite de 1940.

La guerre de 70 et ses suites sont très importantes dans l'histoire diplomatique de l'Europe et dans le développement des circonstances qui amenèrent la guerre en 1914.

Questions

1. Qui a été remis sur le trône de France en 1815? 2. Qu'a fait le peuple français en 1830? en 1848? 3. Qui s'est emparé du pouvoir pendant la Deuxième République? 4. Qu'est-ce que Louis Napoléon s'est proclamé en 1852? 5. Par quoi a été marqué le règne de Napoléon III? 6. Qui a fait percer le canal de Suez? 7. Quelle était la situation politique en Allemagne pendant ces années-là? 8. Qui était devenu le chef de la confédération allemande? 9. Qui a organisé l'armée allemande de cette époque? 10. Quelle est la reine que les Espagnols avaient renversée? 11. A qui avaient-ils offert la couronne d'Espagne? 12. Qu'est-ce que le gouvernement français a fait alors? 13. Et ensuite, qu'est-ce que le gouvernement français a demandé à l'Allemagne? 14. Quelle a été la cause de la guerre avec l'Allemagne? 15. Combien de temps a duré cette guerre? 16. Qui l'a gagnée? 17. Qu'est-ce que la France a perdu après cette guerre? 18. Quelle était la situation politique en France à la fin de la guerre? 19. Qu'a-t-on établi en France en 1875?

Devoirs

® *A. Remplacez les articles en italique par l'adjectif démonstratif. (Voir Grammaire § 15)* Exemple: *Le* professeur et *les* élèves ne connaissent pas *la* ville. *Ce* professeur et *ces* élèves ne connaissent pas *cette* ville.

1. Qui avez-vous trouvé devant *l'*hôtel? 2. *Le* repas m'a beaucoup plu. 3. *Les* pommes de terre frites sont excellentes. 4. *La* viande est

[1] For *than* see § 13 B. [2] This amounted to more than $1,000,000,000 in contemporary American currency.

trop dure. 5. *Les* œufs coûtent cher. 6. J'aime beaucoup *les* légumes et *la* salade.

B. Remplacez les tirets par un pronom démonstratif. (Voir Grammaire §§ 33, 34)

1. Lisez——. 2. Je ne peux pas faire——. 3. Voyez-vous ces deux grands bateaux?——-ci est anglais et——-là est français. 4. Comprenez-vous——? 5. ——qui vont à Paris prennent souvent l'avion. 6. Oui, nous avons deux voitures. ——de mon frère est meilleure que ——de mon père. 7. Vous avez vu les deux sœurs. Laquelle préférez-vous? ——-ci? Non,——qui étudie la musique.

C. Remplacez le tiret par ce, il, elle, ils *ou* elles *selon le cas. (Voir Grammaire §§ 35, 36)*

1. Avez-vous vu cet homme? ——est Français. 2. ——est médecin. 3. ——est un médecin célèbre. 4. ——est très connu. 5. ——est à Bordeaux depuis deux jours. 6. Qui est là? ——est moi. 7. Qui est-——? 8. ——est Marie. 9. ——est une jeune fille. 10. ——est intelligente. 11. ——est en Amérique.

D. Remplacez le tiret par ce *ou* il *selon le cas. (Voir Grammaire § 37)*

1. J'aime beaucoup voyager. ——est intéressant. 2. Parlez-vous couramment? ——est très difficile. 3. Allez-vous en France? —— serait bien agréable. 4. ——est intéressant de voyager. 5. ——est difficile de parler russe. 6. ——est agréable d'aller en France.

E. Remplacez les mots entre parenthèses par l'équivalent français. (Voir Grammaire § 38 A, B, C, D)

1. (*What*) ferez-vous quand il sera parti? 2. Pour (*whom*) écrivez-vous cette lettre? 3. (*Who*) avait frappé à la porte? 4. (*What*) est derrière la maison? 5. A (*whom*) donnerez-vous cet argent? 6. (*What*) vous empêche d'aller en Russie? 7. De (*what*) avez-vous parlé cet après-midi? 8. (*Who*) a fait construire le canal de Suez? 9. (*Whom*) Paul a-t-il vu? 10. (*What*) nous mangerons en sortant du cinéma? 11. (*Whom*) le président enverra-t-il en France? 12. Avec (*what*) avez-vous ouvert la porte? 13. (*What*) vous avez vu à Paris?

*F. Remplacez les tirets par la forme convenable de **quel** ou de **lequel**. (Voir Grammaire §§ 16, 38 E)*

1. —— est le nom de ce livre? 2. ——, celui-ci ou celui-là? 3. —— sont les jours de la semaine? 4. Dans —— ville habite votre oncle? 5. —— sont les saisons les plus agréables? 6. —— est le mot qui désigne le repas de la nuit de Noël? 7. —— est votre nom?

G. Remplacez les tirets par le passé composé du mot convenable qui exprime take. (*Voir Grammaire* § 94 — take)

1. L'année dernière j' —— trois cours. 2. Comme nous n'avons pas voulu que l'enfant reste avec nous, Pierre l' ——. 3. Nous —— les pommes qui étaient sur la table. 4. Hier soir j' —— Charles au restaurant. 5. Vous —— une heure à faire ce travail. 6. Qui —— votre voiture? 7. Je n'ai plus de stylo. Claude l' ——. 8. Marie —— son amie au théâtre. 9. Jean —— tous ses livres à l'école. 10. Pendant deux ans nos voisins —— à trois journaux. 11. Hier soir Jacques et Hélène —— une promenade. 12. Nous —— le train pour Nancy. 13. Ce matin j' —— mon examen de biologie. 14. Pendant les vacances les étudiants —— un grand voyage. 15. Qui vous —— au musée?

® CONVERSATION

1. Demandez à Monsieur I. qui il a mené au cinéma hier soir. 2. Demandez à Monsieur J. où il a porté la valise. 3. Demandez à Monsieur K. combien de cours il suit. 4. Demandez à Monsieur L. quand il passera son examen d'anglais.

VOCABULAIRE — PAGE 363

GRAMMAIRE

A. Demonstrative adjectives. (§ 15)
B. Demonstrative pronouns. (§ 33, 34)
C. The *introductory **ce**.* (§ 35, 36)
D. The *indefinite **ce*** and *impersonal **il**.* (§ 37)
E. Interrogative pronouns. (§ 38 A, B, C, D)
F. The interrogatives ***quel*** and ***lequel***. (§§ 16, 38 E)
G. Ways of expressing *take* in French. (§ 94)

Les Français en Amérique

Les Français créèrent une civilisation et une culture toutes différentes de celles des autres nations d'Europe. D'autre part, bien que la France ait perdu presque toutes ses possessions dans le nouveau monde, elle y a laissé des traces caractéristiques de son influence.

Avant que la France envoyât des explorateurs au Canada, l'Espagne et l'Angleterre en avaient déjà envoyé dans plusieurs régions du nouveau monde. Mais en 1534, Jacques Cartier fut chargé par le roi François Ier de chercher au nord du continent américain un passage vers les Indes. Il traversa l'Atlantique et découvrit le Saint-Laurent. Au cours d'un second voyage, il remonta ce fleuve et prit possession au nom du roi de la «Nouvelle France». En 1608 Champlain fonda la ville de Québec. Peu après, des missionnaires français atteignirent la région des Grands Lacs. Ils avaient renoncé à une vie confortable en France pour convertir les Indiens à leur religion. Ils ne se plaignaient pas des rudes conditions d'existence qu'ils trouvaient dans le nouveau monde. Ils allaient dans les endroits les plus dangereux, s'exposant à la fatigue, à la maladie, à la torture. Ils étaient plus amis des Indiens que les Anglais. Plus que les Anglais, les Français explorèrent les plaines inconnues de l'intérieur du vaste continent. Au milieu du dix-septième siècle la France possédait une grande partie du Canada et tout le centre des États-Unis, connu sous le nom de Louisiane. Après une série de guerres malheureuses, il fallut que la France livrât le Canada à l'Angleterre en 1763.

La perte de ce vaste territoire n'empêcha pas la France de continuer sa lutte contre l'Angleterre dans le nouveau monde. Quoique le gouvernement français n'eût pas reconnu l'indépendance des treize colonies en 1776, peu après il leur envoya des secours. De nombreux enthousiastes français se présentèrent à Washington. Parmi eux se trouvait le marquis de La Fayette. Celui-ci avait eu de grandes difficultés à quitter la France, car Louis XVI craignait que les idées libérales, base de la Révolution américaine, ne[1] se répandissent en France. A la longue, pourtant, il finit par accepter que des ressources matérielles et de l'argent fussent mis à la disposition des Américains. L'aide de la France pendant la Révolution américaine fut très importante, et sans elle l'histoire américaine eût été différente.

[1] For the use of this *ne*, see page 460, note 3.

Au milieu du dix-septième siècle, la France possédait une grande partie du Canada et tout le centre des États-Unis

Après la Révolution française de 1789, la France commença une nouvelle guerre contre l'Angleterre. Cette guerre dura pendant des années; Napoléon craignait que le territoire de la Louisiane ne[1] tombât aux mains des Anglais. C'est pour cette raison, qu'il le vendit aux États-Unis en 1803. Cette cession marqua la fin de la colonisation des Français en Amérique du Nord.

Mais cette période de colonisation laissa beaucoup de traces. On trouve des noms français partout au centre des États-Unis. Il y a Détroit, Saint-Louis, la Nouvelle-Orléans, Bâton-Rouge, etc. L'état de la Louisiane conserve aujourd'hui certaines coutumes françaises. On parle encore français à la Nouvelle-Orléans; la cuisine française de cette ville est

[1] For the use of this *ne,* see page 460, note 3.

renommée. Le système des lois de la Louisiane est basé sur le Code Napoléon. Les «Cajuns» des états de l'Alabama, du Mississippi et de la Louisiane sont les descendants des «Acadiens» que Longfellow célébra dans son poème *Evangeline. Acadien* devint *Cajun.*

Au Canada toute la province de Québec parle français. Montréal est la deuxième ville du monde au point de vue de la langue française. Mais la prononciation du canadien-français est différente du français de Paris, et le vocabulaire du canadien-français a subi l'influence de la langue anglaise. Les Canadiens français se distinguent nettement des autres Canadiens. Ils conservent leurs vieilles traditions. Dans les villes de la province de Québec on trouve partout l'influence de l'architecture française. Aucune ville d'Amérique n'est plus pittoresque que la ville de Québec; aucune ville n'a gardé autant de traces de la colonisation française en Amérique. Tout le pays a un aspect bien particulier qui rappelle la France elle-même.

Questions

1. Quelles sont les nations qui avaient envoyé des explorateurs dans le nouveau monde avant que la France en ait envoyé? 2. Qui a découvert le Saint-Laurent? 3. Quelle est la ville que Champlain a fondée en 1608? 4. Qui a exploré la région des Grands Lacs? 5. Comment la France a-t-elle perdu le Canada? 6. Comment la France a-t-elle aidé les treize colonies américaines pendant la Révolution? 7. Pourquoi Louis XVI craignait-il d'aider ces colonies? 8. Qui est La Fayette? 9. Pourquoi Napoléon a-t-il vendu la Louisiane aux États-Unis en 1803? 10. Quelles traces la civilisation française a-t-elle laissées en Amérique? 11. D'où vient le nom «Cajun»? 12. Quelle est la deuxième ville du monde au point de vue de la langue française? 13. En quoi le canadien-français est-il différent du français de Paris? 14. Comment se manifeste l'influence de la civilisation française dans le Canada français?

Devoirs

® *A. Mettez les verbes suivants* (1) *au présent du subjonctif* (2) *au passé du subjonctif.* EXEMPLE: nous lirions (1) que nous lisions (2) que nous ayons lu (*Voir Grammaire* §§ *80, 82 A*)

1. il finit 2. vous savez 3. ils sortent 4. je pourrai 5. nous faisons 6. vous vous lavez 7. elle viendra 8. je prends 9. vous buvez

B. Remplacez l'infinitif par le présent ou le futur de l'indicatif ou par le présent du subjonctif, selon le cas. (*Voir Grammaire* § *83 A, B, C, D*)

1. Il faut que nous (partir) tout de suite. 2. Il est certain que vous (savoir) cela. 3. Je doute que Charles (venir) ce soir. 4. C'est dommage qu'il (pleuvoir). 5. Il est évident que cette dame (vouloir) acheter une voiture. 6. J'ai peur que vous ne (travailler) pas assez. 7. Il est probable que nous (arriver) après-demain. 8. Il vaut mieux que je (prendre) le train. 9. Nous sommes contents que ces enfants (pouvoir) aller à la plage. 10. Je voudrais que vous (faire) ce voyage demain. 11. Il est important que Jacques (aller) voir son père. 12. Je vois que vous (avoir) une nouvelle robe. 13. Nous savons que vous (lire) beaucoup. 14. Je regrette que mon camarade (écrire) si peu à ses parents. 15. Il est vrai qu'il n'(avoir) pas beaucoup de temps.

C. Remplacez l'infinitif par le présent ou le futur de l'indicatif ou le présent du subjonctif, selon le cas. (*Voir Grammaire* § *83 E, F, G, H, I*)

1. Croyez-vous que vous (pouvoir) trouver quelqu'un qui (vouloir) travailler pour vous? 2. Venez vite pour que je vous (dire) ce qui s'est passé. 3. Je ne connais personne qui (savoir) lire le russe. 4. Nous avons une femme de ménage qui (savoir) parler russe. 5. Je crois que je (prendre) l'avion pour aller en France. 6. Quelles que (être) vos idées, vous pouvez rester dans ce pays. 7. Est-ce que Paris est la plus belle ville que vous (connaître)? 8. Je ne crois pas qu'il (être) aussi intéressant de voyager en avion qu'en bateau. 9. Si riche que (être) votre père, vous ne pourrez pas trouver une place sur le bateau au mois de juin. 10. Je ne vois rien qui (pouvoir) vous empêcher de visiter l'Allemagne. 11. Je partirai à moins que vous (faire) tout ce que je vous demande. 12. La meilleure chose que vous (pouvoir) faire à la frontière c'est de ne rien cacher. 13. Quoi que vous (dire), vous reviendrez ici. 14. Je crois que vous (trouver) Paris charmant. 15. Avant que je (partir), vous me direz où il faut que je (aller) en France. 16. Bien que nous (parler) français, il n'est pas certain que nous (comprendre) tout ce que nous entendrons. 17. Qui que vous (être), vous ne pourrez pas revenir aux États-Unis sans avoir été vaccinés.

D. Remplacez l'infinitif par le présent ou le passé du subjonctif, selon le cas. (*Voir Grammaire* § *84 A, B, E*)

1. Il est possible qu'il (pleuvoir) demain. 2. Il est peu probable

que ma mère (voir) votre voisin hier. 3. Regrettez-vous que Jean ne (venir) pas la semaine prochaine? 4. Je suis désolé que Paul (venir) jeudi dernier. 5. Cherchez-vous quelqu'un qui (apprendre) le français il y a deux ans? 6. Nous nous étonnons que Marie (savoir) toujours ses leçons. 7. Je regrette que Maurice (perdre) sa montre hier. 8. Il n'y a personne qui (pouvoir) vous aider si vous conduisez si vite. 9. Est-ce que le Louvre est le plus beau musée que vous (voir) quand vous étiez en Europe?

E. *Mettez en français les expressions anglaises entre parenthèses. Choisissez entre le subjonctif et l'infinitif, selon le cas. (Voir Grammaire § 85)*

1. Je voudrais (*that I were*) en France. 2. Je voudrais (*that you were*) ici. 3. Nous sommes contents (*that we can*) partir demain. 4. Nous sommes contents (*that you can*) passer vos vacances à Paris. 5. Avez-vous peur (*that I will lose*) votre argent? 6. Avez-vous peur (*that you will arrive*) trop tard? 7. Je fermerai la porte (*in order that I may hear*) la conférence. 8. Je vous donnerai de l'argent (*in order that you may buy*) un cadeau pour ma sœur. 9. Est-ce que Paul partira (*before he sees*) le professeur? 10. Est-ce que vous partirez (*before I write*) cette lettre?

F. *Les verbes suivants sont à l'imparfait ou au plus-que-parfait du subjonctif. Mettez-les au présent du subjonctif.* EXEMPLE: elle fût — elle soit. (*Voir Grammaire §§ 80, 81, 82 B*)

1. il allât 2. il choisît 3. ils eussent 4. ils eussent entendu 5. elle eût connu 6. elle demandât 7. ils eussent cru 8. il eût voulu 9. il dût 10. ils fussent venus 11. j'eusse dit 12. il sût 13. elle eût envoyé 14. il reçût 15. nous fussions 16. il pût 17. il eût fait 18. il fût mort 19. ils eussent mis 20. il eût lu 21. il eût fallu

® G. *Remplacez les formes de l'imparfait et du plus-que-parfait du subjonctif par les formes employées dans la conversation.* EXEMPLE: On avait donné l'ordre que les soldats s'arrêtassent. On avait donné l'ordre que les soldats *s'arrêtent.* (*Voir Grammaire § 84*)

1. Le roi craignait que le peuple se révoltât. 2. Il était important qu'il sût ce que faisaient ses ministres. 3. Il regrettait que La Fayette fût parti pour l'Amérique. 4. Les ministres voulaient que le roi

empêchât les représentants du peuple de faire une nouvelle constitution. 5. Mais ils s'étonnaient que le gouvernement eût perdu son autorité.

H. Remplacez par l'équivalent français l'expression anglaise entre parenthèses. (*Voir Grammaire* § *94*—visit)

1. Pierre (*will visit*) son oncle à Lyon. 2. Hier nous (*visited*) notre voisin, monsieur Lenoir. 3. Cet été nos amis (*will visit*) Paris et Rome. 4. Tous les jours ce garçon (*visited*) un soldat qui était en prison. 5. Voulez-vous que nous (*visit*) vos cousins quand nous serons à Paris? 6. Non, je veux que vous (*visit*) les musées les plus célèbres de Paris. 7. Voulez-vous (*visit*) le Portugal? 8. Pendant les vacances nous (*visited*) nos amis à Strasbourg.

®

Conversation

1. Demandez à Monsieur M. s'il ira voir son correspondant français quand il sera à Paris. 2. Demandez à Monsieur N. s'il a visité Tours pendant son voyage en France. 3. Demandez à Monsieur O. s'il fera une visite à ses parents pendant les vacances de Noël. 4. Demandez à Monsieur P. s'il rendra visite à ses anciens voisins quand il retournera dans la ville où il est né.

Vocabulaire — page 364

Grammaire

A. The formation of the present and past subjunctive. (§§ 80, 82 A)
B, C. The general concept of the subjunctive and the specific cases in which it is used. (§ 83)
D. The use of the present and past subjunctive. (§ 84 A, B, E)
E. The use of the subjunctive vs. the infinitive. (§ 85)
F. The formation of the imperfect and pluperfect subjunctive. (§§ 81, 82 B)
G. The uses of the imperfect and pluperfect subjunctive. (§ 84 B, D, F)
H. Ways of expressing *visit* in French. (§ 94)

Onzième révision — Leçons 51 à 60

Première partie

A. Répondez en français par des phrases complètes aux questions suivantes.

Questions sur l'histoire de France

1. A quelle époque la France est-elle devenue une république? 2. Qu'est devenue la langue française au dix-septième siècle? 3. Qu'est-ce que le roi Louis XIV a fait pour donner plus de prestige à son pays? 4. Quelle différence y a-t-il entre les jardins de Versailles et ceux qui étaient à la mode en Europe au dix-neuvième siècle? 5. Comment s'appelle la salle où a été signé le traité de Versailles après la guerre de 1914? 6. Pourquoi Louis XIV a-t-il fait construire le château de Versailles? 7. Qu'est-ce que vous entendez par l'Ancien régime? 8. Comment les idées des écrivains français du dix-huitième siècle ont-elles influencé les Américains? 9. Pourquoi le 14 juillet est-il la fête nationale de la France? 10. Comment Napoléon a-t-il changé le système administratif français? 11. Pourquoi Napoléon n'a-t-il pas envahi l'Angleterre? 12. A quelle bataille Napoléon a-t-il été vaincu? 13. Qui a fait percer le canal de Suez? 14. Quelle a été la cause de la guerre de 70? 15. Quels territoires la France a-t-elle dû céder à l'Allemagne à la fin de la guerre de 70? 16. Dans quelles régions du nouveau monde les Français ont-ils envoyé des explorateurs? 17. Comment la France a-t-elle aidé les treize colonies pendant la Révolution américaine? 18. Quelles sont les traces que les Français ont laissé sur le continent américain?

Questions sur les autres leçons

19. Citez les découvertes les plus importantes de Pasteur. 20. Racontez l'expérience de Pasteur à Melun. 21. Pourquoi Pasteur a-t-il essayé son traitement contre la rage sur Joseph Meister? 22. Quelle est la saison où les feuilles des arbres jaunissent? 23. Citez des poésies anglaises et américaines qui décrivent l'automne. 24. Quelle est la date de la rentrée des classes en Amérique? 25. Pourquoi ne fait-on pas de publicité à la radio et à la télévision françaises? 26. Quelles sont les émissions les plus suivies en France? 27. Citez des postes émetteurs très écoutés en France qui appartiennent à des sociétés privées. 28. Que fait-on en France la veille de Noël? 29. Décrivez le réveillon. 30. Où les petits Français mettent-ils leurs souliers le soir de Noël?

B. Expliquez en français par une phrase complète les noms suivants.

Anatole France
Ancien régime
André Chénier
Bismarck
Champlain
Clovis
Code civil
Elbe
États-Généraux
l'Expiation
Ferdinand de Lesseps
Galerie des Glaces
Grand Trianon
Grande Armée
Jacques Cartier
Joseph Meister
Lavoisier
Leipzig
Louis Napoléon
Louis-Philippe
Louis XIV
Louis XVI
Louis XVIII
Louisiane
Marie-Antoinette
Montesquieu
Montréal
Napoléon Bonaparte
Napoléon Ier
Napoléon III
Pasteur
Paul Verlaine
Petit Trianon
Pyramides
Québec
romantisme
Rousseau
Saint-Laurent
Sainte-Hélène
Terreur
tiers état
Voltaire
Waterloo

C. Rédigez une composition sur un des sujets suivants.

1. Le dix-septième siècle en France 2. L'automne aux États-Unis 3. La rentrée des classes 4. La Révolution française 5. La radio aux États-Unis 6. Les deux Napoléon 7. Noël chez nous 8. Les Français au Canada et aux États-Unis

DEUXIÈME PARTIE

Voici trois anecdotes. Copiez-les en remplaçant les infinitifs entre parenthèses par la forme convenable du verbe s'il y a lieu.

A

Dans les écoles françaises des fonctionnaires du ministère de l'Éducation nationale (venir) de temps en temps (voir) les classes, et les professeurs (avoir) souvent peur que leurs élèves ne leur (faire) pas honneur.

Dans le lycée d'une petite ville, cependant, il y (avoir) un professeur dont tous les élèves (sembler) toujours (connaître) les réponses à toutes les questions qu'il leur (poser). Les autres professeurs de cette école (s'étonner) que les élèves de ce dernier (savoir) tant de choses. Ils lui (demander) un jour:

— Comment (être)-il possible que vos élèves (être) si forts? Qu'est-ce que vous (faire) pour qu'ils (apprendre) si bien?

—Ce (être) très facile, (répondre) le professeur. Quand je (savoir) qu'il y (avoir) des visiteurs, je (dire) à mes élèves: «Cet après-midi, nous (avoir) des visiteurs. Quand ils (être) ici, (lever) la main droite si vous (savoir) les réponses; si vous ne les (savoir) pas, (lever) la main gauche.» De cette façon, il y (avoir) toujours dans la classe quelqu'un qui (pouvoir) (répondre) à chaque question.

B

La femme d'un pauvre paysan (être) très malade. Son mari (envoyer) chercher le médecin. Quand celui-ci (arriver), le paysan (être) assis à une table où il y (avoir) plusieurs billets de dix francs.

—Docteur, (dire) le paysan, voici cinquante francs. Je vous les (donner) si vous (guérir) ma femme, mais je vous les (donner) également si vous la (tuer).

Malgré tous les soins que le médecin (pouvoir) lui donner, la femme du paysan (mourir).

Comme le médecin, après plusieurs semaines, ne (avoir) pas de nouvelles du paysan à qui il (envoyer) sa note, il (aller) le voir.

—Docteur, (dire) le paysan, je (vouloir) bien vous payer, mais (vouloir)-vous (répondre) d'abord à deux questions?

—Mais oui, (répondre) le médecin.

—Eh bien, (continuer) le paysan, (guérir)-vous ma femme?

—Non, malheureusement, (devoir) répondre l'autre.

—Est-ce que vous la (tuer)?

—Certainement pas.

—Eh bien alors, (se rappeler) nos conditions, (dire) le paysan; je ne (voir) pas pourquoi je (devoir) vous payer les cinquante francs.

C

Un soir dans une ville anglaise un voyageur (arriver) à un hôtel où tout le monde (être) déjà couché. Il (demander) une chambre au propriétaire qui lui (répondre):

—Je ne (avoir) plus qu'une seule chambre. Mais dans la chambre au-dessous (se trouver) un homme très nerveux qui ne (s'endormir) qu'avec peine et qui (se réveiller) au moindre bruit. Je vous (donner) la chambre libre à condition que vous ne (faire) pas de bruit.

Le voyageur (promettre) au propriétaire de (faire) très attention. Il (sortir) du bureau de l'hôtel et (monter) au quatrième étage. En (arriver) à sa chambre, il (sortir) la clé qu'il (mettre) dans sa poche, (ouvrir) la porte très doucement pour qu'on ne (entendre) rien et la (refermer) de la même façon. Comme il (être) très fatigué, il (s'asseoir) dans un grand fauteuil et (commencer) à ôter ses chaussures. (oublier) l'homme qui (dormir) au-dessous de sa chambre, il (laisser) (tomber) un de ses souliers avec bruit. (regretter) cela, il (enlever) l'autre soulier et le (déposer) silencieusement à côté du fauteuil. Ensuite, il (se coucher) et (s'endormir) tout de suite.

Une demi-heure après, le voyageur (se réveiller) en (entendre) (frapper) à sa porte. Étonné, il (dire):

— (entrer).

La porte (s'ouvrir) devant un homme en pyjama[1], pâle et nerveux, qui (demander) à notre voyageur:

— (dire)-moi, s'il vous (plaire), quand vous (aller) (laisser) (tomber) l'autre soulier. Voilà une heure que je le (attendre).

[1] Pronounced [piʒama].

Supplément aux Leçons 51 à 60

CINQUANTE ET UNIÈME LEÇON

Vocabulaire

affirmer
l'alcool *m.*
l'animal *m.*
l'application *f.*
appliquer
la cause
consacrer
contagieux, contagieuse
la contribution
déterminer
diplomatique

domestique
l'effet *m.*
l'évolution *f.*
examiner
expérimenter
la fermentation
le germe
l'inoculation *f.*
inoculer
Joseph Meister

la manœuvre
Melun
Pasteur
la pasteurisation
scientifique
sérieusement
la stérilisation
le symptôme
la théorie
le vaccin
vacciner

le bienfait *benefit*
la blessure *wound*
le bois *wood*
bouleverser *upset*
la chimie *chemistry*

condamner *doom*
les connaissances[a] *f.* *knowledge*
couronner *crown*
la découverte *discovery*
échapper à[b] *escape, avoid*

[a] The word *connaissance,* which means *acquaintance* in the singular, takes on the additional meaning of *knowledge* in the plural.

[b] Distinguish between *échapper à quelque chose,* which means *to escape from something which one has not yet encountered,* therefore, *to avoid,* and *s'échapper de quelque chose,* which means *to escape from something in which one already is.*

l'efficacité *f.* *effectiveness*
enragé *mad*
l'être *m.* *being*
éventuel [a], éventuelle *possible*
l'expérience *f.* *experiment*
frapper *knock*
guérir *cure*
inquiet, inquiète *uneasy*
malade *sick*
le médecin *doctor*
moindre *least*
mordre *bite*
non-vacciné *unvaccinated*
or *now*
la patrie *fatherland*
la preuve *proof*
le procédé *process*
*produire *produce*; produit *produced*
la rage *rabies*
la recherche [b] *research*
sauver *save (a person)*
le savant *scientist*
le secours *help*
*survivre *survive*; survécu *survived*
tenter *attempt*

à partir de ce jour *from that day on*
âgé de neuf ans *nine years old*
couronné de succès *crowned with success*
passer le temps à marcher [c] *spend the time walking*
la Société d'Agriculture *Agricultural Association*

Devoirs

Before doing these exercises, review (a) *the position of French adjectives in § 12;* (b) *the differences in use between* **connaître** *and* **savoir** *in § 94 — know.*

A. *Write the French equivalent of each of the following sentences.*

1. Pasteur had a vague idea of the cause of contagious diseases [1]. 2. Thanks to the work [2] of the French and German scientists, many human lives have been saved. 3. The famous [3] doctor proposed a public experiment of the new method. 4. The unfortunate woman begged the good scientist to save her poor child. 5. The great man spent long hours in the woods. 6. Vacations [1] are an excellent opportunity to [4] get‿acquainted‿with [5] interesting girls. 7. Football [1] is the most popular sport we have. 8. One often hears a lively discussion over [6] the radio.

[1] Use the definite article with this noun. [2] Use the plural. [3] Precedes noun. [4] *de* [5] Use a form of *faire la connaissance de.* [6] *à*

* An asterisk (*) placed before a verb indicates that this verb is irregular.

[a] The French word *éventuel* indicates something which might possibly happen in the future rather than something which will happen, as commonly does the English *eventual.*

[b] *la recherche* means *a piece of research* or *research in general.*

[c] The verb *passer* + **a period of time** is followed by *à* + **infinitive** to express the English *spend time doing.*

B. Say aloud rapidly the French equivalent of each of the following sentences.

1. Do you know the cause of contagious diseases [1]? 2. I know a doctor who has done a great deal of research [2]. 3. He knows how to cure sick [3] people. 4. We know several scientists. 5. Do you know my opinion of [4] that child? 6. I know several cities in [5] Europe where one can study. 7. Pasteur knew that the unfortunate child would die. 8. He was well acquainted with the theory of the cause of diseases [1].

[1] Use the article with this noun. [2] Use the plural form of this noun.
[3] sick people *les malades* [4] *sur* [5] *d'*

CINQUANTE-DEUXIÈME LEÇON

Vocabulaire

absolu
absorber
la centralisation
Clovis
la corruption
le déclin
le degré
despotique
divin
la doctrine
extravagant
gouverner
imiter
le ministre
la monarchie
occasionner
la perfection
personnellement
le prestige
le protestant
la querelle
le représentant
le revenu
territorial
l'unification
unifier

achever *complete*
affaiblir *weaken*
l'apogée *f.* *height*
le conseiller *adviser, counsellor*
coûteux, coûteuse *costly, expensive*
la dépense *expenditure*
Dieu *m.* *God*
diriger *direct*
entraîner *bring on*
l'entretien *m.* *upkeep*
la fête *feast; holiday*
la haine *hate*
haut *high*
lointain *distant*
la marine *navy*
*parvenir *arrive;* parvenu *arrived*
rétablir *reestablish*
le royaume *kingdom*
la sagesse *wisdom*
le seigneur *lord*

en même temps *at the same time*
servir de *serve as*
le train de vie *the pace of life*

Devoirs

A. Write the French equivalent of each of the following sentences.

1. Before the revolution the kings had much power. 2. France has nu-

* An asterisk (*) placed before a verb indicates that this verb is irregular.

merous resources, but she does not have enough gold and she does not have any coffee. 3. The majority of men and many[1] women like music. 4. In Germany, in Denmark, and in Sweden few people[2] speak Russian. 5. We are going to France and we shall stay in Paris. 6. The castle was surrounded by[3] trees. 7. We need writers. Have you found any good writers? 8. Bring me some good milk and some small apples.

[1] Use *bien.* [2] *gens* [3] *de*

B. Say aloud rapidly the French equivalent of each of the following sentences.

1. I'll leave for Paris tomorrow. 2. Do not leave the building. 3. I'm leaving. 4. He left his watch on the table. 5. My mother left just[1] now, but she will soon come[2] back. 6. He left his work. 7. With whom did your sister go out? 8. Where did you leave your friend? 9. They left New York this morning.

[1] just now *tout à l'heure* [2] To express *come back,* use a form of *rentrer.*

CINQUANTE-TROISIÈME LEÇON

Vocabulaire

brillant
le contraste
l'épisode *m.*
géométriquement
Louis XVI
la majesté
Marie-Antoinette
la nature
perpendiculaire
la perspective
le point
proclamer
la Prusse
pur
régulier, régulière[a]
la symétrie
le Trianon
le vestige

à[b] *in the manner of, with*
agrandir *enlarge*
l'aile *f.* *wing*
*s'apercevoir *notice;* aperçu *noticed*
au delà de *beyond*
dessiner *draw, design*
digne *worthy*
disposé *laid out, arranged*
éclairer *light*
l'éclat *m.* *splendor, brilliance, magnificence*
la glace *mirror*
la grille *iron grating, iron fence*
l'intimité *f.* *coziness, intimacy*
jadis[c] *formerly*
manquer *lack*
le marbre *marble*
le miroir *mirror*
ordonné *laid out*
le parterre *flower bed*
le pas *step*
le passé *past*
la perte *loss*
le romantisme *romanticism*
vivement *deeply, vividly*
la vue *view*

* An asterisk (*) placed before a verb indicates that this verb is irregular.
[a] In this lesson *régulier* is used to designate the formal French garden plotted in straight lines in contrast to the informal type associated with English landscapes.
[b] This is the *à* characteristic which is often rendered in English by *in* or *with.*
[c] The *-s* is pronounced [ʒadis].

à la française [a] *in the French style, in the French manner*
à perte de vue *as far as the eye can reach*
aux lignes régulières [a] *with straight lines*
faire contraste avec *contrast with*
la fenêtre donne sur les jardins *the window looks out on the gardens*
la Galerie des Glaces *the Hall of Mirrors*
le Grand Trianon *one of the smaller palaces near the palace of Versailles*
le Petit Trianon *small palace at Versailles, originally built for Mme de Pompadour, later occupied by Marie-Antoinette*

Devoirs

A. Write the French equivalent of each of the following sentences.

1. We have been in Versailles for two hours. 2. Before leaving [1] Paris, I got [2] my ticket at the station. 3. After arriving in Versailles, they went to the gardens. 4. On seeing the beauty of these gardens, we decided to take a walk in the forest. 5. You cannot visit these places without admiring the beauty of the past. 6. Knowing that the palace was constructed by Louis XIV, we read a history of the seventeenth century before coming to this city. 7. After spending a whole day in the rooms [3] of the palace, we returned to Paris. 8. On arriving in the capital, I shall telephone my parents [4].

[1] Use a form of *quitter.* [2] Use a form of *prendre.* [3] *salles*
[4] This is the indirect object of the verb.

B. Say aloud rapidly the French equivalent of each of the following sentences.

1. He lives in Tours. 2. Victor Hugo lived in [1] the nineteenth century. 3. We have been living in a small town for some years. 4. He lives from his work. 5. Does he live well? 6. They live on [1] the ground floor of the apartment house. 7. Where does your sister live? 8. She lives near the railroad station.

[1] *au*

CINQUANTE-QUATRIÈME LEÇON

Vocabulaire

Anatole France	monotone	le sens
la lampe	l'obligation *f.*	solitaire
la mélancolie	Paul Verlaine	transporter

[a] This is the *à* characteristic which is often rendered in English by *in* or *with.*

agité *troubled, stormy*
l'âme *f.* *soul*
blesser *wound*
le bonhomme[a] *good fellow*
chanter *sing*
la chasse *hunt, hunting*
le chasseur *hunter*
écraser *crush*
l'épaule *f.* *shoulder*
éprouver *feel, experience*
la ferme *farm*
la feuille *leaf*
jamais[b] *ever*
jaune *yellow*
l'oiseau *m.* *bird*
l'ombre *f.* *shadow*
*parcourir *move around in; go through;* parcouru *moved around in; gone through*
pareil, pareille *like, similar*
la pensée *thought*
pleurer *weep, cry*
la poche *pocket*
la poésie *poetry*
*se remettre à *begin again, resume;* remis *begun again; resumed*
rouge *red*
*se souvenir de *remember;* souvenu *remembered*
triste *sad*
voler *fly*

à plusieurs points de vue *from several points of view*
alors que *when*
un dîner à la lampe *dinner by lamplight*
il avait le cœur serré *his heart was heavy, he was depressed*
l'heure sonne *the clock strikes*
un à un *one by one*

Devoirs

A. Write the French equivalent of each of the following sentences.

1. Show me that novel. Show it to me. Don't show it to me. 2. Don't read that poem to the children. Don't read it to them. Read it to them. 3. Have you read the works[1] of Anatole France? Yes, I have read some of them. 4. What do you think[2] of them? What do you think of him? 5. We often think of[2] our youth. Do you often think of it? Do you remember it? 6. Do you think of your parents? I think of them, I write to them, and when I am home[3], I go out with them. 7. I found some stamps for my friend; I will send some to him. 8. Who opened the door? They. No, he.

[1] *œuvres*
[2] The verb *penser* requires *de* before a noun when it is used in the sense of *to have an opinion of,* but it requires *à* before a noun when it is used in the sense of *to think of a person or thing.*
[3] Use *chez* with a pronoun object.

* An asterisk (*) placed before a verb indicates that this verb is irregular.
[a] Usually there is in *le bonhomme* the connotation of *a good-natured fellow* or *a simple soul.*
[b] Used in a complete sentence without *ne, jamais* means *ever;* with *ne,* it means *never.* Used in an elliptical sentence without a verb, it means *never* even without *ne.*

B. Say aloud rapidly the French equivalent of each of the following sentences.

1. Charles got married two years ago. 2. He married Louise. 3. Did he marry a rich girl? 4. Mr. Durand married his daughter to a teacher 5. She didn't want to marry a soldier. 6. When will she get married? 7 Whom will she marry? 8. They got married in Paris.

CINQUANTE-CINQUIÈME LEÇON

Vocabulaire

l'abolition *f.*
l'absolutisme *m.*
alarmer
André Chénier
s'armer
l'attitude *f.*
le calendrier
caractériser
la constitution
contribuer
le danger
décisif, décisive
la déclaration
la diffusion
l'effort *m.*
emprisonner
l'extérieur *m.*
la guillotine
guillotiner
l'incompréhension *f.*
influencer
Lavoisier
la liberté
métrique
Montesquieu
la notion
le parti
le poète
la presse
le principe
la prison
le privilège
la proclamation
profondément
refuser
le régime
la religion
républicain
révolutionnaire
Rousseau
ruiner
se séparer
substituer
le suspect
le symbole
total
véritable
la victime
Voltaire

l'abus *m.* *abuse*
accorder *grant, concede, accord*
agir *act*
André *Andrew*
*apparaître *appear;* apparu *appeared*
arriver à *succeed in*
la chute *fall*
le clergé *clergy*
le comité *committee*
convoquer *call together*
le coup *blow*
critiquer *criticize*
la déesse *goddess*
l'échange *m.* *exchange*
enfermer *shut up, imprison*
faible *weak*
le fondateur *founder*
l'impôt *m.* *tax*
*introduire *introduce;* introduit *introduced*
jouir de *enjoy*
jurer *swear*
lourd *heavy*
la misère *poverty; wretchedness*
la mort *death*
la noblesse *nobility*
ouvertement *openly*

* An asterisk (*) placed before a verb indicates that this verb is irregular.

la parole *(spoken) word*
le penseur *thinker*
la prodigalité *extravagance in expenditure*
rassembler *assemble*
se répandre *spread*
reposer *rest*
le salut *safety*
seul *only*
se soulever *rise up*
soupçonner *suspect*
tarder à *delay in*
la Terreur *Reign of Terror*
le trésor *treasury*

à la suite de *after*
en échange *in exchange*
gagner l'étranger *reach foreign lands*
mettre en doute *question*
peu après *soon afterwards*
prendre fin *end*

l'Ancien régime *the Old Regime*
le Comité de Salut public *the Committee of Public Safety*
la Convention nationale *the National Convention*
la Déclaration d'indépendance *the Declaration of Independence*
les États-Généraux *the States General*
le tiers état *the Third Estate*

Devoirs

A. Write the French equivalent of each of the following sentences.

1. The king was forced to call together [1] an assembly which had not met [2] for many years [3]. 2. The people [4] were very unhappy, for they paid very heavy taxes. 3. During the eighteenth century, the principal writers were spreading the idea of the Rights of Man. 4. These ideas influenced the authors of the American Constitution. 5. The representatives of the people [4] refused to vote the taxes which the king had requested. 6. The king decided to act, but it was too [5] late. 7. The people [4] seized the prison where several political prisoners were waiting. 8. Can we see the prison that they attacked? 9. No, no one has seen it, for it no longer exists.

[1] Use a form of *convoquer*. [2] Use a form of *se réunir*. [3] See § 98 for the difference between *ans* and *années*. [4] *le peuple* [5] *trop*

B. Say aloud rapidly the French equivalent of each of the following sentences.

1. Yesterday, I met [1] Louise on [2] the street. 2. Have you met [3] Mrs. Bonneville? 3. We met [3] the president's wife last week. 4. They will meet [4] in front of the library. 5. I will [5] meet you at the station. 6. They met [1] their teacher in the park. 7. I met [4] my father at Bordeaux. 8. He met [6] me with the car. 9. The Parliament meets in the Luxembourg palace.

[1] i.e., to meet accidentally [2] *dans* [3] i.e., to get acquainted with
[4] i.e., to meet by appointment [5] Instead of the future, use the proper form of *aller* with the infinitive. [6] i.e., to go and get

CINQUANTE-SIXIÈME LEÇON

Vocabulaire

l'auditeur *m.*
avide
le bulletin
commenter
le concert
la conséquence
contrôler
culturel, culturelle
le développement
documentaire
l'élite *m.*
évident
la fabrication
favoriser
l'hôpital, *m.*
l'information [a] *f.*
le jazz
littéraire
le match
l'opérette *f.*
physique
le profit
le public
récent
le studio

actuellement *at present*
l'agrément *m.* *pleasure*
l'amateur *m.* *devotee, "fan"*
attirer *draw, attract*
bavarder *chat*
la causerie *chat, talk*
chirurgical *surgical*
entièrement *entirely*
le fond *end; depth*
le foyer [b] *home*
fréquemment *frequently*
le malade *sick person*
ménager *take care of, look after, humor*
se passionner *be enthusiastic*
la portée *import, signification*
quelconque *whatever, whatsoever*
quotidien, quotidienne *daily*
la revue *review*
la société *company; corporation*

à l'heure actuelle *at the present time*
à tout prix *at any price*
au fond de *in the most remote part of*
en famille *in the family circle*
en particulier *in particular*
en revanche *in return*
la grande musique *high-class music*
le grand public *the general public*
l'office religieux *religious service*
allumer / mettre / ouvrir } la radio *turn on the radio*
R.T.F. *French (National) Radio and Television*

Devoirs

A. Write the French equivalent of each of the following sentences.

1. The student whose exercises are written hopes that he will be able to hear his favorite program. 2. The young man with whom my brother went to Paris gets up every morning at seven o'clock. 3. My parents prefer the radio, but yours prefer the television. 4. Our friends were traveling every-

[a] In French this word is normally used in the plural.
[b] The basic meaning of *foyer* is *fireplace.* but it has taken on the additional meaning of *home* or *family circle.*

where while yours were beginning their studies. 5. My name[1] is Charles; yours[1] is Roland. 6. The day when their radio set arrived there was no one at home. 7. Our teacher found nothing on his desk. 8. The friend whose television set I bought has never come to see me. 9. Tell me what your mother heard over[2] the radio. Nothing.

[1] Use a form of *s'appeler*. [2] *à*

B. *Say aloud rapidly the French equivalent of each of the following sentences.*

1. That man must be rich. 2. You must finish your work. 3. I must leave soon. 4. They must listen to the radio every evening. 5. If you must buy a new set, that will cost a great deal of money, won't it? 6. That doctor must have a great deal to do. 7. If we must stay here, we will not arrive on time.

CINQUANTE-SEPTIÈME LEÇON

Vocabulaire

abdiquer
l'admiration *f.*
allié
l'avalanche *f.*
Berlin
le blocus
catholique
le concordat
*conquérir, conquis
le consul
continental
définitivement
diminuer
Elbe *f.*
exiler
l'Expiation f.
grave
le héros
Leipzig
Louis XVIII
la Louisiane
la manière
Moscou
Napoléon Bonaparte
l'organisme *m.*
la possession
les Pyramides *f.*
victorieux, victorieuse
Waterloo

la banque *bank*
la campagne *campaign*
certes *certainly*
se contenter de *be satisfied with*
se débarrasser de *get rid of*
*décrire *describe;* décrit *described*
la faiblesse *weakness*
la flotte *fleet*
harceler *harass*
l'Inde *f.* *India*
jaloux, jalouse *jealous*
le pape *pope*
*parvenir à *succeed in;* parvenu *succeeded*
le produit *product*
reculer *draw back, retreat*
la règle *rule*
le Russe *Russian*
saisissant *thrilling, impressive*
le trône *throne*
s'unir *unite*
*vaincre *conquer;* vaincu *conquered*

* An asterisk (*) placed before a verb indicates that this verb is irregular.

commander en chef *command as chief*
le consul à vie *consul for life*
le coup d'état *unexpected political move, usually connected with seizure of power*
d'une manière saisissante *in a thrilling manner*
monter sur le trône *ascend the throne*

la Bataille des Pyramides *the Battle of the Pyramids*
la Grande Armée *the Great Army, a term used to refer to the army of Napoleon*

Devoirs

A. Write the French equivalent of each of the following sentences.

1. As soon as we read Napoleon's life, we shall describe the battle of Waterloo to you. 2. If the great general had been born one year earlier [1], he would not have been French. 3. When you have finished your work, I shall show you my new car. 4. If those students were in France, they would probably talk with the French girls. 5. If that man continues to work, he will be exhausted. 6. When we have written that letter, we shall mail [2] it. 7. If Napoleon had not invaded Russia, he would never have been conquered. 8. When you go to the bank, you will be able to get some money.

[1] *plus tôt.* [2] Use a form of *mettre à la poste.*

B. Say aloud rapidly the French equivalent of each of the following sentences.

1. My brother left this morning, but he will return this evening. 2. I returned his ticket to him. 3. Our friends were here, but they returned to Bordeaux last week. 4. At what time did you return (home [1]) last evening? 5. Return my book to me. 6. Yesterday my father returned to [2] the city where he works. 7. I'll return (home [1]) late this evening. 8. Mr. Leclerc is in France now, but he'll return here next week.

[1] Included in the verb. [2] *dans*

CINQUANTE-HUITIÈME LEÇON

Vocabulaire

la branche
le cercle
le Christ
le cri
la délivrance
l'émotion *f.*
l'enthousiasme *m.*
la joie
mécanique
multicolore
originel, originelle [a]
se prolonger
traditionnel, traditionnelle

[a] Used chiefly in the expression *péché originel,* meaning *original sin.*

l'argent *m.* *silver*
brillamment *brilliantly, brightly*
la cheminée *fireplace*
chargé *loaded*
le chrétien *Christian*
le coin *corner*
couché *in bed; put to bed; asleep*
dehors *outside*
déposer *place*
l'espérance *f.* *hope*
fidèle *faithful;* les fidèles *the faithful (ones)*
se figurer *imagine*
le gâteau *cake*
illuminer *light, illuminate*
*se joindre à *join;* joint *joined*
minuit *midnight*
la naissance *birth*
la neige *snow*
l'or *m.* *gold*
le pareil *equal*
pousser *push; utter*
propre [a] *clean*
*recouvrir *cover, cover again;* recouvert *covered*
*rejoindre *join, rejoin;* rejoint *joined*
se rendre à *go to*
rêver *dream*
le sol *ground, soil*
solennel, solennelle *solemn*
le soulier *shoe*
le toit *roof*
le vœu *wish; greeting*
le voisin *neighbor*

le gâteau au chocolat *chocolate cake*
le jour de l'an *New Year's Day*
le Père Noël *Santa Claus*
pousser un cri *utter a cry*
sans pareil *without equal*
la tradition veut que *tradition decrees that*
le vœu de Noël *Christmas greeting*

Devoirs

A. Write the French equivalent of each of the following sentences.

1. The children did not hesitate to put their shoes beside the fireplace. 2. Santa Claus brings nothing to children who do not wish to obey their parents. 3. We told the American soldier to marry a French girl. 4. My brother entered the living room and asked my mother to give him his notebook. 5. I tried to remember the words [1] of that song. 6. My little sister thinks of Christmas every day. 7. Our children do not lack toys at Christmas. 8. Do you play [2] golf or do you prefer to play [2] the violin? 9. We promised the children to buy a dog at Easter.

[1] *paroles* [2] Distinguish between *jouer à un jeu* and *jouer d'un instrument.*

B. Say aloud rapidly the French equivalent of each of the following sentences.

1. How much time did you spend in France? 2. We spent three weeks

* An asterisk (*) placed before a verb indicates that this verb is irregular.
[a] When *propre* precedes its noun, it means *own;* when it follows its noun, it means *clean.*

in Germany. 3. Did you spend all your money? 4. He will spend too much money in Paris. 5. He will spend all his time at the library. 6. Where did you spend Christmas vacation? 7. Did you spend a great deal of money during the vacation? 8. I didn't spend much money abroad, because I didn't spend much time in the large cities.

CINQUANTE-NEUVIÈME LEÇON

Vocabulaire

ambitieux, ambitieuse
Bismarck
le canal
la candidature
céder
Charles X
la confédération
le cousin
Ferdinand de Lesseps [a]
l'indemnité [b] *f.*
l'insulte *f.*
interpréter
Isabelle II
Louis Napoléon
Louis-Philippe
matériel, matérielle
Napoléon III
le prince
protester
se révolter
Suez

la couronne *crown*
*élire *elect;* élu *elected*
embellir *beautify, embellish*
habile *clever*
l'ouvrage *m.* *work*
percer *dig, tunnel*
la promesse *promise*
le refus *refusal*
*remettre *put back again;* remis *put back again*
retirer *withdraw*
se sauver *escape, run off*
la suite *consequence*
le trouble *confusion, disorder, turmoil, uneasiness;* les troubles *disturbances* (*much stronger than English "trouble"*)

encore une fois *again, once again*
la France ne pouvait rien *France could do nothing*

Devoirs

A. Write the French equivalent of each of the following sentences.

1. What prevented that emperor from winning those wars? 2. Who had [1] those boulevards constructed? These? No, those. 3. What did the Spanish offer to a cousin of the king of Prussia? 4. Of what did those men dream? 5. Between 1870 and 1920 France had two wars with Germany. The latter lasted longer [2] than the former. 6. Who is that man? He is a teacher. He is an excellent teacher, but he is sick. 7. Do you read well? It is not very difficult. 8. It is impossible to go out this evening. No, you

[1] This is the auxiliary of the causative construction. See § 92 A. [2] *plus longtemps*

* An asterisk (*) placed before a verb indicates that this verb is irregular.
[a] The final *-s* is pronounced [dəlɛsɛps].
[b] The *-em-* is usually pronounced like *-èm-* [ɛ̃dɛmnite].

are wrong; it is not impossible. 9. Show me those flowers. Which ones? These? No, those.

B. Say aloud rapidly the French equivalent of each of the following sentences.

1. We will take a trip next month. 2. Take that chair away. 3. He took his friend to the movie. 4. This morning I took an examination. 5. We take several newspapers. 6. What courses are you taking? 7. He is going to take the lamp to[1] his mother's. 8. Who took my notebook? 9. They will take their guest to a good restaurant.

[1] *chez*

SOIXANTIÈME LEÇON

Vocabulaire

l'Acadien *m.*
Alabama
baser
Bâton-Rouge
le Cajun
canadien, canadienne
Champlain
la colonisation
convertir
le descendant
Détroit
la disposition
l'enthousiaste *m.*
l'explorateur *m.*
exposer
la fatigue
les Indes *f.*
l'Indien *m.*
Jacques Cartier
La Fayette
libéral
le marquis
le missionnaire
le Mississippi
Montréal
le Saint-Laurent
Saint-Louis

célébrer *make famous*
la cession *transfer, cession*
livrer *hand over*
nettement *plainly, clearly, sharply*
*se plaindre *complain;* plaint *pitied, complained*
remonter *go up, ascend*
renommé *noted, famous*
renoncer à *give up, renounce*
rude *rough, harsh*

à la longue *in the long run*
au point de vue de *from the point of view of*
d'autre part *moreover; on the other hand*
les Grands Lacs *the Great Lakes*

Devoirs

A. Write the French equivalent of each of the following sentences.

1. In the long run, it is better that we recognize the differences between the two countries. 2. Are you afraid that there will be a war soon? 3. I believe that we can prevent a war. 4. The government is looking for men

* An asterisk (*) placed before a verb indicates that this verb is irregular.

who know how to speak foreign languages [1]. 5. We must learn foreign languages in order that we may understand other nations [1]. 6. Most of the countries of the world are glad that Germany did not win the last war. 7. Before you leave [2] the university, your teachers will explain to you why it was necessary for us to make war in 1941. 8. We want you to be acquainted with the history of all the important nations of Europe. 9. Whoever you are, you have nothing which can help him.

[1] Supply the definite article. [2] Use a form of *quitter*.

B. Say aloud rapidly the French equivalent of each of the following sentences.

1. Did you visit Dijon when you were in France? 2. We visited our neighbors yesterday evening. 3. He will visit his father in June. 4. What countries will you visit next year? 5. I am going to visit my mother next week. 6. They visited Rome and Paris the last time that they were in Europe. 7. My mother visited Mrs. Dupont yesterday. 8. They often visit their parents.

Il est né, le divin [1] Enfant

Il est né, le divin Enfant, Jouez, haut-bois [2], résonnez [3], musettes [4];
Il est né, le divin Enfant; Chantons tous son avènement [5]!

1. Depuis plus de quatre mille ans, Nous le promettaient les Prophètes;
Depuis plus de quatre mille ans, Nous attendions cet heureux temps.
Il est né, etc.

2. Ah! qu'il est beau, qu'il est charmant, Que ses grâces sont parfaites!
Ah! qu'il est beau, qu'il est charmant, Qu'il est doux, le divin Enfant!
Il est né, etc.

3. Une étable [6] est son logement [7], Un peu de paille [8], sa couchette [9],
Une étable est son logement, Pour un Dieu, quel abaissement [10]!
Il est né, etc.

4. O Jésus! O Roi tout puissant! Tout petit enfant que vous êtes,
O Jésus! O Roi tout puissant! Régnez sur nous entièrement!
Il est né, etc.

[1] Pronounce [divinɑ̃fɑ̃] [2] *oboes* [3] *resound* [4] *bagpipes* [5] *coming*
[6] *stable* [7] *lodging* [8] *straw* [9] *bed* [10] *humiliation*

La Seine

(Refrain)

1. La Seine est [1] aventureuse
De Châtillon à Méry,
Et son [2] humeur voyageuse
Flâne à travers le pays . . .
Elle se [3] fait langoureuse
De Juvisy à Choisy
Pour aborder [4], l'âme heureuse,
L'amoureux [5] qu'elle a choisi!

Ell' roucoule [6], coule, coule
Dès qu'elle entre dans Paris!
Ell' s'enroule [7], roule [8], roule
Autour de ses quais fleuris [9]!
Elle chante, chante, chante, chante,
Chant' le jour et la nuit,
Car la Seine est une amante [10],
Et son amant [10] c'est Paris!

2. Elle traine [11] d'île en île,
Caressant [12] le Vieux-Paris,
Elle ouvre ses bras dociles
Au sourir' du roi Henri . . .
Indifférente aux édiles [13]
De la Mairie de Paris,
Elle court vers les idylles [14]
Des amants des Tuileries!

Ell' roucoule [6], coule, coule
Du Pont-Neuf jusqu'à Passy!
Elle est saoûle [15], saoûle, saoûle
Au souvenir de Bercy!
Elle chante, chante, chante, chante,
Chant' le jour et la nuit . . .
Si sa marche [16] est [17] zigzagante
C'est qu'elle est grise [18] à Paris!

3. Mais la Seine est paresseuse [19],
En passant près de Neuilly,
Ah, comme elle est malheureuse
De quitter son bel ami!
Dans une étreinte [20] amoureuse [21]
Elle enlace [22] encore Paris,
Pour lui laisser, généreuse [23],
Une boucle [24] . . . à Saint-Denis!

Ell' roucoule [6], coule, coule
Sa complainte [25] dans la nuit . . .
Elle roule [8], roule, roule
Vers la Mer où tout finit . . .
Elle chante, chante, chante, chante,
Chant' l'Amour de Paris!
Car la Seine est une amante [10]
Et Paris dort dans son lit [26]!

[1] est aventureuse *likes to roam about* [2] son humeur voyageuse flâne *her desire for traveling takes her* [3] se fait langoureuse *slows down* [4] *meet* [5] *loved one* [6] *coos* [7] *twists about* [8] *rolls* [9] *flowery* [10] *lover* [11] *makes her way* (*lit.* drags) [12] *caressing* [13] *city magistrates* [14] *romantic meeting places* [15] *intoxicated* [16] *course* [17] est zigzagante *zigzags* [18] *tipsy* [19] *lazy* [20] *embrace* [21] *loving* [22] *hugs* [23] *the generous one* [24] *curl, bend* (*in the river*) [25] *sad refrain* [26] *bed*

Grammaire

The Article – L'article

In English the definite article is *the.* The indefinite article is *a* or *an.*

1. *The forms of the definite article — Les formes de l'article défini*

In English the definite article has but one form: *the.* In French the definite article has four forms.

A. The singular forms of the French word for *the* are

le — *le* nord *le* sud *le* Havre *le* héros *le* petit pays

used before a masculine singular noun or adjective beginning with a consonant or an aspirate *h.*[1]

la — *la* capitale *la* mer *la* haine *la* grande ville *la* haute montagne

used before a feminine singular noun or adjective beginning with a consonant or an aspirate *h.*[1]

l' — *l'*est *l'*ouest *l'*Atlantique *l'*hôtel *l'*excellente frontière

used before a masculine or feminine noun or adjective beginning with a vowel or a mute *h.* When a word following the singular form of the definite article begins with a vowel or a mute *h,* this elision must be made.[2]

B. The plural of the French word for *the* is always

les — *les* continents *les* capitales *les* États-Unis *les* hôtels

It is *les* regardless of the gender or initial letter of the following word.

2. *The contractions of the definite article*
Les contractions de l'article défini

A. The definite article always contracts with *de* as follows:

de + le = *du*	le centre *du* pays
de + les = *des*	une partie *des* montagnes

[1] See pages 511–512. [2] See the discussion of elision on page 514.

But *de la* and *de l'* do not contract.

de la	le nord *de la* France
de l'	une partie *de l'*Europe

B. The definite article always contracts with *à* as follows:

à + le = *au*	situé *au* nord de la France
à + les = *aux*	*aux* frontières de la Belgique

But *à la* and *à l'* do not contract.

à la	*à la* capitale du pays
à l'	*à l'*est de l'Espagne

3. *The indefinite article — L'article indéfini*

In English the indefinite article has the forms *a* and *an.* In French the indefinite article has two singular forms and one plural form.

A. The French words for *a* and *an* are

un *un* pays *un* continent *un* endroit *un* hôtel

used before masculine singular nouns or adjectives

une *une* ville *une* partie *une* haute montagne *une* embouchure

used before feminine singular nouns or adjectives

B. The plural of the indefinite article is expressed in French by

des *des* pays *des* continents *des* villes *des* parties

When an indefinite noun is found in the plural in English, often no article is used. Sometimes the indefinite adjectives *some* or *any* express indefiniteness. In French, the indefinite *des* must normally be used with a plural noun to express indefiniteness.

La France et l'Italie sont *des pays.*	France and Italy are *countries.*
Les Pyrénées sont *des montagnes élevées.*	The Pyrenees are *high mountains.*
Citez *des villes* du nord de la France.	Mention *some cities* in the north of France.

4. *Some uses of the article — Quelques emplois de l'article*

A. In both English and French the definite article usually indicates a definite object.

Paris est *la* capitale de la France.	Paris is *the* capital of France.
La Seine est *le* fleuve qui traverse *le* pays.	The Seine is *the* river which crosses *the* country.

B. In French the definite article must be used with a noun to designate an object taken in a general sense. In English only the noun is used.

Le Havre est important pour *le commerce.*	Le Havre is important for *commerce.*
Les fromages français sont bons.	French *cheeses* are good.
On aime *le cidre* en Normandie.	They like *cider* in Normandy.

C. In both English and French the definite article is used with names of *rivers* and *mountains.*

le Rhin	*the* Rhine	*les* Alpes	*the* Alps
la Seine	*the* Seine	*les* Rocheuses	*the* Rockies

But in French the definite article is likewise used with names of *countries* and *continents.* In English only the noun is used.

la France	France	*l'*Europe	Europe
*l'*Espagne	Spain	*l'*Amérique	America

1. When the name of a continent or feminine country is preceded by the preposition *en* (meaning *in* or *to*) or *de* (meaning *from*), no article is used.

en France	*in* France, *to* France	*de* France	*from* France
en Europe	*in* Europe, *to* Europe	*d'*Europe	*from* Europe

2. When the name of a continent or feminine country is preceded by *de* (meaning *of*), usually no article is used *if the phrase may be expressed by an adjective in English.* Otherwise, the article must be used. Compare

un fleuve *de France*	une partie *de la France*
a *French* river	a part of France

However, there are certain expressions where the use or omission of the article has been fixed by usage. For instance:

l'histoire *de France*	French history
le roi *de France*	the king of France
la géographie *de la France*	the geography of France
la capitale *de la France*	the capital of France
l'empereur *des Français*	the French emperor
la littérature *française*	French literature

D. The days of the week are used without the definite article in French as in English to indicate an occurrence which takes place only once.

Il va à Paris *lundi.*	He is going to Paris (*on*) *Monday.*
Ils ont un jour de congé *mardi.*	They have a day off *Tuesday* (just this Tuesday).

But the definite article is used before the days of the week to indicate a regular occurrence each week on the day mentioned. In English, *-s* is often added to the day of the week or the word *every* is placed before the day of the week.

Il va à Paris *le lundi.*	He goes to Paris *Mondays* (every Monday).
Ils ont un jour de congé *le mardi.*	They have a day off *Tuesdays* (every Tuesday).

E. Appositives, that is, nouns which follow other nouns in order to explain them, are used with or without an article, depending on the intention of the speaker.

1. Appositives are used without any article when they supply additional information which is presumably unknown to the reader.

Rouen, *capitale de l'ancienne province de Normandie,* se trouve sur la Seine près du Havre.	Rouen, *the capital of the former province of Normandy,* is located on the Seine near Le Havre.
Nous sommes à Grenoble, *ville pittoresque entourée de montagnes.*	We are at Grenoble, *a picturesque city surrounded by mountains.*
Jean, *étudiant en médecine,* habite à Paris.	John, *a medical student,* lives in Paris.

2. Appositives are used with an article when they distinguish their noun from others or when they state a well-known fact.

Nous lisons un roman de Balzac, *le grand écrivain du dix-neuvième siècle.*	We are reading a novel of Balzac, *the great writer of the nineteenth century.*

F. The definite article is normally used with names of languages in French.

Le français est une langue facile.	*French* is an easy language.

But the name of a language is used without the article when preceded by *en* and often when it follows the verb *parler.*

Comment dit-on "grapes" *en français?*	How do you say "grapes" *in French?*
Mon camarade *parle français.*	My friend *speaks French.*

G. The definite article is generally used instead of the possessive adjective before parts of the body and sometimes with articles of clothing when the noun in question is not the subject of the sentence.[1]

Maurice baisse *la tête* et réfléchit.	Maurice bows *his head* and contemplates.
Nous voyons avec *les yeux.*	We see with *our eyes.*

H. After forms of the verb *être* French designates profession, position, religion, etc., by a noun unmodified by an article. English uses a noun modified by the indefinite article.

Votre père est *professeur.*	Your father is *a teacher.*
Jean est *étudiant en médecine.*	John is *a medical student.*

I. The article is sometimes omitted in enumerations.

Nous avons trouvé toutes sortes de choses: *crayons, stylos, cahiers,* etc.	We found all sorts of things: pencils, fountain pens, notebooks, etc.
Puis on choisit un plat du jour: *poisson* ou *viande.*	Then one chooses the main course: *fish* or *meat.*

5. *The partitive article — L'article partitif*

A. The partitive article is a combination of *de* and **the definite article.**

du	*du* lait (some)[2] milk	*du* beurre (some) butter	*du* fromage (some) cheese

used before a masculine singular noun beginning with a consonant or an aspirate *h.*

de la	*de la* crème (some) cream	*de la* viande (some) meat	*de la* soie (some) silk

used before a feminine singular noun beginning with a consonant or an aspirate *h.*

---

[1] For a complete treatment of the use of the article for the possessive adjective, see Pargment, *Cours supérieur de français,* pp. 193–195. Macmillan, 1951.

[2] English expresses this construction by either the noun or the noun modified by *some.* Thus *du lait* is *milk* or *some milk.*

de l' *de l'*encre (some) ink *de l'*alcool (some) alcohol *de l'*opposition (some) opposition

used before all masculine and feminine singular nouns beginning with a vowel or mute h.

des *des* villes (some) cities *des* pays (some) countries *des* hommes (some) men *des* héros (some) heroes

used before all plural nouns.

B. The partitive article is used with a noun to indicate indefinite quantity (a part of all that exists).[1] It indicates that the noun is indefinite.

La Normandie fournit *du lait* et *de la crème* à tout le pays.	Normandy furnishes *milk* and *cream* to the whole country.
On trouve *des vaches, des bœufs* et *des moutons* dans toute la région.	One finds *cows, steers,* and *sheep* in the whole region.

In the above sentences, *milk, cream, cows, steers,* and *sheep* are all indefinite. In English this indefinite idea is usually expressed by the noun alone. Sometimes *some* or *any* modify the noun to express indefinite quantity. Compare: We find *cows* in the field. —We find *some cows* in the field. In French, this concept of indefiniteness is usually expressed by the noun modified by the partitive articles *du, de la, de l'*, and *des.*

C. Thus in French, ***du, de la, de l',*** and ***des*** sometimes mean *of the* and sometimes mean *some.* In reading French, one must recognize from the context of the sentence whether they mean *of the* or whether they are ***partitive articles.***

Les habitants *des* villes ont ***des*** voitures.	The inhabitants *of the* cities have (***some***) cars.
La capitale *du* pays fournit ***du*** lait aux autres villes.	The capital *of the* country furnishes (***some***) milk to the other cities.

D. Indefinite quantity is indicated after *sans* (without) and *ni . . . ni* (neither . . . nor) by the noun alone without any partitive article.

Paul est arrivé *sans argent.*	Paul arrived *without money.*
Nous n'avons *ni livres ni papier.*	We have *neither books nor paper.*
Ni professeurs ni élèves n'y vont.	*Neither teachers nor pupils* go there.

---

[1] Consider the following historical development in the meaning of the partitive construction: Donnez-moi *du pain.* (1) Give me *of the bread.* (original meaning of du) (2) Give me ***part of the bread.*** (literal partitive sense) (3) Give me *some bread.* (actual English equivalent)

E. Indefinite quantity is indicated by the noun alone in a phrase of manner consisting of *avec* + **unmodified abstract noun.**

Il a parlé *avec difficulté.*	He spoke *with difficulty.*
Daniel a regardé sa femme *avec surprise.*	Daniel looked at his wife *in surprise.*
Les élèves ont écrit *avec soin.*	The pupils wrote *with care.*

6. *Cases in which* de *is found before a noun*[1]
Cas où de *se trouve devant un nom*

A. When an adjective precedes a plural[2] noun, one finds

de + adjective + plural noun

Il y a toujours *de nombreux touristes* dans cette région.	There are always *numerous tourists* in that region.
A Cannes se trouvent *de charmantes plages* et *d'élégants hôtels* dans des paysages agréables.	At Cannes are *charming beaches* and *elegant hotels* in pleasant surroundings.

B. Expressions of quantity are followed by *de* before a noun.[3]

---

[1] In this section, the word *noun* indicates an indefinite noun. The difference between an indefinite and a definite noun may be seen from the following examples:

1. *livres* is indefinite

La table est couverte de *livres.*	The table is covered with *books.*

2. *livres* is definite

La table est couverte des *livres* que nous avons achetés.	The table is covered with *the books* which we bought.

[2] But when an adjective precedes a singular noun, one usually finds

partitive article + adjective + noun

Examples: Nous avons ***du bon vin.*** J'entends ***de la belle musique.***

[3] Note the following cases where certain expressions of quantity are followed by different constructions:

1. *bien* + **partitive article** = many

Nous avons *bien des choses* à faire.	We have *many things* to do.
Il a eu *bien de la peine* à le trouver.	He had a *great deal of trouble* to find it.

2. *la plupart* + *de* + **definite article** = the majority of the

La plupart des élèves sont là.	*The majority of the pupils* are there.

One always finds *la plupart des* except in the expression *la plupart du temps.*

beaucoup de	*much, many*	moins de	*less, fewer*
peu de	*few, little*	tant de	*so much, so many*
assez de	*enough*	autant de	*as much, as many*
trop de	*too many*	combien de	*how many*
plus de	*more*		

On trouve *beaucoup de fruits* dans le Midi.	One finds *many fruits* in the south of France.
Il y a *trop de gens* sur les plages.	There are *too many people* on the beaches.

C. The negative *pas* is normally followed by *de.* In such cases, *pas* is equivalent to the English *not . . . any* or *no.*[1]

Il n'y a *pas de* châteaux aux États-Unis.	There are *no* castles in the United States.
On ne trouve *pas d'*oranges dans le nord du pays.	One does *not* find *any* oranges in the north of the country.

D. Many French verbs, adjectives, and idiomatic expressions are normally followed by the preposition *de.* After such constructions, *de* alone is used before a noun.

La France *se compose de* plaines et *de* montagnes.	France *is composed of* plains and mountains.
Les châteaux sont *entourés de* murailles.	The castles are *surrounded by* walls.
Nous avons *besoin de* timbres.	We *need* stamps.

The noun that follows *de* is always indefinite.

E. French uses a phrase consisting of *de* + **noun** to describe another noun, where English uses an adjective.

une maison *de pierre*	a house *of stone*	= a *stone* house
une robe *de soie*	a dress *of silk*	= a *silk* dress
un chapeau *de paille*	a hat *of straw*	= a *straw* hat
un cours *de conversation*	a course *of conversation*	= a *conversation* course
un compagnon *de voyage*	a companion *of travel*	= a *traveling* companion

[1] Actually in this case, *pas* indicates negative quantity and is followed by *de,* just as are other expressions of quantity. Therefore, in making negative a sentence such as: Cet homme a *un livre,* one must say: Cet homme *n'a pas de livre(s).* When *pas* expresses an absolute negative (usually after the verb *être*), it is followed by the partitive construction before a noun. In such cases, *pas* is equivalent to the English *not:* Ce ne sont pas *des* vaches. These are not cows.

F. The types of constructions considered in sections B, C, D, and E may all be summed up into one rule by saying that whenever the preposition *de* precedes an indefinite noun, no partitive article is used before that noun.

The Noun – Le nom

A noun is a word that names a person, place, or thing. EXAMPLES: *man, girl, Mexico, book*

7. *The gender of nouns — Le genre des noms*

In English, nouns that refer to males are masculine, nouns that refer to females are feminine, and all other nouns are neuter.

man *masculine* girl *feminine* book *neuter*

The gender of English nouns constitutes no difficulty at all.

A. In French nouns are either masculine or feminine. There are no neuters. It is necessary to know the gender of each noun because various forms of the language depend upon the gender of the noun.

le continent *masculine* la capitale *feminine*

The best way to remember the gender of a noun is to associate the article with the noun, learning them together as a word-group.

B. Rules for determining the gender of nouns
While there is no way of determining the gender of all French nouns, the following hints will help to indicate whether a noun is masculine or feminine.

1. Nouns denoting males are masculine; those denoting females are feminine.

MASCULINE		FEMININE	
le roi	*king*	la reine	*queen*
le bœuf	*steer*	la vache	*cow*
l'homme	*man*	la femme	*woman*

2. It is often possible to recognize the gender of a noun by its ending.

COMMON MASCULINE ENDINGS

-age le village, le fromage, le paysage, le visage, le potage, le nuage

-eau le tableau, le château, le plateau, le bureau, le tombeau, le drapeau, le gâteau

-isme	le classicisme, le romantisme
-ment	le changement, le gouvernement, le tempérament, le monument, le département

EXCEPTIONS: **-age:** une image, la page (*of a book*), la plage, la rage
-eau: l'eau, *f.;* **-ment:** la jument (*mare*)

COMMON FEMININE ENDINGS

-ée	la vallée, la dictée, la journée, la pensée, la cheminée, la journée, la soirée
-ie	la partie, la colonie, la vie, la psychologie, la chimie
-ion	la division, la région, l'opinion, la tradition, la permission, la pension
-té	la quantité, la majorité, la difficulté, la possibilité, la rivalité
-ue	la langue, la laitue, la vue, la statue, la musique, la rue, la fatigue
-ure	la voiture, la culture, la peinture, la figure, la blessure, la mesure
double consonant + e	la ville, la forteresse, la muraille, la femme, la pomme, la classe, la coiffe, la richesse, la flotte, la personne

EXCEPTIONS: **-ée:** le lycée, le musée; **-ie;** le génie, un incendie; **-ion:** un avion, un camion, un lion; **-té;** le député; -ue: le manque

3. Names of *months, days, seasons,* and *languages* are always masculine; names of *trees* are usually masculine.

juin	le lundi	le printemps	le français	un olivier
août	le jeudi	un été	le russe	le chêne

4. Place names

a. All **countries** ending in *-e* are feminine; all others are masculine. One important exception: *le Mexique.*

la France	la Chine	le Canada	le Danemark
la Russie	la Bolivie	le Japon	le Portugal

This means that all European countries are feminine except *le Danemark, le Portugal,* and *le Luxembourg,* and that the three major countries of North America are masculine: *le Canada, les États-Unis, le Mexique.*

b. All **continents** end in *-e* and are feminine.

l'Asie	l'Afrique	l'Amérique du Nord	l'Océanie
l'Europe	l'Australie	l'Amérique du Sud	

c. **Cities** are usually masculine, but *Marseille, Bruxelles, la Nouvelle Orléans* and a few others are considered feminine.

5. Nouns which were masculine or neuter in Latin are likely to be masculine in French; nouns which were feminine in Latin tend to be feminine in French.

LATIN	FRENCH	ENGLISH
status *m.*	l'état *m.*	*state*
amicus *m.*	l'ami *m.*	*friend*
villa *f.*	la ville *f.*	*city*
insula *f.*	l'île *f.*	*island*
vinum *n.*	le vin *m.*	*wine*
castellum *n.*	le château *m.*	*castle*
lyceum *n.*	le lycée *m.*	*high school*

8. *The plural of nouns — Le pluriel des noms*

In English most nouns form their plurals by adding *-s* to the singular.

mountain mountains place places

A. In French nouns regularly form their plurals by adding *-s* to the singular. This *-s* is silent.

le continent	la partie	la montagne
les continents	les parties	les montagnes

B. Nouns ending in *-s, -x, -z* do not change in the plural.

le pays	la voix	le nez
les pays	les voix	les nez

C. Nouns ending in *-eau* and in *-eu* add *-x* to the singular form.

le château	un tableau	le neveu	un feu
les châteaux	des tableaux	les neveux	des feux

D. Nouns ending in *-al* and several nouns ending in *-ail* have a plural in *-aux.*

le journal	un animal	le travail	le vitrail
les journaux	des animaux	les travaux	les vitraux

But: le détail les détails

E. Nouns ending in *-ou* generally add *-s* to the singular form.

le sou	le clou	le trou
les sous	les clous	les trous

But seven common nouns in *-ou* add *-x* in the plural.

bijou (x)	*jewel*	chou (x)	*cabbage*	joujou (x)	*toy*
caillou (x)	*pebble*	genou (x)	*knee*	pou (x)	*louse*
		hibou (x)	*owl*		

The Adjective – L'adjectif

An adjective is a word that modifies a noun or pronoun. EXAMPLES: John is a *tall* boy. He is *intelligent.*

9. *The agreement of adjectives — L'accord des adjectifs*

In English the adjective does not change in form to indicate gender and number.

A. In French the adjective agrees with the noun it modifies in gender and number.

le *petit* pays	the *small* country
les *petits* pays	the *small* countries
la *petite* ville	the *small* city
les *petites* villes	the *small* cities

B. When an adjective modifies a masculine and feminine noun or two masculine nouns at the same time, it takes the masculine plural form.

La Seine, la Garonne et *le Rhône* sont ***importants*** pour le commerce.	*The Seine, the Garonne,* and *the Rhone* are ***important*** for commerce.

Here ***importants*** is masculine plural to agree with a masculine singular and two feminine singular nouns.

10. *The feminine of adjectives — Le féminin des adjectifs*

A. Most adjectives form their feminines by adding *-e* to the masculine form.

MASCULINE	FEMININE	
situé	située	*situated*
petit	petite	*small, little*
grand	grande	*large, great*

B. Adjectives whose masculine form ends in (unaccented) *-e* do not change in the feminine.

MASCULINE	FEMININE	
difficile	difficile	*difficult*
facile	facile	*easy*
grave	grave	*serious*

C. Certain adjectives whose masculine form ends in *e* + a **consonant** place a **grave** (`) accent over this *e* (*è*) as well as adding the regular *-e* to form the feminine.

MASCULINE	FEMININE	
premier	première	*first*
étranger	étrangère	*foreign*
complet	complète	*complete*

D. Adjectives whose masculine form ends in *-f* change the *-f* to *-ve*.

MASCULINE	FEMININE	
neuf	neuve	*new*
actif	active	*active*

E. Adjectives whose masculine form ends in *-x* change the *-x* to *-se*.

MASCULINE	FEMININE	
nombreux	nombreuse	*numerous*
heureux	heureuse	*happy*

F. Adjectives whose masculine forms end in *-el, -eil, -ien, -as,* and *-os* double the final consonant before adding *-e*. Thus,

MASCULINE	FEMININE		EXAMPLES	
ENDING	ENDING	MASCULINE	FEMININE	MEANING
-el	-elle	quel	quelle	*which*
-eil	-eille	pareil	pareille	*similar*
-ien	-ienne	ancien	ancienne	*old*
-as	-asse	bas	basse	*low*
-os	-osse	gros	grosse	*large*

G. The adjectives *beau, fou, mou, nouveau,* and *vieux* have a special masculine form—*bel, fol, mol, nouvel,* and *vieil*—which is used when the word it directly precedes begins with a vowel or a mute *h*. These adjectives are also somewhat irregular in the feminine.

Singular			Plural		
MASCULINE		FEMININE	MASCULINE	FEMININE	
beau	**bel**	belle	beaux	belles	*beautiful*
fou	**fol**	folle	fous	folles	*foolish*
mou	**mol**	molle	mous	molles	*soft*
nouveau	**nouvel**	nouvelle	nouveaux	nouvelles	*new*
vieux	**vieil**	vieille	vieux	vieilles	*old*

Forms in the first column are used when they directly precede a word beginning with a consonant; forms in the second column when they immediately precede a word beginning with a vowel or a mute *h*.

In the following illustrations, note how the adjective changes form when it modifies (1) a masculine noun beginning with a consonant (2) a masculine noun beginning with a vowel or a mute *h* (3) a feminine noun.

(1)	(2)	(3)
un beau pays	un bel homme	une belle ville
un nouveau crayon	un nouvel édifice	une nouvelle rue
un vieux pont	un vieil endroit	une vieille église

H. Certain masculine adjectives form their feminines irregularly. The most common irregular adjectives are:

Singular		Plural		
MASCULINE	FEMININE	MASCULINE	FEMININE	
blanc	blanche	blancs	blanches	*white*
bon	bonne	bons	bonnes	*good*
doux	douce	doux	douces	*soft, sweet*
épais	épaisse	épais	épaisses	*thick*
faux	fausse	faux	fausses	*false*
frais	fraîche	frais	fraîches	*fresh*
gentil	gentille	gentils	gentilles	*nice*
grec	grecque	grecs	grecques	*Greek*
long	longue	longs	longues	*long*
public	publique	publics	publiques	*public*
sec	sèche	secs	sèches	*dry*

11. *The plural of adjectives — Le pluriel des adjectifs*

English adjectives do not change their forms in the plural.

A. Most French adjectives form their masculine plurals by adding *-s* to the masculine singular and their feminine plurals by adding *-s* to the feminine singular. This *-s* is not pronounced.

	SINGULAR	PLURAL	
MASCULINE	situé	situés	*situated*
FEMININE	située	situées	
MASCULINE	petit	petits	*small*
FEMININE	petite	petites	
MASCULINE	long	longs	*long*
FEMININE	longue	longues	
MASCULINE	facile	faciles	*easy*
FEMININE	facile	faciles	

B. Adjectives whose masculine singular ends in *-s, -x,* or *-z* do not change in the masculine plural. The feminine plural is formed by adding *-s* to the feminine singular.

	SINGULAR	PLURAL	
MASCULINE	gris	gris	*gray*
FEMININE	grise	grises	
MASCULINE	heureux	heureux	*happy*
FEMININE	heureuse	heureuses	

C. Adjectives whose masculine singular ends in *-eau* add *-x* to form the masculine plural. EXAMPLES: beau, beaux; nouveau, nouveaux.

D. Adjectives whose masculine singular ends in *-al* change the *-al* to *-aux* in the masculine plural.

	SINGULAR	PLURAL	
MASCULINE	national	nationaux	*national*
FEMININE	nationale	nationales	
MASCULINE	principal	principaux	*principal*
FEMININE	principale	principales	

E. The adjective *tout* (all) has a special plural in *tous.*[1] The rest of the forms are regular: *tout* (masculine singular), *toute* (feminine singular), *toutes* (feminine plural).

F. As an adverb, *tout* is usually invariable, but when it modifies a feminine adjective beginning with a consonant or an aspirate *h,* it agrees with that adjective in gender and number. Examples: (a) invariable: Les *tout*

[1] The word *tous* has two distinct pronunciations. The *-s* is silent [tu] when it is used as an adjective. EXAMPLE: *Tous* les pays ont des problèmes. The *-s* is pronounced as *s* [tus] when *tous* is used as a pronoun. EXAMPLE: *Tous* fournissent des produits aux autres nations.

petits dorment dans leurs voitures. (b) variable: Regardez cette église toute blanche qui domine la ville.[1]

G. In French an adjective may be used alone with an article as a noun.

Le bouquiniste renseigne *les curieux* sur le prix des livres.	The book dealer informs *the curious* (*ones*) about the price of the books.

12. *The position of adjectives — La place des adjectifs*

In English, adjectives precede their nouns. EXAMPLES: a *good* book, a *French* citizen, a *green* hat.

In French, the position of the adjective depends on its type, its function, and sometimes on the relative length of the noun and adjective and on the rhythm of the sentence.

A. Descriptive adjectives normally *follow* their nouns. They *distinguish* the object under consideration from others of its kind.

Les Pyrénées sont des montagnes *élevées.*	The Pyrenees are *high* mountains.
Le Rhône a un courant *rapide.*	The Rhone has a *swift* current.
Les vieillards parlent une langue *celtique*.	The old men speak a *Celtic* language.

Adjectives of color, nationality, religion, profession, and past participles used as adjectives always follow their noun.

B. Many descriptive adjectives may precede their noun for stylistic effect. In such cases, the adjective, which usually indicates a quality inherent in the noun, rather adorns its noun than distinguishes it from other objects of its kind.[2]

Chenonceaux est un *magnifique* château de la Renaissance.	Chenonceaux is a *magnificent* Renaissance château.
Dans les romans de Balzac on trouve de *vivantes* descriptions de la pension de famille.	In the novels of Balzac one finds *vivid* descriptions of the boarding house.
Après de *violents* combats, les armées s'établirent solidement.	After (some) *violent* combat(s), the armies gained a solid footing.
Le *malheureux* enfant ne pouvait pas échapper à la rage.	The *unfortunate* child could not escape [the] rabies.

---

[1] In other words, the adverb *tout* agrees in sound like an adjective.

[2] When the adjective follows its noun, it indicates how the noun is different from other nouns of the same class; when the adjective precedes its noun, it shows how the noun is like all others of the same class.

C. Some descriptive adjectives which follow their noun when they have a literal meaning precede their noun when they have a figurative meaning.

un trou [1] *profond*	une salle *obscure* [2]	un goût [3] *amer* [4]
un *profond* sentiment	un *obscur* ressentiment	d'*amers* reproches
un homme *faible*	une figure *sale* [5]	une valise *lourde*
une *faible* résistance	une *sale* [6] figure	une *lourde* responsabilité

D. Certain very frequently used descriptive adjectives have *one* meaning when they precede their noun, *another* meaning when they follow it. Some of the commonest of these are:

ADJECTIVE	MEANING WHEN PRECEDING	MEANING WHEN FOLLOWING
ancien	*former, old*	*old, ancient*
brave [7]	*worthy, fine*	*brave*
cher	*dear* (*loved*)	*dear* (*expensive*)
grand	*great, large*	*tall*
pauvre	*poor* (*unfortunate*)	*poor* (*without money*)

E. The following types of adjectives regularly precede their noun:

1. numerals, both cardinal and ordinal, and demonstrative, interrogative, possessive, and indefinite adjectives

trois livres	*cette* ville	*mon* crayon
la *troisième* leçon	*quel* pays	*quelques* livres

2. a number of common short adjectives, such as

autre	*other*	long	*long*
beau	*beautiful*	mauvais	*bad*
bon	*good*	méchant	*naughty, wicked*
gentil	*nice*	meilleur	*better, best*
grand	*great, large, tall*	moindre	*least*
gros	*big*	nouveau	*new*
haut	*high*	petit	*small, little; short*
jeune	*young*	vieux	*old*
joli	*pretty*	vilain	*ugly, bad*

13. *The comparison of adjectives — La comparaison des adjectifs*

In French as in English, there are three degrees of comparison: the positive, the comparative, and the superlative. The English adjective is com-

[1] *hole* [2] *dark* [3] *taste* [4] *bitter* [5] *dirty* [6] *ugly*
[7] But to express the English *brave,* French normally uses the adjective *courageux.*

pared by adding *-er* (comparative) and *-est* (superlative) to the positive form or by placing *more* or *less* (comparative) and *most* or *least* (superlative) before the positive form.

POSITIVE	COMPARATIVE	SUPERLATIVE
narrow	narrower less narrow	narrowest least narrow
important	more important less important	most important least important

A. The comparative form of the French adjective is obtained by placing *plus* (more) or *moins* (less) before the positive form. The superlative form is obtained by placing the definite article (*le, la, les*) before the comparative form.

POSITIVE	COMPARATIVE	SUPERLATIVE
étroit	plus étroit moins étroit	le plus étroit[1] le moins étroit
important	plus important moins important	le plus important le moins important

The following examples show how these forms are used:

COMPARATIVE

La Russie est *plus grande* que la France.	Russia is *larger* than France.
Les Alpes sont *moins difficiles* à défendre que le Rhin.	The Alps are *less difficult* to defend than the Rhine.

SUPERLATIVE

Orléans, Tours et Nantes sont les trois villes *les plus importantes* situées sur la Loire.	Orleans, Tours, and Nantes are the three *most important* cities situated on the Loire.
De toutes les frontières, les Alpes sont *les moins difficiles* à défendre.	Of all the borders, the Alps are the *least difficult* to defend.

---

[1] This is the masculine singular form. The feminine singular form is *la plus étroite,* the masculine plural *les plus étroits,* and the feminine plural *les plus étroites.*

B. The word *than* is usually expressed by ***que.***

La Loire est plus longue *que* la Seine.	The Loire is longer *than* the Seine.
Les États-Unis sont plus grands *que* l'Italie.	The United States is larger *than* Italy.

But before numerals, *than* is expressed by ***de.***

Tours a plus *de* cent mille habitants.	Tours has more *than* a hundred thousand inhabitants.
Versailles est à moins *de* trente kilomètres de Paris.	Versailles is less *than* thirty kilometers from Paris.

C. Adjectives which usually precede their nouns may precede them in the superlative, but may equally well follow their nouns.

La Loire est *le plus long* fleuve de France.	The Loire is *the longest* river in France.

When adjectives in the superlative follow their nouns, the definite article must always directly precede *plus* (more) or *moins* (least).

La Seine est le fleuve *le plus connu* de France.	The Seine is the *best known* river of France.
Les Alpes et les Pyrénées sont les frontières *les plus faciles* à défendre.	The Alps and the Pyrenees are the *easiest* borders to defend.
Le Havre est un des trois ports *les plus importants* situés sur la Manche.	Le Havre is one of the three *most important* ports situated on the English Channel.

D. In English the superlative is usually followed by *in.* In French ***de*** is regularly used after the superlative.

Paris est la plus grande ville *de* France.	Paris is the largest city ***in*** France.

E. Certain adjectives are compared irregularly. The most common of these are:

POSITIVE	COMPARATIVE	SUPERLATIVE
bon (*good*)	meilleur (*better*)	le meilleur (*best*)
mauvais (*bad*)	plus mauvais / pire (*worse*)	le plus mauvais / le pire (*worst*)

F. In English we say: *Texas is as large as France.* This comparison with *as . . . as* is called the comparative of equality. In French the comparative of equality is expressed by ***aussi . . . que.***

Le Texas est *aussi grand que* la France.	Texas is *as large as* France.
Les Normands ne sont pas *aussi gais que* les habitants du sud de la France.[1]	The Normans are not *as gay as* the inhabitants of the south of France.

14. *Possessive adjectives — Les adjectifs possessifs*

The English possessive adjectives are *my, his, her, its, our, your, their,* and *one's.* They do not change in form. EXAMPLE: *my* uncle, *my* aunt, *my* parents

A. The French possessive adjectives have different masculine and feminine forms in the singular and the same form for both masculine and feminine plural.

The Possessive Adjectives

PERSON		MASCULINE SINGULAR	FEMININE SINGULAR	MASCULINE AND FEMININE PLURAL	
SINGULAR	1	mon	ma	mes	*my*
	2	ton [2]	ta [2]	tes [2]	*your* [2]
	3	son	sa	ses	*his, her, its*
PLURAL	1	notre	notre	nos	*our*
	2	votre	votre	vos	*your*
	3	leur	leur	leurs	*their*

B. The French possessive adjective agrees in gender and number with the noun it modifies.

Roger habite à Paris avec *son* père, *sa* mère, *ses* frères et *sa* sœur.	Roger lives in Paris with *his* father, *his* mother, *his* brothers, and *his* sister.

The third person singular forms *son, sa* and *ses* mean *his, her* or *its,* depending on the person to whom they refer. The following sentences will clarify their usage.

Jean trouve *son* cidre, et Marie trouve *son* lait.	John finds *his* cider, and Mary finds *her* milk.
Jean a *sa* motocyclette, et Marie a *sa* bicyclette.	John has *his* motorcycle, and Mary has *her* bicycle.

[1] In present-day French, the pattern . . . *aussi* . . . *que* . . . is used to express the comparative of equality in negative as well as affirmative sentences.

[2] These forms are used only under the same conditions as the subject pronoun *tu.* (See § 23 B.)

C. The forms *mon, ton* and *son* are used to modify feminine singular nouns when the use of *ma, ta* and *sa* would cause two vowel sounds to come together.

mon amie *f.*	*my* girl friend
ton école *f.*	*your* school
son idée *f.*	*his, her* idea
son histoire *f.*	*his, her* story
mon autre tante *f.*	*my* other aunt

D. For the use of the article to express possession with parts of the body, see § 4 G.

15. *The demonstrative adjectives — Les adjectifs démonstratifs*

Demonstrative adjectives point out objects more definitely than the definite article *the.* Compare: *The* castle is magnificent. ***That*** castle is magnificent. The English demonstrative adjectives are *this, that, these* and *those.*

A. The French demonstrative adjectives are

	SINGULAR	PLURAL
MASCULINE	ce cet	ces
FEMININE	cette	

ce is used before masculine singular nouns and adjectives beginning a consonant or an aspirate *h.* EXAMPLES: *ce* château, *ce* pays, *ce* petit jardin

cet is used before masculine singular nouns and adjectives beginning with a vowel or a mute *h.* EXAMPLES: *cet* endroit, *cet* état, *cet* autre pays, *cet* homme

cette is used before all feminine singular nouns and adjectives. EXAMPLES: *cette* montagne, *cette* ville, *cette* architecture, *cette* grande maison

ces is used before all plural nouns and adjectives. EXAMPLES: *ces* châteaux, *ces* endroits, *ces* villes, *ces* grandes maisons

B. French does not ordinarily distinguish between *this* and *that* and between *these* and *those.*

Ce château tombe maintenant en ruines.	*This* (or *That*) castle is now falling in ruins.

C. But where contrast is desired, to distinguish between *this* and *that, these* and *those* the demonstrative adiective (*ce, cet, cette, ces*) is placed before the noun, and *-ci* (from *ici* meaning *here*) or *-là* (*there*) appended to the noun with a hyphen. To express the contrast between objects which are nearer or farther, French uses in effect *this here* and *that there,* which are incorrect in English. One rarely finds *-ci* in one part of the sentence without *-là* in the other. But *-là* is sometimes used without *-ci,* especially in time expressions.

Cette carte-*ci* est plus moderne que *cette* carte-*là*.	*This* map is more modern than *that* map.
Que faites-vous en *ce* moment?	What are you doing at *this* time?
Il était en France à *ce* moment-*là*.	He was in France at *that* time.

16. *The interrogative adjectives — Les adjectifs interrogatifs*

An interrogative adjective is one that asks a question while modifying a noun. The English interrogative adjectives are *which* and *what.* EXAMPLES: *Which* houses have you seen? *What* work have you done?

A. In French the interrogative adjectives are:

	MASCULINE	FEMININE
SINGULAR	quel	quelle
PLURAL	quels	quelles

B. In French the interrogative adjective agrees in gender and number with the noun it modifies.

Quel cours préférez-vous?	*Which* course do you prefer?
Quelles langues apprenez-vous?	*What* languages are you studying?

C.[1, 2] In sentences such as ***What is the capital of France? What are the principal industries of Spain?***, where the answer requires choosing one or several of a number of possibilities, French uses

quel + *est* + noun.

Quelle est la capitale de la France?	*What* is the capital of France?
Quels sont les pays de l'Amérique du Nord?	*What* are the countries of North America?
Quel est votre nom?	*What* is your name?

---

[1] When the noun has been mentioned before, a form of the interrogative pronoun *lequel* is often used to ask *which one.* EXAMPLE: La Russie, la Suède, la France et l'Espagne sont des nations importantes. *Lesquelles* sont dans l'ouest de l'Europe? (See § 38 E.)

[2] For the use of *Qu'est-ce que* and *Qu'est-ce que c'est que* to express *What is* or *What are* when a definition is required, see § 38 F.

D. The interrogative adjective is also used with the verb *être* followed by the name of a person or thing to ask the nature of that person or thing.

Quel est cet homme?	*Who* is that man? [1]
Quels sont ces édifices?	*What* buildings are those?

17. *The cardinal numerals—Les adjectifs numéraux cardinaux*

A. The cardinal numerals are:

1	un, une	[œ̃] [yn]
2	deux	[dø]
3	trois	[trwɑ]
4	quatre	[katr]
5	cinq	[sɛ̃k]
6	six	[sis]
7	sept	[sɛt]
8	huit	[ɥit]
9	neuf	[nœf]
10	dix	[dis]
11	onze	[õz]
12	douze	[duz]
13	treize	[trɛz]
14	quatorze	[katɔrz]
15	quinze	[kɛ̃z]
16	seize	[sɛz]
17	dix-sept	[dissɛt]
18	dix-huit	[dizɥit]
19	dix-neuf	[diznœf]
20	vingt	[vɛ̃]
21	vingt et un	[vɛ̃teœ̃]
22	vingt-deux	[vɛ̃tdø]
23	vingt-trois	[vɛ̃ttrwɑ]
24	vingt-quatre	[vɛ̃tkatr]
25	vingt-cinq	[vɛ̃tsɛ̃k]
26	vingt-six	[vɛ̃tsis]
30	trente	[trɑ̃t]
31	trente et un	[trɑ̃teœ̃]
32	trente-deux	[trɑ̃tdø]
40	quarante	[karɑ̃t]
50	cinquante	[sɛ̃kɑ̃t]
60	soixante	[swasɑ̃t]
70	soixante-dix	[swasɑ̃tdis]
71	soixante et onze	[swasɑ̃teõz]
72	soixante-douze	[swasɑ̃tduz]
73	soixante-treize	[swasɑ̃ttrɛz]
80	quatre-vingts	[katrəvɛ̃]
81	quatre-vingt-un	[katrəvɛ̃œ̃]
82	quatre-vingt-deux	[katrəvɛ̃dø]
83	quatre-vingt-trois	[katrəvɛ̃trwɑ]
90	quatre-vingt-dix	[katrəvɛ̃dis]
91	quatre-vingt-onze	[katrəvɛ̃õz]
100	cent	[sɑ̃]
101	cent un	[sɑ̃œ̃]
200	deux cents	[døsɑ̃]
201	deux cent un	[døsɑ̃œ̃]
202	deux cent deux	[døsɑ̃dø]
300	trois cents	[trwɑsɑ̃]
400	quatre cents	[katrəsɑ̃]
1000	mille	[mil]
1001	mille un	[milœ̃]
2000	deux mille	[dømil]
100,000	cent mille	[sɑ̃mil]
1,000,000	un million	[œ̃miljõ]
2,000,000	deux millions	[dømiljõ]

B. The pronunciations indicated above are those of the numbers pronounced without any following noun. When the numerals are followed by an adjective or a

[1] Meaning: *What is the nature* of that man?

noun beginning with a consonant or an aspirate *h,* they are pronounced as follows:

un port	[œ̃pɔr]	si(x) ports	[sipɔr]
deu(x) ports	[døpɔr]	sep*t* ports	[sɛtpɔr]
troi(s) ports	[trwapɔr]	hui(t) ports	[ɥipɔr]
quatre ports	[katrəpɔr]	neu*f* ports	[nœfpɔr]
cin(q)[1] ports	[sɛ̃pɔr]	di(x) ports	[dipɔr]

When the numerals are followed by an adjective or a noun beginning with a vowel or a mute *h,* the final consonant of the numeral is generally linked to the next word. Final *-x* is linked as *z.* Final *-f* remains *-f* in most words, but becomes *v* in the expressions *neuf ans* [nœvɑ̃], *neuf heures* [nœvœr], and *neuf hommes* [nœvɔm].

un état	[œ̃neta]	six états	[sizeta]
deux états	[døzeta]	sept états	[sɛteta]
trois états	[trwɑzeta]	huit états	[ɥiteta]
quatre états	[katreta]	neuf états	[nœfeta]
cinq états	[sɛ̃keta]	dix états	[dizeta]

There is a difference of usage as to the pronunciation of the final consonant of numerals in dates. Some Frenchmen say *le dix mai* [lədismɛ]; others *le di(x) mai* [lədimɛ].

Neither elision nor linking occurs before *huit* and *onze.* One says: *le huit février* [ləɥifevrje], *le onze mars* [ləõzmars], *les huit enfants* [leɥitɑ̃fɑ̃], *les onze livres* [leõzlivr].

The final *-t* of *cent* is linked to the following noun, but is not linked to a following *un.* EXAMPLES: cent ans [sɑ̃tɑ̃] *but* cent un [sɑ̃œ̃], deux cent un [døsɑ̃œ̃], quatre cent un [katrəsɑ̃œ̃].

C. From 60 to 100 the French count by 20's. Note the formation of 70 (*soixante-dix*) and of 90 (*quatre-vingt-dix*) and of the other numbers in the same group. Note that the *-s* of *quatre-vingts* is dropped before another numeral. EXAMPLES: quatre-vingt-sept, quatre-vingt-quinze.

D. Multiples of *cent* (*deux cents, trois cents, quatre cents,* etc.) take an *-s* in the plural. There is no *-s* when these multiples are followed by another numeral, nor in dates. EXAMPLES: huit cents étudiants, l'an dix-neuf cent, deux cent trente, trois cent deux, quatre cent soixante-sept, etc. *Mille* does not change in form. EXAMPLES: deux mille, trois mille, quatre mille, etc.

E. The numerals *cent* and *mille* are not preceded by the indefinite article (*un*) in French. EXAMPLES: cent deux (102) (*a hundred and two*), cent quatre-vingts (180) (*a hundred and eighty*); mille soixante (1060) (*a thousand and sixty*), mille quatre-vingt-deux (1082) (*a thousand and eighty-two*).

F. In reading dates between 1000 and 1100 and dates from 2000 on, *mille* is used. For dates between 1100 and 1999, either *mille* or a multiple of *cent* is

[1] It is considered most correct to pronounce this word cin(q) [sɛ̃] when the next word begins with a consonant. But the pronunciation cinq [sɛ̃k] is rapidly gaining ground. Many Frenchmen would say [sɛ̃kpɔr].

used. The latter is somewhat more common. The word *cent* may not be omitted when reading French dates, as it is currently in English. EXAMPLES: 1215 (*douze cent quinze* or *mille deux cent quinze*), 1939 (*dix-neuf cent trente-neuf* or *mille neuf cent trente-neuf*), 1870 (*dix-huit cent soixante-dix* or *mille huit cent soixante-dix*). The French express B.C. by *av. J.-C.* (*avant Jésus-Christ*), and A.D. by *apr. J.-C.* (*après Jésus-Christ*). EXAMPLES: 44 av. J.-C., 476 apr. J.-C.

G. Most numerals are adjectives and directly precede their nouns. EXAMPLES: trois garçons, cinquante et un étudiants, cent personnes, mille francs. But certain numerals, such as *un million* and the approximate numbers in *-aine,* such as *une dixaine* (about ten), *une douzaine* (a dozen), *une vingtaine* (about twenty), etc., are nouns. Such numerals require a *de* before the following noun. EXAMPLES: un million de francs, trois millions de soldats, une douzaine de personnes, une vingtaine d'élèves. But when *million* is not used as a round number, it becomes adjectival and is not followed by *de.* EXAMPLE: deux millions cinq cent mille enfants.

18. *The ordinal numerals — Les adjectifs numéraux ordinaux*

A. In English the ordinals are: first, second, third, fourth, etc. In French the ordinals are regularly formed by adding *-ième* to the corresponding cardinals. Note particularly the method of expressing 1st, 2d, 21st, 31st, etc. The ordinals are abbreviated: 1er, 2e, 3e, etc. There are also the abbreviations 1°, 2°, 3°, etc. (*primo, secundo,* etc.).

B. The ordinal numerals are:

1st	premier, première	18th	dix-huitième
2d	second deuxième	19th	dix-neuvième
		20th	vingtième
3d	troisième	21st	vingt et unième
4th	quatrième	22d	vingt-deuxième
5th	cinquième	23d	vingt-troisième
6th	sixième	30th	trentième
7th	septième	31st	trente et unième
8th	huitième	40th	quarantième
9th	neuvième	50th	cinquantième
10th	dixième	60th	soixantième
11th	onzième	70th	soixante-dixième
12th	douzième	71st	soixante et onzième
13th	treizième	80th	quatre-vingtième
14th	quatorzième	81st	quatre-vingt-unième
15th	quinzième	90th	quatre-vingt-dixième
16th	seizième	100th	centième
17th	dix-septième	101st	cent unième

C. Despite the old rule which states that the English *second* is expressed in French by *second* when there are only two in a series and by *deuxième* when there are more than two, *second* and *deuxième* are interchangeable in actual usage. Note that the *c* in *second* is pronounced *g* [səgõ].

D. In indicating kings and emperors, the French use the ordinal for the *first* and cardinals for *all others* of a house of dynasty.

WRITTEN	READ	
Napoléon Ier	Napoléon premier	*Napoleon I*
Napoléon III	Napoléon trois	*Napoleon III*
Charles Ier	Charles premier	*Charles I*
Charles VII	Charles sept	*Charles VII*
Louis XIV	Louis quatorze	*Louis XIV*
Louis XV	Louis quinze	*Louis XV*

E. To indicate the day of the month, French uses the ordinal for the *first* day and the cardinals for *all the others.* French dates are written without capitals and without commas. EXAMPLES: le 1er février 1969, le 10 mai 1972, le 4 juillet 1776. These are read (but not written) *le premier février dix-neuf cent soixante-neuf, le dix mai dix-neuf cent soixante-douze, le quatre juillet dix-sept cent soixante-seize.*

The Adverb – L'adverbe

An adverb is a word that modifies a verb, adjective, or another adverb. EXAMPLES: They write *clearly* (*clearly* modifies the verb *write*). He is an *unusually* careful driver (*unusually* modifies the adjective *careful*). She speaks *very* distinctly (*very* modifies the adverb *distinctly*).

19. *The formation of adverbs — La formation des adverbes*

In English adverbs are often formed by adding *-ly* to the adjective. EXAMPLES: clear — clearly; usual — usually; correct — correctly

A. French adverbs are often formed by the addition of *-ment* to the masculine form of adjectives ending in a vowel and to the feminine form of adjectives whose masculine form ends in a consonant.

ADJECTIVE	ADVERB	ADJECTIVE	ADVERB
vrai	vraiment	seul	seulement
poli	poliment	sûr	sûrement
absolu	absolument	principal	principalement
décidé	décidément	naturel	naturellement
facile	facilement	complet	complètement
typique	typiquement	relatif	relativement

B. Adverbs are formed from adjectives of more than one syllable ending in *-ent* by changing the *-ent* to *-emment.* The first *e* of this suffix is pronounced *a.* Adjectives of more than one syllable ending in *-ant* change the *-ant* to *-amment.*

ADJECTIVE	ADVERB	ADJECTIVE	ADVERB
évident	évidemment	constant	constamment
récent	récemment	courant	couramment
négligent	négligemment	élégant	élégamment
différent	différemment	suffisant	suffisamment

C. In certain adverbs the final *-e* of the adjective is replaced by *-é:*

aveuglément	*blindly*	conformément	*suitably*
commodément	*properly*	communément	*commonly*
confusément	*confusedly*	énormément	*enormously*
immensément	*immensely*	obscurément	*obscurely*
précisément	*precisely*	profondément	*deeply*
profusément	*profusely*	uniformément	*uniformly*

D. Some adverbs are not so formed from their adjective.

ADJECTIVE	ADVERB	ADJECTIVE	ADVERB
bon	bien	petit	peu
mauvais	mal	vite	vite

20. *The position of adverbs—La place des adverbes*

A. The adverb usually (but not always) follows a simple verb directly. It almost never comes between the subject and the verb.

Nous passons *souvent* la nuit dans une auberge de la jeunesse.	We *often* spend the night in a youth hostel.
Il aime *beaucoup* la France.	He likes France *very much.*

B. In the compound tenses the adverb is usually placed between the auxiliary and the past participle of a compound verb. In negative sentences the adverb follows *pas.*

Nous avons *déjà* acheté la voiture.	We have *already* bought the car.
Vous avez *bien* travaillé.	You have worked *well.*
Il n'a *pas encore* lu le journal.	He has*n't yet* read the newspaper.

C. Many adverbs in *-ment* regularly come between the auxiliary and the past participle of a compound verb, but certain adverbs in *-ment* must follow the past participle and certain others follow the noun object of the sentence.[1]

J'ai *complètement* oublié son adresse.	I *completely* forgot his address.
Elle a parlé *doucement.*	She spoke *softly.*
Marie a écrit la lettre *lentement.*	Marie wrote the letter *slowly.*

D. The adverbs of time and place *aujourd'hui, hier, demain, autrefois, tôt, tard, ici, là, ailleurs,* and *partout* never come between the auxiliary and the past participle. They normally follow the past participle but not always directly. The adverbs of time *aujourd'hui, hier, demain,* and *autrefois* often begin the sentence.

Nous avons fait cela *hier.*	We did that *yesterday.*
Votre ami est arrivé *tôt.*	Your friend arrived *early.*
Il est venu *ici.*	He came *here.*
Aujourd'hui nous sommes partis à huit heures.	*Today* we left at eight o'clock.

E. When *peut-être* (perhaps), *aussi* (meaning *therefore, thus,* or *so* in this position), and the expression *à peine* (scarcely) begin the sentence, the subject and verb are usually inverted.

Peut-être ***viendra-t-il*** ce soir.	*Perhaps* ***he will come*** this evening.
Un voyage en Amérique coûterait trop cher. *Aussi* ***irons-nous*** en Espagne.	A trip to America would cost too much. *Therefore,* ***we'll go*** to Spain.
A peine ***était-il sorti*** qu'il a commencé à pleuvoir.	*Scarcely* ***had he gone out*** when it began to rain.

There is a tendency in conversational French to use *que* followed by normal word order after *peut-être.*

Vous ne pouvez pas trouver votre portefeuille? *Peut-être* ***que*** vous l'avez perdu.	Can't you find your billfold? Perhaps you've lost it.

21. *The comparison of adverbs — La comparaison des adverbes*

The English adverb is compared by placing *more* or *less* (comparative) and *most* or *least* (superlative) before the positive form.

[1] The length of the adverb in *-ment* does not determine its position in the compound tenses.

POSITIVE	COMPARATIVE	SUPERLATIVE
rapidly	more rapidly	most rapidly
	less rapidly	least rapidly

A. French adverbs, like adjectives, are compared by placing *plus* (more) or *moins* (less) before the positive form of the adverb to express the comparative degree and by placing *le plus* or *le moins* before the positive form of the adverb, to express the superlative degree. Since the adverb has no gender, the *le* of the superlative degree is invariable.

POSITIVE	COMPARATIVE	SUPERLATIVE
rapidement	plus rapidement	le plus rapidement
récemment	plus récemment	le plus récemment

B. Certain adverbs are compared irregularly:

POSITIVE	COMPARATIVE	SUPERLATIVE
bien	mieux	le mieux
mal	plus mal pis	le plus mal le pis
peu	moins	le moins
beaucoup	plus	le plus

22. *The negative — Le négatif*

The English sentence is made negative by means of the adverb *not.* EXAMPLE: France is *not* a continent.

A. A French sentence is usually made negative by placing *ne* before and *pas* after the verb. The *ne* becomes *n'* before a word beginning with a vowel or a mute h.

La source de la Garonne *n*'est *pas* en France.	The source of the Garonne *is not* in France.
La Seine *ne* traverse *pas* Lyon.	The Seine does *not* cross Lyons.

B. In a negative statement, the *ne* comes directly after the subject with all its modifiers, that is to say, *ne* precedes all other words which come before the verb. The *pas* follows the simple verb directly.

Berlin *n*'est *pas* en France.	Berlin is *not* in France.
Les fleuves importants de France *ne* sont *pas* au centre du pays.	The important rivers of France are *not* in the center of the land.
La Loire *ne* se jette *pas* dans la Manche.	The Loire does *not* empty into the English Channel.
Je *ne* le lui donne *pas.*	I do *not* give it to him.
Il *n'en* a *pas.*	He *hasn't* any.

C. In a question with a pronoun-subject the following word order is used:

ne VERB–PRONOUN-SUBJECT *pas* FOLLOWING WORDS

*N'*est-il *pas* en France?	Is*n't* it in France?
Ne forment-elles *pas* une frontière entre les deux pays?	Do*n't* they form a frontier between the two countries?
Ne se jette-t-il *pas* dans la Méditerranée?	Does*n't* it empty into the Mediterranean?
Ne la racontez-vous *pas* aux élèves?	Do*n't* you tell it to the pupils?
Ne la leur écrit-il *pas?*	Does*n't* he write it to them?

In a question with a noun-subject, the following word order is used:

NOUN-SUBJECT *ne* VERB–PRONOUN-SUBJECT *pas* FOLLOWING WORDS

Le Rhône *n'*est-il *pas* en France?	Is*n't* the Rhone in France?
Les Alpes *ne* forment-elles *pas* une frontière entre les deux pays?	Do*n't* the Alps form a frontier between the two countries?
Le Rhône *ne* se jette-t-il *pas* dans la Méditerranée?	Does*n't* the Rhone empty into the Mediterranean?
Marie *ne* la raconte-t-elle *pas* à son frère?	Does*n't* Mary tell it to her brother?
Paul *ne* la leur écrit-il *pas?*	Does*n't* Paul write it to them?

D. In the compound tenses, the *auxiliary verb only* is regarded as the verb as far as the position of the negative words is concerned. In other words, *pas* comes directly after the auxiliary verb.

Il *n'*a *pas* acheté ces cahiers.	He did*n't* buy those notebooks.
Nous *n'*avons *pas* trouvé notre journal.	We did*n't* find our newspaper.
Les Français *n'*ont *pas* choisi un président.	The French did*n't* choose a president.

Notice the same negative sentences in interrogative form:

*N'*a-t-il *pas* acheté un cahier?	Has*n't* he bought a notebook?
*N'*avons-nous *pas* trouvé un journal?	Did*n't* we find a newspaper?
Les Français *n'*ont-ils *pas* choisi un président?	Did*n't* the French choose a president?

E. Certain words are always used with *ne* in a complete sentence. Among these are:

ne . . . aucun	*no, not any*	ne . . . plus	*no longer, no more*
ne . . . guère	*scarcely*	ne . . . point	*not at all*
ne . . . jamais	*never*	ne . . . que	*only*
ne . . . ni . . . ni	*neither . . . nor*	ne . . . rien	*nothing*
ne . . . personne	*no one*		

F. In sentences containing these negative combinations

1. *ne* comes where it ordinarily would with *pas* (§ 22 B, C);
2. *guère* (scarcely), *jamais* (never), *plus* (no longer, no more), and *point* (not at all) follow the same rules for position as *pas* (§ 22 A, C, D).

Il *n*'y a *guère* de Français qui se passe de vacances.	There is *scarcely* a Frenchman who does without vacations.
Il *n*'a *jamais* acheté une voiture.	He *never* bought a car.
Les provinces *n*'existent *plus.*	The provinces *no longer* exist.

3. The pronouns *personne* (no one) and *rien* (nothing) begin the sentence if they are used as the subject and follow the verb if they are used as the object.

Personne ne va en Bretagne.	*No one* is going to Brittany.
Il *n*'y a *personne* à Paris.	There is *no one* at Paris.
Rien n'est sur le bureau.	*Nothing* is on the desk.
Je *ne* trouve *rien.*	I find *nothing.*

In sentences with compound tenses, *personne* follows the past participle; *rien* comes between the auxiliary and the past participle.

Il *n*'a vu *personne.*	He saw *no one.*
Il *n*'a *rien* vu.	He saw *nothing.*

4. The word *que* (only) follows the entire verb and immediately precedes the word it modifies.

Nous *n*'avons *que* trois livres.	We have *only* three books.
Vous *n*'avez acheté *que* six crayons.	You bought *only* six pencils.

5. The adjective *aucun* (no, not any) comes directly before its noun.

Il *n*'a trouvé *aucun* élève dans la salle de classe.	He found *no* pupil in the classroom.
Aucune voiture *n*'est dans la rue.	*No* car is in the street.

G. When a negative word is used alone (without a verb) in answer to a question, no *ne* accompanies it.

Devine qui j'ai trouvé après deux heures de recherches. *Personne.*	Guess whom I found after two hours of searching. *No one.*
N'y a-t-il pas toujours un concierge, même en été? *Jamais.*	Isn't there always a janitor, even in summer? *Never.*

H. The second part of the negation follows *ne* directly when the negative modifies a present infinitive.

Il est impossible de *ne pas* parler français en France.	It is impossible *not* to speak French in France.
Elle m'a demandé de *ne jamais* partir.	She asked me *never* to leave.

When the negative modifies a past infinitive, the second part of the negation may either follow *ne* directly or follow the auxiliary.

Il craint de *ne pas* avoir compris le professeur. *or* Il craint de *n'*avoir *pas* compris le professeur.	He fears that he did not understand the teacher.

I. The word *pas* may be omitted after the verbs *pouvoir, savoir, oser,* and *cesser* followed by a dependent infinitive.

Je *ne* savais que faire.	I did*n't* know what to do.
Il *n'*ose le dire.	He does*n't* dare to say it.

The Pronoun – Le pronom

A pronoun is a word used to take the place of a noun. It is used to avoid having to repeat the noun. EXAMPLE: Did you see the boys? *They* (meaning *the boys*) arrived last night.

23. *The subject personal pronouns — Les pronoms personnels — sujet.*

A. The subject personal pronouns are:

PERSON	SINGULAR	PLURAL
1st	je *I*	nous *we*
2d	tu *thou, you*	vous *you*
3d	il *he, it* elle *she, it*	ils *they* m. elles *they* f.

B. In English we no longer use the pronoun *thou* (singular of *you*) except in prayer. The French use the second person singular pronoun *tu* when speaking to intimate friends, relatives, children, pets, sometimes servants. Students, soldiers doing military service, and others in the same general social class, usually speak to each other in the *tu* form. Otherwise *vous* is used in the second person plural to indicate either one or more persons.

24. *The direct object personal pronouns*
Les pronoms personnels — complément direct

In the sentences — He writes *it;* We like *them;* They see *us* — the italicized pronouns are direct objects because they receive the direct action of the verbs *write, like,* and *see.* They are pronoun objects which take the place of some noun object already mentioned.

A. In French the direct object personal pronouns are:

me[1]	*me*	nous	*us*
te[1]	*you*	vous	*you*
le[1]	*him, it*	les	*them*
la[1]	*her, it*		

The reflexive object *se* will be discussed in § 26.

B. These pronouns take the place of *definite noun objects,* that is, noun objects modified by a definite article, a possessive adjective, a demonstrative adjective, or any other definite modifier, just as do *him, her, it, them,* etc. in English.

Il corrige *la faute*.	He corrects *the mistake*.
Il *la* corrige.	He corrects *it.*
Les élèves écrivent *leurs phrases*.	The pupils write *their sentences*.
Les élèves *les* écrivent.	The pupils write *them.*
Explique-t-il *ce mot*?	Does he explain *this word*?
*L'*explique-t-il?	Does he explain *it?*

[1] When the forms *me, te, se, le* or *la* precede a verb beginning with a vowel or a mute *h,* they elide, becoming *m', t', s',* or *l'.* (See Prononciation § 5 A, B, page 514)

Le professeur explique *le mot.*	Le professeur *l'*explique.
Ecrit-il *la phrase?*	L'écrit-il?

25. *The indirect object personal pronouns*
Les pronoms personnels — complément indirect

In the sentences — I write *him* a letter; We show *them* the house; He tells *me* the story — the italicized words receive the indirect action of the verb. They are the indirect objects. They usually answer the question *to* or *for whom?* In each case we might have said: I write a letter *to him;* We show the house *to them,* etc. The preposition *to,* understood or expressed, is the sign of the indirect object in English.

A. In French the indirect object pronouns are:

me [1]	*to me*	nous	*to us*
te [1]	*to you*	vous	*to you*
lui	*to him* / *to her*	leur	*to them*

B. These pronouns indicate an indirect object already mentioned.

Roger écrit une lettre *à son oncle*. — Roger writes a letter *to his uncle*

Roger *lui* écrit une lettre. — Roger writes *him* a letter.

Le professeur parle *aux élèves*. — The teacher speaks *to the pupils*.

Le professeur *leur* parle. — The teacher speaks *to them*.

Lit-il le livre *à sa sœur*? — Does he read the book *to his sister*?

Lui lit-il le livre? — Does he read *her* the book?

26. *The reflexive pronouns — Les pronoms réfléchis*

Reflexive pronouns are those which refer to the subject. In English they are distinguished by the word *-self.* EXAMPLES: myself, himself. The reflexive pronouns may be used as direct or indirect object.

DIRECT OBJECT

Je *me* lave. — I wash *myself.*

[1] When the forms *me, te* or *se* precede a verb beginning with a vowel or a mute *h,* they elide, becoming *m', t',* or *s'.* (See Prononciation § 5 A, B, page 514) EXAMPLES: Le professeur *m'*explique le mot. *T'*écrit-elle souvent?

INDIRECT OBJECT

Elle *se* parle.	She speaks *to herself.*

Reflexive pronouns are used in conjunction with verbs, making the verbs *reflexive verbs.* (See § 88)

A. The French reflexive pronouns are:

me[1]	*myself, to myself*	nous	*ourselves, to ourselves*
te[1]	*yourself, to yourself*	vous	*yourself, to yourself* / *yourselves, to yourselves*
se[1]	*himself, to himself* / *herself, to herself* / *itself, to itself*	se[1]	*themselves, to themselves*

soi *himself, herself, itself, themselves*

B. When the reflexive pronoun is used in the sense of *each other,* it is known as a reciprocal pronoun, but its form in French is the same as if it were a reflexive pronoun. For example, *Ils se parlent,* may mean: They talk *to themselves* (reflexive meaning); or, They talk *to each other* (reciprocal meaning). To make the meaning clearly reciprocal, the French sometimes use *l'un l'autre, l'une l'autre, les uns les autres, les unes les autres* meaning *each other* as direct objects and *l'un à l'autre, l'une à l'autre, les uns aux autres, les unes aux autres* meaning *to each other* as indirect objects.

Ils *s'*aiment *l'un l'autre.*	They love *each other.*
Elles *se parlent l'une à l'autre.*	They speak *to each other.*

27. *The disjunctive pronouns — Les pronoms absolus*

A. The disjunctive pronouns are:

moi	*me*[2]	nous	*us*
toi	*you*	vous	*you*
lui	*him*	eux	*them,* m.
elle	*her*	elles	*them,* f.

B. Disjunctive pronouns are used in emphatic positions such as:

1. after prepositions

Il parle ***de** moi.*	He is speaking ***of** me.*
Elle est ***avec** lui.*	She is ***with** him.*
J'arrive ***après** eux.*	I arrive ***after** them.*
Il le fait ***pour** vous.*	He is doing it ***for** you.*

[1] See footnotes on page 400.

[2] The most common translations of the French disjunctives.

2. in compound subjects and objects when one or more of the compound parts is a pronoun

Pierre et *moi* descendons dans la rue.[1]	Pierre and *I* go down to the street.
Sa sœur et *lui* sont à Paris.	His sister and *he* are in Paris.
Nous rencontrons Marie et *elle.*	We meet Marie and *her.*

3. to emphasize the subject of the sentence or when the subject is separated from the verb

Lui, il connaît très bien Paris.	*He* knows Paris very well.
Eux seuls peuvent le faire.	*They* alone can do it.
Je ne sais pas, *moi.*	*I* don't know.

4. in comparisons after *que* meaning *as* or *than*

Vous êtes aussi intelligent ***que lui.***	You are as intelligent ***as he.***
Nous sommes plus riches ***qu'eux.***	We are richer ***than they.***

5. following *ce* + a form of the verb *être*

C'est *moi.*	*It is **I.***	C'est *nous.*	*It is **we.***
C'est *toi.*	*It is **you.***	C'est *vous.*	*It is **you.***
C'est *lui.*	*It is **he.***	Ce sont *eux.*	*It is **they** (m.).*
C'est *elle.*	*It is **she.***	Ce sont *elles.*	*It is **they** (f.).*

6. alone, in answer to questions

Qui est là? *Moi.*	Who is there? *I.*
Qui voyez-vous? *Lui.*	Whom do you see? *Him.*

7. compound with *-même* (self)

moi-même	*myself*
lui-même	*himself*
elles-mêmes	*themselves,* f.

28. *The pronoun* en — *Le pronom* en

A. The French *en* is a special pronoun which has no English counterpart. It may be expressed in English by *some, any, of it, of them,* etc., depending

[1] One may also say *Pierre et moi nous descendons dans la rue.*

upon the sentence in which it is used. Often, the French *en* does not need to be translated in the English equivalent sentence, but without it many French sentences are not complete. Study the cases where it is used in order to accustom yourself to it.

Avez-vous des timbres? Oui, j'*en* ai.	Have you any stamps? Yes, I have (*some*).
En a-t-il? Il *en* a deux.	Does he have *any?* He has two (*of them*).

B. The word *en* is used as the object pronoun whenever the indefinite nature of the noun object would make *some, any, of it, of them,* etc., expressed or understood, the English pronoun object.[1] Study the following examples, which show the difference between the two types of pronoun objects.

DEFINITE	Nous avons *les livres.* Nous *les* avons.	We have *the books.* We have *them.*
INDEFINITE	Nous avons *des livres.* Nous *en* avons.	We have *some books.* We have *some.*
DEFINITE	A-t-il *ce crayon?* *L'*a-t-il?	Does he have *this pencil?* Does he have *it?*
INDEFINITE	A-t-il *un crayon?* *En* a-t-il *un?*	Does he have a pencil? Does he have *one* (*of them*)?

Note also how *en* is used in the following sentences.

La Normandie a beaucoup de *vaches.*	Normandy has many *cows.*
La Normandie *en* a beaucoup.	Normandy has many (*of them*).
Il a acheté trois *livres.*	He bought three *books.*
Il *en* a acheté trois.	He bought three (*of them*).
Vend-on *du beurre?*	Do they sell (*any*) *butter?*
En vend-on?	Do they sell *any?*

C. The pronoun *en* replaces a phrase introduced by *de* if the object refers to a thing. But if the object is a definite person, *de* is normally used with a disjunctive pronoun.

---

[1] One may say, then, that *en* replaces (1) a noun modified by a partitive article; e.g., Nous avons *des livres.* Nous *en* avons. (2) a noun modified by an indefinite article or a numeral; e.g., Maurice achète *un timbre.* Maurice *en* achète *un.* Louise cherche *six crayons.* Louise *en* cherche *six.* The *en* must be expressed with numbers whenever the noun object is omitted. (3) other indefinite nouns; e.g., Ils vendent beaucoup de *voitures.* Ils *en* vendent beaucoup. Combien de *professeurs* avez-vous? Combien *en* avez-vous? J'ai besoin de *papier.* J'*en* ai besoin.

THING	Elle s'occupe *de la maison.* Elle s'*en* occupe.	She looks after *the house.* She looks after *it.*
DEFINITE PERSON	Elle s'occupe *de son frère.* Elle s'occupe *de lui.*	She looks after *her brother.* She looks after *him.*
THING	Nous parlons *de mes voyages.* Nous *en* parlons.	We speak *of my trips.* We speak *of them.*
DEFINITE PERSON	Nous parlons *de mes amis.* Nous parlons *d'eux.*	We speak *of my friends.* We speak *of them.*
THING	Je me souviens *de votre nom.* Je m'*en* souviens.	I remember *your name.* I remember *it.*
DEFINITE PERSON	Je me souviens *de Marie.* Je me souviens *d'elle.*	I remember *Mary.* I remember *her.*

D. The pronoun *en* does not have gender and number. Normally, then, the past participle in a compound tense with *avoir* remains unchanged after *en.*

Nous avons acheté *des livres.*	We bought *some books.*
Nous *en* avons *acheté.*	We bought *some.*

E. As an adverb of place *en* means *from there.*

Nous sommes sortis *de la forêt.*	We went out *of the forest.*
Nous *en* sommes sortis.	We went out *of it.*
Je reviens *de France.*	I am returning *from France.*
J'*en* reviens.	I am returning *from there.*

29. *The pronoun-adverb* y — *Le pronom-adverbial* y

A. The word *y* is a special pronoun-adverb which indicates a place already mentioned. It means *there.*

Roger va *à la campagne* avec ses frères.	Roger goes *to the country* with his brothers.
Roger *y* va avec ses frères.	Roger goes *there* with his brothers.
Il *y* passe le week-end.	He spends the week end *there.*
Y allez-vous?	Do you go *there?*

B. The pronoun-adverb *y* is contrasted with *là,* which also means *there.* The adverb *là* points out strongly and usually indicates a place which has not been mentioned previously, or emphasizes a place which has been mentioned.

Où est mon livre? (*pointing*) Il est *là*.	Where is my book? (*pointing*) It is (*over*) *there*.
Les auberges de la jeunesse sont destinées à des jeunes gens. *Là* nous rencontrons des garçons de toute nationalité.	Youth hostels are designed for young people. *There* we meet boys of every nationality.

C. After reflexive verbs which are habitually followed by *à* and after certain other verbs and expressions, the most common of which are *penser à* (to think of) and *faire attention à* (watch out for, pay attention to), *y* replaces a phrase introduced by *à* if the object is a thing. But if the object is a definite person, *à* is used with a disjunctive pronoun.

THING	Elle s'intéresse *aux langues.* Elle s'*y* intéresse.	She is interested *in languages.* She is interested *in them.*
DEFINITE PERSON	Elle s'intéresse *aux pensionnaires.* Elle s'intéresse *à eux.*	She is interested *in the boarders.* She is interested *in them.*
THING	Je pense *au travail.* J'*y* pense.	I think *of the work.* I think *of it.*
DEFINITE PERSON	Je pense *à mon ami.* Je pense *à lui.*	I think *of my friend.* I think *of him.*

D. Pronoun objects of the verb *répondre* (*à*) present a special case. When the noun object is a person, the corresponding pronoun object is an ordinary indirect object pronoun which precedes the verb without a preposition.

Je réponds *à mon professeur.*	I answer *my teacher.*
Je *lui* réponds.	I answer *him.*
Nous répondons *à nos amis.*	We answer *our friends.*
Nous *leur* répondons.	We answer *them.*

When the noun object is a thing, the corresponding pronoun object is *y*.

Il répond *à la lettre.*	He answers *the letter.*
Il *y* répond.	He answers *it.*

30. *The position of object pronouns* (relative to the verb)
La place des pronoms compléments

A. The object pronouns usually immediately precede the verb.

Mon frère *y* va.	My brother goes *there.*
Le professeur *la* corrige.	The teacher corrects *her* (*it*).
Vous ne *les* remarquez pas.	You do not notice *them.*
Le lisez-vous?	Do you read *it?*
Je *lui* parle.	I speak *to him.*
Le lui montrons-nous?	Do we show *it to him?*

B. But in the affirmative imperative, object pronouns follow the verb and are appended to the verb by hyphens.

Lisez-*les.*	Read *them.*
Racontez-*le-nous.*	Tell *it to us.*

The object pronoun *me* becomes *moi* and *te* becomes *toi* when placed after the verb.[1]

Donnez-le-*moi.*	Give it *to me.*
Dites-*moi* votre nom.	Tell *me* your name.

Pronoun objects precede verbs in the negative imperative. Notice how the above sentences are made negative.

Ne *les* lisez pas.	Don't read *them.*
Ne *nous le* racontez pas.	Don't tell *it to us.*
Ne *me le* donnez pas.	Don't give *it to me.*
Ne *me* dites pas votre nom.	Don't tell *me* your name.

31. *The order of object pronouns* (relative to each other) *L'ordre des pronoms compléments*

In English we say our object pronouns without concerning ourselves about their order because we learned at an early age to do so automatically. In French we should also try to get the feeling of the order. Repeating sentences with these pronouns helps to make the order become automatic. The order of object pronouns may be learned either by the few simple rules in A, B, C, D, of this section or by the table given in E. You are advised to learn *one* or the *other.*

A. *Y* and *en* follow all other object pronouns.

Je lui *en* parle.	I speak to him of it.
Lui *en* donnez-vous?	Do you give any to him?
Donnez-lui-*en.*	Give him some of them.
Montrez-m'*en.*	Show me some.

[1] The forms *me* and *te* are known as weak forms because very little force is put upon them when pronouncing the sentence as a whole. In the affirmative imperative, where pronouns follow the verb, *me* becomes *moi* and *te* becomes *toi,* because here they are strong forms upon which considerable emphasis is placed in speaking. Note the changes between the affirmative and negative.

WEAK	Ne *me* le donnez pas.	Don't give it *to me.*
STRONG	Donnez-le-*moi.*	Give it *to me.*
WEAK	Ne *me* dites pas ce que vous faites.	Don't tell *me* what you are doing.
STRONG	Dites-*moi* ce que vous faites.	Tell *me* what you are doing.

B. *Y* always precedes *en.*

Il *y en* a.	There are some.

C. Except for *y* and *en,* the object pronouns beginning with *l-* always come nearest the verb.

Elle me *le* dit.	She tells it to me.
Il vous *le* montre.	He shows it to you.
Elle me *les* indique.	She shows them to me.
Me *le* dites-vous?	Do you tell it to me?
Dites-*le*-moi.	Tell it to me.
Donnez-*les*-moi.	Give them to me.
Montrez-*les*-nous.	Show us them.

D. Two *l-* forms in the same sentence come in alphabetical order, that is,

le la les	*always precede*	lui leur

Les élèves *la lui* montrent.	The pupils show it to him.
Il *le leur* raconte.	He tells it to them.
Nous *les lui* indiquons	We indicate them to him.
Les leur donne-t-il?	Does he give them to them?
Montrez-*la-lui.*	Show it to him.
Racontez-*le-leur.*	Tell it to them.
Dites-*les-lui.*	Tell them to him.

E. Table for order of object pronouns.

me te se nous vous	*before*	le la les	*before*	lui leur	*before*	y	*before*	en	*before*	VERB

VERB	*before*	le la les	*before*	moi [1] toi [1] lui nous vous leur	*before*	y	*before*	en

[1] The pronouns *moi* and *toi* become *m'* and *t'* before *en.* EXAMPLE: Donnez-*m'*en.

32. *The possessive pronouns — Les pronoms possessifs*

A possessive pronoun is one which indicates possession. Possessive pronouns should be distinguished from possessive adjectives which modify a noun.

ADJECTIVE	This is *my* book.	The adjective *my* modifies *book.*
PRONOUN	*Yours* is on the table.	The pronoun *yours* takes the place of *book.*

A. The possessive pronouns consist of the definite article and the pronoun itself.

	SINGULAR		PLURAL		
	MASCULINE	FEMININE	MASCULINE	FEMININE	
PERSON					
1st	le mien	la mienne	les miens	les miennes	*mine*
2d	le tien	la tienne	les tiens	les tiennes	*yours*
3d	le sien	la sienne	les siens	les siennes	*his, hers, its*
1st	le nôtre	la nôtre	les nôtres	les nôtres	*ours*
2d	le vôtre	la vôtre	les vôtres	les vôtres	*yours*
3d	le leur	la leur	les leurs	les leurs	*theirs*

B. The forms *nôtre* and *vôtre* differ from the corresponding possessive adjective forms *notre* and *votre* in the pronunciation of the *o.*[1]

C. The possessive pronouns agree with their antecedents in gender and number and with the possessor in person. They do not depend upon the gender of the possessor as is the case in English.

Robert et moi sommes ici. Voici ma bicyclette et voilà *la sienne.*	Robert and I are here. Here is my bicycle and there is *his.*

The possessive *la sienne* is feminine, although referring to Robert, because it agrees with its antecedent *bicyclette.*

D. The possessive pronouns indicate possession in an emphatic manner.

Ce livre est *le mien.*	This book is *mine* (not yours).

The French usually indicate possession either by the verb *être* + *à* + a **disjunctive pronoun** or by using the verb *appartenir* (belong).

Ce livre est *à moi.*	This book is *mine.*
Ce livre *m'appartient.*	This book *belongs to me.*

[1] The *ô* in *nôtre* and *vôtre* is pronounced *ô* [o] and the *o* in *notre* and *votre* is pronounced *o* [ɔ].

33. *The definite demonstrative pronouns*
Les pronoms démonstratifs définis

A demonstrative pronoun is one which points out an aforementioned object without repeating its name. The English demonstrative pronouns are *this, that, these,* and *those.*

In English we say: Look at *those* pencils. *This one* is longer than *that.* Here *this* and *that* are demonstrative pronouns referring to objects with definite gender and number. We also say: *He* who cannot hear is deaf. *One* who cannot see is blind. In these sentences *he* and *one* are demonstrative pronouns in French, although they are not in English.

A. The French definite demonstrative pronouns [1] are:

	lui		celui
ce +	elle	=	celle
	eux		ceux
	elles		celles

	MASCULINE	FEMININE
SINGULAR	celui	celle
PLURAL	ceux	celles

B. The definite demonstrative pronouns agree with their antecedents in gender.

J'ai *mon stylo* et *celui* de Jean.	I have my fountain pen and John's.
Il cherche *ma lettre* et *celles* de mon frère.	He is looking for my letter and those of my brother.

C. The definite demonstrative pronouns *must* be followed by *-ci* or *-là* or by a *relative pronoun* or by a *preposition.* They *cannot* be followed by *-ci* or *là* when they are followed by a relative pronoun or by a preposition.

Cette jeune fille-ci préfère la littérature, *celle-là* les cours pratiques.	This girl prefers literature, *that one* the practical courses.
Ce livre-ci est plus intéressant que *celui qui* est sur la table.	This book is more interesting than *the one which* is on the table.
Celui qui ne peut pas entendre est sourd.	*He who* cannot hear is deaf.
Je préfère les cours de conversation à *ceux de* grammaire.	I prefer the conversation courses to *those of grammar.*

Note that *-ci* and *-là* are really the adverbs *ici* (here) and *là* (there).

---

[1] The French definite demonstratives are a combination of *ce* and the third person disjunctive pronouns. (See §§ 27 and 35)

D. When the definite demonstrative pronouns are used in connection with two previously mentioned nouns, *celui-ci* (or other forms with *-ci*) refers to the nearer of the two nouns (*the latter*) and *celui-là* (or other forms with *-là*) to the more distant of the two (*the former*).

Une Suédoise et une Anglaise parlent des cours qu'elles suivent à Grenoble. *Celle-ci* s'intéresse surtout à la littérature, *celle-là* aux cours pratiques.	A Swedish girl and an English girl are speaking of the courses that they are taking at Grenoble. *The latter* is especially interested in literature, *the former* in practical courses.

There is, however, an increasing tendency to express *the latter* by a form of *ce dernier.*

Je préfère les cours de conversations à ceux de grammaire. *Ces derniers* sont plus difficiles et moins intéressants que les autres.	I prefer the courses in conversation to those in grammar. *The latter* are more difficult and less interesting than the others.

34. *The indefinite demonstrative pronouns*
Les pronoms démonstratifs indéfinis

A. The indefinite demonstrative pronouns are *ceci* and *cela.* The form *ça* is used colloquially for *cela.*

B. *Ceci* and *cela* are used to indicate something general without gender and number, such as an idea or something not definitely mentioned before.

Regardez *cela.*	Look at *that.*
Qu'est-ce que c'est que *ça? Ceci* ou *cela?*	What's *that? This* or *that?*
Achetez *ceci,* pas *cela.*	Buy *this,* not *that* (pointing).
Cela me semble terrible.	*That* (an indefinite idea) seems terrible to me.

In each case, the speaker has not previously mentioned *this* or *that* by name.

C. *Ceci* refers to the nearer, *cela* to the more distant previously unmentioned object.

Faites *ceci,* ne faites pas *cela.*	Do *this,* do not do *that.*

D. When the object has not been mentioned by name, and therefore has no gender and number in the mind of the hearer, the indefinite demonstratives *ceci* and *cela* must be used.

Cela coûte trois francs.	*That* (pointing) costs three francs.

But when the object has already been mentioned by name and therefore has gender and number in the mind of both the speaker and listener, the definite demonstratives *celui, celle, ceux,* or *celles* must be used.

Regardez ces deux livres. *Celui-ci* coûte dix francs, *celui-là* vingt francs.	Look at those two books. *This one* costs ten francs, *that one* twenty francs.

35. *The demonstrative pronoun* ce — *Le pronom démonstratif* ce

A. The demonstrative pronoun *ce* is generally used as the subject of the verb *être*.[1]

C'est le Luxembourg.	It is the Luxembourg.
Ce sont mes livres.	These are my books.
C'était moi.	It was I.
C'est vrai.	It's true.

B. The demonstrative pronoun *ce* is invariable, i.e., its form does not change. *C'est* and its equivalent in other tenses are used with a singular complement or with *nous* and *vous*. *Ce sont* and its equivalent in other tenses are used with plural complements except *nous* and *vous*.

C'est mon père.	*C'est* nous.	*Ce sont* nos parents.
C'est lui.	*Ce sont* eux.	*C'étaient* vos parents.

C. The demonstrative pronoun *ce* has two distinct uses.

1. It may be used as an *introductory word* to indicate a subject to follow the verb *être*. This *ce* we will call the **introductory *ce*.** See § 36.
2. It may be used as an *indefinite* demonstrative to refer back to something already mentioned which has no gender or number. This *ce* we will call the **indefinite *ce*.** See § 37.

36. *The introductory* ce *vs.* il, elle, ils, elles
L'emploi de ce *au lieu d'*il, elle, ils, elles

[1] The pronoun *ce* is also used with *devoir* + *être*. EXAMPLE: *Ce doit être* Paul.

A. The **introductory** ***ce*** is used before a form of the verb *être* when the part of the sentence following *être* could be the subject of the sentence. The part following *être* could be

1. a noun [1]

C'est *le Louvre.*	It is *the Louvre.*
Ce sont *les maîtres* de la peinture française.	They are *the masters* of French painting.
C'est *une femme* qui aime parler français.	She is *a woman* who likes to talk French.

2. a pronoun [2]

C'est *moi.*	It is *I.*
C'est *toi.*	It is *you.*
C'est *lui.*	It is *he.*
C'est *elle.*	It is *she.*
C'est *nous.*	It is *we.*
C'est *vous.*	It is *you.*
Ce sont *eux.*	It is *they m.*
Ce sont *elles.*	It is *they f.*
C'est *un* des musées de Paris.	It is *one* of the museums of Paris.
C'est *celui* que nous avons visité.	It is *the one* that we visited.

3. The **introductory** ***ce*** is sometimes translated by *he, she* or *they,* often by *it.*

B. The personal pronouns *il, elle, ils* and *elles* are used as the subject of the verb *être* when what follows *être* could not be the subject of the sentence. These personal pronouns refer to some definite aforementioned object which has been named and which has gender and number.[3]

---

[1] Unless such a noun is a proper name, it is normally modified by an article or an adjective. EXAMPLES: C'est *Robert.* C'est *un médecin.* C'est *la guerre.* Ce sont *mes livres.*

[2] Sometimes a superlative used as a pronoun follows *ce* + *être.* EXAMPLE: C'est *le plus grand* des musées français. It is *the largest* (*one*) of the French museums.

[3] When the verb *être* is followed by an unmodified noun indicating profession, nationality, religion, etc., it is considered in French as an adjective. Therefore, one would say:

Il est professeur.	but	*C'est* un bon professeur.
Elle est Française.	but	*C'est* une jeune Française.

Voilà *le Louvre. Il* est ***immense.***	There is *the Louvre. It* is ***huge.***
Connaissez-vous *mes frères? Ils* sont ***jeunes.***	Do you know *my brothers? They* are ***young.***
Regardez *Marie. Elle* est ***jolie.***	Look at Mary. *She* is ***pretty.***
Où est *Jean? Il* est ***là.***	Where is *John? He* is **there.**
Nous cherchons *nos camarades.* Sont-*ils* ***ici?***	We are looking for *our friends.* Are *they* ***here?***
Où est *ce tableau? Il* est ***dans le Louvre.***	Where is *this picture? It* is ***in the Louvre.***
Votre mère n'est pas ici. *Elle* est ***à Paris.***	*Your mother* is not here. *She* is ***in Paris.***

In each of the above examples, the word or phrase which followed *être* could not possibly be the subject of the sentence. It is an adjective, adverb, or phrase.

37. *The indefinite* ce *vs. the impersonal* il
Ce *au lieu de l'*il *impersonnel*

A. The indefinite demonstrative *ce* refers to a preceding idea. This idea has neither gender nor number.[1]

On ne peut pas trouver un appartement. *C'*est vrai.	One cannot find an apartment. *It* is true.
Gérard a acheté une voiture. *C'*est bien.	Gérard bought a car. *That*'s good.
Je ne peux pas partir. *C'*est impossible.	I cannot leave. *It* is impossible.
Charles ne veut pas travailler tout le temps. *C'*est trop fatigant.	Charles does not wish to work all the time. *It* is too tiring.

B. But sometimes the speaker begins a sentence without referring to any previous idea but rather with the intention of introducing some idea which is about to follow. He sometimes introduces the thought as follows:

the **impersonal** *il* + a form of *être* + an **adjective** + THE IDEA

In that case, the impersonal pronoun *il* refers to nothing aforementioned.[2]

---

[1] The indefinite *ce* sometimes apparently refers even to a definite noun. In such cases, *ce* actually refers to something vaguer and more all-inclusive than just the noun; e.g., Vous avez un joli appartement! — Oui, mais *c'*est trop petit. Here *ce* includes not only the apartment itself but the crowded living quarters, the family, etc.

[2] In spoken French it is not uncommon to find *ce* used for the impersonal *il;* e.g., *C'*est vrai qu'on ne peut pas trouver un appartement.

Il est vrai qu'on ne peut pas trouver un appartement.	*It* is true that one cannot find an apartment.
Il est bien que Gérard ait acheté une voiture.	*It* is good that Gérard bought a car.
Il est impossible que je parte.	*It* is impossible for me to leave.
Il est trop fatigant de travailler tout le temps.	*It* is too tiring to work all the time.

38. *The interrogative pronouns — Les pronoms interrogatifs*

An interrogative pronoun is one used to ask a question. In English the interrogative pronouns are: *who? whose? whom? which? what?* EXAMPLES: *Who* did that? *What* is he reading?

A. *Qui* is the French interrogative pronoun referring to persons.

Qui écrit les devoirs?	*Who* writes the exercises?
Qui rencontrons-nous?	*Whom* do we meet?
Avec *qui* Roger va-t-il à l'école?	With *whom* does Roger go to school?

Qu'est-ce qui, que, qu'est-ce que, quoi are four French interrogative pronouns referring to things. Their form depends on their use in the sentence.

Qu'est-ce qui est sur la table?	*What* is on the table?
Que faites-vous?	*What* are you doing?
Qu'est-ce que vous faites?	*What* are you doing?
Avec *quoi* écrivez-vous?	With *what* are you writing?

B. The following outline will serve to illustrate the use of the various interrogative pronouns:

FUNCTION	PERSONS	THINGS
subject	qui	qu'est-ce qui
object	qui	{ que qu'est-ce que
after prepositions	qui	quoi

Study these examples:

Qui entre dans la salle de classe?	*Who* enters the classroom?
Qui les élèves regardent-ils?	*Whom* do the pupils look at?
Pour *qui* écrit-il la lettre?	For *whom* is he writing the letter?
Qu'est-ce qui est sur le bureau?	*What* is on the desk?
Que font les élèves?	*What* are the pupils doing?
Qu'est-ce que les élèves font?	*What* are the pupils doing?
De *quoi* parle-t-il?	Of *what* is he speaking?

C. Referring to persons, the alternate forms *qui est-ce qui* may be used for the subject and *qui est-ce que* for the object.

Qui écrit une composition? *Qui est-ce qui* écrit une composition?	*Who* is writing a composition?
Qui regarde-t-il? *Qui est-ce qu'*il regarde?	*Whom* is he looking at?

Note the difference of word order in the second group of sentences. *Qui* is followed by inverted word order; *qui est-ce que* by normal word order. (See § 96 H)

D. Both *que* and *qu'est-ce que* are used as an object referring to things.

Que fait le garçon? *Qu'est-ce que* le garçon fait?	*What* does the boy do?
Que raconte-t-elle? *Qu'est-ce qu'*elle raconte?	*What* does she tell?
Que trouve le professeur derrière la porte? *Qu'est-ce que* le professeur trouve derrière la porte?	*What* does the teacher find behind the door?

In the first sentence of each group, the verb precedes the subject. This is *inverted* word order. In the second sentence of each group, the subject precedes the verb. This is *normal* word order. We may say then:

Que + verb + subject (+ rest of sentence)
Qu'est-ce que + subject + verb (+ rest of sentence)

(See § 96 I.)
The French use the *est-ce que* forms in speaking but avoid them in writing.

E. *Which one,* referring to a definite object already mentioned or mentioned immediately after *which one* (of), is expressed by:

	SINGULAR	PLURAL
MASCULINE	lequel	lesquels
FEMININE	laquelle	lesquelles

Il y a beaucoup de *pays* en Europe. *Lequel* est le plus grand?	There are many *countries* in Europe. *Which* (*one*) is the largest?
La France a beaucoup de *villes.* *Laquelle* est la plus belle?	France has many *cities. Which* (*one*) is the most beautiful?
Connaissez-vous Victor Hugo? *Lesquelles* de ses *œuvres* avez-vous lues?	Do you know Victor Hugo? *Which* (*ones*) of his *works* have you read?

F. The English expressions *What is . . .?* and *What are . . .?* are sometimes used to ask for a definition.[1] One says: *What is* a plateau? *What are* boarding houses? The French express this idea by *Qu'est-ce que . . .?* or by the longer form *Qu'est-ce que c'est que . . .?*

*Qu'est-ce qu'*un plateau? *Qu'est-ce que c'est qu'*un plateau?	*What is* a plateau?
Qu'est-ce que c'est que ça?	*What is* that?

39. *The relative pronouns — Les pronoms relatifs*

A relative pronoun is one which connects the dependent with the independent clause of a sentence. In English the relative pronouns are *who, whose, whom, which,* and *that.* In English, the relative pronoun is sometimes omitted. In French it is never omitted. EXAMPLES: The Seine is a river *which* crosses Paris. There is the friend he saw. (or) There is the friend *whom* he saw.

A. This table presents the relative pronoun in outline form.

FUNCTION	PERSONS	THINGS	THE INDEFINITE "WHAT"
subject	qui	qui	ce qui
object	que	que	ce que
after prepositions	qui lequel [2]	lequel [2]	quoi [3]

de + *relative* = dont   *relative of place (where)* / *relative of time (when)* = où

B. The word *qui* (who, which, that) is used as the **subject** of its own clause.

Le Rhin est un fleuve *qui* sépare la France de l'Allemagne.	The Rhine is a river *which* separates France from Germany.
Les Bretons, *qui* habitent la Bretagne, ne sont pas de la même race que les autres habitants de la France.	The Bretons, *who* inhabit Brittany, are not of the same race as the other inhabitants of France.
J'ai un camarade américain *qui* s'appelle Robert.	I have an American friend *who* is called Robert.

[1] Do not confuse *What is . . .* used to ask for a definition with *What is . . .* used to ask which of a number of possibilities. The latter, expressed by a form of *Quel est . . .*, is explained in § 16 C.

[2] *lequel, laquelle, lesquels* or *lesquelles,* as may be required.

[3] Sometimes *ce* + **preposition** + *quoi* is required.

C. The word *que* (whom, which, that) is used as the **object** of its own clause.

Robert est le camarade *que* je rencontre à Grenoble.	Robert is the friend *whom* I meet at Grenoble.
Apportez au bureau le livre *que* vous cachez.	Bring to the desk the book *that* you are hiding.

The pronoun *que* becomes *qu'* before a following word beginning with a vowel.

L'élève lit un livre *qu'*il semble cacher.	The pupil is reading a book *which* he seems to be hiding.

D. The words *lequel, laquelle, lesquels* and *lesquelles* are used after prepositions to refer to persons and things. The relative *qui* is also used after prepositions to refer to persons. The relative *lequel* agrees with its antecedent in gender and number.

Dans la bouche se trouve la langue avec *laquelle* nous parlons.	In the mouth is the tongue with *which* we speak.
Voilà les étudiants avec *lesquels* je suis allé à Dijon.	There are the students with *whom* I went to Dijon.

E. The word *dont* (whose, of which) usually replaces *de* and any relative pronoun.[1]

Voilà le livre *dont* le professeur a parlé.	There is the book of which the teacher spoke.

When *dont* is linked with the subject of its own clause, this subject is usually modified by an article in French but not in English.

Nous avons vu l'homme *dont le fils* est à Paris.	We saw the man *whose son* is in Paris.
Un pays *dont les habitants* sont nombreux a de graves problèmes.	A country *whose inhabitants* are numerous has serious problems.

When *dont* is linked with the object of its own clause, the French word order is

dont + *subject* + *verb* + *object*

whereas the English word order is **whose** + *object* + *subject* + *verb.*

[1] When a prepositional phrase comes between the relative pronoun and its antecedent, *de* + *relative* must be used instead of *dont*. EXAMPLES: C'est *la rue au bout de laquelle* il habite. Connaissez-vous *la femme à côté de qui* elle est assise?

C'est la jeune fille *dont* vous avez *l'adresse.*	It is the girl *whose address* you have.
Il a parlé d'un pays *dont* nous verrons *les montagnes.*	He spoke of a country *whose mountains* we shall see.

Note that if the English sentence substitutes *of whom* or *of which* for *whose,* the word order of the English sentence is the same as that of the French sentence, as, for example, in the above sentences: It is the girl *of whom* you have *the address.* He spoke of a country *of which* we shall see *the mountains.*

F. The word *où* is a relative pronoun of place.

Ils ont une maison de campagne *où* ils passent leurs week-ends.	They have a country house *where* (*in which*) they spend their week-ends.

The word *où* is also a relative pronoun of time. As a relative of time it is often the equivalent of the English *when.* This *when* has an antecedent. It is used in expressions such as *the day* **when** (*le jour* **où**), *the year* **when** (*l'année* **où**), *the time* **when** (*le moment* **où**, *l'époque* **où**, etc.)

Le jour *où* vous irez en France, vous verrez des choses curieuses.	The day *when* (*that*) you go to France, you will see strange things.
Je parlais de lui au moment *où* il est arrivé.	I was speaking of him at the time *when* he arrived.

Notice that each time that *où* is used as *when* it has an antecedent.

G. The indefinite relative *what* refers back to something without number or gender. The combination *that which* may usually be substituted for *what.* EXAMPLES: *What* (*That which*) he told us is true. Paul always remembers *what* (*that which*) he learns.
In French, the indefinite relatives are *ce qui* (subject), *ce que* (object), and *quoi* (after prepositions). Note that *ce qui* and *ce que* are combinations corresponding to *that which.*[1]

1. In French, *ce qui* expresses *what* or *that which* used as the subject of its clause.

Ce qui est intéressant n'est pas difficile à apprendre.	*What* is interesting is not hard to learn.
Dites-moi *ce qui* vous gêne.	Tell me *what* is troubling you.

[1] The indefinite pronoun *tout* (everything) must be followed by *ce* before a relative; e.g., La concierge sait *tout ce qui* se passe dans la maison. *Tout ce que* vous faites est merveilleux.

2. In French, *ce que* expresses *what* or *that which* used as the object of its clause. This *ce que* elides to *ce qu'* before words beginning with a vowel.

Dites-moi *ce que* vous faites.	Tell me *what* you are doing.
Paul me montrera *ce qu'*il a acheté.	Paul will show me *what* he has bought.

3. The indefinite *quoi* is normally used after a preposition.[1]

Pierre a parlé, après *quoi* tout le monde est parti.	Peter spoke, after *which* everyone left.
Dites-moi de *quoi* il a parlé.	Tell me of *what* he spoke.

40. *The indefinite pronoun* on — *Le pronom indéfini* on

A. The French indefinite pronoun *on,* meaning *one,* refers to *people in general,* and *not* to any particular person. The pronoun *on* is always used with a third person singular verb.

In English *on* may be rendered by **one, people, we, you** or **they** when such pronouns indicate *people in general.* Or in English a sentence with a passive voice may be used. In this case, *on* is not specifically expressed in the English sentence.

The English translations of the following sentences with *on* will illustrate the nature of this indefinite pronoun.

En France *on* parle français.	In France *one* speaks French. In France *people* speak French. In France *we* (*you, they*) speak French. In France French *is spoken.*
On trouve des jardins autour du château.	*One* finds gardens around the castle. Gardens *are found* around the castle.

Just as the French *on* is often expressed in English by the passive voice, the English passive voice is often expressed in French by *on* with the active form of the verb. (See § 87 B 1)

B. The form *l'on* is sometimes used after *si, où, que,* and *et* to prevent two vowels from coming together. This form is almost never used in spoken French and should not be used if there are other words with *l's* near *on.*

[1] In certain types of constructions, *ce* + **preposition** + *quoi* must be used. EXAMPLE: *Ce à quoi* il pense doit être intéressant. What he is thinking of must be interesting.

Si *l'on* part, *on* sera là à neuf heures.	If one leaves, one will get there at nine o'clock.
On peut aller où *l'on* veut.	One can go where one pleases.
but	
On y va et *on l'*entend parler.	They go there and they hear him speak.

The Preposition – La préposition

41. *Possession — Possession*

English expresses possession by *'s* in the singular, *-s'* in the plural, or by the preposition *of*. EXAMPLES: the girl's book, the girls' books, the roof of the house.

French expresses possession by placing the preposition *de* before a proper name or by *de* with the article or some other modifying word before a common noun. The *-'s* and *-s'* do not exist in French.

les industries *de* Lyon	the industries *of* Lyons
le port *de* Marseille	the harbor *of* Marseilles
l'architecture *de* la maison	the architecture *of* the house
les coutumes *de* chaque province	the customs *of* each province
les livres *du* garçon	the boy'*s* books
le crayon *de* Marie	Mary'*s* pencil
les cahiers *des* élèves	the pupil*s'* notebooks

42. ***The prepositions of place* to, in, at**
Les prépositions de lieu à, en, dans, chez

A. The English prepositions *in, at,* and *to* are usually expressed by one preposition with any given place (proper noun) in French. These prepositions vary with the gender and type of noun with which they are used.[1]

Il va *en* France.	He goes *to* France.
Il est *en* France.	He is *in* France.
Elle va *à* Paris.	She goes *to* Paris.
Elle est *à* Paris.	She is *in* Paris.

B. *en* is used with names of feminine countries.[2]

Pierre va *en* France.	Peter goes *to* France.
Je suis *en* Angleterre.	I am *in* England.

[1] For the genders of places, see § 7 B 4.

[2] The pronoun *en* is also used with continents. One says: *en Europe, en Asie, en Afrique, en Australie, en Amérique.* It is much more common to hear *en Amérique* than *en Amérique du Nord.*

C. *à* + the definite article is used with names of masculine countries.

Il va *au* Mexique.	He goes *to* Mexico.
Il est *au* Canada.	He is *in* Canada.
Nous vous verrons *aux* États-Unis.	We'll see you *in* the United States.

D. *à* is used with all cities.

Elle est *à* Tours.	She is *in* Tours.
Nous allons *à* Bordeaux.	We are going *to* Bordeaux.

E. *dans* with the article is often used to express *in* when the name of the place is qualified by an adjective.[1]

Nous sommes *dans la* belle France.	We are *in* beautiful France.
Elles voyagent *dans la* vieille Espagne.	They are traveling *in* old Spain.

F. *chez* is a preposition of place which is always used with persons. It has no exact English counterpart. Its translation, varying with the context, may be *at the house of, at the place of business of, in the country of,* etc. Often we say in English *at the doctor's, at the Browns',* etc. Try to understand the French usage by studying the following examples.

Allez *chez notre professeur.*	Go *to our teacher's.*
Vous pouvez venir *chez moi* ce soir.	You can come *to my house* this evening.
On trouve cela *chez le boucher.*	One finds that *at the butcher's.*
Chez nous on va à l'école à l'âge de cinq ans.	*In our country* one goes to school at the age of five.

43. *The preposition of place* from — *La préposition de lieu* de

A. In French *from* is expressed by *de* or by *de* + the definite article.

B. *de* is used with cities and feminine countries.

Il vient *de* Paris.	He comes *from* Paris.
Il revient *de* France.	He is returning *from* France.
Nous partons *d'*Italie.	We are leaving Italy.

[1] Today expressions such as *l'Afrique du Nord* and *l'Amérique du Sud* are considered as units and *en* is used with them to express *in* or *to,* as *en Afrique du Nord, en Amérique du Sud.*

C. *de + the article* is used with masculine countries or with places modified by an adjective.

Il vient *du* Canada.	He comes *from* Canada.
Il revient *du* Mexique.	He is returning *from* Mexico.
Ils partent *des* États-Unis.	They go out *of* the United States.
Sortons-nous *de la* vieille Espagne?	Are we going out *of* old Spain?
Partez-vous *de la* belle France?	Are you leaving beautiful France?

44. *The prepositions governing dependent infinitives*
Les prépositions qui précèdent les infinitifs

In English some verbs are followed directly by a dependent infinitive (He can come); many take the preposition *to* before a dependent infinitive (He wants *to* come; They refuse *to* leave); still others require some other construction (We insist *on* coming). The construction used must be learned for each verb.[1]

A. In French, verbs are also connected to a dependent infinitive in various ways. In French, one says:

Nous allons écrire.	No preposition between *allons* and *écrire.*
Il apprend *à* lire.	The preposition *à* connects *apprend* and *lire.*
Ils refusent *de* sortir.	The preposition *de* connects *refusent* and *sortir.*
Elle insiste *pour* venir.	The preposition *pour* connects *insiste* and *venir.*

Verbs of motion (*aller, venir*) and **verbs of wishing** (*vouloir, désirer, souhaiter*) are followed directly by the infinitive; **verbs of telling, asking, ordering, advising** (someone to do something) and most **verbs of emotion** (*craindre, avoir peur, regretter,* etc.) are followed by *de* before an infinitive.

But aside from these generalities, the construction used after each verb must be learned.[2]

B. Some verbs require no preposition before an infinitive. The most common of these are:

---

[1] The construction following a given verb may be found in the French-English and English-French vocabularies at the end of the book.

[2] The construction used after a verb may be found directly after this verb in the French-English and English-French vocabularies.

aimer	*like*	falloir	*be necessary*
aimer mieux	*prefer*	laisser	*leave, allow, let*
aller	*go, be going*	oser	*dare*
compter	*intend*	pouvoir	*can, be able*
croire	*believe*	préférer	*prefer*
désirer	*desire, wish*	savoir	*know, know how*
devoir	*am to, must*	sembler	*seem*
entendre	*hear*	venir	*come*
espérer	*hope*	voir	*see*
faire	*do, make, have*	vouloir	*want, wish*

Je vais jouer avec mon ami.	I am going to play with my friend.
Nous voulons aller en classe.	We want to go to class.
Vous pouvez entrer.	You can enter.

C. Some verbs require *de* before an infinitive. The most common of these are:

avoir peur de	*be afraid*	finir de	*finish*
cesser de	*cease*	ordonner de	*order*
craindre de	*fear*	oublier de	*forget*
décider de	*decide*	permettre de	*permit*
défendre de	*forbid*	prier de	*beg, ask, pray*
demander de[1]	*ask*	promettre de	*promise*
se dépêcher de	*hurry*	refuser de	*refuse*
dire de	*tell*	regretter de	*regret*
écrire de	*write*	remercier de	*thank*
empêcher de	*prevent*	tâcher de	*try*
essayer de	*try*		

Nous avons décidé *de* partir.	We have decided to leave.
J'ai oublié *de* vous le montrer.	I forgot to show it to you.

D. Some verbs require *à* before an infinitive. The most common of these are:

aider à	*help*	enseigner à	*teach*
s'amuser à	*amuse oneself*	s'habituer à	*accustom oneself*
apprendre à	*learn, teach*	hésiter à	*hesitate*
arriver à	*succeed*	inviter à	*invite*
avoir à	*have*	se mettre à	*begin*
chercher à	*seek, try*	recommencer à	*begin again*
commencer à	*begin*	réussir à	*succeed*
consentir à	*consent*	songer à	*think, dream*
continuer à	*continue*	tarder à	*delay in*
se décider à	*decide*		

[1] The verb *demander* + an indirect object requires *de* before an infinitive. Compare: Il demande *à* venir. Il demande à son ami *de* venir.

Je vous invite *à* dîner.	I invite you to dine.
Il apprend *à* lire.	He is learning to read.

E. The prepositions *de* and *à* are regularly used before infinitives in these two very common constructions:

Il (impersonal) + *être* + adjective + *de* + IDEA.

Il est impossible *de* **partir demain.**	It is impossible to leave tomorrow.
Il est difficile *de* **lire le latin.**	It is hard to read Latin.

IDEA + *être* + adjective + *à* + *infinitive*

Le latin *est* difficile *à* lire.	Latin is hard to read.
Vous chantez bien. C'*est* agréable *à* entendre.	You sing well. It is pleasant to hear.

45. *Verbs governing nouns with or without prepositions*
Les verbes suivis d'une préposition devant un nom ou suivi d'un nom

A. It is impossible to write correct French without learning whether or not the verb takes a preposition before the noun it governs. These prepositions are not always the same as in English.

Consider the italicized expressions in the following sentences:

Je *cherche* mon stylo.	I *look for* my fountain pen.
Il *entre dans* le bureau.	He *enters* the office.
Elle *dit à Paul de* fermer la porte.	She *tells Paul to* close the door.
Vous *pensez à* vos leçons.	You *think of* your lessons.

The prepositional constructions in the above sentences are different in the two languages. These constructions must be learned.[1] They may be classified into three groups.

B. Certain verbs require a direct object in French but a preposition before the object in English. Among these are:

attendre	*wait for*	Paul *attend* son ami.
chercher	*look for*	Marie *cherche* son livre.
demander	*ask for*	Pierre *demande* cinq cents francs.
écouter	*listen to*	Nous *écoutons* la musique.
payer [2]	*pay for*	Il *a payé* cet objet mille francs.
regarder	*look at*	Je *regarde* le plan de Paris.

[1] The construction used after a verb may be found directly after this verb in the French-English and English-French vocabularies at the end of the book.

[2] In certain cases, the French do use *pour* after the verb *payer;* e.g., Les Français ne

C. Certain verbs require a preposition before the object in French but a direct object in English. Among these are:

s'approcher de	*approach*	Nous nous *approchons de* la ville.
assister à	*attend*	Il *assiste à* la réunion.
changer de	*change*	Elle *a changé de* robe.
entrer dans	*enter*	Qui *entre dans* la salle?
échapper à	*escape* [1]	Le soldat *a échappé à* la mort.
s'échapper de	*escape* [1]	Le prisonnier *s'est échappé* du bateau.
jouer à	*play* [2]	Je *joue au* football et *aux* échecs.
jouer de	*play* [2]	Elle *joue du* piano et *du* violon.
manquer de	*lack*	Je *manque de* savon.
se marier avec	*marry*	Denise *se marie avec* Guy.
obéir à	*obey*	Paul *obéit à* son père.
plaire à	*please*	Yvonne *plaît à* sa tante.
répondre à	*answer*	Je *réponds à* la lettre.
résister à	*resist*	Il *résiste à* la tentation.
ressembler à	*resemble*	Maurice *ressemble à* son frère.
se servir de	*use*	Ils *se servent de* la machine à écrire.
se souvenir de	*remember*	Je *me souviens de* la guerre.

D. Certain verbs require one preposition in French and another in English. Among these are:

s'intéresser à	*be interested in*	Il *s'intéresse à* la musique.
s'occuper de	*busy oneself with*	Je *m'occupe de* la pension.
penser à	*think of* [3]	Il *pense à* son travail.
penser de	*think of* [3]	Que *pensez-vous de* cet homme?
remercier de	*thank for* [4]	Il *a remercié* sa mère *de* son cadeau.
rire de	*laugh at*	Nous *rions de* cet enfant.
songer à	*think of*	Il *songe à* son voyage en France.

---

paient pour leur logement qu'un petit pourcentage de leur salaire. But in other cases, they use only the direct object. It seems impossible to generalize on these usages.

[1] The verb *échapper à* means *to escape getting into something, s'échapper de* means *to escape from something one has gotten into.*

[2] The construction *jouer à* means *to play a game,* the construction *jouer de* means *to play a musical instrument.*

[3] The construction *penser à* means *to think of someone or something,* the construction *penser de* is used in questions *to ask one's opinion of someone or something.*

[4] The verb *remercier* may also be followed by *pour* before a noun. EXAMPLE: Il *a remercié* sa mère *pour* son cadeau.

E. Certain verbs require *à* before a noun object and *de* before a following infinitive in French but not necessarily in English. These may be called the *à* + *de* verbs. Among these are:

conseiller à quelqu'un de	*advise someone to*	Je *conseille à Paul de* partir.
défendre à quelqu'un de	*forbid someone to*	Il *défend à Marie de* sortir.
demander à quelqu'un de	*ask someone to*	Elle *demande à sa mère de* venir.
dire à quelqu'un de	*tell someone to*	Je *dis à mon frère de* parler.
écrire à quelqu'un de	*write someone to*	Nous *écrivons à Guy de* rester.
ordonner à quelqu'un de	*order someone to*	Il *ordonne au soldat de* se taire.
permettre à quelqu'un de	*permit someone to*	Je *permets à Jean d'*entrer.
promettre à quelqu'un de	*promise someone to*	Elle *promet à Henri de* lui écrire.
téléphoner à quelqu'un de	*telephone someone to*	Il *téléphone à Claude de* s'en aller.

The Verb – Le verbe

I. *The organization of the French verb*
L'organisation du verbe français

46. *The French verb — Le verbe français*

A. The French verb is divided into three main groups of regular verbs: [1]

1. *-er* verbs
2. *-ir* verbs
3. *-re* verbs

B. There are also certain verbs in *-er, -ir,* and *-re* which do not follow the general tendencies of these verbs in all tenses. Such verbs are called irregular verbs. There is also a group of verbs whose infinitives end in *-oir.* They are sometimes considered as regular verbs, but they are so irregular within the group that we shall consider them all irregular. Irregular verbs usually follow a certain pattern, even in their irregularities. These patterns will be discussed with each tense in which they occur. A table of common irregular verbs is found in § 95. In the final vocabulary, references are made to paragraphs of the *Grammaire* dealing with irregularities and to the table of paradigms.

[1] For the conjugation of regular verbs, see § 95.

C. The tenses of the verbs are formed on the stems. Regular verbs have only a main stem. Irregular verbs have a main stem and sometimes several others. These are discussed in § 48 under the caption "The Principal Parts of Verbs."

D. The main stem of a verb is found by taking the infinitive ending *-er, -ir, -re,* or *-oir* from the infinitive.

INFINITIVE	STEM
parler	parl-
choisir	chois-
répondre	répond-
recevoir	recev-

47. *The tenses of the French verb — Les temps du verbe français*

A. The French verb is divided into simple and compound tenses, as follows:

SIMPLE TENSES	COMPOUND TENSES
PRESENT	COMPOUND PAST
IMPERFECT	PLUPERFECT
SIMPLE PAST	PAST ANTERIOR
FUTURE	FUTURE PERFECT
CONDITIONAL	PAST CONDITIONAL

B. These tenses are commonly translated as follows:

TENSE	FRENCH *il*-FORM	ENGLISH TRANSLATION
	SIMPLE TENSES	
PRESENT	il parle	*he speaks, he is speaking, he does speak*
IMPERFECT	il parlait	*he spoke, he was speaking*
SIMPLE PAST	il parla	*he spoke, he did speak*
FUTURE	il parlera	*he will speak*
CONDITIONAL	il parlerait	*he would speak*
	COMPOUND TENSES	
COMPOUND PAST	il a parlé	*he spoke, he has spoken*
PLUPERFECT	il avait parlé	*he had spoken*
PAST ANTERIOR	il eut parlé	*he had spoken*
FUTURE PERFECT	il aura parlé	*he will have spoken*
PAST CONDITIONAL	il aurait parlé	*he would have spoken*

48. *The principal parts of the verb*
Les temps primitifs du verbe français

A. Each verb has five principal parts, from which the various stems of the verb are derived:

1. the infinitive
2. the present participle
3. the past participle
4. the first person singular of the present indicative
5. the first person singular of the simple past

B. All stems of all regular *-er* and *-re* verbs are the same as that of the main (infinitive) stem. The present participle of most *-ir* verbs inserts an *-iss-* between the infinitive stem and the endings. The second class *-ir* verbs drop the final consonant of the main stem in the singular of the present. Irregular verbs sometimes have five different stems.

INFINITIVE	PRESENT PARTICIPLE	PAST PARTICIPLE	SINGULAR OF PRESENT	SIMPLE PAST
parl-er	parl-ant	parlé	parl-e	parl-ai
perd-re	perd-ant	perdu	perd-s	perd-is
fin-ir	fin-iss-ant	fini	fin-is	fin-is
dorm-ir	dorm-ant	dormi	dor-s	dorm-is
boi-re	buv-ant	bu	boi-s	bu-s
prend-re	pren-ant	pris	prend-s	pri-s
ven-ir	ven-ant	venu	vien-s	vin-s
mour-ir	mour-ant	mort	meur-s	mour-us

C. Certain tenses are usually formed on each of these stems as shown in the arrangement on page 429.

INFINITIVE	PRESENT PARTICIPLE	PAST PARTICIPLE	PRESENT	SIMPLE PAST
future conditional	plural of present [1] imperfect indicative present subjunctive [2]	compound past pluperfect indicative future perfect past conditional past anterior past subjunctive pluperfect subjunctive	singular of present	simple past imperfect subjunctive

[1] In a number of verbs, the third person plural of the present follows the stem of the singular of the present indicative. EXAMPLES: je bois, ils boivent; je meurs, ils meurent.

[2] Where the stem of the third person plural present indicative is different from that of the imperfect indicative, the present subjunctive usually has two stems. See § 80 B.

D. In § 95, common irregular verbs are conjugated by tenses. This is practical for easy reference, but the verbs will be easier to learn if you will rearrange them by stems, as shown below.

INFINITIVE
boire

FUTURE
je boirai
tu boiras
il boira
nous boirons
vous boirez
ils boiront

CONDITIONAL
je boirais
tu boirais
il boirait
nous boirions
vous boiriez
ils boiraient

PRESENT PARTICIPLE
buvant

PLURAL OF PRESENT INDICATIVE
nous buvons
vous buvez
ils boivent

IMPERFECT INDICATIVE
je buvais
tu buvais
il buvait
nous buvions
vous buviez
ils buvaient

PRESENT SUBJUNCTIVE
que je boive
que tu boives
qu'il boive
que nous buvions
que vous buviez
qu'ils boivent

PAST PARTICIPLE
bu

COMPOUND PAST INDICATIVE
j'ai bu, etc.

PLUPERFECT INDICATIVE
j'avais bu, etc.

FUTURE PERFECT
j'aurai bu, etc.

PAST CONDITIONAL
j'aurais bu, etc.

PAST ANTERIOR
j'eus bu, etc.

PAST SUBJUNCTIVE
que j'aie bu, etc.

PLUPERFECT SUBJUNCTIVE
que j'eusse bu, etc.

PRESENT INDICATIVE
je bois
tu bois
il boit

SIMPLE PAST
je bus
tu bus
il but
nous bûmes
vous bûtes
ils burent

IMPERFECT SUBJUNCTIVE
que je busse
que tu busses
qu'il bût
que nous bussions
que vous bussiez
qu'ils bussent

II. *The formation and use of tenses and other parts of the verb*
La formation et l'emploi des temps et des autres parties du verbe

49. *The formation of the present tense — La formation du présent*

A. *-er* verbs form their present tense by adding to the stem (——) the following endings:

je ——e	nous ——ons
tu ——es	vous ——ez
il ——e	ils ——ent

EXAMPLES: demander, parler, aimer, trouver, traverser, couler.[1]

[1] For the conjugation of an *-er* verb, see § 95, page 482.

B. *-ir* verbs generally insert *-iss-* between the stem and endings of the plural:

je ——is	nous ——iss-ons
tu ——is	vous ——iss-ez
il ——it	ils ——iss-ent

EXAMPLES: punir, finir, obéir, choisir, réussir.[1]

C. Side by side with the large class of *-ir* verbs already studied in (B) is a small but important group of six verbs and their compounds. These we shall call *-ir* verbs of the second class. They are different from other *-ir* verbs in that they do not insert *-iss-* in certain tenses. In other words, they are essentially like the verbs taken up in (D). The *six* verbs which make up this group with their compounds[2] are: (1) *dormir* (to sleep); (2) *mentir* (to tell a lie); (3) *partir* (to go away); (4) *sentir* (to feel, to smell); (5) *servir* (to serve); (6) *sortir* (to go out). Each of these verbs has only two syllables in the infinitive and has a stem ending in two consonants.

In the singular of the present indicative, these verbs drop the final consonant of the stem before adding the endings. Letting (-) represent the absent consonant at the end of the stem, the endings are:

je ——(-)s	nous ——ons
tu ——(-)s	vous ——ez
il ——(-)t	ils ——ent

dormir:	je dors, tu dors, il dort, nous dormons, vous dormez, ils dorment
sentir:	je sens, tu sens, il sent, nous sentons, vous sentez, ils sentent
servir:	je sers, tu sers, il sert, nous servons, vous servez, ils servent
sortir:	je sors, tu sors, il sort, nous sortons, vous sortez, ils sortent

D. *-re* verbs form their present tense by adding to the stem the following endings:

je ——s	nous ——ons
tu ——s	vous ——ez
il ——	ils ——ent

EXAMPLES: répondre, entendre, attendre, perdre.[3, 4]

---

[1] For the conjugation of an *-ir* verb, see § 95, page 482.

[2] By compounds are meant other verbs having one of these verbs as the essential part of the stem. EXAMPLES: s'en*dormir*, re*partir*, se *servir*.

[3] For the conjugation of an *-re* verb, see § 95, page 482.

[4] A few verbs, such as *rompre,* add *-t* to the stem in the third person singular of the present. EXAMPLE: il rompt.

E. Many common verbs are irregular in the present. A certain number of these, such as *avoir, aller, être* and *faire* follow no common pattern. The forms of such verbs must simply be learned. But most of the verbs which are irregular in the present follow one pattern or another. Of these, one of the most frequent is that in which *the entire singular and the third person plural forms have one stem vowel,* whereas *the first and second persons plural have another, usually that of the infinitive.* This change is due to a shift in stress. (Cf. Latin de′beo, de′bes, de′bet, debe′mus, debe′tis, de′bent.)

devoir	pouvoir	mourir	recevoir	voir	vouloir
je dois	peux	meurs	reçois	vois	veux
tu dois	peux	meurs	reçois	vois	veux
il doit	peut	meurt	reçoit	voit	veut
nous devons	*pouvons*	*mourons*	*recevons*	*voyons*	*voulons*
vous devez	*pouvez*	*mourez*	*recevez*	*voyez*	*voulez*
ils doivent	peuvent	meurent	reçoivent	voient	veulent

50. *The use of the present tense — L'emploi du présent*

A. In French, as in English, the present is used to express a simple present action or a state or action which always exists.

Nous *visitons* la France.	We *are visiting* France.
Il *aime* beaucoup la France.	He *likes* France a great deal.

But in English there are *three* forms of the present, whereas in French only *one* form exists:

SIMPLE PRESENT	he lives	all expressed	
PROGRESSIVE PRESENT	he is living	in French by	il habite
EMPHATIC PRESENT	he does live	the form	

This is true not only of the present but of all other tenses. The French have no ordinary progressive and emphatic forms of the verb. The verbs *être* and *faire* should never be used as auxiliaries to express these ideas.

B. The French present tense is used with *depuis, il y a . . . que, voici . . . que,* and *voilà . . . que* to express an action which has begun in the past and continues down to the present. The English here normally uses the present perfect.[1]

[1] When the action was completed in the past, the past tenses are used with *pendant.*

J'*ai été* à Paris **pendant** dix semaines.	I *was* at Paris *for ten weeks.*
Nous *avons attendu* le train *pendant* trois minutes.	We *waited for* the train *for* three minutes.

Je *suis* à Paris *depuis* dix semaines.	I *have been* at Paris *for* ten weeks. (and I am still there)
Il y a trois minutes *que* nous *attendons* le train.	We *have been waiting* for the train *for* three minutes. (and we are still waiting)
Voilà trois ans *que* la guerre *dure.*	The war *has been going on for* three years. (and it is still going on)

C. The present is sometimes used to express an action which is to take place in the near future. English uses the present in the same way.

Demain nous *commençons* à explorer les Alpes.	Tomorrow we *begin* to explore the Alps.

51. *The formation of the imperfect tense—La formation de l'imparfait*

A. The imperfect of *-er* verbs, of second class *-ir* verbs, or *-re* verbs, and of most irregular verbs is formed by adding to the stem these endings:

je ——ais	nous ——ions
tu ——ais	vous ——iez
il ——ait	ils ——aient

B. The class of *-ir* verbs which inserts *-iss-* between the stem and the ending in the plural of the present does likewise throughout the imperfect.

je ——iss-ais	nous ——iss-ions
tu ——iss-ais	vous ——iss-iez
il ——iss-ait	ils ——iss-aient

C. The imperfect stem of all verbs, regular or irregular (except *être* and *falloir*), may be found by taking *-ons* from the first person plural of the present indicative.

INFINITIVE	FIRST PERSON PLURAL PRESENT	IMPERFECT
avoir	nous avons	j'avais
connaître	nous connaissons	je connaissais
croire	nous croyons	je croyais
devoir	nous devons	je devais
dire	nous disons	je disais
écrire	nous écrivons	j'écrivais

52. *The use of the imperfect—L'emploi de l'imparfait*

A. The imperfect tense is so called because it describes an incomplete action or state of being, that is, one that was going on when another action took place. French imperfects are often expressed by *was* (or *were*) + ——*ing* in English.

The imperfect is used for background states or actions which set the scene for principal actions. Actions in the imperfect have no beginning or end in reference to the time of the particular situation at hand. They simply go on.

Note in the following example how the italicized verbs, which are in the imperfect, form a background for what happened but do not themselves indicate any forwarding action.

Il *était* déjà presque cinq heures quand nous sommes arrivés à la gare. Un employé *se tenait* près de la porte qui donne accès aux quais. Beaucoup de voyageurs *attendaient* le train. Quelques-uns d'entre eux *causaient,* d'autres *se promenaient* le long du quai.	It *was* already five o'clock when we arrived at the station. An employee *was standing* near the door which leads to the platforms. Many travelers *were awaiting* the train. Some of them *were chatting,* others *were walking* along the platform.

B. Two ways in which the imperfect forms a background for the principal actions are:

1. to express a condition, often a description or a state of mind, during a period of time in the past.

Notre wagon *était* plein de voyageurs. Les gens qui n'*avaient* pas de place *se tenaient* dans le couloir. Ils *étaient* debout ou assis sur leurs valises. Dans notre compartiment une femme *causait* avec son mari, une jeune fille *lisait* un roman policier, un enfant *mangeait* du pain, sa petite sœur *dormait* et un vieillard qui *parlait* avec un accent prononcé *disait* à une dame: «Oui, je suis Alsacien.»	Our coach *was* full of travelers. The people who *had* no seat *were* in the aisles. They *were* standing or *were* seated on their suitcases. In our compartment a woman *was talking* with her husband, a girl *was reading* a detective story, a child *was eating* some bread, his little sister *was sleeping,* and an old man who *spoke* with a pronounced accent *was saying* to a lady: "Yes, I am Alsatian."

2. to express a continued[1] past action which was interrupted by some other action.[2]

---

[1] Learners often believe erroneously that all continued past actions should be in the imperfect. This is false. The criterion for the imperfect is not whether the action was continued (for all actions, however short, are continued over some period of time), but whether the action did or did not have a definite beginning and end in the particular situation at hand. If the beginning or end existed, then the imperfect would not be used.

[2] Imperfect actions, in the examples, are in italics, interrupting actions in boldface.

Les gens qui *attendaient* sur le quai sont montés dans les wagons.	The people who *were waiting* on the platform got into the coaches.
Je *finissais* mes études à Strasbourg quand la guerre a éclaté.	I *was finishing* my studies at Strasbourg when the war broke out.
Ce monsieur *commençait* à m'en parler quand le contrôleur est venu demander les billets.	This man *was beginning* to speak to me of it when the conductor came to ask for the tickets.

Notice that this type of imperfect is ordinarily expressed in English by *was* (or *were*) + —— *ing.*

C. The imperfect is sometimes used to express a customary, habitual or repeated action in the past. Such customary, habitual or repeated actions are expressed in English by *used to* or *would* [1] with the infinitive.

A huit heures, la cloche *annonçait* le souper. Après le souper, dans les beaux jours, on *s'asseyait* sur le perron . . . Ma mère, Lucile et moi, nous *regardions* le ciel, les bois, les derniers rayons du soleil, les premières étoiles. A dix heures, on *rentrait* et l'on *se couchait.*	At eight o'clock, the bell *would announce* supper. After supper, in good weather, we *used to sit* on the steps . . . My mother, Lucile and I *would look at* the sky, the woods, the last rays of the sun, the first stars. At ten o'clock, we *used to go back into the house* and *go to bed.*

D. The imperfect is used with *depuis* and *il y avait . . . que* to express an action which began in the remote past and continued down to a point in the past at which another action began or took place. English uses the pluperfect to express the same idea and usually the progressive form of the pluperfect.

J'habitais ***depuis*** quelques jours dans une famille où je préparais l'un des fils au baccalauréat quand la mobilisation est venue me surprendre.	I *had been living* ***for*** several days in a family where I was preparing one of the sons for his baccalaureate examination when the mobilization took me by surprise.
Il y avait une demi-heure ***que*** le train *parcourait* une campagne âpre.	The train *had been crossing* a desolate country ***for*** a half hour.

E. The imperfect is also used with *si* in conditional sentences. (See § 72, B 2)

[1] Note that the English sentence *They **would** go to Paris* might mean *They **used** to go to Paris* (in which case French would say *Ils **allaient** à Paris*), or it might mean *They **would** go to Paris **if they could*** (in which case French would say *Ils **iraient** à Paris*).

53. *The combined uses of the compound past and the imperfect*
L'emploi du passé composé et de l'imparfait dans le même récit

A. In conversational narration of past events, there are usually two types of action: those which recount the main events of the story and those which supply the background to what happens but have nothing to do with the actual forwarding of the action of the story. The **main events** are in the *compound past,* the **background actions** are in the *imperfect.*

Since the imperfect supplies a background, imperfect actions have no beginning or end in reference to the particular situation at hand. The actions of the compound past, on the other hand, forward the narrative and are therefore limited as to the length of time in which they take place. Actions which are limited in time and actions whose beginning and end are indicated must, therefore, be put into the compound past.

In the following example, the italicized verbs, which are in the *imperfect,* create a **background** for the main action. The verbs in boldface, which are in the *compound past,* **narrate what happened and are main actions.** Keep in mind that it is the speaker who determines which actions or states are background, and which forward the action.

Nous **avons entendu** siffler le train. Il *était* encore loin, mais il *approchait* à toute vitesse. Il **est arrivé, s'est arrêté** et quelques voyageurs **sont descendus.** Les gens qui *attendaient* sur le quai **sont montés** dans les wagons.	We **heard** the train whistle. It *was* still far away, but it *was approaching* at full speed. It **arrived, stopped,** and some travelers **got off.** The people who *were waiting* on the platform **got into** the coaches.

B. The use of the imperfect and the compound past to express mental and physical states is of particular importance.

MENTAL STATES

Imperfect	*Compound Past*
The imperfect describes a state of mind not specifically limited in time.	The compound past often indicates a change in state of mind.
Je *savais* que vous étiez là.	J'**ai su** par votre frère que vous étiez là.
I knew that you were there.	I **learned** through your brother that you were there.
Guy *pensait* que nous arriverions bientot.	Tout d'un coup Guy **a pensé** que nous arriverions bientot.
Guy *thought* that we would soon arrive.	Suddenly **it occurred** to Guy that we would soon arrive.

Roger *avait peur* que vous partiez.	Roger **a eu peur** que vous partiez.
Roger *was afraid* that you would leave.	Roger **became afraid** that you would leave.

PHYSICAL STATES

Imperfect	*Compound Past*
The imperfect describes a physical state which forms a background for something else which happened.	The compound past often describes a change of physical state which may be expressed in English by **got** or **became.**
J'*avais très chaud* quand nous sommes entrés dans la maison.	J'ai **eu très chaud** quand nous sommes entrés dans la maison.
I *was very warm* when we entered the house.	I **became very warm** when we entered the house.
Il faisait froid hier soir quand nous sommes rentrés.	**Il a fait froid** hier soir après que nous sommes rentrés.
It was cold last evening when we returned home.	**It got cold** last evening after we returned home.

When the physical state is definitely limited in time, it is normally expressed by the compound past even though it takes place over a period of time.

Marie *a eu mal à la gorge* pendant trois jours.	Marie **had a sore throat** for three days.
Il a fait chaud toute la semaine.	**It was warm** the whole week.

54. *The formation of the future — La formation du futur*[1]

A. The future (I shall speak, you will speak, he will speak, etc.) is formed by adding to the infinitive a set of endings which are really the present tense of *avoir* (*avons* shortened to *-ons, avez* to *-ez*).

---

[1] The future, like all other French tenses except the present, the imperfect, and the simple past, is in reality a compound tense. It consists of the *infinitive* and the appended present of *avoir* (*je parler -ai,* etc.); we can trace it back to before 1000 A.D. when it was sometimes written "je parler ai, tu parler as," etc. Compare English "I have to speak" with our own future "I shall speak," and you will find it easier to understand how the feeling for this type of future grew in French and in the other Romance languages (Spanish, Italian, Portuguese, etc.). Compare the future with the *passé composé* (*j'ai parlé*), where the auxiliary is used with the past participle to form the compound tenses.

je *infinitive* -ai	nous *infinitive* -ons
tu *infinitive* -as	vous *infinitive* -ez
il *infinitive* -a	ils *infinitive* -ont

Verbs in *-re* drop the *-e* before adding the endings. EXAMPLE: je perdrai.

B. The endings of the future are always the same, but eighteen common verbs have a slightly modified infinitive stem in the future. The stems of certain of these verbs are formed in a similar manner. These verbs might be arranged into groups as follows:

1		2		3	
avoir	il aura	voir	il verra	tenir	il tiendra
savoir	il saura	envoyer	il enverra	venir	il viendra

4		5		6		7	
aller	il ira	courir	il courra	devoir	il devra	falloir	il faudra
faire	il fera	mourir	il mourra	pleuvoir	il pleuvra	valoir	il vaudra
être	il sera	pouvoir	il pourra	recevoir	il recevra	vouloir	il voudra

55. *The use of the future — L'emploi du futur*

A. The French future, like the English, is used to express actions which will take place at some future time.

Vous *trouverez* les rues de Paris différentes des rues américaines.	You *will find* the streets of Paris different from the American streets.

B. The future is used in French after such expressions as *quand* (when), *lorsque* (when), *aussitôt que* (as soon as), and *dès que* (as soon as) to indicate a future action.[1] English usually uses the present tense in the same type of sentence.

Quand vous *arriverez* à Paris, vous remarquerez des choses curieuses.	***When*** you *arrive* at Paris, you will notice strange things.
Lorsque vous *répondrez* à ma lettre, dites-moi ce que vous faites.	***When*** you *answer* my letter, tell me what you are doing.
Aussitôt que vous *aurez* le temps, lisez ce livre.	***As soon as*** you *have* the time, read this book.
Dès que nous *arriverons* en France, nous vous écrirons.	***As soon as*** we *arrive* in France, we shall write you.

[1] Such expressions are *not* followed by the future to indicate *present* or *past* actions; e.g., ***Quand*** je *suis arrivé* à Paris, j'ai remarqué des choses curieuses. ***Dès que*** nous *arrivons* en France, nous écrivons toujours à nos parents.

C. The future is also used in the conclusion of certain conditional sentences. (See § 72 B.)

56. *The formation of the conditional — La formation du conditionnel*[1]

A. The French conditional (I should speak, you would speak, he would speak, etc.) is formed by adding to the infinitive the imperfect endings, which are, in reality, shortened forms of the imperfect indicative of *avoir.*

je *infinitive* -ais	nous *infinitive* -ions
tu *infinitive* -ais	vous *infinitive* -iez
il *infinitive* -ait	ils *infinitive* -aient

Verbs in *-re* drop the *-e* before adding the endings. EXAMPLE: je perdrais.

B. The endings of the conditional are always the same, and the eighteen common verbs which have an irregular infinitive stem in the future have the same irregular stem in the conditional. For example: avoir — il aurait; venir — il viendrait; aller — il irait, etc. See § 54 B for the stems of the verbs which are irregular in the conditional.

57. *The use of the conditional — L'emploi du conditionnel*

A. The conditional is used to express a future action dependent upon another and usually past action.

Il a dit qu'il *parlerait* aux élèves.	He said that he *would speak* to the pupils.

B. The conditional is often used to soften the present. Note the differences between these sentences:

Je *veux* un verre d'eau.	I *want* a glass of water.
Je *voudrais* un verre d'eau.	I *should like* a glass of water.
Aimez-vous aller au théâtre?	*Do* you *like* to go to the theater?
Aimeriez-vous aller au théâtre?	*Would* you *like* to go to the theater?

C. The conditional is used in the conclusion of certain conditional sentences. (See § 72 B.)

---

[1] Just as the French future is formed by adding the present indicative of *avoir* to the infinitive, so the conditional is formed by adding shortened forms of the imperfect indicative of *avoir* to the infinitive. It partakes of the quality of a past future. For example, if the main verb in the example in § 57 A is put into the present, the sentence will read:

Il dit qu'il *parlera* aux élèves.	He says that he *will speak* to the pupils.

58. *The formation of the simple past—La formation du passé simple*

A. The simple past is formed by adding a given set of endings to a special stem. In regular verbs this stem is the same as the main stem; in irregular verbs, the special stem must be learned for each verb. The endings are as follows:

-er VERBS	*-ir* AND *-re* VERBS	MANY IRREGULAR AND MOST *-oir* VERBS
je ——ai	je ——is	je ——us
tu ——as	tu ——is	tu ——us
il ——a	il ——it	il ——ut
nous ——âmes	nous ——îmes	nous ——ûmes
vous ——âtes	vous ——îtes	vous ——ûtes
ils ——èrent	ils ——irent	ils ——urent

B. A number of very common verbs have irregular stems in the simple past.

1. The stem of the simple past of many verbs resembles its irregular past participle. Among these verbs are:

INFINITIVE	PAST PARTICIPLE	SIMPLE PAST	INFINITIVE	PAST PARTICIPLE	SIMPLE PAST
boire	bu	je bus	pleuvoir	plu	il plut
connaître	connu	je connus	pouvoir	pu	je pus
courir	couru	je courus	prendre	pris	je pris
croire	cru	je crus	rire	ri	je ris
devoir	dû	je dus	savoir	su	je sus
dire	dit	je dis	suivre	suivi	je suivis
falloir	fallu	il fallut	valoir	valu	je valus
lire	lu	je lus	vivre	vécu	je vécus
mettre	mis	je mis	vouloir	voulu	je voulus
plaire	plu	je plus			

2. The simple past of certain verbs is completely irregular and must be learned. The most common of these are:

INFINITIVE	SIMPLE PAST	INFINITIVE	SIMPLE PAST	INFINITIVE	SIMPLE PAST
avoir	j'eus	être	je fus	ouvrir	j'ouvris
conduire	je conduisis	faire	je fis	tenir	je tins
craindre	je craignis	mourir	je mourus	venir	je vins
écrire	j'écrivis	naître	je naquis	voir	je vis

59. *The use of the simple past — L'emploi du passé simple*

A. The simple past is a literary tense used only in narration whose action takes place distinctly in the past to express actions which are quite definitely completed. It is rarely used in spoken French.

Le 28 juin 1914 un jeune Serbe *assassina* l'archiduc héritier d'Autriche-Hongrie.	The 28th of June 1914, a young Serb *assassinated* the heir to the throne of Austria-Hungary.

B. Where the French use the simple past in a literary narration, they would use the compound past to express the same type of action in a conversation.

LITERARY STYLE	CONVERSATIONAL STYLE
Pour gagner la guerre le plus vite possible, l'Allemagne *décida* d'attaquer la France par le nord.	Pour gagner la guerre le plus vite possible, l'Allemagne *a décidé* d'attaquer la France par le nord.
Heureusement les Français *réussirent* à les arrêter sur la Marne.	Heureusement les Français *ont réussi* à les arrêter sur la Marne.
Mais finalement, avec l'aide des États-Unis, qui *entrèrent* en guerre en 1917, les Alliés *remportèrent* la victoire.	Mais finalement, avec l'aide des États-Unis, qui *sont entrés* en guerre en 1917, les Alliés *ont remporté* la victoire.

60. *The compound tenses — Les temps composés*

A compound tense is one which is made up of an auxiliary verb and some part of the main verb. EXAMPLES: he has seen, they will go

In French the principal compound tenses and their composition are as follows:

Compound Past	Passé Composé	present of *avoir* or *être*		past
Pluperfect	Plus-que-parfait	imperfect of *avoir* or *être*		participle
Past Anterior	Passé Antérieur	simple past of *avoir* or *être*	+	of
Future Perfect	Futur Antérieur	future of *avoir* or *être*		main
Past Conditional	Conditionnel Passé	conditional of *avoir* or *être*		verb

61. *The formation of the compound past—La formation du passé composé*

A. The *passé composé* is a tense which consists of the present of an auxiliary verb (*avoir* or *être*) and the past participle of the main verb. EXAMPLES: elle a parlé, nous avons fini, j'ai répondu, elle est entrée, ils sont arrivés.

B. All transitive verbs [1] and many others are conjugated with the auxiliary *avoir* in the *passé composé* and other compound tenses.

j'ai ——	nous avons ——	(where there is a dash, the
tu as ——	vous avez ——	past participle is required)
il a ——	ils ont ——	

C. Most intransitive verbs of motion require *être* as an auxiliary verb.[2]

je suis ——(e)	nous sommes ——(e)s	
tu es ——(e)	vous êtes ——(e)(s)	(where —— is the
il est ——	ils sont ——s	past participle)
elle est ——e	elles sont ——es	

The agreements which are indicated here are discussed in § 77 B.

D. The following verbs are conjugated with *être* in the compound tenses when they are used intransitively: *aller, arriver, descendre,*[3] *devenir, entrer, monter,*[3] *mourir, naître, partir, passer,*[3] *rentrer, rester, retourner, revenir, sortir,*[3] *tomber,* and *venir.*

Le lendemain nous *sommes allés* à la gare.	The next day we *went* to the station.
Nous *sommes montés* dans le train.	We *got into* the train.
Le train *est parti* de la gare à neuf heures dix.	The train *left* the station at ten after nine.
Après une heure de voyage nous *sommes arrivés* à Fontainebleau.	After a trip of one hour we *arrived* at Fontainebleau.

E. All reflexive verbs are conjugated with *être* as auxiliary verb. This applies not only to verbs always used reflexively, such as *se souvenir de* (remember), but to any ordinary verb used reflexively, such as *se parler* (speak to oneself) and *s'aimer* (like oneself).

je me suis ——(e)	nous nous sommes ——(e)s	(where there is a
tu t'es ——(e)	vous vous êtes ——(e)(s)	dash, the past
il s'est ——	ils se sont ——s	participle is re-
elle s'est ——e	elles se sont ——es	quired)

The agreements which are indicated here are discussed in § 77 D.

---

1 Except the reflexive verbs, which are discussed in § 61 E.

2 However, the verbs *marcher* (to walk), *courir* (to run), and some others are conjugated with *avoir.*

3 These verbs are conjugated with *avoir* when used transitively; e.g., Je *suis sorti* de la maison. (I left the house.) J'*ai sorti* mon cahier. (I took out my notebook.) Elle *est passée* par Tours. (She went through Tours.) Elle *a passé* un examen. (She took an examination.) Nous *sommes montés* dans la chambre. (We went up to the room.) Nous *avons monté* l'escalier. (We climbed the stairs.)

Je *me suis couché* vers dix heures du soir.	I *went to bed* about ten o'clock in the evening.
Je *me suis endormi* tout de suite.	I *went to sleep* immediately.
Il *s'est réveillé* vers sept heures.	He *woke up* at about seven o'clock.
Nous *nous sommes levés,* nous *nous sommes habillés.*	We *got up,* we *dressed.*

62. *The word order in the compound past*
La place des mots au passé composé

A. The order of a normal affirmative sentence in the compound past is:

SUBJECT AUXILIARY VERB PAST PARTICIPLE OTHER WORDS

Nous *avons demandé* du cidre.	We asked for some cider.
Pierre *a acheté* un cahier.	Pierre bought a notebook.

B. The order of an interrogative sentence with a pronoun-subject is:

AUXILIARY VERB–PRONOUN-SUBJECT PAST PARTICIPLE OTHER WORDS

Avez-vous *travaillé* cette année?	Did you work this year?
A-t-il *rencontré* Jean Brissaud?	Did he meet John Brissaud?

C. The order of an interrogative sentence with a noun-subject is:

NOUN-SUBJECT AUXILIARY VERB –PRONOUN-SUBJECT PAST PARTICIPLE OTHER WORDS

Les étudiants *ont*-ils *passé* des examens?	Did the students take examinations?
Jean *a*-t-il *parlé* de l'Université de Paris?	Did John speak of the University of Paris?

D. Pronoun objects, which precede the main verb in the present tense, precede the auxiliary verb in compound tenses.

Nous *en avons demandé.*	We asked for *some.*
Pierre *en a acheté.*	Pierre bought *some.*
L'a-t-il *rencontré?*	Did he meet *him?*
Jean *le lui a*-t-il *donné?*	Did John give *it to him?*
Vous *me les avez montrés.*	You showed *them to me.*

E. For negative word-order in the compound tenses, see § 22 D.

63. *The use of the compound past — L'emploi du passé composé*

A. The compound past is commonly used to express a simple completed past action. In English the past tense usually describes the same type of action.

Maurice *a quitté* le lycée à quatre heures.	Maurice *left* the high school at four o'clock.
Nous *avons trouvé* beaucoup de monde au Luxembourg.	We *found* many people in the Luxembourg.

B. The compound past is used in conversation and in non-literary written style, as in letters for instance, to recount successive main actions in a narrative. Each successive main action serves to forward the plot of a narrative.
Note in the following paragraph how the italicized forms of the compound past form a series of successive actions, each one of which contributes to forwarding the narrative.

Un matin Maurice m'*a rencontré* dans la rue. Il m'*a salué* et m'*a demandé* l'heure. J'*ai regardé* ma montre et lui *ai répondu:*

— Il est huit heures moins le quart.

Maurice m'*a invité* à l'accompagner au lycée. J'*ai accepté* et nous *avons marché* jusqu'à son école. Peu après, nous *avons aperçu* le lycée, un grand bâtiment gris, au bout de la rue.

Une fois dans la cour du lycée, Maurice *a retrouvé* plusieurs de ses camarades devant la porte de la classe. Il leur *a dit* bonjour, il m'*a présenté* à son ami Jacques, et nous *avons parlé* de sports jusqu'à l'arrivée du professeur.

C. The compound past sometimes corresponds to the English present perfect tense.

Avez-vous déjà *acheté* un journal?	*Have* you already *bought* a newspaper?
Elles *ont* toujours *parlé* espagnol.	They *have* always *spoken* Spanish.
J'*ai vu* des cours suivis par huit cents étudiants.	I *have seen* courses with eight hundred students.

64. *The formation of the pluperfect — La formation du plus-que-parfait*

A. The pluperfect is a compound tense which is formed as follows:

imperfect of *avoir* or *être*	+	past participle of main verb

It is rendered in English by *had* + the past participle. EXAMPLES: I had spoken, you had left, he had washed himself

B. The pluperfect is conjugated with the same auxiliary verb as the compound past. (Reread § 61 B, C, D, E)

TRANSITIVE VERBS AND MANY OTHERS	INTRANSITIVE VERBS OF MOTION	REFLEXIVE VERBS
j'avais parlé	j'étais parti(e)	je m'étais couché(e)
tu avais parlé	tu étais parti(e)	tu t'étais couché(e)
il avait parlé	il était parti	il s'était couché
nous avions parlé	nous étions parti(e)s	nous nous étions couché(e)s
vous aviez parlé	vous étiez parti(e)(s)	vous vous étiez couché(e)(s)
ils avaient parlé	ils étaient partis	ils s'étaient couchés

65. *The use of the pluperfect — L'emploi du plus-que-parfait*

A. The pluperfect is used to indicate a past action which took place before another past action.

Nous *étions restés* au Louvre presque deux heures et j'*avais vu* beaucoup d'œuvres d'art quand Maurice est venu me chercher.	We *had remained* at the Louvre for almost two hours and I *had seen* many works of art when Maurice came for me.

The pluperfect should not ordinarily be used in a clause introduced by *quand, lorsque, aussitôt que, dès que* or *après que.* (See § 69)

B. The pluperfect is also used with *si* in conditional sentences. (See § 72)

66. *The formation of the future perfect — La formation du futur antérieur*

A. The future perfect is a compound tense which is formed as follows:

future of *avoir* or *être* + past participle of main verb

It is rendered in English by *shall have* or *will have* + **the past participle.**

EXAMPLES: I shall have spoken, you will have left, he will have washed himself, etc.

B. The future perfect is conjugated with the same auxiliary verb as the compound past. (Reread § 61 B, C, D, E)

TRANSITIVE VERBS AND MANY OTHERS	INTRANSITIVE VERBS OF MOTION	REFLEXIVE VERBS
j'aurai parlé	je serai parti(e)	je me serai couché(e)
tu auras parlé	tu seras parti(e)	tu te seras couché(e)
il aura parlé	il sera parti	il se sera couché
nous aurons parlé	nous serons parti(e)s	nous nous serons couché(e)s
vous aurez parlé	vous serez parti(e)(s)	vous vous serez couché(e)(s)
ils auront parlé	ils seront partis	ils se seront couchés

67. *The use of the future perfect — L'emploi du futur antérieur*

A. The French future perfect, like the English, is used to indicate an action which will have taken place when another future action occurs.

They *will have written* the letter when Paul arrives.	Ils *auront écrit* la lettre quand Paul arrivera.

B. The French use the future perfect to express the exact shade of time much more often than English. Often the English-speaking person is content to use the present perfect in a clause where exactness compels the French to use the future perfect.

Quand j'*aurai fini* mes devoirs, je sortirai.	When I *have finished* my exercises, I'll go out.
Dès que mon mari *sera revenu* d'Angleterre, je lui en parlerai.	As soon as my husband *returns* (or *has returned*) from England, I'll speak to him about it.

In these sentences, the italicized verbs describe actions which have not yet taken place but which will take place before the action of the second verb, which is in the future. Therefore, they are put in the future perfect in French.

68. *The formation of the past anterior — La formation du passé antérieur*

A. The past anterior is a compound tense which is formed as follows:

simple past of *avoir* or *être*	+	past participle of main verb

The past anterior does not exist in English, but the French past anterior is translated by the English pluperfect. EXAMPLES: I had spoken, you had left, he had washed himself, etc.

B. The past anterior is conjugated with the same auxiliary verb as the compound past. (Reread § 61 B, C, D, E)

TRANSITIVE VERBS AND MANY OTHERS	INTRANSITIVE VERBS OF MOTION	REFLEXIVE VERBS
j'eus parlé	je fus parti(e)	je me fus couché(e)
tu eus parlé	tu fus parti(e)	tu te fus couché(e)
il eut parlé	il fut parti	il se fut couché
nous eûmes parlé	nous fûmes parti(e)s	nous nous fûmes couché(e)s
vous eûtes parlé	vous fûtes parti(e)(s)	vous vous fûtes couché(e)(s)
ils eurent parlé	ils furent partis	ils se furent couchés

69. *The use of the past anterior — L'emploi du passé antérieur*

A. The past anterior is used in literary style with *quand, lorsque, dès que, aussitôt que* and *après que* to indicate an action which took place immediately before another action when this second action is expressed by the simple past.

Dès qu'il *eut fermé* la porte, sa femme entra.	As soon as he *had closed* the door, his wife entered.
Après que les armées américaines *eurent envahi* l'Allemagne, quelques généraux allemands signèrent la capitulation.	After the American armies *had invaded* Germany, some German generals signed the capitulation.

The French pluperfect cannot be used in these sentences.

B. In non-literary style, a special tense known as the *passé surcomposé* (*passé composé* of *avoir* or *être* + past participle of main verb) is used with *quand, lorsque, dès que, aussitôt que* and *après que* to indicate an action which took place immediately before another action when this second action is expressed by the *passé composé.*

Dès que j'*ai eu fini* mon travail, je suis sorti.	As soon as *I had finished* my work, I left.

70. *The formation of the past conditional*
La formation du conditionnel passé

A. The past conditional is a compound tense which is formed as follows:

conditional of *avoir* or *être* + past participle of main verb

It is rendered in English by *should have* or *would have* + **the past participle.**

EXAMPLES: I should have spoken, you would have left, he would have washed himself, etc.

B. The past conditional is conjugated with the same auxiliary verb as the compound past. (Reread § 61 B, C, D, E)

TRANSITIVE VERBS AND MANY OTHERS	INTRANSITIVE VERBS OF MOTION	REFLEXIVE VERBS
j'aurais parlé	je serais parti(e)	je me serais couché(e)
tu aurais parlé	tu serais parti(e)	tu te serais couché(e)
il aurait parlé	il serait parti	il se serait couché
nous aurions parlé	nous serions parti(e)s	nous nous serions couché(e)s
vous auriez parlé	vous seriez parti(e)(s)	vous vous seriez couché(e)(s)
ils auraient parlé	ils seraient partis	ils se seraient couchés

71. *The use of the past conditional — L'emploi du conditionnel passé*

The past conditional is most frequently used in contrary-to-fact conditions.

Si Napoléon Bonaparte était né un an avant, il *aurait été* Italien.	If Napoleon Bonaparte had been born one year earlier, he *would have been* Italian.
Si Napoléon n'avait pas fait la campagne désastreuse en Russie, il *aurait pu* rester empereur plus longtemps.	If Napoleon had not undertaken the disastrous Russian campaign, he *would have been able* to remain emperor longer.

72. *Conditional sentences — Les phrases conditionnelles*

A. Conditional sentences normally consist of two parts: the condition (*si*-clause) and the conclusion.

Si nous allons à Paris, nous verrons la Tour Eiffel.	If we go to Paris, we shall see the Eiffel Tower.

B. Often French uses the same combination of tenses as English in the parts of the conditional sentences.

CONDITION (*si*-clause)	CONCLUSION
1. present indicative	1. future
2. imperfect indicative	2. conditional
3. pluperfect indicative	3. past conditional

French	*English*
1. *si* + PRESENT — FUTURE Si nous *allons* en France, nous *parlerons* français.	1. *if* + PRESENT — FUTURE If we *go* to France, we *will speak* French.
2. *si* + IMPERFECT — CONDITIONAL Si vous *étiez* en France, vous *parleriez* français.	2. *if* + PAST — CONDITIONAL If you *were* in France, you *would speak* French.
3. *si* + PLUPERFECT — PAST CONDITIONAL Si vous *aviez été* en France, vous *auriez parlé* français.	3. *if* + PLUPERFECT — PAST CONDITIONAL If you *had been* in France, you *would have spoken* French.

C. In any condition of the third type, either the pluperfect or the past conditional or both may be replaced in literary style by the pluperfect subjunctive.

NORMAL STYLE: *literary and spoken*

Si Napoléon *avait gagné* la bataille de Waterloo, toute l'histoire de l'Europe *aurait été* changée.

LITERARY STYLE ONLY

S'il *eût gagné* la bataille de Waterloo, toute l'histoire de l'Europe aurait été changée.
S'il avait gagné la bataille de Waterloo, toute l'histoire de l'Europe *eût été* changée.
S'il *eût gagné* la bataille de Waterloo, toute l'histoire de l'Europe *eût été* changée.

D. Almost any combination used in English conditional sentences may also be used in French except that in French *si* (meaning *if*) may never be followed by the future or the conditional.

Si Roger *a écrit* la lettre, nous la *recevrons.*	If Roger *has written* the letter, we *will receive* it.
S'il *pleut,* nous *restons* à la maison.	If it *rains,* we *stay* in the house.
Si vous *aviez travaillé* hier, vous *seriez* libre aujourd'hui.	If you *had worked* yesterday, you *would be* free today.

but

S'il *arrivait* ce soir, nous ne *serions* pas prêts.	If he *should arrive* this evening, we *would* not *be* ready.

73. *The formation of the present participle*
La formation du participe présent

In English the verbal form ending in *-ing* is called a present participle if it is used partly as a verb, partly as an adjective. EXAMPLE: We found the boys *eating* apples.

A. In French the present participle ends in *-ant.* EXAMPLES: parl*ant* (speak*ing*), dorm*ant* (sleep*ing*)

B. For all verbs, both regular and irregular, the present participle is formed by adding *-ant* to the stem formed by dropping the ending *-ons* from the *nous*-form of the present indicative.

	INFINITIVE	PRESENT INDICATIVE	PRESENT PARTICIPLE	
-er verb	donner	nous donn*ons*	donn*ant*	*giving*
-ir verb I	finir	nous finiss*ons*	finiss*ant*	*finishing*
-ir verb II	dormir	nous dorm*ons*	dorm*ant*	*sleeping*
-re verb	perdre	nous perd*ons*	perd*ant*	*losing*
irregular verbs	pouvoir	nous pouv*ons*	pouv*ant*	*being able*
	prendre	nous pren*ons*	pren*ant*	*taking*
	venir	nous ven*ons*	ven*ant*	*coming*
	voir	nous voy*ons*	voy*ant*	*seeing*
	vouloir	nous voul*ons*	voul*ant*	*wishing*
verbs with spelling changes	commencer	nous commenç*ons*	commenç*ant*	*beginning*
	manger	nous mange*ons*	mange*ant*	*eating*

But there are three exceptions:

avoir	*ayant*	*having*
être	*étant*	*being*
savoir	*sachant*	*knowing*

74. *The use of the present participle—L'emploi du participe présent*

A. The present participle indicates an action which takes place at the same time as the main action of the sentence. It cannot be used without another verb in the same sentence.

Se tournant vers le professeur, Robert lui a dit son nom.	*Turning* toward the teacher, Robert told him his name.
Sortant de la bibliothèque, j'ai rencontré un ami.	Leaving the library, I met a friend.

B. The present participle is often used with *en; en* is the only preposition which is used with the present participle. (See § 78 A.) When *en* is used with the present participle, this construction always refers to the subject of the sentence and expresses an action very closely connected in time with the action of the main verb.

Je l'ai vu *en sortant* de la bibliothèque.	I saw him *while leaving* the library.
On prépare la salade *en* y *mettant* du sel, du poivre, du vinaigre et de l'huile et *en mélangeant* le tout.	One prepares the salad *by putting* salt, pepper, vinegar, and oil in it and *by mixing* the whole.

C. The present participle is invariable when used partly as a verb, partly as an adjective.

Une femme *habitant* Paris . . . A woman *living* in Paris . . .

It agrees with the noun it modifies in gender and number when it is used entirely as an adjective.

une femme *vivante*	a *living* woman
des jeunes filles *charmantes*	*charming* girls

75. *The formation of the past participle*
La formation du participe passé

In English the past participle of regular verbs ends in *-ed.* EXAMPLES: avoided, obtained, erased. The past participles of irregular verbs are often distinguished by a change of stem vowel. EXAMPLES: write, written; buy, bought; sell, sold.

A. Past participles of regular verbs are formed as follows in French:

INFINITIVE	PAST PARTICIPLE	EXAMPLES INFINITIVE	EXAMPLES PAST PARTICIPLE
-er	-é	demander	demandé
-ir	-i	punir	puni
-re	-u	répondre	répondu
-oir	-u	recevoir	reçu

B. Many verbs have an irregular past participle. The most common are listed below.

INFINITIVE	PAST PARTICIPLE	INFINITIVE	PAST PARTICIPLE	INFINITIVE	PAST PARTICIPLE
avoir	eu	faire	fait	*prendre	pris
boire	bu	falloir	fallu	rire	ri
†conduire	conduit	lire	lu	savoir	su
*connaître	connu	*mettre	mis	suivre	suivi
courir	couru	mourir	mort	*tenir	tenu
†craindre	craint	naître	né	valoir	valu
croire	cru	†ouvrir	ouvert	*venir	venu
devoir	dû	plaire	plu	vivre	vécu
dire	dit	pleuvoir	plu	*voir	vu
écrire	écrit	pouvoir	pu	vouloir	voulu
être	été				

† These verbs belong to a family with the same stem, all of which follow the same conjugation pattern.

* These verbs have compounds formed by adding prefixes to the verb. The compounds follow the same conjugation pattern as the simple verb.

76. *The use of the past participle — L'emploi du participe passé*

In English the past participle is used with auxiliary verbs to form the compound tenses.

He *has **walked*** a great deal.	I *have **met*** many students.
We *have **lived*** in many countries.	You *will have **eaten*** at three.
They *had **seen*** their friends.	He *would have **written*** sooner.

A. The French past participle is also used with auxiliary verbs to form compound tenses:

COMPOUND PAST:	il *a **demandé***	he *has **asked***
PLUPERFECT:	vous *aviez **choisi***	you *had **chosen***
FUTURE PERFECT:	j'*aurai **répondu***	I *shall have **answered***
PAST CONDITIONAL:	ils *auraient **reçu***	they *would have **received***
PAST ANTERIOR:	nous *fûmes **venus***	we *had **come***

B. The past participle is frequently used as a pure adjective. In such cases, it agrees with its noun in number and gender and always follows its noun when used attributively.

Paul s'est caché derrière la porte *fermée.*	Paul hid himself behind the *closed* door.
Qui a trouvé les enfants *perdus?*	Who found the *lost* children?

77. *The agreement of the past participle — L'accord du participe passé*

A. *avoir* + PAST PARTICIPLE

When a compound tense is conjugated with a form of *avoir,* the past participle normally is invariable (does not change its form).

avoir + INVARIABLE PAST PARTICIPLE

Maurice *a fini* sa journée au lycée.	Maurice *finished* his day at the lycée.
Nous *avons attendu* ses camarades.	We *waited for* his friends.
Vous *avez continué* votre promenade.	You *continued* your walk.

But when a **direct object** precedes the verb in the compound tense, the past participle agrees in gender and number with the **preceding direct object.**

DIRECT OBJECT + *avoir* + PAST PARTICIPLE WHICH AGREES

Maurice ***les** a finis.*	Maurice *finished **them.***
Voilà les camarades ***que*** nous *avons attendus.*	There are the friends ***whom*** we *awaited.*
Quelle porte *avez*-vous *fermée?*	***Which door*** *did* you *close?*

The pronoun *en* does not have gender and number. Normally, then, the past participle in a compound tense with *avoir* remains unchanged after *en*.

Avez-vous *trouvé des livres?*	Oui, j'*en ai trouvé* à la bibliothèque.

B. Verbs of motion: *être* + PAST PARTICIPLE
The past participles of verbs of motion conjugated with *être* (see § 61 C, D) always agree with the subject of the sentence in gender and number.

SUBJECT + *être* +	PAST PARTICIPLE OF VERB OF MOTION WHICH AGREES WITH SUBJECT
Nous sommes allés à Fontainebleau.	*We went* to Fontainebleau.
Ils sont arrivés à la gare.	*They arrived* at the station.
Elle est entrée dans le château.	*She entered* the château.
Il est retourné à Paris.	*He returned* to Paris.

C. Since *vous* may be masculine or feminine, singular or plural, the past participle may have one of four forms, depending upon what the speaker means by *vous*.

Vous êtes allé à l'école.	You (masculine singular) went to school.
Vous êtes allée à l'école.	You (feminine singular) went to school.
Vous êtes allés à l'école.	You (masculine plural) went to school.
Vous êtes allées à l'école.	You (feminine plural) went to school.

D. Reflexive verbs: REFLEXIVE OBJECT + *être* + PAST PARTICIPLE
The past participle of a reflexive verb usually agrees with the reflexive object.

Marie *s'est couchée* à dix heures.	Mary went to bed at ten o'clock.
Nous *nous sommes salués.*	We greeted each other.
Elles *se sont réveillées.*	They woke up.
Ils *se sont lavés.*	They washed themselves.
Nous *nous sommes souvenus* [1] de la guerre.	We remembered the war.

But if the reflexive object is indirect, then the past participle remains invariable (unchanged).[2]

---

[1] Verbs such as *se souvenir, s'emparer,* etc., are inherently reflexive verbs, that is, they do not exist in the non-reflexive form. Their reflexive object is neither direct nor indirect, but inherent.

[2] The advanced student only should note that when the reflexive object is indirect, the past participle of the verb is invariable unless there is a preceding direct object, in which case the past participle of the reflexive verb agrees with the preceding direct object; e.g., Elle *s'est parlé.* Avez-vous vu la maison qu'ils *se sont achetée?*

Marie *s'est parlé.* — Mary spoke to herself.
Ils *se sont lavé* les mains. — They washed their hands. (Lit., They washed the hands to themselves.)

In other words, the past participle of a reflexive verb agrees with the reflexive object unless the reflexive object is indirect, in which case it remains unchanged.

78. *The infinitive — L'infinitif*

A. The infinitive may be used after *all* prepositions except *en.*

Il est parti *sans* ***parler.*** — He left *without* ***speaking.***
Nous avons téléphoné *au lieu d'****écrire*** une lettre. — We telephoned *instead of* ***writing*** a letter.

English uses a present participle in these cases.

B. With the two time expressions *before —ing* and *after —ing,* special constructions are used.

1. The expression *before —ing* is conveyed in French by the compound preposition *avant de* + **infinitive**

avant de parler	*before speaking*
avant de choisir	*before choosing*
avant d'entrer	*before entering*
avant de se tourner	*before turning*

2. The expression *after —ing* is conveyed in French by the preposition *après* + **compound infinitive**

après avoir parlé	*after speaking*
après avoir choisi	*after choosing*
après être entré	*after entering*
après s'être tourné	*after turning*

3. These expressions are substituted for clauses whenever possible.

Avant de venir en classe, il a préparé sa leçon. — *Before he came* to class, he prepared his lesson.
Il est parti *après avoir vu* le président. — He left *after he had seen* the president.

C. The preposition *pour* (and in literary style *afin de*) is used with the infinitive to denote purpose.

Nous avons acheté une voiture *pour* voir tous les pays d'Europe.	We bought a car (*in order*) *to* see all the countries of Europe.

Purpose is expressed after the verbs *aller* and *venir* and occasionally other verbs of motion with or without *pour.*

Je suis venu *chercher* ma valise.	I came *to get my* suitcase.

When *pour* is used with these verbs, the idea of purpose is more emphatic or the infinitive is separated from the main verb by several words.

Il est venu *pour demander* son argent.	He came (*in order*) *to ask for* his money.
Paul est allé en France cet été *pour apprendre* le français.	Paul went to France this summer *to learn* French.

79. *The imperative — L'impératif*

The imperative is a special form of the verb used to give a command. In English the ordinary imperative is distinguished by the absence of any pronoun subject. EXAMPLES: *Read* the letter. *Wash* the dishes.

A. The commonest imperative in French, which we may call the *vous*-**imperative,** corresponds exactly to the second person plural of the present indicative. Like the English imperative, this French imperative has no pronoun subject. This imperative always ends in *-ez* except for the verbs *dire* and *faire.*

INFINITIVE	2D PERSON PLURAL PRESENT INDICATIVE	IMPERATIVE
demander	vous demandez	demandez
punir	vous punissez	punissez
dormir	vous dormez	dormez
répondre	vous répondez	répondez
dire	vous dites	dites
faire	vous faites	faites

There are four verbs with irregular imperatives which are subjunctive forms.

INFINITIVE	2D PLURAL SUBJUNCTIVE	IMPERATIVE	
être	que vous soyez	soyez	*be*
avoir	que vous ayez	ayez	*have*
savoir	que vous sachiez	sachez	*know*
vouloir	que vous vouliez	veuillez [1]	*be willing*

[1] The form *veuillez* is a remnant of an old subjunctive form.

Note these negative forms:

ne demandez pas	*don't ask*
ne perdez pas	*don't lose*

B. We have a first person plural imperative in English which is: Let us speak; Let us finish; Let us answer. This *let us* **imperative** is expressed in French by the *-ons* (first person plural) present indicative form of the verb. Like the *vous-imperative,* the pronoun subject is not expressed.

INFINITIVE	*nous*-IMPERATIVE	
demander	demandons	*let us ask*
punir	punissons	*let us punish*
dormir	dormons	*let us sleep*
répondre	répondons	*let us answer*
dire	disons	*let us say*
faire	faisons	*let us do*
parler	ne parlons pas	*let us not speak*
choisir	ne choisissons pas	*let us not choose*

There are three verbs with irregular imperatives which are subjunctive forms:

INFINITIVE	1ST PLURAL SUBJUNCTIVE	*nous*-IMPERATIVE	
être	que nous soyons	soyons	*let us be*
avoir	que nous ayons	ayons	*let us have*
savoir	que nous sachions	sachons	*let us know*

C. The French **familiar imperative** corresponds to the second person singular present indicative in all but *-er* verbs. In *-er* verbs, this imperative ends in *-e.*

INFINITIVE	FAMILIAR-IMPERATIVE	
demander	demande	*ask*
punir	punis	*punish*
dormir	dors	*sleep*
répondre	réponds	*answer*
dire	dis	*say*
faire	fais	*do*
parler	ne parle pas	*don't speak*
choisir	ne choisis pas	*don't choose*

There are four verbs with irregular familiar imperatives which are subjunctive forms:

INFINITIVE	2D SINGULAR SUBJUNCTIVE	IMPERATIVE	
être	que tu sois	sois	*be*
avoir	que tu aies	aie	*have*
savoir	que tu saches	sache	*know*

The familiar imperative is used only under conditions explained in § 23 B.

D. In the imperative of reflexive verbs, the reflexive object pronoun follows the verb in the affirmative imperative and precedes it in the negative. (See § 30 A, B.)

INFINITIVE	AFFIRMATIVE	NEGATIVE
se tourner	tourne-toi (*turn*)	ne te tourne pas (*don't turn*)
se promener	promenons-nous (*let's walk*)	ne nous promenons pas (*let's not walk*)
se lever	levez-vous (*get up*)	ne vous levez pas (*don't get up*)

80. *The formation of the present subjunctive*
La formation du présent du subjonctif

A. The present subjunctive may be formed by taking as a stem the third person plural present indicative minus the *-ent* termination and adding the present subjunctive endings:

INFINITIVE	3D PERSON PLURAL PRESENT INDICATIVE	PRESENT SUBJUNCTIVE STEM
donner	ils donnent	donn-
punir	ils punissent	puniss-
dormir	ils dorment	dorm-
répondre	ils répondent	répond-

PRESENT SUBJUNCTIVE ENDINGS

que je ——e	que nous ——ions
tu ——es	vous ——iez
il ——e	ils ——ent

-er VERBS	MOST -ir VERBS	2D CLASS -ir VERBS	-re VERBS
que je donn*e*	que je puniss*e*	que je dorm*e*	que je répond*e*
que tu donn*es*	que tu puniss*es*	que tu dorm*es*	que tu répond*es*
qu'il donn*e*	qu'il puniss*e*	qu'il dorm*e*	qu'il répond*e*
que nous donn*ions*	que nous puniss*ions*	que nous dorm*ions*	que nous répond*ions*
que vous donn*iez*	que vous puniss*iez*	que vous dorm*iez*	que vous répond*iez*
qu'ils donn*ent*	qu'ils puniss*ent*	qu'ils dorm*ent*	qu'ils répond*ent*

B. To form the present subjunctive, most irregular verbs (all except *aller, avoir, être, faire, pouvoir, savoir, valoir* and *vouloir*) use the same stem as regular verbs except in the *nous* and *vous* forms. The *nous* and *vous* forms of the present subjunctive of these verbs are exactly like the *nous* and *vous* forms of the imperfect indicative.

INFINITIVE	3D PERSON PLURAL PRESENT INDICATIVE	PRESENT SUBJUNCTIVE STEM
boire	ils boivent	boiv-
venir	ils viennent	vienn-

que je boive	que je vienne	the *je, tu, il* and *ils* forms have a stem derived from the *ils* form of the present indicative
que tu boives	que tu viennes	
qu'il boive	qu'il vienne	
que nous buvions	**que nous venions**	the **nous** and **vous** forms are exactly like the imperfect indicative
que vous buviez	**que vous veniez**	
qu'ils boivent	qu'ils viennent	

C. Note the present subjunctives of the verbs which do not follow the rule:

	aller	**avoir**	**être**	**faire**	falloir
que	j' aille	j'aie	je sois	je fasse	
	tu ailles	aies	sois	fasses	
	il aille	ait	soit	fasse	faille
	nous allions	ayons	soyons	fassions	
	vous alliez	ayez	soyez	fassiez	
	ils aillent	aient	soient	fassent	

	pouvoir	**savoir**	**valoir**	**vouloir**
que je	puisse	sache	vaille	veuille
tu	puisses	saches	vailles	veuilles
il	puisse	sache	vaille	veuille
nous	puissions	sachions	valions	voulions
vous	puissiez	sachiez	valiez	vouliez
ils	puissent	sachent	vaillent	veuillent

81. *The formation of the imperfect subjunctive*
La formation de l'imparfait du subjonctif

The imperfect subjunctive is regularly formed by adding to the second person singular of the simple past the following endings:

je ——se	nous ——sions
tu ——ses	vous ——siez
il ——^t	ils ——sent

The third person singular places a circumflex accent (^) over the last stem vowel, eliminates the *-s* from the stem, and adds *-t*.

The first form in the paradigms below is the second person singular of the simple past. The following forms constitute the conjugation of the verb in the imperfect subjunctive.

parler	**punir**	**dormir**
tu parlas	*tu punis*	*tu dormis*
je parlasse	je punisse	je dormisse
tu parlasses	tu punisses	tu dormisses
il parlât	il punît	il dormît
nous parlassions	nous punissions	nous dormissions
vous parlassiez	vous punissiez	vous dormissiez
ils parlassent	ils punissent	ils dormissent

perdre	**recevoir**	**venir**
tu perdis	*tu reçus*	*tu vins*
je perdisse	je reçusse	je vinsse
tu perdisses	tu reçusses	tu vinsses
il perdît	il reçût	il vînt
nous perdissions	nous reçussions	nous vinssions
vous perdissiez	vous reçussiez	vous vinssiez
ils perdissent	ils reçussent	ils vinssent

82. *The formation of the compound tenses of the subjunctive*
La formation des temps composés du subjonctif

A. The past subjunctive (passé du subjonctif) is a combination of the present subjunctive of the auxiliary verb with which that verb is usually conjugated and the past participle.

que j'aie parlé	que nous ayons fini	que je sois parti
que tu aies perdu	que vous ayez vu	que tu te sois levé
qu'il ait dormi	qu'ils aient trouvé	que nous nous soyons dépêchés

B. The pluperfect subjunctive (plus-que-parfait du subjonctif) is a combination of the imperfect subjunctive of the auxiliary with which the compound tenses of the verb are conjugated and the past participle.

que j'eusse parlé	que nous eussions fini	que je fusse parti
que tu eusses perdu	que vous eussiez vu	que tu te fusses levé
qu'il eût dormi	qu'ils eussent trouvé	que nous nous fussions dépêchés

83. *The use of the subjunctive — L'emploi du subjonctif*

In French, as in English, the two chief modes are the *indicative* and the *subjunctive.* The indicative deals with objective facts, with reality. The subjunctive suggests hypothetical actions or states which are in the realm of conjecture or it indicates the subjective attitude or feeling of the speaker toward something which might happen, is happening, or has happened.

Consider the **boldface** (indicative) and *italicized* (subjunctive) verb forms in the following English sentences:

Indicative — object fact	Subjunctive — subjective attitude or feeling of speaker toward a possible action or state
He **is** there.	It is important that he *be* there.
He **writes** a letter.	We suggest that he *write* a letter.
He **goes** to school.	They insist that he *go* to school.

Each **boldface** (indicative) verb is in a main clause and states a fact. Each *italicized* (subjunctive) verb is in a dependent clause and indicates the speaker's subjective feeling or attitude toward a possible action or state. The sentences on the right represent a use of the subjunctive which is relatively rare in English but extremely common in French. The French use this type of subjunctive after many more verbs and expressions than does English.

Sections A, B, C, and D are specific cases in which the attitude or feeling of the subject of the main clause toward an action or state, either actual or only contemplated, is expressed by a subjunctive in French. In each of these cases, it is the emphasis on the attitude of the subject of the main clause toward an action rather than the emphasis on the factual nature of the action which prompts the French speaker to use a subjunctive rather than an indicative.

The subjunctive is used specifically, then:

A. after verbs of wishing

Mon père **veut** que je *sois* à la maison à neuf heures.	My father wants[1] me to be at home at nine o'clock.
Je **voudrais** que vous *imaginiez* une conversation entre deux personnes.	I should like[1] to have you imagine a conversation between two persons.

B. after certain impersonal expressions[2] where not a fact[3] but an opinion, attitude or feeling concerning an action or state is expressed; among these expressions are:

---

[1] After verbs of wishing, French uses a *que*-clause. English uses an entirely different construction. To express the correct French construction of these two sentences, one would have to use the awkward English: *My father wants that I be home at nine o'clock. I should like that you imagine a conversation between two persons.*

[2] An impersonal expression is one which is devoid of any mention of persons. It begins with the impersonal *il,* meaning *it.* This *il* refers to nothing which has already been mentioned.

[3] Impersonal expressions which imply a fact are followed by the indicative. Among these are: *il est certain, il est clair, il est évident, il est exact, il est probable, il est sûr, il est vrai.*

il est bon	*it is good*	il est possible	*it is possible*
il est douteux	*it is doubtful*	il est préférable	*it is preferable*
il est étonnant	*it is surprising*	il est peu probable [1]	*it is unlikely*
il est étrange	*it is strange*	il est rare	*it is rare*
il est important	*it is important*	il est temps	*it is time*
il est impossible	*it is impossible*	il faut	*it is necessary*
il est juste	*it is right*	il se peut	*it is possible*
il est naturel	*it is natural*	il semble [2]	*it seems*
il est nécessaire	*it is necessary*	il vaut mieux	*it is better*

Il faut que vous *étudiiez* le subjonctif.	It is necessary that you study the subjunctive.
Il est possible que *j'aille* en France.	It is possible that I may go to France.
Il est bon que vous *sachiez* saluer un ami.	It is good that you know how to greet a friend.

Note in each example how the verb in the subjunctive in the subordinate clause does not express a fact.

C. after verbs of doubting and fearing [3]

Le professeur **doute** que vous *sachiez* votre leçon.	The teacher doubts that you know your lesson.
J'ai **peur** que vous n'en *trouviez* pas facilement.	I am afraid that you won't find any easily.
Nous **craignons** qu'il ne *soit* pas venu.	We fear that he has not come.

D. after verbs and expressions of emotion, such as *regretter* (regret), *être désolé* (regret), *être content* (be glad), *être heureux* (be happy), *s'étonner* (be surprised), *être étonné* (be surprised), and *c'est dommage* (it's too bad)

Je **m'étonne** que cela ne *soit* pas plus facile.	I am surprised that that is not easier.
Nous **sommes contents** que vous *ayez fait* cela.	We are glad that you did that.

[1] But *il est probable* is followed by the indicative.

[2] But *il me semble* is followed by the indicative.

[3] Often in literary French and occasionally in spoken French, *ne* alone is used before subjunctive forms in clauses after verbs of fearing. This *ne* is not negative and must not be translated into English; e.g., Elle **craint** qu'il *n'*ait perdu son livre. She fears that he has lost her book.

C'est dommage que vous ne *puissiez* pas sortir. — It is too bad that you cannot go out.

Note that in each case, although the verb in the dependent clause states a fact, it is not the fact which is important but the attitude of the subject of the main clause toward the fact.

Closely connected with the above uses of the subjunctive to indicate the attitude or feeling of the speaker toward an action is the use of the subjunctive to indicate an action or state which in the mind of the speaker may not exist or have the possibility of existing, or to indicate some doubt in the mind of the speaker concerning the attainment of such an action. Consider the following sentences:

J'ai un chauffeur qui **sait** parler français.

In this sentence *qui sait parler français* refers to a chauffeur who exists. Therefore, the indicative expresses this fact.

Je cherche un chauffeur qui *sache* parler français.

In this sentence *qui sache parler français* refers to a chauffeur who does not yet exist and whose attainability is uncertain. Therefore the subjunctive expresses this as yet non-existent state.

C'est le premier roman qu'il *a écrit.*

This sentence simply states a fact, and the indicative expresses the fact.

Est-ce que c'est la première pièce qu'il *ait écrite?*

Here, there is an element of doubt in the mind of the speaker, who expresses this doubt by the subjunctive.

The subjunctive is used then

E. in relative clauses where there is doubt or denial of the existence or attainability of the antecedent.

Je cherche une jeune fille qui *veuille* bien sortir avec moi. — I am looking for a girl who would be willing to go out with me.

Nous ne connaissons personne qui *puisse* nous accompagner. — We know no one who can accompany us.

F. sometimes, but not always, in clauses introduced by a relative pronoun whose antecedent is modified by the superlative form of an adjective, by *seul, premier* or *dernier.* In such cases, if the speaker is simply stating an objective fact, he uses the indicative. If he is stating a subjective opinion or if some element of doubt is introduced into the clause, then the subjunctive serves to emphasize the subjectivity or the doubt.

C'est la seule chose que vous *avez faite* ce matin.	Est-ce que c'est la seule chose que vous *ayez faite* ce matin?
Here the speaker simply states a fact. He therefore uses the indicative.	Here the speaker introduces an element both of doubt and of subjectivity. The subjunctive brings out these elements of doubt and subjectivity.

G. often, but not always, after **negative** and **interrogative** verbs of thinking and hoping, and in expressions of uncertainty such as *je ne suis pas sûr que . . .*, when the speaker wishes to stress the element of doubt or uncertainty.

Je ne crois pas que Charles *ait fait* cela.	I do not think that Charles did that.
Croyez-vous qu'il *puisse* faire cela?	Do you think that he can do that?
Je ne suis pas sûr que Marie *soit partie.*	I am not sure that Marie has left.

When the element of doubt is not foremost in the speaker's mind, the indicative is often used. When the action is future, the future is almost always used, even after negative and interrogative verbs of believing.

Je ne crois pas qu'il *viendra.*	I do not think that he will come.

On the contrary, **the indicative is *always* used after affirmative forms of verbs of thinking and believing.**

Je pense que le professeur *est* là.	I think that the teacher is there.
Nous croyons que Paul *a écrit* la lettre.	We believe that Paul wrote the letter.

In French, dependent clauses are sometimes introduced by conjunctions which emphasize a given attitude toward the verb of the clause or which indicate the speaker's point of view toward the hypothetical action of the clause. In such cases, the subjective nature of the action is brought out by the use of a subjunctive in French. For instance:

PURPOSE

Je conduirai vite **pour que** vous *arriviez* tout de suite.	I will drive rapidly in order that you may arrive immediately.

CONDITION

Nous ferons le voyage **pourvu que** Michel *conduise* la voiture.	We'll take the trip provided that Michael will drive the car.

CONCESSION

Je partirai **bien que** vous *soyez* encore là.	I'll leave although you may still be there.
Si riche **qu'il** *soit,* il n'est pas heureux.	However rich he may be, he is not happy.
Quoi qu'il *fasse,* nous ne le verrons pas.	Whatever he may do, we'll not see him.

RESTRICTION

Il écrira la lettre **à moins que** vous lui *disiez* de ne pas le faire.	He'll write the letter unless you tell him not to do so.
Je ne le ferai pas **sans que** vous m'*aidiez.*	I'll not do it without your helping me.

ACTIONS DEPENDING ON TIME

Je le ferai **avant que** vous *arriviez.*	I'll do it before you arrive.
Nous travaillerons **jusqu'à ce que** vous *téléphoniez.*	We'll work until you telephone.

Sections H and I take up specific cases in which dependent clauses are introduced by a relative which embodies the above ideas.

The subjunctive is used specifically, then:

H. after certain subordinate conjunctions expressing purpose, condition, concession, restriction, etc. The commonest of these are:

afin que	*in order that*	à condition que	*on the condition that*
pour que	*in order that*	à moins que	*unless*
bien que	*although*	sans que	*without*
quoique	*although*	avant que	*before*
pourvu que	*provided that*	jusqu'à ce que	*until*

Dépêchez-vous **pour que** nous *arrivions* à l'heure.	Hurry so that we may arrive on time.
Faites-le **avant qu'**elle *meure.*	Do it before she dies.

For the use of equivalent expressions with the infinitive, see § 85 D.

I. when an indefinite combines with *que* to introduce a relative clause indicating concession. The principal indefinites are:

qui que	*whoever*	quoi que	*whatever*
quel que	*whoever, whatever*	si . . . que[1]	*however*

[1] si riche que = *however rich that*

Qui que vous *soyez,* vous ne pouvez pas entrer.	Whoever you are, you cannot enter.
Quelle que *soit* sa profession, il gagne peu d'argent.	Whatever his profession may be, he earns little.
Si intelligents **que** *soient* vos élèves, ils ne parlent pas français.	However intelligent your pupils may be, they do not speak French.

The subjunctive is also used:

J. in a third person imperative introduced by *que* and translated *let him, let her,* or *let them;*

Qu'il *se taise!*	Let him keep still!
Qu'elles *viennent* chez moi.	Let them come to my house.

The subjunctive is also used without *que.*

Vive la France!	Long live France!
Soit!	So be it!

K. in literary French, the pluperfect subjunctive is often used in either or both parts of a contrary-to-fact condition. See § 72 C.

L'aide de la France pendant la Révolution fut très importante, et sans ces secours, l'histoire américaine *eût été* différente.	French aid during the Revolution was very important, and without this aid, American history *would have been* different.

84. *The sequence of tenses of the subjunctive*
La concordance des temps du subjonctif

A. The present subjunctive is used in a subordinate clause after the present, future, or conditional tenses in the main clause to relate an action which takes place at the same time or after the action of the main verb.

Je *suis* content (I am glad)
Je *serai* content (I shall be glad) que vous ***veniez*** (that you are coming).
Je *serais* content (I should be glad)

B. The past subjunctive is used in the subordinate clause after the present, future, or conditional tenses in the main clause to relate an action which has gone on before the action of the main verb.

Je *suis* content (I am glad)
Je *serai* content (I shall be glad) que ***vous soyez venu*** (that you came).
Je *serais* content (I should be glad)

C. The imperfect subjunctive is used in literary style after any past tense or the conditional to relate an action which took place at the same time or after the action of the main verb. In conversation, the imperfect subjunctive is replaced by the present subjunctive.[1]

J'*étais* content	(I was glad)	
Je *fus* content	(I was glad)	
J'*ai été* content	(I was glad)	que vous ***vinssiez*** (that you came).
J'*avais été* content	(I had been glad)	
Je *serais* content	(I should be glad)	
J'*aurais été* content	(I should have been glad)	

D. The pluperfect of the subjunctive is used in literary language after any past tense or the conditional in the main clause to express an action which had gone on before the action of the main verb. In conversation, the pluperfect subjunctive is replaced by the past subjunctive.[1]

J'*étais* content	(I was glad)	
Je *fus* content	(I was glad)	
J'*ai été* content	(I was glad)	que vous ***fussiez venu***
J'*avais été* content	(I had been glad)	(that you had come).
Je *serais* content	(I should be glad)	
J'*aurais été* content	(I should have been glad)	

E. The sequence of tenses of the subjunctive in spoken and written non-literary French may be outlined as follows:

MAIN CLAUSE (in indicative)		SUBORDINATE CLAUSE (in subjunctive)	
ANY TENSE	*que*	PRESENT	if the action of the subordinate clause occurs at the same time as or after that of the main clause
	que	PAST	if the action of the subordinate clause occurred before that of the main clause

F. The sequence of the subjunctive in literary French may be outlined as follows:

[1] The French dislike the imperfect subjunctive forms in *-ss-*. They avoid the subjunctive as much as possible by using the infinitive (§ 85) where feasible, and otherwise use the present and past subjunctive. The third person singular of the imperfect and pluperfect subjunctives are found more frequently than the other forms.

MAIN CLAUSE (in indicative)	SUBORDINATE CLAUSE (in subjunctive)		
PRESENT FUTURE CONDITIONAL	*que*	PRESENT	if the action of the subordinate clause occurs at the same time as or after that of the main clause
	que	PAST	if the action of the subordinate clause occurred before that of the main verb
ALL PAST TENSES CONDITIONAL	*que*	IMPERFECT	if the action of the subordinate clause occurred at the same time or after that of the main clause
	que	PLUPERFECT	if the action of the subordinate clause occurred before that of the main verb

85. *The use of the infinitive instead of the subjunctive*
L'emploi de l'infinitif au lieu du subjonctif

A. The subjunctive is used after expressions and constructions which require it *only* when the subject of the dependent clause is not the same as the subject of the main clause.[1]

Je suis content que *Paul* soit ici.	*I* am glad that *Paul* is here.
Il craint que *vous* ne sachiez pas la leçon.	*He* is afraid that *you* do not know the lesson.
Nous regrettons qu'*elle* ait vu le médecin.	*We* are sorry that *she* saw the doctor.
Je veux que *vous* fassiez ce travail.	*I* want *you* to do this work.

B. The infinitive must be used instead of a dependent clause with the subjunctive when the subject of the main clause would also be the subject of the dependent clause if the subjunctive construction were used. Study the following examples, comparing both the French and English versions with those above.[1]

[1] In a few cases, such as in sentences with *bien que, quoique, pourvu que,* and *jusqu'à ce que,* it is impossible to replace a clause in the subjunctive by an infinitive construction even when the subject of the main clause and that of the dependent clause would be the same, since there is no prepositional construction which corresponds to the subordinate conjunctions. In these few special cases only, the subjunctive may be used even when the subject of the main clause and

Je suis content d'être ici.	*I* am glad that *I* am here.
Il craint de ne pas savoir la leçon.	*He* is afraid that *he* does not know the lesson.
Nous regrettons d'avoir vu le médecin.	*We* are sorry that *we* saw the doctor.
Je veux faire ce travail.	*I* want to do this work.

Verbs of emotion and most impersonal expressions are followed by *de* + infinitive, but verbs of wishing are followed directly by an infinitive without any preposition.

C. Applying the above principles in reverse, the subjunctive must be used instead of the infinitive if there are different subjects in the main and in the dependent clause. Study the following pairs of examples to understand when the infinitive and when the subjunctive is used.

Je voudrais *savoir* le français.	I should like to know French.
Je voudrais que **vous** *sachiez* le français.	I should like to have you know French.
Il est possible d'*écrire* cette lettre.	It is possible to write that letter.
Il est possible que **nous** *écrivions* cette lettre.	It is possible that we shall write that letter.
Nous craignons de *traverser* la mer.	We are afraid to cross the sea.
Nous craignons que **vous** *traversiez* la mer.	We are afraid that you will cross the sea.
Elle est contente d'*avoir trouvé* sa clé.	She is glad that she found her key.
Elle est contente qu'**ils** *aient trouvé* leur clé.	She is glad that they found their key.

D. Many conjunctions which are followed by the subjunctive (§ 83 H) have corresponding prepositions which are followed by the infinitive in cases where the subjunctive must be avoided because the subject of the dependent clause would be the same as the subject of the main clause.[1]

CONJUNCTION FOLLOWED BY SUBJUNCTIVE	PREPOSITION FOLLOWED BY INFINITIVE
afin que	afin de
pour que	pour
à moins que	à moins de
avant que	avant de
sans que	sans

that of the dependent clause are the same. EXAMPLES: *Je* resterai ici *jusqu'à ce que je finisse* ce travail. *Bien que Jacques soit* très occupé, *il* aura le temps de vous accompagner à la gare. *Nous* viendrons *pourvu que nous puissions* voir le président.

[1] See footnote 1 on page 466.

Compare the following pairs of examples:

J'ai acheté une voiture pour que **ma mère** *puisse* voyager.	I bought a car in order that my mother might be able to travel.
J'ai acheté une voiture pour *pouvoir* voyager.	I bought a car in order to be able to travel. (i.e., in order that I may be able . . .)
Je vous écrirai avant que **ma mère** *parte.*	I'll write you before my mother leaves.
Je vous écrirai avant de *partir.*	I'll write you before leaving (i.e., before I leave).
Je ne peux pas faire cela sans que **Paul** *soit* à Paris.	I cannot do that without Paul's being in Paris.
Je ne peux pas faire cela sans *être* à Paris.	I cannot do that without being in Paris.

86. *The formation of the passive voice — La formation de la voix passive*

A sentence in the active voice is one in which the subject is acting; a sentence in the passive voice is one in which the subject is acted upon. In English the passive voice is composed of some form of the auxiliary verb *be* and the **past participle.**

ACTIVE	PASSIVE
The thief *kills* the man.	The man *is killed* by the thief.
The boy *wrote* that letter.	That letter *was written* by the boy.

A. The French verb is made passive exactly as the English verb, that is, by a form of the verb *être* and the **past participle.**

L'état *est gouverné* par le gouverneur.	The state *is governed* by the governor.
Le président *sera choisi* demain.	The president *will be chosen* tomorrow.
La maison *a été vendue.*	The house *has been sold.*

B. The tenses of the passive correspond to the tenses of the verb *être* used:

PRESENT	elle est choisie	she is chosen
IMPERFECT	elle était choisie	she was chosen
COMPOUND PAST	elle a été choisie	she was chosen
PASSÉ SIMPLE	elle fut choisie	she was chosen
FUTURE	elle sera choisie	she will be chosen
CONDITIONAL	elle serait choisie	she would be chosen
PLUPERFECT	elle avait été choisie	she had been chosen
FUTURE PERFECT	elle aura été choisie	she will have been chosen
PAST CONDITIONAL	elle aurait été choisie	she would have been chosen

PRESENT SUBJUNCTIVE	qu'elle soit choisie	that she be chosen
IMPERFECT SUBJUNCTIVE	qu'elle fût choisie	that she were chosen
PAST SUBJUNCTIVE	qu'elle ait été choisie	that she has been chosen
PLUPERFECT SUBJUNCTIVE	qu'elle eût été choisie	that she had been chosen

C. The past participle of the passive voice agrees with the subject of the sentence in gender and number, because it is essentially an adjective.

Elle est *nommée* par le président.	She is named by the president.

87. *The use of the passive voice — L'emploi de la voix passive*

A. French and English both use the passive voice in sentences where the subject is acted upon rather than acting.

Le pays *est attaqué* par l'ennemi.	The country *is attacked* by the enemy.
La cathédrale *a été commencée* au treizième siècle.	The cathedral *was begun* in the thirteenth century.

B. French does not use the passive voice as frequently as English. There are many cases where it would be awkward to use the passive voice in French. The two principal means of avoiding the passive voice are:

1. by the use of the indefinite pronoun *on* (see § 40);

On appelle la Touraine le jardin de la France.	Touraine is called the garden of France.
On parle anglais ici.	English is spoken here.

2. by using the reflexive form of the verb.

La France *se compose* de plaines et de montagnes.	France *is composed* of plains and mountains.
Ça ne *se fait* pas ici.	That *is*n't *done* here.

Often the French use the *se* reflexive forms of the verb to express an English passive when the action in question is general, whereas a real passive is normally used when the action is specific. Compare the types of action indicated in the following sentences.

Ce livre *se vend* partout.	This book *is sold* everywhere.
Ce livre *a été* vendu hier.	This book *was sold* yesterday.

C. After the passive voice the preposition *par* is used to indicate the agent acting upon the subject if the action is real.

Le préfet est recommandé *par* le Ministre de l'Intérieur.	The prefect is recommended *by* the Minister of the Interior.

If the action is only apparent and indicates rather a condition or state, the preposition *de* is often used instead of *par* to indicate the agent.

Jeanne d'Arc était aimée *du* peuple.	Joan of Arc was loved *by* the people.

III. *Special types of verbs*
Des catégories spéciales de verbes

88. *The reflexive verb — Le verbe pronominal*

Reflexive verbs are those whose subject acts upon itself. English reflexive verbs have reflexive objects ending in *-self* which refer to the subject. Reflexive objects may be direct or indirect. EXAMPLES: I see myself; he killed himself; she will speak to herself.

Any verb which is capable of having an object and whose meaning permits may be made reflexive by the addition of the reflexive pronoun object.

ORDINARY VERB	REFLEXIVE VERB
he washes	he washes himself
I cut	I cut myself
she speaks	she speaks to herself

A reflexive verb is conjugated: I wash myself, you wash yourself, he washes himself, etc. The reflexive object must correspond to the subject. One would not say: *I wash himself.*

A. In French, any verb which is capable of having an object and whose meaning permits becomes reflexive when it is used with a reflexive pronoun (see § 26 A).

ORDINARY VERB	REFLEXIVE VERB
je lave	je me lave
il coupe	il se coupe
elle parle	elle se parle

B. Reflexive verbs are used far more frequently in French than in English. French reflexive verbs fall into several classes in relation to their non-reflexive English equivalents.

1. Some verbs which have a reflexive connotation in both French and English are used with or without a reflexive pronoun in English but are reflexive in French. One may say equally well in English: *we dress* or *we dress ourselves,* and *I shave* or *I shave myself.* In French these ideas are expressed by reflexive forms of verbs and cannot be expressed by the simple non-reflexive form of the verb. For instance, *nous habillons* and *je rase* are incomplete in French. One must say: *nous*

nous habillons and *je me rase.* If one said only: *Je rase,* the Frenchman would ask: *Qui rasez-vous?* (Whom are you shaving?).

2. Certain reflexive verbs whose ordinary English equivalent is non-reflexive betray their reflexive nature when they are translated literally.

FRENCH VERB	LITERAL TRANSLATION	USUAL ENGLISH EQUIVALENT
il se couche	*he puts himself to bed*	*he goes to bed*
je me promène	*I take myself walking*	*I take a walk*
nous nous levons	*we raise ourselves*	*we get up*
le fleuve se jette	*the river throws itself*	*the river empties*

3. Some verbs have no non-reflexive form in French; they are always found in a reflexive form. Such verbs are called inherently reflexive verbs. Their English equivalent is usually non-reflexive.

je me souviens	*I remember*
il s'empare	*he seizes*

C. In French, as in English, the reflexive object of a reflexive verb must correspond with the subject of the verb.

je me lave	nous nous lavons
tu te laves	vous vous lavez
il se lave	ils se lavent

One cannot say: *je se lave,* which would mean: *I wash himself.*

D. The French reflexive verb is conjugated in the simple tenses like the non-reflexive verb, but in addition it has a reflexive object, which usually immediately precedes its verb.[1] In the compound tenses, the reflexive verb is conjugated with the auxiliary *être.*

1. See § 95 (7) for the complete conjugation of the model reflexive verb *se laver.*
2. See § 61 E for the discussion of the formation of the passé composé of a reflexive verb.
3. See § 77 D for the agreement of the past participle of a reflexive verb.

E. In French, reflexive verbs often express an action or state which would be rendered by the passive voice in English. This is especially true when the

[1] The reflexive object follows the verb in the affirmative imperative. See § 30 for the position of object pronouns.

se form of the reflexive is used and when the verb states a general fact or condition rather than one limited to a specific instance or time.

Les plaines *se trouvent* à l'intérieur de la France.	The plains *are located* in the interior of France.
La France *se compose* de plusieurs régions historiques.	France *is composed* of several historical regions.
Ces régions historiques *s'appellent* des provinces.	These historical regions *are called* provinces.

For further discussion of the reflexive used for an English passive, see § 87 B 2.

89. *The orthographical changing verbs*
Les verbes à alternance du radical

A. Since *c* is pronounced like *s* only before *e* and *i* and like *k* before *a, o,* and *u,*[1] verbs whose infinitives end in *-cer* change *c* to *ç* when the *c* is followed by *a, o,* or *u,* in order to preserve the *s* sound of the *c.* Changes are made then in the tenses below and in the imperfect subjunctive. EXAMPLE: *effacer.*

PRESENT PARTICIPLE	PRESENT INDICATIVE	IMPERFECT INDICATIVE	SIMPLE PAST
effaçant	j'efface	j'effaçais	j'effaçai
	tu effaces	tu effaçais	tu effaças
	il efface	il effaçait	il effaça
	nous effaçons	nous effacions	nous effaçâmes
	vous effacez	vous effaciez	vous effaçâtes
	ils effacent	ils effaçaient	ils effacèrent

B. Since *g* is pronounced like *g* in *get* before *a, o,* and *u,* and like *s* in *pleasure* before *e* and *i,*[1] verbs whose infinitives end in *-ger* insert *e* between *g* and the next vowel whenever that vowel is not *e* or *i.* Changes are made then, in the tenses below and in the imperfect subjunctive. EXAMPLE: *changer.*

PRESENT PARTICIPLE	PRESENT INDICATIVE	IMPERFECT INDICATIVE	SIMPLE PAST
changeant	je change	je changeais	je changeai
	tu changes	tu changeais	tu changeas
	il change	il changeait	il changea
	nous changeons	nous changions	nous changeâmes
	vous changez	vous changiez	vous changeâtes
	ils changent	ils changeaient	ils changèrent

[1] See page 528.

C. Verbs in *-yer* (*-ayer*,[1] *-oyer*, *-uyer*) change *y* to *i* before a mute *e* in the following syllable. This change occurs throughout the present except for the *nous* and *vous* forms and throughout the entire future and conditional. EXAMPLE: *nettoyer.*

PRESENT INDICATIVE	PRESENT SUBJUNCTIVE	FUTURE	CONDITIONAL
je nettoie	que je nettoie	je nettoierai	je nettoierais
tu nettoies	que tu nettoies	tu nettoieras	tu nettoierais
il nettoie	qu'il nettoie	il nettoiera	il nettoierait
nous nettoyons	que nous nettoyions	nous nettoierons	nous nettoierions
vous nettoyez	que vous nettoyiez	vous nettoierez	vous nettoieriez
ils nettoient	qu'ils nettoient	ils nettoieront	ils nettoieraient

D. Many verbs, such as *mener, lever,* and *acheter,* whose stems end in unaccented *e* plus a single consonant, place a grave accent (`) over this *e* whenever the following syllable also has a mute *e.* This indicates that the pronunciation of the *e* [ə] of the stem becomes *è* [ɛ]. The grave accent is found throughout the singular and in the third person plural of the present indicative and subjunctive and throughout the entire future and conditional of all these verbs. EXAMPLE: *mener.*

PRESENT INDICATIVE	PRESENT SUBJUNCTIVE	FUTURE	CONDITIONAL
je mène	que je mène	je mènerai	je mènerais
tu mènes	que tu mènes	tu mèneras	tu mènerais
il mène	qu'il mène	il mènera	il mènerait
nous menons	que nous menions	nous mènerons	nous mènerions
vous menez	que vous meniez	vous mènerez	vous mèneriez
ils mènent	qu'ils mènent	ils mèneront	ils mèneraient

E. Verbs whose stems end in *é* followed by a single consonant change this *é* to *è* throughout the singular and in the third person plural of the present indicative and present subjunctive.
In the future and conditional, the *é* is retained in writing, but this *é* is usually pronounced *è* because a vowel tends to open in a closed syllable.[2]
EXAMPLE: *espérer*

---

[1] See Bruneau et Heulluy, *Grammaire Française et Exercices, Classe de 4e,* (1937), Sec. 533.

[2] The fact that the mute *e* of the infinitive drops out in pronunciation closes the preceding syllable, thus tending to open the *e;* e.g., j'espérerai [ʒɛspɛrre]; il espérerait [ilɛpɛrrɛ]; tu céderas [tysɛdra].

PRESENT INDICATIVE	PRESENT SUBJUNCTIVE	FUTURE	CONDITIONAL
j'espère	j'espère	j'espérerai	j'espérerais
tu espères	tu espères	tu espéreras	tu espérerais
il espère	il espère	il espérera	il espérerait
nous espérons	nous espérions	nous espérerons	nous espérerions
vous espérez	vous espériez	vous espérerez	vous espéreriez
ils espèrent	ils espèrent	ils espéreront	ils espéreraient

F. Verbs in *-eler* and a few verbs in *-eter* double the *l* or *t* when the next syllable contains a mute *e.* This change takes place in the singular and third person plural of the present indicative and of the present subjunctive and throughout the future and conditional. EXAMPLE: appeler.

PRESENT INDICATIVE	PRESENT SUBJUNCTIVE	FUTURE	CONDITIONAL
j'appelle	que j'appelle	j'appellerai	j'appellerais
tu appelles	que tu appelles	tu appelleras	tu appellerais
il appelle	qu'il appelle	il appellera	il appellerait
nous appelons	que nous appelions	nous appellerons	nous appellerions
vous appelez	que vous appeliez	vous appellerez	vous appelleriez
ils appellent	qu'ils appellent	ils appelleront	ils appelleraient

IV. *The uses of certain verbs*
La façon d'employer certains verbes

90. *Some uses of the verb* avoir
Certaines façons d'employer le verbe avoir

A. Age is expressed in French with the verb *avoir.*

Quel âge *avez*-vous?	How old are you?
Marie *a* seize ans.	Mary is sixteen (years old).

B. The verb *avoir* is used in many idiomatic expressions in which the subject is a person:

Elle *a beau* parler; elle ne peut rien faire.	She *speaks in vain;* she cannot do anything.
Nous *avons besoin* d'argent.	We *need* money.
Avez-vous *chaud?*	*Are* you *warm?*
Il *avait envie* de sortir.	He *felt like* going out.
J'*ai mal* à la tête.	I have a headache.
Vous *aurez mal* aux pieds.	Your feet will hurt.
Il *a mal* à la gorge.	He has a sore throat.
Ils *ont eu soif.*	They *were thirsty.*

The most common expressions containing *avoir* and used with a person as the subject are:

avoir beau + *infinitive*	*do something in vain*
avoir besoin (de)	*need*
avoir chaud	*be hot*
avoir envie (de)	*feel like*
avoir faim	*be hungry*
avoir froid	*be cold*
avoir honte	*be ashamed*
avoir mal	*have a pain, hurt*
avoir peur (de)	*be afraid*
avoir raison	*be right*
avoir soif	*be thirsty*
avoir sommeil	*be sleepy*
avoir tort	*be wrong*

91. *Il y a, voici, voilà*

A. The expression *il y a* (there is, there are) indicates the existence of something.

Il y a une cathédrale à Tours.	*There is* a cathedral at Tours.
Il y a des voitures dans la rue.	*There are* cars in the street.

It has only one form in each tense, but it is used with both singular and plural nouns. Note its forms in other tenses:

IMPERFECT	il y avait	*there was, there were*
COMPOUND PAST	il y a eu	*there was, there were*
FUTURE	il y aura	*there will be*
CONDITIONAL	il y aurait	*there would be*
SIMPLE PAST	il y eut	*there was, there were*
PLUPERFECT	il y avait eu, etc.	*there had been*

In the combination of *il y a* + an expression of time, *il y a* means *ago.*

Il y a trois ans nous sommes allés en Suisse.	*Three years ago* we went to Switzerland.

B. *Voici*[1] (here is, here are) and *voilà*[2] (there is, there are) point out objects. *Voici* indicates objects nearer the speaker; *voilà* points out more dis-

[1] *Voici* is made up of *vois* and *ici* (see here).
[2] *Voilà* is made up of *vois* and *là* (see there).

tant objects. These words include the verb, which should not be expressed a second time. *Voici* and *voilà* are both singular and plural.

Voici la carte de France.	*Here is* the map of France.
Voilà mon livre.	*There is* my book.

C. Direct object pronouns are placed directly before *voici* and *voilà.*

Voici *mon livre.*	Here is *my book.*
Le voici.	Here *it* is.
Voilà *les journaux.*	There are *the newspapers.*
Les voilà.	There *they* are.
Voilà *du papier.*	There is *some paper.*
En voilà.	There is *some.*

92. *Some uses of the verb* faire
Certaines façons d'employer le verbe faire

A. The causative construction (*to have something done*) is expressed in French by a combination of the verb *faire* and the infinitive.[1]

Il *fait construire* une maison.	He *has* a house *built.*
L'empereur *fit embellir* Paris.	The emperor *had* Paris *beautified.*

B. The verb *faire* is used with the impersonal subject *il* to indicate the condition of the weather in expressions such as:

il fait froid	*it is cold*
il fait chaud	*it is warm*
il fait frais	*it is cool*
il fait doux	*it is mild*
il fait beau (temps)	*it is good weather*
il fait mauvais temps	*it is bad weather*
il fait du vent	*it is windy*
il fait sec	*it is dry*
Quel temps fait-il?	*What kind of weather is it?*
il fait jour	*it is day*
il fait nuit	*it is night*

93. *The various meanings of the verb* devoir
Les divers sens du verbe devoir

A. With a noun or pronoun object, the verb devoir means *owe.*

Je lui dois de l'argent.	I owe him some money.

[1] When the causative construction has only one object, it is always a direct object. When there are two objects (a person and a thing), the thing is the direct object, the person the indirect object; e.g., La vendeuse fait respirer *le parfum à madame Bonneville.* The saleswoman has *Mrs. Bonneville* smell *the perfume.*

B. When followed by an infinitive, *devoir* must be translated in various ways, depending on the context and the tense in which it is used. In the present and past tenses, *devoir* has the meanings of *am to* and *must.* But when translating *devoir, must* itself has two entirely different connotations. For example:

He must work.	=	He *has to* work. He *probably* works.

C. In the following translations of *devoir* by tenses, meanings overlap because of the double connotation of *must* in English.

PRESENT	ils doivent partir	*they are to leave* *they must leave* *they have to leave* *they probably leave*
IMPERFECT	ils devaient partir	*they were to leave* *they had to leave* *they probably used to leave* *they must have left*
COMPOUND PAST SIMPLE PAST	ils ont dû partir ils durent partir	*they had to leave* *they must have left* *they probably left*
FUTURE	ils devront partir	*they will have to leave*
CONDITIONAL	ils devraient partir	*they should leave* *they ought to leave*
PAST CONDITIONAL	ils auraient dû partir	*they should have left* *they ought to have left*

D. The English word *must* is expressed by both the present of *devoir* and by the impersonal expression *il faut:*

you must work	vous devez travailler il faut que vous travailliez

But *il faut que vous travailliez* is much stronger than *vous devez travailler,* which is only slightly stronger than *you should work.*

E. The English *should,* denoting obligation, is expressed by the conditional of *devoir.*

We *should go* to France.	Nous *devrions aller* en France.
I *should write* a letter.	Je *devrais écrire* une lettre.

94. *Verbs with several meanings — Verbes à plusieurs sens*

Certain English verbs are expressed by two or more different French verbs, depending on the specific meaning of the English verb. In order to speak and write French correctly, it is very important to use the proper French equivalent of the English verb.

The following are the verbs which cause the greatest difficulty to the English-speaking person.

KNOW

connaître	be acquainted with a person or thing	Je *connais* plusieurs étudiants français.
	be familiar with	Nous *connaissons* bien les romans de Balzac. *Connaissez*-vous Paris?
	meet	Où *avez*-vous *connu* cette jeune fille?
savoir	know from memory	Je *sais* ce poème (par cœur).
	know through study	Cet élève *sait* sa leçon.
	be aware of	Charles *sait* où se trouve Fontainebleau.
	know how to	Andrée *sait* conduire la voiture.

LEAVE

laisser	leave something or someone behind somewhere (always followed by a direct object)	J'*ai laissé* mon stylo sur la table. Il *a laissé* son ami devant le magasin.
quitter	leave a person or place (always followed by a direct object)	Nous *avons quitté* nos amis. Jean *a quitté* le lycée à quatre heures.
s'en aller	go away, go off (never followed by a place)	Je *m'en vais.* Il *s'en ira* tout de suite.

partir	go away	Louise *est partie* ce matin.
	leave (from) a place (always followed by *de* + place)	Je *pars* de Paris tout de suite.
	leave (for) (followed by *pour, à, en* + place)	Il *est parti* pour la France.[1] Il *est parti* en France.
sortir	go out (in general)	Je *suis sorti* hier soir.
	go out with someone	Il *est sorti* avec Marie.
	go out of a place (always followed by *de* + place)	Il *est sorti* de la maison.
	LIVE	
demeurer[2]	dwell in a place	La concierge *demeure* dans sa loge.
habiter	inhabit a place, live in a place (either with direct object or preposition + place)[3]	Nous *habitons* Paris. Nous *habitons* à Paris.
vivre	exist	Il *vit* de ses rentes. Il *a vécu* au dix-neuvième siècle.
	MARRY	
épouser	marry someone (always with direct object)	Roger *a épousé* Geneviève.
marier	marry someone to someone	M. Dupont *a marié* sa fille à un médecin.

[1] Both *Il est parti pour la France* and *Il est parti en France* are commonly heard in French.

[2] At present, the verb *demeurer,* which also means *remain,* is used relatively infrequently with the sense of *live.* It is preferable to use *habiter.*

[3] Although purists prefer to use *habiter* with a direct object, the use of a preposition of place after *habiter* is very common.

se marier	get married (without an object)	Charles et Andrée *se sont mariés* au mois de décembre.
	marry someone (always followed by *avec* + person)	Roger *s'est marié avec* Geneviève.
	MEET	
faire la connaissance de[1]	make the acquaintance of	Nous *avons fait la connaissance de* madame Chevalier.
rencontrer	meet (by chance)	Ah! ce matin *j'ai rencontré* votre sœur dans la rue.
retrouver	meet (by appointment)	Je vous *retrouverai* devant le cinéma.
se réunir	meet (gather together)	Les élèves *se réunissent* dans la cour.
	MUST	
devoir	am to (not strong), have to	Demain je *dois* parler avec votre père.
	must (probably does)	Cet étudiant sait tout. Il *doit* étudier tout le temps!
falloir	must, have to (strong necessity)	*Il faut que* j'aille au laboratoire.
être obligé de	must (be obliged to)	Je *suis obligé* de partir.
	RETURN	
rendre	give back	Maurice m'*a rendu* ce livre.
rentrer	return home	Je *suis rentré* très tard hier soir.
retourner	go back	Il *retournera* à sa ville natale.
revenir	come back	Jacques est parti ce matin, mais il *reviendra* demain.
	SPEND	
dépenser	spend money	Charles *a dépensé* tout son argent.
passer	spend time	Nous *avons passé* deux jours à la campagne.

[1] It is also possible to use *faire connaissance avec*.

	TAKE	
prendre	seize, take in one's hand (always a thing)	*Avez*-vous *pris* mon stylo?
porter[1]	carry something to a person or place	Je vais *porter* votre valise à la gare. Françoise *a porté* ce livre à un voisin.
emporter	carry off (something)	Jacques *a emporté* notre ventilateur.
mener	take a person (destination must be indicated)	Paul *a mené* Louise au cinéma.
emmener	take a person away	Paul *a emmené* Louise. Paul *a emmené* Louise au cinéma.
mettre	take time	J'*ai mis* cinq jours à traverser l'Atlantique.
faire	take (in many idiomatic expressions)	Nous *avons fait* un voyage. Nous *avons fait* une promenade.
passer	take (an examination)	Je *passe* mon examen demain.
suivre	take (a course)	Robert *suit* un cours d'histoire.
s'abonner	take, subscribe to (followed by *à*)	Je *m'abonne* à ce journal.
	VISIT	
aller voir[2]	go to see a person (a casual visit)	Je *suis allé voir* M. Ledoux.
faire une visite à	visit a person (more formal)	J'*ai fait une visite à* M. Ledoux.
rendre visite à	visit a person (more formal)	J'*ai rendu visite à* M. Ledoux.
visiter	visit a place (only)	Nous *avons visité* Paris.

[1] Some Frenchmen also use *apporter* in the sense of *take.* It usually is used in the sense of *bring;* e.g., *Apportez*-moi votre livre.

[2] The important details to note are: (1) the verb *visiter* is used only with places, never with persons; (2) the commonest way of expressing the idea of visiting a person is by *aller voir.*

95. *The conjugation of the verb*

INFINITIVE AND PARTICIPLES	INDICATIVE			
	PRESENT	IMPERFECT	SIMPLE PAST	FUTURE
1. *-er* verbs parler (*speak*) parlant parlé	parle parles parle parlons parlez parlent	parlais parlais parlait parlions parliez parlaient	parlai parlas parla parlâmes parlâtes parlèrent	parlerai parleras parlera parlerons parlerez parleront
	COMPOUND PAST	PLUPERFECT	PAST ANTERIOR	FUTURE PERFECT
	ai parlé as parlé a parlé avons parlé avez parlé ont parlé	avais parlé avais parlé avait parlé avions parlé aviez parlé avaient parlé	eus parlé eus parlé eut parlé eûmes parlé eûtes parlé eurent parlé	aurai parlé auras parlé aura parlé aurons parlé aurez parlé auront parlé
	PRESENT	IMPERFECT	SIMPLE PAST	FUTURE
2. *-ir* verbs finir (*finish*) finissant fini	finis finis finit finissons finissez finissent	finissais finissais finissait finissions finissiez finissaient	finis finis finit finîmes finîtes finirent	finirai finiras finira finirons finirez finiront
	COMPOUND PAST	PLUPERFECT	PAST ANTERIOR	FUTURE PERFECT
	ai fini as fini a fini avons fini avez fini ont fini	avais fini avais fini avait fini avions fini aviez fini avaient fini	eus fini eus fini eut fini eûmes fini eûtes fini eurent fini	aurai fini auras fini aura fini aurons fini aurez fini auront fini
	PRESENT	IMPERFECT	SIMPLE PAST	FUTURE
3. *-re* verbs perdre (*lose*) perdant perdu	perds perds perd perdons perdez perdent	perdais perdais perdait perdions perdiez perdaient	perdis perdis perdit perdîmes perdîtes perdirent	perdrai perdras perdra perdrons perdrez perdront
	COMPOUND PAST	PLUPERFECT	PAST ANTERIOR	FUTURE PERFECT
	ai perdu as perdu a perdu avons perdu avez perdu ont perdu	avais perdu avais perdu avait perdu avions perdu aviez perdu avaient perdu	eus perdu eus perdu eut perdu eûmes perdu eûtes perdu eurent perdu	aurai perdu auras perdu aura perdu aurons perdu aurez perdu auront perdu

La conjugaison du verbe

CONDITIONAL	IMPERATIVE	SUBJUNCTIVE	
PRESENT CONDITIONAL		PRESENT	IMPERFECT
parlerais		parle	parlasse
parlerais	parle	parles	parlasses
parlerait		parle	parlât
parlerions	parlons	parlions	parlassions
parleriez	parlez	parliez	parlassiez
parleraient		parlent	parlassent
PAST CONDITIONAL		PAST	PLUPERFECT
aurais parlé		aie parlé	eusse parlé
aurais parlé		aies parlé	eusses parlé
aurait parlé		ait parlé	eût parlé
aurions parlé		ayons parlé	eussions parlé
auriez parlé		ayez parlé	eussiez parlé
auraient parlé		aient parlé	eussent parlé
PRESENT CONDITIONAL		PRESENT	IMPERFECT
finirais		finisse	finisse
finirais	finis	finisses	finisses
finirait		finisse	finît
finirions	finissons	finissions	finissions
finiriez	finissez	finissiez	finissiez
finiraient		finissent	finissent
PAST CONDITIONAL		PAST	PLUPERFECT
aurais fini		aie fini	eusse fini
aurais fini		aies fini	eusses fini
aurait fini		ait fini	eût fini
aurions fini		ayons fini	eussions fini
auriez fini		ayez fini	eussiez fini
auraient fini		aient fini	eussent fini
PRESENT CONDITIONAL		PRESENT	IMPERFECT
perdrais		perde	perdisse
perdrais	perds	perdes	perdisses
perdrait		perde	perdît
perdrions	perdons	perdions	perdissions
perdriez	perdez	perdiez	perdissiez
perdraient		perdent	perdissent
PAST CONDITIONAL		PAST	PLUPERFECT
aurais perdu		aie perdu	eusse perdu
aurais perdu		aies perdu	eusses perdu
aurait perdu		ait perdu	eût perdu
aurions perdu		ayons perdu	eussions perdu
auriez perdu		ayez perdu	eussiez perdu
auraient perdu		aient perdu	eussent perdu

95. *The conjugation of the ve*

INFINITIVE AND PARTICIPLES	INDICATIVE			
	PRESENT	IMPERFECT	SIMPLE PAST	FUTURE
4. 2d class	dors	dormais	dormis	dormirai
-ir verbs	dors	dormais	dormis	dormiras
dormir	dort	dormait	dormit	dormira
(*sleep*)	dormons	dormions	dormîmes	dormirons
dormant	dormez	dormiez	dormîtes	dormirez
dormi	dorment	dormaient	dormirent	dormiront
	COMPOUND PAST	PLUPERFECT	PAST ANTERIOR	FUTURE PERFECT
	ai dormi	avais dormi	eus dormi	aurai dormi
	as dormi	avais dormi	eus dormi	auras dormi
	a dormi	avait dormi	eut dormi	aura dormi
	avons dormi	avions dormi	eûmes dormi	aurons dormi
	avez dormi	aviez dormi	eûtes dormi	aurez dormi
	ont dormi	avaient dormi	eurent dormi	auront dormi
	PRESENT	IMPERFECT	SIMPLE PAST	FUTURE
5. *-oir* verbs	reçois	recevais	reçus	recevrai
recevoir	reçois	recevais	reçus	recevras
(*receive*)	reçoit	recevait	reçut	recevra
recevant	recevons	recevions	reçûmes	recevrons
reçu	recevez	receviez	reçûtes	recevrez
	reçoivent	recevaient	reçurent	recevront
	COMPOUND PAST	PLUPERFECT	PAST ANTERIOR	FUTURE PERFECT
	ai reçu	avais reçu	eus reçu	aurai reçu
	as reçu	avais reçu	eus reçu	auras reçu
	a reçu	avait reçu	eut reçu	aura reçu
	avons reçu	avions reçu	eûmes reçu	aurons reçu
	avez reçu	aviez reçu	eûtes reçu	aurez reçu
	ont reçu	avaient reçu	eurent reçu	auront reçu
	PRESENT	IMPERFECT	SIMPLE PAST	FUTURE
6. *Intransitive*	entre	entrais	entrai	entrerai
verb of	entres	entrais	entras	entreras
motion	entre	entrait	entra	entrera
entrer	entrons	entrions	entrâmes	entrerons
(*enter*)	entrez	entriez	entrâtes	entrerez
entrant	entrent	entraient	entrèrent	entreront
entré				
	COMPOUND PAST	PLUPERFECT	PAST ANTERIOR	FUTURE PERFECT
	suis entré(e)	étais entré(e)	fus entré(e)	serai entré(e)
	es entré(e)	étais entré(e)	fus entré(e)	seras entré(e)
	est entré(e)	était entré(e)	fut entré(e)	sera entré(e)
	sommes entré(e)s	étions entré(e)s	fûmes entré(e)s	serons entré(e)
	êtes entré(e)(s)	étiez entré(e)(s)	fûtes entré(e)(s)	serez entré(e)
	sont entré(e)s	étaient entré(e)s	furent entré(e)s	seront entré(e)

La conjugaison du verbe

CONDITIONAL	IMPERATIVE	SUBJUNCTIVE	
PRESENT CONDITIONAL		PRESENT	IMPERFECT
dormirais		dorme	dormisse
dormirais	dors	dormes	dormisses
dormirait		dorme	dormît
dormirions	dormons	dormions	dormissions
dormiriez	dormez	dormiez	dormissiez
dormiraient		dorment	dormissent
PAST CONDITIONAL		PAST	PLUPERFECT
aurais dormi		aie dormi	eusse dormi
aurais dormi		aies dormi	eusses dormi
aurait dormi		ait dormi	eût dormi
aurions dormi		ayons dormi	eussions dormi
auriez dormi		ayez dormi	eussiez dormi
auraient dormi		aient dormi	eussent dormi
PRESENT CONDITIONAL		PRESENT	IMPERFECT
recevrais		reçoive	reçusse
recevrais	reçois	reçoives	reçusses
recevrait		reçoive	reçût
recevrions	recevons	recevions	reçussions
recevriez	recevez	receviez	reçussiez
recevraient		reçoivent	reçussent
PAST CONDITIONAL		PAST	PLUPERFECT
aurais reçu		aie reçu	eusse reçu
aurais reçu		aies reçu	eusses reçu
aurait reçu		ait reçu	eût reçu
aurions reçu		ayons reçu	eussions reçu
auriez reçu		ayez reçu	eussiez reçu
auraient reçu		aient reçu	eussent reçu
PRESENT CONDITIONAL		PRESENT	IMPERFECT
entrerais		entre	entrasse
entrerais	entre	entres	entrasses
entrerait		entre	entrât
entrerions	entrons	entrions	entrassions
entreriez	entrez	entriez	entrassiez
entreraient		entrent	entrassent
PAST CONDITIONAL		PAST	PLUPERFECT
serais entré(e)		sois entré(e)	fusse entré(e)
serais entré(e)		sois entré(e)	fusses entré(e)
serait entré(e)		soit entré(e)	fût entré(e)
serions entré(e)s		soyons entré(e)s	fussions entré(e)s
seriez entré(e)(s)		soyez entré(e)(s)	fussiez entré(e)(s)
seraient entré(e)s		soient entré(e)s	fussent entré(e)s

95. *The conjugation of the*

INFINITIVE AND PARTICIPLES	INDICATIVE			
	PRESENT	IMPERFECT	SIMPLE PAST	FUTURE
7. *Reflexive*	me lave	me lavais	me lavai	me lavera
verb	te laves	te lavais	te lavas	te lavera
	se lave	se lavait	se lava	se lavera
se laver	nous lavons	nous lavions	nous lavâmes	nous laverc
(*wash*	vous lavez	vous laviez	vous lavâtes	vous lavere
oneself)	se lavent	se lavaient	se lavèrent	se laverc
se lavant				
lavé	COMPOUND PAST	PLUPERFECT	PAST ANTERIOR	FUTURE PERF
	me suis lavé(e)	m'étais lavé(e)	me fus lavé(e)	me serai lav
	t'es lavé(e)	t'étais lavé(e)	te fus lavé(e)	te seras lav
	s'est lavé(e)	s'était lavé(e)	se fut lavé(e)	se sera lav
	nous sommes lavé(e)s	nous étions lavé(e)s	nous fûmes lavé(e)s	nous serons lav
	vous êtes lavé(e)(s)	vous étiez lavé(e)(s)	vous fûtes lavé(e)(s)	vous serez lavé
	se sont lavé(e)s	s'étaient lavé(e)s	se furent lavé(e)s	se seront lav
	PRESENT	IMPERFECT	SIMPLE PAST	FUTURE
8. *Auxiliary*	ai	avais	eus	aurai
verb	as	avais	eus	auras
	a	avait	eut	aura
avoir	avons	avions	eûmes	aurons
(*have*)	avez	aviez	eûtes	aurez
ayant	ont	avaient	eurent	auront
eu				
	COMPOUND PAST	PLUPERFECT	PAST ANTERIOR	FUTURE PERF
	ai eu	avais eu	eus eu	aurai e
	as eu	avais eu	eus eu	auras e
	a eu	avait eu	eut eu	aura e
	avons eu	avions eu	eûmes eu	aurons e
	avez eu	aviez eu	eûtes eu	aurez e
	ont eu	avaient eu	eurent eu	auront e
	PRESENT	IMPERFECT	SIMPLE PAST	FUTURE
9. *Auxiliary*	suis	étais	fus	serai
verb	es	étais	fus	seras
	est	était	fut	sera
être	sommes	étions	fûmes	serons
(*be*)	êtes	étiez	fûtes	serez
étant	sont	étaient	furent	seront
été				
	COMPOUND PAST	PLUPERFECT	PAST ANTERIOR	FUTURE PERF
	ai été	avais été	eus été	aurai ét
	as été	avais été	eus été	auras ét
	a été	avait été	eut été	aura ét
	avons été	avions été	eûmes été	aurons ét
	avez été	aviez été	eûtes été	aurez ét
	ont été	avaient été	eurent été	auront ét

La conjugaison du verbe

CONDITIONAL	IMPERATIVE	SUBJUNCTIVE	
PRESENT CONDITIONAL		PRESENT	IMPERFECT
me laverais		me lave	me lavasse
te laverais	lave-toi	te laves	te lavasses
se laverait		se lave	se lavât
nous laverions	lavons-nous	nous lavions	nous lavassions
vous laveriez	lavez-vous	vous laviez	vous lavassiez
se laveraient		se lavent	se lavassent
PAST CONDITIONAL		PAST	PLUPERFECT
me serais lavé(e)		me sois lavé(e)	me fusse lavé(e)
te serais lavé(e)		te sois lavé(e)	te fusses lavé(e)
se serait lavé(e)		se soit lavé(e)	se fût lavé(e)
nous serions lavé(e)s		nous soyons lavé(e)s	nous fussions lavé(e)s
vous seriez lavé(e)(s)		vous soyez lavé(e)(s)	vous fussiez lavé(e)(s)
se seraient lavé(e)s		se soient lavé(e)s	se fussent lavé(e)s
PRESENT CONDITIONAL		PRESENT	IMPERFECT
aurais		aie	eusse
aurais	aie	aies	eusses
aurait		ait	eût
aurions	ayons	ayons	eussions
auriez	ayez	ayez	eussiez
auraient		aient	eussent
PAST CONDITIONAL		PAST	PLUPERFECT
aurais eu		aie eu	eusse eu
aurais eu		aies eu	eusses eu
aurait eu		ait eu	eût eu
aurions eu		ayons eu	eussions eu
auriez eu		ayez eu	eussiez eu
auraient eu		aient eu	eussent eu
PRESENT CONDITIONAL		PRESENT	IMPERFECT
serais		sois	fusse
serais	sois	sois	fusses
serait		soit	fût
serions	soyons	soyons	fussions
seriez	soyez	soyez	fussiez
seraient		soient	fussent
PAST CONDITIONAL		PAST	PLUPERFECT
aurais été		aie été	eusse été
aurais été		aies été	eusses été
aurait été		ait été	eût été
aurions été		ayons été	eussions été
auriez été		ayez été	cussiez été
auraient été		aient été	eussent été

95. *The conjugation of the verb*

INFINITIVE AND PARTICIPLES	INDICATIVE			
	PRESENT	IMPERFECT	SIMPLE PAST	COMPOUND PAST
10. acquérir	acquiers	acquérais	acquis	ai acquis
(*acquire*)	acquiers	acquérais	acquis	as acquis
acquérant	acquiert	acquérait	acquit	a acquis
acquis	acquérons	acquérions	acquîmes	avons acquis
	acquérez	acquériez	acquîtes	avez acquis
	acquièrent	acquéraient	acquirent	ont acquis
11. aller	vais	allais	allai	suis allé(e)
(*go*)	vas	allais	allas	es allé(e)
allant	va	allait	alla	est allé(e)
allé	allons	allions	allâmes	sommes allé(e)s
	allez	alliez	allâtes	êtes allé(e)(s)
	vont	allaient	allèrent	sont allé(e)s
12. asseoir[1,2]	assieds	asseyais	assis	me suis assis(e)[1]
(*seat*)	assieds	asseyais	assis	t'es assis(e)
asseyant	assied	asseyait	assit	s'est assis(e)
assis	asseyons	asseyions	assîmes	nous sommes assis(es)
	asseyez	asseyiez	assîtes	vous êtes assis(e)(s)
	asseyent	asseyaient	assirent	se sont assis(es)
assoyant	assois	assoyais		
	assois	assoyais		
	assoit	assoyait		
	assoyons	assoyions		
	assoyez	assoyiez		
	assoient	assoyaient		
13. battre	bats	battais	battis	ai battu
(*beat*)	bats	battais	battis	as battu
battant	bat	battait	battit	a battu
battu	battons	battions	battîmes	avons battu
	battez	battiez	battîtes	avez battu
	battent	battaient	battirent	ont battu
14. boire	bois	buvais	bus	ai bu
(*drink*)	bois	buvais	bus	as bu
buvant	boit	buvait	but	a bu
bu	buvons	buvions	bûmes	avons bu
	buvez	buviez	bûtes	avez bu
	boivent	buvaient	burent	ont bu

[1] This verb is usually used in its reflexive form *s'asseoir* (to sit). For this reason, the reflexive forms of the compound past and imperative are given.
[2] Certain tenses of this verb have two forms.

La conjugaison du verbe

	CONDITIONAL	IMPERATIVE	SUBJUNCTIVE	
FUTURE			PRESENT	IMPERFECT
acquerrai	acquerrais		acquière	acquisse
acquerras	acquerrais	acquiers	acquières	acquisses
acquerra	acquerrait		acquière	acquît
acquerrons	acquerrions	acquérons	acquérions	acquissions
acquerrez	acquerriez	acquérez	acquériez	acquissiez
acquerront	acquerraient		acquièrent	acquissent
irai	irais		aille	allasse
iras	irais	va	ailles	allasses
ira	irait		aille	allât
irons	irions	allons	allions	allassions
irez	iriez	allez	alliez	allassiez
iront	iraient		aillent	allassent
assiérai	assiérais		asseye	assisse
assiéras	assiérais	assieds-toi[1]	asseyes	assisses
assiéra	assiérait		asseye	assît
assiérons	assiérions	asseyons-nous	asseyions	assissions
assiérez	assiériez	asseyez-vous	asseyiez	assissiez
assiéront	assiéraient		asseyent	assissent
assoirai	assoirais		assoie	
assoiras	assoirais	assois-toi	assoies	
assoira	assoirait		assoie	
assoirons	assoirions	assoyons-nous	assoyions	
assoirez	assoiriez	assoyez-vous	assoyiez	
assoiront	assoiraient		assoient	
battrai	battrais		batte	battisse
battras	battrais	bats	battes	battisses
battra	battrait		batte	battît
battrons	battrions	battons	battions	battissions
battrez	battriez	battez	battiez	battissiez
battront	battraient		battent	battissent
boirai	boirais		boive	busse
boiras	boirais	bois	boives	busses
boira	boirait		boive	bût
boirons	boirions	buvons	buvions	bussions
boirez	boiriez	buvez	buviez	bussiez
boiront	boiraient		boivent	bussent

[1] This verb is usually used in its reflexive form *s'asseoir* (to sit). For this reason, the reflexive forms of the compound past and imperative are given.

95. *The conjugation of the verb*

INFINITIVE AND PARTICIPLES	INDICATIVE			
	PRESENT	IMPERFECT	SIMPLE PAST	COMPOUND PAST
15. conduire	conduis	conduisais	conduisis	ai conduit
(*lead*)	conduis	conduisais	conduisis	as conduit
conduisant	conduit	conduisait	conduisit	a conduit
conduit	conduisons	conduisions	conduisîmes	avons conduit
	conduisez	conduisiez	conduisîtes	avez conduit
	conduisent	conduisaient	conduisirent	ont conduit
16. connaître	connais	connaissais	connus	ai connu
(*be acquainted*)	connais	connaissais	connus	as connu
connaissant	connaît	connaissait	connut	a connu
connu	connaissons	connaissions	connûmes	avons connu
	connaissez	connaissiez	connûtes	avez connu
	connaissent	connaissaient	connurent	ont connu
17. courir	cours	courais	courus	ai couru
(*run*)	cours	courais	courus	as couru
courant	court	courait	courut	a couru
couru	courons	courions	courûmes	avons couru
	courez	couriez	courûtes	avez couru
	courent	couraient	coururent	ont couru
18. craindre	crains	craignais	craignis	ai craint
(*fear*)	crains	craignais	craignis	as craint
craignant	craint	craignait	craignit	a craint
craint	craignons	craignions	craignîmes	avons craint
	craignez	craigniez	craignîtes	avez craint
	craignent	craignaient	craignirent	ont craint
19. croire	crois	croyais	crus	ai cru
(*believe*)	crois	croyais	crus	as cru
croyant	croit	croyait	crut	a cru
cru	croyons	croyions	crûmes	avons cru
	croyez	croyiez	crûtes	avez cru
	croient	croyaient	crurent	ont cru
20. devoir	dois	devais	dus	ai dû
(*owe, have to*)	dois	devais	dus	as dû
devant	doit	devait	dut	a dû
dû, due[1]	devons	devions	dûmes	avons dû
	devez	deviez	dûtes	avez dû
	doivent	devaient	durent	ont dû

[1] The masculine singular form of the past participle is written with the circumflex accent to distinguish it from the word *du*. All other forms are written without the accent (*dû, due, dus, dues*).

La conjugaison du verbe

			SUBJUNCTIVE	
FUTURE	CONDITIONAL	IMPERATIVE	PRESENT	IMPERFECT
conduirai	conduirais		conduise	conduisisse
conduiras	conduirais	conduis	conduises	conduisisses
conduira	conduirait		conduise	conduisît
conduirons	conduirions	conduisons	conduisions	conduisissions
conduirez	conduiriez	conduisez	conduisiez	conduisissiez
conduiront	conduiraient		conduisent	conduisissent
connaîtrai	connaîtrais		connaisse	connusse
connaîtras	connaîtrais	connais	connaisses	connusses
connaîtra	connaîtrait		connaisse	connût
connaîtrons	connaîtrions	connaissons	connaissions	connussions
connaîtrez	connaîtriez	connaissez	connaissiez	connussiez
connaîtront	connaîtraient		connaissent	connussent
courrai	courrais		coure	courusse
courras	courrais	cours	coures	courusses
courra	courrait		coure	courût
courrons	courrions	courons	courions	courussions
courrez	courriez	courez	couriez	courussiez
courront	courraient		courent	courussent
craindrai	craindrais		craigne	craignisse
craindras	craindrais	crains	craignes	craignisses
craindra	craindrait		craigne	craignît
craindrons	craindrions	craignons	craignions	craignissions
craindrez	craindriez	craignez	craigniez	craignissiez
craindront	craindraient		craignent	craignissent
croirai	croirais		croie	crusse
croiras	croirais	crois	croies	crusses
croira	croirait		croie	crût
croirons	croirions	croyons	croyions	crussions
croirez	croiriez	croyez	croyiez	crussiez
croiront	croiraient		croient	crussent
devrai	devrais		doive	dusse
devras	devrais	dois	doives	dusses
devra	devrait		doive	dût
devrons	devrions	devons	devions	dussions
devrez	devriez	devez	deviez	dussiez
devront	devraient		doivent	dussent

95. *The conjugation of the verb*

INFINITIVE AND PARTICIPLES	INDICATIVE			
	PRESENT	IMPERFECT	SIMPLE PAST	COMPOUND PAST
21. dire	dis	disais	dis	ai dit
(*say, tell*)	dis	disais	dis	as dit
disant	dit	disait	dit	a dit
dit	disons	disions	dîmes	avons dit
	dites	disiez	dîtes	avez dit
	disent	disaient	dirent	ont dit
22. écrire	écris	écrivais	écrivis	ai écrit
(*write*)	écris	écrivais	écrivis	as écrit
écrivant	écrit	écrivait	écrivit	a écrit
écrit	écrivons	écrivions	écrivîmes	avons écrit
	écrivez	écriviez	écrivîtes	avez écrit
	écrivent	écrivaient	écrivirent	ont écrit
23. envoyer	envoie	envoyais	envoyai	ai envoyé
(*send*)	envoies	envoyais	envoyas	as envoyé
envoyant	envoie	envoyait	envoya	a envoyé
envoyé	envoyons	envoyions	envoyâmes	avons envoyé
	envoyez	envoyiez	envoyâtes	avez envoyé
	envoient	envoyaient	envoyèrent	ont envoyé
24. faire	fais	faisais[1]	fis	ai fait
(*do, make*)	fais	faisais	fis	as fait
faisant[1]	fait	faisait	fit	a fait
fait	faisons	faisions	fîmes	avons fait
	faites	faisiez	fîtes	avez fait
	font	faisaient	firent	ont fait
25. falloir[2]	il faut	il fallait	il fallut	il a fallu
(*be necessary*)				
fallu				
26. fuir	fuis	fuyais	fuis	ai fui
(*flee*)	fuis	fuyais	fuis	as fui
fuyant	fuit	fuyait	fuit	a fui
fui	fuyons	fuyions	fuîmes	avons fui
	fuyez	fuyiez	fuîtes	avez fui
	fuient	fuyaient	fuirent	ont fui
27. lire	lis	lisais	lus	ai lu
(*read*)	lis	lisais	lus	as lu
lisant	lit	lisait	lut	a lu
lu	lisons	lisions	lûmes	avons lu
	lisez	lisiez	lûtes	avez lu
	lisent	lisaient	lurent	ont lu

[1] The *ai* of the stem of these forms is pronounced like mute *e* [ə].
[2] Used in third person singular only.

La conjugaison du verbe

	CONDITIONAL	IMPERATIVE	SUBJUNCTIVE	
FUTURE			PRESENT	IMPERFECT
dirai	dirais		dise	disse
diras	dirais	dis	dises	disses
dira	dirait		dise	dît
dirons	dirions	disons	disions	dissions
direz	diriez	dites	disiez	dissiez
diront	diraient		disent	dissent
écrirai	écrirais		écrive	écrivisse
écriras	écrirais	écris	écrives	écrivisses
écrira	écrirait		écrive	écrivît
écrirons	écririons	écrivons	écrivions	écrivissions
écrirez	écririez	écrivez	écriviez	écrivissiez
écriront	écriraient		écrivent	écrivissent
enverrai	enverrais		envoie	envoyasse
enverras	enverrais	envoie	envoies	envoyasses
enverra	enverrait		envoie	envoyât
enverrons	enverrions	envoyons	envoyions	envoyassions
enverrez	enverriez	envoyez	envoyiez	envoyassiez
enverront	enverraient		envoient	envoyassent
ferai	ferais		fasse	fisse
feras	ferais	fais	fasses	fisses
fera	ferait		fasse	fît
ferons	ferions	faisons	fassions	fissions
ferez	feriez	faites	fassiez	fissiez
feront	feraient		fassent	fissent
il faudra	il faudrait		il faille	il fallût
fuirai	fuirais		fuie	fuisse
fuiras	fuirais	fuis	fuies	fuisses
fuira	fuirait		fuie	fuît
fuirons	fuirions	fuyons	fuyions	fuissions
fuirez	fuiriez	fuyez	fuyiez	fuissiez
fuiront	fuiraient		fuient	fuissent
lirai	lirais		lise	lusse
liras	lirais	lis	lises	lusses
lira	lirait		lise	lût
lirons	lirions	lisons	lisions	lussions
lirez	liriez	lisez	lisiez	lussiez
liront	liraient		lisent	lussent

95. *The conjugation of the verb*

INFINITIVE AND PARTICIPLES	INDICATIVE			
	PRESENT	IMPERFECT	SIMPLE PAST	COMPOUND PAST
28. mettre	mets	mettais	mis	ai mis
(*put*)	mets	mettais	mis	as mis
mettant	met	mettait	mit	a mis
mis	mettons	mettions	mîmes	avons mis
	mettez	mettiez	mîtes	avez mis
	mettent	mettaient	mirent	ont mis
29. mourir	meurs	mourais	mourus	suis mort(e)
(*die*)	meurs	mourais	mourus	es mort(e)
mourant	meurt	mourait	mourut	est mort(e)
mort	mourons	mourions	mourûmes	sommes mort(e)s
	mourez	mouriez	mourûtes	êtes mort(e)(s)
	meurent	mouraient	moururent	sont mort(e)s
30. naître	nais	naissais	naquis	suis né(e)
(*be born*)	nais	naissais	naquis	es né(e)
naissant	naît	naissait	naquit	est né(e)
né	naissons	naissions	naquîmes	sommes né(e)s
	naissez	naissiez	naquîtes	êtes né(e)(s)
	naissent	naissaient	naquirent	sont né(e)s
31. ouvrir	ouvre	ouvrais	ouvris	ai ouvert
(*open*)	ouvres	ouvrais	ouvris	as ouvert
ouvrant	ouvre	ouvrait	ouvrit	a ouvert
ouvert	ouvrons	ouvrions	ouvrîmes	avons ouvert
	ouvrez	ouvriez	ouvrîtes	avez ouvert
	ouvrent	ouvraient	ouvrirent	ont ouvert
32. peindre	peins	peignais	peignis	ai peint
(*paint*)	peins	peignais	peignis	as peint
peignant	peint	peignait	peignit	a peint
peint	peignons	peignions	peignîmes	avons peint
	peignez	peigniez	peignîtes	avez peint
	peignent	peignaient	peignirent	ont peint
33. plaire	plais	plaisais	plus	ai plu
(*please*)	plais	plaisais	plus	as plu
plaisant	plaît	plaisait	plut	a plu
plu	plaisons	plaisions	plûmes	avons plu
	plaisez	plaisiez	plûtes	avez plu
	plaisent	plaisaient	plurent	ont plu
34. pleuvoir[1]	il pleut	il pleuvait	il plut	il a plu
(*rain*)				
pleuvant				
plu				

[1] Used only in third person singular.

La conjugaison du verbe

	CONDITIONAL	IMPERATIVE	SUBJUNCTIVE	
FUTURE			PRESENT	IMPERFECT
mettrai	mettrais		mette	misse
mettras	mettrais	mets	mettes	misses
mettra	mettrait		mette	mît
mettrons	mettrions	mettons	mettions	missions
mettrez	mettriez	mettez	mettiez	missiez
mettront	mettraient		mettent	missent
mourrai	mourrais		meure	mourusse
mourras	mourrais	meurs	meures	mourusses
mourra	mourrait		meure	mourût
mourrons	mourrions	mourons	mourions	mourussions
mourrez	mourriez	mourez	mouriez	mourussiez
mourront	mourraient		meurent	mourussent
naîtrai	naîtrais		naisse	naquisse
naîtras	naîtrais	nais	naisses	naquisses
naîtra	naîtrait		naisse	naquît
naîtrons	naîtrions	naissons	naissions	naquissions
naîtrez	naîtriez	naissez	naissiez	naquissiez
naîtront	naîtraient		naissent	naquissent
ouvrirai	ouvrirais		ouvre	ouvrisse
ouvriras	ouvrirais	ouvre	ouvres	ouvrisses
ouvrira	ouvrirait		ouvre	ouvrît
ouvrirons	ouvririons	ouvrons	ouvrions	ouvrissions
ouvrirez	ouvririez	ouvrez	ouvriez	ouvrissiez
ouvriront	ouvriraient		ouvrent	ouvrissent
peindrai	peindrais		peigne	peignisse
peindras	peindrais	peins	peignes	peignisses
peindra	peindrait		peigne	peignît
peindrons	peindrions	peignons	peignions	peignissions
peindrez	peindriez	peignez	peigniez	peignissiez
peindront	peindraient		peignent	peignissent
plairai	plairais		plaise	plusse
plairas	plairais	plais	plaises	plusses
plaira	plairait		plaise	plût
plairons	plairions	plaisons	plaisions	plussions
plairez	plairiez	plaisez	plaisiez	plussiez
plairont	plairaient		plaisent	plussent
il pleuvra	il pleuvrait		il pleuve	il plût

95. *The conjugation of the verb*

INFINITIVE AND PARTICIPLES	INDICATIVE			
	PRESENT	IMPERFECT	SIMPLE PAST	COMPOUND PAST
35. pouvoir	peux, puis	pouvais	pus	ai pu
(*be able*)	peux	pouvais	pus	as pu
pouvant	peut	pouvait	put	a pu
pu	pouvons	pouvions	pûmes	avons pu
	pouvez	pouviez	pûtes	avez pu
	peuvent	pouvaient	purent	ont pu
36. prendre	prends	prenais	pris	ai pris
(*take*)	prends	prenais	pris	as pris
prenant	prend	prenait	prit	a pris
pris	prenons	prenions	prîmes	avons pris
	prenez	preniez	prîtes	avez pris
	prennent	prenaient	prirent	ont pris
37. rire	ris	riais	ris	ai ri
(*laugh*)	ris	riais	ris	as ri
riant	rit	riait	rit	a ri
ri	rions	riions	rîmes	avons ri
	riez	riiez	rîtes	avez ri
	rient	riaient	rirent	ont ri
38. savoir	sais	savais	sus	ai su
(*know*)	sais	savais	sus	as su
sachant	sait	savait	sut	a su
su	savons	savions	sûmes	avons su
	savez	saviez	sûtes	avez su
	savent	savaient	surent	ont su
39. suivre	suis	suivais	suivis	ai suivi
(*follow*)	suis	suivais	suivis	as suivi
suivant	suit	suivait	suivit	a suivi
suivi	suivons	suivions	suivîmes	avons suivi
	suivez	suiviez	suivîtes	avez suivi
	suivent	suivaient	suivirent	ont suivi
40. tenir	tiens	tenais	tins	ai tenu
(*hold, keep*)	tiens	tenais	tins	as tenu
tenant	tient	tenait	tint	a tenu
tenu	tenons	tenions	tînmes	avons tenu
	tenez	teniez	tîntes	avez tenu
	tiennent	tenaient	tinrent	ont tenu

La conjugaison du verbe

FUTURE	CONDITIONAL	IMPERATIVE	SUBJUNCTIVE PRESENT	SUBJUNCTIVE IMPERFECT
pourrai	pourrais		puisse	pusse
pourras	pourrais		puisses	pusses
pourra	pourrait		puisse	pût
pourrons	pourrions		puissions	pussions
pourrez	pourriez		puissiez	pussiez
pourront	pourraient		puissent	pussent
prendrai	prendrais		prenne	prisse
prendras	prendrais	prends	prennes	prisses
prendra	prendrait		prenne	prît
prendrons	prendrions	prenons	prenions	prissions
prendrez	prendriez	prenez	preniez	prissiez
prendront	prendraient		prennent	prissent
rirai	rirais		rie	risse
riras	rirais	ris	ries	risses
rira	rirait		rie	rît
rirons	ririons	rions	riions	rissions
rirez	ririez	riez	riiez	rissiez
riront	riraient		rient	rissent
saurai	saurais		sache	susse
sauras	saurais	sache	saches	susses
saura	saurait		sache	sût
saurons	saurions	sachons	sachions	sussions
saurez	sauriez	sachez	sachiez	sussiez
sauront	sauraient		sachent	sussent
suivrai	suivrais		suive	suivisse
suivras	suivrais	suis	suives	suivisses
suivra	suivrait		suive	suivît
suivrons	suivrions	suivons	suivions	suivissions
suivrez	suivriez	suivez	suiviez	suivissiez
suivront	suivraient		suivent	suivissent
tiendrai	tiendrais		tienne	tinsse
tiendras	tiendrais	tiens	tiennes	tinsses
tiendra	tiendrait		tienne	tînt
tiendrons	tiendrions	tenons	tenions	tinssions
tiendrez	tiendriez	tenez	teniez	tinssiez
tiendront	tiendraient		tiennent	tinssent

95. *The conjugation of the verb*

INFINITIVE AND PARTICIPLES	INDICATIVE			
	PRESENT	IMPERFECT	SIMPLE PAST	COMPOUND PAST
41. vaincre	vaincs	vainquais	vainquis	ai vaincu
(*conquer*)	vaincs	vainquais	vainquis	as vaincu
vainquant	vainc	vainquait	vainquit	a vaincu
vaincu	vainquons	vainquions	vainquîmes	avons vaincu
	vainquez	vainquiez	vainquîtes	avez vaincu
	vainquent	vainquaient	vainquirent	ont vaincu
42. valoir	vaux	valais	valus	ai valu
(*be worth*)	vaux	valais	valus	as valu
valant	vaut	valait	valut	a valu
valu	valons	valions	valûmes	avons valu
	valez	valiez	valûtes	avez valu
	valent	valaient	valurent	ont valu
43. venir	viens	venais	vins	suis venu(e)
(*come*)	viens	venais	vins	es venu(e)
venant	vient	venait	vint	est venu(e)
venu	venons	venions	vînmes	sommes venu(e)s
	venez	veniez	vîntes	êtes venu(e)(s)
	viennent	venaient	vinrent	sont venu(e)s
44. vivre	vis	vivais	vécus	ai vécu
(*live*)	vis	vivais	vécus	as vécu
vivant	vit	vivait	vécut	a vécu
vécu	vivons	vivions	vécûmes	avons vécu
	vivez	viviez	vécûtes	avez vécu
	vivent	vivaient	vécurent	ont vécu
45. voir	vois	voyais	vis	ai vu
(*see*)	vois	voyais	vis	as vu
voyant	voit	voyait	vit	a vu
vu	voyons	voyions	vîmes	avons vu
	voyez	voyiez	vîtes	avez vu
	voient	voyaient	virent	ont vu
46. vouloir	veux	voulais	voulus	ai voulu
(*wish, want*)	veux	voulais	voulus	as voulu
voulant	veut	voulait	voulut	a voulu
voulu	voulons	voulions	voulûmes	avons voulu
	voulez	vouliez	voulûtes	avez voulu
	veulent	voulaient	voulurent	ont voulu

La conjugaison du verbe

FUTURE	CONDITIONAL	IMPERATIVE	SUBJUNCTIVE PRESENT	SUBJUNCTIVE IMPERFECT
vaincrai	vaincrais		vainque	vainquisse
vaincras	vaincrais	vaincs	vainques	vainquisses
vaincra	vaincrait		vainque	vainquît
vaincrons	vaincrions	vainquons	vainquions	vainquissions
vaincrez	vaincriez	vainquez	vainquiez	vainquissiez
vaincront	vaincraient		vainquent	vainquissent
vaudrai	vaudrais		vaille	valusse
vaudras	vaudrais	vaux	vailles	valusses
vaudra	vaudrait		vaille	valût
vaudrons	vaudrions	valons	valions	valussions
vaudrez	vaudriez	valez	valiez	valussiez
vaudront	vaudraient		vaillent	valussent
viendrai	viendrais		vienne	vinsse
viendras	viendrais	viens	viennes	vinsses
viendra	viendrait		vienne	vînt
viendrons	viendrions	venons	venions	vinssions
viendrez	viendriez	venez	veniez	vinssiez
viendront	viendraient		viennent	vinssent
vivrai	vivrais		vive	vécusse
vivras	vivrais	vis	vives	vécusses
vivra	vivrait		vive	vécût
vivrons	vivrions	vivons	vivions	vécussions
vivrez	vivriez	vivez	viviez	vécussiez
vivront	vivraient		vivent	vécussent
verrai	verrais		voie	visse
verras	verrais	vois	voies	visses
verra	verrait		voie	vît
verrons	verrions	voyons	voyions	vissions
verrez	verriez	voyez	voyiez	vissiez
verront	verraient		voient	vissent
voudrai	voudrais		veuille	voulusse
voudras	voudrais	veuille	veuilles	voulusses
voudra	voudrait		veuille	voulût
voudrons	voudrions		voulions	voulussions
voudrez	voudriez	veuillez	vouliez	voulussiez
voudront	voudraient		veuillent	voulussent

Miscellany – Traits Divers

96. *Interrogative word order — L'ordre interrogatif*

A. An affirmative sentence may be made interrogative by placing *Est-ce que* . . , before it. This becomes *Est-ce qu'* . . . before a word beginning with a vowel.[1]

Est-ce que la capitale de la France est une grande ville?	Is the capital of France a large city?
*Est-ce qu'*elle est située sur la Seine?	Is it situated on the Seine?

The question with *Est-ce que* . . . is used especially in conversation.

B. A sentence with a personal pronoun subject may be made interrogative by placing the verb before the subject.[2] The verb is then connected to the pronoun-subject by a hyphen (-).

VERB - PRONOUN-SUBJECT	REST OF SENTENCE
Sont-elles faciles à défendre?	Are they easy to defend?
Forment-ils une partie de la frontière du pays?	Do they form a part of the boundaries of the country?

C. A sentence with a noun-subject may have this interrogative word order:

NOUN-SUBJECT VERB - PRONOUN-SUBJECT REST OF SENTENCE

The verb is connected to the pronoun-subject by a hyphen.

La France est-elle un pays?	Is France a country?
Les montagnes séparent-elles la France de l'Italie?	Do the mountains separate France from Italy?

D. Whenever the verb-form ends in a vowel and the pronoun begins with a vowel, a *-t* is inserted between them to prevent two vowels from coming together in pronunciation.

---

[1] In French, as in English, a statement may be made interrogative simply by placing a question mark at the end of the sentence; e.g., La capitale de la France est une grand ville? Elle est située sur la Seine? In saying such a sentence, the French use one type of intonation for the statement, quite a different one for the question. See Prononciation § 9 B 2 a.

[2] The *Est-ce que* . . . form must be used in the first person singular of the present of *-er* verbs. EXAMPLE: Est-ce que je parle? Est-ce que je voyage? In poetry, however, the inverted form may be used, but an acute accent is placed over the *-e:* parlé-je? Voyagé-je? The *Est-ce que* . . . form is also normally used instead of the inverted form of most other verbs in the first person singular of the present except the forms *Suis-je* . . . and *Puis-je*. . . . EXAMPLES: Est-ce que je punis . . . , Est-ce que j'entends . . . , Est-ce que je veux . . . , etc.

Sépare-t-il les deux pays?	Does it separate the two countries?
La Seine traverse-t-elle Paris?	Does the Seine cross Paris?

This *-t-* must be inserted even when the final consonant of the verb stem is *-t-*, if the verb-form ends in *-e*. EXAMPLE: limite-t-il? se jette-t-elle?

E. When a sentence with a personal pronoun-subject begins with *où, quand, comment, combien, quoi, pourquoi,* or *quel* modifying some noun, the word order may be

INTERROGATIVE WORD   VERB - PRONOUN-SUBJECT   REST OF SENTENCE

or

INTERROGATIVE WORD   *est-ce que*   PRONOUN-SUBJECT   VERB   REST OF SENTENCE

Où se trouve-t-il? Où *est-ce qu'*il se trouve?	Where is it?
Quand écrit-il une composition? Quand *est-ce qu'*il écrit une composition?	When does he write a composition?
Par où entrent-ils dans la salle de classe? Par où *est-ce qu'*ils entrent dans la salle de classe?	By what do they enter the classroom?
Pourquoi apprend-elle la leçon? Pourquoi *est-ce qu'*elle apprend la leçon?	Why does she learn the lesson?
Dans quel pays habite-t-elle? Dans quel pays *est-ce qu'*elle habite?	In what country does she live?

F. When a sentence with a noun-subject but without a direct noun-object begins with *où, quand, comment, quoi, combien,* or *quel* modifying a noun, the word order may be:

INTERROGATIVE WORD   VERB   NOUN-SUBJECT   REST OF SENTENCE [1]

or

INTERROGATIVE WORD   NOUN-SUBJECT   VERB - PRONOUN-SUBJECT   REST OF SENTENCE

or

INTERROGATIVE WORD   *est-ce que*   NOUN-SUBJECT   VERB   REST OF SENTENCE

---

[1] This form is not used when the rest of the sentence would make it lack rhythm. The second form would then be used.

Où se trouvent les Pyrénées? Où les Pyrénées se trouvent-elles? Où *est-ce que* les Pyrénées se trouvent?	Where are the Pyrenees located?
Quand sortira votre mère? Quand votre mère sortira-t-elle? Quand *est-ce que* votre mère sortira?	When will your mother go out?
Combien coûte le billet? Combien le billet coûte-t-il? Combien *est-ce que* le billet coûte?	How much does the ticket cost?

G. When a sentence with a noun-subject and a noun-object begins with *où, quand, comment, quoi, combien,* or *quel* modifying a noun, the word order may be:

INTERROGATIVE WORD — NOUN-SUBJECT — VERB - PRONOUN-SUBJECT — REST OF SENTENCE

or

INTERROGATIVE WORD — *est-ce que* — NOUN-SUBJECT — VERB — REST OF SENTENCE

The above word order is always used with *pourquoi* in a sentence with a noun-subject.

Où Pierre trouvera-t-il du papier? Où *est-ce que* Pierre trouvera du papier?	Where will Pierre find some paper?
Quand Marie écrira-t-elle une lettre à son frère? Quand *est-ce que* Marie écrira une lettre à son frère?	When will Mary write a letter to her brother?
A quelle heure cet homme a-t-il pris son billet? A quelle heure *est-ce que* cet homme a pris son billet?	At what time did this man buy his ticket?
Pourquoi cet élève est-il ici? Pourquoi *est-ce que* cet élève est ici?	Why is this pupil here?

H. When the interrogative pronoun-object *qui* is used with a noun-subject, the order is

Qui NOUN-SUBJECT VERB - PRONOUN-SUBJECT REST OF SENTENCE

or

Qui est-ce que NOUN-SUBJECT VERB REST OF SENTENCE

Qui le professeur punit-il? *Qui est-ce que* le professeur punit?	Whom does the teacher punish?

I. When the interrogative pronoun-object *que* is used with a noun subject, the order is

Que VERB NOUN-SUBJECT REST OF SENTENCE

or

Qu'est-ce que NOUN-SUBJECT VERB REST OF SENTENCE

Que fait cet élève? *Qu'est-ce que* cet élève fait?	What is this pupil doing?

(See § 38 C, D.)

J. The expression *n'est-ce pas* placed after a statement asks for confirmation of that statement. This expression has no one English equivalent. We say *isn't it, doesn't she, aren't they,* etc., depending on the preceding verb. This *n'est-ce pas* corresponds to the German *nicht wahr* and the Spanish *¿verdad?*

Vous parlez français, *n'est-ce pas?*	You speak French, *don't you?*
Ils y vont, *n'est-ce pas?*	They are going there, *aren't they?*

97. *Time — L'heure*

A. The days [1] of the week are:

lundi	*Monday*	vendredi	*Friday*
mardi	*Tuesday*	samedi	*Saturday*
mercredi	*Wednesday*	dimanche	*Sunday*
jeudi	*Thursday*		

[1] In French, a small letter is used to begin the days of the week and the months of the year. This is the form normally found in print, but there is a tendency on the part of many Frenchmen to begin the days of the week and the months of the year with capitals in their personal correspondence.

B. The months [1] of the year are:

janvier	*January*	juillet	*July*
février	*February*	août	*August*
mars	*March*	septembre	*September*
avril	*April*	octobre	*October*
mai	*May*	novembre	*November*
juin	*June*	décembre	*December*

C. The seasons of the year are:

le printemps	*spring*
l'été	*summer*
l'automne	*autumn*
l'hiver	*winter*

One says:

au printemps	*in spring*
en été	*in summer*
en automne	*in autumn*
en hiver	*in winter*

D. The French tell time as follows:

Il est deux heures.	*It is two o'clock.*
Il est trois heures et quart.	*It is quarter after three.*
Il est cinq heures et demie.	*It is half past five.*
Il est sept heures moins le quart.	*It is quarter to seven.*
Il est neuf heures moins dix.	*It is ten minutes to nine.*
Il est dix heures quatre.	*It is four minutes after ten.*
Il est midi.	*It is twelve o'clock noon.*
Il est minuit.	*It is twelve o'clock midnight.*
Il est midi et demi.	*It is half past twelve* (afternoon).
Il est minuit et demi.	*It is half past twelve* (night).

E. The adjective *demi* agrees in gender with the noun it follows. It is invariable when it precedes.

une heure et *demie*	*half past one*	or	*an hour and a half*
huit heures et *demie*	*half past eight*	or	*eight hours and a half*
une *demi* heure	*a half hour*		

[1] In French, a small letter is used to begin the days of the week and the months of the year. This is the form normally found in print, but there is a tendency on the part of many Frenchmen to begin the days of the week and the months of the year with capitals in their personal correspondence.

F. In formal announcements of meetings, timetables, etc., the French use the twenty-four-hour method of telling time, but in current conversation, the twelve-hour method is usually employed.

dix-sept heures trente cinq heures et demie de l'après-midi	5:30 P.M.

A.M. and P.M. are not used in French. One says: *huit heures du matin, trois heures de l'après-midi, neuf heures du soir.*

98. *English words with several French translations*
Mots anglais à plusieurs traductions françaises

Sometimes a given English word is expressed in French by two or more words, depending on the use of the word in the sentence. Examples of the uses of many of these words may be found in the section entitled *Les fautes favorites* (pp. 541–546).

A certain number of these words occasion a great deal of difficulty to English-speaking people and therefore merit special treatment. Verbs of this type are explained in § 94. Other words which most frequently cause difficulty are treated here.

The choice of the proper French word sometimes depends on whether the word in question is a *preposition* (a word which introduces a phrase) or a *subordinate conjunction* (a word used to introduce a dependent clause). The following outline may help to distinguish a phrase from a clause:

phrase	=	preposition + noun or preposition + pronoun	*after* the party *after* him
dependent clause	=	subordinate conjunction + subject + verb	*after* my friend left *after* we saw him

If the French word in the first column of the following outline is a preposition, it will be followed by + *noun or pronoun;* if it is a subordinate conjunction, it will be followed by + *clause.*

AFTER

après	+ noun or pronoun	Nous partirons *après* le concert. Robert est arrivé *après* moi.

après que	**+ clause**	Roger arrive *après que* le professeur a expliqué la leçon. *Après que* nous aurons gagné assez d'argent, nous partirons en Europe.

BECAUSE

parce que	**+ clause**	Je vais en France *parce que* je veux parler français.
à cause de (because of)	**+ noun** or **pronoun**	Je vais en France *à cause des* possibilités de parler français. Louise est restée à la maison *à cause de* moi.

BEFORE

devant	**+ noun** or **pronoun** indicates place	Il y a un étranger *devant* votre porte.
avant	**+ noun** or **pronoun** usually indicates time	Les élèves arrivent en classe *avant* le professeur. Le sénateur parlera *avant* moi.
avant de	**+ infinitive** equivalent to English *before —ing*	Travaillez *avant de* venir en classe. J'ai fermé la porte *avant de* partir.
avant que	**+ clause** (whose verb is always in the subjunctive)	Je serai sorti *avant que* vous puissiez me téléphoner.

BETTER

meilleur	an adjective which modifies a noun or a pronoun	Jacqueline est une *meilleure* élève qu'Hélène. Le lait est *meilleur* pour la santé que le vin.
mieux	an adverb which usually modifies a verb	Jacqueline comprend *mieux* que Denise. Mes amis chantent *mieux* que moi.

DAY

jour	The usual word for *day.* Indicates a unit of time.	J'ai passé trois *jours* à Paris. Lundi est le premier *jour* de la semaine.
journée	Focuses attention on the duration of the day and on how the day was spent.	J'ai passé toute la *journée* à la bibliothèque.

FOR

pour	+ **noun** or **pronoun**	Paul a acheté un cadeau *pour* Louise.
car	+ **clause** *for* in the sense of *because*	La France est un grand pays, *car* elle est très riche.
puisque	+ **clause** *for* in the sense of *since*	Je viendrai, *puisque* (*car*) je suis obligé de venir.
depuis	+ **noun of time** Usually found with a verb in the present tense to indicate the duration of an action begun in the past and still continuing.	Nous écrivons *depuis* une heure. Je suis ici *depuis* un an. Vous parlez *depuis* dix minutes. Nous habitons ici *depuis* notre mariage.
pendant	+ **noun of time** Most often used to indicate the duration of a completed past action.	Nous avons écrit *pendant* une heure. J'ai habité Paris *pendant* un an. Vous avez parlé *pendant* dix minutes.

NEXT

prochain	The usual word for *next.* Used in speaking of the present and future. Not normally used when speaking of the past.	La semaine *prochaine* nous irons à Paris.
suivant	Used instead of *prochain* when speaking of past occurrences.	La semaine *suivante* nous sommes allés à Paris.

PEOPLE

gens	The usual word for *people.*	Il y a trop de *gens* sur les plages.
personnes	Often used for *people* when it is a question of number.	Combien de *personnes* y avait-il à la soirée?
peuple	(a) "the masses" (b) a national group	*Le peuple* s'est révolté. Les italiens sont *un peuple* qui aime la musique.
on	Indicates *people* in a general sense.	*On* n'aime pas travailler le dimanche.
monde	Indicates *people* in the sense of a *gathering* or a *crowd.*	Il y avait beaucoup de *monde* à ce concert. Il y aura du *monde* dans le jardin dimanche.

TIME

temps	The usual word for *time.*	Je n'ai pas beaucoup de *temps* ce matin. En même *temps,* il fait d'autres choses.
fois	Used with numbers.	Une *fois* j'ai vu un éléphant blanc. Avez-vous lu la leçon trois *fois?*
moment	Indicates a point in time.	*A ce moment-là* nous sortions beaucoup. *En ce moment* je suis très occupé.
époque	Indicates a longer period in past time than does *moment.*	*A cette époque-là* il n'y avait pas d'automobiles.
heure	Used in connection with telling time.	Quelle *heure* est-il? Il est cinq *heures.* Avez-vous *l'heure?*
s'amuser	Equivalent to the English *have a good time.*	*Ils se sont* bien *amusés* à Paris. *Amusez-vous* bien.

WHILE

pendant que	Shows duration of time. Means *when.*	Roger lit un roman policier *pendant que* le professeur parle.
tandis que	Shows contrast. Means *while on the contrary, whereas.*	Les autres élèves écoutent le professeur *tandis que* Roger lit un roman policier.

WITH

avec	The usual word for *with.*	Hélène est venue *avec* son ami.
à	Indicates a characteristic.	C'est un garçon *aux* yeux bleus.
de	(a) manner (b) after certain adjectives (c) after certain verbs	Il a parlé *d'*une voix douce. Je suis content *de* mon voyage. Nous avons rempli la boîte *de* chocolats.
chez	Meaning *at the house of.*	Jean habite *chez* son oncle.

YEAR

année	Used in most cases.	Il a passé quelques *années* en France. C'est ma première *année* à Paris.
an	Used with cardinal numbers and in the expressions *par an* and *tous les ans.*	Il a passé trois *ans* à Tours. Il y va tous les *ans.* J'y vais deux fois par *an.*

YES

oui	The usual word for *yes.*	—Fait-il froid? —*Oui,* il fait très froid. —Êtes-vous Français? —*Oui,* je suis Français.
si	The word for *yes* which follows a negative question or statement. It contradicts the expected negative reply.	—Il ne fait pas très froid. —*Si,* il fait très froid. —N'êtes-vous pas Français? —*Si,* je suis Français.

Prononciation

Remarks on the French language
Diverses notions sur la langue française

1. *The Alphabet — L'alphabet*

LETTER	NAME	PRONUNCIATION [1]	LETTER	NAME	PRONUNCIATION
a	a	[a]	n	enne	[ɛn]
b	bé	[be]	o	o	[o]
c	cé	[se]	p	pé	[pe]
d	dé	[de]	q	ku	[ky]
e	e	[ə] [2]	r	erre	[ɛr], [ɛʀ]
f	effe	[ɛf]	s	esse	[ɛs]
g	gé	[ʒe]	t	té	[te]
h	ache	[aʃ]	u	u	[y]
i	i	[i]	v	vé	[ve]
j	ji	[ʒi]	w	double vé	[dubləve]
k	ka	[ka]	x	iks	[iks]
l	elle	[ɛl]	y	i grec	[igrɛk]
m	emme	[ɛm]	z	zède	[zɛd]

The letters of the alphabet are the same in French as in English. However, *k* and *w* are used practically only in words of foreign origin. EXAMPLES: le *k*iosque, le *w*agon, le tram*w*ay.

The French alphabet, like the English, is divided into vowels and consonants. The vowels (*voyelles*) are *a, e, i, o, u,* and *y.* All the other letters are consonants (*consonnes*).

There are two types of *h* in French. Both are silent.

A. Mute *h* (h-muet), which causes the word which it begins to be treated as if that word began with the following vowel, thus permitting linking and elision. EXAMPLES: l'*h*abitant, l'*h*iver, l'*h*eure, l'*h*omme, les *h*abitants, les *h*ivers, les *h*eures, les *h*ommes.

B. Aspirate *h* (h-aspiré), which, although silent, prevents either elision or linking of the final letter of the preceding word with the initial vowel of

[1] Represented in the International Phonetic Alphabet. See page 532 [2] Also written é and called [e].

the word beginning with the aspirate *h*. EXAMPLES: le Havre, le hors-d'œuvre, le héros, les||hors-d'œuvre, les||héros.

C. Words beginning with aspirate *h* are usually indicated in the dictionary by an asterisk (*) or by a dagger (†). There is no simple rule for determining which type of *h* begins a word, but mute *h* is far more frequent than aspirate *h*. The *h* of words derived from Latin is usually a mute *h*; the *h* of words derived from the Germanic languages is usually an aspirate *h*.

2. *The accents — Les accents*

In addition to the letters of the alphabet, three accents are currently used in French:

A. The accents are:
   1. the acute accent (´) (l'accent aigu), used only over *e*. EXAMPLES: situé, Méditerranée, divisé.
   2. the grave accent (`) (l'accent grave), used on *a, e,* or *u*. EXAMPLES: où, à, très, frontière, problème.
   3. the circumflex accent (^) (l'accent circonflexe), used on *a, e, i, o,* or *u*. EXAMPLES: château, âge, extrême, même, île, Rhône, côte, sûr. It is frequently used to show the disappearance of an *s*. EXAMPLES: forêt (forest), île (isle), hôte (host).

B. The accents do *not* indicate stress in French. They are pronunciation marks. They are used:
   1. to indicate the pronunciation of a vowel. Compare the sounds of the italicized vowels in the following groups of words: p*a*tte, p*â*te; m*e*n*e*r, *é*cole, *é*l*è*ve, t*ê*te; n*o*tre, n*ô*tre.
   2. to distinguish between two words of the same pronunciation but different meaning. EXAMPLES: a (*has*), à (*to*); la (*the*), là (*there*); ou (*or*), où (*where*); sur (*on*), sûr (*sure*).

3. *Other signs — Autres signes orthographiques*

Several other signs are used to aid spelling and pronunciation of French words:

A. the cedilla (¸) (la cédille), which is placed under *c* (ç) when followed by *a, o,* or *u* to indicate that it sounds like *s* instead of *k*. EXAMPLES: français, garçon, reçu.

B. the apostrophe (') (l'apostrophe), which indicates the omission of a vowel (see Pr. § 5). EXAMPLES: l'Atlantique, l'ouest, qu'il.

C. the hyphen (-) (le trait d'union), which is used, as in English, to separate parts of a word, and also to connect certain words. (See *Grammaire* § 96 B, C, D) EXAMPLES: Est-il? A-t-il?

D. the diaeresis (¨) (le tréma) shows that the vowel over which it is placed forms an additional syllable; it causes the immediately preceding vowel to be pronounced independently. EXAMPLES: naïve, haïr, héroïne, aiguë.

4. *Punctuation — La ponctuation*

A. The punctuation marks (signes de ponctuation) are:

(.)	le point	(—)	le tiret
(,)	la virgule	(!)	le point d'exclamation
(;)	le point et virgule	(...)	les points de suspension
(:)	les deux points	(« »)	les guillemets
(?)	le point d'interrogation	( )	les parenthèses
(-)	le trait d'union		

B. Two of the most notable differences in punctuation are:

1. In French no comma is used between the last two words in a series, whereas in English it usually is.

Nous avons des bœufs, des vaches et des moutons.	We have steers, cows, and sheep.

2. The French use of quotation marks and dashes to indicate direct quotations is different from ours and not completely uniform. Also, French quotation marks are written in a slightly different way than are English quotation marks.

«Allez-vous à l'école? m'a-t-il demandé.	"Are you going to school?" he asked me.
— Je ne sais pas.	"I don't know."
— Quand le saurez-vous?»	"When will you know?"

C. The French use capital letters less often than English. Small letters are used:

1. for *je* (I) in the interior of a sentence;
2. to begin the days of the week and the months of the year;

Nous sommes partis *lundi.*	We left *Monday.*
Il fait chaud en *juillet.*	It is warm in *July.*

3. to begin adjectives of nationality; [1]

un fleuve *allemand;* une rue *anglaise;* la langue *française;* une femme *russe*	a *German* river; an *English* street; the *French* language; a *Russian* woman

---

[1] When referring to persons, adjectives of nationality used in the predicate after a form of *être* are capitalized. EXAMPLES: Paul est *Français.* Ces femmes sont *Russes.*

4. usually to begin any but the first important word or noun of the title of a work, but this usage is not uniform.

Avez-vous lu *le Livre de mon ami?*	Have you read *The Book of My Friend?*

5. *Elision — Élision*

Elision is the dropping of the final vowel of one word before a following word beginning with a vowel or a mute *h*. Elision is made both in speaking and writing. An apostrophe marks the omission of the vowel. EXAMPLE: l'Atlantique.

The following are the most frequent elisions:

A. The final *-e* of words of one syllable (que, me, je, ne, se, te, etc.) is dropped before words beginning with a vowel or a mute *h*. EXAMPLES: l'est, l'ouest, d'Amérique, m'est, j'ai, l'homme

B. The *-a* of *la* is elided before words beginning with a vowel or mute *h*. EXAMPLES: l'Espagne, l'Atlantique, l'importance

C. The *-i* is elided only in the combinations *si il* and *si ils* which become *s'il* and *s'ils*.

6. *Division of words into syllables* *La division des mots en syllabes*

Not many of us are sure where to divide English words into syllables. French words may be divided more easily, because three simple rules may be applied to govern their division. These rules are:

A. A single consonant between vowels always goes with the following vowel. EXAMPLES: Pa-ris, ca-pi-ta-le, di-vi-sé, ci-tez, ma-da-me, pe-ti-te, pla-teau, trou-ver, sé-pa-rez

B. Two consonants of which the second is *l* or *r,* both belong in the following syllable, as well as combinations pronounced as a single sound, such as *ch, gn, ill, ph,* and *th*. EXAMPLES: pro-blè-me, au-tre, é-troi-te, cé-lè-bre, ca-thé-dra-le, ci-dre, ta-bleau, a-che-ter, mon-ta-gne, Mar-se-ille, tra-va-iller.

C. In other combinations of two consonants, the first goes with the preceding and the second with the following syllable. EXAMPLES: par-tie, tra-ver-ser, con-ti-nent, nom-bre, Bel-gi-que, for-mer, im-por-tant, cons-truc-tion.

It is important that you know how to divide a French word into syllables for the following three reasons:

A. In pronouncing, the French sound the consonants with the following rather than the preceding syllable. Whereas we say: Par-is, the French say: Pa-ris; and whereas we say: ge-og-ra-phy, the French say: gé-o-gra-phie.

B. In determining whether or not a vowel is nasalized, it is necessary to know whether the *m* or *n* goes with the preceding or following syllable. See page 527.

C. In separating words at the ends of a line, these rules for syllabication are followed.

Pronunciation – Prononciation

Whether or not you speak French like a Frenchman will depend largely on three factors: (1) rhythm; (2) the intonation of your sentences; (3) your articulation of individual sounds.

7. *Accentuation — L'accentuation*

A. The position of the stress in an isolated word

In an isolated word the stress is always placed on the last pronounced vowel. In the following examples the stressed vowel is italicized.

Par*i*s	Cal*ai*s	Mass*i*f	auss*i*
conn*u*	Strasb*ou*rg	pet*i*t	étrang*er*

If the word ends in a mute *e* (final *-e* without a written accent), this *e* is not pronounced in an isolated word.

capit*a*l(e)	Méditerran*é*(e)	fronti*è*r(e)
trav*e*rs(e)	mont*a*gn(e)	V*o*sg(es)

B. The nature of the stress

The stress in an English word consists above all in an increase in force on the accented syllable. The stress in a French word is *very light.* There is very little difference in force between the various syllables of a given word. In a French word stress consists essentially in the lengthening of the stressed vowel and in a change in the tone with which that vowel is spoken. The length and position of tone of the following words are indicated by the accompanying diagrams, which indicate (1) the rising and falling of the voice; (2) the relative length of each syllable.

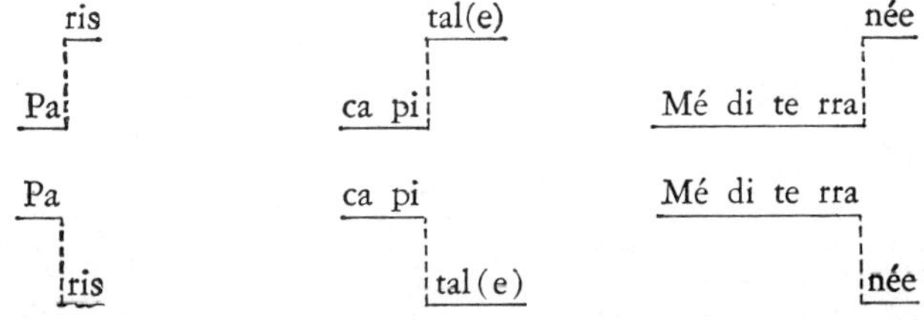

C. The sentence stress

In a sentence, the stress of the isolated word disappears and is replaced by a stress of the word-group. Compare the intonation of the isolated word and of the same word in the word-group in the following combinations:

ISOLATED WORD	SAME WORD IN WORD GROUP
pe tit(e)	un(e) pe tit(e) vill(e)
mon sieur	mon sieur Du pont
au ssi	au ssi im por tant

In speaking, French sentences are separated into word-groups, which are determined by the meaning of the sentence.

As shown above, each word-group consists of a number of unstressed syllables which are very closely linked and, at the end of the group, of an accented syllable. It is only the vowel of the stressed syllable which has a rising or falling inflection.

Notice the division of the following sentences into word-groups and the stressed syllables of those groups.

Par*is* est situ*é* sur la S*ei*ne.

La S*ei*ne trav*e*rse Par*is*.

Cal*a*is est une petite v*i*lle qui n'est pas aussi import*an*te que Par*is*.

8. *Rhythm — Le rythme*

All the unstressed vowels of a French word have the same length. Only the stressed vowels are longer. A stressed vowel is about twice as long as an unstressed vowel. Compare the place and length of the syllables in the following French words and their English equivalents.

FRENCH	ENGLISH
ca pi tale	cap i tal
con ti nent	con ti nent
im por tant	im por tant
am bi tieux	am bi tious
ad mi ni stra tion	ad min is tra tion
re pré sen ta tion	rep re sen ta tion

Note the regularity of the French rhythm as compared to the English. In French, the only vowel which can be slurred over in pronunciation is the mute *e*. The extent to which it can be slurred depends on its position in relation to the surrounding consonants.

la pe̸tite̸	la fe̸nêtre̸	une̸ nation
une̸ montagne̸	une̸ frontière̸	un che̸val

9. *Intonation — L'intonation*

A. Word and word-group intonation
In general, the intonation of the French word and word-group is rising.

But at the end of the sentence, when the idea is finished, the intonation of a word generally falls.

Je vais à Pa
ris

B. Sentence intonation[1]

1. declarative sentences
   a. a short sentence
      Paris est la capitale de la France.

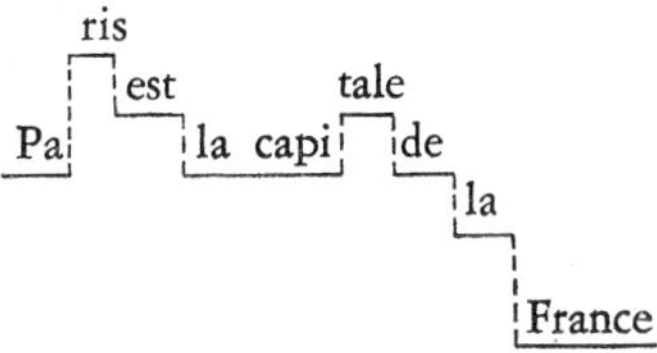

[1] These diagrams show typical French intonation patterns for different types of sentences. The patterns given here have been checked with the spectrograph. Since intonation depends on the intention with which the speaker says the sentence and on the emphasis he desires, other intonation patterns are possible for the same types of sentences. But these basic patterns will serve as a guide to the learner of French.

b. a series of increasingly longer sentences. to indicate change in intonation as the sentence grows longer

1. La Seine est très connue.

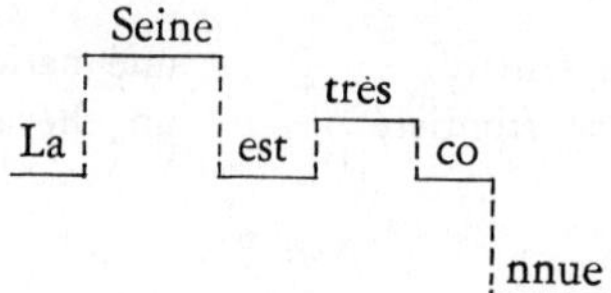

2. La Seine est plus connue que les autres fleuves de France.

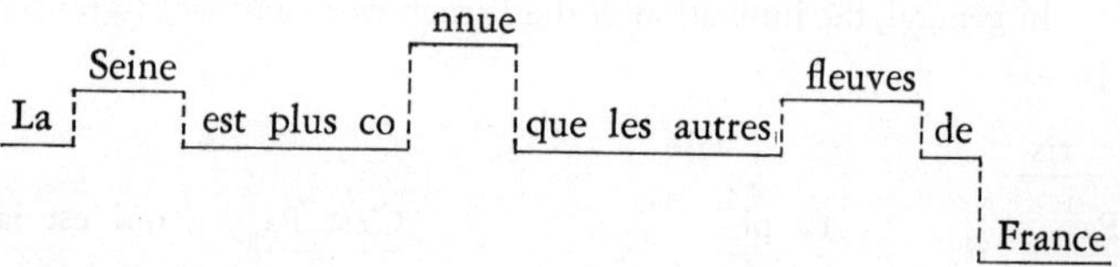

3. La Seine est plus connue que les autres fleuves de France, parce que Paris est situé sur la Seine.

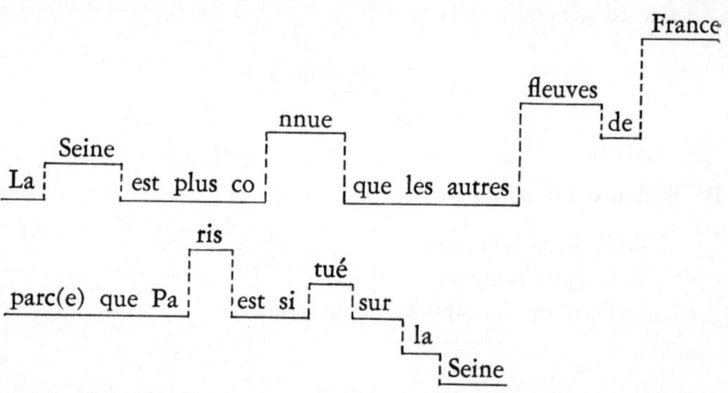

2. The interrogative sentence

a. a statement made interrogative by a question mark
Cette ville est la capitale de la France?

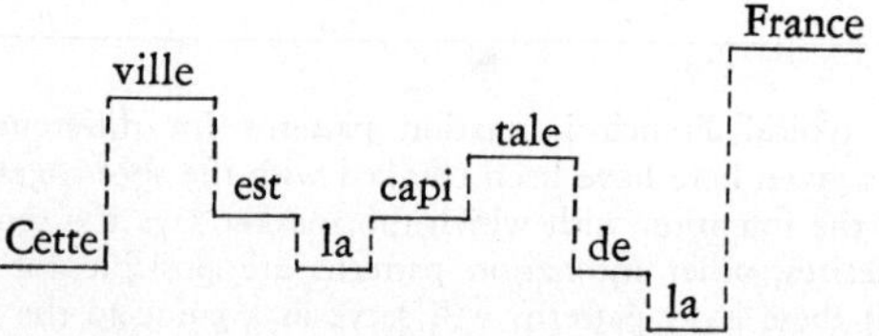

b. a statement made interrogative by inversion

Cette ville est-elle la capitale de la France?

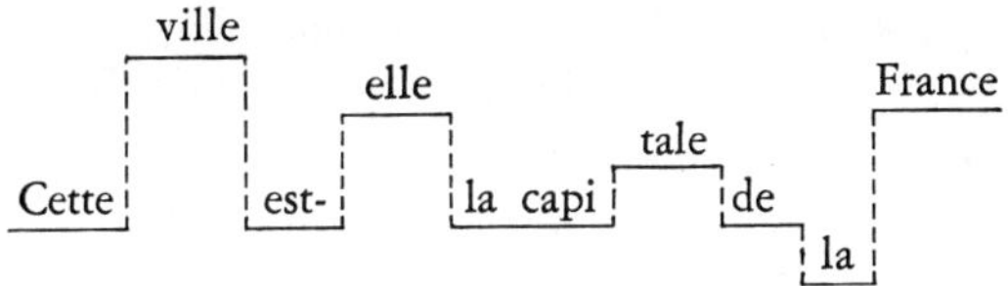

c. a statement made interrogative by *Est-ce que* . . .

Est-ce que cette ville est la capitale de la France?

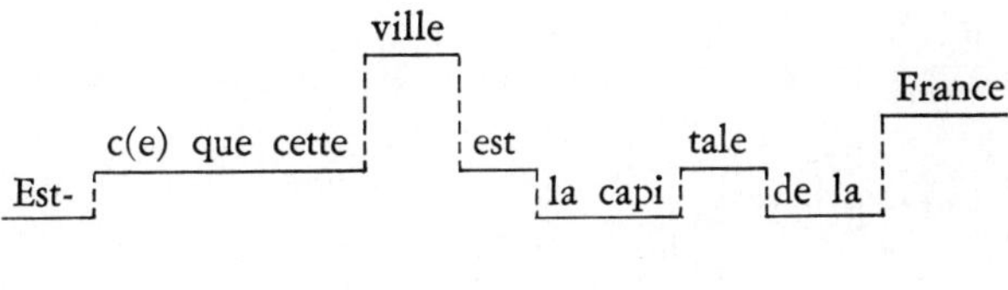

or

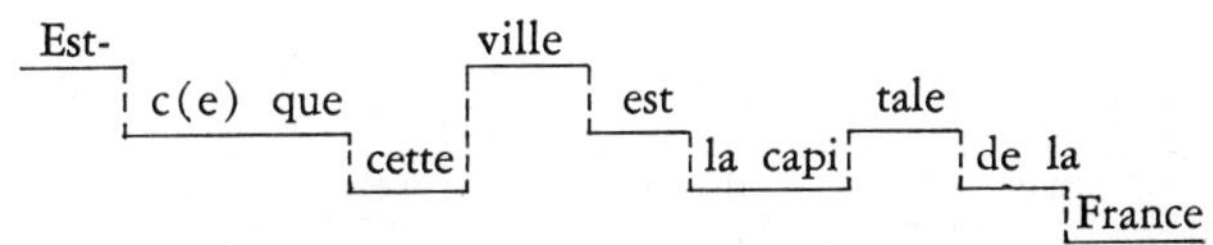

d. sentences with interrogative words

1. Où est la capitale de la France?

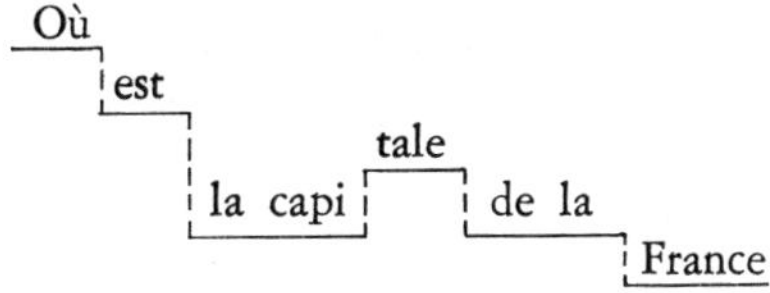

2. Que faites-vous?

Que
faites
vous

3. Quelle est la ville la plus importante du Portugal?

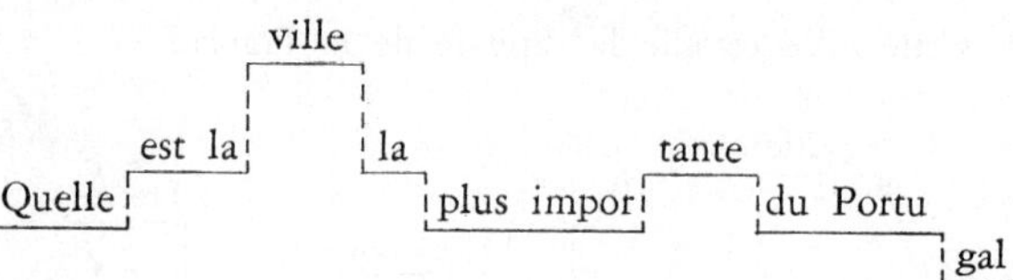

Interrogative sentences which begin with an interrogative word often stress the interrogative word and tend to end with a falling intonation.

3. The imperative sentence

a. Récitez votre leçon.

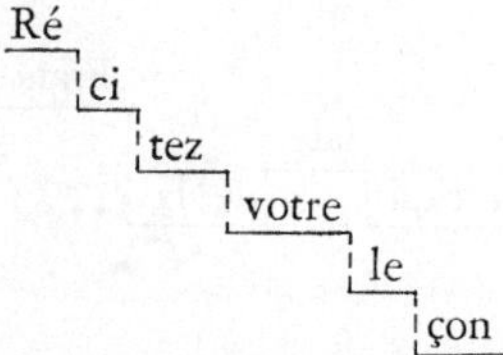

b. Demandez à mademoiselle si Paris est en France.

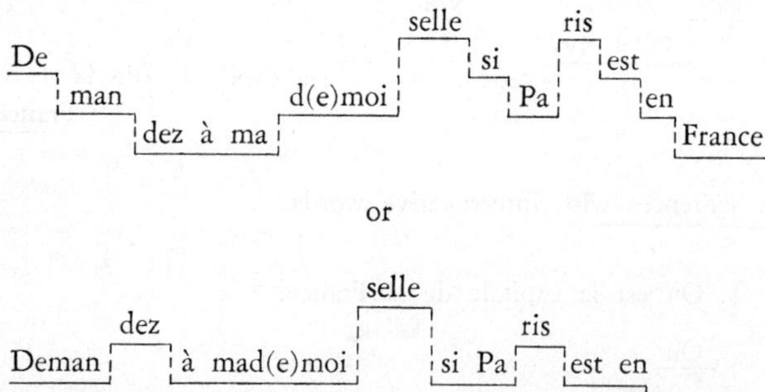

c. Dites à monsieur Guy quelle est la capitale de la France.

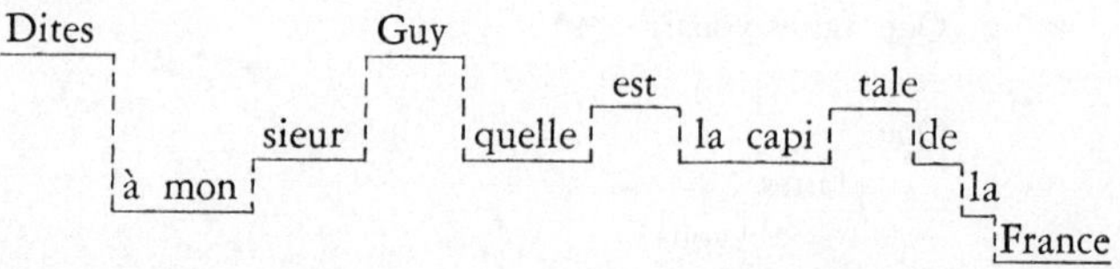

10. *Enchaînement — Enchaînement*

When a word ending in a final pronounced consonant immediately precedes a word of the same word-group beginning with a vowel or a mute *h,* the final consonant of the first word is pronounced with the initial vowel of the second word. This is called *enchaînement.*

il‿est partir‿en classe neuf‿enfants bec‿ouvert

Enchaînement takes place even if a mute *e* separates the final pronounced consonant of the first word from the initial vowel of the second word.

une dame̸‿âgée une̸‿action la première̸‿année

The final consonant of the first word is pronounced as part of the second word. One says: i lest *and not* il||est; une̸ da me̸âgée *and not* une̸ dame̸||âgée.

11. *Linking — Liaison*

Most final consonants are silent. But when a final silent consonant of one word immediately precedes a word in the same word group beginning with a vowel or mute *h,* the final consonant of the first word is often pronounced and linked with the initial vowel of the following word. This is called linking or *liaison.*

The final consonant of the first word is pronounced as part of the second word.

There are certain combinations of words where *liaison* is absolutely necessary, others where it is absolutely forbidden, and then a number of cases where it is optional. Where *liaison* is optional, it is largely a personal matter and a question of one's background. Educated people link more than uneducated. More linkings are made when reading than when speaking. People now link in fewer combinations than formerly. To make a great many of the optional *liaisons* gives the impression of affectation.

A. The necessary *liaisons* are those made from a less important to a more important word, from an unstressed to a stressed word. The following *liaisons* are absolutely necessary:

1. articles and adjectives with a following noun

les‿Alpes un‿endroit trois‿olives des‿ennemis
petit‿état ces‿états mon‿oncle un grand‿homme

2. the pronoun subject and the inflected verb-form

ils‿entrent est‿il nous‿avons
vous‿êtes rend‿il parlent‿ils

3. usually invariable words of one syllable, such as adverbs and prepositions, with the following word

bien‿aimé	trop‿élevé	plus‿étroit	chez‿eux
sans‿intérêt	très‿intéressant	sous‿un lit	dans‿une ville

4. certain set expressions, regardless of their nature

les États‿Unis	accent‿aigu	les Champs‿Élysées	tout‿à coup
de temps‿en temps	sang‿impur	comment‿allez-vous	fait‿accompli

B. The forbidden *liaisons* are often those from a more important to a less important word, from a stressed to an unstressed word. The following combinations must not be linked.

1. words not in the same group

Les plaines se trouvent surtout||à l'intérieur de la France.
Y a-t-il des montagnes||entre les deux pays?
Au centre des États-Unis||il y a une grande plaine.

2. *et* and the following word [1]

Roger a deux frères||et||une sœur.
Le pays est grand||et||il a beaucoup de ressources naturelles.

3. a singular noun with a following adjective

un port||important	un monument||historique	une région||intéressante
un pays||étranger	un endroit||agréable	une opinion||extrême

4. a noun-subject and its verb

Le pays||est très important.	Le garçon||entre dans la maison.
Les villes||ont des monuments.	Ces régions||occupent une vallée fertile.

5. The monosyllables *en, on, ils,* and *elles* preceded by a verb, followed by another verb-form or another word.

a-t-on||eu peur	sont-ils||allées	ont-elles||assez de temps
prenez-en||encore	donne m'en||aussi	ont-ils||écrit la lettre

6. groups in which the second word begins with an aspirate *h* or with *un, onze, huit* or *oui*

les||héros	cent||un	les||onze pays	les||huit pays
mais||oui	les||hautes montagnes	deux cent||un	ces||onze élèves

7. in conversation an infinitive ending in *-er* and a following word

Il veut aller||à l'école.	Vous pouvez parler||allemand.

---

[1] Usually a preceding word is not linked with *et* either, but in reading such a *liaison* is sometimes made. One normally says: les plaines||et les montagnes.

C. The following liaisons are optional.

1. a plural noun with a following adjective

   des montagnes||élevées des frontières||artificielles des amis||américains

2. a verb-form plus a following word, depending on whether the greater stress is on the first or second word

LIAISON PROBABLE	LIAISON POSSIBLE	LIAISON IMPROBABLE
je suis||arrivé	je dois||en parler	il vient||à quatre heures

3. invariable words of more than one syllable, such as adverbs and prepositions, with the following word

toujours||aimable	après||une heure	depuis||un an
beaucoup||à faire	jamais||à l'heure	pendant||une semaine

12. *Methods of learning sounds — Méthodes pour apprendre les sons*

There are two common methods of learning to pronounce French: imitation of the teacher or of recordings of voices of Frenchmen and the assimilation of certain principles of pronunciation which will enable you to pronounce words without having heard them pronounced before. Both methods should be used.

There are two ways of learning how to pronounce a French word you have never seen before: (1) You may learn the value of the various letters and combinations of letters of the French alphabet; (2) You may learn the sounds of the symbols of the International Phonetic Alphabet and look up the pronunciation of the words in the vocabulary or in a pronouncing dictionary. French pronunciation is now presented first by the letters and combinations of letters of the alphabet, then by the phonetic symbols. In the French-English vocabulary at the end of the text the phonetic symbols of each word are supplied.

The pronunciation of the French letters
La prononciation des lettres françaises

13. *The vowels — Les voyelles*

Pronounce the English word *made.* Note that you say "m-a-ee-d." The *a* is made up of the sound *a* plus the glide-sound *ee.* French vowels do not have the glide-sound. Their pronunciation is constant, the jaws, lips, and tongue being held in the same position throughout the time required for making the sound. The French would pronounce *made* "m-é-d" which would cause it to sound foreign, for it would be too abrupt. You must pronounce your French vowels without the glide-sound to make them sound truly French.

a

a is written *a* and *â*. It has two common pronunciations.

a is most often pronounced by a sound between the *a* of English f*a*ther and the *a* of English c*a*t. This sound is much nearer the *a* of f*a*ther than the *a* of c*a*t. EXAMPLES: capitale, partie, traverser, la, madame, plateau, montagne, séparer, grave, allemand, facile, relativement.

a is pronounced somewhat like the *a* in English f*a*ther, (1) usually when it is written *â*, (2) nearly always when it is followed by *s*. EXAMPLES: château, âge, pas, passer, classe, phrase, bas, basse.

The distinction in sound between *a* and *â* is becoming rarer and rarer in French. Many Frenchmen pronounce all *a* sounds like the first *a* described above.

e

e is written *é, è, ê,* and *e*. It has three distinct and common pronunciations. In certain cases, *e* (unaccented) is silent.

é is comparable to the *a* in the English word *a*te but without the glide. EXAMPLES: situé, divisé, élevé, défendre, défense, étroit, différent, édifice, élégant, intéressant, économe.

è is comparable to *e* in the English word m*e*t. EXAMPLES: très, frontière, près, célèbre, après, caractère, élève.

ê is comparable to *e* in the English word m*e*t but is prolonged before certain consonants. EXAMPLES: même, empêcher, extrême.

e has three pronunciations; at times, it is silent.

1. It is pronounced *é*
   a. in final *-er* and *-ez* verb endings. EXAMPLES: travers*e*r, travers*e*z, cit*e*r, cit*e*z, compos*e*r, compos*e*z, trouv*e*r, trouv*e*z.
   b. in monosyllables ending in *-es*. EXAMPLES: l*e*s, c*e*s, d*e*s, m*e*s.
   c. in most words ending in *-ier* and in many words ending in *-er*. EXAMPLES: premi*e*r, papi*e*r, quarti*e*r, étrang*e*r.
2. It is pronounced *è* in a syllable ending in a pronounced consonant. EXAMPLES: qu*e*lle, comm*e*rce, f*e*rtile, av*e*c, *e*spagnol, pr*e*sque, corr*e*ction.
3. It is known as mute *e* and pronounced something like *e* in the English word oth*e*r.
   a. in words of one syllable not followed by a pronounced consonant. EXAMPLES: l*e*, d*e*, qu*e*, m*e*, s*e*, t*e*, c*e*.

b. in most other words in which it is the last letter of any syllable except the last syllable. EXAMPLES: p*e*tit, r*e*garder, d*e*voir, f*e*nêtre, d*e*vant, d*e*bout, r*e*commencer.

c. in complete sentences whether or not the mute *e* is pronounced generally depends on the number of preceding consonants in the word or word-group. When mute *e* is preceded by *more than one pronounced consonant* and followed by another consonant, whether the consonants are in the same word or in the immediately preceding or following word of the same group, the mute *e* is pronounced. EXAMPLES: fort*e*resse, quelqu*e*fois, gouvern*e*ment, départ*e*ment, direct*e*ment, appart*e*ment, un(e) p*e*tite ville, le nord d*e* la France.

e is silent

1. at the end of words of more than one syllable.[1] EXAMPLES: quell*e*, madam*e*, trouv*e*, fleuv*e*, un*e*, capital*e*.
2. when the final syllable ends in an *-es* of which the *-s* is a plural or an *-ent* which is a third person plural present verb-ending. EXAMPLES: quell*es*, mesdam*es*, trouv*ent*, fleuv*es*. These entire endings are silent.
3. when, in other than the first syllable of a word, it is preceded by a single consonant sound and is the final letter in the syllable. EXAMPLES: app*e*ler, all*e*mand, ach*e*ter, mèn*e*rai, él*e*vé, seul*e*ment, méd*e*cin, emp*e*reur, prom*e*nade, mad*e*moiselle.

Under certain conditions, the final stressed syllable of a word causes the sound *è* of the preceding syllable to change to *é*. This phenomenon is known as regressive vowel assimilation or *harmonisation vocalique*. See § 20.

i

i is written *i* or *î*. It is usually pronounced like the *i* in the English word pol*i*ce. EXAMPLES: capitale, partie, situé, continent, divisé, citez, ville, petit, qui, constituer, limité, difficile, limite, il.

Often when *i* is followed by another pronounced vowel, it has the sound of the English *y* in *y*ou, but is pronounced more rapidly. EXAMPLES: front*i*ère, intér*i*eur, quest*i*on, artific*i*el.

o

o is written *o* and *ô*. It has two pronunciations.

o is most frequently pronounced somewhat like the *o* in English *o*ught. EXAMPLES: nord, former, problème, important, colonie, espagnol, costume, prononciation, historique, encore, occuper, fortifié, joli, produit.

[1] Although *-e* is silent at the end of words, it is considered part of a separate syllable. Thus, we divide *capitale* ca-pi-ta-le. This is important in determining nasal vowels.

o is pronounced somewhat like the *o* in the English c*o*ld but without the glide: (a) when written *ô*. EXAMPLES: côte, tôt, côté, plutôt; (b) when *o* is followed by a *z* sound. EXAMPLES: comp*o*ser, exp*o*sition, ch*o*se; (c) when *o* is the final pronounced sound in a word. EXAMPLES: tr*o*p, styl*o*, v*o*s, vet*o*, gr*o*s, numér*o*.

u

u is written *u* and *û*. It has no English equivalent. It is made by rounding the lips as if to pronounce *oo* in *tool*, then, keeping the lips in that position, saying *i* as in *police*. Practice rounding your lips before a mirror and saying the *i* in pol*i*ce. (Compare German *ü*.) EXAMPLES: sud, sur, une, naturel, connu, plus, du, embouchure, sûr.

u, when followed immediately by another vowel, is often pronounced as French *u* very rapidly followed by the full value of the following vowel. EXAMPLES: situé, constitué, Suisse, ensuite.

14. *Vowel combinations — Combinaisons de voyelles*

ou

ou is pronounced something like the English *oo* in *tool*, but without the glide described on pages 523–524. Keep this sound pure. The lips are rounded in making the French *ou*. EXAMPLES: où, trouver, pour, couler, embouchure, source.

ou when followed by another pronounced vowel usually has the sound of *w* in the English word *w*est. EXAMPLES: oui, ouest.

ai

ai is most often pronounced like *è*. EXAMPLES: pl*ai*ne, milit*ai*re, m*ai*son, m*ai*s, *ai*r, sem*ai*ne, *ai*m*ai*t, pl*ai*s*ai*t.

ai is pronounced like *é* when it comes at the end of a verb-ending. EXAMPLES: j'*ai*, je parler*ai*, je finir*ai*, je trouv*ai*.

ei

ei is usually pronounced like *è*. EXAMPLES: r*ei*ne, n*ei*geait, S*ei*ne.

oi

oi is pronounced like a combination of the English *w* and the French *a*. EXAMPLES: endr*oi*t, tr*oi*s, étr*oi*t, pourqu*oi*, s*oi*e, r*oi*, r*oy*aliste,[1] quelquef*oi*s.

eu, œu

eu, also written *œu*, has two distinct pronunciations, neither of which occurs in English.

---

[1] y between two vowels is equivalent to *ii*. Thus *royaliste* = *roi-ialiste*.

eu and *œu* are most often pronounced by placing the lips in the position for the French *o* and pronouncing *è*. EXAMPLES: intéri*eu*r, fl*eu*ve, plusi*eu*rs, l*eu*rs, b*eu*rre, h*eu*re, err*eu*r, s*œu*r, c*œu*r, b*œu*f.

eu and *œu* as final sounds in a word or before a final *z* sound are pronounced by placing the lips in the position for *ô* and pronouncing *é*. The sound approaches that of *e* in the English word oth*e*r. It is not very different from the French mute *e* in l*e*. EXAMPLES: d*eu*x, b*œu*fs, nombr*eux,* nombr*eu*se, p*eu,* séri*eu*x, bl*eu.*

au, eau

au and *eau* are usually pronounced like *ô*. EXAMPLES: aussi, au, plateau, aujourd'hui, automne, faute, haut, gauche, nouveau, bateau, pauvre.

au followed by *r* is usually pronounced as the French *o*. EXAMPLE: aura.

-ill-, *vowel* + -il, *vowel* + -ille

The combination *-ill-* is pronounced as French *i* + *y* (as in English *y*ou). EXAMPLES: fille, famille. But the combination *-ill-* is pronounced as French *il* in *ville, mille, tranquille,* and their derivatives, such as *village, million, tranquillité.* It is also so pronounced at the beginning of words. EXAMPLE: illustrer.

The vowels + final *-il* and the vowels + *-ill-* are pronounced as a combination of the vowel in question + *y* (as in English *y*ou). Avoid pronouncing the endings of words in *-ail* and *-aille* like the English *i* in n*i*ce. EXAMPLES: trava*il,* trava*ille,* déta*il,* bata*ille,* Marse*ille,* conse*il,* appare*il,* conse*ill*er, sole*il,* œ*il,* grenou*ille,* feu*ille.*

15. *The nasal vowels — Les voyelles nasales*

In French, any vowel followed by *m* or *n* in the same syllable is made in such a way as to issue partly from the nose instead of entirely from the mouth. This is called nasalization. In these combinations the *m* and the *n* are not pronounced. These are no English equivalents for the French nasal vowels.

There is no nasalization (a) when the *m* or *n* following a vowel does not belong to the same syllable; (b) when *m* or *n* is doubled.

Turn back to page 514, § 6 and review syllabication for a complete understanding of when a vowel is nasalized.

con-ti-n*ent*, n*om*-bre, *im*-por-t*ant*, *em*-bou-chu-re; ma-de-moi-sel-le, li-mi-te, en-ne-mi (*no nasal here because of double* n), im-mo-bi-le.

am, an, em, en *in the same syllable*

Each of the above nasals has the same pronunciation.

EXAMPLES: d*an*s, gr*an*d, import*an*t, c*en*tre, contin*en*t, déf*en*dre, *en,* excell*en*t, relativem*en*t.

im, in, aim, ain, eim, ein, *and* (i)en *in the same syllable*

All of these combinations are pronounced in the same way.
EXAMPLES: *im*portant, *in*térieur, prov*in*ce, cert*ain,* m*ain,* pe*in*tre, bi*en,* ri*en,* jard*in.*

om, on *in the same syllable*

EXAMPLES: n*om*bre, c*om*poser, c*on*tinent, nati*on,* s*on*t, fr*on*tière, m*on*tagne, c*on*stituer, questi*on.*

um, un *in the same syllable*

These combinations are both pronounced in the same way.
EXAMPLES: *un,* l*un*di, chac*un,* parf*um.*

oin

This combination is pronounced as a combination of the English *w* + French nasalized *in.*
EXAMPLES: m*oin*s, c*oin,* s*oin,* l*oin,* bes*oin,* p*oin*t.

16. *The consonants — Les consonnes*

Most consonants are more nearly alike in French and English than are the vowels. The following consonants require special attention:

c is pronounced:

1. like English *k* before *a, o,* and *u,* and at the end of words. EXAMPLES: capitale, continent, constituer, connu.
2. like English *s* in *s*it before *e, i,* and *y.* EXAMPLES: centre, citez, facile, difficile, effacer.

To soften the *c* before *a, o,* and *u* a cedilla (¸) is placed under the *c* (ç). EXAMPLES: garçon, façade, français.

g is pronounced:

1. like English *g* in *g*ot before *a, o, u,* or a consonant. EXAMPLES: grand, grave, magasin.
2. like English *s* in plea*s*ure before *e, i,* and *y.* EXAMPLES: large, région, étranger.

To soften the *g* before *a, o,* and *u,* an *e* is inserted between the *g* and the vowel. EXAMPLES: mang*e*ons, charg*e*ais.

h is completely silent in French; see pages 511–512.

j is pronounced like the English *s* in plea*s*ure. EXAMPLES: jette, aujourd'hui, joli, jeune, déjà, jour, jusqu'à, je.

l constitutes a special difficulty, since it does not correspond to the English *l*. It approaches initial *l* in *leap*. Imitate your teacher's *l*, and avoid making the *l* of the English word *bell*. EXAMPLES: capitale, les, quelle, ville, il, elle, facile.

q is always followed by *u* except when final. *q* and *qu* are ordinarily pronounced as *k*. EXAMPLES: quelle, qui, que, presque, marque, historique, politique, pittoresque, quelque, cinq, coq.

r has no English equivalent. To pronounce a French word containing *r* with an American *r* is the surest possible way of betraying an American accent. The sound *r* is made in various ways in different parts of France, but the most elegant French *r* and the standard in cultivated pronunciation is considered to be the Parisian *r*. The articulation of the Parisian *r* varies somewhat, depending on the position of the *r* in the word.

How to pronounce the Parisian r

Place the tip of your tongue against your lower teeth and pronounce the *ch* in the German word *Bach*.[1] The result is a rasping sound produced by the air hitting the back of the tongue, which is in a raised position. Pronounce the *r* in this way in the combinations *pra, tra, fra, cra, s(e)ra, prè, trè, frè.* In saying these combinations, do not try to pronounce the *r* as the sound you normally associate with *r*.

Now pronounce the following words, which contain the sound *r* in various combinations.

1. *consonant + r + vowel*

In this position, *r* is pronounced as described above. It is a relatively strong rasping sound almost like the sound made when one clears one's throat.

très, trouve, trois, entrer, étroit, étranger, industrie

près, pris, prend, presque, principal, prononcer, province, après, approcher, grand, grave, gris, grêle

frais, fréquent, France, français, Afrique

2. *vowel + r + vowel*

Intervocalic *r* is essentially the sound described above but much softer. Practice saying *r* in the combinations *ara, arè, ari, aro, aru.* The *r* in these combinations has nothing of the nature of the American *r*. The tip of the tongue is against the lower teeth, the back of the tongue is raised, and the sound of the *r* is produced by the air hitting the back of the tongue.

Paris, Garonne, caractère, varié, comparaison, séparer

différence, tempérament, intéressant, Amérique

Pyrénées, Gironde, Europe

Jura, naturel, historique, pittoresque, Touraine, muraille

---

[1] This is the same sound as the *j* in the Spanish word *bajo*.

3. *vowel + r (final)*

Final *-r* is pronounced very lightly. Pronounce the following words first without *-r,* then with *r,* but as if *r* were part of a following syllable: mer (mè-, mè-r), court (cou-, cou-rt).

mer, frontière, militaire, Angleterre, hiver, divers, pierre, estuaire
souvenir, finir, punir, choisir
nord, fort, port, encore
Tours, court, toujours, Luxembourg, Strasbourg
embouchure, architecture, voiture, intérieur
Loire, histoire

4. *r + consonant*

Usually the consonant belongs to a following syllable. Pronounce the syllable ending in *r* clearly, as though it were final *r* as described above, before beginning to pronounce the following syllable.

partie, Marseille, artificiel, marqué, parle
Cherbourg, commerce, fertile, certain, conservé
former, important, Normandie, Orléans, forteresse, fortifié
surtout, source, fournir

5. *initial r*

Keep in mind that *r* is a rasping sound always made with the tip of the tongue against the lower teeth. It is pronounced in this same way when it comes at the beginning of a word.

race, radio, rage, raconter
relativement, Renaissance, région, rendre, Reims, Rhin
rive, rivalité
robe, roman, Rome, Rhône
rue, rude, Russie, ruine
roi, royal

6. *consonant + -re (at end of word)*

In combinations of *consonant* + **-re** at the end of a word, the *r* is almost whispered. It is still a rasping sound.

autre, centre, le Havre, célèbre, nombre, être, défendre, kilomètre

s has two distinct pronunciations.

1. that of English *s* in *sit* in all cases except when it comes between two vowels. EXAMPLES: situé, traverser, sud, séparer.
2. that of English *z* in *zero* when it comes between two vowels. EXAMPLES: composer, division, rose.

w is found chiefly in foreign words. It is most often pronounced like the English *v*. EXAMPLE: wagon. In some words, it is pronounced like the English *w*. EXAMPLE: tramway.

x has four sounds:

1. *ks* usually in words resembling English words where *x* has the same pronunciation. EXAMPLES: excellent, excepté, expérience, expliquer, extrême, exprès.
2. *gz* usually in words resembling English words where *x* has the same pronunciation. EXAMPLES: examen, examiner, exact, exagérer, exemple, exister.
   Caution: The *x* of *exercise* is pronounced *gz.*
3. *s* in *soixante* and in *six* and *dix* when not used to modify a noun.
4. *z* in *deux, six,* and *dix* when linked to a following word beginning with a vowel or a mute *h,* in *dix-huit, dix-neuf, deuxième, sixième, dixième,* and in words ending in *-x* when linked to a following word.

17. *Consonant combinations — Les combinaisons de consonnes*

cc: Pronounced like *k* before *a, o,* and *u,* and like *ks* before *e, i,* and *y.* EXAMPLES: accabler, accord, accuser, accent, accès, accident.

ch: Pronounced like English *ch* in *machine.* EXAMPLES: architecture, empêcher, château, chef, charme, choisir, marcher.

Occasionally it is pronounced like *k.* EXAMPLES: orchestre, écho, Michel-Ange.

gn: Pronounced like English *ny* in ca*ny*on. EXAMPLES: montagne, champagne.

ph: Pronounced like English *f.* EXAMPLES: géographie, phrase, pharmacie.

qu: Pronounced like English *k.* EXAMPLES: quelle, qui, que, presque, marqué.

ti, not initial, and not preceded by *-s-,* is often pronounced like English *see.* EXAMPLES: nation, diplomatie, patience, balbutier. In the *-stion-* group the *-t-* is pronounced as *t.* EXAMPLES: question, bastion, congestion.

th: Pronounced like French *t.* EXAMPLES: théoriquement, thé.

18. *Final consonants — Les consonnes finales*

Final consonants are often silent in French.

1. *-s* and *-es* as a mark of the plural are usually silent. EXAMPLES: nations, fleuves.
2. *-ent* of verb-endings is always silent. EXAMPLES: traversent, forment, coulent.
3. The consonants in the word *"careful,"* i.e., *c, r, f,* and *l* are often pronounced when they are final, as is final *-ct.* EXAMPLES: ave*c,* be*c,* fe*r,* me*r,* che*f,* œu*f,* que*l,* ba*l,* dire*ct,* distri*ct.*
4. *-c* is sounded except after nasals. EXAMPLES: ban*c,* blan*c,* (*-c is silent*).

5. *-r* is normally sounded. EXAMPLES: fini*r*, pou*r*, autou*r*, du*r*, ca*r*, fleu*r*. In the ending *-er*, *-r* is usually silent, the *-er* being pronounced like *-é*. EXAMPLES: parl*er*, donn*er*, boulang*er*, lég*er*, premi*er*, étrang*er*. By exception, the *-r* of the following words in *-er* is pronounced: me*r*, fe*r*, ve*r*, hive*r*, ame*r*, éthe*r*, cuille*r*, enfe*r*, hie*r*, fie*r*, and the *-r* of all learned words such as Jupite*r*.

Pronunciation by phonetic symbols
La prononciation par les symboles phonétiques

To represent the pronunciation of various languages, an international phonetic alphabet has been devised. The French language contains thirty-seven sounds, represented by thirty-seven symbols of this phonetic alphabet. Most of these symbols correspond to letters of the English alphabet. Only where one letter of our alphabet represents several sounds does this alphabet use a different symbol. The phonetic alphabet, with examples taken from early lessons of the book, is:

SYMBOL	EXAMPLE		SYMBOL	EXAMPLE	
1. a	c*a*pit*a*le	[kapital]	20. o	p*o*se	[poz]
2. ɑ	*â*ge	[ɑʒ]	21. ɔ	n*o*rd	[nɔr]
3. ɑ̃	d*ans*	[dɑ̃]	22. õ	nati*on*	[nɑsjõ]
4. b	ha*b*itant	[abitɑ̃]	23. ø	p*eu*	[pø]
5. d	*d*e	[də]	24. œ	intéri*eu*r	[ɛ̃terjœr]
6. e	*é*t*é*	[ete]	25. œ̃	*un*	[œ̃]
7. ɛ	tr*è*s	[trɛ]	26. p	*p*artie	[parti]
8. ɛ̃	*in*térieur	[ɛ̃terjœr]	27. ʀ, r	pa*r*tie	[paʀti, parti]
9. ə	p*e*tit	[pəti]	28. s	*s*itué	[sitɥe]
10. f	*f*ort	[fɔr]	29. ʃ	*ch*âteau	[ʃɑto]
11. g	*g*rand	[grɑ̃]	30. t	*t*raverse	[travɛrs]
12. h	a*h*a!	[ɑ(h)ɑ]	31. u	tr*ou*ve	[truv]
13. i	cap*i*tale	[kapital]	32. w	*ou*est	[wɛst]
14. j	front*i*ère	[frõtjɛr]	33. v	tra*v*erse	[travɛrs]
15. k	*c*apitale	[kapital]	34. y	s*u*d	[syd]
16. l	capita*l*e	[kapital]	35. ɥ	sit*ué*	[sitɥe]
17. m	*m*ada*m*e	[madam]	36. z	compo*s*e	[kõpoz]
18. n	*n*ation	[nɑsjõ]	37. ʒ	*j*eter	[ʒəte]
19. ɲ	monta*gn*e	[mõtaɲ]			

19. *The vowels — Les voyelles*

Pronounce the English word *made.* Note that you say "m-a-ee-d" [meid]. The *a* is made up of the sound [e] plus the glide-sound [i]. French vowels do not have the glide-sound. Their pronunciation is constant, the jaws, lips, and tongue being held in the same position throughout the time required for making the sound. The French would pronounce *made* [med], which would cause it to sound foreign, for it would be too abrupt. You must pronounce your French vowels in this way to make them sound truly French.

[a]

[a] is most often pronounced by a sound between the *a* of f*a*ther and the *a* of c*a*t. This sound is much nearer the *a* of f*a*ther than the *a* of c*a*t.

capitale	[kapital]	la	[la]
traverse	[travɛrs]	grave	[grav]
facile	[fasil]	allemand	[almɑ̃]
madame	[madam]	relativement	[rəlativmɑ̃]
montagne	[mõtaɲ]	séparer	[separe]

[ɑ]

[ɑ] is pronounced somewhat like the *a* in f*a*ther. It is represented in French by *â* and often by *a* followed by *s*. The distinction between [a] and [ɑ] is becoming rarer and rarer in French. Many Frenchmen pronounce all *a* sounds as [a].

château	[ʃɑto]	pas	[pɑ]	passer	[pɑse]	phrase	[frɑz]
âge	[ɑʒ]	bas	[bɑ]	classe	[klɑ̈s]	basse	[bɑs]

[e]

[e] is comparable to the *a* in the English word *a*te but without the glide. This sound is represented in French in various ways:

1. by *é;*

situé	[sitɥe]	divisé	[divize]
été	[ete]	défendre	[defɑ̃dr]
élégant	[elegɑ̃]	édifice	[edifis]
défense	[defɑ̃s]	intéressant	[ɛ̃terɛsɑ̃]
étroit	[etrwɑ]	différent	[diferɑ̃]
économe	[ekɔnɔm]	modéré	[mɔdere]

2. by *-er* and *-ez* in verb-endings;

traverser	[travɛrse]	citer	[site]
traversez	[travɛrse]	citez	[site]
composer	[kõpoze]	trouver	[truve]
composez	[kõpoze]	trouvez	[truve]

3. in monosyllables by final *-es;*

les	[le]	ces	[se]	des	[de]	mes	[me]

4. In most words ending in *-ier* and in many words ending in *-er;*

premier [prəmje] papier [papje] quartier [kartje] étranger [etrɑ̃ʒe]

5. by *ai* at the end of verbs.

j'ai [ʒe] je parlerai [ʒəparləre] je finirai [ʒəfinire] je trouvai [ʒətruve]

[ɛ]

[ɛ] is comparable to the *e* in the English word m*e*t.
This sound is represented in French by:

1. *è;*

très	[trɛ]	après	[aprɛ]	célèbre	[selɛbr]	caractère	[karaktɛr]
près	[prɛ]	élève	[elɛv]	frontière	[frɔ̃tjɛr]	sévère	[sevɛr]
pièce	[pjɛs]	crème	[krɛm]	matière	[matjɛr]	troisième	[trwɑzjɛm]

2. *ê;*

même [mɛm] empêche [ɑ̃pɛʃ] extrême [ɛkstrɛm] conquête [kɔ̃kɛt]

3. *e* in a syllable ending in a pronounced consonant;

quelle	[kɛl]	fertile	[fɛrtil]
verte	[vɛrt]	avec	[avɛk]
commerce	[kɔmɛrs]	espagnol	[ɛspaɲɔl]
presque	[prɛsk]	celtique	[sɛltik]
correction	[kɔrɛksjɔ̃]	fermenté	[fɛrmɑ̃te]
pittoresque	[pitɔrɛsk]	question	[kɛstjɔ̃]

4. *ai* except at the end of verbs.

plaine	[plɛn]	maison	[mɛzɔ̃]	mais	[mɛ]	aime	[ɛm]
militaire	[militɛr]	semaine	[səmɛn]	air	[ɛr]	plaisait	[plɛzɛ]

5. *ei*

pleine [plɛn] reine [rɛn] veine [vɛn] peine [pɛn]

[ə]

[ə] is pronounced something like the *e* in the English word oth*e*r. This sound is represented in French by *e*

1. in isolated words of one syllable not followed by a pronounced consonant;

le [lə] de [də] que [kə] me [mə] se [sə] te [tə] ce [sə]

2. in most other isolated words in which it is the final letter of the syllable (except the last syllable, where it is silent);

petit	[pəti]	devoir	[dəvwar]
regarder	[rəgarde]	fenêtre	[fənɛtr]
devant	[dəvɑ̃]	recommencer	[rəkɔmɑ̃se]
debout	[dəbu]	Breton	[brətɔ̃]

3. in a word or in groups of words in which the *e* is preceded by more than one consonant and followed by another consonant, whether the consonants are in the same word or in the immediately preceding or following word of the same group;

forteresse	[fɔrtərɛs]	département	[departəmɑ̃]
quelquefois	[kɛlkəfwa]	directement	[dirɛktəmɑ̃]
gouvernement	[guvɛrnəmɑ̃]	appartement	[apartəmɑ̃]

une petite ville	[ynpətitvil]
le nord de la France	[lənɔrdəlafrɑ̃s]
sur le fleuve	[syrləflœv]

[i]

[i] is pronounced like *i* in the English word pol*i*ce. It is represented in French by *i* and *î*.

capitale	[kapital]	continent	[kɔ̃tinɑ̃]	ville	[vil]	constituer	[kɔ̃stitɥe]
partie	[parti]	divisé	[divize]	petit	[pəti]	limite	[limit]
situé	[sitɥe]	citez	[site]	qui	[ki]	difficile	[difisil]
il	[il]	limité	[limite]	île	[il]	corrige	[kɔriʒ]

[o]

[o] is pronounced like *o* in the English word c*o*ld but without the glide. It is represented in French in several ways.

1. *ô*

côte [kot] tôt [to] côté [kote] plutôt [plyto]

2. *o* followed by a *z* sound

composer [kɔ̃poze] exposition [ɛkspozisjɔ̃] chose [ʃoz] pose [poz]

3. *o* when it is the final pronounced sound in a word.

trop [tro] stylo [stilo] vos [vo] veto [veto] gros [gro]

4. *au* and *eau*

au	[o]	autour	[otur]	plateau	[plato]	tableau	[tablo]
aussi	[osi]	gauche	[goʃ]	Bordeaux	[bɔrdo]	beau	[bo]
autre	[otr]	aujourd'hui	[oʒurdɥi]	château	[ʃɑto]	bateau	[bato]

[ɔ]

[ɔ] is pronounced somewhat as *o* in English *o*ught. It is represented by *o* in French in most cases where *o* is not pronounced [o].

nord	[nɔr]	important	[ɛ̃pɔrtɑ̃]	costume	[kɔstym]
former	[fɔrme]	colonie	[kɔlɔni]	prononciation	[prɔnɔ̃sjasjɔ̃]
problème	[prɔblɛm]	espagnol	[ɛspaɲɔl]	historique	[istɔrik]
encore	[ɑ̃kɔr]	occuper	[ɔkype]	fortifié	[fɔrtifje]
joli	[ʒɔli]	produit	[prɔdɥi]	professeur	[prɔfɛsœr]

[u]

[u] is pronounced something like the English *oo* in *too*l but without the glide. The sound is made by rounding the lips. Be sure that the sound is pure. [u] is expressed by *ou* in French.

où	[u]	trouver	[truve]	pour	[pur]
couler	[kule]	embouchure	[ɑ̃buʃyr]	source	[surs]

[y]

[y] has no English equivalent. Round your lips (before a mirror) as if to pronounce [u]. Keep your lips in that position but say [i]. That produces the sound [y]. [y] is represented by *u* in French.

sud	[syd]	une	[yn]	naturel	[natyrɛl]	du	[dy]
sur	[syr]	connu	[kɔny]	plus	[ply]	embouchure	[ɑ̃buʃyr]

[ø]

[ø] is pronounced by placing the lips in the position for [o] and pronouncing [e]. This sound does not exist in English, but it approaches the *e* in oth*e*r. It is represented in French by *eu* and *œu* final, before a silent letter, or before a *z* sound.

deux	[dø]	nombreux	[nɔ̃brø]	peu	[pø]	sérieux	[serjø]	veut	[vø]
bœufs	[bø]	nombreuse	[nɔ̃brøz]	bleu	[blø]	sérieuse	[serjøz]	peut	[pø]

[œ]

[œ] is pronounced by placing the lips in the position for [ɔ] and pronouncing [ɛ]. This sound does not exist in English. It is represented in French by *eu* or *œu* except in the cases explained under ø.

intérieur	[ɛ̃terjœr]	plusieurs	[plyzjœr]	beurre	[bœr]	erreur	[ɛrœr]
fleuve	[flœv]	leurs	[lœr]	heure	[œr]	sœur	[sœr]
cœur	[kœr]	pleure	[plœr]	bœuf	[bœf]	peuvent	[pœv]

20. *Regressive vowel assimilation — Harmonisation vocalique*

In general, *harmonisation vocalique* is the result of the influence of a following vowel (usually final and stressed) on the immediately preceding vowel of a word. There are several following vowels which, under certain conditions, can modify the sound of the preceding vowel, but the one we are most concerned about is the change of the [ɛ] of the preceding syllable to [e].

Under certain conditions, the final stressed syllable of a word causes the [ɛ] of the preceding syllable to change to [e].

Consider the pronunciation of the following groups of words:

adresse	[adrɛs]	adresser	[adrese]
aident	[ɛd]	aidez	[ede]
aime	[ɛm]	aimer	[eme]
arrête	[arɛt]	arrêtai	[arete]
baigne	[bɛɲ]	baigner	[beɲe]
blessent	[blɛs]	blessez	[blese]
cesse	[sɛs]	cessé	[sese]
dépêchent	[depɛʃ]	dépêcher	[depeʃe]

Each word in the first column has a stressed syllable which ends in [ɛ]. Most words derived from these words retain the [ɛ] in pronunciation even when it is in an unstressed syllable. For instance:

adressons	[adrɛsõ]	aidera	[ɛdra]	arrêtais	[arɛtɛ]
baignions	[bɛɲõ]	blesserait	[blɛsrɛ]	cessait	[sɛsɛ]

But when the [ɛ] of such words is followed by a final syllable whose stressed vowel is [i], [e] or [y], then the influence of this final stressed vowel causes the [ɛ] of the preceding syllable to become [e].

This assimilation does not take place when the preceding syllable whose vowel is [ɛ] ends in a consonant; e.g., perd [pɛr], perdez [pɛrde], perdit [pɛrdi], perdu [pɛrdy].

The modifications brought about by *harmonisation vocalique* are found in the pronunciation of the unaffected cultivated Frenchman of today. This modification has therefore been incorporated into the phonetic transcriptions of the words in the French-English vocabulary.

21. *The nasal vowels — Les voyelles nasales*

In French, any vowel followed by *m* or *n* in the same syllable, is made in such a way as to issue partly from the nose instead of entirely from the mouth. This is called nasalization. In these combinations the *m* and the *n* are not pronounced. There are no English equivalents for the French nasal vowels. There is no nasalization (*a*) when the *m* or *n* following a vowel do not belong to the same syllable; (*b*) when *m* or *n* are doubled.

Turn back to page 514, Pr. § 6 and review syllabication for a complete understanding of when a vowel is nasalized.

Phonetic script uses the tilde (˜) over [ɑ], [ɛ], [o], and [œ] to indicate the nasal vowels.

[ɑ̃]

[ɑ̃] is represented in French by *am, an, em,* or *en* in the same syllable.

dans	[dɑ̃]	important	[ɛ̃pɔrtɑ̃]	centre	[sɑ̃tr]
grand	[grɑ̃]	continent	[kõtinɑ̃]	défendre	[defɑ̃dr]
en	[ɑ̃]	Normandie	[nɔrmɑ̃di]	relativement	[rəlativmɑ̃]

[ɛ̃]

[ɛ̃] is represented in French by *im, in, aim, ain, eim, ein,* or by *en* after *i* in the same syllable.

important	[ɛ̃pɔrtɑ̃]	certain	[sɛrtɛ̃]	bien	[bjɛ̃]
intérieur	[ɛ̃terjœr]	main	[mɛ̃]	rien	[rjɛ̃]
province	[prɔvɛ̃s]	peintre	[pɛ̃tr]	jardin	[ʒardɛ̃]

[õ]

[õ] is represented in French by *om* or *on* in the same syllable.

nombre	[nõbr]	nation	[nasjõ]	montagne	[mõtaɲ]
composer	[kõpoze]	sont	[sõ]	constituer	[kõstitɥe]
continent	[kõtinɑ̃]	frontière	[frõtjɛr]	question	[kɛstjõ]

[œ̃]

[œ̃] is represented in French by *um* or *un* in the same syllable.

un [œ̃] lundi [lœ̃di] chacun [ʃakœ̃]

22. *The semi-vowels — Les semi-voyelles*

[j]

[j] is pronounced like *y* in English *you.* It is represented in French by *i* followed by another pronounced vowel and by *y.*

frontière	[frõtjɛr]	question	[kɛstjõ]	payer	[peje]
intérieur	[ɛ̃terjœr]	artificiel	[artifisjɛl]	voyez	[vwaje]

[j] is also represented by *-ill-,* by final *-il* preceded by a vowel, and by *-ill-* preceded by a vowel. Avoid pronouncing the phonetic [aj] like the English *i* in n*i*ce.

fille	[fij]	travail	[travaj]	Marseille	[marsɛj]
famille	[famij]	détail	[detaj]	conseil	[kõsɛj]
travaille	[travaj]	bataille	[batɑj]	grenouille	[grənuj]
appareil	[aparɛj]	soleil	[sɔlɛj]	œil	[œj]

But in *ville, mille, tranquille,* and their derivatives, and at the beginning of words, *-ill-* is pronounced [il].

ville	[vil]	village	[vilaʒ]	illustrer	[ilystre]
mille	[mil]	million	[miljõ]	illisible	[ilizibl]
tranquille	[trɑ̃kil]	tranquillité	[trɑ̃kilite]	illuminer	[ilymine]

[w]

[w] is pronounced like the *w* in the English word *w*est. It is represented in French by *ou* followed directly by a pronounced vowel.

oui [wi] ouest [wɛst]

[w] also makes up a part of the pronunciation of the digraph *oi.* It is pronounced *wa* and *wɑ*.

endroit	[ɑ̃drwa]	étroit	[etrwa]	soie	[swɑ]	quelquefois	[kɛlkəfwa]
trois	[trwɑ]	pourquoi	[purkwa]	roi	[rwa]	royaliste	[rwajalist]

[ɥ]

[ɥ] is pronounced almost like *y* but more rapidly. It is represented in French by the letter *u* followed by another pronounced vowel.

situé [sitɥe] constitué [kõstitɥe] suisse [sɥis] ensuite [ɑ̃sɥit]

23. *The consonants — Les consonnes*

French consonants are more apt to resemble English consonants than French vowels English vowels. The following consonants require special attention:

[f] is represented in French both by *f* and by *ph.*
frontière [frõtjɛr] géographie [ʒeɔgrafi] phrase [frɑz] pharmacie [farmasi]

[g] is represented in French by *g* followed by *a, o,* and *u,* and by the combination *gu* followed by *e* or *i.* It is pronounced as English *g* in got.
grand [grɑ̃] grave [grav] magasin [magazɛ̃] guerre [gɛr] guide [gid]

[h] This sound does not exist in French; see pages 511–512, § 1 A, B.

[k] is represented in French by *c* followed by *a, o,* and *u,* by final *q,* and by *qu* followed by a vowel.

capitale	[kapital]	constituer	[kõstitɥe]	connu	[kɔny]
continent	[kõtinɑ̃]	commerce	[kɔmɛrs]	quelle	[kɛl]
historique	[istɔrik]	politique	[pɔlitik]	quelque	[kɛlkə]
qui	[ki]	marqué	[marke]	kiosque	[kjɔsk]
que	[kə]	presque	[prɛsk]	coq	[kɔk]

[l] constitutes a special difficulty, since it does not correspond to the English *l.* It approaches initial *l* in *leap.* Imitate your teacher's *l,* and avoid making the *l* [ɫ] of the English word *bell* [bɛɫ].

capitale	[kapital]	ville	[vil]	facile	[fasil]
quelle	[kɛl]	elle	[ɛl]	il	[il]

[ɲ] is represented in French by *gn.* It is pronounced somewhat like *ny* in the English word ca*ny*on, but in French constitutes a single sound.

montagne	[mõtaɲ]	champagne	[ʃɑ̃paɲ]

[r], [ʀ] have no English equivalent. Especially the American *r,* represented by [ɹ] in phonetic script, is completely unsuitable for pronouncing French. The Parisian *r,* represented by [ʀ] in phonetic script, is the most elegant and the one used by the majority of Frenchmen in the region of France of which Paris is the center. The trilled *r,* represented by [r] in phonetic script, is common in many of the provinces and especially in the south of France. Following the practice of most American French books, the French *r* is represented by [r] in the phonetic transcription of this text. However, it might be advisable for the student to learn to pronounce *r* as [ʀ.] The method of pronouncing [ʀ] is described in detail on pages 529–530.

[s] is pronounced like the *s* in the English word *sit.* It is represented in French by *s,* except when between vowels, and by *c* followed by *e* or *i,* and by *ç.* It is represented by *ss* between vowels.

situé	[sitɥe]	séparer	[separe]	facile	[fasil]	façade	[fasad]
traverser	[travɛrse]	centre	[sɑ̃tr]	difficile	[difisil]	garçon	[garsõ]
sud	[syd]	citez	[site]	commerce	[kɔmɛrs]	français	[frɑ̃sɛ]

[ʃ] is pronounced as *ch* in ma*ch*ine. It is represented in French by *ch.*

architecture	[arʃitɛktyr]	château	[ʃɑto]	charme	[ʃarm]	marcher	[marʃe]
empêche	[ɑ̃pɛʃ]	chef	[ʃɛf]	choisir	[ʃwazir]		

[z] is pronounced as the *z* of the English *zero.* It is represented by *z,* and by *s* between vowels.

gaz	[gɑz]	composer	[kõpoze]	division	[divizjõ]	rose	[roz]

[ʒ] is pronounced like the English *s* in plea*s*ure. It is represented in French by *j* and by *g* followed by *e* and *i.*

jette	[ʒɛt]	jeune	[ʒœn]	déjà	[deʒa]	je	[ʒə]	région	[reʒjõ]
joli	[ʒɔli]	jour	[ʒur]	jusqu'à	[ʒyska]	large	[larʒ]	étranger	[etrɑ̃ʒe]

Les fautes favorites
The favorite mistakes

Almost every English-speaking person who is still in the process of learning the language makes certain errors in French because of the influence of English vocabulary and English constructions. To eliminate such errors, one must first become aware that they exist, then set about to learn how the French express such words and constructions.

The following 148 English sentences contain words and constructions which present problems when expressed in French. The English list is alphabetized by the italicized keyword, which entails the difficulty. The French list gives the correct way of expressing the English sentences in French.

To study these sentences, it is suggested that the student cover the French list, then try to write the French equivalent of a limited number of the English sentences, check his sentence against the French list in the book, then learn the correct form of sentences in which he has made errors. Also study *Grammaire* §§ 94, 98.

1. Paul has *about* ten books.	1. Paul a dix livres *environ.*
2. Paul will see Louise at *about* three o'clock.	2. Paul verra Louise *vers* trois heures.
3. Paul writes a story *about* (*concerning*) his trip.	3. Paul écrit une histoire *sur* son voyage.
4. Paul *actually* works.	4. Paul travaille *vraiment.* Paul travaille *réellement.*
5. Paul gives *advice* to Louise.	5. Paul donne *des conseils* à Louise.
6. Paul leaves *after*[1] Louise has spoken.	6. Paul part *après que*[1] Louise a parlé.
7. Paul will leave *after*[2] he speaks.	7. Paul partira *après*[2] avoir parlé.
8. Paul writes to Louise *again.*	8. Paul écrit *encore une fois* à Louise. Paul écrit *de nouveau* à Louise.
9. Paul does *not* write to Louise *again.*	9. Paul *n'*écrit *plus* à Louise.
10. Paul sees Louise *again.*	10. Paul *re*voit Louise.
11. Paul *agrees* with Louise.	11. Paul *est d'accord* avec Louise.
12. Paul and Louise *agree* on the importance of French.	12. Paul et Louise *sont d'accord* sur l'importance du français.
13. Paul walks *along* the Seine.	13. Paul se promène *le long de* la Seine.

[1] Here, *after* is a conjunction and must be expressed by *après que.* Also study *Grammaire* §§ 94, 98. (§ 98 — *after*)

[2] Here, *after* is a preposition and is expressed by *après.* (§ 78 B 2)

14. Paul *answers* the question.	14. Paul *répond à* la question.
15. Paul *approaches* Louise.	15. Paul *s'approche de* Louise.
16. Paul *asks Louise for a book.*	16. Paul *demande un livre à Louise.*
17. Paul *asks her for a book.*	17. Paul *lui demande un livre.*
18. Paul *asks Louise a question.*	18. Paul *pose une question à Louise.*
19. Paul admires Louise *because* she is intelligent.	19. Paul admire Louise *parce qu'*elle est intelligente.
20. Paul admires Louise *because of* her intelligence.	20. Paul admire Louise *à cause de* son intelligence.
21. Paul leaves *before*[1] Louise is ready.	21. Paul part *avant que*[1] Louise soit prête.
22. Paul leaves *before*[2] he has finished his work.	22. Paul part *avant de*[2] finir son travail.
23. All come *but* (*except*) Paul.	23. Tous viennent *sauf* Paul. Tous viennent *à part* Paul.
24. Paul sees *but* (*only*) two books.	24. Paul *ne* voit *que* deux livres.
25. Paul is the most important *character* in that play.	25. Paul est le *personnage* le plus important de cette pièce.
26. Paul has a rather gentle *character.*	26. Paul a le *caractère* assez doux.
27. Paul will leave at the *end* of the week.	27. Paul partira à la *fin* de la semaine.
28. Paul lives at the *end* of the street.	28. Paul habite au *bout* de la rue.
29. There is a table at the *end* (*back*) of the room.	29. Il y a une table au *fond* de la salle.
30. Paul *enters* the store.	30. Paul *entre dans* le magasin.
31. Paul has *everything* Louise brought back from France.	31. Paul a *tout ce que* Louise a rapporté de France.
32. Paul *feels* good.	32. Paul *se sent* bien.
33. Paul sings *for* Louise.	33. Paul chante *pour* Louise.
34. Paul sings, *for* (*because*) he is happy.	34. Paul chante, *car* il est heureux.
35. Paul sang *for*[3] an hour.	35. Paul a chanté *pendant*[3] une heure.
36. Paul has been singing *for*[4] an hour.	36. Paul chante *depuis*[4] une heure. *Voilà* une heure *que* Paul chante. *Il y a une* heure *que* Paul chante.
37. Paul *goes up to* his room.	37. Paul *monte dans* sa chambre.
38. *He is*[5] an intelligent young man.	38. *C'est*[5] un jeune homme intelligent.
39. Paul *hears of* Louise.	39. Paul *entend parler de* Louise.
40. Paul *hears that* Louise is sick.	40. Paul *entend dire que* Louise est malade.

---

[1] Here, *before* is a conjunction and must be expressed by *avant que* + **subjunctive.** (§§ 83 H, 98 — *before*)

[2] Here, *before* is a preposition and is expressed by *avant de* + **infinitive.** (§ 78 B 1)

[3] § 98 — *for* [4] § 50 B [5] § 36 A

41. *In the morning* Paul gets up and *in the evening* he goes to bed.	41. *Le matin* Paul se lève et *le soir* il se couche.
42. Paul *intends* to go to France.	42. Paul *pense* aller en France. Paul *a l'intention d'*aller en France. Paul *compte* aller en France.
43. Paul *is interested in* music.	43. Paul *s'intéresse à* la musique.
44. Paul *introduces* Robert to Louise.	44. Paul *présente* Robert à Louise.
45. Paul hears *a knock* at the door.	45. Paul entend *frapper* à la porte.
46. Paul *knows* [1] his lesson.	46. Paul *sait*[1] sa leçon.
47. Paul *knows* [1] Louise.	47. Paul *connaît*[1] Louise.
48. Paul *knows* [1] *how to swim.*	48. Paul *sait*[1] nager.
49. Paul *lacks* books.	49. Paul *manque de* livres. Les livres *manquent à* Paul.
50. Paul *laughs at* Louise.	50. Paul *rit de* Louise.
51. Paul *leaves* [2] the book on the table.	51. Paul *laisse* [2] le livre sur la table.
52. Paul *leaves* [2] the house.	52. Paul *sort* [2] *de* la maison. Paul *quitte* la maison. Paul *part* [2] *de* la maison.
53. Paul *leaves* [2] France.	53. Paul *part* [2] de France. Paul *quitte* la France.
54. Paul *leaves for* [3] France.	54. Paul *part pour* [3] la France.
55. Paul *listens to* Louise.	55. Paul *écoute* Louise.
56. Paul *lived* in the nineteenth century.	56. Paul *a vécu* au dix-neuvième siècle.
57. Paul *lives* [4] from his work.	57. Paul *vit* [4] de son travail.
58. Paul *lives* [4, 5] in Paris.	58. Paul *habite* [4, 5] à Paris. Paul *habite* Paris.
59. Paul reads *a long time.*	59. Paul lit *longtemps.*
60. Paul *looks at* Louise.	60. Paul *regarde* Louise.
61. Paul *looks for* Louise.	61. Paul *cherche* Louise.
62. Paul *makes* Louise *happy.*	62. Paul *rend* Louise *heureuse.*
63. The teacher *gave* Paul *a* good *mark.*	63. Le professeur *a mis une* bonne *note* à Paul.
64. Paul *got a* good *mark.*	64. Paul *a eu une* bonne *note.*
65. Paul *marries.*[6] Paul *gets married.*	65. Paul *se marie.*[6]
66. Paul *marries* [6] Louise.	66. Paul *se marie avec* [6] Louise. Paul *épouse* [6] Louise.
67. Paul *means* that Louise has arrived.	67. Paul *veut dire* que Louise est arrivée.
68. Paul *meets* (by chance) [7] Louise on the street.	68. Paul *rencontre* [7] Louise dans la rue.
69. Paul *meets* (by appointment) [7] Louise at the library.	69. Paul *retrouve* [7] Louise à la bibliothèque.

[1] § 94 — *know* [2] § 94 — *leave*

[3] One also hears *Paul part en France.* This is considered less correct.

[4] § 94 — *live*

[5] Also correct but much less frequently used is *Paul demeure à Paris.*

[6] § 94 — *marry* [7] § 94 — *meet..*

70. The pupils *meet* (together) [1] in the church.	70. Les élèves *se réunissent* [1] à l'église.
71. Paul *meets* (is introduced to) [1] Louise.	71. Paul *fait la connaissance de* [1] Louise.
72. Paul left *the next day.*	72. Paul est parti *le lendemain.* Paul est parti *le jour suivant.*
73. Paul left *the next morning.*	73. Paul est parti *le lendemain matin.* Paul est parti *le matin suivant.*
74. Paul *notices* (catches sight of) Louise.	74. Paul *aperçoit* Louise.
75. The teacher *notices* (realizes) *that* Paul has not prepared his lesson.	75. Le professeur *s'aperçoit que* Paul n'a pas préparé sa leçon.
76. Louise *obeys* Paul.	76. Louise *obéit à* Paul.
77. Paul is *on the other side* of the street.	77. Paul est *de l'autre côté* de la rue.
78. Paul is *on* [2] Dupont *Street,* Louise is *on* [2] Durand *Avenue,* and Robert is *on* [2] Saint-Michel *Boulevard.*	78. Paul est *dans* [2] *la rue* Dupont, Louise est *dans* [2] *l'avenue* Durand et Robert est *sur* [2] *le boulevard* Saint-Michel.
79. Paul is *on* the train.	79. Paul est *dans* le train.
80. Paul takes advantage of the *opportunity* to speak French.	80. Paul profite de *l'occasion* de parler français.
81. Paul has the *opportunity* to go to France.	81. Paul a la *possibilité* d'aller en France.
82. Some students speak English, *others* speak French.	82. Quelques (Certains) étudiants parlent anglais, *d'autres* parlent français.
83. Paul reads the *paper.*	83. Paul lit le *journal.*
84. Hand in your *papers.*	84. Remettez les *copies.*
85. Paul *pays two hundred dollars for the car.*	85. Paul *paie la voiture deux cents dollars.*
86. Those *people* don't work very often.	86. Ces *gens* ne travaillent pas souvent.
87. There were many *people* there.	87. Il y avait beaucoup de *monde.* Il y avait *du monde.*
88. The *people* [3] revolted.	88. Le *peuple* [3] se révolta.
89. Paul looks for a *piece* of chalk.	89. Paul cherche un *morceau* de craie.
90. Paul looks for a *piece* of paper.	90. Paul cherche une *feuille* de papier.
91. There is the *place* [4] where Paul lives.	91. Voilà l'*endroit* [4] où Paul habite.
92. Paul *plays* [5] tennis and chess.	92. Paul *joue au* [5] tennis et *aux* échecs.
93. Paul *plays* [5] the violin and the piano.	93. Paul *joue du* [5] violon et *du* piano.

[1] § 94 — *meet*

[2] In French, one says *dans la rue, dans* (or *sur*) *l'avenue, sur le boulevard, sur la place.*

[3] Here *people* in the sense of *common people.*

[4] The English word *place* is regularly expressed by *endroit* in French. The French word *place* indicates a public square or a place in a theater or train.

[5] One says *jouer à* a game, *jouer de* a musical instrument.

94. Paul is *rather* tired.
95. Paul would fail *rather* than study.
96. Paul would *rather* go to France.
97. What is the *reason for* his absence?
98. Tell me the *reason that* he left.
99. Paul *resembles* his father.
100. Paul often *rests.*
101. Paul *returns*[1] (*comes back*) here in the afternoon.
102. Paul *returns*[1] (*goes back*) to Paris.
103. Paul *returns*[1] (*gives back*) the book.
104. Paul rented a *room.*[2]
105. Paul has a house with eight *rooms.*
106. Can you find a *room* for the meeting?
107. Paul receives the visitors in the *living room.*
108. Paul *is sitting* (*seated*) behind us.
109. Paul *is sitting down* (*seating himself*).
110. Paul *spends* a great deal of money.
111. Paul *spends* a week in Paris.
112. Paul *spends*[3] an hour *writing.*
113. Paul *should*[4] (*ought to*) go to France.
114. Paul is working, *since* (*because*) he needs money.
115. Paul has been working *since*[5] yesterday.
116. Paul *takes*[6] a book from the table.
117. Paul *takes*[6] a book to Louise.
118. Paul *takes*[6] Louise to the movies.
119. Paul *takes*[6] a course.
120. Paul *takes*[6] a walk.
121. Paul *takes*[6] an examination.
122. Paul *takes*[6] two hours to do his work.

94. Paul est *assez* fatigué.
95. Paul échouerait *plutôt* que de travailler.
96. Paul *aimerait mieux* aller en France.
97. Quelle est la *raison de* son absence?
98. Dites-moi la *raison pour laquelle* il est parti.
99. Paul *ressemble à* son père.
100. Paul *se repose* souvent.
101. Paul *revient*[1] ici l'après-midi.
102. Paul *retourne*[1] à Paris.
103. Paul *rend*[1] le livre.
104. Paul a loué une *chambre.*[2]
105. Paul a une maison de huit *pièces.*
106. Pouvez-vous trouver une *salle* pour la réunion?
107. Paul reçoit les visiteurs dans le *salon.*
108. Paul *est assis* derrière nous.
109. Paul *s'assoit* (*s'assied*).
110. Paul *dépense* beaucoup d'argent.
111. Paul *passe* huit jours à Paris.
112. Paul *passe*[3] une heure *à écrire.*
113. Paul *devrait*[4] aller en France.
114. Paul travaille, *puisqu'*il a besoin d'argent.
115. Paul travaille *depuis*[5] hier.
116. Paul *prend*[6] un livre sur la table.
117. Paul *apporte*[6] un livre à Louise.
118. Paul *mène*[6] (*conduit*) Louise au cinéma.
119. Paul *suit*[6] un cours.
120. Paul *fait*[6] une promenade.
121. Paul *passe*[6] un examen.
122. Paul *met*[6] deux heures à (pour) faire son travail.

---

[1] § 94 — *return*

[2] The word *chambre* usually means *bedroom.*

[3] To express manner of spending time, French uses *à* + **infinitive** after *passer.*

[4] The conditional of the verb *devoir* must be used to express *should* or *ought* in this sense. See § 93 E.

[5] The preposition *depuis* is used to express *since* when an action began in the past and continues up to the present.

[6] § 94 — *take*

123. Paul *tells Louise to* speak to him.	123. Paul *dit à Louise de* lui parler.
124. Paul *tells her to* speak.	124. Paul *lui dit de* parler.
125. Paul *thinks of* [1] Louise.	125. Paul *pense à* [1] Louise.
126. What *does* Paul *think of* [1] Louise?	126. Qu'est-ce que Paul *pense de* [1] Louise?
127. Paul has *time* to read.	127. Paul a le *temps* de lire.
128. Paul knocked three *times.*	128. Paul a frappé trois *fois.*
129. What *time* is it?	129. Quelle *heure* est-il?
130. Paul reads at a *time* when he has nothing else to do.	130. Paul lit à un *moment* où il n'a rien d'autre à faire.
131. Paul *has a good time.*	131. Paul *s'amuse.* Paul *se distrait.*
132. Paul goes *to* [2] his friend's.	132. Paul va *chez* [2] son ami.
133.[3] Paul goes *to* Paris, *to* Spain, *to* Canada and *to* old Mexico.	133.[3] Paul va *à* Paris, *en* Espagne, *au* Canada et *dans le* vieux Mexique.
134. Paul *visits* [4] Paris.	134. Paul *visite* [4] Paris.
135. Paul *visits* Louise.	135. Paul *fait une visite à* Louise. Paul *rend visite à* Louise. Paul *va voir* Louise.
136. Paul *waits for* Louise.	136. Paul *attend* Louise.
137. Paul *wants Louise to read.*	137. Paul *veut que Louise lise.*
138. Paul leaves *when* Louise arrives.	138. Paul part *quand* Louise arrive.
139. Paul leaves the day *when* [5] Louise arrives.	139. Paul part le jour *où* [5] Louise arrive.
140. Paul reads *while* Louise is talking to her mother.	140. Paul lit *pendant que* Louise parle avec sa mère.
141. Paul works *while* (on the other hand) Louise plays.	141. Paul travaille *tandis que* Louise joue.
142. Paul goes out *with* Louise.	142. Paul sort *avec* Louise.
143. The table is covered *with* [6] books.	143. La table est couverte *de* [6] livres.
144. Paul speaks *with* [7] a gentle voice.	144. Paul parle *d'*une [7] voix douce.
145. Paul is a boy *with* [8] dark hair.	145. Paul est un garçon *aux* [8] cheveux bruns.
146. Paul *would play* [9] if he had the time.	146. Paul *jouerait* [9] s'il avait le temps.
147. Paul *would play* [9] (*used to play*) every day.	147. Paul *jouait* [9] tous les jours.
148. The *young men* [10] speak French.	148. Les *jeunes gens* [10] parlent français.

[1] Distinguish between *penser à* (to think of) and *penser de* (to have an opinion of).

[2] § 42 F [3] § 42 A, B, C, D, E [4] § 94 — *visit* [5] § 39 F

[6] This example is to illustrate verbs and adjectives always followed by *de.*

[7] This is an example of the *de* of manner.

[8] This is an example of the *à* characteristic.

[9] The English *would* has two distinct meanings: one to indicate a condition, in which case the conditional is used if it is in the conclusion of a condition; the other to indicate habitual action, in which case the imperfect is used.

[10] The plural of *le jeune homme* is regularly *les jeunes gens.*

Vocabulaire anglais-français

ABBREVIATIONS:

adj.	adjective	p.	page
adv.	adverb	pl.	plural
conj.	conjugate	pp	past participle
f.	feminine	prep.	preposition
inf.	infinitive	pron.	pronoun
m.	masculine	sing.	singular

§ — References to the *Grammaire*
* aspirate *h* (*Prononciation* § 1 B)

(2) *-ir* verb of the second class (§ 49 C)

Verbs whose principal parts are given are irregular and are conjugated in § 95 of the *Grammaire* or are conjugated like some verb found in § 95. The principal parts of the verb are the infinitive, present participle, past participle, first person singular present indicative, first person singular simple past. The importance of the principal parts of a verb is explained in § 48.

A

a *un, une*
able, be *pouvoir* (*pouvant, pu, je peux, je pus*)
about (approximately) *environ;* (concerning) *sur;* (in expressions of time) *vers*
abroad *à l'étranger*
accompany *accompagner*
acquaintance *connaissance* f.
acquainted, be *connaître* (*connaissant, connu, je connais, je connus*)
  get acquainted *connaître*
act *agir*
address *adresse* f.
administrative *administratif, administrative*
admire *admirer*
afraid, be *avoir peur*
Africa *Afrique* f.
after *après*
afternoon *après-midi* m. or f.
against *contre*
age *âge* m.
  Middle Ages *moyen âge* m.
  at the age of three *à trois ans*
ago *il y a* (§ 91 A)
  two years ago *il y a deux ans*
aim *but* m.
airmail, by *par avion*
airplane *avion* m.
all *tout, toute, tous, toutes*
  not at all *ne . . . point* (§ 22 F), *pas du tout*
ally *allié* m.
almost *presque*
alone *seul*
along *le long de*
aloud *à haute voix*
Alps *Alpes* f. pl.
already *déjà*
Alsace *Alsace* f.
Alsatian *Alsacien, Alsacienne* m., f.
also *aussi*
although *bien que* (+ subjunctive), *quoique* (+ subjunctive)
always *toujours*
am *suis*
ambition *ambition* f.
America, North *Amérique du Nord* f.
American (noun) *Américain;* (adj.) *américain*
among *parmi; entre*
  among themselves *entre eux*
ancestor *ancêtre* m.
and *et*
announcement *annonce* f.
another *un autre, une autre*

answer *répondre* (*à* + noun)
any (adj.) *du, de la, de l', des* (§ 5); *quelque;* (object pron.) *en* (§ 28)
any more, not *plus* (§ 22 F 2)
apartment house *immeuble* m.
apple *pomme* f.
approve *approuver*
April *avril* m.
architecture *architecture* f.
are *sont; se trouvent*
 are to *doivent* (§ 93)
 there are *il y a* (§ 91 A)
army *armée* f.
around *autour de*
arrival *arrivée* f.
arrive *arriver*
article *article* m.
artist *artiste* m.
as *comme*
 as much as *autant que*
 as soon as *dès que, aussitôt que*
Asia *Asie* f.
ask *demander* (*quelque chose à quelqu'un*)
 ask a question *poser une question*
asleep, be *dormir* (2)
assembly *assemblée* f.
 National Assembly *Assemblée Nationale* f.
at *à*
 at about two o'clock *vers deux heures*
 at + *city* *à* + city (§ 42 D)
 at home *chez moi, chez vous,* etc. (§ 42 F); *à la maison*
 at least *au moins*
 at once *tout de suite*
 at the table *à table*
 at what time *à quelle heure*
Atlantic *Atlantique* m.
attack *attaquer*
attain *atteindre* (*atteignant, atteint, j'atteins, j'atteignis*) (conj. like *peindre*)
August *août*
aunt *tante* f.
author *auteur* m.
autumn *automne* m.
avenue *avenue* f.

B

bad *mauvais*
 it is too bad *c'est dommage*
 the weather is bad *il fait mauvais temps*
ball *balle* f.
Balzac *Balzac*
Baton Rouge *Bâton-Rouge* m.
battle *bataille* f.
be *être* (*étant, été, je suis, je fus*)
 be able *pouvoir*
 be afraid of *avoir peur*
 be better *valoir mieux*
 be born *naître*
 be forced to *être forcé de*
 be seated *être assis*
 be sorry *regretter, être désolé*
 be still (imperative) *taisez-vous*
 be willing *vouloir bien*
 be worth *valoir*
beach *plage* f.
beautiful *beau, bel, belle* (§ 10 G)
beauty *beauté* f.
because *parce que* (+ clause)
 because of *à cause de* (+ noun or pron.)
become *devenir* (*devenant, devenu, je deviens, je devins*) (conj. like *venir*)
bed, go to *se coucher*
beer *bière* f.
before (time) *avant* (+ noun or pron.), *avant de* (+ inf.) (§78 B 1), *avant que* (+ subjunctive); (place) *devant*
beg *prier* (+ noun object + *de* + inf.)
begin *commencer* (*à* + inf.) (§ 89 A)
 begin with *commencer par*
beginning *commencement* m.
Belgium *Belgique* f.
believe *croire* (*croyant, cru, je crois, je crus*) (§ 83 G)
bell *cloche* f.
belong *appartenir* (*appartenant, appartenu, j'appartiens, j'appartins*) (conj. like *tenir*)
beside *à côté de*
best (adj.) *meilleur;* (adv.) *mieux*
better (adj.) *meilleur;* (adv.) *mieux*
 be better *valoir mieux*
between *entre*
bicycle *bicyclette* f.
bill *addition* f.
blind *aveugle*
Blois *Blois*

blue *bleu*
board *tableau* m.
boarding house *pension* (*de famille*) f.
body *corps* m.
bomb *bombarder*
Bonneville *Bonneville*
book *livre* m.
telephone book *annuaire* m.
booth, telephone *cabine téléphonique* f.
Bordeaux *Bordeaux* m.
border *limiter*
border *frontière* f.
born, be *naître* (*naissant, né, je nais, je naquis*)
bottle *flacon* m.
boulevard *boulevard* m.
boundary *frontière* f.
boy *garçon* m.
brand *marque* f.
bread *pain* m.
breakfast *petit déjeuner* m.
have breakfast *prendre le petit déjeuner*
Brest *Brest* m.
Breton *Breton* m.
bridge *pont* m.
bring (a thing) *apporter;* (a person) *mener* (§ 89 D), *amener* (§ 89 D), *conduire* (§ 95, no. 15)
bring about *amener* (§ 89 D)
Britain, Great *Grande Bretagne* f.
Brittany *Bretagne* f.
brother *frère* m.
build *construire* (*construisant, construit, je construis, je construisis*) (conj. like *conduire*)
building *édifice* m., *bâtiment* m.
burn *brûler*
bus *autobus* m.
but *mais*
butter *beurre* m.
buy *acheter* (§ 89 D)
buyer *acheteur* m.
by *par, de* (§ 87 C)

C

Caen *Caen* m.
café *café* m.
Calais *Calais* m.
call *appeler* (§ 89 F)
be called *s'appeler*
make a telephone call *donner un coup de téléphone*
telephone call *coup de téléphone* m.
call together *convoquer*
camp, concentration *camp de concentration* f.
can *pouvoir* (*pouvant, pu, je peux, je pus*)
Canada *Canada* m.
Cannes *Cannes* m.
capital *capitale* f.
car *voiture* f., *auto* f., *automobile* f.
carry *porter*
carry on one's studies *faire ses études*
castle *château* m.
cathedral *cathédrale* f.
cause *cause* f.
Central, Massif *Massif Central* m.
center *centre* m.
century *siècle* m.
ceremony *cérémonie* f.
certain *certain*
chair *chaise* f.
Channel, English *Manche* f.
Charles *Charles*
chat *causer*
cheaper *meilleur marché*
cheese *fromage* m.
Cherbourg *Cherbourg* m.
child *enfant* m. or f.
China *Chine* f.
Chinon *Chinon* m.
choice *choix* m.
choose *choisir*
Christmas *Noël* m.
church *église* f.
Cid *Cid* m.
cider *cidre* m.
cigarette *cigarette* f.
city *ville* f.
city hall *mairie* f.
class *classe* f.
to class *en classe*
classroom *salle* f.; *classe* f.
clean *nettoyer* (§ 89 C)
clerk *employé* m.
close *fermer*
cloudy, it is *le ciel est couvert*
club, night *boîte de nuit* f.
coast *côte* f.
coffee *café* m.
cold *froid*
be cold (referring to a person)

avoir froid; (referring to weather) *faire froid*
colony *colonie* f.
come *venir* (*venant, venu, je viens, je vins*)
come back *revenir* (§ 94); *rentrer*
commerce *commerce* m.
commercial *commercial*
common *répandu*
compartment *compartiment* m.
composed, be *se composer* (*de* + noun)
concentration camp *camp de concentration* m.
concerning *sur*
conductor *contrôleur* m.
conquer *vaincre* (*vainquant, vaincu, je vaincs, je vainquis*)
Conqueror, William the *Guillaume le Conquérant*
consider *considérer* (*comme* + adj. or noun)
considerable *considérable*
constitution *constitution* f.
construct *construire* (*construisant, construit, je construis, je construisis*) (conj. like *conduire*)
contagious *contagieux, contagieuse*
contain *contenir* (*contenant, contenu, je contiens, je contins*) (conj. like *tenir*)
continent *continent* m.
continue *continuer* (*à* + inf.)
conversation *conversation* f.
cool *frais, fraîche*
it is cool *il fait frais*
copy *copier*
Corneille *Corneille*
correct *corriger* (§ 89 B)
cost *coûter*
country (nation) *pays* m.; (opposite of city) *campagne* f.
course (in school) *cours* m.; (of a meal) *plat* m.
take a course *suivre un cours*
courtyard *cour.* f.
cousin *cousin* m.
cow *vache* f.
cream *crème* f.
cross *traverser*
cultivate *cultiver*
curious *curieux, curieuse*
custom *coutume* f.

D

date *dater*
date *date* f.
daughter *fille* f.
day (§ 98) *jour* m., *journée* f.
every day *tous les jours*
deaf *sourd*
deal, a great *beaucoup*
decide *décider* (*de* + inf.), *se décider* (*à* + inf.)
declare *déclarer*
deep *profond*
defense *défense* f.
Denmark *Danemark* m.
dentist *dentiste* m.
departure *départ* m.
depression *crise financière* f.
deputy *député* m.
describe *décrire* (*décrivant, décrit, je décris, je décrivis*) (conj. like *écrire*)
desk *bureau* m.
destroy *détruire* (*détruisant, détruit, je détruis, je détruisis*) (conj. like *conduire*)
detail *détail* m.
detective story *roman policier* m.
die *mourir* (*mourant, mort, je meurs, je mourus*)
difference *différence* f.
different *différent*
difficult *difficile*
Dijon *Dijon*
dine *dîner*
dinner *dîner* m.
direct *diriger* (§ 89 B)
disappear *disparaître* (*disparaissant, disparu, je disparais, je disparus*) (conj. like *connaître*)
discuss *discuter, parler* (*de* + noun)
discussion *discussion* f.
disease *maladie* f.
dish, main *plat du jour* m.
division *division* f.
do *faire* (*faisant, fait, je fais, je fis*)
do without *se passer de*
doctor *médecin* m.
dog *chien* m.
dollar *dollar* m.
door *porte* f.
dream *rêver*
dress, dress oneself *s'habiller*

drive (a car) *conduire* (*conduisant, conduit, je conduis, je conduisis*)
Dupont *Dupont*
during *pendant*

E

each *chaque*
each other *se* (§ 26 B)
ear *oreille* f.
earlier *plus tôt*
early *de bonne heure, tôt*
east *est* m.
easy *facile*
eat *manger* (§ 89 B)
edition *édition* f.
eighteenth *dix-huitième*
eight *huit*
eighty *quatre-vingts*
either *non plus*
emperor *empereur* m.
employee *employé* m.
empty *se jeter* (§ 89 F)
empty *vide*
end *fin* f.
put an end to *mettre fin à*
engage in sports *faire du sport*
engagement *fiançailles* f. pl.
England *Angleterre* f.
English (noun) *Anglais;* (adj.) *anglais*
English Channel *Manche* f.
English language *anglais* m.
enormous *énorme*
enough *assez*
enter *entrer* (*dans* + noun)
erase *effacer* (§ 89 A)
especially *surtout*
Europe *Europe* f.
evening *soir* m., *soirée* f.
evening party *soirée* f.
yesterday evening *hier soir*
every *tout*
every day *tous les jours*
everyone *tout le monde*
everywhere *partout*
examination *examen* m.
pass an examination *réussir à un examen*
take an examination *passer un examen*
evidently *évidemment*
excellent *excellent*
except *sauf*
exhausted *épuisé*
exercise *devoir* m.
exist *exister*
expensive *cher, chère*
experiment *expérience* f.
explain *expliquer*
explanation *explication* f.
export *exporter*
extract *extrait* m.
eye (sing) *œil;* (pl.) *yeux* m.

F

fail *échouer*
fail an examination *échouer à un examen*
family *famille* f.
famous *célèbre*
far *loin*
far away *loin*
father *père* m.
favorite *préféré*
fear *avoir peur; craindre* (*craignant, craint, je crains, je craignis*)
February *février*
feel *sentir* (2), *se sentir*
feel good *se sentir bien*
feel like *avoir envie* (*de* + inf.)
few *peu* (*de* + noun)
fifty *cinquante*
fill *remplir*
finally *enfin*
find *trouver*
finish *finir*
fire *feu* m.
first *premier, première*
fireplace *cheminée* f.
five *cinq*
floor *étage* m.
ground floor *rez-de-chaussée* m.
second floor *premier étage*
flow *couler*
flower *fleur* f.
foot *pied* m.
on foot *à pied*
football *football* m.
for (§ 98) *pour; depuis; pendant; car*
forbid *interdire* (*interdisant, interdit, j'interdis, j'interdis*) (conj. like *dire*)
force *forcer* (*à* + inf.), *obliger* (*à* + inf.) [1]

[1] But *être forcé de* (+ inf.), *être obligé de* (+ inf.).

forced, be *être forcé de*
foreign *étranger, étrangère*
foreigner *étranger* m.
forest *forêt* f.
forget *oublier*
form *former*
formality *formalité* f.
former *celui-là, etc.* (§ 33 D)
fortunately *heureusement*
found, be *se trouver*
fountain pen *stylo* m.
four *quatre*
France *France* f.
Francis *François*
Franco-Prussian War *guerre franco-allemande* f.
French (noun) *Français;* (adj.) *français*
French fried potatoes (*pommes de terre*) *frites* f. pl.
French history *histoire de France* f.
French language *français* m.
Frenchman *Français* m.
fried *frit*
French fried potatoes (*pommes de terre*) *frites* f. pl.
friend *ami* m., *amie* f.
from *de* (§ 43)
front: in front of *devant*
fruit *fruit* m.
full *plein*
furnish *fournir*
furniture *meubles* m. pl.

G

game *jeu* m.; *match* m., *partie* f.
garden *jardin* m.
Garonne *Garonne* f.
gather *se réunir*
general *général* m.
geography *géographie* f.
Gerard *Gérard*
German (noun) *Allemand;* (adj.) *allemand*
Germany *Allemagne* f.
get (become) *devenir* (*devenant, devenu, je deviens, je devins*) (conj. like *venir*)
(obtain) *obtenir* (*obtenant, obtenu, j'obtiens, j'obtins*) (conj. like *tenir*)
get acquainted *connaître, faire la connaissance* (*de* + noun)
get married *se marier*
get off *descendre*
get on a bus *monter dans un autobus*
get a ticket *prendre un billet*
get up *se lever*
gift *cadeau* m.
girl *jeune fille* f.
give *donner*
glad *content; heureux, heureuse*
go *aller* (*allant, allé, je vais, j'allai*), *se diriger* (§ 89 B)
go back *retourner*
go to bed *se coucher*
go home *rentrer*
go off *s'en aller*
go out *sortir* (2)
gold *or* m.
golf *golf* m.
good *bon, bonne*
good bye *au revoir*
good morning *bonjour*
it is good weather *il fait beau*
government *gouvernement* m.
grammar *grammaire* f.
great *grand*
great deal *beaucoup*
great many *beaucoup*

H

half past . . . *. . . et demie* (§ 97 D)
hall *couloir* m.
city hall *mairie* f.
hand *main* f.
hand in, hand to *remettre* (*remettant, remis, je remets, je remis*) (conj. like *mettre*)
happen *arriver*
has *a*
have *avoir* (*ayant, eu, j'ai, j'eus*)
have something written *faire écrire quelque chose* (causative construction, § 92 A)
Havre, le *le Havre* m.
he *il; lui* (§ 27 B)
he who *celui qui*
head *tête* f.
headache *mal de tête* m.
have a headache *avoir mal à la tête*
hear *entendre*
heavy *lourd*
Helen *Hélène*
help *aider*

her (direct object) *la;* (indirect object) *lui;* (with prep.) *elle;* (adj.) *son, sa, ses*
here *ici*
hesitate *hésiter* (*à* + inf.)
hide *cacher*
high *élevé,* **haut*
him (direct object) *le;* (indirect object) *lui;* (with prep.) *lui*
his (adj.) *son, sa, ses;* (pron.) *le sien, la sienne, etc.*
history *histoire* f.
 French history *histoire de France*
Hitler *Hitler*
home, at *à la maison, chez moi, chez lui, etc.* (§ 42 F)
hope *espérer* (§ 89 E)
hostel, youth *auberge de la jeunesse* f.
hot *chaud*
 be hot (referring to a person) *avoir chaud;* (referring to weather) *faire chaud*
hotel *hôtel* m.
hour *heure* f.
house *maison* f.
 apartment house *immeuble* m.
 boarding house *pension* (*de famille*) f.
how *comment*
 How are you? *Comment allez-vous?*
 how long *depuis quand; combien de temps*
 how many *combien* (*de* + noun)
 how much *combien* (*de* + noun)
 how old is he? *Quel âge a-t-il?*
Hugo *Hugo*
human *humain*
hundred *cent*
hungry, be *avoir faim*
hurry *se dépêcher*
husband *mari* m.

I

I *je; moi* (§ 27 B)
 I am very well *je vais très bien*
idea *idée* f.
if *si*
immediately *immédiatement, tout de suite*
import *importer*
importance *importance* f.
important *important*
impossible *impossible*
in *dans, en, à* (§ 42); *de* (§ 13 D)
 in front of *devant*
 in vain (do) *avoir beau* (+ inf.)
industry *industrie* f.
influence *influencer* (§ 89 A)
inhabit *habiter*
inhabitant *habitant* m.
ink *encre* f.
intellectual *intellectuel, intellectuelle*
instead of *au lieu de*
intend *avoir l'intention* (*de* + inf.)
interesting *intéressant*
interior *intérieur* m.
into *dans, en*
invade *envahir*
is *est*
island *île* f.
it (subject) *il, elle;* (direct object) *le, la*
 it is (+ expressions of weather) *il fait*
Italy *Italie* f.
its *son, sa, ses*

J

Jack *Jacques*
January *janvier* m.
Japan *Japon* m.
Joan of Arc *Jeanne d'Arc*
John *Jean*
July *juillet* m.
just *juste*
 have just *venir de* (+ inf.)

K

kind *sorte* f.
 What kind of weather is it? *Quel temps fait-il?*
king *roi* m.
 king of France *roi de France*
knapsack *sac* m.
know (§ 94) (something) *savoir* (*sachant, su, je sais, je sus*); (be acquainted with someone or something) *connaître* (*connaissant, connu, je connais, je connus*)
 know how *savoir* (+ inf.)
known *connu*

L

lack *manquer* (*de* + noun)
lamp *lampe* f.
language *langue* f.

large *grand*
last *dernier, dernière*
  last night *cette nuit*
late (not early) *tard*
Latin *latin* m.
latter *celui-ci,* etc. (§ 33 D)
laugh *rire* (*riant, ri, je ris, je ris*)
Law School *la Faculté de Droit*
learn *apprendre* (*apprenant, appris, j'apprends, j'appris*) (*à* + inf.) (conj. like *prendre*)
leave (§ 94) (something somewhere) *laisser;* (a place) *quitter; partir* (*de* + noun) (2); *sortir* (*de* + noun) (2)
left *gauche* f.
  to the left *à gauche*
less *moins*
lesson *leçon* f.
let us (verb stem) + *-ons* (§ 79 B)
letter *lettre* f.
liberate *libérer*
library *bibliothèque* f.
life *vie* f.
like *aimer*
  feel like *avoir envie* (*de* + inf.)
lip *lèvre* f.
listen *écouter*
  listen to *écouter* (+ noun)
literature *littérature*
little (adj.) *petit;* (adv.) *peu*
live (§ 94) *habiter* (+ noun, or, *à* + noun, or, *dans* + *noun*); *vivre* (*vivant, vécu, je vis, je vécus*)
lively *vif, vive*
living room *salon* m.
located, be *se trouver, être situé*
Loches *Loches*
Loire *Loire* f.
London *Londres* m.
long *long, longue*
  how long *depuis quand*
  in the long run *à la longue*
  no longer *ne . . . plus* (§ 22 F 2)
  not any longer *plus*
look at *regarder* (+ noun)
look for *chercher* (+ noun)
Lorraine *Lorraine* f.
lose *perdre*
Louis *Louis*
Louise *Louise*
Louvre *Louvre* m.
luck *chance* f.
Luxembourg *Luxembourg* m.
lycée *lycée* m.

M

Madrid *Madrid* m.
magnificent *magnifique*
mail *mettre à la poste*
mail *courrier* m.
main dish *plat du jour* m.
majority *plupart* f. (page 373, note 3)
make *faire* (*faisant, fait, je fais, je fis*); *constituer*
  make a telephone call *donner un coup de téléphone*
  make the acquaintance of *faire la connaissance de*
man *homme* m.
  old man *vieillard* m.
  working man *ouvrier* m.
many *beaucoup* (*de* + noun)
  how many *combien* (*de* + noun)
  too many *trop* (*de* + noun)
map (of a country, state) *carte* f.; (of a city) *plan* m.
  map of France *carte de France*
March *mars* m.
Marie *Marie*
marriage *mariage* m.
married, get *se marier*
marry (§ 94) *épouser* (+ noun), *se marier* (*avec* + noun)
Marseilles *Marseille* f.
match *allumette* f.
Mathilda *Mathilde*
Maurice *Maurice*
may *pouvoir* (*pouvant, pu, je peux, je puis*)
mayor *maire* m.
me *me, moi*
meal *repas* m.
mean *vouloir dire*
meat *viande* f.
medical school *Faculté de Médecine* f.
Mediterranean *Méditerranée* f.
meet (§ 94) (by appointment) *retrouver;* (by chance) *rencontrer;* (together) *se réunir*
menu *carte* f.; *menu* m.
method *méthode* f.
Mexico *Mexique* m.
middle *milieu* m.
  Middle Ages *moyen âge* m.
mild *doux, douce*

it is mild, the weather is mild *il fait doux*
military *militaire*
milk *lait* m.
mine *le mien, la mienne,* etc.
minute *minute* f.
mistake *faute* f.
modern *moderne*
modern language *langue vivante* f.
moment *moment* m.
Monday *lundi* m.
month *mois* m.
monument *monument* m.
more *plus;* (comparative of adj.) *plus* + adj. (§ 13 A)
morning *matin* m.
the next morning *le lendemain matin*
most *le plus;* (superlative + adj.) *le* (*la, les*) *plus* + adj. (§ 13 A); *la plupart des* (see page 373, note 3)
mother *mère* f.
motorcycle *moto* f.
mountain *montagne* f.
Rocky Mountains, the *les montagnes Rocheuses* f.
to the mountains *à la montagne*
mouth *bouche* f. (of a river) *embouchure* f.
movie *cinéma* m.
Mr. *monsieur* m.; (abbr.) M.
Mrs. *madame* f.; (abbr.) Mme
much *beaucoup* (*de* + noun)
how much *combien* (*de* + noun)
too much *trop* (*de* + noun)
museum *musée* m.
musique *musique* f.
must (§ 94) *devoir* (*devant, dû, je dois, je dus*) (§ 93); *falloir* (*fallant, fallu, il faut, il fallut*)
he must *il doit, il faut qu'il* (+ subjunctive), *il est obligé de*
my *mon, ma, mes*

N

name *nom* m.
whose name is *qui s'appelle*
Nantes *Nantes*
Napoleon *Napoléon*
nation *nation* f.
national *national*
National Assembly *Assemblée Nationale* f.
nationality *nationalité* f.
natural *naturel, naturelle*
near *près* (*de* + noun)
nearly *presque*
necessary *nécessaire*
it is necessary *il faut, il est nécessaire*
need *avoir besoin* (*de* + noun)
neglect *négliger* (§ 89 B)
neighbor *voisin* m.
neither . . . nor *ni . . . ni* (§5 D)
nephew *neveu* m.
never *jamais, ne . . . jamais* (§ 22 F2)
new *nouveau, nouvel, nouvelle* (§ 10 G)
news (piece of) *nouvelle* f.; (in general) *les nouvelles* f. pl.
newspaper *journal* m.
next (§ 98) *prochain; suivant*
the next morning *le lendemain matin*
Nice *Nice*
night *nuit* f.
last night *cette nuit*
night club *boîte de nuit* f.
nine *neuf*
nineteenth *dix-neuvième*
ninety-three *quatre-vingt-treize*
no *aucun; ne . . . aucun* (§ 22 F 5)
no longer *plus, ne . . . plus* (§ 22 F 2)
no one *personne; ne . . . personne* (§ 22 F 3)
noise *bruit* m.
none *aucun*
noon *midi* m.
Norman *normand*
Normandy *Normandie* f.
north *nord* m.
northeast *nord-est* m.
North America *Amérique du Nord* f.
nose *nez* m.
not *ne . . . pas, pas* (§ 22)
not at all *ne . . . point*
not any longer *ne . . . plus*
notebook *cahier* m.
nothing *rien, ne . . . rien* (§ 22 F 3)
notice *remarquer, s'apercevoir* (*s'apercevant, aperçu, je m'aperçois, je m'aperçus*) (conj. like *recevoir*) (*de* + noun)
novel *roman* m.
November *novembre* m.

now *maintenant*
numerous *nombreux, nombreuse*

O

obey *obéir* (*à* + noun)
oblige *obliger* (*à* + verb)
 be obliged *être obligé* (*de* + verb)
obtain *obtenir* (*obtenant, obtenu, j'obtiens, j'obtins*) (conj. like *tenir*)
occupy *occuper*
o'clock *heure*(*s*) (§ 97 D)
of *de* (§ 41)
offer *offrir* (*offrant, offert, j'offre, j'offris*) (conj. like *ouvrir*)
office *bureau* m.
 post office *poste* f., *bureau de poste* m.
often *souvent*
old *vieux, vieil, vieille;* pl. *vieux* (§ 10 G)
 How old are you? *Quel âge avez-vous?*
 I am twenty years old. *J'ai vingt ans.*
 old man *vieillard* m.
on *sur; à; dans*
 on foot *à pied*
 on time *à l'heure*
once, at *tout de suite*
one *un, une;* (indefinite pron.) *on* (§ 40)
 that one *celui-là*
only (adj.) *seul;* (adv.) *seulement, ne . . . que* (§ 22 F 4)
open *ouvrir* (*ouvrant, ouvert, j'ouvre, j'ouvris*)
opera *opéra* m.
Opéra-Comique *Opéra-Comique* m.
opinion *opinion* f.; *avis* m.
opportunity *occasion* f.
orange *orange* f.
order (in a restaurant) *commander*
 in order that *pour que* (+ subjunctive)
 in order to *pour* (+ inf.)
organization *organisation* f.
other *autre*
ought *devrais, devrait, etc.* (§ 93 E)
our *notre, nos*
ours *le nôtre, la nôtre,* etc.

P

package *paquet* m.
painting *tableau* m.
palace *château* m.
pardon *pardonner* (*à* + noun)
parent *parent* m.
Paris *Paris* m.
park *parc* m.
Parliament *Parlement m.*
part *partie* f.
party *soirée* f.
pass an examination *réussir à un examen*
passenger *voyageur* m.
past *passé* m.
Pasteur *Pasteur*
pay *payer* (§ 89 C)
 pay for *payer* (§ 45 B)
pen, fountain *stylo* m.
pencil *crayon* m.
people (§ 98) *gens* m.; *peuple* m.
 many people *beaucoup de gens, beaucoup de monde*
 sick people *les malades* m. or f. pl.
performance *représentation* f.
perhaps *peut-être*
period *époque* f.
person *personne* f.
philosophy *philosophie* f.
picture *tableau* m.
picturesque *pittoresque*
place *endroit* m.
 take place *avoir lieu*
plain *plaine* f.
plateau *plateau* m.
platform *quai* m.
play *jouer* (*à* + game; *de* + musical instrument)
play *pièce* (*de théâtre*) f.
poem *poème* m., *poésie* f.
Poland *Pologne* f.
political *politique*
politics *politique* f. sing.
poor *pauvre*
popular *populaire*
port *port* m.
Portugal *Portugal* m.
possible *possible*
post office *poste* f., *bureau de poste* m.
potato *pomme de terre* f.
 French fried potatoes (*pommes de terre*) *frites* f. pl.
power *pouvoir* m.
prefer *préférer* (+ inf.) (§ 89 E)
prepare *préparer, se préparer* (*à* + inf.)

president *président* m.
pretty *joli*
prevent *empêcher* (*de* + inf.)
price *prix* m.
principal *principal*
prison *prison* f.
prisoner *prisonnier* m.
professional *professionnel, professionnelle*
program (radio) *programme* m., *émission* f.
promise *promettre* (*promettant, promis, je promets, je promis*) (conj. like *mettre*) (*à* + noun, *de* + inf.)
pronounce *prononcer* (§ 89 A)
propose *proposer*
provided that *pourvu que, à condition que* (+ subjunctive)
province *province* f.
public *public, publique*
punish *punir*
pupil *élève* m., f.
put *mettre* (*mettant, mis, je mets, je mis*)
  put an end to *mettre fin à*
Pyrenees *Pyrénées* f. pl.

Q

quantity *quantité* f.
quarter *quartier* m.
  Latin Quarter *Quartier latin*
  quarter to ... *... moins le quart*
  quarter after ... *... et quart*
queen *reine* f.
question *question* f.
  ask a question *poser une question*

R

radio *radio* f.; (adj.) *de radio*
railroad station *gare* f.
rain *pleuvoir* (*pleuvant, plu, il pleut, il plut*)
  it rains, it is raining *il pleut*
raise *lever* (§ 89 D)
rapid *rapide*
rapidly *rapidement, vite*
rather *plutôt*
  rather than *plutôt que*
read *lire* (*lisant, lu, je lis, je lus*)
reading *lecture* f.
realize *se rendre compte* (*de* + noun)
receive *recevoir* (*recevant, reçu, je reçois, je reçus*)
recognize *reconnaître* (*reconnaissant, reconnu, je reconnais, je reconnus*) (conj. like *connaître*)
refuse *refuser* (*de* + inf.)
region *région* f.
regret *regretter*
relative *parent* m.
remain *rester*
remember *se souvenir* (*se souvenant, souvenu, je me souviens, je me souvins*) (conj. like *venir*) (*de* + noun; *de* + inf.); *se rappeler* (+ noun) (§ 89 F)
reply *répondre* (*à* + noun)
representative *représentant* m.
request *demander*
research *recherche* f. (often used in pl.)
resemble *ressembler* (*à* + noun)
resource *ressource* f.
rest *se reposer*
restaurant *restaurant* m.
result *résultat* m.
return (§ 94) (come back) *revenir* (*revenant, revenu, je reviens, je revins*) (conj. like *venir*); (go back) *retourner;* (go back home) *rentrer;* (give back) *rendre*
revolution *révolution* f.
Rhine *Rhin* m.
Rhone *Rhône* m.
rich *riche*
right (adj.) *droit;* (the right to do something) *le droit;* (opposite of left) *la droite*
  to be right *avoir raison*
  to the right *à droite*
ring *bague* f.
river *fleuve* m.
Riviera *Côte d'Azur* f.
Robert *Robert*
Rocky Mountains *montagnes Rocheuses* f.
Roger *Roger*
Roland *Roland*
Rome *Rome*
room (bedroom) *chambre* f.; (general) *salle* f., *pièce* f.; (living room) *salon* m.
ruin *ruine* f.
  in ruins *en ruines*

run *courir* (*courant, couru, je cours, je courus*)
in the long run *à la longue*
rush *se précipiter*
Russia *Russie* f.
Russian (noun) *Russe;* (adj.) *russe*
Russian language *russe* m.

S

saleswoman *vendeuse* f.
same *même*
Santa Claus *Père Noël* m.
Saturday *samedi* m.
save (a person) *sauver;* (money) *économiser*
say *dire* (*disant, dit, je dis, je dis*)
scarcely *ne . . . guère* (§ 22 E); *à peine*
school *école* f.; (college of a university) *faculté* f.
Law School *Faculté de Droit* f.
Medical School *Faculté de Médecine* f.
to school *à l'école*
scientist *savant* m., *homme de science* m.
seated *assis*
second *second, deuxième*
second floor *premier étage* m.
see *voir* (*voyant, vu, je vois, je vis*)
seem *sembler*
Seine *Seine* f.
seize *s'emparer* (*de* + noun)
sell *vendre*
send *envoyer* (*envoyant, envoyé, j'envoie, j'envoyai*)
sentence *phrase* f.
separate *séparer*
serious *sérieux, sérieuse*
servant *domestique* m., f.
service *service* m.
set *poste* m.
radio set *poste de radio* m.
television set *poste de télévision* m.
seven *sept*
seventeenth *dix-septième*
several *plusieurs*
she *elle*
sheep *mouton* m.
shoe *soulier* m.; (pl.) *les souliers* m., *les chaussures* f.
shop *boutique* f.
tobacco shop *bureau de tabac* m.
should *devrais, devrait,* etc. (§ 93 E)
show *montrer*
shut up *enfermer*
sick *malade*
sick people *les malades* m. or f. pl.
sidewalk *trottoir* m.
silk *soie* f.
simple *simple*
sister *sœur*
sit down *s'asseoir* (*s'asseyant, assis, je m'assieds, je m'assis*); (imperative) *asseyez-vous*
situated *situé*
six *six*
skyscraper *gratte-ciel* m.
sleep *dormir* (2)
sleepy, be *avoir sommeil*
slowly *lentement*
small *petit*
smell *sentir* (2)
snow *neiger* (§ 89 B)
it snows, it is snowing *il neige*
so that *pour que* (+ subjunctive)
some (adj.) *du, de la, de l', des* (§ 5) *quelque;* (subject pron.) *quelques-uns;* (object pron.) *en* (§ 28)
something *quelque chose*
sometimes *parfois*
soon *tôt; bientôt*
as soon as *dès que, aussitôt que*
sorry, be *regretter, être désolé*
soup *potage* m.
south *sud* m.; *le Midi* (*de la France*)
southeast *sud-est* m.
southwest *sud-ouest* m.
Spain *Espagne* f.
Spanish (adj.) *espagnol;* (noun) *Espagnol* m.
speak *parler*
specialist *spécialiste* m.
spend (§ 94) (money) *dépenser;* (time) *passer*
sport *sport* m.
engage in sports *faire du sport*
spread *répandre*
spring *printemps* m.
in spring *au printemps*
St. Louis *Saint-Louis* m.
stairs *escalier* m.
stamp *timbre* m.
stand *se tenir* (*se tenant, tenu, je me tiens, je me tins*) *se tenir debout, être debout*
state *état* m.

station *gare* f.
 railroad station *gare* f.
stay *rester*
steak *bifteck* m.
steer *bœuf* m.
still *encore*
 be still (imperative) *taisez-vous*
stop *s'arrêter*
store *magasin* m.
story *histoire* f.
 detective story *roman policier* m.
Strasbourg *Strasbourg* m.
street *rue* f.
 on the street *dans la rue*
strike *grève* f.
student *étudiant* m.; *étudiante* f.
study *étudier, apprendre* (*apprenant, appris, j'apprends, j'appris*) (conj. like *prendre*)
study *étude* f.
 carry on studies *faire des études*
subject *sujet* m.; (of study) *matière* f.
subway *métro* m.
 subway station *station de métro* f.
succeed *réussir*
summer *été* m.
 in summer *en été*
Sunday *dimanche* m.
sure *sûr*
surprise *étonner*
surprised, be *être étonné, s'étonner*
surround *entourer*
Susan *Suzanne*
Sweden *Suède* f.
sweep *balayer* (§ 89 C)
Switzerland *Suisse* f.

T

table *table* f.
take (§ 94) *prendre* (*prenant, pris, je prends, je pris*)
 take away (a thing) *emporter*
 take a course *suivre un cours*
 take a person *mener, conduire une personne*
 take a train *prendre un train*
 take a trip *faire un voyage*
 take a walk *faire une promenade; se promener*
talk *parler*
tax *impôt* m.
taxi *taxi* m.
tea *thé* m.
teacher *professeur* m.
team *équipe* f.
telephone *téléphoner; donner un coup de téléphone*
 telephone book *annuaire* m.
 telephone booth *cabine téléphonique* f.
 telephone call *coup de téléphone* m.
television *télévision* f.
 television set *poste de télévision* m.
tell *dire* (*disant, dit, je dis, je dis*); *raconter*
ten *dix*
tennis *tennis* m.
territory *territoire* m.
test *épreuve* f.
text *texte* m.
than *que* (§ 13 B)
thanks to *grâce à*
that (adj.) *ce* (§ 15); (pron.) *celui-là, celle-là* (§ 33); *cela* (§ 34); *que; où* (§ 39 F)
 that one *celui-là* (§ 33)
the *le, la, l', les*
theater *théâtre* m.
their *leur, leurs*
theirs *le leur, la leur, etc.*
them (direct object) *les;* (indirect object) *leur;* (with prep.) *eux, elles*
then *puis; ensuite*
theory *théorie* f.
there (§ 29 B) *y; là*
 there is, there are *il y a; voilà* (§ 91)
therefore *donc*
these (adj.) *ces* (§ 15); (pron.) *ceux-ci, celles-ci* (§ 33)
they *ils, elles; eux* (§ 27 B 2, 3)
thing *chose* f.
think *penser* (à + noun); *croire* (*croyant, cru, je crois, je crus*)
 What do you think of him? *Que pensez-vous de lui?*
third *troisième*
this (adj.) *ce* (§ 15); (pron.) *celui-ci, celle-ci* (§ 33); *ceci* (§ 34)
those (adj.) *ces* (§ 15); (pron.) *ceux-là, celles-là* (§ 33)
thousand *mille*
three *trois*
Thursday *jeudi* m.

ticket *billet* m.
get a ticket *prendre un billet*
time (§ 98) *heure* f.; *temps* m.; *fois* f.; *époque* f.
on time *à l'heure*
What time is it? *Quelle heure est-il?*
tired *fatigué*
to *à;* (with place names) *à, en* (§ 42); *chez* (§ 42 F)
in order to *pour*
to the *au, à la, à l', aux*
up to *jusqu'à*
tobacco shop *bureau de tabac* m.
today *aujourd'hui*
tomorrow *demain*
too *trop*
it is too bad *c'est dommage*
too many *trop* (*de* + noun)
too much *trop* (*de* + noun)
Touraine *Touraine* f.
tourist *touriste* m.
Tours *Tours* m.
toward *vers*
toy *jouet* m.
trailer *remorque* (*de camping, pour le camping*) f.
train *train* m.
get on a train *monter dans un train*
training *formation* f.
travel *voyager* (§ 89 B)
traveler *voyageur* m.
treaty *traité* m.
tree *arbre* m.
trip *voyage* m.
take a trip *faire un voyage*
troop *troupe* f.
true *vrai*
try *essayer* (*de* + inf.) (§ 89 C)
Tuesday *mardi* m.
turn *se tourner*
twelve *douze*
twelve o'clock (noon) *midi;* (midnight) *minuit*
two *deux*
type *genre* m.

U

uncle *oncle* m.
understand *comprendre* (*comprenant, compris, je comprends, je compris*) (conj. like *prendre*)
unemployment *chômage* m.
unfortunate *malheureux, malheureuse*
United States *États-Unis* m. pl.
university *université* f.
unless *à moins que* (+ subjunctive)
unlikely *peu probable*
until *jusqu'à ce que* (+ subjunctive)
up and down *le long de*
up to *jusqu'à*
us *nous*
use *se servir* (*de* + noun) (2)
use *emploi* m.
used to (+ inf.) a form of the imperfect tense (§ 52 C)
usher *ouvreuse* f.
utilize *utiliser*

V

vacation *vacances* f. pl.
vague *vague*
vain, in (do) *avoir beau* (+ inf.)
valley *vallée* f.
verb *verbe* m.
Versailles *Versailles*
very *très*
very much *beaucoup*
violin *violon* m.
visit (§ 94) (a place) *visiter;* (a person) *faire une visite à, rendre visite à, aller voir*
Vosges *Vosges* f. pl.
vote *voter*

W

wait *attendre*
wait for *attendre* (+ noun)
waiter *garçon* m.
wake up *se réveiller*
walk *se promener* (§ 89 D); *marcher*
take a walk *se promener, faire une promenade*
wall *mur* m., *muraille* f.
want *vouloir* (*voulant, voulu, je veux, je voulus*)
war *guerre* f.
the war breaks out *la guerre éclate*
warm *chaud*
be warm (referring to a person) *avoir chaud;* (referring to weather) *faire chaud*
watch *montre* f.
Waterloo *Waterloo* m.
way, this *par ici*
we *nous*
wear *porter*

weather *temps* m.
the weather is bad *il fait mauvais temps*
the weather is good *il fait beau (temps)*
What kind of weather is it? *Quel temps fait-il?*
Wednesday *mercredi* m.
week *semaine* f.
weekend *week-end* m.
well *bien*
I am very well *Je vais très bien*
well-known *connu*
west *ouest* m.
wharf *quai* m.
what (interrogative) *qu'est-ce qui; que, qu'est-ce que; quoi* (§ 38 A–D); *quel, quelle* (§ 16); *qu'est-ce que, qu'est ce que c'est que* (§ 38 F); (relative) *ce qui; ce que* (§ 39 G)
when *quand; où* (§ 39 F)
where *où*
which (interrogative) *quel, quelle* (§ 16); *lequel, laquelle* (§ 38 E); (relative) *qui; que; lequel; quoi* (§ 39 A–D)
which one *lequel, laquelle*
while (§ 98) (at the same time) *pendant que;* (whereas) *tandis que*
who *qui*
whole *tout, toute, tous, toutes; entier, entière*
whom (interrogative) *qui;* (relative) *que*
whose *dont* (§ 39 E)
why *pourquoi*
wide *large*
wife *femme* f.
William the Conqueror *Guillaume le Conquérant*
willing, be *vouloir bien*
win *gagner*
windy, it is *il y a du vent*
wine *vin* m.
winter *hiver* m.
in winter *en hiver*
wish *vouloir (voulant, voulu, je veux, je voulus)*
with *avec*
without *sans* (§ 5 D)
do without *se passer de*
woman *femme* f.
woods *bois* m.
word *mot* m.; (spoken word, words of a song) *parole* f.
work *travailler*
work *travail* m. (*travaux*, pl.)
literary work *œuvre* f.
working man *ouvrier* m.
workman *ouvrier* m.
world *monde* m.
World War I *la guerre de 14; la Première Guerre mondiale*
World War II *la guerre de 39; la Deuxième Guerre mondiale*
write *écrire (écrivant, écrit, j'écris, j'écrivis)*
writer *écrivain* m.
wrong, be *avoir tort*

Y

year (§ 98) *an* m., *année* f.
yesterday *hier*
yesterday evening *hier soir*
yet *encore*
you *vous;* (indefinite) *on* (§ 40)
young *jeune*
your *votre, vos*
yours *le vôtre, la vôtre,* etc.
youth *jeunesse* f.
youth hostel *auberge de la jeunesse* f.

Vocabulaire français-anglais

ABBREVIATIONS:

abbr.	abbreviation	*m.*	masculine	*pers.*	person
adj.	adjective	*no.*	number	*pres.*	present
conj.	conjugate	*p.*	page	*pron.*	pronoun
f.	feminine	*pl.*	plural	*sing.*	singular
fut.	future	*pp*	past participle	*sp*	simple past
inf.	infinitive				

§ References to the *Grammaire*
* aspirate h (*Prononciation* § 1 B)
(2) *-ir* verb of second class (§ 49 C)

Verbs whose principal parts are given are irregular and are conjugated in § 95 of the *Grammaire* or are conjugated like some verb found in § 95. The principal parts of the verb are the *infinitive, present participle, past participle, first person singular present indicative, first person singular simple past.* The importance of the principal parts of a verb is explained in § 48.

Following the latest practice in French pronunciation, *harmonisation vocalique* or regressive vowel assimilation is respected in the phonetic transcriptions. For an explanation of this phenomenon, see *Prononciation* § 20.

The length sign [:] and the reflexive pronoun of reflexive verbs are omitted in the phonetic transcriptions.

A

a [a] (avoir) *has*
 il y a *there is, there are; ago*
à [a] *to, in, at*
 à cause de *because of*
 à l'étranger {*in* / *to*} *a foreign country, abroad*
 à la fois *at the same time*
 à la française *in the French style*
 à haute voix *aloud*
 à jeudi *until Thursday*
 à la mode *in style*
 à moins que *unless*
 à nouveau *again*
 à part *except, except for*
 à partir de . . . *from . . . on*
 à peine *scarcely*
 à perte de vue *as far as the eye can reach*
 à peu près *about*
 à pied *on foot*
 à présent *at present*
 à propos de *in regard to*
 à suivre *to be continued*
 à ce sujet *on this subject*
 à table *at the table*
 à son tour *in (his) turn*
 à tout à l'heure *until later, "so long"*
 à travers *through*
 à vie *for life*
 à voix basse *in a low voice, in a whisper*
abdiquer [abdike] *abdicate*
abolition [abɔlisjõ] *f.* *abolition*
d'abord [dabɔr] *first, at first*
aboutir [abutir] (à + noun) *end in*
absolu [apsɔly] *absolute*
absolument [apsɔlymɑ̃] *absolutely*
absolutisme [apsɔlytism] *m.* *absolutism*
absorber [apsɔrbe] *absorb*
abus [aby] *m.* *abuse*
abuser [abyze] *abuse*
Acadien [akadjɛ̃] *m.* *Acadian*
accent [aksɑ̃] *m.* *accent*
accepter [aksɛpte] *accept*

accès [aksɛ] *m.* *access, approach*
accident [aksidɑ̃] *m.* *accident*
accompagner [akõpaɲe] *accompany*
accord [akɔr] *m.* *agreement; accord*
 d'accord *in agreement; agreed, OK*
accorder [akɔrde] *grant*
accroître [akrwatr] *increase*
acharné [aʃarne] *desperate, obstinate, intense, stubborn*
acheter [aʃte] (§ 89 D) *buy*
acheteur [aʃtœr] *m.* *buyer*
achever [aʃve] (§ 89 D) *finish*
acquérir [akerir] (acquérant, acquis, j'acquiers, j'acquis) *acquire*
acquis [aki] (*pp and sp of* acquérir) *acquired*
acteur [aktœr] *m.* *actor*
actif, active [aktif, aktiv] *active*
action [aksjõ] *f.* *action*
activité [aktivite] *f.* *activity*
actuel, actuelle [aktɥɛl] *present*
 à l'heure actuelle *now, at present*
actuellement [aktɥɛlmɑ̃] *now, at present*
s'adapter [adapte] *adapt itself*
addition [adisjõ] f. *bill; addition*
adjectif [adʒɛktif] *m.* *adjective*
admettre [admɛtr] (admettant, admis, j'admets, j'admis) (*conj. like* mettre) *admit*
administratif, administrative [administratif, administrativ] *administrative*
administration [administrɑsjõ] *f.* *administration*
admirable [admirabl] *admirable*
admiration [admirɑsjõ] *f.* *admiration*
admirer [admire] *admire*
adopter [adɔpte] *adopt*
adresse [adrɛs] *f.* *address*
s'adresser [adrese] *be directed to, appeal to, go to speak to*
adverbe [advɛrb] *m.* *adverb*
aérien, aerienne [aerjɛ̃, aerjɛn] *aerial, air* (adj.), *from the air*
affaiblir [afeblir] *weaken*
affaire [afɛr] *f.* *affair, matter, business*
 les affaires *f. pl.* *business*
 Ministre des Affaires Étrangères *Minister of Foreign Affairs*
 voyage d'affaires *business trip*
affectueux, affectueuse [afɛktɥø, afɛktɥøz] *affectionate*
affiche [afiʃ] *f.* *notice, sign*
affirmer [afirme] *affirm*
afin de [afɛ̃də] *in order to*
africain [afrikɛ̃] *African*
Afrique [afrik] *f.* *Africa*
 Afrique du Nord *North Africa*
âge [ɑʒ] *m.* *age*
 d'un certain âge *middle-aged*
 le moyen âge *Middle Ages*
 Quel âge avez-vous? *How old are you?*
âgé [ɑʒe] *old, aged*
 âgé de neuf ans *nine years old*
agir [aʒir] *act, do*
 s'agir de *be a question of*
agitation [aʒitɑsjõ] *restlessness; agitation*
agité [aʒite] *agitated, rough; troubled*
s'agiter [aʒite] *be restless*
 le pays s'agite *there is unrest in the country*
agrandi [agrɑ̃di] *enlarged, lengthened*
s'agrandir [agrɑ̃dir] *become larger*
agréable [agreabl] *agreeable, pleasant*
agrément [agremɑ̃] *m.* *pleasure*
agricole [agrikɔl] *agricultural*
agriculture [agrikyltyr] *f.* *agriculture*
ah [ɑ] *ah!, oh!*
ai [e] (*1st pers. sing. pres. of* avoir) *have*
aide [ɛd] *f.* *aid, help*
aider [ede] (à + inf.) *help*
aigle [ɛgl] *m.* *eagle*
aile [ɛl] *f.* *wing*
aille [aj] (aller) *go*
ailleurs [ajœr] *elsewhere*
d'ailleurs [dajœr] *besides, moreover*
aimer [eme] (+ inf.) *love, like*
 aimer mieux (+ inf.) *prefer, like better*
ainsi [ɛ̃si] *thus, so*
 ainsi que *in the same way, as well as*
air [ɛr] *m.* *air*
 avoir l'air de *seem, have the appearance*
 d'un air surpris *in a surprised manner*
 plein air *open air*
aise [ɛz] *f.* *ease*
 à l'aise *at ease, comfortably*
Aix-les-Bains [ɛksləbɛ̃] *Aix-les-Bains*
ajouter [aʒute] *add*
Alabama [alabama] *f.* *Alabama*

alarmer [alarme] *alarm*
Albert [albɛr] *m.* *Albert*
alcool [alkɔl] *m.* *alcohol*
algèbre [alʒɛbr] *f.* *algebra*
allée [ale] *f.* *path, passage, walk*
Alleghanys [alegani] *Allegheny Mountains*
allégresse [alegrɛs] *f.* *happiness*
Allemagne [almaɲ] *f.* *Germany*
allemand [almɑ̃] *German*
aller [ale] (allant, allé, je vais, j'allai) (+ inf.) *go*
  aller chercher *go to get*
  Comment allez-vous? *How are you?*
  Comment ça va? *How are you?*
  Je vais bien. *I'm fine.*
s'en aller [ɑ̃nale] (§§ 94, 95, no. 11) *go away, go off*
alliance [aljɑ̃s] *f.* *alliance*
allié, alliée [alje], *ally, allied*
  les Alliés *France, England, and Russia, and later Italy; the United States, and all other countries who fought against Germany in World War I; England, the United States, and all other countries who fought against Germany in World War II*
allô [alo] *"hello"* (at the beginning of a telephone conversation)
allocation [alɔkɑsjɔ̃] *f.* *allocation, allowance*
  allocation familiale *family allowance given by the French government to families*
allons [alɔ̃] *come now, let's go*
  allons donc *well now, you don't say*
allumer [alyme] *light*
allumette [alymɛt] *f.* *match*
alors [alɔr] *then*
  alors que *while*
Alpes [alp] *f.* *Alps*
Alsace [alzas] *f.* *Alsace, province in eastern France.*
Alsace-Lorraine [alzaslɔrɛn] *f.* *Alsace-Lorraine, territory taken by Germany from France in 1871 and returned to France in 1918*
Alsacien [alzasjɛ̃] *m.* *Alsatian*
amateur [amatœr] *m.* *amateur; devotee, "fan"*
Amazone [amazɔn] *m.* *Amazon*
ambassadeur [ɑ̃basadœr] *m.* *ambassador*
ambitieux, ambitieuse [ɑ̃bisjø, ɑ̃bisjøz] *ambitious*
ambition [ɑ̃bisjɔ̃] *f.* *ambition*
âme [ɑm] *f.* *soul*
améliorer [ameljɔre] *better*
amener [amne] (§ 89 D) *lead, take (a person), bring on, bring about*
américain [amerikɛ̃] *American*
Amérique [amerik] *f.* *America*
  Amérique du Nord *f.* *North America*
  Amérique du Sud *f.* *South America*
ami [ami] *m.* *friend*
amicalement [amikalmɑ̃] *in a friendly way*
amie [ami] *f.* *(girl) friend*
Amiens [amjɛ̃] *city of northern France in ancient province of Picardy*
amitié [amitje] *f.* *friendship*
amour [amur] (*m.* in sing. *f.* in pl.) *love*
amuser [amyze] *amuse*
  s'amuser (à + inf.) *enjoy oneself, amuse oneself, have a good time*
an [ɑ̃] *m.* *year*
  le jour de l'an *New Year's day*
  j'ai vingt ans *I am twenty years old*
Anatole [anatɔl] *Anatole*
ancêtre [ɑ̃sɛtr] *m.* *ancestor*
ancien, ancienne [ɑ̃sjɛ̃, ɑ̃sjɛn] *old, ancient; former*
Ancien régime [ɑ̃sjɛ̃reʒim] *m.* *Old Regime, used in reference to the period when France was under an absolute monarchy, before 1789*
Andes [ɑ̃d] *f.* *principal mountain chain of South America*
André [ɑ̃dre] *Andrew*
anecdote [anɛkdɔt] *f.* *anecdote*
anglais [ɑ̃glɛ] *English*
Anglais [ɑ̃glɛ] *m.* *Englishman*
Anglaise [ɑ̃glɛz] *f.* *English girl*
Angleterre [ɑ̃glətɛr] *f.* *England*
anglo-américain [ɑ̃gloamerikɛ̃] *anglo-american*
animal, animaux [animal, animo] *m.* *animal*
animé [anime] *gay, animated, enlivened*
Anne [an] *f.* *Anne*
année [ane] *f.* *year*
annexer [anɛkse] *annex*
annonce [anɔ̃s] *f.* *announcement*

annuaire [anɥɛr] *m.* *telephone book, telephone directory*
antérieur [ɑ̃terjœr] *anterior*
futur antérieur *future perfect*
passé antérieur *past anterior* (*a second pluperfect*)
antique [ɑ̃tik] *antique, ancient*
Antoine [ɑ̃twan] *proper name*
août [u] *m.* *August*
apaiser [apeze] *calm*
apercevoir [apɛrsəvwar] (apercevant, aperçu, j'aperçois, j'aperçus) (*conj. like* recevoir) *perceive, see, notice*
s'apercevoir (de + noun) *perceive, notice*
aperçu, aperçus [apɛrsy] (*pp and sp of* apercevoir) *perceived, noticed*
apéritif [aperitif] *m.* *appetizer, drink taken before a meal*
apogée [apɔʒe] *m.* *height, apex*
apparaître [aparɛtr] (apparaissant, apparu, j'apparais, j'apparus) (*conj. like* connaître) *appear*
appareil [aparɛj] *m.* *apparatus; (radio or television) set*
apparence [aparɑ̃s] *f.* *appearance, looks*
appartement [apartəmɑ̃] *m.* *apartment*
appartenir [apartənir] (appartenant, appartenu, j'appartiens, j'appartins) (*conj. like* tenir) *belong*
apparu, apparus [apary] (*pp and sp of* apparaître) *appeared*
appel [apɛl] *m.* *appeal*
faire appel à *call on*
appelé [aple] *called, named*
appeler [aple] (§ 89 F) *call*
s'appeler *be called*
application [aplikɑsjɔ̃] *f.* *application*
appliquer [aplike] *apply*
s'appliquer *apply oneself to, strive to, work hard at, try*
apporter [apɔrte] *bring*
apprécié [apresje] *popular, well-liked*
apprendre [aprɑ̃dr] (apprenant, appris, j'apprends, j'appris) (thing + à + person; à + inf.) *learn; teach*
approcher [aprɔʃe] *approach*
s'approcher (de + noun) *approach*
approuver [apruve] *approve*
appuyer [apɥije] (§ 89 C) *press down on, support*
âpre [ɑpr] *harsh*
après [aprɛ] *after*
après que *after* + clause
d'après *according to*
peu après *a little later, soon after*
après-demain [aprɛdmɛ̃] *day after tomorrow*
après-midi [aprɛmidi] (*m.* or *f.*) *afternoon*
Arabe [arab] *m.* *Arab*
arbre [arbr] *m.* *tree*
arc [ark] *m.* *arch*
Arc de Triomphe [arkdətrijɔ̃f] *Triumphal Arch* (referring to the one at *the Place de l'Étoile*)
Arc de Triomphe du Carrousel, *arch situated between the Louvre and the Tuileries*
archiduc [arʃidyk] *m.* *archduke*
archiduc-héritier *crown prince; heir to the throne*
architecture [arʃitɛktyr] *f.* *architecture*
argent [arʒɑ̃] *m.* *money; silver*
Argentine [arʒɑ̃tin] *f.* *Argentina*
Arles [arl] *city on the Rhone noted for its Roman ruins*
arme [arm] *f.* *arm, weapon*
armée [arme] *f.* *army*
la Grande Armée *army of Napoleon I*
Ministre des Forces Armées *Minister of Defense*
s'armer [arme] *arm oneself, take arms*
armistice [armistis] *m.* *armistice*
arrêter [arete] *stop*
s'arrêter *stop*
arrivée [arive] *f.* *arrival*
arriver [arive] (à + inf.) *arrive; happen; succeed in*
art [ar] *m.* *art*
artère [artɛr] *f.* *artery*
article [artikl] *m.* *article*
artificiel, artificielle [artifisjɛl] *artificial*
artiste [artist] *m.f.* *artist*
artistique [artistik] *artistic*
Asie [azi] *f.* *Asia*
aspect [aspɛ] *m.* *aspect*
assassiner [asasine] *assassinate*
assemblée [asɑ̃ble] *f.* *assembly*
Assemblée Nationale [asɑ̃blenasjɔnal]

National Assembly, the lower house in the French Parliament, formerly called the Chamber of Deputies
s'asseoir [aswar] (s'asseyant, assis, je m'assieds, je m'assis) *sit down*
asseyez-vous [asejevu] (*imperative of* s'asseoir) *sit down*
assez [ase] *enough; rather*
assis [asi] (*pp and sp of* asseoir) *seated*
assistance [asistɑ̃s] *f.* *assistance*
assister [asiste] (à + noun) *be present at*
associer [asɔsje] *associate, mix*
assurer [asyre] *insure, assure*
astronomique [astrɔnɔmik] *astronomical*
atelier [atəlje] *m.* *(work)shop; factory; studio*
athlétisme [atletism] *m.* *track and field*
Atlantique [atlɑ̃tik] *m.* *Atlantic*
atmosphère [atmɔsfɛr] *f.* *atmosphere*
attacher [ataʃe] *attach*
attaquer [atake] *attack*
atteindre [atɛ̃dr] (atteignant, atteint, j'atteins, j'atteignis) (*conj. like* peindre) *attain, reach*
attendant: en attendant que *until*
attendre [atɑ̃dr] (+ noun) *wait for, await, wait*
  j'attends de vos nouvelles *I am waiting for news from you*
  s'attendre à *expect*
attentat [atɑ̃ta] *m.* *attempt at crime, attempted murder*
attention [atɑ̃sjõ] *f.* *attention*
  attention! *look out!*
  attention à *look out for, pay attention to*
  faire attention *pay attention; be careful, watch out*
  retenir l'attention *attract attention*
attentivement [atɑ̃tivmɑ̃] *attentively*
attirer [atire] *attract*
attitude [atityd] *f.* *attitude*
au [o] (§ 2 B) *to the, at the*
  au contraire *on the contrary*
  au delà de *beyond*
  au fond de *in the remotest part of, in the depths of; at the back of*
  au loin *in the distance*
  au maximum *at most*
  au moins *at least*
  au revoir *good bye*
auberge [obɛrʒ] *f.* *inn*
  auberge de la jeunesse *youth hostel*
aucun [okœ̃] *any*
  ne . . . aucun *not any, no, none*
au-dessous [odsu] *below, underneath*
au-dessus [odsy] *above*
auditeur [oditœr] *m.* *auditor, listener*
augmentation [ɔgmɑ̃tɑsjõ] *f.* *increase*
aujourd'hui [oʒurdɥi] *today*
auparavant [oparavɑ̃] *formerly, before*
auquel [okɛl] (*contraction of* à lequel) *to which*
aurai [ɔre] (*1st pers. sing. fut. of* avoir) *shall have*
aussi [osi] *also, too*
  aussi . . . que (§ 13 F) *as . . . as*
Aussi . . . (§ 20 E) *so, therefore*
aussistôt [osito] *immediately*
  aussitôt que *as soon as*
autant [otɑ̃] *as much, as many*
  d'autant plus . . . que *so much the more . . . because*
  autant que *as much as*
auteur [otœr] *m.* *author*
auto [ɔto] *f.* *auto*
autobus [ɔtɔbys] *m.* *bus*
  monter dans un autobus *get on a bus*
automatique [ɔtɔmatik] *automatic*
automatiquement [ɔtɔmatikmɑ̃] *automatically*
automne [otɔn, ɔtɔn] *m.* *autumn*
autorité [ɔtɔrite] *f.* *authority*
autour [otur] *around*
  autour de *around*
autre [otr] *other*
  de l'autre côté *on the other side*
  d'autre part *on the other hand, moreover, likewise*
autrefois [otrəfwa] *formerly*
Autriche [otriʃ] *f.* *Austria*
Autriche-Hongrie [otriʃõgri] *f.* *Austria-Hungary*
aux [o] (§2 B) *to the, at the, in the*
  aux lignes régulières *with regular lines*
auxiliaire [ɔksiljɛr] *auxiliary*
avalanche [avalɑ̃ʃ] *f.* *avalanche*
avance [avɑ̃s] *f.* *advance*
  à l'avance *in advance*
avancer [avɑ̃se] (§ 89 A) *advance*
avant [avɑ̃] *before*
  avant de *before* (+ inf.)
  avant que *before* (+ clause)

avantage [avɑ̃taʒ] *m.* *advantage*
avec [avɛk] *with*
avenue [avny] *f.* *avenue*
aveugle [avœgl] *blind*
aveuglément [avœglemɑ̃] *blindly*
avez [ave] (avoir) *(you) have*
aviation [avjɑsjõ] *f.* *aviation*
avide [avid] (de + noun) *avid for, eager for*
Avignon [aviɲõ] *city in southern France on the Rhone, noted for its papal palace*
avion [avjõ] *m.* *airplane*
avis [avi] *m.* *opinion*
avocat [avɔka] *m.* *lawyer*
avoir [avwar] (ayant, eu, j'ai, j'eus) (à + inf.) *have*
 avoir l'air *seem, have the appearance*
 avoir (quinze) ans *be (fifteen) years old*
 avoir beau *do (something) in vain*
 avoir besoin (de) *need*
 avoir chaud *be warm, hot*
 avoir envie *feel like, desire*
 avoir faim *be hungry*
 avoir froid *be cold*
 avoir honte (de + noun; de + inf.) *be ashamed of*
 avoir l'intention (de + inf.) *intend*
 avoir lieu *take place*
 avoir mal *hurt, have a pain*
 avoir mal à la tête *have a headache*
 avoir peur (de + noun; de + inf.) *be afraid*
 avoir raison *be right*
 avoir soif *be thirsty*
 avoir sommeil *be sleepy*
 avoir tort *be wrong*
 il y a (§ 90 A) *there is, there are; ago*
 il y en a pour *it will last for*
 Quel age avez-vous? *How old are you?*
avons [avõ] (avoir) *(we) have*
avril [avril] *m.* *April*
azur [azyr] *blue*
Côte d'Azur [kotdazyr] *strip of coast along the Mediterranean from Toulon to the Italian border known as the French Riviera*

B

Baccalauréat [bakalɔrea] *m.* *baccalaureate, degree obtained by French lycée student after passing two series of state examinations*
Bachot [baʃo] *m.* *nickname for* Baccalauréat
bague [bag] *f.* *ring*
se baigner [beɲe] *bathe, go bathing*
baiser [beze] *m.* *kiss*
baisser [bese] *lower*
bal [bal] *m.* *ball, dance*
balayer [baleje] (§ 89 C) *sweep*
balle [bal] *f.* *ball*
ballon [balõ] *m.* *football*
Balzac, Honoré de [balzak] (*1799–1850*) *great French realistic novelist of the nineteenth century*
ban [bɑ̃] *m.* *public announcement of marriage, bann*
banque [bɑ̃k] *f.* *bank*
banquette [bɑ̃kɛt] *f.* *bench* (in a railroad compartment)
bar [bar] *m.* *bar; snack bar*
barrière [barjɛr] *f.* *barrier*
bas, basse [bɑ, bɑs] *low*
 à voix basse *in a low voice, in a whisper*
 en bas *downstairs*
base [bɑz] *f.* *basis, base*
base-ball [bɛzbɔl] *m.* *baseball*
baser [bɑze] *base*
basket-ball [baskɛtbɔl] *m.* *basketball*
Basque [bask] *m.* *inhabitant of the Basque provinces in the French and Spanish Pyrenees*
bassin [basɛ̃] *m.* *basin, fountain in a park*
Bastille [bastij] *f.* *state prison taken and destroyed by the people of Paris on July 14, 1789*
bataille [batɑj] *f.* *battle*
bateau [bato] *m.* *boat*
bâtiment [bɑtimɑ̃] *m.* *building*
Bâton-Rouge [bɑtõruʒ] *m.* *capital of Louisiana*
battre [batr] (battant, battu, je bats, je battis) *beat*
 battre en retraite *retreat*
 se battre *fight*
bavard [bavar] *talkative*
bavarder [bavarde] *converse, chat; gossip*
Bayeux [bajø] *town in Normandy in*

which may be seen the tapestry of Queen Mathilda
beau (*pl.* beaux) [bo] (§ 10 G) *beautiful, handsome*
avoir beau *to do (something) in vain*
faire beau *be good weather*
beaucoup [boku] (de + noun) *much, many, a great deal*
beauté [bote] *f.* *beauty*
Beaux-Arts, École des [ekɔldebozar] *school of fine arts at Paris*
bel, belle [bɛl] (§ 10 G) *beautiful*
Belfort [bɛfɔr [1], bɛlfɔr] *only city of Alsace which remained French after the Franco-Prussian war*
belge [bɛlʒ] *Belgian*
Belgique [bɛlʒik] *f.* *Belgium*
bénéficier [benefisje] (de + noun) *benefit, be the recipient of*
berceau [bɛrso] *m.* *cradle*
Berlin [Bɛrlɛ̃] *capital of Germany*
Bernard [bɛrnar] *m.* *Bernard*
besoin [bəzwɛ̃] *m.* *need*
avoir besoin (de + noun; de + inf.) *need*
bête [bɛt] *f.* *beast, creature, animal*
beurre [bœr] *m.* *butter*
bibliothèque [biblijɔtɛk] *f.* *library*
biblique [biblik] *biblical*
bicyclette [bisiklɛt] *f.* *bicycle*
bien [bjɛ̃] *well; well-off, comfortable; good; indeed; very, very much*
bien des *many*
bien entendu *of course*
eh bien *well, very well*
être bien *be comfortable*
ou bien *or, or indeed*
si bien que *so that*
vouloir bien *be willing, be quite willing*
bien que [bjɛ̃kə] *although*
bienfait [bjɛ̃fɛ] *m.* *benefit*
bientôt [bjɛ̃to] *soon*
bière [bjɛr] *f.* *beer*
bifteck [biftɛk] *m.* *steak*
billet [bijɛ] *m.* *ticket; bills, banknotes*
prendre un billet *buy a ticket*
biologie [bjɔlɔʒi] *f.* *biology*
Bismarck [bismark] (*1815–1898*) *German statesman*
blanc, blanche [blɑ̃, blɑ̃ʃ] *white*

[1] *Ainsi prononcé dans le pays même.*

blanchisseuse [blɑ̃ʃisøz] *f.* *washwoman*
blême [blɛm] *pale*
blesser [blese] *wound, hurt*
blessure [blesyr] *f.* *wound*
bleu [blø] *blue*
blindé [blɛ̃de] *armored, Panzer*
blocus [blɔkys] *m.* *blockade*
blond [blɔ̃] *blond*
bœuf [*sing.* bœf, *pl.* bø] *m.* *ox, steer*
boire [bwar] (buvant, bu, je bois, je bus) *drink*
bois [bwɑ] *m.* *wood, woods*
boisson [bwasɔ̃] *f.* *beverage*
boîte [bwat] *f.* *box; special type of box used to display books and pictures, found along the parapets overlooking the wharves of the Seine*
boîte aux lettres *mail box*
boîte de nuit *night club*
bombarder [bɔ̃barde] *bombard*
bon, bonne [bɔ̃, bɔn] *good*
bon marché *cheap*
de bonne heure *early*
tenir bon *hold out*
Bonaparte [bɔnapart] *family name of Napoleon I*
bonbon [bɔ̃bɔ̃] *m.* *candy*
bonhomme [bɔnɔm] *m.* *fellow*
bonjour [bɔ̃ʒur] *good day, good morning, good afternoon, hello*
Bonneville [bɔnvil] *family name*
bord [bɔr] *m.* *shore, edge*
au bord de la mer *at the seashore*
Bordeaux [bɔrdo] *French port situated at the junction of the Garonne and the Gironde*
border [bɔrde] *border on, border*
borgne [bɔrɲ] *blind in one eye*
bouche [buʃ] *f.* *mouth*
bougie [buʒi] *f.* *candle*
Boul' Mich' [bulmiʃ] *nickname given by students to the Boulevard Saint-Michel*
boulanger [bulɑ̃ʒe] *m.* *baker*
boulevard [bulvar] *m.* *boulevard*
les grands boulevards *certain of the wide boulevards in the center of Paris, such as the Boulevard Haussmann*
bouleverser [bulvɛrse] *upset; cause a revolution in*
bouquiniste [bukinist] *m.* *man who*

sells books in one of the "boîtes" along the Seine
Bourbon, Palais [palɛburbõ] *building in which the Assemblée Nationale meets*
bout [bu] *m.* *end*
boutique [butik] *f.* *shop*
bouton [butõ] *m.* *button*
boxe [bɔks] *f.* *boxing*
combat de boxe *boxing bout*
boy-scout [bɔjskut] *m.* *boy scout*
branche [brɑ̃ʃ] *f.* *branch*
bras [bra] *m.* *arm*
Brest [brɛst] *military port in the extreme west of France*
Bretagne [brətaɲ] *f.* *Brittany*
Grande-Bretagne *Great Britain*
Breton [brətõ] *m.* *inhabitant of Brittany*
breton, bretonne [brətõ, brətɔn] *Breton*
Brie [bri] *m.* *kind of cheese*
brillant [brijɑ̃] *brilliant*
brillamment [brijamɑ̃] *brilliantly*
britannique [britanik] *British*
bruit [brɥi] *m.* *noise*
brûler [bryle] *burn*
brun, brune [brœ̃, bryn] *brunette; dark haired; dark complexioned*
bu, bus [by] (*pp and sp of* boire) *drunk, drank*
bûche [byʃ] *f.* *large piece of firewood, log*
bulletin [byltɛ̃] *m.* *bulletin*
bureau [byro] *m.* *desk; office*
bureau de poste *post office*
bureau de tabac *tobacco shop*
buste [byst] *m.* *bust*
but [byt, by] *m.* *aim*
byzantin [bizɑ̃tɛ̃] *Byzantine*

C

ça [sa] (§ 34 A) *that*
Comment ça va? *How are you?*
C'est ça *That's right*
Ça m'est égal *it's all the same to me*
Qu'est-ce que c'est que ça? *What's that?*
Ça va bien *I'm fine*
cabine [kabin] *f.* *cabinet*
cabine téléphonique *telephone booth*
cabinet [kabinɛ] *m.* *cabinet*
cacher [kaʃe] *hide*
cadeau [kado] *m.* *gift*
faire un cadeau *give a gift*
Caen [kɑ̃] *city in Normandy*
café [kafe] *m.* *type of café where only drinks are sold; sometimes combined with restaurant and called* café-restaurant; *coffee*
cahier [kaje] *m.* *notebook*
caisse [kɛs] *f.* *cashier's*
Cajun [kadʒœ̃] (*from* Acadien) *in Louisiana a person reputed to be of French Canadian descent*
Calais [kalɛ] *French port on North Sea*
calendrier [kalɑ̃drije] *m.* *calendar*
Californie [kalifɔrni] *f.* *California*
calme [kalm] *calm*
camarade [kamarad] *m.* *comrade, chum, school-friend*
Camembert [kamɑ̃bɛr] *m.* *type of cheese*
camp [kɑ̃] *m.* *camp*
camp de concentration *concentration camp*
campagne [kɑ̃paɲ] *f.* *country* (opposite of city); (*military*) *campaign*
à la campagne *to the country, in the country*
camping [kɑ̃piŋ] *m.* *camping*
Canada [kanada] *m.* *Canada*
canadien, canadienne [kanadjɛ̃, kanadjɛn] *Canadian*
canal [kanal] *m.* *canal*
canal de Suez *Suez Canal*
candidat [kɑ̃dida] *m.* *candidate*
candidature [kɑ̃didatyr] *f.* *candidacy*
Cannes [kan] *French city on the Riviera*
cantique [kɑ̃tik] *m.* *carol, religious song, hymn*
capitale [kapital] *f.* *capital*
capitulation [kapitylɑsjõ] *f.* *capitulation*
car [kar] *for, because*
caractère [karaktɛr] *m.* *character*
caractériser [karakterise] *characterize*
caractéristique [karakteristik] *characteristic*
caravane [karavan] *f.* *caravan, company*
Carcassonne [karkasɔn] *picturesque walled city in southern France*
carrefour [karfur] *m.* *crossroad*
Carrousel, Arc de Triomphe du [arkdətrijõfdykaruzɛl] *m.* *Arch of*

Triumph placed between the Jardin des Tuileries *and the* Louvre.
carte [kart] *f.* *map; menu*
Cartier, Jacques [kartje] (*1491–1557*), *French explorer*
cas [kɑ] *m.* *case*
en tout cas *in any case*
selon le cas *as the case may be, depending on the case, whichever may be needed*
cathédrale [katedral] *f.* *cathedral*
catholique [katɔlik] *Catholic*
causatif, causative [kozatif, kozativ] *causative*
cause [koz] *f.* *cause*
à cause de *because of*
causer [koze] *talk, chat; cause*
causerie [kozri] *f.* *talk, chat*
ce, cet, cette, ces [sə, sɛt, sɛt, se] (§ 15) *this, that*
ce [sə] (§§ 35–37) *it; he; she; they*
ce que [skə] (§ 39 A, G) *what, that which, which*
ce qui [ski] (§ 39 A, G) *what, that which, which*
ceci [səsi] (§ 34) *this*
céder [sede] (§ 89 E) *give over to, cede*
cela [səla, sla] (§ 34) *that*
célèbre [selɛbr] *famous, noted*
célébrer [selebre] *make famous, celebrate*
célibataire [selibatɛr] *m.* *bachelor*
celle [sɛl] (§ 33) *this one, that one, the one*
celle-ci (§ 33 D) *this one, the latter*
celle-là (§ 33 D) *that one, the former*
celle qui *she who*
celtique [sɛltik] *Celtic*
celui [səlɥi] (§ 33) *this one, that one, the one*
celui-ci (§ 33 D) *this one, the latter*
celui-là (§ 33 D) *that one, the former*
celui qui *he who*
censure [sɑ̃syr] *f.* *censure, blame, disapprobation*
cent [sɑ̃] (§ 17 D, E) *(one) hundred*
centaine [sɑ̃tɛn] *f.* *a hundred; about a hundred*
central, centraux [sɑ̃tral, sɑ̃tro] *central*
centralisation [sɑ̃tralizɑsjɔ̃] *f.* *centralization*
centre [sɑ̃tr] *m.* *center*
cependant [spɑ̃dɑ̃, səpɑ̃dɑ̃] *however*
cercle [sɛrkl], *m.* *circle*
cérémonie [seremɔni] *f.* *ceremony*
certain [sɛrtɛ̃] *certain*
certains *certain ones*
d'un certain âge *middle-aged*
certainement [sɛrtɛnmɑ̃] *certainly*
certes [sɛrt] *certainly; indeed*
cerveau [sɛrvo] *m.* *brain*
ces [se] (§ 15) *these, those*
César [sezar] *m.* *Caesar, referring to Julius Caesar, the Roman general who conquered Gaul between 59–51 B.C.*
cesse [sɛs] *f.* *ceasing*
sans cesse *without cease, ceaselessly*
cesser [sese] (de + inf.) *stop, cease*
cession [sɛsjɔ̃] *f.* *transfer, cession*
c'est [sɛ] *that is; it is; he is; she is*
c'est-à-dire *that is to say*
c'est ça *that's right*
c'est dommage *that's too bad*
cet, cette [sɛt] (§ 15) *this, that*
ceux (sø) (§ 33) *these, those*
ceux-ci (§ 33 D) *these, the latter*
ceux-là (§ 33 D) *those, the former*
ceux qui *they who*
chacun [ʃakœ̃] *each, each one*
chaîne [ʃɛn] *f.* *chain; (radio) network*
chaise [ʃɛz] *f.* *chair*
chambre [ʃɑ̃br] *f.* *room, bedroom*
Chamonix [ʃamɔni, ʃamɔniks] *French city at the foot of Mont Blanc*
champ [ʃɑ̃] *m.* *field*
Champlain [ʃɑ̃plɛ̃] (*1567–1635*) *French explorer and founder of Quebec*
Champs-Elysées [ʃɑ̃zelize] *m.* *avenue in Paris leading from the* Place de la Concorde *to the* Place de l'Étoile
chance [ʃɑ̃s] *f.* *chance; luck*
changement [ʃɑ̃ʒmɑ̃] *m.* *change*
changer [ʃɑ̃ʒe] (§ 89 B) (de + noun) *change*
changer de train *change trains*
chanson [ʃɑ̃sɔ̃] *f.* *song*
chansonnier [ʃɑ̃sɔnje] *m.* *writer and performer of popular songs or songs dealing with political satire*

chanter [ʃɑ̃te] *sing*
chapeau [ʃapo] *m.* *hat*
chaque [ʃak] *each*
charcuterie [ʃarkytri] *f.* *pork, sausage meat, all pork products; market where pork is sold*
charger [ʃarʒe] (§ 89 B) *charge, load, load with*
se charger de *take charge of, take upon oneself, undertake, look after*
Charlemagne [ʃarləmaɲ] (742–814), *king of France and emperor of the West*
Charles [ʃarl] *m.* *Charles*
Charles X *king of France* (1824–1830)
Charlotte [ʃarlɔt] *f.* *Charlotte*
charmant [ʃarmɑ̃] *charming, delightful, lovely*
charme [ʃarm] *m.* *charm*
chasse [ʃas] *f.* *hunting; hunt*
chasseur [ʃasœr] *m.* *hunter*
château [ʃɑto] *m.* *château, castle*
Châtelet [ʃɑtlɛ] *m.* *subway station, theater, and square on the right bank of the Seine in Paris*
chaud [ʃo] *warm, hot*
avoir chaud (§ 90 B) *be warm, hot*
faire chaud (§ 92 B) *be warm, hot*
chaussures [ʃosyr] *f. pl.* *shoes*
chef [ʃɛf] *m.* *chief, head*
chemin [ʃəmɛ̃] *m.* *road*
chemin de fer *railroad*
cheminée [ʃəmine] *f.* *fireplace*
Chénier, André [ʃenje] *(1762–1794) French poet guillotined during the Reign of Terror*
Chenonceaux [ʃənɔ̃so] *Renaissance château built under Francis I; later the château of Diane de Poitiers, then of Catherine de Medici*
cher, chère [ʃɛr] *dear*
coûter cher *be expensive*
revenir cher *be expensive*
Cherbourg [ʃɛrbur] *French port on the English Channel*
chercher [ʃɛrʃe] (+ noun; à + inf.) *look for, get; try to, seek to*
envoyer chercher *send for*
cheval [ʃəval] *m.* *horse*
cheveux [ʃəvø] *m. pl.* *hair*
chez [ʃe] (§ 42 F) *at the house of*
chez Jean *at John's house*
chez nous *at our house; in our country*
chic [ʃik] *m.* *elegance, smartness*
Chicago [ʃikago] *m.* *second largest city in the United States*
chien [ʃjɛ̃] *m.* *dog*
chiffre [ʃifr] *m.* *figure, number, cipher*
chimie [ʃimi] *f.* *chemistry*
chimique [ʃimik] *chemical*
Chine [ʃin] *f.* *China*
Chinon [ʃinɔ̃] *city in Touraine, site of a medieval castle, now in ruins*
chirurgical [ʃiryrʒikal] *surgical*
chocolat [ʃɔkɔla] *m.* *chocolate*
choisir [ʃwɑzir] *choose*
choix [ʃwɑ] *m.* *choice*
chômage [ʃomaʒ] *m.* *unemployment*
chose [ʃoz] *f.* *thing*
quelque chose *something*
Chou-chou [ʃuʃu] *dog's name*
chrétien, chrétienne [kretjɛ̃, kretjɛn] *Christian*
Christ [krist] *m.* *Christ*
chroniqueur [krɔnikœr] *m.* *chronicler*
chute [ʃyt] *f.* *fall*
Cid [sid] *m.* *famous play by Corneille written in 1636*
cidre [sidr] *m.* *cider*
ciel [sjɛl] *m.* *sky; heaven*
cigare [sigar] *m.* *cigar*
cigarette [sigarɛt] *f.* *cigarette*
cinéma [sinema] *m.* *movie*
cinq [sɛ̃k, sɛ̃] *five*
cinquante [sɛ̃kɑ̃t] *fifty*
cinquante et un *fifty-one*
cinquième [sɛ̃kjɛm] *fifth*
circonstance [sirkɔ̃stɑ̃s] *f.* *circumstance*
circulation [sirkylɑsjɔ̃] *f.* *circulation; traffic*
circuler [sirkyle] *circulate*
cité [site] *f.* *walled city*
île de la Cité *island in the middle of the Seine on which Paris was first built*
Cité Universitaire *student dormitories situated on the Boulevard Jourdan at the southern extremity of Paris*
citer [site] *name; cite*
citoyen [sitwajɛ̃] *m.* *citizen*
civil [sivil] *civil*
civilisation [sivilizɑsjɔ̃] *f.* *civilization*
clair [klɛr] *clear*

clairement [klɛrmɑ̃] *clearly*
classe [klɑs] *f.* *class; classroom*
classique [klɑsik] *classical*
Claude [klod] *m.* *Claude*
clé [kle] *f.* *key*
clergé [klɛrʒe] *m.* *clergy*
client [klijɑ̃] *m.* *customer*
cloche [klɔʃ] *f.* *bell*
Clovis [klɔvis] (465?–511) *first king of France, reigning from 481 to 511*
club [klyb, klœb] *m.* *club*
code [kɔd] *m.* *code*
Code civil / Code Napoléon *system of French laws drawn up under the direction of Napoleon I*
cœur [kœr] *m.* *heart*
coiffeur [kwafœr] *m.* *barber*
coin [kwɛ̃] *m.* *corner*
collection [kɔlɛksjɔ̃] *f.* *collection; collection of dresses and coats*
  jour de la collection *opening day of a style show*
collège [kɔlɛʒ] *m.* *French school corresponding to American grammar and high school; it may be under direction of a municipality, or it may be privately owned*
  collège électoral *electoral college*
Cologne [kɔlɔɲ] *city in Western Germany*
  eau de Cologne *perfumed toilet water*
colonial [kɔlɔnjal] *colonial*
colonie [kɔlɔni] *f.* *colony*
colonisation [kɔlɔnizɑsjɔ̃] *f.* *colonization*
colonne [kɔlɔn] *f.* *column*
  cinquième colonne *fifth column*
coloré [kɔlɔre] *colorful*
combat [kɔ̃ba] *m.* *combat*
  combat de boxe *boxing bout*
combattre [kɔ̃batr] (combattant, combattu, je combats, je combattis) (*conj. like* battre) *fight*
combien [kɔ̃bjɛ̃] (de + noun) *how much, how many; how*
  tous les combien *how often*
combiner [kɔ̃bine] *combine*
comédie [kɔmedi] *f.* *comedy, play*
Comédie-Française [kɔmedifrɑ̃sɛz] *French State Theater, also called* le Théâtre-Français
comité [kɔmite] *m.* *committee*
Comité de Salut public [kɔmitedsalypyblik] *Committee of Public Safety*
commander [kɔmɑ̃de] *order; command*
  commander en chef *be in supreme command*
comme [kɔm] *like, as*
  comme je peux *however I can*
commencer [kɔmɑ̃se] (§ 89 A) (à + inf.) *begin*
  commencer par *begin with*
comment [kɔmɑ̃] *how, what; What!*
  Comment allez-vous? *How are you?*
  Comment appelle-t-on . . . ? *What does one call . . . ?*
  Comment ça va? *How are you?*
  Comment vous appelez-vous? *What is your name?*
commenter [kɔmɑ̃te] *comment, comment on*
commerçant [kɔmɛrsɑ̃] *m.* *merchant*
commerce [kɔmɛrs] *m.* *commerce*
commercial [kɔmɛrsjal] *commercial*
communication [kɔmynikɑsjɔ̃] *f.* *communication*
compagnon [kɔ̃paɲɔ̃] *m.* *companion*
comparaison [kɔ̃parɛzɔ̃] *f.* *comparison*
comparatif, comparative [kɔ̃paratif, kɔ̃parativ] *comparative*
comparer [kɔ̃pare] *compare*
compartiment [kɔ̃partimɑ̃] *m.* *compartment*
complément [kɔ̃plemɑ̃] *m.* *complement, object*
  complément direct *direct object*
  complément indirect *indirect object*
complet, complète [kɔ̃plɛ, kɔ̃plet] *complete*
complètement [kɔ̃plɛtmɑ̃] *completely*
compliment [kɔ̃plimɑ̃] *m.* *compliment*
comporter [kɔ̃pɔrte] *include; comprise*
composé [kɔ̃poze] (*pp of* composer) *composed, compound*
  passé composé *m.* *compound past, past indefinite*
composer [kɔ̃poze] *compose, consist, make up*
  se composer de *consist of, be composed of*

composition [kõpozisjõ] *f.* *composition*
comprendre [kõprɑ̃dr] (comprenant, compris, je comprends, je compris) (*conj. like* prendre) *understand; include; comprise*
compris [kõpri] (*pp and sp of* comprendre) *understood*
compte [kõt] *m.* *account, profit*
 se rendre compte de *realize*
compter [kõte] (+ inf.) *count; intend*
concentration [kõsɑ̃trɑsjõ] *f.* *concentration*
 camp de concentration *concentration camp*
conception [kõsɛpsjõ] *f.* *conception*
concert [kõsɛr] *m.* *concert*
concierge [kõsjɛrʒ] *m. f.* *house-porter, janitor*
conclu, conclus [kõkly] (*pp and sp of* conclure) *concluded*
conclure [kõklyr] *conclude*
concordat [kõkɔrda] *m.* *agreement*
Concorde [kõkɔrd] *f.* *Concord*
 Place de la Concorde *large square on the right bank of the Seine directly opposite the* Palais Bourbon
condamner [kõdɑne] *condemn; doom*
condition [kõdisjõ] *f.* *circumstance, condition, walk of life*
 à condition que *provided that, on the condition that*
conditionnel [kõdisjɔnɛl] *m.* *conditional*
conduire [kõdɥir] (conduisant, conduit, je conduis, je conduisis) *take* (a person), *lead; conduct*
 conduire une voiture *drive a car*
conduit [kõdɥi] (*pp and sp of* conduire) *took, taken; led*
confection [kõfɛksjõ] *f.* *manufacture*
 maison de confection *factory*
confectionner [kõfɛksjɔne] *manufacture*
confédération [kõfederɑsjõ] *f.* *confederation*
conférence [kõferɑ̃s] *f.* *lecture*
 salle de conférences *lecture hall*
conflit [kõfli] *m.* *conflict*
confortable [kõfɔrtabl] *comfortable*
confus [kõfy] *embarrassed*
confusion [kõfyzjõ] *f.* *confusion*
congé [kõʒe] *m.* *holiday, day off, vacation*
 les congés payés *vacations with pay*
 jour de congé *m.* *holiday, day off*
connaissance [kɔnɛsɑ̃s] *f.* *acquaintance;*
 connaissances *knowledge*
 faire la connaissance de *get acquainted with*
connaître [kɔnɛtr] (connaissant, connu, je connais, je connus) (§ 94) *know, be acquainted with*
 se connaître à *be acquainted with, be informed on*
 je n'y connais rien *I know nothing about it*
connu, connus [kɔny] (*pp and sp of* connaître) *known*
conquérir [kõkerir] (conquérant, conquis, je conquiers, je conquis) (*conj. like* acquérir) *conquer*
conquête [kõkɛt] *f.* *conquest*
conquis [kõki] (*pp and sp* of conquérir) *conquered*
consacrer [kõsakre] *consecrate*
conseil [kõsɛj] *m.* *advice; council*
 Conseil Constitutionnel *Constitutional Council, the body which decides on the constitutionality of French laws*
 Conseil des Ministres *Council of Ministers, Cabinet*
 Conseil Économique et Sociale *Economic and Social Council, the body which confers concerning economic and social aspects of governmental problems*
conseiller [kõseje] (à + person + de + inf.) *advise*
conseiller [kõseje] *m.* *councilor; adviser*
conséquence [kõsekɑ̃s] *f.* *consequence, result*
conséquent, par [parkõsekɑ̃] *therefore*
conservé [kõsɛrve] *preserved*
conserver [kõsɛrve] *preserve, save*
considérable [kõsiderabl] *considerable*
considérer [kõsidere] *consider*
consister [kõsiste] *consist*
constamment [kõstamɑ̃] *constantly*
constater [kõstate] *ascertain; notice*
constituer [kõstitɥe] *constitute, set up*

Constitution [kõstitysjõ] *f.* *Constitution*
constitutionnalité [kõstitysjɔnalite] *f.* *constitutionality*
constitutionnel, constitutionnelle [kõstitysjɔnɛl] *constitutional*
construction [kõstryksjõ] *f.* *construction; word order*
construire [kõstrɥir] (construisant, construit, je construis, je construisis (*conj. like* conduire) *construct*
construit [kõstrɥi] (*pp of* construire) *constructed*
consul [kõsyl] *m.* *consul*
consulter [kõsylte] *consult*
contagieux, contagieuse [kõtaʒjø, kõtaʒjøz] *contagious*
contempler [kõtɑ̃ple] *contemplate*
contemporain [kõtɑ̃pɔrɛ̃] *contemporary*
contenir [kõtnir] (contenant, contenu, je contiens, je contins) (*conj. like* tenir) *contain, hold*
content [kõtɑ̃] *glad, content, happy*
contentement [kõtɑ̃tmɑ̃] *m.* *contentment, happiness*
se contenter [kõtɑ̃te] (de + noun; de + inf.) *be content (with)*
continent [kõtinɑ̃] *m.* *continent*
continental [kõtinɑ̃tal] *continental*
continuel, continuelle [kõtinɥɛl] *continual*
continuellement [kõtinɥɛlmɑ̃] *continually*
continuer [kõtinɥe] (à + inf.) *continue*
contourner [kõturne] *outflank, go around*
contraction [kõtraksjõ] *f.* *contraction*
contraire [kõtrɛr] *m.* *contrary*
au contraire *on the contrary*
contraste [kõtrast] *m.* *contrast*
faire contraste avec *contrast with, make a contrast with*
contre [kõtr] *against*
par contre *on the contrary*
contribuer [kõtribɥe] *contribute*
contribution [kõtribysjõ] *f.* *contribution*
contrôle [kõtrol] *m.* *control*
contrôler [kõtrole] *control*
contrôleur [kõtrolœr] *m.* *conductor*
convenable [kõvnabl] *proper, suitable*
convenance [kõvnɑ̃s] *f.* *convenience*
mariage de convenance *marriage for money or position*
convenir [kõvnir] (convenant, convenu, je conviens, je convins) (*conj. like* venir) (à + noun) *suit*
Convention Nationale [kõvɑ̃sjõnɑsjɔnal] *National Convention, revolutionary assembly which came into being in 1792 and made way for the Directory in 1795*
conversation [kõvɛrsɑsjõ] *f.* *conversation*
convertir [kõvɛrtir] *convert*
convient, conviennent [kõvjɛ̃, kovjɛn] (à + noun) *suit(s)*
convoquer [kõvɔke] *convoke, call together*
copier [kɔpje] *copy*
cordialement [kɔrdjalmɑ̃] *cordially*
Corneille [kɔrnɛj] (*1606–1684*) *French dramatist*
Corot [kɔro] (*1796–1875*) *French landscape painter*
corps [kɔr] *m.* *body*
correctement [kɔrɛktəmɑ̃] *correctly*
correspondance [kɔrɛspõdɑ̃s] *f.* *transfer (in streetcar, bus, or subway); correspondence*
prendre une correspondance *change cars, transfer*
correspondre [kɔrɛspõdr] *correspond*
corriger [kɔriʒe] (§ 89 B) *correct*
corruption [kɔrypsjõ] *f.* *corruption*
Corse [kɔrs] *f.* *Corsica*
costume [kɔstym] *m.* *dress, costume*
côte [kot] *f.* *coast; hill, slope*
Côte d'Azur [kotdazyr] *territory along the southeast coast of France, also known as the French Riviera*
côté [kote] *m.* *side*
à côté *nearby, next door*
à côté *beside*
de chaque côté *on each side*
de l'autre côté *on the other side*
de son côté *for his part*
des deux côtés *on both sides*
du côté de *on the side of, in the direction of*
d'un côté *on one side*
mettre de côté *set aside*
côtelette [kotlɛt] *f.* *chop, cutlet*

cou [ku] *m.* *neck*
Coubertin, Pierre de [kubɛrtɛ̃] (*1863–1937*) *founder of the modern Olympic Games*
couché [kuʃe] *in bed; asleep; put to bed*
coucher [kuʃe] *pass the night, sleep*
se coucher *go to bed, lie down*
coude [kud] *m.* *elbow*
couler [kule] *flow; sink*
couleur [kulœr] *f.* *color*
couloir [kulwar] *m.* *corridor, hall; passageway*
coup [ku] *m.* *stroke, blow*
coup d'état *sudden and often violent change of state policy; seizure of political power by violent means*
coup d'œil *glance*
coup de téléphone *"ring," telephone call*
donner un coup de téléphone *call someone on the telephone*
couper [kupe] *cut*
cour [kur] *f.* *court, courtyard*
couramment [kuramɑ̃] *currently; fluently; commonly*
courant [kurɑ̃] *m.* *current*
courant [kurɑ̃] *ordinary, common*
coureur [kurœr], *m.* *runner, racer*
courir [kurir] (courant, couru, je cours, je courus) *run*
couronne [kurɔn] *f.* *crown*
couronner [kurɔne] *crown*
couronner de succès *crown with success*
courrier [kurje] *m.* *mail*
courroux [kuru] *m.* *anger*
cours [kur] *m.* *course of study; class*
au cours de *in the course of*
travailler un cours *work on a course*
course [kurs] *f.* *race, running*
course-cycliste *bicycle racer*
court [kur] *short*
couru, courus [kury] (*pp and sp of* courir) *run, ran*
cousin [kuzɛ̃], *m.* *cousin*
coûter [kute] *cost*
coûter cher *be expensive*
coûteux, coûteuse [kutø, kutøz] *costly, expensive*
coutume [kutym] *f.* *custom, habit*
couture [kutyr] *f.* *sewing*
la maison de couture *fashion house*
couturier [kutyrje] *m.* *dressmaker, ladies' tailor, fashion designer*
couvert [kuvɛr] (*pp of* couvrir) *covered*
le ciel est couvert *it is cloudy, the sky is overcast*
couvrir [kuvrir] (couvrant, couvert, je couvre, je couvris) (*conj. like* ouvrir) (de + noun) *cover*
craindre [krɛ̃dr] (craignant, craint, je crains, je craignis) (+ noun; de + inf.) *fear, be afraid*
crainte [krɛ̃t] *f.* *fear*
crayon [krɛjõ] *m.* *pencil*
créateur [kreatœr] *m.* *creator; artist*
création [kreɑsjõ] *f.* *creation; model*
créer [kree] *create*
crème [krɛm] *f.* *cream*
cri [kri] *m.* *cry, shout*
pousser un cri *utter a cry*
crise [kriz] *f.* *crisis; depression*
crise financière *financial depression*
crise de logement *housing shortage*
critique [kritik] *m.* *critic*
critiquer [kritike] *criticize*
croire [krwar] (croyant, cru, je crois, je crus) (+ inf.; à + *thing;* en[1] + *person*) *believe, think*
croquis [krɔki] *m.* *first sketch; rough draft*
croyance [krwajɑ̃s] *f.* *belief*
cru, crus [kry] (*pp and sp* of croire) *believed*
cuisine [kɥizin] *f.* *cooking*
cultiver [kyltive] *cultivate*
culture [kyltyr] *f.* *culture*
culturel, culturelle [kyltyrɛl] *cultural*
curieux, curieuse [kyrjø, kyrjøz] *curious*

D

d'abord [dabɔr] *first, at first*
d'ailleurs [dajœr] *besides, moreover*
dame [dam] *f.* *lady*
Danemark [danmark] *m.* *Denmark*
danger [dɑ̃ʒe] *m.* *danger*
dangereux, dangereuse [dɑ̃ʒrø, dɑ̃ʒrøz] *dangerous*
dans [dɑ̃] *in, into*
dansant [dɑ̃sɑ̃] *dancing*
la soirée dansante *dance*

[1] With the sense of *to have faith in.*

danse [dɑ̃s] *f.* *dance*
salle de danse *dance hall*
danser [dɑ̃se] *dance*
Dantzig [dɑ̃tzig] *German city, established as a Free City at the mouth of the Polish Corridor by the Treaty of Versailles, reseized by the Germans in September, 1939*
date [dat] *f.* *date*
dater [date] *date*
davantage [davɑ̃taʒ] *more*
de [də] *of, from; in* (§ 13 D); *than* (§ 13 B)
de cette façon *in that way*
de l'autre côté *on the other side*
de même *in the same way, likewise*
de nouveau *again*
de plus en plus *more and more*
de sorte que *so that*
de temps en temps *from time to time*
de ville en ville *from city to city*
d'un côté *on one side*
quelque chose de défini *something definite*
débarquement [debarkəmɑ̃] *m.* *landing* (used instead of *invasion* to refer to landings of allied forces in France and in Africa in World War II)
se débarrasser [debarase] (de + noun) *get rid of*
debout [dəbu] *standing*
début [deby] *m.* *beginning; debut*
deçà [dəsa] *here, on this side*
décembre [desɑ̃br] *m.* *December*
décider [deside] (de + inf.) *decide*
se décider (à + inf.) *make up one's mind*
décisif, décisive [desizif, desiziv] *decisive*
déclaration [deklarɑsjɔ̃] *f.* *declaration*
Déclaration d'indépendance *f.* *Declaration of Independence*
déclarer [deklare] *declare*
déclin [deklɛ̃] *m.* *decline*
découvert [dekuvɛr] (*pp of* découvrir) *discovered*
découverte [dekuvɛrt] *f.* *discovery*
découvrir [dekuvrir] (découvrant, découvert, je découvre, je découvris) (*conj. like* ouvrir) *discover*
décret [dekrɛ] *m.* *decree*
décrire [dekrir] (décrivant, décrit, je décris, je décrivis) (*conj. like* écrire) *describe*
déesse [deɛs] *f.* *goddess*
défaire [defɛr] (défaisant, défait, je défais, je défis) (*conj. like* faire) *undo*
défaite [defɛt] *f.* *defeat*
défendre [defɑ̃dr] *defend;* (à + person + de + inf.) *forbid*
défense [defɑ̃s] *f.* *defense*
défiler [defile] *march past, file past, go past; parade*
défini [defini] *definite*
définitivement [definitivmɑ̃] *definitely*
dégager [degaʒe] *clear, disengage*
degré [dəgre] *m.* *degree*
dehors [dəɔr] *outside*
déjà [deʒa] *already*
déjeuner [deʒøne] *eat the noon meal, eat lunch*
déjeuner [deʒøne] *m.* *lunch; noon meal*
le petit déjeuner *breakfast*
de Lesseps [dəlesɛps] (*1804–1894*) *French engineer who constructed the Suez Canal and began the construction of the Panama Canal*
delà [dəla] *beyond there, on that side*
au delà de *beyond*
délibération [deliberɑsjɔ̃] *f.* *deliberation*
délicat [delika] *delicate*
délivrance [delivrɑ̃s] *f.* *deliverance*
demain [dəmɛ̃] *tomorrow*
demander [dəmɑ̃de] (à + person + de + inf.) *ask, ask for*
se demander *wonder*
demandez [dəmɑ̃de] (*imperative of* demander) *ask*
demeurer [dəmœre] (§ 94) *live, reside*
demi [dəmi] (§ 97 E) *half*
démission [demisjɔ̃] *f.* *resignation*
démocratique [demɔkratik] *democratic*
démonstratif, démonstrative [demɔ̃stratif, demɔ̃strativ] *demonstrative*
démontrer [demɔ̃tre] *demonstrate, prove, point out*
Denise [dəniz] *f.* *Denise*
dénoncer [denɔ̃se] (§ 89 A) *denounce*
dent [dɑ̃] *f.* *tooth*
dentiste [dɑ̃tist] *m.* *dentist*
d'entre eux [dɑ̃trø] *of them*

départ [depar] *m.* *departure*
département [departəmɑ̃] *m.* *department, political division of modern France for administrative purposes*
dépasser [depɑse] *by-pass*
se dépêcher [depeʃe] (de + inf.) *hurry*
dépense [depɑ̃s] *f.* *expense*
dépenser [depɑ̃se] (§ 94) *spend*
déplacement [deplasmɑ̃] *m.* *moving*
se déplacer [deplase] *get around*
déporter [depɔrte] *deport*
déposer [depoze] *place, leave*
depuis [dəpɥi] (§§ 50 B, 52 D) *since, from, for*
  depuis . . . jusqu'à *from . . . to*
  depuis quand *how long*
député [depyte] *m.* *deputy*
dernier, dernière [dɛrnje, dɛrnjɛr] *last*
  ce dernier *the latter*
derrière [dɛrjɛr] *behind*
des [de] (§§ 2 A, 3 B, 5) *of the; some*
dès [dɛ] *from, since, as early as*
  dès que *as soon as*
désagréable [dezagreabl] *disagreeable*
désapprouver [dezapruve] *disapprove*
descendant [desɑ̃dɑ̃] *m.* *descendant*
descendre [desɑ̃dr] *go down; get off*
  descendre d'un train *get off a train*
description [dɛskripsjõ] *f.* *description*
désert [dezɛr] *deserted*
désespoir [dezɛspwar] *m.* *despair*
désigner [deziɲe] *designate, name, call*
désir [dezir] *m.* *desire, wish*
désirer [dezire] (+ inf.) *desire, wish*
désolé [dezɔle] *sorry, very sorry*
désorganisation [dezɔrganizɑjõ] *f.* *disorganization*
despotique [dɛspɔtik] *despotic*
dessert [desɛr] *m.* *dessert*
dessinateur [desinatœr] *m.* *designer; model designer, who designs or suggests new styles to the "créateur" of a fashion house*
dessiner [desine] *design, lay out*
destination [dɛstinɑsjõ] *f.* *destination*
  arriver à destination *arrive at one's destination*
destiné à [dɛstinea] *designed to*
destruction [dɛstryksjõ] *f.* *destruction*
détail [detaj] *m.* *detail*
déterminer [detɛrmine] *determine*
Détroit [detrwa] *city in United States*
détruire [detrɥir] (détruisant, détruit, je détruis, je détruisis) (*conj. like* conduire) *destroy*
détruit [detrɥi] (*pp of* détruire) *destroyed*
deux [dø] *two*
  tous les deux *both*
deuxième [døzjɛm] *second*
devant [dəvɑ̃] *in front of, before*
développement [devlɔpmɑ̃] *m.* *development*
devenir [dəvnir] (devenant, devenu, je deviens, je devins) (*conj. like* venir) *become*
  Qu'est-ce que Robert est devenu? *What became of Robert?*
devenu [dəvny] (*pp. of* devenir) *become*
deviner [dəvine] *guess*
devise [dəviz] *f.* *motto*
devoir [dəvwar] (devant, dû, je dois, je dus) (+ inf.) (§§ 93, 94) *have to, must, ought to, should;* (+ noun) *owe*
devoir [dəvwar] *m.* *exercise; duty*
dialecte [djalɛkt] *m.* *dialect*
dictature [diktatyr] *f.* *dictatorship*
dictée [dikte] *f.* *dictation*
dicter [dikte] *dictate*
Dieu [djø] *m.* *God*
différemment [diferamɑ̃] *differently*
différence [diferɑ̃s] *f.* *difference*
différent [diferɑ̃] *different*
difficile [difisil] *difficult*
difficulté [difikylte] *f.* *difficulty*
diffuser [difyze] *diffuse*
diffusion [difyzjõ] *f.* *diffusion*
digne [diɲ] *worthy*
Digne [diɲ] *city in extreme southeastern France*
Dijon [diʒõ] *city in eastern France, capital of ancient province of Burgundy*
dimanche [dimɑ̃ʃ] *m.* *Sunday*
diminuer [diminɥe] *diminish, lessen*
dinde [dɛ̃d] *f.* *turkey*
dîner [dine] *dine*
dîner [dine] *m.* *dinner*
diplomatique [diplɔmatik] *diplomatic*
diplôme [diplom] *m.* *diploma*
dire [dir] (disant, dit, je dis, je dis) (à + person + de + inf.) *say, tell*

c'est à dire *that is to say*
vouloir dire *mean*
direct [dirɛkt] *direct*
directement [dirɛktəmɑ̃] *directly*
directeur, directrice [dirɛktœr, dirɛktris] (adj.) *guiding, controlling*
direction [dirɛksjɔ̃] *f.* *direction*
Directoire [dirɛktwar] *m.* *Directory, body governing France just before Napoleon I*
diriger [diriʒe] (§ 89 B) *direct*
se diriger *go toward*
discret, discrète [diskrɛ, diskrɛt] *discreet*
discussion [diskysjɔ̃] *f.* *discussion*
discuter [diskyte] *discuss*
disparaître [disparɛtr] (disparaissant, disparu, je disparais, je disparus) (*conj. like* connaître) *disappear*
se disperser [dispɛrse] *disperse, be dispersed*
disposé [dispoze] *laid out*
disposer [dispoze] *dispose; incline*
disposition [dispozisjɔ̃] *f.* *disposition*
dissoudre [disudr] *dissolve;* (*pp*) dissolu *dissolved*
distinction [distɛ̃ksjɔ̃] *f.* *distinction*
distinguer [distɛ̃ge] *distinguish*
se distinguer *be distinguished, distinguish oneself*
distribuer [distribɥe] *distribute*
dit [di] (*pp of* dire) *said*
proprement dit *properly speaking*
dites [dit] (*imperative of* dire) *tell, say*
divers [divɛr] *various, different*
divin [divɛ̃] (*but* [divin] *in the combination* divin enfant) *divine*
divisé [divize] (*pp of* diviser) *divided*
diviser [divize] *divide*
division [divizjɔ̃] *f.* *division*
dix [dis, di, diz] *ten*
dix-huit *eighteen*
dix-neuf *nineteen*
dix-sept *seventeen*
dix-septième *seventeenth*
dix-sept cent quatre-vingt-neuf *seventeen hundred eighty nine*
dixième [dizjɛm] *tenth*
doctrine [dɔktrin] *f.* *doctrine*
documentaire [dɔkymɑ̃tɛr] *m.* *documentary film*
documentaire [dɔkymɑ̃tɛr] (adj.) *documentary*
doigt [dwa] *m.* *finger; toe*
domaine [dɔmɛn] *m.* *domain*
dôme [dom] *m.* *dome*
domestique [dɔmɛstik] *m. f.* *servant*
domestique [dɔmɛstik] *domestic*
domination [dɔminɑsjɔ̃] *f.* *domination*
dominer [dɔmine] *dominate*
dommage [dɔmaʒ] *m.* *harm*
c'est dommage *it's too bad*
donc [dɔ̃k, dɔ̃] *then, thus*
allons donc! *come now! I declare! you don't say!*
donner [dɔne] *give*
donner sur *look out upon, open on*
donner un coup de téléphone *give a "ring," telephone*
pour voir ce que cela donne *to see how that looks*
dont [dɔ̃] (§ 39 E) *of which, whose*
d'ordinaire [dɔrdinɛr] *ordinarily*
doré [dɔre] *golden*
dormir [dɔrmir] (2) *sleep*
dos [do] *m.* *back*
dot [dɔt] *f.* *dowry*
d'où [du] *from where, whence*
doucement [dusmɑ̃] *softly*
doute [dut] *m.* *doubt*
mettre en doute *question*
douter [dute] *doubt*
doux, douce [du, dus] *soft, sweet, gentle, mild*
il fait doux (§ 92 B) *it is mild weather*
douze [duz] *twelve*
douzième [duzjɛm] *twelfth*
dramatique [dramatik] *dramatic*
drapeau [drapo] *m.* *flag*
draper [drape] *drape*
droit [drwa] *m.* *law; right*
payer des droits *pay for the right to*
droit [drwa] *right*
droite [drwat] *f.* *right*
à droite *to the right*
du [dy] (§ 2 A, 5) *of the, from the; some*
du moins *at least*
du reste *moreover*
dû, due [dy] (*pp of* devoir) (§ 93) *had to, etc.;* (adj.) *due to*
Dupont [dypɔ̃] *family name*
duquel [dykɛl] *of which*
dur [dyr] *hard*
un œuf dur *hard-boiled egg*

Durand [dyrɑ̃] *family name*
durant [dyrɑ̃] *during*
durement [dyrmɑ̃] *severely*
durer [dyre] *last*

E

eau [o] *f.* *water*
  eau de Cologne *perfumed toilet water*
échange [eʃɑ̃ʒ] *m.* *exchange*
  en échange *in exchange*
échanger [eʃɑ̃ʒe] *exchange*
échantillon [eʃɑ̃tijɔ̃] *m.* *sample*
échapper [eʃape] (à + noun) *escape*
  s'échapper (de + noun) *escape (from)*
échouer [eʃwe] (à un examen) *fail (an examination)*
éclairer [eklere] *light*
éclat [ekla] *m.* *renown, brilliance*
éclater [eklate] *break out*
école [ekɔl] *f.* *school*
  à l'école *at school*
  les grandes écoles *term used to refer to colleges of engineering, dentistry, education, etc., which are not among the five traditional* facultés *of the University of Paris, but which are either attached to the University or exist independent of it*
  École des Beaux-Arts *School of Fine Arts, a school for artists in Paris on the left bank of the Seine*
  École Centrale *engineering school*
  École Normale Supérieure *school at Paris which prepares its students for teaching positions at the secondary level*
  École Polytechnique *school in Paris which trains its students to become engineers*
écolier [ekɔlje] *m.* *schoolboy*
économe [ekɔnɔm] *economical*
économie [ekɔnɔmi] *f.* *economy; savings*
économique [ekɔnɔmik] *economic*
économiser [ekɔnɔmize] *save*
écouter [ekute] (+ noun) *listen*
  écoutez plutôt *listen for yourself*
écraser [ekrɑze] *crush*
écrire [ekrir] (écrivant, écrit, j'écris, j'écrivis) (à + person + de + inf.) *write*
  écrire à l'encre *write in ink*
  écrire au crayon *write in pencil*
écris, écrit [ekri] (*sp and pp of* écrire) *wrote, written*
écrivain [ekrivɛ̃] *m.* *writer, author*
écrivez [ekrive] (*imperative of* écrire) *write*
édifice [edifis] *m.* *building*
édition [edisjɔ̃] *f.* *edition*
éducation [edykɑsjɔ̃] *f.* *education; bringing up*
  Ministre de l'Éducation Nationale *Minister of Education*
effacer [efase] (§ 89 A) *erase; wipe out*
effet [efɛ] *m.* *effect*
  en effet *in fact*
efficacité [efikasite] *f.* *efficacy*
effort [efɔr] *m.* *effort*
effrayer [efreje] *frighten*
égal [egal] *equal*
  ça m'est égal *that's all the same to me*
également [egalmɑ̃] *equally, also*
égalité [egalite] *f.* *equality*
égard [egar] *m.* *regard*
  à cet égard *in that respect*
église [egliz] *f.* *church*
Egypte [eʒipt] *f.* *Egypt*
eh bien [ebjɛ̃] *well, very well*
Eiffel [efɛl] (*1832–1923*) *French engineer who constructed the Eiffel Tower*
Elbe [ɛlb] *f.* *Elba, Italian island in the Mediterranean where Napoleon was exiled in 1814*
électeur [elɛktœr] *m.* *elector*
élection [elɛksjɔ̃] *f.* *election*
électoral [elɛktɔral] *electoral*
  collège électoral *electoral college*
électrique [elɛktrik] *electric*
élégant [elegɑ̃] *elegant, cultivated*
élève [elɛv] *m. f.* *pupil*
élevé [ɛlve] *high*
s'élever [ɛlve] (§ 89 D) *rise*
élire [elir] (élisant, élu, j'élis, j'élus) (*conj. like* lire) *elect*
élision [elizjɔ̃] *f.* *elision, the dropping of the last vowel of one word before the initial vowel of a following word*

élite [elit] *f.* *elite, best, choice*
elle [ɛl] *she; it; her*
elles [ɛl] *f.* *they; them*
élu [ely] (*pp of* élire) *elected*
Embarquement pour Cythère [ɑ̃barkəmɑ̃pursitɛr] *"Embarkation for Cytherea," a famous painting by Watteau*
embellir [ɑ̃belir] *beautify*
embouchure [ɑ̃buʃyr] *f.* *mouth of a river*
émetteur [emɛtœr] *m.* *station*
poste émetteur *broadcasting station*
émission [emisjɔ̃] *f.* *broadcast; program*
emmener [ɑ̃mne] (§§ 89 D, 94) *take away (a person)*
émotion [emosjɔ̃] *f.* *emotion*
s'emparer [ɑ̃pare] (de + noun) *take possession of, seize*
empêcher [ɑ̃peʃe] (+ noun + de + inf.) *prevent, hinder*
empereur [ɑ̃prœr] *m.* *emperor*
empire [ɑ̃pir] *m.* *empire*
Empire [ɑ̃pir] *m.* *Empire*
Premier Empire *First Empire (1804–1815), set up by Napoleon I*
Second Empire *Second Empire (1852–1870), set up by Napoleon III*
Saint Empire romain *Holy Roman Empire*
emploi [ɑ̃plwa] *m.* *use*
employant [ɑ̃plwajɑ̃] *using*
employé [ɑ̃plwaje] *m.* *clerk, employee*
employer [ɑ̃plwaje] (§ 89 C) *use*
s'employer *be used*
emporter [ɑ̃pɔrte] (§ 94) *carry off*
emprisonner [ɑ̃prizɔne] *imprison*
en [ɑ̃] *in, into* (§ 42 A, B); *some, of it, of them* (§ 28 A, B, C, D); *from it, from there* (§ 28 E); *while* (§ 74 B); *as*
en bas *downstairs*
en effet *in fact, indeed, in reality*
en face (de + noun) *opposite*
en famille *in the family circle*
en haut de *at the top of*
en même temps *at the same time*
en outre *moreover*
en revanche *on the other hand*
en somme *in brief, in short*
en tout cas *in any case*
en vacances *on a vacation*
encens [ɑ̃sɑ̃] *m.* *incense*
enchanter [ɑ̃ʃɑ̃te] *delight, enchant*
encombrer [ɑ̃kɔ̃bre] *encumber, load*
encore [ɑ̃kɔr] *still, still more*
encore une fois *again*
encourager [ɑ̃kuraʒe] (§ 89 B) *encourage*
encre [ɑ̃kr] *f.* *ink*
s'endormir [ɑ̃dɔrmir] (2) *go to sleep, fall asleep*
endroit [ɑ̃drwa] *m.* *place*
énergique [enɛrʒik] *energetic*
enfance [ɑ̃fɑ̃s] *f.* *childhood*
enfant [ɑ̃fɑ̃] *m. f.* *child*
enfantin [ɑ̃fɑ̃tɛ̃] *childish*
enfermer [ɑ̃fɛrme] *shut in, imprison*
enfin [ɑ̃fɛ̃] *at last, finally*
enfoncer [ɑ̃fɔ̃se] *break into*
enlever [ɑ̃lve] (+ thing + à + person) *take away*
ennemi [ɛnmi] *m.* *enemy;* (adj.) *enemy*
énorme [enɔrm] *enormous*
enragé [ɑ̃raʒe] *mad*
ensemble [ɑ̃sɑ̃bl] *m.* *whole*
ensemble [ɑ̃sɑ̃bl] *together*
ensuite [ɑ̃sɥit] *then*
entendre [ɑ̃tɑ̃dr] (+ inf.) *hear; understand*
entendre parler de *hear of*
qu'entendez-vous par *what do you understand by*
enthousiasme [ɑ̃tuzjasm] *m.* *enthusiasm*
enthousiaste [ɑ̃tuzjast] *enthusiastic*
entier, entière [ɑ̃tje, ɑ̃tjɛr] *entire*
entièrement [ɑ̃tjɛrmɑ̃] *entirely*
entourer [ɑ̃ture] *surround*
entr'acte [ɑ̃trakt] *m.* *intermission*
entraîner [ɑ̃trene] *bring on; draw in, drag in*
entre [ɑ̃tr] *between, among*
d'entre eux *of them*
entre eux *among themselves*
entrée [ɑ̃tre] *f.* *entrance*
entreprendre [ɑ̃trəprɑ̃dr] (entreprenant, entrepris, j'entreprends, j'entrepris) (*conj. like* prendre) *undertake*
entreprise [ɑ̃trəpriz] *f.* *enterprise*
entrer [ɑ̃tre] (dans + noun) *enter*
entretien [ɑ̃trətjɛ̃] *m.* *upkeep*

envahir [ɑ̃vair] *invade*
enverrai [ɑ̃vɛre] (*1st pers. sing. fut. of* envoyer) *shall send*
envie [ɑ̃vi] *f.* *wish, desire*
avoir envie de (§ 90 B) *feel like, want to*
environ [ɑ̃virɔ̃] *about, approximately*
s'envoler [ɑ̃vɔle] *fly away, fly off*
envoyer [ɑ̃vwaje] (envoyant, envoyé, j'envoie, j'envoyai) *send*
envoyer chercher *send for*
épatant [epatɑ̃] *fine, wonderful, "swell!", "terrific"*
épaule [epol] *f.* *shoulder*
épisode [epizɔd] *m.* *episode*
époque [epɔk] *f.* *period*
épouser [epuze] (§ 94) *marry, wed*
époux [epu] *m. pl.* *husband and wife*
épreuve [eprœv] *f.* *test*
éprouver [epruve] *feel, experience*
épuisant [epɥizɑ̃] *exhausting*
épuiser [epɥize] *exhaust*
équipe [ekip] *f.* *team*
équivalent [ekivalɑ̃] *m.* *equivalent*
ériger [eriʒe] (§ 89 B) *erect*
escalier [ɛskalje] *m.* *stairway*
espace [ɛspas] *m.* *space, room*
Espagne [ɛspaɲ] *f.* *Spain*
espagnol [ɛspaɲɔl] *Spanish*
espérance [ɛsperɑ̃s] *f.* *hope*
espérer [ɛspere] (§ 89 E) (+ inf.) *hope*
esprit [ɛspri] *m.* *spirit*
esquisse [ɛskis] *f.* *sketch*
essai [esɛ] *m.* *try, attempt*
essayer [eseje] (§ 89 C) (de + inf.) *try*
est [ɛ] (*3d pers. sing. pres. of* être) *is*
est-ce que . . . (§ 96 A) (*method of asking a question*)
est [ɛst] *m.* *east*
estomac [ɛstɔma] *m.* *stomach*
estuaire [ɛstɥɛr] *m.* *estuary, a narrow arm of the sea at the mouth of a river*
et [e] *and*
établir [etablir] *establish*
s'établir *establish oneself*
établissement [etablismɑ̃] *m.* *establishment*
étage [etaʒ] *m.* *floor, story*
premier étage *second floor*
deuxième étage *third floor, etc.*

étant [etɑ̃] (*pres. participle of* être) *being*
étape [etap] *f.* *stage, stop*
état [eta] *m.* *state*
coup d'état *m.* *sudden and often violent change of state policy; seizure of political power by violent means*
États-Généraux [etaʒenero] *States-General*
États-Unis [etazyni] *m.* *United States*
etc. [ɛtsetera] (*abbr. for* et cetera) *and so forth*
été [ete] (*pp of* être) *been*
été [ete] *m.* *summer*
en été *in summer*
éteindre [etɛ̃dr] (éteignant, éteint, j'éteins, j'éteignis) (*conj. like* peindre) *put out, turn out, extinguish*
éteint [etɛ̃] (*pp of* éteindre) *put out, turned out, extinguished*
s'étendre [etɑ̃dr] *extend*
étendu [etɑ̃dy] (*pp of* étendre) *extensive, extended*
êtes [ɛt] (être) (*you*) *are*
étoile [etwal] *f.* *star*
Étoile *used to designate* la Place de l'Étoile *because the streets converging at that square give it the appearance of a star*
étonné [etɔne] *surprised*
étonner [etɔne] *surprise, astonish*
s'étonner *be surprised*
étrange [etrɑ̃ʒ] *strange*
étranger [etrɑ̃ʒe] *m.* *foreigner*
étranger, étrangère, [etrɑ̃ʒe, etrɑ̃ʒɛr] *foreign*
à l'étranger {*to* / *in*} *a foreign country, abroad*
gagner l'étranger *reach foreign lands*
être [ɛtr] (étant, été, je suis, je fus) *be*
être d'accord *be in agreement*
être [ɛtr] *m.* *being*
étroit [etrwa] *narrow*
étude [etyd] *f.* *study*
faire des études *carry on one's studies*
étudiant [etydjɑ̃] *m.* *student (of college level)*
étudiante [etydjɑ̃t] *f.* *girl student*
étudier [etydje] *study*

eu, eus [y] (*pp and sp of* avoir) *had*
Europe [œrɔp] *f.* *Europe*
Europe Nº 1 *French language private radio station whose studios are in Paris but which broadcasts from the Saar*
européen, européenne [œrɔpeɛ̃, œrɔpeɛn] *European*
eux [ø] *them*
événement [evɛnmɑ̃] *m.* *event*
éventuel, éventuelle [evɑ̃tɥɛl] *eventual*
Évian [evjɑ̃] *m.* *small French town situated on Lake Geneva*
évidemment [evidamɑ̃] *evidently; obviously, clearly*
évident [evidɑ̃] *evident*
évolution [evɔlysjõ] *f.* *evolution*
évoquer [evɔke] *evoke, call forth*
exagérer [egzaʒere] *exaggerate*
examen [egzamɛ̃] *m.* *examination*
passer un examen *take an examination*
réussir à un examen *pass an examination*
examiner [egzamine] *examine*
excellent [ɛkselɑ̃] *excellent*
excursion [ɛkskyrsjõ] *f.* *excursion*
exécution [egzekysjõ] *f.* *execution*
exemple [egzɑ̃pl] *m.* *example*
par exemple *for example*
exercer [egzɛrse] *exercise*
exiger [ɛgziʒe] *demand, require*
exiler [ɛgzile] *exile*
existence [ɛgzistɑ̃s] *f.* *existence*
exister [ɛgziste] *f.* *exist*
exotique [ɛgzɔtik] *exotic, foreign*
expérience [ɛksperjɑ̃s] *f.* *experiment*
expérimenter [ɛksperimɑ̃te] *experiment*
expiation [ɛkspjɑsjõ] *f.* *expiation, atonement*
explication [ɛksplikɑsjõ] *f.* *explanation*
expliquer [ɛksplike] *explain*
explorateur [ɛksplɔratœr] *m.* *explorer*
explorer [ɛksplɔre] *explore*
exporter [ɛkspɔrte] *export*
s'exposer [ɛkspoze] *expose oneself*
expression [ɛksprɛsjõ] *f.* *expression*
exprimer [ɛksprime] *express*
extérieur [ɛksterjœr] *m.* *exterior;* (adj.) *exterior*
extrait [ɛkstrɛ] *m.* *extract*
extraordinaire [ɛkstraɔrdinɛr] *extraordinary*
extravagant [ɛkstravagɑ̃] *extravagant*
extrême [ɛkstrɛm] *extreme*

F

fabrication [fabrikɑsjõ] *f.* *manufacture*
fabriquer [fabrike] *manufacture*
fabriquer en série *manufacture in quantity*
façade [fasad] *f.* *façade, front of a building*
face [fas] *f.* *face*
en face (de + noun) *opposite, facing*
faire face à *confront*
facile [fasil] *easy*
facilement [fasilmɑ̃] *easily*
facilité [fasilite] *f.* *facility, ease*
faciliter [fasilite] *facilitate, make easy*
façon [fasõ] *f.* *fashion, manner, way*
de cette façon *in this way, in that way*
de façon à *so as to, so that they*
de la même façon *in the same way*
faculté [fakylte] *f.* *college or school of a university, including buildings and teaching staff*
faible [fɛbl] *weak*
faiblesse [fɛblɛs] *f.* *weakness*
faim [fɛ̃] *f.* *hunger*
avoir faim (§ 90 B) *be hungry*
faire [fɛr] (faisant, fait, je fais, je fis) (+ inf.) (§ 92) *make, do*
faire appel à *call on*
faire attention *pay attention; be careful, watch out*
faire beau *be fine, be pleasant*
faire un cadeau *give a gift*
faire chaud *be hot, be warm*
faire la connaissance de *make the acquaintance of, get acquainted with*
faire doux *be mild*
faire des études *carry on studies*
faire face à *confront*
faire froid *be cold*
faire mauvais temps *be bad weather*
faire partie de *be a part of*
faire part *inform*
faire une promenade *take a walk*
faire signe *make a sign*

faire du ski *go skiing*
faire du sport *practice sports*
faire du vent *be windy*
faire une visite *pay a visit*
faire un voyage *take a trip*
fait [fɛ] *m. fact, deed*
tout à fait *quite, completely, entirely*
fait [fɛ] (*pp of* faire) *made, done*
faites [fɛt] (*imperative of* faire) *make, do*
faites attention *pay attention*
falloir [falwar] (—, fallu, il faut, il fallut) (+ inf.) (§ 94) *must, be necessary*
familial [familjal] *family* (adj.)
famille [famij] *f. family*
allocation familiale *family allowance*
en famille *in the family circle*
pension de famille *boarding house*
fasse [fas] (*pres. subjunctive of* faire) *make*
fatigue [fatig] *f. fatigue, weariness*
fatigué [fatige] *tired*
faut [fo] (*3d pers. sing. pres. of* falloir) *it is necessary, one must*
faute [fot] *f. mistake*
fauteuil [fotœj] *m. armchair*
faux, fausse [fo, fos] *false*
favorable [favɔrabl] *favorable*
favori, favorite [favɔri, favɔrit] *favorite*
favoriser [favɔrize] *favor*
féliciter [felisite] *congratulate*
femme [fam] *f. woman; wife*
femme de ménage, *f. charwoman, maid, woman who comes in to do housework*
fenêtre [fənɛtr] *f. window*
féodal [feɔdal] *feudal*
fer [fɛr] *m. iron*
chemin de fer *m. railroad*
ferai [fre] (*1st pers. sing. fut. of* faire) shall do, shall make
Ferdinand [fɛrdinɑ̃] *given name of de Lesseps*
ferme [fɛrm] *f. farm*
fermentation [fɛrmɑ̃tɑsjɔ̃] *f. fermentation*
fermenté [fɛrmɑ̃te] *fermented*
fermer [fɛrme] *close*
féroce [ferɔs] *fierce, ferocious*
fertile [fɛrtil] *fertile*
fête [fɛt] *f. holiday; festivity*
feu [fø] *m. fire*
feuille [fœj] *f. sheet, leaf*
feuilleter [fœjte] (§ 89 F) *leaf, run through rapidly*
février [fevrije] *m. February*
fiançailles [fjɑ̃sɑj] *f. pl. engagement, betrothal*
fiancé [fjɑ̃se] *m. fiancé*
fiancé [fjɑ̃se] *engaged*
fiancée [fjɑ̃se] *f. fiancée*
fidèle [fidɛl] *faithful*
les fidèles *the faithful (ones)*
figure [figyr] *f. face*
se figurer [figyre] *imagine*
fille [fij] *f. daughter; girl*
jeune fille *f. girl*
film [film] *m. film*
fin [fɛ̃] *f. end*
mettre fin à *put an end to*
prendre fin *end, come to an end*
final [final] *final*
finalement [finalmɑ̃] *finally*
financier, financière [finɑ̃sje, finɑ̃sjɛr] *financial*
crise financière *financial depression*
finir [finir] *finish*
finir par *end up by, finally*
fis [fi] (*sp of* faire) *made, did*
flacon [flakɔ̃] *m. bottle (with glass stopper)*
flamand [flamɑ̃] *Flemish*
flamme [flam] *f. flame*
fleur [flœr] *f. flower*
fleuve [flœv] *m. river*
flotte [flɔt] *f. navy; fleet*
fois [fwa] *f. time*
encore une fois *once more, again*
fonctionnaire [fɔ̃ksjɔnɛr] *m. government worker, government official, civil service employee*
fonctionnement [fɔ̃ksjɔnmɑ̃] *m. functioning*
fond [fɔ̃] *m. end, back, rear, bottom*
au fond (de) *at the end (of), at the rear (of), at the bottom (of); in the depths of; in the most remote part of*
fondateur [fɔ̃datœr] *m. founder*
Fondation [fɔ̃dasjɔ̃] *f. term used to designate part of the buildings of the* Cité Universitaire, *and in par-*

ticular the Fondation des États-Unis

fonder [fõde] *found, establish*

font [fõ] (*3d pers. pl. pres. of* faire) *make, do*

fontaine [fõtɛn] *f. fountain*

Fontainebleau [fõtɛnblo] *city and forest south of Paris*

football [futbɔl] *m. football*

force [fɔrs] *f. force, strength*

Forces françaises libres *Free French forces fighting outside of France for the liberation of the country during World War II*

Ministre des Forces Armées *Minister of Defense*

forcer [fɔrse] (§ 89 A) (à + inf.; être forcé de + inf.)[1] *force*

forêt [fɔrɛ] *f. forest*

formalité [fɔrmalite] *f. formality*

formation [fɔrmɑsjõ] *f. training*

forme [fɔrm] *f. form*

former [fɔrme] *form; train, educate*

fort [fɔr] *strong; (intellectually) good*

forteresse [fɔrtərɛs] *f. fortress, stronghold*

fortifié [fɔrtifje] *fortified*

fortifier [fɔrtifje] *fortify*

foule [ful] *f. crowd*

fournir [furnir] *furnish*

foyer [fwaje] *m. lobby*

frais [frɛ] *m. (usually pl.) expense*

frais, fraîche [frɛ, frɛʃ], *fresh, cool*

il fait frais *it is cool*

franc [frɑ̃] *m. franc; French monetary unit*

français [frɑ̃sɛ] *French*

le français *French language*

Français [frɑ̃sɛ] *m. Frenchman*

Française [frɑ̃sɛz] *f. French girl, French woman*

France [frɑ̃s] *f. France*

la France métropolitaine *France proper, France without her colonies*

France, Anatole (*1844–1924*) *French novelist and short story writer noted for his simple but ironic style*

Francine [frɑ̃sin] *f. Francine*

franco-allemand [frɑ̃koalmɑ̃] *Franco-German*

franco-belge [frɑ̃kobɛlʒ] *Franco-Belgian*

François Ier [frɑ̃swɑprəmje] *Francis I, king of France (1515–1547)*

Françoise [frɑ̃swaz] *f. Frances*

frapper [frape] *strike, knock*

fraternité [fratɛrnite] *f. brotherhood*

fréquemment [frekamɑ̃] *frequently*

fréquenter [frekɑ̃te] *frequent, go to regularly*

frère [frɛr] *m. brother*

frigidaire [friʒidɛr] *m. frigidaire*

frissonner [frisɔne] *shiver, tremble*

frit [fri] *fried*

frites [frit] *f. pl. French-fried potatoes*

froid [frwa] *m. cold*

avoir froid (§ 90 B) *be cold*

faire froid (§ 92 B) *be cold*

fromage [frɔmaʒ] *m. cheese*

front [frõ] *m. front*

front populaire [frõpɔpylɛr] *Popular Front, coalition French government which came into power under Léon Blum by the elections of May, 1936*

frontière [frõtjɛr] *f. frontier, boundary*

fruit [frɥi] *m. fruit*

fumer [fyme] *smoke*

fus [fy] (*sp of* être) *was*

fusiller [fyzije] *shoot*

futur [fytyr] *m. future*

G

gagner [gaɲe] *win, gain; earn*

gagner l'étranger *reach foreign lands*

gai [ge] *gay*

galerie [galri] *f. gallery*

Galerie des Glaces [galrideglas] *Hall of Mirrors in the palace at Versailles*

garantir [garɑ̃tir] *guarantee, pledge*

garçon [garsõ] *m. boy; waiter*

garder [garde] *keep, watch, guard; hold*

gare [gar] *f. (railroad) station*

Gare de Lyon [gardəljõ] *important railway station at Paris for trains leaving for Lyon, Marseilles, and the Riviera*

Garonne [garɔn] *f. river in southern France*

gâteau [gɑto] *m. cake*

gâteau au chocolat *chocolate cake*

[1] Louise *force* Paul *à* parler; Paul *est forcé de* parler.

gauche [goʃ] *f.* *left*
à gauche *to the left, on the left hand*
Gaule [gol] *f.* *ancient territory comprising France and Belgium*
Gaulle, Charles de [dəgol] (*1890–*) *French general in World War II who long before the war advocated mechanization of weapons, who organized the Free French Forces in London to carry on the war in the colonies and abroad, who became the chief of state after the "Liberation," who was called back to power in 1958 and became the first president of the Fifth Republic*
gendarme [ʒɑ̃darm] *m.* *policeman* (*usually state police*)
gêner [ʒene] *impede, bother*
général [ʒeneral] *m.* *general*
général, généraux [ʒeneral, ʒenero] *general*
généralement [ʒeneralmɑ̃] *generally*
Genève [ʒənɛv] *Geneva*
lac de Genève *Lake Geneva*
genou [ʒənu] *m.* *knee*
genre [ʒɑ̃r] *m.* *kind, class; gender*
gens [ʒɑ̃] *m. pl.* *people*
jeunes gens *young men; young people*
gentil, gentille [ʒɑ̃ti, ʒɑ̃tij] *nice*
géographie [ʒeɔgrafi] *f.* *geography*
géométrie [ʒeɔmetri] *f.* *geometry*
géométriquement [ʒeɔmetrikmɑ̃] *geometrically*
Georges [ʒɔrʒ] *m.* *George*
Gérard [ʒerar] *m.* *Gerard, Jerry*
germanique [ʒɛrmanik] *Germanic*
germe [ʒerm] *m.* *germ*
gibecière [ʒipsjɛr] *f.* *booksack, hunting sack*
gigantesque [ʒigɑ̃tɛsk] *gigantic*
Gilbert [ʒilbɛr] *m.* *Gilbert*
Gironde [ʒirɔ̃d] *f.* *estuary of Garonne*
glace [glas] *f.* *glass; mirror; ice; ice cream*
Galerie des Glaces *Hall of Mirrors in the palace at Versailles*
gloire [glwar] *f.* *glory*
golf [gɔlf] *m.* *golf*
gothique [gɔtik] *gothic*
goût [gu] *m.* *taste*
goûter [gute] *taste*
gouvernement [guvɛrnəmɑ̃] *m.* *government*
gouvernemental [guvɛrnəmɑ̃tal] *governmental*
gouverner [guvɛrne] *govern*
grâce (à) [grɑs] *thanks* (*to*)
gracieux, gracieuse [grɑsjø, grɑsjøz] *gracious*
grammaire [gramɛr] *f.* *grammar*
grand [grɑ̃] *great, large; grown-up*
le grand magasin *department store*
les grandes écoles *term used to refer to colleges of engineering, dentistry, etc., which are not among the traditional* facultés *of the University of Paris*
les grandes vacances *summer vacation*
Grand Trianon [grɑ̃trijanɔ̃] *m.* *palace built at Versailles under the direction of Louis XIV by Hardouin-Mansard*
Grande-Bretagne [grɑdbrətaɲ] *f.* *Great Britain*
grandiose [grɑ̃djoz] *grandiose, imposing*
grappe [grap] *f.* *bunch* (*of grapes*)
gratte-ciel [gratsjɛl] *m.* *skyscraper*
gratuit [gratɥi] *free, without charge*
grave [grav] *grave, serious*
gravure [gravyr] *f.* *etching, print*
grec, greque [grɛk] *Greek*
le grec *Greek language*
Grenoble [grənɔbl] *m.* *French city*
grès [grɛ] *m.* *sandstone*
grève [grɛv] *f.* (*labor*) *strike*
se mettre en grève *strike*
grille [grij] *f.* *iron grating*
gros, grosse [gro, gros] *large, great*
groupe [grup] *m.* *group*
se grouper [grupe] *gather in groups*
Gruyère [gryjɛr] *m.* *kind of French cheese*
guère [gɛr] *scarcely*
ne . . . guère *scarcely*
guérir [gerir] *cure*
guerre [gɛr] *f.* *war*
guerre de 70 *Franco-Prussian War* (*1870–71*)
guerre de 14 *World War I* (*1914–18*)
guerre de 39 *World War II* (*1939–45*)

guerre franco-allemande *Franco-Prussian War (1870–71)*
deuxième guerre mondiale *World War II (1939–45)*
première guerre mondiale *World War I (1914–18)*
guichet [giʃɛ] *m.* *ticket window; window in post office to serve customers*
guide [gid] *m.* *guide*
Guillaume [gijom] *William*
Guillaume le Conquérant *William the Conqueror*
guillotine [gijɔtin] *f.* *guillotine*
guillotiner [gijɔtine] *guillotine, execute by the guillotine*
Guy [gi] *m.* *Guy*

H

An * indicates an aspirate *h*. See pages 511–512, *Prononciation* § 1 B, C.
habile [abil] *clever*
s'habiller [abije] *dress, dress oneself*
habitant [abitɑ̃] *m.* *inhabitant*
habiter [abite] (§ 94) (+ place, à + place) *live in, inhabit*
habitude [abityd] *f.* *habit, custom*
s'habituer [abitɥe] (à + inf.) *become accustomed to, accustom oneself to*
*haine [ɛn] *f.* *hate*
harceler [arsəle] *harass*
*haricot [ariko] *m.* *bean*
les haricots verts *green beans*
*haut [o] *m.* *top, height*
*haut [o] *high*
en haut *at the top*
à haute voix *aloud*
tout haut *out loud*
*hauteurs [otœr] *f. pl.* *heights*
*Havre, le [ləɑvr] *m.* *port in northwestern France on English Channel*
Hélène [elɛn] *f.* *Helen*
Henri [ɑ̃ri] *m.* *Henry*
Henriette [ɑ̃rjɛt] *f.* *Henrietta*
héritier [eritje] *m.* *heir*
archiduc-héritier *crown prince, heir to the throne*
*héros [ero] *m.* *hero*
hésiter [ezite] (à + inf.) *hesitate*
heure [œr] *f.* *hour; time; o'clock*
à l'heure actuelle *at the present time*
à quelle heure *at what time*
à tout à l'heure *so long, see you later*
de bonne heure *early*
l'heure sonne *the clock is striking*
Il est (deux) heures *It is (two) o'clock*
Quelle heure est-il? *What time is it?*
tout à l'heure *in a little while; just now; a little while ago*
heureusement [œrøzmɑ̃] *fortunately*
heureux, heureuse [œrø, œrøz] *happy*
hier [ijɛr, jɛr] *yesterday*
histoire [istwar] *f.* *history*
histoire sainte *sacred history, history of the Bible*
historique [istɔrik] *historical*
Hitler [itlɛr] *(1889–1945?) German Chancellor (1933–1945)*
hiver [ivɛr] *m.* *winter*
en hiver *in winter*
*hockey [ɔkɛ] *m.* *hockey*
*hollandais [ɔlɑ̃dɛ] *Dutch*
*Hollande [ɔlɑ̃d] *f.* *Holland*
homme [ɔm] *m.* *man*
homme d'affaires *m.* *business man*
honneur [ɔnœr] *m.* *honor*
Honoré [ɔnɔre] *Balzac's given name*
*honte [ɔ̃t] *f.* *shame*
hôpital [ɔpital] *m.* *hospital*
horloge [ɔrlɔʒ] *f.* *clock (in a tower)*
*hors-d'œuvre [ɔrdœvr] *m.* *relish; radishes, tomato salad, sardines, pastry containing cold spiced meat, etc.*
hôtel [otɛl, ɔtɛl] *m.* *hotel*
Hugo, Victor [ygo] *(1802–1885) noted French novelist, dramatist, and poet*
huile [ɥil] *f.* *oil*
*huit [ɥit, ɥi] *eight*
huit jours *a week*
*huitième [ɥitjɛm] *eighth*
huître [ɥitr] *f.* *oyster*
humain [ymɛ̃] *human*

I

ici [isi] *here*
par ici *this way*
idéal [ideal] *ideal*
idée [ide] *f.* *idea*
il [il] *he, it; there*
il y a (§ 91 A) *there is, there are*

il y a (trois ans) *(three years) ago*
il y en a pour . . . *there will be . . . for, it will last . . .*
s'il y a lieu *if it is necessary*
île [il] *f.* *island*
île d'Elbe *Island of Elba*
île de la Cité *island in the Seine on which the cathedral of Notre Dame is situated*
Ile-de-France *former province of which Paris is the center*
île de Sainte-Hélène *St. Helena, island in the Atlantic*
illuminer [ilymine] *light*
ils [il] *they*
imaginer [imaʒine] *imagine*
imiter [imite] *imitate*
immédiatement [imedjatmɑ̃] *immediately*
immense [imɑ̃s] *immense*
immeuble [imœbl] *m.* *building; apartment house*
imparfait [ɛ̃parfɛ] *m.* *imperfect*
impatience [ɛ̃pasjɑ̃s] *f.* *impatience*
s'impatienter [ɛ̃pasjɑ̃te] *be impatient, get impatient*
impératif [ɛ̃peratif] *m.* *imperative*
importance [ɛ̃pɔrtɑ̃s] *f.* *importance*
important [ɛ̃pɔrtɑ̃] *important*
importer [ɛ̃pɔrte] *import*
imposer [ɛ̃poze] *impose*
impossible [ɛ̃pɔsibl] *impossible*
impôt [ɛ̃po] *m.* *tax*
imprégner [ɛ̃preɲe] *imbue*
impression [ɛ̃prɛsjɔ̃] *f.* *impression*
impressionnant [ɛ̃prɛsjɔnɑ̃] *impressive*
impressionner [ɛ̃prɛsjɔne] *impress*
incessant [ɛ̃sɛsɑ̃] *continual*
incident [ɛ̃sidɑ̃] *m.* *incident*
incompréhension [ɛ̃kɔ̃preɑ̃sjɔ̃] *f.* *lack of understanding*
inconnu [ɛ̃kɔny] *unknown*
Inde [ɛ̃d] *f.* *India*
les Indes *the Indies; India*
indéfini [ɛ̃defini] *indefinite*
indemnité [ɛ̃dɛmnite] *f.* *indemnity*
indépendance [ɛ̃depɑ̃dɑ̃s] *f.* *independence*
indépendant [ɛ̃depɑ̃dɑ̃] *independent*
indicatif [ɛ̃dikatif] *m.* *indicative*
indication [ɛ̃dikɑsjɔ̃] *f.* *directions, instructions; indications; "tips"*
Indien [ɛ̃djɛ̃] *m.* *Indian*
indiqué [ɛ̃dike] (*pp of* indiquer) *indicated, shown*
indiquer [ɛ̃dike] *indicate*
indirect [ɛ̃dirɛkt] *indirect*
indispensable [ɛ̃dispɑ̃sabl] *indispensable*
individualiste [ɛ̃dividɥalist] *individualistic*
individuel, individuelle [ɛ̃dividɥɛl] *individual*
indivisible [ɛ̃divisibl] *indivisible*
industrialiser [ɛ̃dustrialize] *industrialize*
industrie [ɛ̃dystri] *f.* *industry*
industriel, industrielle [ɛ̃dystriɛl], *industrial*
inertie [inɛrsi] *f.* *inertia*
inévitable [inevitabl] *inevitable*
infime [ɛ̃fim] *infinitesimal, minute*
infinitif [ɛ̃finitif] *m.* *infinitive*
inflation [ɛ̃flɑsjɔ̃] *f.* *inflation*
infliger [ɛ̃fliʒe] (§ 89 B) *inflict*
influence [ɛ̃flyɑ̃s] *f.* *influence*
influencer [ɛ̃flyɑ̃se] (§ 89 A) *influence*
information [ɛ̃fɔrmɑsjɔ̃] *f.* *information*
Ministre de l'Information *Minister of Information*
ingénieur [ɛ̃ʒenjœr] *m.* *engineer*
innombrable [inɔ̃brabl] *innumerable*
inoculation [inɔkylɑsjɔ̃] *f.* *inoculation*
inoculer [inɔkyle] *inoculate*
inquiet, inquiète [ɛ̃kjɛ, ɛ̃kjɛt] *uneasy, anxious, worried*
s'inscrire [ɛ̃skrir] (s'inscrivant, inscrit, je m'inscris, je m'inscrivis) (*conj. like* écrire) *register, enroll*
inspiration [ɛ̃spirɑsjɔ̃] *f.* *inspiration*
inspirer [ɛ̃spire] *inspire*
s'inspirer *be inspired*
installer [ɛ̃stale] *install*
s'installer *install oneself, settle, settle down*
instant [ɛ̃stɑ̃] *m.* *instant*
instinct [ɛ̃stɛ̃] *m.* *instinct*
institut [ɛ̃stity] *m.* *institute*
instituer [ɛ̃stitɥe] *institute; set up, establish*
insulte [ɛ̃sylt] *f.* *insult*
insurgé [ɛ̃syrʒe] *m.* *insurgent*
intégration [ɛ̃tegrɑsjɔ̃] *f.* *integration*
intégrer [ɛ̃tegre] *integrate*

intellectuel, intellectuelle [ɛ̃telɛktɥɛl] *intellectual*
intelligence [ɛ̃teliʒɑ̃s] *f.* *intelligence*
intention [ɛ̃tɑ̃sjɔ̃] *f.* *intention*
avoir l'intention de *have the intention of, intend to*
interdire [ɛ̃tɛrdir] (interdisant, interdit, j'interdis, j'interdis) (*conj. like* dire) *forbid*
intéressant [ɛ̃terɛsɑ̃] *interesting*
intéresser [ɛ̃terese] *interest*
s'intéresser (à + noun) *be interested in*
intérêt [ɛ̃terɛ] *m.* *interest*
porter plus d'intérêt *have more interest*
intérieur [ɛ̃terjœr] *m.* *interior;* (adj.) *interior*
international [ɛ̃tɛrnasjɔnal] *international*
interpréter [ɛ̃tɛrprete] *interpret*
interrogatif, interrogative [ɛ̃tɛrɔgatif, ɛ̃tɛrɔgativ] *interrogative*
interroger [ɛ̃tɛrɔʒe] (§ 89 B) *question*
intervenir [ɛ̃tɛrvənir] (intervenant, intervenu, j'interviens, j'intervins) (*conj. like* venir) *intervene; occur*
intimité [ɛ̃timite] *f.* *intimacy, coziness*
intonation [ɛ̃tɔnɑsjɔ̃] *f.* *intonation*
introduire [ɛ̃trɔdɥir] (introduisant, introduit, j'introduis, j'introduisis) (*conj. like* conduire) *introduce*
introduisez [ɛ̃trɔdɥize] (*imperative of* introduire) *introduce; put into*
Invalides, les [ɛ̃valid] *building on left bank of the Seine where Napoleon I is buried*
invasion [ɛ̃vɑzjɔ̃] *f.* *invasion*
inversion [ɛ̃vɛrsjɔ̃] *f.* *inversion, inverted word order*
invité [ɛ̃vite] *m.* *guest*
Irlande [irlɑ̃d] *f.* *Ireland*
irai [ire] (*1st sing. fut. of* aller) *shall go*
irrégulier, irrégulière [iregylje, iregyljɛr] *irregular*
irresponsabilité [irɛspɔ̃sabilite] *f.* *lack of responsibility*
Isabelle II [izabɛldø] *Isabella II, Queen of Spain from 1833 until she was deposed in 1868*
isolé [izɔle] *isolated*
Italie [itali] *f.* *Italy*
italien, italienne [italjɛ̃, italjɛn] *Italian*
italique [italik] *italic(s)*
itinéraire [itinerɛr] *m.* *itinerary; route*

J

Jacqueline [ʒaklin] *f.* *Jacqueline*
Jacques [ʒak, ʒɑk] *m.* *Jack*
jadis [ʒadis] *formerly*
jalousement [ʒaluzmɑ̃] *jealously*
jaloux, jalouse [ʒalu, ʒaluz] *jealous, envious*
jamais [ʒamɛ] *ever, never*
ne . . . jamais *never*
jambe [ʒɑ̃b] *f.* *leg*
janvier [ʒɑ̃vje] *m.* *January*
Japon [ʒapɔ̃] *m.* *Japan*
jardin [ʒardɛ̃] *m.* *garden*
jaune [ʒon] *yellow*
jaunir [ʒonir] *turn yellow*
javelot [ʒavlo] *m.* *javelin*
lancement du javelot *javelin throw*
jazz [dʒaz] *m.* *jazz*
je [ʒə] *I*
je n'en sais rien *I know nothing about it*
Jean [ʒɑ̃] *m.* *John*
Jeanne [ʒan] *f.* *Jean*
Jeanne d'Arc [ʒandark] *Joan of Arc*
jeter [ʒəte] (§ 89 F) *throw*
se jeter *empty into* (*said of river*)
jeu [ʒø] *m.* *game*
jeu radiophonique *quiz program*
jeudi [ʒødi] *m.* *Thursday*
à jeudi *until Thursday*
jeune [ʒœn] *young*
jeune fille *f.* *girl*
jeunes gens *m.* *young men; young people*
jeunesse [ʒœnɛs] *f.* *youth*
Jeux Olympiques [ʒøzɔlɛ̃pik] *m. pl.* *the Olympic Games*
joie [ʒwɑ] *f.* *joy*
se joindre [ʒwɛ̃dr] (se joignant, joint, je me joins, je me joignis) (*conj. like* craindre) *join*
joli [ʒɔli] *pretty*
Joseph [ʒozɛf] *Joseph*
joue [ʒu] *f.* *cheek*
jouer [ʒwe] (de + instrument, à + game) *play*
jouet [ʒwɛ] *m.* *toy*

joueur [ʒwœr] *m.* *player*
jouir [ʒwir] (de + noun) *enjoy*
jour [ʒur] *m.* *day*
  huit jours *a week*
  le jour de l'an *New Year's Day*
  quinze jours *two weeks*
  tous les jours *every day*
Jourdan [ʒurdɑ̃] *m.* *boulevard in the southern part of Paris on which the* Cité Universitaire *is located*
journal [ʒurnal] *m.* *newspaper*
journaliste [ʒurnalist] *m.* *journalist*
journée [ʒurne] *f.* *day*
juger [ʒyʒe] *judge, try*
juillet [ʒɥijɛ] *m.* *July*
juin [ʒɥɛ̃] *m.* *June*
Jura [ʒyra] *m.* *chain of mountains in eastern France*
jurer [ʒyre] *swear*
jus [ʒy] *m.* *juice*
jusqu'à [ʒyska] *until, to, as far as, to the time of*
jusqu'à ce que [ʒyskask(ə)] *until*
jusque [ʒysk] *to, up to, until*
juste [ʒyst] *right, just, exactly*
justement [ʒystəmɑ̃] *precisely; just now*
justice [ʒystis] *f.* *justice*

K

kilomètre [kilɔmɛtr] *m.* *kilometer (about five-eighths of a mile)*

L

la [la] *f.* *the; her, it*
là [la] *there*
  là-bas *yonder, over there*
  là-haut *up there*
laboratoire [labɔratwar] *m.* *laboratory*
lac [lak] *m.* *lake*
  les Grands Lacs *Great Lakes*
  lac de Genève *Lake Geneva*
LaFayette [lafajɛt] (*1757–1834*) *French general and statesman who helped the thirteen colonies during the American Revolution*
laïque [laik] *secular, not of the church*
laisser [lese] (+ inf.) (§ 94) *leave; let*
  laisser tomber *drop*
lait [lɛ] *m.* *milk*
laitue [lety] *f.* *lettuce*
  salade de laitue *lettuce salad*

lampe [lɑ̃p] *f.* *lamp*
lancement [lɑ̃smɑ̃] *m.* *throwing*
  lancement du javelot *javelin throw*
  lancement du poids *shot-put*
lancer [lɑ̃se] (§ 89 A) *launch*
langue [lɑ̃g] *f.* *language; tongue*
  langue vivante *modern language*
langueur [lɑ̃gœr] *f.* *languor*
large [larʒ] *wide*
largement [larʒəmɑ̃] *largely*
La Rochelle [larɔʃɛl] *f.* *French city situated on the Atlantic noted for its Huguenot uprisings in the seventeenth century*
latin [latɛ̃] *m.* *Latin (language)*
  Quartier latin *Latin Quarter, the student quarter of Paris*
Lausanne [lozan] *Swiss city situated on Lake Geneva*
laver [lave] *wash*
  se laver *wash oneself*
Lavoisier [lavwazje] (*1743–1794*) *father of modern chemistry*
le [lə] *the; him, it*
Le Chevalier [ləʃvalje] *family name*
leçon [ləsɔ̃] *f.* *lesson*
lecture [lɛktyr] *f.* *reading*
léger, légère [leʒe, leʒɛr] *light*
légèrement [leʒɛrmɑ̃] *slightly*
législatif, législative [leʒislatif, leʒislativ] *legislative*
légume [legym] *m.* *vegetable*
Leipzig [lɛpsig] *city in central Germany at which a famous battle was fought in 1813*
lendemain [lɑ̃dmɛ̃] *m.* *next day*
  le lendemain matin *the next morning*
  le lendemain soir *the next evening*
lentement [lɑ̃tmɑ̃] *slowly*
Léonard [leɔnar] *m.* *Leonard, given name of Leonardo da Vinci*
lequel, laquelle, lesquels, lesquelles [ləkɛl, lakɛl, lekɛl, lekɛl] (§§ 38 E, 39 D) *which, which one; who, whom*
les [le] *the; them*
Lesseps, Ferdinand de [dəlesɛps] (*1804–1894*) *engineer who constructed the Suez Canal and started the construction of the Panama Canal*
lettre [lɛtr] *f.* *letter*

la boîte aux lettres *mailbox*
lettres *"letters", literature and art*
leur [lœr] *them, to them; their, theirs*
lever [ləve] (§ 89 D) *raise*
se lever *rise, get up*
lèvre [lɛvr] *f.* *lip*
libéral [liberal] *liberal*
libérer [libere] *free*
liberté [libɛrte] *f.* *liberty*
libre [libr] *free*
licence [lisɑ̃s] *f.* *first college degree in the French university*
lieu [ljø] *m.* *place*
au lieu de *instead of*
avoir lieu *take place*
s'il y a lieu *if it is necessary*
ligne [liɲ] *f.* *line*
Ligne Maginot [liɲmaʒino] *series of fortifications in eastern France*
Lille [lil] *city in northern France*
limité [limite] (*pp of* limiter) *limited, bordered*
limiter [limite] *limit, border, bound*
liqueur [likœr] *f.* *cordial*
lire [lir] (lisant, lu, je lis, je lus) *read*
lis, lit [li] (lire) *read, reads*
lisez [lize] (lire) *read*
littéraire [literɛr] *literary*
littérature [literatyr] *f.* *literature*
livre [livr] *m.* *book*
livrer [livre] *give over to*
local, locaux [lɔkal, lɔko] *local*
locataire [lɔkatɛr] *m. f.* *renter, tenant*
Loches [lɔʃ] *city in Touraine noted for its medieval château*
loge [lɔʒ] *f.* *small apartment, usually on ground floor of the French apartment house, in which the concierge lives*
logement [lɔʒmɑ̃] *m.* *housing*
loger [lɔʒe] (§ 89 B) *live*
loi [lwa] *f.* *law*
projet de loi *bill*
loin [lwɛ̃] *far*
au loin *in the distance*
lointain [lwɛ̃tɛ̃] *distant*
Loire [lwar] *f.* *river in central and western France*
loisir [lwazir] *m.* *leisure*
les loisirs *leisure time*
Londres [lɔ̃dr] *m.* *London*
long, longue [lɔ̃, lɔ̃g] *long*
à la longue *in the long run*
le long de *along*
tout le long *all along*
longer [lɔ̃ʒe] (§ 89 B) *go along, skirt*
longtemps [lɔ̃tɑ̃] *for a long time*
longuement [lɔ̃gmɑ̃] *for a long time*
longueur [lɔ̃gœr] *f.* *length*
Lorraine [lɔrɛn] *f.* *Lorraine*
lors [lɔr] *that moment, then*
lorsque [lɔrskə] *when*
Louis [lwi] *m.* *Louis*
Louis IX, XI, XIII, XIV, XV, XVI, XVIII *various kings of France from the Middle Ages to 1824*
Louis-le-Grand *lycée at Paris noted for its literary courses*
Louis Napoléon (1808–1873) *Napoleon III, emperor of France from 1852 to 1870*
Louis-Philippe (1773–1850) *king of France from 1830 to 1848*
Saint-Louis (1215–1270) *king of France during the Middle Ages, Louis IX; city of the United States*
Louise [lwiz] *f.* *Louise*
Louisiane [lwizjan] *f.* *territory explored by the French in the central part of the United States; sold by Napoleon I to the United States in 1803*
lourd [lur] *heavy*
Louvre [luvr] *m.* *museum in Paris*
loyer [lwaje] *m.* *rent*
lu, lus [ly] (*pp and sp* of lire) *read*
Lucienne [lysjɛn] *f.* *Lucy*
lui [lɥi] *him, to him; her, to her; it, to it*
lui-même [lɥimɛm] *himself*
lumière [lymjɛr] *f.* *light*
lundi [lœ̃di] *m.* *Monday*
lutte [lyt] *f.* *struggle*
lutter [lyte] *struggle*
Luxembourg [lyksɑ̃bur] *m.* *garden and palace at Paris; tiny European state*
luxueux, luxueuse [lyksɥø, lyksɥøz] *luxurious*
lycée [lise] *m.* *French secondary school equivalent to the American high school and junior college*
Lyon [ljɔ̃] *m.* *Lyons, city on the Rhone*

M

ma [ma] *my*
mâcher [mɑʃe] *chew*
madame [madam] *f.* *Mrs., madam*
Madeleine [madlɛn] *f.* *church planned by Vignon in classical style, visible from the* Place de la Concorde; *girl's name*
mademoiselle [madmwazɛl] *f.* *Miss*
Madrid [madrid] *m.* *capital of Spain*
magasin [magazɛ̃] *m.* *store*
  le grand magasin *department store*
Maginot [maʒino] (*1877–1932*) *Minister of War under whom the defense system in eastern France was constructed after World War I*
  la ligne Maginot *system of fortifications constructed after World War I along the Franco-German border*
magnifique [maɲifik] *magnificent*
mai [mɛ] *m.* *May*
main [mɛ̃] *f.* *hand*
  à la main *in (his, her, my, our, etc.) hand*
maintenant [mɛ̃tnɑ̃] *now*
maintenir [mɛ̃tnir] (maintenant, maintenu, je maintiens, je maintins) *conj. like* tenir) *maintain*
maire [mɛr] *m.* *mayor*
mairie [meri] *f.* *town hall, city hall*
mais [mɛ] *but*
maison [mɛzõ] *f.* *house*
  à la maison *at home, home*
  maison de campagne *country house*
  maison de commerce *business house*
  maison de couture *fashion house*
maître [mɛtr] *m.* *master*
majesté [maʒɛste] *f.* *majesty*
majorité [maʒɔrite] *f.* *majority*
mal [mal] *m.* *hurt, pain; difficulty, trouble; evil*
  avoir mal à la tête (§ 90 B) *have a headache*
malade [malad] *sick, ill*
  le malade *the sick person*
maladie [maladi] *f.* *sickness, disease*
malgré [malgre] *in spite of*
malheureux, malheureuse [malœrø, malœrøz] *unhappy, unfortunate*
maman [mamɑ̃] *f.* *mamma, mother*
Manche [mɑ̃ʃ] *f.* *English Channel*
manger [mɑ̃ʒe] (§ 89 B) *eat*
  salle à manger *f.* *dining-room*
manière [manjɛr] *f.* *manner, way*
manipulation [manipylɑsjõ] *f.* *manipulation, process*
mannequin [mankɛ̃] *m.* *dressmaker's artificial model, used to display clothing; woman hired to display gowns by wearing them*
manœuvre [manœvr] *f.* *maneuver, move, tactics*
manquer [mɑ̃ke] *lack*[1] (de + noun); *fail to keep* (à + noun); *miss* (+ noun)
manteau [mɑ̃to] *m.* *coat; overcoat*
marbre [marbr] *m.* *marble*
Marc [mark] *m.* *Mark*
marché [marʃe] *m.* *market*
  à bon marché *cheaply*
  bon marché *cheap*
  meilleur marché *cheaper*
marcher [marʃe] *walk*
mardi [mardi] *m.* *Tuesday*
maréchal [mareʃal] *m.* *marshal*
mari [mari] *m.* *husband*
mariage [marjaʒ] *m.* *marriage*
  mariage de convenance *marriage of convenience, marriage made for social or financial advantages acquired*
Marie [mari] *f.* *Mary*
Marie-Antoinette [mariɑ̃twanɛt] (*1755–1793*) *queen of France, wife of Louis XVI*
se marier [marje] (avec + noun) (§ 94) *marry*
marine [marin] *f.* *navy*
Marne [marn] *f.* *a tributary of the Seine which joins it near Paris; scene of famous battles of World War I*
marque [mark] *f.* *trade-mark, product; brand*
marqué [marke] (*pp of* marquer) *marked*
marquer [marke] *mark; indicate*
marquis [marki] *m.* *marquis*
mars [mars] *m.* *March*
Marseillaise [marsɛjɛz] *f.* *French national anthem*
Marseille [marsɛj] *f.* *Marseilles,*

[1] *Paul lacks money* may be expressed by *Paul manque d'argent* or *L'argent manque à Paul.*

largest French port on the Mediterranean; second largest city in France
marteau [marto] *m.* *hammer*
se masser [mɑse] *be massed, be gathered*
massif [masif] *m.* *flower-bed*
Massif Central [masifsɑ̃tral] *plateau in south-central France*
match [matʃ] *m.* *match, game*
matériel, matérielle [materjɛl] *material*
mathématiques [matematik] *f. pl.* *mathematics*
Mathilde [matild] *Mathilda, wife of William the Conqueror*
matière [matjɛr] *f.* *subject; matter*
matin [matɛ̃] *m.* *morning*
matinée [matine] *f.* *morning*
Maurice [mɔris] *m.* *Maurice*
mauvais [mɔvɛ] *bad*
  il fait mauvais temps *it is bad weather*
maximum [maksimɔm] *m.* *maximum*
me [mə] *me, to me*
mécanique [mekanik] *mechanical*
mécanisme [mekanism] *m.* *mechanism*
mécontent [mekɔ̃tɑ̃] *unhappy, malcontent*
médecin [mɛd(t)sɛ̃] *m.* *doctor*
médecine [med(t)sin] *f.* *medicine*
  étudiant en médecine *medical student*
médical [medikal] *medical*
Méditerranée [mediterane] *f.* *Mediterranean*
meilleur [mɛjœr] (§ 13 E) *better, best*
  meilleur marché *cheaper*
Meister, Joseph [ʒozɛfmɛstɛr] *first person to receive Pasteur treatment for rabies*
mélancolie [melɑ̃kɔli] *f.* *melancholy*
mélanger [melɑ̃ʒe] *mix*
mêler [mele] *mix*
Melun [məlœ̃] *m.* *French town a short distance southeast of Paris*
membre [mɑ̃br] *m.* *member*
même [mɛm] (§ 27 B 7) *self; same; even; itself*
  en Alsace même *in Alsace itself*
  en même temps *at the same time*
  les principes mêmes *the very principles*
  quand même *even so*
  tout de même *all the same*
mémoire [memwar] *f.* *memory*
menacer [mənase] (§ 89 A) *threaten*
ménage [menaʒ] *m.* *household, housework*
  femme de ménage *charwoman, maid, woman who comes in to do the housework*
ménager [menaʒe] *treat with respect, take care of, humor*
mener [məne] (§§ 89 D, 94) *lead, take (a person)*
mentalité [mɑ̃talite] *f.* *nature, psychological make-up*
mentionner [mɑ̃sjɔne] *mention*
menton [mɑ̃tɔ̃] *m.* *chin*
menu [məny] *m.* *menu*
mer [mɛr] *f.* *sea*
  mer du Nord *North Sea*
merci [mɛrsi] *thanks, thank you*
mercredi [mɛrkrədi] *m.* *Wednesday*
mère [mɛr] *f.* *mother*
mériter [merite] *deserve*
merveille [mɛrvɛj] *f.* *wonder*
merveilleux, merveilleuse [mɛrvɛjø, mɛrvɛjøz] *marvelous*
mes [me] *my*
messe [mɛs] *f.* *mass*
mesure [məzyr] *f.* *measure*
métallique [metalik] *metallic*
méthode [metɔd] *f.* *method*
mètre [mɛtr] *m.* *meter (39.37 inches)*
métrique [metrik] *metric*
métro [metro] (*abbrev. for* Métropolitain) *m.* *subway (of Paris)*
métropolitain [metrɔpɔlitɛ̃] *metropolitan*
  la France métropolitaine *France proper, European France, referring to France without her colonies*
mettez [mete] (*imperative of* mettre) *put*
mettre [mɛtr] (mettant, mis, je mets, je mis) *put*
  mettre à la poste *mail*
  mettre de côté *set aside, save*
  mettre en doute *question*
  mettre fin à *end*
  se mettre *place oneself*
  se mettre à *begin to*
  se mettre à table *sit at table, begin to eat*
Metz [mɛs] *most important city in the*

part of the Lorraine that became German in 1870
meuble [mœbl] *m.* *(piece of) furniture*
meurs, meurt, meurent [mœr] (*pres. of* mourir) *die, dies, die*
Mexique [mɛksik] *m.* *Mexico*
Michel [miʃɛl] *m.* *Michael*
Michel-Ange [mikɛlɑ̃ʒ] (*1475–1564*) *Michelangelo, famous painter and sculptor of the Italian Renaissance*
midi [midi] *m.* *noon*
Midi [midi] *m.* *south (used especially in speaking of southern France)*
mien, mienne [mjɛ̃, mjɛn] *mine*
mieux [mjø] (§§ 21 B, 98) *better, best*
aimer mieux *like better, prefer*
valoir mieux (+ inf.) *be better to*
milieu [miljø] *m.* *middle, center; society; sphere, environment*
au milieu *in the midst; in the middle*
militaire [militɛr] *military*
mille [mil] (§ 17 D, E, F) *thousand*
Millet [milɛ, mijɛ] (*1815–1875*) *French painter*
milliard [miljar] *m.* *billion*
millier [milje] *m.* *thousand*
million [miljõ] *m.* *million*
minéral [mineral] *mineral*
ministère [ministɛr] *m.* *ministry, department*
ministre [ministr] *m.* *minister*
Conseil des Ministres *Cabinet*
Premier Ministre *Prime Minister*
Ministre des Affaires Étrangères *Foreign Minister, Secretary of State*
Ministre de l'Agriculture *Secretary of Agriculture*
Ministre de l'Éducation Nationale *Minister of Public Instruction*
Ministre de l'Information *Minister of Information*
Ministre de l'Intérieur *Secretary of the Interior*
Ministre de la Justice *Minister of Justice, Attorney General*
Ministre des Forces Armées *Secretary of Defense*
minuit [minɥi] *m.* *midnight*
minute [minyt] *f.* *minute*
miroir [mirwar] *m.* *mirror*
mis [mi] (*pp and sp of* mettre) *put*
«Misérables, les» [lemizerabl] *famous sociological novel of Victor Hugo (1862), of which Jean Valjean is the hero*
misère [mizɛr] *f.* *wretchedness, poverty, distress, want*
missionnaire [misjɔnɛr] *m.* *missionary*
Mississippi [misisipi] *m.* *Mississippi*
mode [mɔd] *f.* *mode, manner, style*
à la mode *in style*
modèle [mɔdɛl] *m.* *model*
modéliste [mɔdelist] *m.* *pattern stylist; modelist, who executes the ideas of the "créateur" in fabrics*
moderne [mɔdɛrn] *modern*
modeste [mɔdɛst] *modest*
modifier [mɔdifje] *modify*
modiste [mɔdist] *f.* *milliner*
moi [mwa] *me, to me; self*
moindre [mwɛ̃dr] *least, slightest*
moineau [mwano] *m.* *sparrow*
moins [mwɛ̃] *less, least*
à moins que *unless*
au moins *at least*
du moins *at least*
mois [mwɑ] *m.* *month*
moisson [mwasõ] *f.* *harvest*
moitié [mwatje] *f.* *half*
Molière [mɔljɛr] (*1622–1673*) *great French dramatist*
moment [mɔmɑ̃] *m.* *moment*
à ce moment-là *at that time*
au moment où *at the time when*
en ce moment *now, at this time*
mon, ma, mes [mõ, ma, me] *my*
mon vieux *"old fellow," "old top"*
monarchie [mɔnarʃi] *f.* *monarchy*
monde [mõd] *m.* *world; people*
beaucoup de monde *many people*
tout le monde *everybody, everyone*
mondial [mõdjal] *world-wide*
la deuxième guerre mondiale *World War II (1939–45)*
la première guerre mondiale *World War I (1914–18)*
monnaie [mɔnɛ] *f.* *small change; change*
Monnot [mɔno] *family name*
monopole [mɔnɔpɔl] *m.* *monopoly*
monotone [mɔnɔtɔn] *monotonous*

monsieur [məsjø] *m.* (*pl.* messieurs) *sir, Mr.*
montagne [mõtaɲ] *f.* *mountain*
montagnes Rocheuses *Rocky Mountains*
mont Blanc [mõblɑ̃] *m.* *highest peak of the Alps*
monter [mõte] *go up, climb*
monter dans un train *board a train*
monter sur le trône *ascend the throne*
Montesquieu [mõtɛskjø] (*1689–1755*) *eighteenth century writer, author of* Les Lettres persanes *and* l'Esprit des lois
Montmartre [mõmartr] *m.* *quarter situated in northern part of Paris noted for its cafés, night clubs, etc.*
Montparnasse [mõparnɑs] *m.* *quarter of Paris noted for its cafés*
Montpellier [mõpelje] *m.* *city in southern France*
montre [mõtr] *f.* *watch*
Montréal [mõreal] *m.* *largest city in French Canada*
montrer [mõtre] *show*
monument [mɔnymɑ̃] *m.* *monument*
morceau [mɔrso] *m.* *piece*
mordre [mɔrdr] *bite*
Moreau [mɔro] *family name*
Morel [mɔrɛl] *family name*
mort [mɔr] (*pp of* mourir) *died, dead*
mort [mɔr] *m.* *the dead person*
mort [mɔr] *f.* *death*
Moscou [mɔsku] *m.* *Moscow*
mot [mo] *m.* *word*
motion [mosjõ] *f.* *motion*
moto [mɔto] *f.* (*abbr. for* motocyclette) *motorcycle*
mourir [murir] (mourant, mort, je meurs, je mourus) *die*
mouton [mutõ] *m.* *sheep*
mouvement [muvmɑ̃] *m.* *movement*
moyen [mwajɛ̃] *m.* *means*
moyen âge *Middle Ages*
moyen, moyenne [mwajɛ̃, mwajɛn] *medium; average*
muet, muette [mɥɛ, mɥɛt] *mute, dumb*
Mulhouse [myluz] *m.* *large city of Alsace*
multicolore [myltikɔlɔr] *many-colored, variegated*
multiple [myltipl] *multiple, many*
mur [myr] *m.* *wall*
muraille [myraj] *f.* *wall*
muscle [myskl] *m.* *muscle*
musée [myze] *m.* *museum*
musique [myzik] *f.* *music*
la grande musique *high class music, classical music*
mutuel, mutuelle [mytɥɛl] *mutual*
mystère [mistɛr] *m.* *mystery*

N

naissance [nɛsɑ̃s] *f.* *birth*
naître [nɛtr] (naissant, né, je nais, je naquis) *be born*
Nancy [nɑ̃si] *city in eastern France*
Nantes [nɑ̃t] *French port near the mouth of the Loire*
Napoléon [napɔleõ] *Napoleon*
Napoléon Ier *Napoleon Bonaparte* (*1769–1821*), *general and French emperor*
Napoléon III *Louis Napoleon* (*1808–1873*), *emperor of France from 1852 to 1870*
Louis Napoléon *Napoleon III*
naquis, naquit [naki] (*sp of* naître) *was born*
narration [narɑsjõ] *f.* *narration*
natalité [natalite] *f.* *birth rate*
nation [nasjõ] *f.* *nation, country*
national, nationaux [nasjɔnal, nasjɔno] *national*
nationalité [nasjɔnalite] *f.* *nationality*
National-Socialiste [nasjɔnalsɔsjalist] *m.* *National-Socialist, Nazi*
nature [natyr] *f.* *nature*
naturel, naturelle [natyrɛl] *natural*
navigable [navigabl] *navigable*
navire [navir] *m.* *ship*
nazi [nazi] *Nazi; term used contemptuously to refer to the National-Socialist followers of Hitler*
ne [nə] (§ 22) *not*
ne ... aucun *none*
ne ... guère *scarcely*
ne ... jamais *never*
ne ... ni ... ni *neither ... nor*
ne ... pas *not*
ne ... personne *no one*
ne ... plus *no longer*
ne ... point *not at all*
ne ... que *only*
ne ... rien *nothing*
né [ne] (*pp of* naître) *born*

nécessaire [nesesɛr] *necessary*
négatif, négative [negatif, negativ] *negative*
négligemment [negliʒamɑ̃] *negligently, carelessly*
négligent [negliʒɑ̃] *negligent*
neige [nɛʒ] *f.* *snow*
neiger [neʒe] (§ 89 B) *snow*
nerf [nɛr] *m.* *nerve*
nerveux, nerveuse [nɛrvø, nɛrvøz] *nervous*
n'est-ce pas [nɛspɑ] (§ 96 J) *isn't it so, etc.*
net, nette [nɛt, nɛt] *clear*
nettement [nɛtmɑ̃] *clearly, plainly, sharply*
nettoyer [netwaje] (§ 89 C) *clean*
neuf [nœf] *nine*
neutralité [nøtralite] *f.* *neutrality*
neuvième [nœvjɛm] *ninth*
neveu [nəvø] *m.* *nephew*
nez [ne] *m.* *nose*
ni [ni] (§ 5 D) *neither*
  ni . . . ni *neither . . . nor*
Nice [nis] *French city on the Riviera*
Nîmes [nim] *city in southern France noted for Roman ruins, especially* la Maison carrée
niveau [nivo] *m.* *level, standard*
  niveau de vie *standard of living*
noblesse [nɔblɛs] *f.* *nobility*
Noël [nɔɛl] *m.* *Christmas*
  le Père Noël *Santa Claus*
noir [nwar] *black*
  tableau noir *blackboard*
nom [nɔ̃] *m.* *name; noun*
nombre [nɔ̃br] *m.* *number*
nombreux, nombreuse [nɔ̃brø, nɔ̃brøz] *numerous*
nommer [nɔme] *name, choose*
non [nɔ̃] *no; not*
  non-agression *non-aggression*
  non plus [nɔ̃ply] *either*
  non-vacciné *unvaccinated*
nord [nɔr] *m.* *north*
nord-ouest [nɔrwɛst] *m.* *northwest*
normal [nɔrmal] *normal*
Normale Supérieure, École [ekɔlnɔrmalsyperjœr] *f.* *distinguished French Normal School at Paris for training of teachers*
normand [nɔrmɑ̃] *m.* *Norman*
Normandie [nɔrmɑ̃di] *f.* *Normandy*
Norvège [nɔrvɛʒ] *f.* *Norway*
nos [no] *our*
notamment [nɔtamɑ̃] *especially*
notion [nosjɔ̃] *f.* *notion*
note [nɔt] *f.* *bill, statement; pattern*
notre [nɔtr] *our*
nôtre [notr] *ours*
Notre-Dame de Paris [nɔtrədamdəpari] *f.* *cathedral on the* île de la Cité *in Paris*
nous [nu] *we; us, to us*
nouveau, nouvel, nouvelle [nuvo, nuvɛl] (§ 10 G) *new, another*
  à nouveau *again*
  de nouveau *again, once more*
  nouveau monde *New World, referring to Western hemisphere*
  nouveau venu *newcomer*
nouveauté [nuvote] *f.* *novelty, new thing*
nouvelle [nuvɛl] *f.* *piece of news*
nouvelle [nuvɛl] *f.* (adj.) *new*
  les nouvelles *news*
Nouvelle-Calédonie [nuvɛlkaledɔni] *f.* *New Caledonia, French island in Pacific Ocean to the east of Australia*
Nouvelle-Orléans (la) [lanuvɛlɔrleɑ̃] *f.* *New Orleans*
novembre [nɔvɑ̃br] *m.* *November*
nuit [nɥi] *f.* *night*
  boîte de nuit *night club*
  cette nuit *last night*
nul, nulle [nyl] *no*
  nulle part ailleurs *nowhere else*
numéro [nymero] *m.* *number*

O

obéir [ɔbeir] (à + noun) *obey*
obélisque [ɔbelisk] *m.* *obelisk*
objet [ɔbʒɛ] *m.* *object*
obligation [ɔbligɑsjɔ̃] *f.* *obligation*
obliger [ɔbliʒe] (§ 89 B) (à + inf.; être obligé de + inf.) [1] *oblige*
observer [ɔpsɛrve] *observe*
obtenir [ɔptənir] (obtenant, obtenu, j'obtiens, j'obtins) (*conj. like* tenir) *obtain*
obtenu [ɔptəny] (*pp of* obtenir) *obtained*
occasion [ɔkɑzjɔ̃] *f.* *opportunity; occasion*

[1] Louis *oblige* Paul *à* sortir; Paul *est obligé de* sortir.

occasionner [ɔkazjɔne] *occasion, require*
occupation [ɔkypasjõ] *f.* *occupation; period from 1940 to 1945 when the Germans occupied France*
occuper [ɔkype] *occupy*
s'occuper (de + noun) *take charge of, busy oneself with*
octobre [ɔktɔbr] *m.* *October*
odeur [ɔdœr] *f.* *odor*
odorant [ɔdɔrɑ̃] *odoriferous, fragrant*
œil [œj] *m. sing.* (*pl.* les yeux) *eye*
coup d'œil *glance*
œuf [*sing.* œf, *pl.* ø] *m.* *egg*
œuf dur *hard-boiled egg*
œuvre [œvr] *f.* *work* (*often literary*)
offert [ɔfɛr] (*pp of* offrir) *offered*
office [ɔfis] *m.* *service*
offices religieux *religious services, church services*
officiel, officielle [ɔfisjɛl] *official*
offrir [ɔfrir] (offrant, offert, j'offre, j'offris) (*conj. like* ouvrir) (à + person) *offer; give* (*a gift*)
oh! [o] (*exclamation*) *oh!*
oie [wa] *f.* *goose*
oiseau [wazo] *m.* *bird*
olive [ɔliv] *f.* *olive*
olivier [ɔlivje] *m.* *olive tree*
Olympiques, les Jeux [leʒøzɔlɛ̃pik] *the Olympic Games*
ombre [õbr] *f.* *shadow; shade*
omission [ɔmisjõ] *f.* *omission*
on [õ] (§ 40) *one, people, you, they*
oncle [õkl] *m.* *uncle*
ont [õ] (avoir) *have*
onze [õz] *eleven*
onzième [õzjɛm] *eleventh*
opéra [ɔpera] *m.* *opera*
l'Opéra [ɔpera] *m.* *National Opera of France by Gabriel; also name of square and subway station*
l'Opéra-Comique [lɔperakɔmik] *National Theater on the right bank of the Seine*
Opéra, Place de l' [plasdəlɔpera] *large square in center of Paris before the Opéra*
opération [ɔperasjõ] *f.* *operation*
opérette [ɔperɛt] *f.* *operetta*
opinion [ɔpinjõ] *f.* *opinion*
opposé [ɔpoze] *opposed*
or [ɔr] *m.* *gold*
or [ɔr] *now*
oral [ɔral] *oral*
oralement [ɔralmɑ̃] *orally*
orange [ɔrɑ̃ʒ] *f.* *orange*
orchestre [ɔrkɛstr] *m.* *orchestra*
ordinaire [ɔrdinɛr] *ordinary*
d'ordinaire *ordinarily*
ordonnance [ɔrdɔnɑ̃s] *f.* *decree*
ordonné [ɔrdɔne] *laid out in order*
ordonner [ɔrdɔne] *order*
ordre [ɔrdr] *m.* *order, command*
oreille [ɔrɛj] *f.* *ear*
organe [ɔrgan] *m.* *organ*
organique [ɔrganik] *organic*
organisation [ɔrganizasjõ] *f.* *organization*
organiser [ɔrganize] *organize*
s'organiser *be organized*
organisme [ɔrganism] *m.* *organism*
s'orienter [ɔrjɑ̃te] *orient oneself, find one's bearings*
origine [ɔriʒin] *f.* *origin*
à l'origine *originally*
originel, originelle [ɔriʒinɛl] *original* (*use usually confined to* le péché originel)
Orléans [ɔrleɑ̃] *French city between Paris and Tours*
la Nouvelle-Orléans *New Orleans*
orner [ɔrne] *ornament*
orthographe [ɔrtɔgraf] *f.* *spelling*
os [*sing.* ɔs, *pl.* o] *m.* *bone*
oser [oze] (+ inf.) *dare*
ou [u] *or*
ou bien *or otherwise, or else*
où [u] *where; when* (§ 39 F)
au moment où *at the time when*
oublier [ublije] (de + inf.) *forget*
ouest [wɛst] *m.* *west*
outre [utr] *further*
en outre *besides*
outre-mer *abroad, beyond the seas, overseas*
oui [wi] *yes*
ouvert [uvɛr] (*pp of* ouvrir) *opened; open*
ouvertement [uvɛrtəmɑ̃] *openly*
ouvrage [uvraʒ] *m.* *work*
ouvreuse [uvrøz] *f.* *woman usher*
ouvrez [uvre] (ouvrir) *open*
ouvrier [uvrije] *m.* *worker, working man*

ouvrier, ouvrière [uvrije, uvrijɛr] (adj.) *working*
ouvrir [uvrir] (ouvrant, ouvert, j'ouvre, j'ouvris) *open*
 ouvrir le poste *turn on the radio*
 s'ouvrir *open*

P

Pacifique [pasifik] *m.* *Pacific Ocean*
page [paʒ] *f.* *page*
pain [pɛ̃] *m.* *bread*
paix [pɛ] *f.* *peace*
palais [palɛ] *m.* *palace*
Palais Bourbon [palɛburbɔ̃] *building in which the* Assemblée Nationale *meets*
Palais de Justice [palɛdʒystis] *Courthouse*
Palais du Luxembourg [palɛdylyksɑ̃bur] *building in the Luxembourg Garden in which the Senate meets*
pâle [pɑl] *pale*
Panthéon [pɑ̃teɔ̃] *m.* *building in the Latin Quarter now used to honor national heroes*
papa [papa] *m.* *papa*
pape [pap] *m.* *pope*
papier [papje] *m.* *paper*
Pâques [pɑk] *m.* *Easter*
paquet [pakɛ] *m.* *package*
par [par] *by; through; for; per*
 par conséquent *therefore*
 par contre *on the contrary*
 par exemple *for example*
 par ici *this way*
parachuter [paraʃyte] *parachute*
paraît, il [ilparɛ] (*3d pers. sing. of* paraître) *it seems, it appears*
paraître [parɛtr] (paraissant, paru, je parais, je parus) (*conj. like* connaître) *appear, seem, look*
parc [park] *m.* *park*
parce que [parsk(ə)] *because*
parcourir [parkurir] (parcourant, parcouru, je parcours, je parcourus) (*conj. like* courir) *go through*
parcours [parkur] *m.* *route, road, way, line, course*
parcouru [parkury] (*pp of* parcourir) *run through*
pardonner [pardɔne] (à + person + de + inf.) *pardon*
pareil, pareille [parɛj] *alike, similar*
pareil [parɛj] *m.* *equal*
 sans pareil *without equal*
parent [parɑ̃] *m.* *relative; parent*
parenthèse [parɑ̃tɛz] *f.* *parenthesis*
parfait [parfɛ] *m.* *perfect (tense)*
parfois [parfwa] *sometimes*
parfum [parfœ̃] *m.* *perfume*
parfumer [parfyme] *perfume*
parfumerie [parfymri] *f.* *perfume shop*
Paris [pari] *m.* *Paris*
Parisien [parizjɛ̃] *m.* *Parisian, inhabitant of Paris*
parisien, parisienne [parizjɛ̃, parizjɛn] *Parisian*
Parisii [parizi] *m. pl.* *tribe that settled the* île de la Cité
Parlement [parləmɑ̃] *m.* *Parliament*
parler [parle] (à + person; de + noun) *speak, talk*
 entendre parler de *hear of*
parmi [parmi] *among*
parole [parɔl] *f.* *word (usually spoken)*
part [par] *f.* *part*
 à part *except, except for*
 d'autre part *on the other hand, moreover; likewise*
 faire part à *inform someone, announce to*
 nulle part ailleurs *nowhere else*
 quelque part *somewhere*
parterre [partɛr] *m.* *flower bed*
parti [parti] *m.* *(political) party*
participe [partisip] *m.* *participle*
participer [partisipe] *participate*
particulier, particulière [partikylje, partikyljɛr] *particular; peculiar; private*
 en particulier *in particular*
particulièrement [partikyljɛrmɑ̃] *particularly*
partie [parti] *f.* *part; game*
 faire partie de *be a part of*
partir [partir] (2) (§ 94) *leave, go away, depart*
 à partir de . . . *from . . . on*
partitif [partitif] *m.* (§ 5) *partitive*
partout [partu] *everywhere*
paru, parus [pary] (*pp and sp of* paraître) *appeared*
parvenir [parvənir] (parvenant, parvenu, je parviens, je parvins) (*conj. like* venir) (à + inf.) *arrive; succeed in*

pas [pɑ] *m.* *step*
pas [pɑ] *not*
pas du tout *not at all*
passage [pɑsaʒ] *m.* *passage*
passé [pɑse] *m.* *past*
passé composé *compound past*
passé simple *simple past*
passer [pɑse] (à + inf.) (§ 94) *pass, spend (time); advance*
un film passe *a film is being shown*
passer un examen *take an examination*
passer le temps à faire *spend one's time doing*
se passer *happen, take place*
se passer de *do without*
passif, passive [pasif, pasiv] *passive*
passion [pɑsjõ] *f.* *passion*
se passionner [pɑsjɔne] *become enthusiastic, "go wild over"*
Pasteur, Louis [pastœr] (*1822–1895*) *great French scientist*
pasteurisation [pastœrizɑsjõ] *f.* *pasteurization*
pâté [pɑte] *m.* *pastry containing cold spiced meat*
patient [pasjã] *patient*
pâtisserie [pɑtisri] *f.* *pastry*
patrie [patri] *f.* *native land, fatherland, country*
patriote [patrijɔt] *m.* *patriot*
Pau [po] *m.* *city in the French Pyrenees*
Paul [pɔl] *m.* *Paul*
pauvre [povr] *poor*
pavillon [pavijõ] *m.* *pavilion, term used to refer to certain buildings of the* Cité Universitaire
payer [peje] (§ 45 B, § 89 C) *pay, pay for*
payer des droits *pay for the right to*
pays [pei, peji] *m.* *country, land*
Pays Basque [peibask] *m.* *the Basque country situated in the French Pyrenees*
paysage [peizaʒ] *m.* *landscape*
paysan [peizã] *m.* *peasant*
le péché [peʃe] *m.* *sin*
peine [pɛn] *f.* *trouble, difficulty; pain*
à peine (§ 20 E) *scarcely, hardly*
valoir la peine *be worth the trouble*
peintre [pɛ̃tr] *m.* *painter*
peinture [pɛ̃tyr] *f.* *painting*
peloton [plɔtõ] *m.* *group, line of racers*
pendant [pãdã] *during*
pendant que *while*
pénétrer [penetre] *penetrate*
pensée [pãse] *f.* *thought*
penser [pãse] *think*
penser (+ inf.) *intend*
penser (à + inf.) *consider*
penser (à + noun) *think about, think of*
penser (de + noun) *have an opinion of*
penseur [pãsœr] *m.* *thinker*
pension [pãsjõ] *f.* *boarding-house*
pension de famille *boarding-house*
pensionnaire [pãsjɔnɛr] *m. f.* *boarder, roomer*
perception [pɛrsɛpsjõ] *f.* *perception*
percer [pɛrse] (§ 89 A) *dig, excavate (a canal)*
perdre [pɛrdr] *lose*
père [pɛr] *m.* *father*
le père Noël *Santa Claus*
perfection [pɛrfɛksjõ] *f.* *perfection*
perfectionner [pɛrfɛksjɔne] *perfect*
période [perjɔd] *f.* *period*
permettre [pɛrmɛtr] (permettant, permis, je permets, je permis) (*conj. like* mettre) (à + person + de + inf.) *permit*
permission [pɛrmisjõ] *f.* *permission*
perpendiculaire [pɛrpãdikylɛr] *perpendicular*
personne [pɛrsɔn] *f.* *person*
personne [pɛrsɔn] *no one, nobody*
ne . . . personne *no one, nobody*
personnel [pɛrsɔnɛl] *m.* *personnel*
personnel, personnelle [pɛrsɔnɛl] *personal*
personnellement [pɛrsɔnɛlmã] *personally*
perspective [pɛrspɛktiv] *f.* *perspective*
perte [pɛrt] *f.* *loss*
à perte de vue *as far as the eye can see*
Pétain, Philippe [petɛ̃] (*1856–1951*) *general during World War I, Chief of State during the period of German occupation of France in World War II*
petit [pəti] *small*
petit déjeuner *m.* *breakfast*
Petit Trianon [pətitrijanõ] *m.* *small*

palace built at Versailles by Gabriel for Marie Antoinette
peu [pø] *little, few*
peu à peu *little by little*
à peu près *about, approximately*
peu après *a little later, soon after*
peu probable *unlikely*
un petit peu *a little bit*
peuple [pœpl] *m.* *people, the masses*
peur [pœr] *f.* *fear*
avoir peur (§ 90 B) *be afraid*
peut-être [pœtɛtr, pøtɛtr] *perhaps*
peux, peut, peuvent [pø, pø, pœv] (*pres. of* pouvoir) *can*
pharmacie [farmasi] *f.* *pharmacy*
Philippe [filip] *m.* *Philip*
philosophie [filɔzɔfi] *f.* *philosophy*
photographie [fɔtɔgrafi] *f.* *photograph*
phrase [frɑz] *f.* *sentence*
physique [fizik] *f.* *physics*
physique [fizik] *physical*
pièce [pjɛs] *f.* *play; room*
pièce de théâtre *play*
pied [pje] *m.* *foot*
à pied *on foot*
Pierre [pjɛr] *Peter*
piscine [pisin] *f.* *swimming pool*
pittoresque [pitɔrɛsk] *picturesque*
place [plas] *f.* *seat; public square; place (space)*
plage [plaʒ] *f.* *beach*
se plaindre [plɛ̃dr] (se plaignant, plaint, je me plains, je me plaignis) (*conj. like* craindre) (de + noun) *complain*
plaine [plɛn] *f.* *plain*
plaire [plɛr] (plaisant, plu, je plais, je plus) (à + person) *please*
plaisanter [plezɑ̃te] *joke*
plaisir [plezir] *m.* *pleasure*
plaît [plɛ] (*3d pers. sing. pres. of* plaire) *pleases*
s'il vous plaît *please, if you please*
plan [plɑ̃] *m.* *plan; map (of city)*
planter [plɑ̃te] *plant*
plat [pla] *m.* *dish*
plat du jour *special dish for the day*
plateau [plato] *m.* *plateau*
plein [plɛ̃] *full, filled*
plein air *open air*
pleurer [plœre] *cry*
pleut [plø] (*3d pers. sing. pres. of* pleuvoir) *rains*
pleuvoir [plœvwar] (pleuvant, plu, il pleut, il plut) *rain*
plier [plie] *fold*
plu [ply] (*pp of* pleuvoir) *rained*
plu, plus [ply] (*pp. and sp of* plaire) *pleased*
plupart [plypar] *f.* *majority*
pluriel [plyrjɛl] *m.* *plural*
plus [ply] *more, most*
de plus *moreover; in addition*
de plus en plus *more and more*
ne . . . plus *no more, no longer*
ne . . . plus que *no longer anything but*
non plus *either*
plusieurs [plyzjœr] *several*
plus-que-parfait [plyskəparfɛ] *m.* *pluperfect*
plutôt [plyto] *rather, more likely*
écoutez plutôt *listen for yourself*
poche [pɔʃ] *f.* *pocket*
poème [pɔɛm] *m.* *poem*
poésie [pɔezi] *f.* *poetry*
poète [pɔɛt] *m.* *poet*
poids [pwɑ] *m.* *weight, weights*
lancement du poids *shot-put*
point [pwɛ̃] *m.* *point, period*
au point de vue *from the point of view*
à plusieurs points de vue *from several points of view*
point [pwɛ̃] (§ 22 E) *not at all*
ne . . . point *not at all*
poisson [pwasɔ̃] *m.* *fish*
poitrine [pwatrin] *f.* *chest*
poivre [pwɑvr] *m.* *pepper*
policier, policière [pɔlisje, pɔlisjɛr] *detective*
roman policier *detective story*
politique [pɔlitik] *f.* *policy, political policy;* (adj.) *political*
Pologne [pɔlɔɲ] *f.* *Poland*
Polytechnique, École [ekɔlpɔlitɛknik] *school in Paris which trains its students to become engineers*
pomme [pɔm] *f.* *apple*
pomme de terre *potato*
pommes de terre frites *French fried potatoes*
pont [pɔ̃] *m.* *bridge*
populaire [pɔpylɛr] *popular*
le front populaire *"Popular Front," referring to the coalition govern-*

ment of the working classes set up by Léon Blum in May, 1936
population [pɔpylɑsjõ] *f.* *population; people*
porc [pɔr] *m.* *pork*
côtelette de porc *pork chop*
port [pɔr] *m.* *seaport, harbor, port*
porte [pɔrt] *f.* *door, gate*
portée [pɔrte] *f.* *range, reach; import, signification*
à longue portée *long range*
à sa portée *at his disposition; within range of*
porter [pɔrte] (§ 94) *carry, bear; wear; take*
porter plus d'intérêt *have more interest*
portillon [pɔrtijõ] *m.* *little door*
portrait [pɔrtrɛ] *m.* *portrait*
Portugal [pɔrtygal] *m.* *Portugal*
poser [poze] *put; pose*
poser une question *ask a question*
position [pozisjõ] *f.* *position*
posséder [pɔsede] (§ 89 E) *possess*
possessif, possessive [pɔsesif, pɔsesiv] *possessive*
possession [pɔsɛsjõ] *f.* *possession*
possible [pɔsibl] *possible*
possibilité [pɔsibilite] *f.* *possibility*
poste [pɔst] *m.* *radio station; radio set*
poste émetteur *broadcasting station*
éteindre le poste *turn off the radio*
fermer le poste *turn off the radio*
mettre le poste *turn on the radio*
ouvrir le poste *turn on the radio*
poste de radio *radio set*
poste de télévision *television set*
poste [pɔst] *f.* *post office, postal service*
bureau de poste *m.* *post office*
potage [pɔtaʒ] *m.* *soup*
poudre [pudr] *f.* *powder*
poumon [pumõ] *m.* *lung*
poupée [pupe] *f.* *doll*
pour [pur] *for; in order to*
pour que *in order that*
pourboire [purbwar] *m.* *tip*
pour-cent [pursɑ̃] *m.* *percent*
pourquoi [purkwa] *why*
pourrai [pure] (*1st pers. sing. fut. of* pouvoir) *shall be able*
poursuivre [pursɥivr] (poursuivant, poursuivi, je poursuis, je poursuivis) (*conj. like* suivre) *pursue*
pourtant [purtɑ̃] *however*
pourvu que [purvyk(ə)] *provided that*
pousser [puse] *push, drive, impel; grow*
pousser un cri *cry out, utter a cry*
pouvoir [puvwar] (pouvant, pu, je peux, je pus) (+ inf.) *can, be able*
ne pouvoir rien *be powerless*
pouvoir [puvwar] *m.* *power*
pratique [pratik] *practical*
pratiquement [pratikmɑ̃] *practically, actually*
pratiquer [pratike] *practice, exercise*
pratiquer un sport *participate in a sport*
pré [pre] *m.* *meadow*
précédent [presedɑ̃] *preceding*
se précipiter [presipite] *rush*
préférable [preferabl] *preferable*
préférer [prefere] (§ 89 E) (+ inf.) *prefer*
préfet [prefɛ] *m.* *prefect*
préliminaires [preliminɛr] *m. pl.* *preliminaries*
premier, première [prəmje, prəmjɛr] *first*
premier étage *second floor*
Premier Ministre *Prime Minister*
prendre [prɑ̃dr] (prenant, pris, je prends, je pris) [+ thing + à (from) + person] *take*
prendre un billet *buy a ticket*
prendre une correspondance *transfer*
prendre dans *take (something) from*
prendre fin *end*
prendre part à *participate in*
prendre le petit déjeuner *have breakfast*
prendre quelque chose *have a drink, have a bit to eat*
prendre un repas *eat a meal*
prendre sa responsabilité *assume one's own responsibility*
préparatif [preparatif] *m.* *preparation*
préparer [prepare] *prepare*
se préparer (à + noun; à + inf.) *prepare*
préposition [prepozisjõ] *f.* *preposition*
près [prɛ] (de + noun) *near, close*

à peu près *about, approximately*
tout près *right near*
présent [prezɑ̃] *m.* *present*
à présent *at present*
présentation [prezɑ̃tɑsjɔ̃] *f.* *presentation; style show*
présenter [prezɑ̃te] *present; introduce*
se présenter *appear; present oneself*
président [prezidɑ̃] *m.* *president*
Président de la République *President of France*
présider [prezide] *preside*
presque [prɛsk(ə)] *almost, nearly*
presse [prɛs] *f.* *press*
pression [prɛsjɔ̃] *f.* *pressure*
prestige [prɛstiʒ] *m.* *prestige*
prêt [prɛ] *ready*
prêtre [prɛtr] *m.* *priest*
preuve [prœv] *f.* *proof*
prie, je vous en [ʒəvuzɑ̃pri] (prier) *I beg of you, don't mention it*
prier [prije] (+ person + de + inf.) *ask, pray, beg*
primaire [primɛr] *primary*
primitif, temps [tɑ̃primitif] *m.* *principal part (of a verb)* (§ 48)
prince [prɛ̃s] *m.* *prince*
principal, principaux [prɛ̃sipal, prɛ̃sipo] *principal*
principe [prɛ̃sip] *m.* *principle*
printemps [prɛ̃tɑ̃] *m.* *spring*
au printemps *in the spring*
pris [pri] (*pp and sp of* prendre) *taken, took*
prison [prizɔ̃] *f.* *prison*
prisonnier, prisonnière [prizɔnje, prizɔnjɛr] *m. f.* *prisoner*
privé [prive] *private*
privilège [privilɛʒ] *m.* *privilege*
prix [pri] *m.* *price; prize*
à prix réduits *at reduced prices*
à tout prix *at any price*
probable [prɔbabl] *probable*
peu probable *unlikely*
problème [prɔblɛm] *m.* *problem*
procédé [prɔsede] *m.* *process*
prochain [prɔʃɛ̃] *next, following*
proclamation [prɔklamɑsjɔ̃] *f.* *proclamation*
proclamer [prɔklame] *proclaim*
prodigalité [prɔdigalite] *f.* *prodigality, extravagance in expenditure, excessive liberality*
produire [prɔdɥir] (produisant, produit, je produis, je produisis) (*conj. like* conduire) *produce*
produit [prɔdɥi] *m.* *product*
produit [prɔdɥi] *pp of* produire *produced*
professeur [prɔfɛsœr] *m.* *teacher at secondary or college level*
professionnel, professionnelle [prɔfɛsjɔnɛl] *professional*
professionnel [prɔfɛsjɔnɛl] *m.* *professional*
profit [prɔfi] *m.* *profit*
profitable [prɔfitabl] *profitable*
profiter [prɔfite] (de + noun) *profit, take advantage of*
profond [prɔfɔ̃] *profound, deep*
profondément [prɔfɔ̃demɑ̃] *profoundly*
programme [prɔgram] *m.* *program, radio program; course of study, curriculum*
progrès [prɔgrɛ] *m.* *progress*
projet [prɔʒɛ] *m.* *project*
se prolonger [prɔlɔ̃ʒe] (§ 89 B) *extend, continue*
promenade [prɔmnad] *f.* *walk*
faire une promenade *walk, take a walk*
se promener [prɔmne] (§ 89 D) *take a walk*
promesse [prɔmɛs] *f.* *promise*
promulguer [prɔmylge] *promulgate, make known to the public formally and officially*
pronom [prɔnɔ̃] *m.* *pronoun*
pronominal, verbe [vɛrbprɔnɔminal] *m.* *reflexive verb*
prononcer [prɔnɔ̃se] (§ 89 A) *pronounce*
prononciation [prɔnɔ̃sjɑsjɔ̃] *f.* *pronunciation*
propos [prɔpo] *m.* *subject; matter*
à ce propos *concerning this subject*
à propos de *in regard to*
proposer [prɔpoze] *propose*
propre [prɔpr] *own; clean*
proprement dit [prɔprəmɑ̃di] *properly speaking*
propriétaire [prɔprietɛr] *m. f.* *landlord, landlady, owner*
prospère [prɔspɛr] *prosperous*
protestant [prɔtɛstɑ̃] *protestant*
protester [prɔtɛste] *protest*

Provence [prɔvɑ̃s] *f. Provence, province in southern France*
province [prɔvɛ̃s] *f. province*
de province *from the provinces*
en province *anywhere in France outside of Paris*
«Provincia» [prɔvɛ̃sja] *part of southern France most thoroughly conquered by the Romans, called* "Provincia nostra"
Prusse [prys] *f. Prussia*
psychologie [psikɔlɔʒi] *f. psychology*
pu, pus [py] (*pp and sp of* pouvoir) *been able, was able*
public [pyblik] *m. the public*
public, publique [pyblik] *public*
publicitaire [pyblisitɛr] *pertaining to publicity; publicity*
publicité [pyblisite] *f. publicity; advertising*
publier [pyblije] *publish*
puis [pɥi] *then*
puis, puisse [pɥi, pɥis] (*1st pers. pres. indic. and subjunctive of* pouvoir) *can, am able; be able*
puisque [pɥisk(ə)] *since*
puissance [pɥisɑ̃s] *f. power*
puissant [pɥisɑ̃] *powerful*
punir [pynir] *punish*
punition [pynisjõ] *f. punishment*
pur [pyr] *pure*
pureté [pyrte] *f. purity; pureness*
pyjama [piʒama] *m. pajamas*
Pyramides [piramid] *f. Pyramids*
Bataille des Pyramides *Battle of the Pyramids, fought by Napoleon in Egypt (1799)*
Pyrénées [pirene] *f. Pyrenees*

Q

quai [ke, kɛ] *m. wharf, (railway or subway) platform*
qualité [kalite] *f. quality; (pl.) favorable qualities*
quand [kɑ̃] *when*
depuis quand *since when, how long*
quand même *even so*
quant à [kɑ̃ta] *as for*
quantité [kɑ̃tite] *f. quantity*
quarante [karɑ̃t] *forty*
quart [kar] (§ 97 D) *m. quarter*
quartier [kartje] *m. quarter, district*
Quartier latin [kartjelatɛ̃] *Latin Quarter, the student quarter of Paris*
quatorze [katɔrz] *fourteen*
quatre [katr] *four*
quatre-vingts [katrəvɛ̃] (§ 17 C) *eighty*
quatre-vingt-dix [katrəvɛ̃di(s)] *ninety*
quatre-vingt-onze [katrəvɛ̃õz] *ninety-one*
quatrième [katrijɛm] *fourth*
Quatrième République *Fourth French Republic (1946–58)*
que [kə] (§ 38 D, § 39 C) *what; which, that, whom; that; than; how many*
ne . . . que (§ 22 F 4) *only*
que de *how many*
qu'est-ce que [kɛskə] (§ 38 D, F) *what*
qu'est-ce que c'est que ça? *what is that?*
qu'est-ce qui [kɛski] (§ 38 B) *what*
Québec [kebɛk] *province in eastern Canada; also capital of the same*
quel, quelle [kɛl] *which, what*
quelconque [kɛlkõk] *whatever, whatsoever*
quelque [kɛlk(ə)] *some, any, a few*
quelque chose [kɛlkəʃoz] *something*
quelque chose d'intéressant *something interesting*
quelquefois [kɛlkəfwa] *sometimes*
quelque part [kɛlkəpar] *somewhere*
quelqu'un [kɛlkœ̃] *someone, somebody*
quelqu'un d'autre *someone else*
querelle [kərɛl] *f. quarrel*
question [kɛstjõ] *f. question*
poser une question *ask a question*
qui [ki] *who, whom; that, which*
quinze [kɛ̃z] *fifteen*
quinze jours *two weeks*
quitter [kite] (§ 94) *leave*
quoi [kwa] (§ 38 B) *what*
quoi que *whatever*
quoi que ce soit *anything whatever*
quoi qu'il arrive *come what may, whatever happens*
quoique [kwak(ə)] *although*
quotidien [kɔtidjɛ̃] *m. daily paper*
quotidien, quotidienne [kɔtidjɛ̃, kɔtidjɛn] *daily*

R

race [ras] *f.* *race*
Racine [rasin] (*1639–1699*) *famous French dramatist*
raconter [rakõte] *tell* (*a story*)
radio [radjo] *f.* *radio*
  Radio Luxembourg *private radio station whose studios are in Paris but which broadcasts French language programs from the country of Luxembourg*
  poste de radio *radio set*
radiodiffusion [radjodifyzjõ] *f.* *radio broadcast*
radiophonique, jeu [ʒøradjofɔnik] *m.* *quiz program*
radis [radi] *m.* *radish*
rage [raʒ] *f.* *rabies*
raisin [rɛzɛ̃] *m.* *grape*
raison [rɛzõ] *f.* *reason*
  avoir raison (§ 90 B) *be right*
ranger [rɑ̃ʒɛ] (§ 89 B) *arrange, put in order*
Raphaël [rafaɛl] (*1483–1520*) *famous painter of the Italian Renaissance*
rapide [rapid] *rapid*
rapidement [rapidmɑ̃] *rapidly*
rappeler [raple] (§ 89 F) *recall, remind*
  se rappeler (+ noun) *remember*
rapport [rapɔr] *m.* *connection, relation*
  être en rapport avec *be in relation with*
rapporter [rapɔrte] *bring back*
rassembler [rasɑ̃ble] *assemble*
ravi [ravi] *delighted*
rayon [rɛjõ] *m.* *department* (*of a store*)
rebâtir [rəbɑtir] *rebuild*
récent [resɑ̃] *recent*
récemment [resamɑ̃] *recently*
récepteur [resɛptœr] *m.* *telephone receiver;* (*radio or television*) *receiving set*
recevoir [rəsəvwar] (recevant, reçu, je reçois, je reçus) *receive*
recherche [rəʃɛrʃ] *f.* *search, quest; research*
récit [resi] *m.* *story*
reçois, reçoit, reçoivent [rəswa, rəswav] (*pres. of* recevoir) *receive, receives, receive*
recommander [rəkɔmɑ̃de] *recommend*
recommencer [rəkɔmɑ̃se] (§ 89 A) (à + inf.) *begin again*
reconnaître [rəkɔnɛtr] (reconnaissant, reconnu, je reconnais, je reconnus) (*conj. like* connaître) *recognize*
recouvrir [rəkuvrir] (recouvrant, recouvert, je recouvre, je recouvris) (*conj. like* ouvrir) *cover; cover over*
récréation [rekreɑsjõ] *f.* *recreation*
reçu, reçus [rəsy] (*pp and sp of* recevoir) *received*
reculer [rəkyle] *retreat*
Rédempteur [redɑ̃ptœr] *m.* *Redeemer*
redevenir [rədəvnir] (redevenant, redevenu, je redeviens, je redevins) (*conj. like* venir) *become again*
redevenu [rədəvny] (*pp of* redevenir) *become again*
rédiger [rediʒe] *write, compose*
réduire [redɥir] (réduisant, réduit, je réduis, je réduisis) (*conj. like* conduire) *reduce*
réduit [redɥi] (*pp of* réduire) *reduced*
redoubler [rəduble] *take over*
  redoubler une classe *take a year of school over*
réel, réelle [reɛl] *real, true*
refermer [rəfɛrme] *close again*
réfléchi [refleʃi] *reflexive*
réforme [refɔrm] *f.* *reform*
refus [rəfy] *m.* *refusal*
refuser [rəfyze] (de + inf.) *refuse*
regagner [rəgaɲe] *regain, win back*
regarder [rəgarde] (+ noun) *look at*
régime [reʒim] *m.* *regime, rule*
région [reʒjõ] *f.* *region*
registre [rəʒistr] *m.* *register*
règle [rɛgl] *f.* *rule*
régler [regle] *determine, decide, regulate; pay; settle an account*
règne [rɛɲ] *m.* *reign*
regretter [rəgrete] (de + inf.) *regret*
régulier, régulière [regylje, regyljɛr] *formal, symmetrical*
Reich [rɛʃ] *m.* *Reich* (*referring to the German empire*)
reine [rɛn] *f.* *queen*
rejoindre [rəʒwɛ̃dr] (rejoignant, rejoint, je rejoins, je rejoignis) (*conj. like* craindre) *join*

relatif, relative [rəlatif, rəlativ] *relative*
relativement [rəlativmɑ̃] *relatively*
relèvement [rəlɛvmɑ̃] *m.* *recovery*
relier [rəlje] *connect*
religieux, religieuse [rəliʒjø, rəliʒjøz] *religious*
religion [rəliʒjõ] *f.* *religion*
remarquable [rəmarkabl] *remarkable*
remarquer [rəmarke] *notice*
rembourser [rɑ̃burse] *reimburse*
remercier [rəmɛrsje] (de *or* pour + thing; de + verb) *thank*
remettre [rəmɛtr] (remettant, remis, je remets, je remis) (*conj. like* mettre) *hand in, turn in; put back; postpone*
  se remettre (à + inf.) *begin again, resume*
remis [rəmi] (*pp and sp of* remettre) *handed in; put back; postponed*
remonter [rəmõte] *date from, go back, go up (stream)*
remorque [rəmɔrk] *f.* *trailer*
remplacer [rɑ̃plase] (§ 89 A) *fill in, replace; take the place of*
remplacez [rɑ̃plase] *fill in*
  remplacez les tirets *fill in the blanks*
remplir [rɑ̃plir] *fill*
remporter [rɑ̃pɔrte] *bring back, carry away*
  remporter la victoire *win the victory*
Renaissance [rənɛsɑ̃s] *f.* *revival of learning following the Middle Ages. It flourished in France from the early years of the sixteenth century to the end of the reign of Henry IV (1610).*
rencontre [rɑ̃kõtr] *f.* *meeting*
rencontrer [rɑ̃kõtre] (§ 94) *meet*
  se rencontrer *meet (each other)*
rendre [rɑ̃dr] (§ 94) *return, make, render*
  rendre célèbre *make famous*
  se rendre compte de *realize*
  rendre visite *pay a visit*
  se rendre (§ 94) *surrender; go to; return*
René [rəne] *m.* *boy's name*
renommé [rənɔme] *famous, renowned*
renoncer [rənõse] (§ 89 A) (à + thing) *renounce, give up*
renseignement [rɑ̃sɛɲmɑ̃] *m.* *information*
renseigner [rɑ̃seɲe] *inform*
rentrée [rɑ̃tre] *f.* *return; opening of school*
  rentrée des classes *opening of school*
rentrer [rɑ̃tre] (§ 94) *return, go back (home); bring in*
renverser [rɑ̃vɛrse] *overthrow, overturn*
réorganiser [reɔrganize] *reorganize*
répandre [repɑ̃dr] *spread*
  se répandre *spread*
répandu [repɑ̃dy] *widespread, common*
réparation [reparɑsjõ] *f.* *reparation*
réparer [repare] *repair*
repas [rəpɑ] *m.* *meal*
  prendre un repas *eat a meal*
répondre [repõdr] (à + noun) *answer, reply*
réponse [repõs] *f.* *reply*
reportage [rəpɔrtaʒ] *m.* *reporting*
reposer [rəpoze] *rest*
  se reposer *rest*
reprendre [rəprɑ̃dr] (reprenant, repris, je reprends, je repris) (*conj. like* prendre) *take again, retake, recapture*
représentant [rəprezɑ̃tɑ̃] *m.* *representative*
représentation [rəprezɑ̃tɑsjõ] *f.* *presentation*
représenter [rəprezɑ̃te] *show, represent, give (a play)*
repris [rəpri] (*pp and sp of* reprendre) *retook*
reproduire [rəprɔdɥir] (reproduisant, reproduit, je reproduis, je reproduisis) (*conj. like* conduire) *reproduce*
républicain [repyblikɛ̃] *republican*
république [repyblik] *f.* *republic*
  Première République (*1792–1804*)
  Deuxième République (*1848–1852*)
  Troisième République (*1870–1940*)
  Quatrième République (*1946–1958*)
  Cinquième République (*1958–*)
réputé [repyte] *famous, reputed*

réserver [rezɛrve] *reserve*
résidence [rezidɑ̃s] *f.* *residence*
résistance [rezistɑ̃s] *f.* *resistance, especially referring to the resistance organized by the French against the Germans during the "occupation"*
résister [reziste] (à + noun) *resist*
résoudre [rezudr] *resolve;* (*pp*) résous, résolu, *resolved*
respecter [rɛspɛkte] *respect*
respiration [rɛspirɑsjɔ̃] *f.* *respiration, breathing*
respirer [rɛspire] *breathe; inhale*
responsable [rɛspɔ̃sabl] (de + noun) *responsible*
responsabilité [rɛspɔ̃sabilite] *f.* *responsibility*
prendre sa responsabilité *assume one's responsibility*
ressembler [rəsɑ̃ble] (à + noun) *resemble*
ressentir [rəsɑ̃tir] (2) *feel*
ressource [rəsurs] *f.* *resource*
restaurant [rɛstɔrɑ̃] *m.* *restaurant*
reste [rɛst] *m.* *remainder, rest*
du reste *moreover*
rester [rɛste] *remain*
résultat [rezulta] *m.* *result*
rétablir [retablir] *re-establish*
retenir [rətnir] (retenant, retenu, je retiens, je retins) (*conj. like* tenir) *keep, hold*
retenir l'attention *attract attention*
retenir une place *reserve a seat*
retirer [rətire] *withdraw, remove, take away*
retour [rətur] *m.* *return*
retourner [rəturne] (§ 94) *return, go back; turn again*
se retourner *turn around*
retraite [rətrɛt] *f.* *retreat; retirement; retirement pension*
battre en retraite *retreat*
retransmission [rɛtrɑ̃smisjɔ̃] *f.* *broadcast; rebroadcast*
retrouver [rətruve] (§ 94) *meet; find again*
se retrouver *be; meet; meet each other*
réunir [reynir] *assemble, unite, reunite; gather together*
se réunir *assemble, meet*
réussir [reysir] (à + inf.) *succeed*
réussir à un examen *pass a test*
réussir dans un cours *pass a course*
revanche, en [ɑ̃rvɑ̃ʃ] *in return*
se réveiller [reveje] *wake up, awaken*
réveillon [revɛjɔ̃] *m.* *a meal eaten in the middle of the night, especially the night before Christmas*
révéler [revele] *reveal*
revenir [rəvnir] (revenant, revenu, je reviens, je revins) (*conj. like* venir) (§ 94) *return, come back*
revenir cher *be expensive*
revenu [rəvny] (*pp of* revenir) *returned, come back*
revenu [rəvny] *m.* *revenue, income*
rêver [reve] *dream*
revoir [rəvwar] (revoyant, revu, je revois, je revis) (*conj. like* voir) *see again*
au revoir *good-by*
se révolter [revɔlte] *revolt*
révolution [revɔlysjɔ̃] *f.* *revolution*
Révolution française *French Revolution. The great French Revolution began in 1789. There were minor revolutions in 1830, 1848, and 1870–1871.*
révolutionnaire [revɔlysjɔnɛr] *revolutionary*
revue [rəvy] *f.* *magazine*
revue de presse *press review*
Rex [rɛks] *popular name for moviehouse in France*
rez-de-chaussée [redʃose] *m.* *ground floor, first floor*
Rhin [rɛ̃] *m.* *Rhine*
Rhône [ron] *m.* *Rhone*
riche [riʃ] *rich*
richesse [riʃɛs] *f.* *riches*
rien [rjɛ̃] *nothing*
je n'en sais rien *I know nothing about it*
la France ne pouvait rien *France couldn't do anything*
ne . . . rien *nothing*
rien de défini *nothing definite*
rire [rir] (riant, ri, je ris, je ris) (de + noun) *laugh*
rivalité [rivalite] *f.* *rivalry*
rive [riv] *f.* *bank (of river)*
Riviera [rivjɛra] *f.* *Riviera, a short stretch of land, along the southeast*

coast of France known by the French as the Côte d'Azur
robe [rɔb] *f.* *dress, gown*
Robert [rɔbɛr] *m.* *Robert*
rocher [rɔʃe] *m.* *rock*
Rocheuses [rɔʃøz] *f. pl.* *Rockies, mountain chain in western United States*
Roger [rɔʒe] *m.* *Roger*
roi [rwa] *m.* *king*
rôle [rol] *m.* *role*
Romain [rɔmɛ̃] *m.* *Roman*
romain [rɔmɛ̃] *Roman*
roman [rɔmɑ̃] *m.* *novel*
roman policier *detective story*
romancier [rɔmɑ̃sje] *m.* *novelist*
romantisme [rɔmɑ̃tism] *m.* *romanticism*
Rome [rɔm] *capital of Italy*
ronde [rɔ̃d] *f.* *round*
Roquefort [rɔkfɔr] *m.* *type of French cheese*
rosace [rozas] *f.* *rose window*
rose [roz] *rose-color, reddish*
rôtir [rotir] *roast*
Rouen [rwɑ̃] *m.* *important city in Normandy situated on the Seine*
rouge [ruʒ] *red*
roulotte [rulɔt] *f.* *trailer*
Rousseau, Jean-Jacques [ruso] (*1712–1778*) *French writer of the eighteenth century, author of* la Nouvelle Héloïse, Émile, le Contrat social, *etc.*
route [rut] *f.* *way, road, route*
en route *on the way*
royal, royaux [rwajal, rwajo] *royal*
rue Royale *Paris street leading from the* Place de la Concorde *to the* Madeleine
royaliste [rwajalist] *royalist*
royaume [rwajom] *m.* *kingdom*
ruban [rybɑ̃] *m.* *ribbon*
rude [ryd] *harsh, rough*
rue [ry] *f.* *street*
rugby [rygbi] *m.* *rugby*
ruine [rɥin] *f.* *ruin*
ruiner [rɥine] *ruin*
Russe [rys] *m.* *Russian*
russe [rys] *Russian*
Russie [rysi] *f.* *Russia*

S

sa [sa] *his, her, its*
sabot [sabo] *m.* *wooden shoe*
sabotage [sabɔtaʒ] *m.* *sabotage; malicious waste or destruction of an employer's property by workmen*
sac [sak] *m.* *sack, knapsack*
sachant, sache [saʃɑ̃, saʃ] (*pres. participle and subjunctive of* savoir) *knowing, know*
Sacré Cœur [sakrekœr] *m.* *Church of the Sacred Heart, located in the Montmartre section of Paris, in Byzantine style*
sagesse [saʒɛs] *f.* *wisdom*
saint [sɛ̃] *sacred, holy*
histoire sainte *sacred history, history of the Bible*
Saint Empire romain *Holy Roman Empire*
Saint-Laurent *St. Lawrence, river in Canada*
Saint-Louis *city of the United States located on Mississippi*
Saint-Malo *picturesque walled city on the coast of Brittany*
Saint-Michel *main boulevard in the Latin Quarter of Paris*
Sainte-Hélène *St. Helena, island in the Atlantic*
sais, sait [se, sɛ] (*pres.* of savoir) *know*
je n'en sais rien *I know nothing about it*
saisir [sezir] *seize*
saison [sɛzɔ̃] *f.* *season*
saisissant [sezisɑ̃] *gripping, thrilling*
salade [salad] *f.* *salad*
saladier [saladje] *m.* *salad bowl*
salaire [salɛr] *m.* *salary*
salle [sal] *f.* *room, large room*
salle à manger *dining-room*
salle de conférence *lecture room*
salle de danse *dance hall*
salon [salɔ̃] *m.* *living-room*
saluer [salɥe] (+ noun) *greet; say "hello" to*
salut [saly] *m.* *safety*
samedi [samdi] *m.* *Saturday*
Samothrace [samɔtras] *island of the Greek Archipelago, near Thrace*
Victoire de Samothrace *famous statue in the Louvre, sometimes called the Winged Victory*
sang [sɑ̃] *m.* *blood*

sanglot [sɑ̃glo] *m.* *sob*
sans [sɑ̃] *without*
sans cesse *without cease*
sans pareil *without equal*
sapin [sapɛ̃] *m.* *pine tree*
sardine [sardin] *f.* *sardine*
saurai [sɔre] (*1st pers. sing. fut. of* savoir) *shall know*
saut [so] *m.* *high jump*
sautiller [sotije] *jump about*
sauvage [sovaʒ] *wild*
sauver [sove] *save*
se sauver *run away, escape, flee*
Sauveur [sovœr] *m.* *Savior*
savant [savɑ̃] *m.* *scientist, scholar*
savoir [savwar] (sachant, su, je sais, je sus) (+ inf.) (§ 94) *know (something); know how*
savon [savɔ̃] *m.* *soap*
scène [sɛn] *f.* *scene*
science [sjɑ̃s] *f.* *science*
scientifique [sjɑ̃tifik] *scientific*
scooter [skutɛr] *m.* *scooter*
scout [skut] *m.* *scout*
sculpture [skyltyr] *f.* *sculpturing*
se [sə] (§ 26 A) *himself, herself, itself, oneself, themselves; each other*
second [səgɔ̃, zgɔ̃] *m.* *second*
secours [səkur] *m.* *help, aid*
secret, secrète [səkrɛ, səkrɛt] *secret*
secrètement [səkrɛtmɑ̃] *secretly*
sécurité [sekyrite] *f.* *security, safety*
Sedan [sədɑ̃] *m.* *city in northeastern France where Napoleon III surrendered in the Franco-Prussian war and where the Germans outflanked the Maginot line in 1940*
seigneur [sɛɲœr] *m.* *lord*
Seine [sɛn] *f.* *Seine*
seize [sɛz] *sixteen*
seizième [sɛzjɛm] *sixteenth*
séjour [seʒur] *m.* *stay, sojourn*
séjourner [seʒurne] *sojourn, reside*
sel [sɛl] *m.* *salt*
selon [səlɔ̃] *according to*
selon le cas *as the case may be, depending on the case, whichever may be needed*
semaine [səmɛn] *f.* *week*
sembler [sɑ̃ble] (+ inf.) *seem*
semestre [səmɛstr] *m.* *semester*
sénat [sena] *m.* *senate*
sénateur [senatœr] *m.* *senator*
sens [sɑ̃s] *m.* *sense, direction*
en tous sens *in every direction*
sensation [sɑ̃sɑsjɔ̃] *f.* *sensation*
sensiblement [sɑ̃sibləmɑ̃] *considerably*
sentiment [sɑ̃timɑ̃] *m.* *sentiment*
sentir [sɑ̃tir] (2) *feel; smell*
se sentir *feel*
séparer [separe] *separate*
se séparer *become separated, be separated*
sept [sɛt] *seven*
septembre [sɛptɑ̃br] *m.* *September*
septième [sɛtjɛm] *seventh*
serai [səre] (*1st pers. sing. fut. of* être) *shall be*
Serbe [sɛrb] *m.* *Serbian*
Serbie [sɛrbi] *f.* *Serbia, country in the Balkan peninsula before World War I, now a part of Yugoslavia*
série [seri] *f.* *series*
fabriquer en série *manufacture in quantity*
sérieusement [serjøzmɑ̃] *seriously*
sérieux, sérieuse [serjø, serjøz] *serious*
sermon [sɛrmɔ̃] *m.* *sermon*
serré [sɛre] *heavy*
serrer [sɛre] *shake; press, squeeze*
se serrer la main *shake hands*
service [sɛrvis] *m.* *service*
servir [sɛrvir] (2) *serve*
servir à (+ inf.) *be used to (for)*
servir de (+ unmodified noun) *serve as*
se servir de *use, make use of*
ses [se] *his, her, its*
seul [sœl] *alone, only, solely, only one; single*
seulement [sœlmɑ̃] *only*
non seulement *not only*
sévère [sevɛr] *severe*
Shakespeare [ʃɛkspir] (*1564–1616*) *great English dramatist*
si [si] *if, whether; so*
si bien que *so that*
s'il vous plaît *please*
s'il y a lieu *if it is necessary*
si [si] (§ 98) *yes*
siècle [sjɛkl] *m.* *century*
siège [sjɛʒ] *m.* *siege; seat*
sien, sienne [sjɛ̃, sjɛn] *his, her, its*
siffler [sifle] *whistle*
signe [siɲ] *m.* *sign*
faire signe *make a sign*

signer [siɲe] *sign*
silence [silɑ̃s] *m.* *silence*
silencieusement [silɑ̃sjøzmɑ̃] *silently*
simple [sɛ̃pl] *simple*
simplement [sɛ̃pləmɑ̃] *simply*
singulier [sɛ̃gylje] *m.* *singular*
situation [sitɥɑsjɔ̃] *f.* *situation*
situé [sitɥe] *situated, located*
six [si, sis, siz] *six*
sixième [sizjɛm] *sixth*
ski [ski] *m.* *skiing*
 faire du ski *go skiing*
social, sociaux [sɔsjal, sɔsjo] *social*
société [sɔsjete] *f.* *society; company, corporation*
 Société d'Agriculture *Agricultural Association*
sœur [sœr] *f.* *sister*
soi [swa] (§ 27) *oneself*
soie [swɑ] *f.* *silk*
soif [swaf] *f.* *thirst*
 avoir soif (§ 90 B) *be thirsty*
soin [swɛ̃] *m.* *care*
soir [swar] *m.* *evening*
 le lendemain soir *the next evening*
soirée [sware] *f.* *evening; party*
 soirée dansante *dance*
sois, soit, soient [swa] (*pres. subjunctive of* être) *be*
soit . . . soit [swa . . . swa] *either . . . or, whether . . . whether*
soixante [swasɑ̃t] *sixty*
 soixante-dix *seventy*
 soixante et onze *seventy-one*
 soixante et un *sixty-one*
sol [sɔl] *m.* *ground, soil*
soldat [sɔlda] *m.* *soldier*
soleil [sɔlɛj] *m.* *sun*
solidement [sɔlidmɑ̃] *solidly*
solitaire [sɔlitɛr] *lonely, solitary*
solennel, solennelle [sɔlanɛl] *solemnly*
solution [sɔlysjɔ̃] *f.* *solution*
sombre [sɔ̃br] *dark, sombre*
somme [sɔm] *f.* *sum*
 en somme *in short*
sommeil [sɔmɛj] *m.* *sleep*
 avoir sommeil (§ 90 B) *be sleepy*
sommes [sɔm] (*1st pers. pl. pres. of* être) *are*
sommet [sɔmɛ] *m.* *summit, top*
son, sa, ses [sɔ̃, sa, se] *his, her, its, one's*
songer [sɔ̃ʒe] (§ 89 B) (à + noun; à + inf.) *think of, dream of*
sonner [sɔne] *sound, ring*
 l'heure sonne *the clock strikes*
sont [sɔ̃] (*3d pers. pl. pres of* être) *are*
Sorbonne [sɔrbɔn] *f.* *College of Arts and College of Sciences of the University of Paris*
sorte [sɔrt] *f.* *sort, kind*
 de sorte que *so that*
sortir [sɔrtir] (2) (§ 94) *go out, leave*
souci [susi] *m.* *care*
soudain [sudɛ̃] *suddenly*
se soulever [sulve] *revolt, rise up in insurrection*
soulier [sulje] *m.* *shoe*
soulignez [suliɲe] *imperative of* souligner *underline*
soumettre [sumɛtr] (soumettant, soumis, je soumets, je soumis) (*conj. like* mettre) *submit*
soupçonner [supsɔne] *suspect*
soupe [sup] *f.* *soup*
source [surs] *f.* *source*
sourd [sur] *deaf*
 sourd-muet *deaf-mute;* (adj.) *deaf and dumb*
sourire [surir] (souriant, souri, je souris, je souris) (*conj. like* rire) *smile*
sourire [surir] *m.* *smile*
sous [su] *under*
soutenir [sutnir] (soutenant, soutenu, je soutiens, je soutins) (*conj. like* tenir) *support*
souterrain [sutɛrɛ̃] *underground*
souvenir [suvnir] *m.* *souvenir, remembrance*
 en souvenir de *in memory of*
se souvenir [suvnir] (se souvenant, souvenu, je me souviens, je me souvins) (*conj. like* venir) (de + noun; de + inf.) *remember*
souvent [suvɑ̃] *often*
spécial, spéciaux [spesjal, spesjo] *special*
spécialement [spesjalmɑ̃] *especially*
se spécialiser [spesjalize] *specialize*
spécialiste [spesjalist] *m.* *specialist*
spectacle [spɛktakl] *m.* *spectacle, sights*
spectateur [spɛktatœr] *m.* *spectator*
splendeur [splɑ̃dœr] *f.* *splendor*
splendide [splɑ̃did] *splendid*

sport [spɔr] *m.* *sport*
faire du sport *participate in sports*
sportif, sportive [spɔrtif, spɔrtiv] *sports-loving, inclined to sports,* (adj.)
station [stɑsjõ] *f.* *station*
statue [staty] *f.* *statue*
stérilisation [sterilizɑsjõ] *f.* *sterilization*
Strasbourg [strasbur] *m.* *principal city of Alsace*
structure [stryktyr] *f.* *structure*
studio [stydjo] *m.* (*radio, television*) *studio*
style [stil] *m.* *style*
stylo [stilo] (*abbr. for* stylographe) *m.* *fountain pen*
su, sus [sy] (*pp and sp of* savoir) *knew, learned*
subir [sybir] *undergo*
subjonctif [sybʒõktif] *m.* *subjunctive*
subsister [sybziste] *stand, exist, continue to exist*
substance [sypstɑ̃s] *f.* *substance*
substituer [sypstitɥe] *substitute*
subventionner [sybvɑ̃sjɔne] *subsidize*
succès [syksɛ] *m.* *success*
sud [syd] *m.* *south,* (*also adj.*)
sud-est *southeast*
sud-ouest *southwest*
Suède [sɥɛd] *f.* *Sweden*
Suédoise [sɥedwaz] *f.* *Swedish girl, Swedish woman*
Suez, canal de [sɥɛz] *m.* *Suez Canal*
suffire [syfir] (suffisant, suffi, je suffis, je suffis) *suffice*
suffisamment [syfizamɑ̃] *sufficiently*
suffisamment de *enough*
suffisant [syfizɑ̃] *sufficient*
suffocant [syfɔkɑ̃] *stifling*
suffrage [syfraʒ] *m.* *suffrage*
au suffrage indirect *by indirect suffrage*
se suicider [sɥiside] *commit suicide*
suis [sɥi] (*1st pers. sing. pres. of* être) *am*
suis [sɥi] (*1st pers. sing. pres. of* suivre) *follow*
Suisse [sɥis] *f.* *Switzerland*
suisse [sɥis] *Swiss*
suite [sɥit] *f.* *continuation; aftermath, consequence; suite*
à la suite de *after*
tout de suite *immediately*
suivant [sɥivɑ̃] *following*
suivez [sɥive] (*imperative of* suivre] *follow*
suivre [sɥivr] (suivant, suivi, je suis, je suivis) *follow*
à suivre *to be continued*
suivre un cours *take a course*
sujet [syʒɛ] *m.* *subject*
à ce sujet *on this subject*
superbe [sypɛrb] *superb*
supérieur [syperjœr] *superior, upper*
les études supérieures *advanced studies*
superlatif, superlative [sypɛrlatif, sypɛrlativ] *superlative*
supplémentaire [syplemɑ̃tɛr] *supplementary*
supprimer [syprime] *suppress; omit*
suprématie [sypremasi] *f.* *supremacy*
sur [syr] *on, over, above; about, concerning*
sûr [syr] *sure, certain, safe*
sûrement [syrmɑ̃] *surely*
surpris [syrpri] (*pp of* surprendre) *surprised*
surprise [syrpriz] *f.* *surprise*
surtout [syrtu] *especially, above all*
surveiller [syrveje] *watch, superintend*
survivre [syrvivr] (survivant, survécu, je survis, je survécus) (*conj. like* vivre) *survive*
suspect [syspɛ] *m.* *suspect*
Suzanne [syzan] *f.* *Susan*
symbole [sɛ̃bɔl] *m.* *symbol*
symétrie [simetri] *f.* *symmetry*
symétrique [simetrik] *symmetrical*
symptôme [sɛ̃ptom] *m.* *symptom*
système [sistɛm] *m.* *system*

T

ta [ta] *your*
tabac [taba] *m.* *tobacco*
table [tabl] *f.* *table*
à table *at the table*
se mettre à table *sit down at the table*
table de travail *work-table*
tableau [tablo] *m.* *picture, painting; blackboard*
tableau noir *blackboard*
tache [taʃ] *f.* *blemish, stain*
tâcher [tɑʃe] (de + inf.) *try*

taille [taj] *f.* *size, shape, height*
se taire [tɛr] (se taisant, tu, je me tais, je me tus) (*conj. like* plaire[1]) *be silent*
taisez-vous *keep still*
tandis que [tɑ̃dikə, tɑ̃diskə] *while (on the other hand)*
tant [tɑ̃] *so much, as much, so many, as many*
tant de *so much, as much, so many, as many*
tant que *as long as*
tant . . . que *as much . . . as*
tante [tɑ̃t] *f.* *aunt*
tantôt . . . tantôt [tɑ̃to . . . tɑ̃to] *now . . . now, sometimes . . . other times*
tapisserie [tapisri] *f.* *tapestry*
tard [tar] *late*
tarder [tarde] (à + inf.) *delay, put off*
tarif [tarif] *m.* *rate*
à tarif réduit *at a reduced rate*
tasse [tɑs] *f.* *cup*
taxi [taksi] *m.* *taxicab, taxi*
Tchécoslovaquie [tʃekɔslɔvaki] *f.* *Czechoslovakia, country created by the Treaty of Versailles*
te [tə] *to you, you*
tel, telle [tɛl] *such*
tel que *such as*
télégramme [telegram] *m.* *telegram*
télégraphe [telegraf] *m.* *telegraph*
téléphone [telefɔn] *m.* *telephone*
donner un coup de téléphone *give a "ring," telephone to*
téléphoner [telefɔne] (à + person + de + inf.) *telephone*
télévision [televizjɔ̃] *f.* *television*
tellement [tɛlmɑ̃] *so; so much*
témoin [temwɛ̃] *m.* *witness*
temple [tɑ̃pl] *m.* *temple; church*
temps [tɑ̃] *m.* *time; weather; tense*
de temps en temps *from time to time*
en même temps *at the same time*
temps primitif *principal part (of a verb)*
tout le temps *all the time, all the while*
tendance [tɑ̃dɑ̃s] *f.* *tendency*
tendre [tɑ̃dr] *extend*
tenir [tənir] (tenant, tenu, je tiens, je tins) *hold*
tenir à (+ noun) *depend on; be due to*
tenir à (+ inf.) *insist on*
j'y tiens *I insist on it*
se tenir *be, stand*
tennis [tenis] *m.* *tennis*
tenter [tɑ̃te] *attempt, try*
terminaison [tɛrminɛzɔ̃] *f.* *ending (of a word)*
terminer [tɛrmine] *finish, end*
se terminer *finish, end*
terrain [tɛrɛ̃] *m.* *tract of land, field*
terrasse [tɛras] *f.* *outdoor part of café, chairs and tables (of a café) set out on sidewalk*
terre [tɛr] *f.* *land, territory, earth*
Terreur [tɛrœr] *f.* *Reign of Terror, the period of the Revolution which began in 1793 and ended 1794, marked by numerous executions under the direction of the Committee of Public Safety*
territoire [tɛritwar] *m.* *territory*
territorial [tɛritɔrjal] *territorial*
tes [te] *your*
tête [tɛt] *f.* *head*
avoir mal à la tête *have a headache*
Texas [tɛksɑs] *m.* *largest state in the United States except Alaska*
texte [tɛkst] *m.* *text; excerpt*
thé [te] *m.* *tea*
théâtre [teɑtr] *m.* *theater; (collection of) plays*
pièce de théâtre *play*
Théâtre-Français *French National Theatre on the right bank of the Seine, also called* la Comédie Française
Théâtre de France *French national theater established in 1959 and housed on the left bank of the Seine in the former Odéon*
Théâtre National Populaire *theater held in the* Palais de Chaillot, *located at the* Place du Trocadéro
théologie [teɔlɔʒi] *f.* *theology*
théorie [teɔri] *f.* *theory*
Thérèse [terɛz] *f.* *Theresa*
tiers [tjɛr] *m.* *third*
Tiers-Etat *Third Estate, the common*

[1] Conjugated like *plaire* except that the 3d pers. sing. pres. ind. is *il tait.*

people of France, the class which was neither the nobility nor the clergy
timbre [tɛ̃br] *m.* *stamp*
tiret [tirɛ] *m.* *blank, dash*
tissu [tisy] *m.* *fabric*
toi [twa] *you, to you*
toit [twɑ] *m.* *roof*
tolérer [tɔlere] *tolerate*
tomate [tɔmat] *f.* *tomato*
tombeau [tõbo] *m.* *tomb*
tomber [tõbe] *fall*
  laisser tomber *drop*
ton [tõ] *m.* *tone*
  donner le ton *set the pace*
ton, ta, tes [tõ, ta, te] *your*
tort [tɔr] *wrong*
  avoir tort (§ 90 B) *be wrong*
torture [tɔrtyr] *f.* *torture*
tôt [to] *soon, quickly, early*
total [tɔtal] *total*
toucher [tuʃe] *touch; receive (money)*
toujours [tuʒur] *always*
Toulouse [tuluz] *city in southern France characterized by its brick structures*
tour [tur] *m.* *turn*
  à son tour *in his turn*
  Tour de France *annual bicycle race across France*
tour [tur] *f.* *tower*
  Tour Eiffel *steel structure on the left bank of the Seine in Paris, erected by Eiffel for the Exposition of 1889*
Touraine [turɛn] *f.* *small province southwest of Paris*
touriste [turist] *m. f.* *tourist*
touristique [turistik] *tourist* (adj.)
tourner [turne] *turn*
  se tourner *turn (around)*
Tours [tur] *m.* *capital of Touraine*
tous [tus] (pron.) *everyone*
tous [tu] (adj.) *all*
  tous les combien *how often*
  tous les deux *both*
  tous les jours *every day*
  tous les trois *all three*
tout [tu] (pron.) *everything*
  pas du tout *not at all*
tout, toute, tous, toutes [tu, tut, tu, tut] (adj.) *all, every, whole*
  à toute vitesse *rapidly, at full speed*
  en tout cas *in any case*
  tout le monde *everyone, everybody*
  toutes les heures *every hour*
  tous les jours *every day*
tout [tu] (adv.) *quite, very (see* § 11 F, *for agreement)*
  à tout à l'heure *until later, "so long"*
  tout à coup *suddenly*
  tout à fait *entirely, completely*
  tout à l'heure *a little while ago; in a little while*
  tout de même *all the same*
  tout de suite *immediately*
  tout le long *all along*
  tout près *right near, near by*
trace [tras] *f.* *trace*
tradition [tradisjõ] *f.* *tradition*
  la tradition veut que *tradition decrees that*
traditionnel, traditionnelle [tradisjɔnɛl] *traditional*
traduire [tradɥir] (traduisant, traduit, je traduis, je traduisis) (*conj. like* conduire) *translate*
traduisez [tradɥize] (*imperative of* traduire) *translate*
tragique [traʒik] *tragic*
train [trɛ̃] *m.* *train*
  monter dans le train *get on the train*
  train de vie *pace of life*
traîner [trene] *pull, drag*
trait d'union [trɛdynjõ] *m.* *hyphen*
traité [trete] *m.* *treaty*
  Traité de Versailles *Treaty of Versailles (1919), establishing the conditions of peace after World War I*
traitement [trɛtmɑ̃] *m.* *treatment; salary*
traiter [trete] *treat; deal with*
tranquille [trɑ̃kil] *quiet, calm*
transformer [trɑ̃sfɔrme] *transform*
  se transformer *transform oneself, change*
transmission [trɑ̃smisjõ] *f.* *broadcast, transmission*
transport [trɑ̃spɔr] *m.* *transportation*
transporter [trɑ̃spɔrte] *transport*
travail [travaj] *m.* *work*
travailler [travaje] *work*
  travailler un cours *work on a course*

travailleur [travajœr] *m.* *worker*
travaux [travo] *m.* (*pl.* *of* travail) *works*
travers, à [atravɛr] *across, through*
traverser [travɛrse] *cross*
treize [trɛz] *thirteen*
treizième [trɛzjɛm] *thirteenth*
trentaine [trɑ̃tɛn] *f.* *about thirty*
trente [trɑ̃t] *thirty*
trente-deux *thirty-two*
trente et un *thirty-one*
très [trɛ] *very*
trésor [trezɔr] *m.* *treasury*
tressaillir [tresajir] *tremble*
Trianon, le Grand [ləgrɑ̃trijanõ] *small castle at Versailles, built by Louis XIV in 1687*
Trianon, le Petit [ləptitrijanõ] *small castle at Versailles, built under Louis XV and later occupied by Marie Antoinette*
tribu [triby] *f.* *tribe*
tribut [triby] *m.* *tribute*
triomphe [trijõf] *m.* *triumph*
l'arc de triomphe *triumphal arch*
triste [trist] *sad*
tristesse [tristɛs] *f.* *sadness*
trois [trwɑ] *three*
troisième [trwɑzjɛm] *third*
tronc [trõ] *m.* *trunk*
trône [tron] *m.* *throne*
monter sur le trône *ascend the throne*
trop [tro] (de + noun) *too much, too many, too*
trottoir [trɔtwar] *m.* *sidewalk*
troubadour [trubadur] *m.* *troubadour, minstrel of southern France during the Middle Ages*
trouble [trubl] *m.* *confusion, disorder, turmoil, uneasiness;* (*pl.*) *disturbances* (*much stronger than English* trouble)
troubler [truble] *trouble*
troupe [trup] *f.* *troop*
troupeau [trupo] *m.* *flock, herd*
trouver [truve] *find*
se trouver *be found, be located, be*
tu [ty] (§ 23 B) *you*
tuer [tɥe] *kill, slay*
Tuileries [tɥilri] *f. pl.* *garden situated in Paris between* Place de la Concorde *and the* Louvre, *formerly the site of a royal palace*
typique [tipik] *typical*
typiquement [tipikmɑ̃] *typically*

U

un, une [œ̃, yn] *a, an; one*
l'un l'autre (§ 26 B) *each other*
un à un *one by one*
unification [ynifikɑsjõ] *f.* *unification*
unifier [ynifje] *unite*
s'unifier *unite, become united*
union [ynjõ] *f.* *union*
Union française *f.* *name indicating European France and French territories abroad which was used during the Fourth Republic 1946–58) and which was replaced during the Fifth Republic by the term* Communauté française.
uniquement [ynikmɑ̃] *only, solely*
unir [unir] *unite*
s'unir *unite*
universitaire [ynivɛrsitɛr] *pertaining to the university*
Cité Universitaire *student dormitories situated on the Boulevard Jourdan at the southern extremity of Paris*
université [ynivɛrsite] *f.* *university*
Université de Paris *University of Paris*
usage [yzaʒ] *m.* *custom, practice, usage*
d'un usage courant *widespread*
d'usage *customary*
usine [yzin] *f.* *factory*
usuel, usuelle [yzɥɛl] *usual, common*
utile [ytil] *useful*
utiliser [ytilize] *use, make use of, utilize, employ*

V

va, vas [va] (*pres. of* aller) *goes, go, is going*
Ça va bien *I'm fine*
Comment ça va? *How are you?*
vacances [vakɑ̃s] *f. pl.* *vacation*
en vacances *on a vacation*
les grandes vacances *long vacation, summer vacation*
vaccin [vaksɛ̃] *m.* *vaccine*
vacciner [vaksine] *vaccinate*
vache [vaʃ] *f.* *cow*
vague [vag] *vague, hazy*
vaincre [vɛ̃kr] (vainquant, vaincu, je

vaincs, je vainquis) *conquer, vanquish*
vaincu [vɛ̃ky] (*pp of* vaincre) *conquered, vanquished*
vais [ve, vɛ] (*1st pers. sing. pres. of* aller) *go, am going*
valeur [valœr] *f. value, worth*
valise [valiz] *f. valise, suitcase*
vallée [vale] *f. valley*
valoir [valwar] (valant, valu, je vaux, je valus) *be worth*
valoir la peine (de + inf.) *be worth the trouble*
valoir mieux (+ inf.) *be better*
varié [varje] *varied*
variété [varjete] *f. variety; feature (on radio program)*
vaste [vast] *vast, wide, spacious*
vaudra, vaudrait [vodra, vodrɛ] (*fut. and cond. of* valoir) *will, would be better*
vaut [vo] (valoir) *is worth*
il vaut la peine (de + inf.) *it is worth while, it is worth the trouble*
il vaut mieux (+ inf.) *it is better*
vécu, vécus [veky] (*pp and sp of* vivre) *lived*
végétal [veʒetal] *vegetable* (adj.)
véhicule [veikyl] *m. vehicle*
veille [vɛj] *f. eve, day before*
veiller [veje] *watch over*
veine [vɛn] *f. vein*
en veine d'inspiration *in a moment of inspiration*
vendange [vɑ̃dɑ̃ʒ] *f. grape-gathering season*
vendangeur [vɑ̃dɑ̃ʒœr] *m. grape-gatherer*
vendeuse [vɑ̃døz] *f. saleswoman; clerk*
vendre [vɑ̃dr] *sell*
vendredi [vɑ̃drədi] *m. Friday*
venir [vənir] (venant, venu, je viens, je vins) (+ inf.) *come*
venir de *have just* (il vient d'arriver *he has just arrived*)
vent [vɑ̃] *m. wind*
il y a beaucoup de vent *it is very windy*
venu [vəny] (*pp of* venir) *come*
nouveau venu *newcomer*
Vénus de Milo [venysdəmilo] *f. famous statue in the Louvre*
verbe [vɛrb] *m. verb*
verbe pronominal *reflexive verb*
véritable [veritabl] *veritable, true*
Verlaine, Paul [vɛrlɛn] (*1844*–96) *French poet, one of the chief members of the symbolistic school*
verrai [vɛre] (*1st pers. sing. fut. of* voir) *shall see*
vers [vɛr] *m. verse; line of poetry*
vers [vɛr] *toward; about (of time)*
Versailles [vɛrsɑj] *city some eighteen kilometers southwest of Paris, noted for its château*
vert [vɛr] *green*
vestige [vɛstiʒ] *m. vestige, trace*
vêtement [vɛtmɑ̃] *m. dress, garment; pl. clothing*
veto [veto] *m. veto*
veuillez [vœje] (*imperative of* vouloir) *please*
veux, veut, veulent [vø, vœl] (*pres. of* vouloir) *wish, wishes*
viande [vjɑ̃d] *f. meat*
Vichy [viʃi] *thermal city in the* Massif Central *which was the seat of government of the* zone libre *during the* occupation *of France by the Germans*
victime [viktim] *f. victim*
victoire [viktwar] *f. victory*
remporter la victoire *win the victory*
Victor [viktɔr] *m. Victor*
victorieux, victorieuse [viktɔrjø, viktɔrjøz] *victorious*
vide [vid] *empty*
vider [vide] *empty*
se vider *become empty*
vie [vi] *f. life*
à vie *for life*
niveau de vie *standard of living*
vieil, vieille [vjɛj] (§ 10G) *old*
vieillard [vjɛjar] *m. old man, old people*
viendrai [vjɛ̃dre] (*1st pers. sing. fut. of* venir) *shall come*
viens, vient, viennent [vjɛ̃, vjɛn] (*pres. of* venir) *come, comes*
vieux [vjø] (§ 10 G) *old;* (noun) *m. old person*
mon vieux *"old fellow," "old chap," "old top," used familiarly between friends, even school children*
vif, vive [vif, viv] *lively*

village [vilaʒ] *m.* *village*
ville [vil] *f.* *city, town*
de ville en ville *from city to city*
vin [vɛ̃] m. *wine*
vinaigre [vinɛgr] *m.* *vinegar*
Vinci, Léonard de [leɔnardəvɛ̃si] (1452–1519) *Leonardo da Vinci, celebrated painter of the Italian Renaissance*
vingt [vɛ̃] *twenty*
vingt et un *twenty-one*
violant [vjɔlɑ̃] *violent*
violer [vjɔle] *violate*
violon [vjɔlɔ̃] *m.* *violin*
vis, vit [vi] (*pres. of* vivre) *live, lives*
vis, vit [vi] (*sp of* voir) *saw*
visage [vizaʒ] *m.* *face*
visite [vizit] *f.* *visit*
faire une visite (§ 94) *visit, pay a visit* (*used with persons*)
rendre visite (§ 94) *visit, pay a visit* (*used with persons*)
visiter [vizite] (§ 94) *visit* (*a town, place, etc.*) (*not used with persons*)
visiteur [vizitœr] *m.* *visitor*
vite [vit] *fast, quickly*
vitesse [vitɛs] *f.* *speed*
à toute vitesse *at top speed, at high speed*
vitrail [vitraj] *m.* *stained-glass window*
vitraux [vitro] *m. pl.* *stained-glass windows*
vitrine [vitrin] *f.* *show-window*
vivant [vivɑ̃] *vivid, life-like*
langue vivante *modern language*
vivement [vivmɑ̃] *deeply, acutely*
vivre [vivr] (vivant, vécu, je vis, je vécus) (§ 94) *live*
vocabulaire [vɔkabylɛr] *m.* *vocabulary, word-list*
vœu [vø] *m.* *wish, greeting*
voici [vwasi] (§ 91 B) *here is, here are*
voie [vwɑ] *f.* *route, way; means*
voilà [vwala] (§ 91 B) *there is, there are*
voir [vwar] (voyant, vu, je vois, je vis) (+ inf.) *see*
pour voir ce que cela donne *to see what that looks like*
voisin, voisine [vwazɛ̃, vwazin] *m. f.* *neighbor;* (adj.) *neighboring*

voiture [vwatyr] *f.* *car* (*the ordinary word used to designate an automobile*); *carriage, coach*
conduire une voiture *drive a car*
voix [vwɑ] *f.* *voice*
à haute voix *aloud, in a loud voice*
à voix basse *softly, in a low voice, in a whisper*
voler [vɔle] *fly; steal*
Volga [vɔlga] *f.* *river in Russia*
volontiers [vɔlɔ̃tje] *willingly*
Voltaire [vɔltɛr] (1694–1778) *eighteenth century writer of philosophical novels, essays, poems, and plays*
vont [vɔ̃] (*3d pers. pl. of* aller) *go*
vos [vo] *your*
Vosges [voʒ] *f. pl.* *chain of mountains in eastern France*
voter [vɔte] *vote; pass* (*a law*)
votre [vɔtr] *your*
vôtre [votr] *yours*
voudrai [vudre] (*1st pers. sing. fut. of* vouloir) *shall wish, shall want*
voudrais, voudrait [vudrɛ] (*cond. of* vouloir) *would like*
vouloir [vulwar] (voulant, voulu, je veux, je voulus) (+ inf.) *wish, want, be willing*
la tradition veut que *tradition decrees that*
vouloir bien *be willing*
vouloir dire *mean*
vous [vu] *you*
voûté [vute] *vaulted, arched*
voyage [vwajaʒ] *m.* *trip, voyage* (*referring to travel by land as well as by sea*); *traveling*
faire un voyage *travel, take a trip*
voyage d'affaires *business trip*
voyager [vwajaʒe] (§ 89 B) *travel, take a trip*
voyageur [vwajaʒœr] *m.* *traveler*
voyelle [vwajɛl] *f.* *vowel*
voyons [vwajɔ̃] *look here! let's see*
vrai [vrɛ] *true, real*
vraiment [vrɛmɑ̃] *truly, really*
vu [vy] (*pp. of* voir) *seen*
vue [vy] *f.* *sight, view*

à perte de vue *as far as the eye can reach*

W

wagon [vagõ] *m.* *(train) coach*
wagon-restaurant [vagõrɛstɔrɑ̃] *m.* *diner, dining-car*
Waterloo [vatɛrlo] *Belgian village, site of the famous battle at which Napoleon was defeated by the combined armies of the English and Prussians on June 18, 1815*
Watteau [vato] *(1684–1721) eighteenth-century French painter, noted especially for his* l'Embarquement pour Cythère
week-end [wikɛnd] *m.* *week end*

Y

y [i] (§ 29) *there, in it*
il y a (§ 91 A) *there is, there are*
yeux [jø] *m.* *(pl. of* œil*) eyes*
Yves [iv] *m.* *boy's name*
Yvetot [ivto] *small town in Normandy*
Yvonne [ivɔn] *f.* *girl's name*

Z

zone [zon] *f.* *zone*

INDEX

References without any sign refer to pages.
References preceded by § refer to sections in the *Grammaire* (pages 367–509).
References preceded by L refer to lessons.
Regular and irregular verbs are conjugated in § 95 (pages 482–99).

A

à
  à + *de* verbs § 46 E, L 44, L 58
  characteristic 310, note 1
  contractions § 2 B, L 3, L 7
  + places § 42 A, C, D, L 39, L 52
  possession § 32 D, L 48
  verb + *à* + infinitive § 44 D, L 41, L 43, L 58
accent marks 512
accentuation (stress) 515–16
adjectives §§ 9–18
  adjectival *de* + noun § 6 E, L 29
  agreement § 9, L 2, L 9, L 16, L 51
  beau, nouveau, vieux, etc. § 10 G, L 35
  comparison § 13, L 5, L 51
  de + adjective + noun § 6 A, L 10, L 44, L 52
  demonstrative § 15, L 8, L 18, L 59
  feminine § 10, L 2, L 4, L 9, L 16, L 35, L 51
  interrogative § 16, L 16, L 59
  irregular §§ 10 C–H, 11 B–E, L 9, L 16, L 35, L 51
  nationality 412, note 3, 513, § 4 H, L 36
  as noun § 11 G
  numerals §§ 17–18, L 12, L 15, L 18, L 20, L 36
  plural § 11, L 3, L 9, L 16, L 35, L 51
  position § 12, L 7, L 9, L 35, L 51
  possessive § 14, L 12, L 56
adverbs §§ 19–22, L 39–40, L 50, L 56–57
  aussi (as) § 13 F, L 9; (therefore) § 20 E, L 50, L 57
  comparison § 21
  formation § 19, L 39
  mieux 506, § 21 B, L 27
  negative § 22, L 6, L 40, L 56
  peut-être § 20 E, L 50, L 57
  position § 20, L 50, L 57
  quantity § 6 B, L 10, L 44, L 52
  tout § 11 F
age § 90 A, L 12
agent, after passive § 87 C, L 42
ago § 91 A, L 39
agreement
  adjectives § 9, L 2, L 9, L 16, L 51
  past participles (adjective) § 76 B; (verb) § 77, L 25–27, L 55; (passive) § 86 C, L 42
  possessive adjectives § 14 B, L 12, L 56
  possessive pronouns § 32 C, L 48. L 56
  present participles § 74 C, L 34, L 53
  tout (adverb) § 11 F
alphabet 511
an, année 509, L 16
appositive § 4 E, L 9, L 52
après + infinitive § 78 B, L 34, L 53
après que 506, § 69, L 43
article §§ 1–6
  contractions § 2, L 3, L 7
  definite §§ 1–2, 4, L 1, L 3, L 52
  dont + article § 39 E, L 33
  elision 514, § 1 A, L 1
  indefinite §§ 3–4, L 2–3, L 52
  partitive §§ 5–6, L 9–10, L 44, L 52
  use and omission § 4; (countries) L 1, (appositive, general sense) L 9, (languages) L 11, (days of week) L 12, (parts of body) L 14, L 30, (profession) L 36, (all) L 52
as ... as § 13 F, L 9
aspirate *h* 511–12, L 5
asseoir, s'asseoir 159, 488–89
at § 42 D, F, L 21, L 39, L 52

aucun § 22 E, F 5, L 40, L 56
aussi (therefore) § 20 E, L 50, L 57
aussi . . . que § 13 F, L 9
auxiliaries §§ 61, 86 A, B, L 23–27, L 42, L 55
  avoir § 61 B, L 23–24, L 55
  être (verbs of motion) § 61 C, D, L 26, L 55; (reflexives) § 61 E, L 27, L 55; (passive) § 86 A, B, L 42
avant de + infinitive 506, § 78 B, L 34, L 53
avant que + subjunctive 506, § 83 H, L 49, L 60
avec (phrase of manner) § 5 E
avoir
  age § 90 A, L 12
  auxiliary § 61 B, L 23–24, L 55
  conjugation 486–87
  expressions with § 90 B, L 39
-ayer verbs § 89 C, L 32, L 56

B

beau, bel, belle § 10 G, L 35
because 506, L 27
believing, verbs of § 83 G, L 50, L 60
before 506, §§ 78 B, 83 H, L 34, L 49, L 53, L 60
better 506, §§ 13 E, 21 B, L 27
bien (comparison) § 22 B
bien des 373, note 3 (1), L 44, L 52
body, parts of § 4 G, L 14, L 30
bon
  comparison § 13 E, L 27
  feminine § 10 H, L 9
by (agent) § 87 C, L 42

C

ça § 34 A, L 37
capitalization 513
cardinal numbers § 17, L 12, L 18, L 20
causative (have something done) § 92 A, L 42
ce (pronoun) §§ 35–37, L 15, L 36, L 44, L 59
ce, cet, cette, ces § 15, L 8, L 18, L 59
ce qui, ce que § 39 G, L 32–33, L 56
ceci, cela § 34, L 37, L 59
cedilla 512
celui, celle, ceux, celles §§ 33, 34 D, L 30, L 37, L 59
cent § 17 D–F, L 20
-cer verbs § 89 A, L 11, L 28, L 41, L 56
c'est, il est §§ 35–37, L 15, L 36, L 44, L 59
chez § 42 F, L 21
-ci, -là
  after demonstrative pronouns § 33 C, L 30
  after nouns § 15 B, C, L 18
cities
  at, in, to § 42 A, L 39, L 52
  gender § 7 B 4 c
comma 513
commands § 79, L 13, L 32, L 35, L 53
comparison
  adjectives § 13, L 5, L 51
  adverbs § 21
  of equality § 13 F, L 9
compound past §§ 53, 61–63, L 23–29, L 55, Review 11 (349–51)
  auxiliaries § 61
  formation § 61, L 23–27
  intransitive verbs of motion § 61 C, D, L 26, L 55
  reflexive verbs § 61 E, L 27, L 55
  transitive verbs § 61 B, L 23–24, L 55
  use §§ 53, 63, L 23, L 28–29, L 55
  word order § 62, L 24
compound subjects and objects § 27 B 2, L 15
compound tenses (also see names of tenses) §§ 60–71, 82, 84 B, D
  auxiliaries § 61
  definition § 60, L 23
  subjunctive §§ 82, 84 B, D, L 47, L 60
conditional §§ 56–57, L 38, L 57
conditional sentences § 72, L 45, L 57
conjugations § 95
  irregular verbs 486–98
  orthographical changing verbs § 89
  regular verbs 482–86
connaître, savoir 478, L 24, L 51
consonants 511, 528–32, 539–40
continents §§ 4 C, 7 B 4 b, L 2, L 52
contractions of article § 2, L 3, L 7
counting §§ 17–18, L 12, L 15, L 18, L 20, L 36
contrary-to-fact conditions § 72 B, C, L 45, L 57
countries
  articles § 4 C, L 1, L 51

from § 43, L 39, L 52
gender § B 4 a, L 2, L 39, L 51
in, to § 42 A, B, C, E, L 2, L 39, L 52

D

dans + place § 42 E
dates
how to read years § 17 F, L 20
pronunciation of day of month § 17 B
writing day of month § 18 E
days of week
article § 4 D, L 12, L 52
capitalization 504, note 1, 513
gender § 7 B 3
list § 97 A, L 12
de
+ adjective + noun § 6A, L 10, L 44, L 52
adjectival *de* + noun § 6 E, L 29
contractions § 2 A, L 3, L 7
from + place § 43, L 39, L 52
in after superlative § 13 D, L 5, L 51
million + *de* § 17 G
partitive (instead of) § 6, L 10, L 44, L 52; (part of) § 5 A, L 9, L 52
passive + *de* § 87 C, L 42
possession § 41
+ relative pronoun = *dont* § 39 E, L 33, L 56
than after comparative § 13 B, L 5, L 51
verb + *de* + infinitive § 44 C, L 41, L 43, L 58
use with or without article § 4 C 2
definite article §§ 1–2, 4
contractions § 2, L 3, L 7
ni . . . ni §§ 5 D, 22 E, L 40, L 44, L 56
plural § 1 B, L 3
singular § 1 A, L 1
+ superlative § 13 A, L 5, L 51
use and omission § 4, (countries) L 1, (appositive, general sense) L 9, (languages) L 11, (days of week) L 12, (parts of body) L 14, L 30, (profession) L 36, (all) L 52
demi § 97 E, L 17
demonstrative adjectives
forms § 15 A, L 8, L 59
with *-ci* and *-là* § 15 B, C, L 18, L 59
demonstrative pronouns
ce §§ 35–37, L 15, L 36, L 44, L 59
ceci, cela § 34, L 37, L 59
celui, celle, ceux, celles §§ 33, 34 D, L 30, L 37, L 59
former, latter § 33 D, L 30
with *-ci* and *-là* § 33 C, L 30
depuis
+ imperfect § 52 D, L 43
+ present 507, § 50 B, L 33, L 53
dernier + subjunctive § 83 B, L 48, L 60
dès que
+ future § 55 B, L 31, L 57
+ past anterior § 69 A, L 43
deuxième, second § 18 C
devoir
conjugation 490–91
meanings § 93, L 38, L 56
diaeresis 513
diphthongs (vowel combinations) 526–27
direct object pronouns §§ 24, 30–31; L 13, L 18, L 21, L 25, L 32, L 54
list and use § 24
order § 31
position § 30
+ *voici, voilà* § 91 C
disjunctive pronouns § 27, L 15, L 54
division of words into syllables 514–15
dont § 39 E, L 33, L 56

E

each other § 26 B, L 31
-e-er verbs § 89 D, L 22, L 56
-é-er verbs § 89 E, L 30, L 56
-eler, -eter verbs § 89 F, L 22, L 56
elision 514
en
agreement of past participle with § 28 D, L 25
+ place § 42 A, B, L 2, L 39, L 52
+ present participle § 74 B, L 34, L 53
pronoun (use) § 28, (position) § 30, (order) § 31; L 21, L 54
+ seasons § 97 C, L 15
enumerations, omission of article § 4 I
-er verbs
conjugation 482–83
orthographical changes § 89, L 11, L 22, L 30, L 32, L 56
present § 49 A, L 11
enchaînement 521
errors, favorite 541–46
est-ce que § 96 A, L 2, L 11

être
auxiliary (verbs of motion) § 61 C, D, L 26, L 55; (reflexives) § 61 E, L 27, L 55
c'est, il est, etc. §§ 35–37, L 15, L 36, L 44, L 59
conjugation 486–87
passive § 86 A, B, L 42
possession with *à* § 32 D, L 48
quel est, etc. § 16 E, D, L 16, L 59

F

faire
causative § 92 A, L 42
conjugation 492–93
weather § 92 B, L 15
favorite mistakes 541–46
feminine of adjectives § 10, L 2, L 4, L 9, L 16, L 35, L 51
feminine noun endings § 7 B, L 7, L 45, L 51
former, latter § 33 D, L 30
from + place § 43, L 39, L 52
future §§ 54–55, L 31, L 57
conditions § 72 A, B, C, L 45, L 57
formation § 54 A
irregular § 54 B
present used to express future § 50 C
use § 55
future perfect (also called *futur antérieur*) §§ 66–67, L 57

G

gender § 7, L 1, L 7, L 45, L 51
general sense, noun taken in § 4 B, L 9, L 52
-ger verbs § 89 B, L 11, L 28, L 41, L 56

H

h 511
harmonisation vocalique 537
have something done (causative) § 92 A, L 42
hyphen 512

I

il est, c'est §§ 35–37, L 15, L 36, L 44, L 59
il y a
ago § 91 A, L 39
existence § 91 A, L 8
il y a . . . que + present § 50 B, L 33, L 53
voilà § 91 B, L 18
il y avait . . . que + imperfect § 53 D, L 43
imperative § 79
affirmative § 30 B, L 32, L 54
intonation 520
nous § 79 B, L 35, L 53
pronoun objects § 30 B, L 32, L 54
reflexive verbs § 79 D, L 35, L 53
vous § 79 A, L 13, L 35, L 53
imperfect indicative §§ 51–53, L 28–29, L 55, Review 11 (349–51)
conditions § 72 B, L 45, L 57
depuis, il y avait . . . que § 52 D, L 43
formation § 51, L 28
use §§ 52–53, L 28–29, L 55, Review 11 (349–51)
imperfect subjunctive
formation § 81
use § 84 C, F, L 60
impersonal expressions
il est + adjective §§ 37 B, 44 E, L 44, L 59
with subjunctive § 83 B, L 46, L 60
weather § 92 B, L 15
in
+ place § 42, L 2, L 39, L 52
with superlative § 13 D, L 5, L 51
indefinite antecedent + subjunctive § 83 E, L 47, L 60
indefinite + *que* + subjunctive § 83 I, L 60
indefinite article §§ 3–4, L 2, L 3, L 52
indefinite pronoun *on* § 40, L 8
indefinite quantity § 5–6, L 9–10, L 44, L 52
indicative (see VERBS, TENSES, and various tenses)
indirect object pronouns §§ 25, 30–31, L 14, L 18, L 32, L 54
list and use § 25
order § 31
position § 30
infinitive
après, avant de § 78 B, L 34, L 53
faire (causative) § 92 A, L 42
negatives § 22 H, L 27, L 48
pour, afin de § 78 C
use after prepositions § 78 A, L 34, L 53
verb + preposition + infinitive § 44, L 41, L 43, L 58
vs. subjunctive § 85, L 46–47, L 49, L 60

interrogation (see QUESTIONS)
interrogative
adjectives § 16, L 16, L 59
intonation 518–20
je + present 500, note 1
pronouns § 38, L 17, L 19, L 38, L 59
word order (compound past) § 62 B, C, L 24; (sentences with interrogative words) § 96, L 2, L 4, L 43
intonation 517–20
intransitive verbs of motion § 61 C, D, L 26, L 55
inverted word order §§ 20 E, 96 B, C, L 4, L 11, L 50, L 57
-ir verbs
1st class (conjugation) 482–83, (present) § 49 B, L 14
2d class (conjugation) 484–85, (present) § 49 C, L 22
irregular verbs
conjugation 486–99
future § 54 B, L 31, L 57
past participles § 75 B, L 24
present indicative § 49 E, L 11–22, L 53
present subjunctive § 80 B, C, L 46–50, L 60
simple past § 58 B, L 41

J

jamais § 22 E, F 2, L 40
jour, journée 507, L 23

K

know 478, L 24, L 51

L

l'
definite article § 1 A, L 1
direct object pronoun 399, note 1, L 13
elision 514
là
position § 20 D, L 50
use 95, note *a,* § 29 B, L 12
languages
article § 4 F, L 11, L 52
gender § 7 B 3
latter, former § 33 D, L 30
le, la, les
definite article §§ 1–2, 4, L 1, L 3, L 52
direct object pronouns §§ 24, 30–31, L 13, L 18, L 21, L 25, L 32, L 54
leave 478, L 52
lequel, laquelle, lesquels, lesquelles
interrogative pronoun § 38 E, L 38, L 59
relative pronoun § 39 A, D, L 30, L 33, L 56
let's imperative § 79 B, L 35, L 53
leur
indirect object pronoun §§ 25, 30–31, L 14, L 18, L 32, L 54
possessive adjective § 14, L 12, L 56
possessive pronoun § 32, L 48, L 56
liaison or linking 521–23
live 479, L 53
l'on § 40 B
lorsque
+ future § 55 B, L 31, L 57
+ past anterior §§ 65 A, 69 A, L 43
lui
disjunctive pronoun § 27, L 15, L 54
indirect object pronoun §§ 25, 30–31, L 14, L 18, L 32, L 54

M

mal §§ 19 D, 21 B
masculine noun endings § 7 B, L 7, L 45, L 51
meet 480, L 55
meilleur 506, § 13 E, L 27
-même § 27 B 7, L 25
mieux 506, § 21 B, L 27
mille § 17 D–F, L 20
million de § 17 G
mistakes, favorite 541–46
modes (see INDICATIVE, SUBJUNCTIVE. IMPERATIVE, INFINITIVE)
moi
disjunctive pronoun § 27, L 15, L 54
instead of *me* § 30 B, L 32, L 54
moins
adverb of quantity § 6 B, L 10
comparative of *peu* § 21 B
used in comparisons (adjectives) § 13 A; (adverbs) § 21 A
months of year
capitalization 504, note 1, 513
gender § 7 B 3
list § 97 B, L 15
motion, intransitive verbs of § 61 C, D, L 26, L 55
must 480, § 93 B, C, D, L 38, L 56

N

nasals 526–28, 537–39
ne (also see NEGATIVE)
  omission of § 22 G, L 40
  pleonastic 460, note 3
negative
  + *de* § 6 C, L 10, L 44, L 52
  imperative § 30 B, L 32, L 54
  + infinitive § 22 H, L 27, L 48
  sentences § 22 A, L 6
  word order (simple tenses) § 22 A–C, L 6; (compound tenses) § 22 D, L 24; (negative combinations other than *ne . . . pas*) § 22 F, L 40, L 56
  words other than *pas* § 22 E, L 40, L 56
n'est-ce pas § 96 J, L 11
ni . . . ni
  article § 5 D, L 44
  negative § 22 E, L 40, L 56
nouns
  adjectival *de* + noun § 6 E, L 29
  adjective used as noun § 11 G
  appositive § 4 E, L 9, L 52
  gender § 7, L 1, L 7, L 45, L 51
  general sense § 4 B, L 9, L 52
  places (article) § 4 C, L 1; (preposition used with) § 42–43, L 2, L 39, L 52
  plural § 8, L 3, L 8, L 51
  profession, etc. 412, note 3 § 4 H, L 36, L 59
  verb + preposition + noun § 45, L 58
numerals
  cardinals § 17, L 12, L 18, L 20
  cent § 17 D–F, L 20
  in dates §§ 17 B, F, 18 E
  mille § 17 D–F, L 20
  million de § 17 G
  ordinals § 18, L 15, L 36
  position § 12 E 1
  pronunciation § 17 A, B
  quatre-vingt(s) § 17 C

O

object pronouns
  direct (list and use) §§ 24, L 13, L 54; (position and order) §§ 30–31, L 18, L 21, L 25, L 32, L 54
  en § 28, L 21, L 54
  indirect (list and use) §§ 25, L 14, L 54; (position and order) §§ 30–31, L 18, L 21, L 32, L 54
on, l'on 508, § 40, L 8
order (see WORD ORDER and various grammatical terms)
ordinals § 18, L 15, L 36
orthographical changing verbs
  -cer verbs § 89 A, L 11, L 28, L 41, L 56
  -e-er verbs § 89 D, L 22, L 56
  -é-er verbs § 89 E, L 30, L 56
  -ger verbs § 89 B, L 11, L 28, L 41, L 56
  -eler and *-eter* verbs § 89 F, L 22, L 56
  -yer (*-ayer, -oyer, -uyer*) verbs § 89 C, L 32, L 56
où (relative) § 39 F, L 33, L 56
ought to § 93 C, E, L 38
oui, si 509, L 17
-oyer verbs § 89 C, L 32, L 56

P

par (agent) § 87 C, L 42
participle
  past (form) § 75, (use) § 76, (agreement) § 77; L 23–27, L 42, L 55
  present §§ 73–74, L 34, L 53
partitive
  de instead of § 6, L 10, L 44, L 52
  formation § 5 A, L 9, L 52
  use § 5 B, C, L 9, L 52
parts of body § 4 G, L 14, L 30
pas
  + *de* § 6 C, L 10, L 52
  omission § 22 I
  position (adverbs) § 20 B, L 50; (compound tenses) § 22 D, L 24; (infinitive) § 22 H, L 27, L 48; (in negative sentence) § 22 A, L 6
passé composé §§ 53, 61–63, L 23–29, L 55, Review 11 (349–51)
passé simple §§ 58–59, L 41
passé surcomposé § 69 B
passive voice §§ 86–87, L 42
past anterior (also called *passé antérieur*) §§ 68, 69 A, L 43
past conditional (also called *conditionnel passé*)
  conditions § 72 B, C, L 45, L 57
  formation § 70, L 45, L 57
  use § 71, L 45, L 57
past definite §§ 58–59, L 41

past indefinite §§ 53, 61–63, L 23–29, L 55, Review 11 (349–51)
past participle
adjective § 76 B
agreement (adjective) § 76 B; *(avoir)* § 77 A, L 25; (motion) § 77 B, L 26; (passive) § 86 C, L 42; (reflexive) § 77 D, L 27; *(vous)* § 77 C
formation § 75, L 23
irregular § 75 B, L 24
use § 76, L 23–27, L 55
past subjunctive
formation § 82, L 47, L 60
use § 84 B, F, L 47–50, L 60
peine, à § 20 E
pendant 507
people 508
personal pronouns
direct object §§ 24, 30–31, L 13, L 18, L 21, L 25, L 32, L 54
disjunctive § 27, L 15, L 54
indirect object §§ 25, 30–31, L 14, L 18, L 32, L 54
order § 31, L 18, L 32, L 54
position § 30, L 13, L 14, L 32, L 54
reciprocal § 26 B, L 31
reflexive § 26, L 22
subject § 23 A, L 4, L 11
tu § 23 B, L 39
personne § 22 F 3, L 40, L 56
peut-être § 20 E, L 50, L 57
peux, puis 105, note *d*
phonetic symbols 532
place
adverbs § 20 D, L 50, L 57
article § 4 C, L 1, L 39, L 52
gender § 7 B 4, L 39, L 52
prepositions (**at, in, to**) § 42, (**from**) § 43, L 2, L 39, L 52
pleonastic *ne* 460, note 3
plupart, la 373, note 3 (2), L 52
pluperfect indicative
conditions § 72 B–D, L 45, L 57
formation § 64, L 37
imperfect, expressed by § 52 D, L 43
use § 65, L 37
pluperfect subjunctive
conditions § 72 C, L 60
formation § 82 B, L 60
use § 84 D, L 60
plural
adjectives § 11, L 3, L 9, L 16, L 35, L 51
nouns § 8, L 3, L 8, L 51
plus
adverbs of quantity § 6 B, L 10
comparative of *beaucoup* § 21 B
used in comparisons (adjectives) § 13 A, L 5, L 51; (adverbs) § 21 A
no more, no longer § 22 E, F 2, L 7, L 40, L 56
position
adjectives § 12, L 7, L 9, L 35, L 56
adverbs § 20, L 50, L 57
object pronouns § 30–31, L 13, L 18, L 21, L 25, L 32, L 54
possession
de § 41
être à § 32 D, L 48
possessive adjectives § 14, L 12, L 56
possessive pronouns § 32, L 48, L 56
pour
to express **for** 507
+ infinitive § 78 C
+ *que* + subjunctive § 83 H, L 49, L 60
pourquoi, word order with § 96 E, G, L 43
premier
feminine § 10 C, L 16
ordinal § 18, L 15, L 36
+ subjunctive § 83 F, L 48, L 60
prepositions (also see various prepositions)
+ disjunctive pronouns § 27 B 1, L 15, L 54
place (**at, in, to**) § 42, (**from**) § 43; L 2, L 39, L 52
verb + preposition + infinitive § 44, L 41, L 43, L 58
verb + preposition + noun § 45, L 58
verbal constructions following § 78 A, L 34, L 53
present indicative
depuis etc. 507, § 50 B, L 33, L 53
-er verbs § 49 A, L 11
-ir verbs of 1st class § 49 B, L 14
-ir verbs of 2d class § 49 C, L 22
irregular verbs § 49 E, L 11–22, L 53
-re verbs § 49 D, L 17
translation § 50 A, B
use § 50, L 53

present participle
  agreement § 74 C, L 34, L 53
  en used with § 74 B, L 34, L 53
  formation § 73, L 34, L 53
  use § 74, L 34, L 53
present subjunctive (formation) § 80, L 46, (use) §§ 83, 84 A, E, F, L 46–50, L 60
principal parts of verbs § 48, L 35
profession, nouns of 412, note 3, § 4 H, L 36, L 59
progressive tenses
  imperfect § 52 A, B 2, L 28–29, L 34, L 43, L 55
  present § 50 A, L 34, L 53
pronouns
  demonstrative *(ce)* §§ 35–37, L 15, L 36, L 44, 59; *(ceci)* § 34, L 37, L 59; *(celui,* etc.) §§ 33, 34 D, L 30, L 37, L 59
  direct object § 24, L 13, L 18, L 21, L 32, L 54
  disjunctive § 27, L 15, L 54
  en § 28, L 21, L 54
  indirect object § 25, L 14, L 18, L 32, L 54
  interrogative § 38, L 17, L 19, L 38, L 59
  order § 31
  position § 30
  possessive § 32, L 48, L 56
  reciprocal § 26 B, L 31
  reflexive § 26 A, L 22
  relative § 39, *(qui, que)* L 14, *(lequel)* L 30, *(ce qui)* L 32, (all) L 33, L 56
  subject § 32, L 4, L 11
  y § 29, L 12, L 54
pronunciation
  by conventional spelling 523–32
  by phonetic script 532–40
  numerals § 17, A, B
  tous 381, note 1
punctuation 513
purpose §§ 78 C, § 83 H, L 49, L 60

Q

quand
  + future § 55 B, L 31, L 57
  interrogative word order § 96 E–G, L 43
  + past anterior §§ 65 A, 69 A, L 43
quantity, expressions of § 6 B, L 10, L 44, L 52
quatre-vingt(s) § 17 C
que
  interrogative § 38 A, B, D, L 17, L 19, L 59
  ne . . . que § 22 F 4, L 16, L 40
  relative § 39 C, L 14, L 33, L 56
  than § 13 B, L 5, L 51
qu'est-ce que
  definition § 38 F, L 16
  interrogative pronoun § 38 D, L 16, L 19, L 59
qu'est-ce que c'est que § 38 F, L 16
quel § 16, L 16, L 59
questions
  compound past § 62 B, C, L 24
  est-ce-que § 96 A, L 2, L 11
  inverted form § 96 B–D, L 4, L 11
  je + present 500, note 2
  with interrogative words § 96 E–I, L 43
  n'est-ce-pas § 96 J, L 11
qui
  interrogative §§ 38 A–C, 96 H, L 19, L 59
  relative § 39 A, B, L 14, L 33, L 56
quoi
  interrogative § 38 A, B, L 19, L 59
  relative § 39 A, G 3
quoi que § 83 I, L 60
quoique § 83 H, L 49, L 60
quotation marks 513

R

r, pronunciation 530–31
-re verbs
  conjugation 482–83
  present § 49 D, L 17
reciprocal pronouns § 26 B, L 31
reflexive pronouns § 26 A, L 22
reflexive verbs § 88, L 22
  agreement of past participle § 77 D, L 27, L 55
  compound past § 61 E, L 27, L 55
  conjugation 486–87, § 88 D
  imperative § 79 D, L 35, L 53
  present § 88 C, L 22
  use §§ 87 B 2, 88 B, E, L 3, L 22, L 42
relative pronouns § 39, *(qui, que)* L 14, *(lequel)* L 30, *(ce que)* L 32, (all) L 33, L 56

dont § 39 C
où § 39 F
what § 39 G
return 480, L 57
rhythm 516
rien § 22 F 3, L 40, L 56

S

sans § 5 D, L 44
savoir, connaître 478, L 24, L 51
se
reciprocal § 26 B, L 31
reflexive § 26 A, L 3, L 22
seasons
gender § 7 B 3
list § 97 C, L 10, L 15
second, deuxième § 18 C
semi-vowels 538–39
sequence of tenses § 84, L 47–50, L 60
seul + subjunctive § 83 F, L 48, L 60
should § 93 C, E, L 38
si
conditions § 72, L 45, L 57
elision with *il, ils* 514
+ imperfect 206, note 1
yes 509, L 17
simple past §§ 58–59, L 41
spelling changes § 89, L 11, L 22, L 28, L 30, L 41, L 56
spend 480, L 58
stems of verbs §§ 46 C, D, 48, L 11, L 35
stress 515–16
subject pronouns
compound subjects § 27 B 2, L 15
emphatic positions § 27 B 3, L 15, L 54
list § 23 A; *(il, ils)* L 4, (all) L 11
tu § 23 B, L 39
subjunctive (also see TENSES and various tenses) §§ 80–85, L 46–50, L 60
imperfect (formation) § 81, (uses) § 84 C, F, L 60
vs. infinitive § 85, L 46–49, L 60
irregular verbs § 80 B, C, L 46, L 49, L 60
past (formation) § 82 A, (use) § 84 B, E, F, L 47–50, L 60
pluperfect (formation) § 82 B, (uses) §§ 83 K, 84 D, F, L 60
present (formation) § 80, L 46, (use) §§ 83, 84 A, E, F, L 46–50, L 60
sequence of tenses § 84, L 47–50, L 60
use (verbs of wishing) § 83 A, L 46, (impersonal expressions) § 83 B, L 46, (verbs of fearing) § 83 C, L 47, (verbs of emotion) § 83 D, L 47, (indefinite antecedent) § 83 E, L 47, (superlative, *seul, premier, dernier*) § 83 F, L 48, (verbs of believing) § 83 G, L 50, (certain subordinate conjunctions) § 83 H, L 49, (indefinites + *que*) § 83 I, L 60, (3d person imperative) § 83 J, (contrary-to-fact conditions) §§ 72 C, 83 K
superlative
+ *de* § 13 D, L 5, L 51
formation and use § 13 A, C–E, L 5, L 51
+ subjunctive § 83 F, L 48, L 60
syllabification 514–15
symbols, phonetic 532

T

take 481, L 59
tenses (also see name of tense)
compound §§ 60–70, 82
conjugation 486–98, § 95
listed and translated § 47
sequence of § 84, L 47–50, L 60
simple §§ 49–59, L 11–22
subjunctive §§ 80–82, L 46, L 47, L 60
than § 13 B, L 5, L 51
time
adverbs § 20 D, L 50, L 57
dates §§ 17 B, F, 18 E, L 20
days of week § 97 A, L 12
months of year § 97 B, L 15
seasons § 97 C, L 10, L 15
telling time § 97 D–F, L 17
time 508
to § 42, L 39, L 52
tous, pronunciation of 381, note 1
tout
adjective § 11 E, L 9
adverb § 11 F, L 21
trees, gender of § 7 B 3
tu § 23 B, L 39

U

un, une §§ 3–4, L 2
l'un l'autre § 26 B, L 31
-uyer verbs § 89 C, L 32, L 56

V

verbs (also see SUBJUNCTIVE, IMPERATIVE, and names of various tenses and other parts of verbs)
auxiliary (compound tenses) § 61, L 23–27, L 55; (passive) § 86 A, B, L 42
conjugation (types) § 46, (by principal parts) § 48, (of regular and irregular verbs) § 95
formation and use of tenses §§ 49–87
irregular (present) § 49 E, (future) § 54 B, (simple past) § 58 B, (past participle) § 75 B, (subjunctive) § 80 B, C, (tables) 486–99
motion § 61 C, D, L 26, L 55
organization §§ 46–48
orthographical changing § 89, L 11, L 22, L 28, L 30, L 41, L 56
passive voice §§ 86–87, L 42
principal parts § 48, L 35
reflexive § 88, L 22
stems §§ 46 C, D, 48
verbs + preposition + infinitive § 44, L 41, L 43, L 58
verb + preposition + noun § 45, L 58
vieux, vieil, vieille, § 10 G, L 35
visit 481, L 60
voice, passive §§ 86–87, L 42
voici § 91 B, C, L 18
voici . . . que + present § 50 B, L 33, L 53
voilà
il y a § 91 A, L 18
pronoun objects § 91 C
voici § 91 B, L 18
voilà . . . que + present § 50 B, L 33, L 53
vous
agreement with past participle § 77 C, L 26
tu § 23 B, L 39
vowel assimilation 537
vowels 511, 523–28, 532–39

W

weather § 92 B, L 15
week, days of § 97 A, L 12
what
interrogative adjective § 16, L 16, L 59
interrogative pronoun § 38, L 17, L 19, L 59
relative pronoun § 39 C, L 14, L 33, L 56
what is . . . (*quel est . . .*) § 16 C, D, (*qu'est-ce que,* etc.) § 38 F, L 16
when
où § 39 F, L 33, L 56
quand (future) § 55 B, L 31, L 57; (past anterior) §§ 65 A, 69 A, L 43; (interrogative word order) § 96 E–G, L 43
while 509
word order
adjectives § 12, L 7, L 9, L 35, L 51
adverbs § 20, L 50, L 57
compound past § 62, L 24
interrogative §§ 62 B, C, 96, L 2, L 4, L 24, L 43
negative § 22, L 6, L 24, L 40, L 56
pronoun objects §§ 30–31, 62 D, L 13, L 14, L 18, L 21, L 32, L 54
reflexive imperative § 78 D, L 35, L 53

Y

y
à + thing § 29 C, L 54
là 95, note *a,* § 29 B, L 12
pronoun of place § 29 A, L 12, L 54
word order §§ 30–31, L 12, L 21, L 32, L 54
year
an, année 509, L 16
months of § 97 B, L 15
reading of dates § 17 F, L 20
-yer verbs § 89 C, L 32, L 56
yes 509, L 17
you § 23 B, L 11, L 39

HIJ–R–73210/698765